Supervision
Concepts and Practices of Management
Second Canadian Edition

Supervision

Concepts and Practices of Management
Second Canadian Edition

Raymond L. Hilgert
Washington University

Edwin C. Leonard, Jr.
Indiana University—Purdue University Fort Wayne

Jackie Shemko
Durham College

Gary Docherty
St. Clair College

NELSON / EDUCATION

NELSON / EDUCATION

Supervision: Concepts and Practices of
Management, Second Canadian Edition

by Raymond L. Hilgert, Edwin C. Leonard, Jr.,
Jackie Shemko, and Gary Docherty

Editorial Director and Publisher:
Evelyn Veitch

Acquisitions Editor:
Anthony Rezek

Executive Marketing Manager:
Don Thompson

Senior Developmental Editor:
Joanne Sutherland

Photo Researchers:
Mary Rose MacLachlan,
Mary Stangolis

Permissions Coordinator:
Mary Rose MacLachlan

Senior Production Editor:
Natalia Denesiuk

Copy Editor and Proofreader:
Karen Rolfe

Indexer:
Edwin Durbin

Senior Production Coordinator:
Kathrine Pummell

Creative Director:
Angela Cluer

Interior Design:
Ramsdell Design

Interior Design Modifications:
Tammy Gay

Cover Design:
Katherine Strain

Cover Image:
© Sharon Green/Corbis/Magma

Compositor:
Nelson Gonzalez

Printer:
Webcom

**Library and Archives Canada
Cataloguing in Publication Data**

Supervision : concepts and
practices of management /
Raymond L. Hilgert ... [et al.]. —
2nd Canadian ed.

Includes bibliographical references
and index.

ISBN 0-17-640603-4

1. Supervision of employees.
2. Personnel management.
I. Hilgert, Raymond L.

HF5549.12.H54 2004   658.3'02
C2004-903604-1

P | Preface

TO THE INSTRUCTOR

If there is one constant in today's business world, it is change. Wholesale changes in technologies, in organizational and competitive structure, and in the social, economic, and political environments all seem to be accelerating more rapidly than ever before. To operate successfully in this changing environment, organizations need supervisors with the managerial skills and creativity to turn uncertainty into opportunity. This edition of *Supervision: Concepts and Practices of Management* will equip students with the knowledge and skills they need to become and succeed as supervisors in the present and future business world.

A Text That Is Skills-Focused

This comprehensive textbook on supervisory management is focused on helping students develop supervisory skills they can really use. While learning important supervisory management concepts, students will also learn how to be supervisors—how to apply the principles of management in the rapidly changing world.

The text is introductory in that it assumes no previous management knowledge. However, it presents challenging material in language that students can understand. The concepts are presented in direct, practical terms.

A major goal of the book is to help the student, the potential supervisor, or the newly appointed supervisor analyze the many problems supervisors face, and the book offers practical advice for their solutions. For experienced supervisors, the text is intended to refresh their thinking, widen their horizons, and challenge them to examine how they are relating to employees, other supervisors, and higher management.

Materials for this text have been drawn from writings and research of scholars in management, leadership, and the behavioural sciences and from reported experiences of many supervisors, managers, and administrators. In addition to the authors' own experiences in management, the text reflects their backgrounds in teaching supervisory management courses, in participating in many stimulating discussions in supervisory development programs, and in consulting for numerous organizations.

Text Features

Current Topics and Concepts

Supervision contains up-to-date material on organizational structure, motivation, communication, ethics, supervisory leadership, positive discipline, supervision of a diverse workforce, performance appraisal, and group dynamics and work teams. Among the many current topics and concepts discussed are

- Organizational downsizing (restructuring and its impact).
- Ethical tests in decision making.

- Employee empowerment.
- Total quality management (TQM).
- Participative management and the collaborative workplace.
- Self-managed (self-directed) work teams.
- Supervising a diverse workforce and compliance with applicable legislation.
- The supervisor as coach and facilitator.
- Encouraging positive employee motivation.
- Employee demotivators, stress, and workplace violence.
- Workplace spirituality and wellness programs.
- Employment and labour legislation that require supervisory understanding and application.
- Supervising in a unionized environment, including the appropriate response to an organizing campaign and establishing positive relationships with shop stewards.
- Managing upward.
- Conducting effective employment interviews.
- Appraising employee performance and managing the outcomes of the appraisal process.

An Integrated Teaching and Testing System

The text and supplements are organized around the learning objectives to enhance a comprehensive teaching and testing system. Each text chapter begins with a series of learning objectives covering the key concepts. The objectives then appear in the text margins, identifying where each objective is fulfilled. The key concepts are reinforced at the end of the chapter, where they are summarized under their learning objectives.

The integrated system creates a close tie between the text and the Instructor's Manual that accompanies the text. Since both are organized around the learning objectives, you can customize your lectures and exams to emphasize the concepts that you feel your students need most. The extensive lecture outlines in the Instructor's Manual identify the materials that fulfill each objective so that you can be sure your lectures cover the key concepts.

"You Make the Call" Opening Vignettes

To stimulate student interest, each chapter begins with an opening scenario titled "You Make the Call." Each scenario presents a real-world supervisory situation that students will learn to handle from studying the chapter. These case-like scenarios, written in the second person, draw students into a problem situation and ask them to decide what to do. At the conclusion of the chapter, a section titled "What Call Did You Make?" appears just before the chapter summary. Here students are provided with suggestions about how to approach the problem in the scenario, using the concepts they just learned in the chapter. Students can then compare their own approaches and decisions to those suggested by the authors and perhaps also by you, their instructor. By applying chapter concepts to these opening problems and then comparing their results to those provided, students are also learning how to tackle the end-of-chapter cases.

Contemporary Issue Boxes

To better comprehend today's business world, students need to recognize and understand complex issues facing supervisors now and in the future. In the "Contemporary Issue" boxes within each chapter, issues and debates surrounding selected current management and supervisory topics are presented. These include

- Surviving in the "nimble" organization (Chapter 1).
- The need for planning (Chapter 2).
- Strategies for improving creative problem solving and decision making (Chapter 3).
- Lean manufacturing (Chapter 4).
- Unusual interview questions (Chapter 5).
- Practices of Canada's top-rated employers (Chapter 6).
- Servant-leadership (Chapter 7).
- Corporate e-mail and Internet policies (Chapter 8).
- Upward performance appraisals (Chapter 9).
- A sampling of Canadian wrongful dismissal cases (Chapter 10).
- Managing virtual teams (Chapter 11).
- Union organizing attempts at Wal-Mart (Chapter 12).
- Open-book management (Chapter 13).
- Innovative diversity program at Loblaws Supermarkets (Chapter 14).

Some of these contemporary issues are controversial and include areas of contention concerning application of supervisory principles in current business practice. Many of these boxes cite specific examples of Canadian companies and illustrate how contemporary issues in supervisory management affect Canadian organizations.

Skills Applications

To develop skills, students need practice. Therefore, two to four skills application activities are provided at the end of each chapter. These hands-on tasks require students to apply what they have learned. Some projects ask students to compare their own experiences with those of practising supervisors. Others provide opportunities for small-group work within or outside class, or require self-assessment, interviews with practising supervisors, and other interesting applications. Each chapter contains at least one skills application that requires students to conduct Internet research to learn more about contemporary issues in supervisory management. Internet-related projects are designated by an icon in the margin as shown here.

Cases

Case studies are excellent tools for teaching and learning supervisory skills. This edition includes 28 cases, which highlight recent issues and trends. Cases have been included at the end of each chapter to help you assign cases for discussion or submission after students have studied specific concepts from the chapter.

Most cases are short—some less than a page. Yet they are challenging without being overwhelming for students. The cases are based on actual experiences of supervisors in work environments. End-of-case discussion questions help students focus their thinking. Expanded commentaries on the case questions appear in the Instructor's Manual to provide helpful guidance in implementing the cases and evaluating student responses.

Some cases include optional Internet-based assignments. These optional assignments provide opportunities for students to search the Internet for current information that may be associated with or included within the concepts of the case and text. Students are urged to further apply their critical thinking and analysis of the case toward broader aspects of current business information. These assignments are identified by an icon in the margin. For ease of recognition, this is the same icon used with skills applications that utilize the Internet.

You may use the cases in several ways: as fuel for class or seminar discussions, as written homework assignments, or as examinations. Case assignments are an excellent way for students to practise their skills on real supervisory problems and to assess their ability to apply what they have learned.

The Skills Development Modules Video

Today's students like the stimulation of visual presentation. Each video available with the text contains seven short segments, with each segment depicting an ineffective and a more effective way of handling a particular supervisory situation. Questions about the video modules are provided at the end of the relevant chapter:

Module 2-1: Planning and Time Management
Module 3-1: Decision Making
Module 5-1: Employee Selection and Interviewing Protocol
Module 6-1: Motivation
Module 7-1: Delegation
Module 8-1: Communication
Module 9-1: Coaching and Performance Appraisal

Questions for discussion require students to integrate the text material into their answers. The Instructor's Manual contains a complete description of each module, including running time, as well as all the information required to integrate the Skills Development Modules into your class presentation. The Skills Development Modules are identified by an icon at the margin as shown here.

Other Pedagogical Features

In addition to those previously described, the text provides a number of other features to enhance student learning. Among these are

Marginal Definitions

In an introductory supervision course, students need to learn the language of business. Therefore, concise definitions of all key terms are placed in the margins of the text where they are first introduced. The key terms and their definitions are also compiled in a glossary at the end of the book for quick reference.

Summary Points

The major chapter concepts are summarized at the end of each chapter, organized around the learning objectives. By reviewing these summaries, students can quickly identify areas where they need further review. Then, using the learning objectives in the text margins, they can easily locate the discussion of the concepts they want to review.

Questions for Discussion

The end-of-chapter discussion questions are designed to help students check their understanding of chapter material.

Supplements to Ease the Teaching Load

The integrated learning system extends to the text's supplementary package. The Instructor's Manual is organized by learning objectives so you can easily customize your lectures to emphasize the concepts your students need the most. The extensive lecture outlines in the manual identify the materials that fulfill each objective so you can be sure your lectures cover key concepts.

The comprehensive Test Bank and Microsoft® PowerPoint® presentation slides are also keyed to the learning objectives for your convenience. All these materials can add immeasurably to classroom lectures and discussions.

Instructor's Resource CD-ROM (0-17-641451-7)

The Instructor's Resource CD-ROM contains the Instructor's Manual with transparency masters, a computerized test bank, and a complete set of Microsoft® PowerPoint® presentation slides. This CD is a one-stop resource for all your ancillary support needs.

Instructor's Manual

Instructors always have more to do than there are hours in a day. To make your class preparations easier, this text has an expanded Instructor's Manual available on the Instructor's Resource CD-ROM. First, the manual contains extensive lecture outlines, which form the core of the integrated teaching system. These outlines provide ample materials for faster and easier lecture preparations, including references to supplementary materials next to the chapter concepts to which they apply. There are also suggestions for when to show each transparency, use the cases, bring in discussion of the chapter's boxed features, and more—all organized around the learning objectives. The outlines also contain discussion suggestions for the transparencies, "You Make the Call" features, and "Contemporary Issue" boxes.

In addition to the lecture outlines, the comprehensive Instructor's Manual includes:

- Summaries of key concepts by learning objective.
- Commentaries on all cases, which will help you guide discussions or evaluate students' written analyses.
- Commentaries on the skills development module video cases.
- Commentaries on the skills applications, including solutions and follow-up approaches.
- Solution guidelines for all end-of-chapter discussion questions.
- A bibliography of additional published resources.

Computerized Test Bank

The computerized test bank for this edition will serve as a valuable resource for you in the preparation of the objective portion of your testing alternatives. The test bank contains at least 50 true/false and multiple-choice questions with answers for each chapter. Each test bank question is categorized according to question type: Definition, Conceptual, or Application. These types will help you identify involvement and difficulty levels.

The test bank is in Examview®Pro format. This computerized testing software enables you to quickly create printed tests, Internet tests, and online (LAN-based) tests. You can also enter your own questions using the word processor provided, as well as customize the appearance of the tests you create. The QuickTest Wizard allows you to use an existing test bank to create a test in minutes, using a step-by-step selection process that gives you exactly what you want.

Microsoft® PowerPoint® Slides

New to this edition is an extensive set of over 250 PowerPoint® presentation slides, available on the Instructor's Resource CD-ROM. All of these have been developed to correlate closely with the text materials and learning objectives. The slides are easy to read and apply, and should be very helpful in adding focus to classroom lectures and discussions.

Supervision, Second Canadian Edition Website http://www.supervision2e.nelson.com

The text now has a brand new supporting website, which includes a variety of resources for both instructors and students. The site includes all the Internet Skills Applications with complete live links to websites, additional chapter links, quiz questions, and crossword puzzles. The Instructor's Manual, transparency masters, and PowerPoint® slides are also available here for download by instructors. References to our website are indicated by the WWW icon.

Acknowledgments

In the preparation of this second Canadian edition, I would like to thank the reviewers who shared with me their insights and constructive criticism: Michael L. Hockenstein, Vanier College; Peggy L. Noble, Southern Alberta Institute of Technology (SAIT); Michael Rock, Seneca College; Pat Rogin, Durham College; William E. Rowberry, Lambton College; Ron Storey, Georgian College; and Anne M. Wylie-Bowman, Niagara College.

I would also like to thank the team at Nelson for their outstanding support and encouragement throughout the process of this revision. The guidance and feedback provided by Anthony Rezek, Acquisitions Editor; Joanne Sutherland, Senior Developmental Editor; and Natalia Denesiuk, Production Editor, were invaluable. Their advice and suggestions have made this a better text.

Thanks to the administration, faculty, and students of Durham College who provided moral support for this project. A special thanks to my colleague, Pat Rogin of Durham College, for her expert advice and perspective on the revision process.

Finally, thanks to my family—Paul, Patrick, and Liam—for their patience and understanding during my work on this project.

Jackie Shemko

About the Authors

Dr. Edwin C. Leonard, Jr. is Professor of Business Administration at Indiana University–Purdue University Fort Wayne (IPFW). He received his bachelor's, master's, and doctor's degrees from Purdue University. Since joining the faculty 35 years ago, Dr. Leonard has held various faculty and administrative positions, including chair of the Management and Marketing Department in the School of Business and Management Sciences. Dr. Leonard has designed and conducted workshops and seminars for thousands of supervisors and managers. He currently serves as academic advisor and coordinator of Do It Best Corp.'s Retail Management Training Course; this comprehensive program is for management personnel of one of the largest hardware and building materials retailers in the United States.

Dr. Leonard's primary research interests are in the areas of employee involvement, teaming, organizational climate and leadership, human resource management interventions, and case development. He has published in varied academic and professional journals, instructional supplement manuals, and proceedings. He is editor of the *Business Case Journal*. Dr. Leonard has authored or co-authored four books dealing with supervisory management, two of which are in their third and ninth editions. His professional memberships include the Society for Case Research, the Midwest Society for Human Resources/Industrial Relations, the Organizational Behavior Teaching Society, and the North American Case Research Association.

Dr. Leonard received the National University Continuing Education Association's Service Award for Continuing Education for the Professions, and he received the Award of Teaching Excellence from the Indiana University School of Continuing Studies. Dr. Leonard has received several "best paper" and "distinguished case" awards from various organizations.

Dr. Raymond L. Hilgert is Professor Emeritus of Management and Industrial Relations at the Olin School of Business of Washington University. He graduated from Westminster College, Fulton, Missouri, with a bachelor of arts degree and received his master's and doctor's degrees from Washington University. His business experience includes management positions at Southwestern Bell Telephone Company and a market research position with an advertising company. Dr. Hilgert taught at Washington University for 40 years, including serving as assistant dean and director of management development programs. He has published over 90 articles and has authored or co-authored six books on human resource management, collective bargaining, industrial relations, and business ethics, three of which are in the sixth, eighth, and tenth editions.

Dr. Hilgert has been a member of the Academy of Management, the Industrial Relations Research Association, the Society for Human Resource Management, the American Compensation Association, and the American Management Association. He has participated in or directed numerous management, supervisory, and business ethics programs and seminars. As an arbitrator certified by the Federal Mediation and Conciliation Service, Dr. Hilgert heard and decided hundreds of union/management grievance-arbitration cases. He holds the Senior Professional in Human Resources (SPHR) accreditation from the Personnel Accreditation Institute. He has received a number of teaching awards from students at Washington University.

Jackie Shemko is a faculty member of the School of Business at Durham College where she teaches a wide range of business courses, including supervision, labour relations, operations management, and management simulation. She received an honours bachelor of business administration from Wilfrid Laurier University, and a bachelor of education from Nipissing University. She has a background in corporate banking, as well as over 10 years of experience teaching at the college.

W. Gary Docherty is a member of the Faculty of Business, Management Studies, at St. Clair College, where he focuses primarily on human resource management courses. He received his bachelor of commerce and M.B.A. from the University of Windsor. Since joining the faculty of St. Clair College some 30 years ago, he has held a variety of faculty and administrative positions, including supervisor, human resource manager, dean, and vice president. He was also the recipient of the Teaching Excellence Award at St. Clair College.

As a consultant, Mr. Docherty has designed and conducted workshops and seminars for hundreds of supervisors and managers in large, small, private, and public Canadian organizations. He has also contributed extensively in the review of management texts and acted as a nominee in labour arbitration cases.

B Brief Contents

C Contents

Chapter 1: The Supervisory Challenge and Management Functions

After studying this chapter you will be able to

1 Explain the demands and rewards of being a supervisor.

2 Identify and discuss the major demographic and societal trends that will affect supervisors.

3 Summarize the challenges supervisors face in fulfilling managerial roles.

4 Explain why effective supervisors should possess a variety of skills.

5 Define management and discuss how the primary managerial functions are interrelated.

Every chapter in this text begins with a section titled "You Make the Call." After reading each case, decide which decision(s) you would make or the course(s) of action you would take as the person described in the case. As you read each chapter, think about how the concepts apply to the opening scenario. After you finish each chapter, compare your ideas to the suggestions in the section titled "What Call Did You Make?" This section appears just before the summary for each chapter.

You are Leslie McGuire, a recent graduate of the business administration program at Shelbourne Community College.

During your three years at college, you worked part-time in the production department of Brant Coatings Ltd., a manufacturer of industrial paints and adhesives. The work was physically demanding and tedious, but the pay was good and your supervisor adjusted your hours to accommodate your school schedule.

Since graduating three months ago, you have continued to work part-time at Brant while conducting a search for full-time employment. You have applied for jobs in a variety of fields, but are not really sure where your strongest interests lie. You studied a wide range of business subjects in college, and found most of them very interesting. Many of your friends specialized in areas such as accounting or marketing, but you preferred to take a general business program, thinking that perhaps some day you would like to run a business of your own.

Yesterday, your supervisor, Colleen Grenier, took you aside during your shift. "Leslie," she began, "I've always been impressed by your good judgment and your hard work. You get along well with your co-workers and you're always looking for better ways to get the job done. The production supervisor on the night shift is retiring next month and I would like you to apply for the job. I think with your front-line production experience and your business administration diploma, you'd really be a good match for the job. There are some long-time production people who might want the job, but I don't think they've shown the initiative and work ethic that you have. I've already talked to the plant manager, and he'd like to interview you tomorrow afternoon if you're interested. What do you think?"

You have mixed feelings about the possibility of being a night shift supervisor. You have enjoyed working at Brant, but always intended to leave the company once you finished college. You have a lot of good ideas about how to improve production methods, and the opportunity to lead a group could be very rewarding. On the other hand, you know that most of the production employees have been at Brant for many years, and seem very set in their ways. You wonder how well you would be accepted and whether the transition to supervisor would be difficult, especially since you were always viewed as the "part-time kid."

This conversation has taken you by surprise. You need to decide whether to meet with the plant manager tomorrow afternoon. If you decide to attend the meeting, you wonder how you should go about preparing for it. Finally, if offered the job, you must decide whether you will accept it.

You make the call!

<table>
<tr><td>

1

Explain the demands and rewards of being a supervisor.

</td><td>

WHAT DOES IT MEAN TO BE A SUPERVISOR IN UNCERTAIN TIMES?

</td></tr>
</table>

Virtually every aspect of life has undergone major changes during the past several decades. Technology has altered the way we communicate, live, and work. "Surfing the Net" is a daily activity for people of all ages. The stock market has seen wide fluctuations that have left many investors shaken. Long-time pillars of Canadian business such as Nortel Networks Corp. and Air Canada have struggled to reorganize and survive in the face of new competition and rapidly changing market conditions.[1]

There is little doubt that change will continue to challenge every organization. But change brings not only uncertainty and chaos, but also opportunities to the organizations and individuals who can best adapt to the new landscape (see Contemporary Issue box).

If they and their organizations are to survive, managers at all levels must be at the forefront of planning for and coping with trends, factors, and problems requiring more effective management.

This book focuses primarily on the first tier of management, which generally is referred to as the supervisory level, or supervisory management. **Supervisors** are first-level managers in charge of entry-level and other departmental employees.

Supervisor
First-level manager in charge of entry-level and other departmental employees.

Critical commentaries on the North American business system indicate that the traditional notions of getting a job done through power and positional authority are no longer effective. Today's managers and supervisors, whether in factories, nursing care units, business offices, retail stores, or government agencies, must realize that reliance on authoritarian direction and close control will not bring about the desired results. Supervisors are being challenged to improve their skills and to obtain better productivity from all of their human resources. In many organizations the role of the supervisor will continue to change drastically. The term *supervisor* may even be eliminated from the vocabulary of some firms, being replaced by terms such as *team leader, facilitator,* or *coach.*

Supervisory work has become more complex, sophisticated, and demanding, and it requires professional and interpersonal skills.[2] Supervisors are in the unique position of being the only managers in the organization who oversee front-line workers. Supervisors are instrumental in ensuring that the goals and strategies formulated by middle and upper-level managers are actually implemented "in the trenches." In many organizations, supervisors are typically the only representatives of management with whom workers have contact on a daily basis. Effective supervisory practices, therefore, are critical to ensuring that the workforce will support and work to achieve management's goals and objectives.

As depicted in Figure 1-1 on page 5, the job of the supervisor is both rewarding and stressful. The ideas presented are not all-inclusive, but they illustrate some of the rewards and challenges associated with the supervisory role.

Although the first-line supervisory position is one of the three levels on the management hierarchy (see Figure 1-2 on page 6), it is the level in which most people obtain their first management experience. You have probably already developed a picture of what supervisory management is all about. Your past experiences as a student, customer, employee, and/or supervisor have allowed you to observe some of the prevailing supervisory practices. In all likelihood,

CONTEMPORARY ISSUE
Lace up Your Nikes™—Do You Have What It Takes to Thrive in the Nimble Organization?

Managing your career in the new millennium feels a lot like playing tennis. You arrive at the courts expecting a friendly game of amateur tennis, only to find both Williams sisters lined up on the other side of the net! Surviving and thriving in today's "nimble corporations" require that employees at all levels must learn to be quick on their feet, ready to adapt to change, and quick to embrace opportunities created during times of upheaval.

It's easy to find examples of Canadian businesses that have struggled to survive in the past decade. On April 1, 2003, Air Canada filed for bankruptcy protection in the wake of dramatic turbulence in the global airline industry following the terrorist attacks of September 11, 2001. Canada's telecommunication giant, Nortel Networks Corp., laid off 50,000 people in 2001 alone. In September 2003, JDS Uniphase, a fibre-optic components maker, moved its headquarters from Ottawa's "Silicon Valley North" to San Jose, California. The relocation reduced the company's Ottawa workforce to 600, down from a peak of 10,000 people.

But on the other side of the ledger, there are examples of Canadian businesses that have been able to survive—and even thrive—in a rapidly changing business environment. During the same time that Air Canada suffered dramatic losses, Calgary-based WestJet's performance soared. WestJet began as a "scrawny, very local, fledgling"[1] in 1996 and has never looked back. WestJet has earned a profit in each of its 26 budget quarters, and is expanding its routes to include international destinations. It is widely known for the quirky corporate sense of humour that accompanies its no-frills approach to travel. WestJet has demonstrated an ability to find market opportunities and thrive when others are struggling. "It's part of our culture to have fun and do things a little bit differently," says Siobhan Vinish, head of public relations.[2]

Daryl R. Conner, author of *Leading at the Edge of Chaos: How to Create the Nimble Organization*, says that successful organizations must learn to operate in a state of "perpetual unrest." He advises organizations to learn to "adapt quickly to changing market conditions, while at the same time conducting human due diligence—a measure of people's capacity to absorb change … so there is enough momentum to face the next change and the one after."[3]

But striving to be nimble has resulted in a significant shift in the employment relationship. Gone are the days of "jobs for life" when employers thought "if you show loyalty to the employee, the employee shows loyalty to you and you both benefit."[4] The need to react quickly to changing market conditions often means that organizations cut jobs, contract out, and hire temporary workers instead of permanent staff—changes that have left many Canadian workers wondering about the security of their jobs.

Supervisors will be affected significantly when organizations strive to become more nimble. The increase in contract and temporary workers will challenge a supervisor's ability to keep the entire workforce motivated to excel. The pace of change will increase and the supervisor will have to guide his or her employees through some unsettling periods of unrest. Change will be the rule, not the exception and the line between rapid change and chaos may not always be clear. Leading in this environment will clearly challenge any supervisor's skills.

So, lace up your shoes and get your tennis racket ready. Here comes the next serve!

Sources: (1) Colby Cosh, "WestJet Seriously Wounds Air Canada," *Citizens Centre Report* (March 17, 2003), p. 28; (2) Mike Pettapiece, "WestJet's throwin' a party; Invitation only barn dance will launch airline's new hangar," *The Hamilton Spectator* (August 12, 2003), p. B1; (3) Daryl R. Conner, "Nimble Organizations," *Executive Excellence* (February 2000), p. 18; (4) Anil Verma, Professor at the University of Toronto's Rotman School of Management as quoted by Ann Perry, "Adjusting to the tough new world of work," *Toronto Star* (April 10, 2003), p. K5.

FIGURE 1-1 The "pluses" and "minuses" of supervision.

THE SUPERVISOR'S JOB IS SATISFYING AND REWARDING

- Supervisors can find considerable satisfaction when they work with motivated employees and help those employees develop their abilities and potential.
- A promotion to supervisor usually means more status and a higher salary that is not based on an hourly wage.
- Supervisors have the opportunity to make many decisions and be held accountable for those decisions. They can manage their departments with some degree of authority.
- Achievement of challenging goals and objectives provides great satisfaction and usually is rewarded in various ways by higher management.
- Being a supervisor provides opportunities for professional and personal growth and possible advancement.

THE SUPERVISOR'S JOB IS DIFFICULT AND STRESSFUL

- Supervisors generally work long hours. The number of hours worked tends to increase as a person climbs the organizational ladder.
- Supervisors promoted from their work groups often find the transition to supervision to be difficult as former peer relationships change. Supervisors must develop a professional rather than a personal relationship with former coworkers.
- Supervisory work is characterized by interruptions, problems, crises, and complaints from various sources.
- Information is the basic ingredient of the supervisor's work. Supervisors spend much of their time obtaining, interpreting, and giving information.
- Supervisors are usually under considerable pressure from the often conflicting demands of higher management, employees, and customers. The constant shifting of priorities can be particularly stressful.

your observations have made you aware that there are distinct differences among supervisors in terms of how they apply supervisory concepts and in how effectively they manage their departments.

In the past, many managers achieved their positions on the basis of practical experience they obtained as a first-level supervisor. Today, the study of management has become more formalized, and many prospective supervisors learn management concepts and principles in a classroom setting. This book is intended for both practising and potential supervisors, especially students who are studying the field of management. It is designed to help you develop the supervisory skills needed to succeed in today's rapidly changing organizations.

As an Appendix to this chapter, we include a section called "Getting into Supervision," which will identify and discuss some of the important factors to consider if seeking a supervisory or management position. The Appendix also includes a number of career tips that are essential for those aspiring to be supervisors and for almost any type of career planning.

FIGURE 1-2
The supervisory or team leader position is where most people begin their management careers.

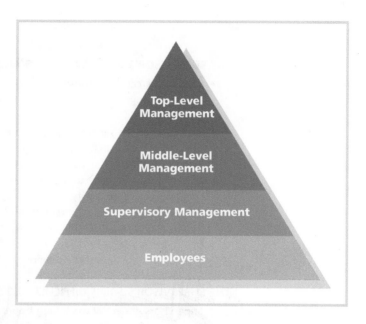

2

FACTORS AND TRENDS AFFECTING THE ROLE OF THE SUPERVISOR

Identify and discuss the major demographic and societal trends that will affect supervisors.

As highlighted in this chapter's Contemporary Issue box (page 4), rapid change is no longer the exception—it is the rule in today's organizations. In order to keep their organizations responsive to changing market conditions, supervisors must understand and respond to many complex environmental factors and trends (see Figure 1.3). Therefore, we will examine some major demographic and societal considerations that are likely to affect the supervisory management position. Although every supervisor is responsible for managing numerous resources, unquestionably the most important, overriding aspect of supervision is the management of people. Therefore, the nature of the workforce should be of vital concern to the supervisor who plans for the future. Finding and developing qualified people have always been among the most important supervisory responsibilities. However, the traditional challenges of attracting and retaining the most qualified employees may be superseded by the more acute supervisory challenge of leading and motivating an increasingly changing workforce. The most significant characteristic of this changing workforce will be its **diversity**. Work groups will be composed of employees who differ in culture, ethnic background, gender, age, educational level, race, and lifestyle characteristics. The supervisor will need to get people from many different cultures to work together.

Diversity
Differences in culture, ethnic background, gender, age, educational level, race, and lifestyle characteristics among employees.

Population and Workforce Growth[3]

Despite the rather low birth rates of recent decades, both the population and the workforce are growing. It is estimated that the Canadian population will grow at a modest rate from a 1996 level of about 30 million people to nearly 32.2 million people by 2006. Assuming a 60 percent employment/population ratio, the workforce can be projected to increase by 1.3 million during this period.

FIGURE 1-3
Effective supervisors must be adaptable and be able to maintain their perspective in the face of rapidly changing conditions.

Immigration continues to add a significant portion to the workforce growth in Canada. In 2001, 5.4 million people, or 18 percent of Canada's total population, reported that they were born outside the country, the highest level in 70 years. Eighty-five percent of immigrants to Canada came from developing countries (see Figure 1-4) and bring a variety of skills and experience with them. Racial minorities in Canada are expected to increase significantly from the present level of 13 percent of the population. Canadian organizations and their supervisors must continue to find ways to capitalize on the talents of this diverse workforce.

While managing a diverse workforce may present some challenges, it also presents numerous opportunities for supervisors to build on the strengths of individuals and groups. In the following sections, we intend not only to create an awareness of the differences to be expected but also to raise consciousness. Supervisors must understand the rights of both their employees and their employers, regardless of workforce differences. Supervisors must recognize the value of a diverse workforce and their own need to become more adaptable to

FIGURE 1-4   Immigrants come increasingly from Asia and the Middle East.

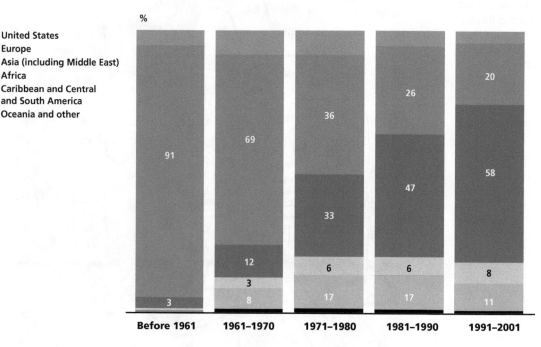

United States
Europe
Asia (including Middle East)
Africa
Caribbean and Central
and South America
Oceania and other

%

91

69

36

33

12

3

3

8

17

26

47

6

17

20

58

8

11

6

Before 1961   1961–1970   1971–1980   1981–1990   1991–2001

Place of birth by period of immigration

Source: Statistics Canada, Census of Population, 2001.

change. Further, perhaps more than ever before, supervisors will have to be scrupulously fair in supervising diverse groups of employees through nondiscriminatory and progressive practices.

Changing Age Patterns

Both the population and the workforce in Canada are getting older. The average age of the workforce in 2001 was 39 years of age compared with an average of 35.8 years in 1981. In 2001, about 62 percent of the workforce was over 35, up from about 47 percent 20 years earlier. This age group normally provides the highest percentage of people who occupy supervisory and other management positions. In the future, therefore, more people will be available to fill these positions, and the competition for supervisory jobs will be keen.

The growth in the 37 to 55 age group poses potential problems for younger workers who are waiting to progress into supervisory positions; there may be a glut of younger employees looking for opportunities as they wait for the large group of older workers to retire. In Ontario, legislators are debating the merits of abolishing mandatory retirement at age 65. Proponents of this change argue that the Canadian economy will be strengthened if the skills of older workers can be retained in the workforce. Critics argue that this move would reduce opportunities for younger workers.[4] Mismatches between the number of employees desiring advancement and the number of opportunities available may lead to increased dissatisfaction and greater turnover as younger workers leave to seek positions elsewhere.

Despite low birthrates in recent decades, both the population and the workforce are growing in Canada.

Jeremy Woodhouse/Photodisc Green/Getty Images

At the opposite end of the spectrum, there will be relatively fewer young people in the workforce as a result of the historical decline in Canada's birth rate. Statistics Canada data show that the 20 to 34 age group has declined from 5.7 million to 4.9 million between 1991 and 2001. Although it is unfair to make sweeping generalizations, many younger workers today are struggling with the fact that their generation will have to work harder for the lifestyle that their parents may have attained relatively easily. Some younger workers become disillusioned when they realize that the effort "that earned their parents two cars, a nice house and cottage at the lake hardly wins them a job flipping burgers."[5] Younger workers are realizing that there are no "jobs for life" and that they must become more entrepreneurial and self-reliant in the changing world of work. Neil Howe and William Strauss, authors of the book *Millennials Rising,* state that young people born since 1982 prefer group activities and want clear rules set for them— a combination that is distinctly different from their mostly **baby-boomer** parents. The researchers believe that this group of new entrants to the workforce, called by some "Y-ers" or "millennials" are more spiritual and less individualistic than their parents,[6] characteristics that should be considered when trying to understand their work motivations. There is little question that the success of supervisors will depend to a considerable extent on those supervisors' abilities to tap into the interests and motivations of all members of the workforce.

Baby-boomers
A large wave of the population born between 1946 and 1963.

Women in the Workforce and Related Issues

Probably the most dramatic change has been the rapid increase in both the number and percentage of women in the workforce. The number of employed women soared by close to 50 percent in the last two decades to more than 7.5 million, while the number of men working rose only 18 percent to 8.5 million.

The participation rate (the percentage of working women who are in the workforce) rose from 56.8 percent in 1995 to 65.2 percent in 2001. In recent years, women have assumed many jobs formerly dominated by men.

While the movement of women into the workforce has significantly increased the skills available to Canadian corporations, this trend has also brought with it a number of challenges for employers that are likely to continue. Two-income families face conflict between work and home, and both male and female employees may bring their family concerns to work. Supervisors need to understand that their employees' work performance may be negatively affected by this conflict between job and family obligations. In order to attract and retain the most qualified employees, employers may need to provide high-quality child-care facilities and continue to experiment with different types of workdays and work weeks, such as **flextime** (in which employees choose their work schedules within certain limits), **job sharing** (in which two or more employees share a job position), **telecommuting** (in which the employee works at home and is linked to the office by computer and modem), and the four-day, 10-hour-a-day work week. Given the increasing numbers of single working parents and the concern over the quality of child-care services, progressive firms are likely to implement these types of working arrangements in an effort to retain talented employees.

A recent study indicates that working mothers go to great lengths to keep family matters out of the workplace, and that it is more likely that work-related issues will intrude on their home lives. A demanding job leaves almost half of parents too tired to do things with their children; 60 percent of working mothers say they have to put work ahead of family at least some of the time and feel less successful in their relationships with spouses, children, and friends. Efforts to help employees balance the responsibilities of home and job will require better supervisory skills and training to help all employees handle work/life issues.[7]

Another major challenge for supervisors will be to ensure that sexual harassment does not occur in the work environment. Sexual harassment has been perpetrated against both men and women, but the latter occurs much more frequently. Recent court decisions have reinforced the fact that supervisors must take action to prevent harassment and must respond immediately when incidents of harassment are reported.

Growth of Racial Minorities in the Workforce

Figure 1-5 outlines the importance of immigration in Canada by region and the percentage of immigrants who arrived in 1991 to 2001.

The growth in the proportion of visible minorities in selected cities shows significant increases as noted in Figure 1-6.

Many immigrants come to Canada with professional designations and advanced skills. The challenge for Canadian organizations will be to tap into this source of talented workers. One of the many responsibilities of supervisors is to attract and retain qualified employees. Yet "there is a tendency to hire what you know. If you have two identical resumes, you may tend to go with a domestic candidate"[8] says Barbara Nowers, director of Career Bridge, an organization overseeing a pilot project in Ontario to help immigrants obtain paid internships in Canadian organizations. Announced in 2003, the pilot project aims to help immigrants break into the Canadian job market in their field of expertise. "Part of the project's goal will be to educate employers. That means taking a chance on a candidate whose language skills may not be perfect but will change exponen-

Flextime
Policy that allows employees to choose their work hours within stated limits.

Job sharing
Policy that allows two or more employees to perform a job normally done by one full-time employee.

Telecommuting
Working at home with links to the office via computer and modem.

FIGURE 1-5 Importance of immigration.

REGION	LABOUR FORCE	PERCENT IMMIGRANTS	PERCENT WHO ARRIVED 1991–2001
Canada	15,872,070	19.9	6.2
Nfld. and Lab.	241,500	1.9	0.4
P.E.I.	73,635	3.0	0.5
Nova Scotia	451,375	4.9	1.1
New Brunswick	371,805	3.4	0.6
Quebec	3,742,485	10.5	3.3
Ontario	6,086,820	29.1	9.2
Manitoba	585,425	13.6	3.1
Saskatchewan	512,240	5.0	1.2
Alberta	1,696,760	16.2	4.4
British Columbia	2,059,945	27.1	9.0
Yukon	17,945	12.4	2.7
N.W.T.	20,785	9.0	2.5
Nunavut	11,355	3.4	0.7

Source: Statistics Canada.

FIGURE 1-6 Percentage of visible minorities in relation to population, 1981–2001.

	1981	1991	2001
Canada	4.7	9.4	13.4
Montreal	5.2	11.0	13.6
Toronto	13.6	25.8	36.8
Vancouver	13.9	24.0	36.9

Source: Statistics Canada.

tially once in the workplace."[9] Some sectors of the Canadian economy face chronic shortages of skilled workers, and supervisors who recognize the potential of the immigrant talent pool may find a way to relieve these shortages.

Opportunities for Women and Minorities

Glass ceiling
Invisible barrier that limits advancement of women and minorities.

Glass walls
Invisible barriers that compartmentalize or segregate women and minorities into certain occupational classes.

Historically, some firms relegated women and minorities to lower-skilled and lower-paying jobs and did not fully utilize the potential contributions that many had to offer. For some people, there was an invisible barrier—a **glass ceiling**—that limited advancement. While women have been appointed to the CEO or president position in companies such as Home Depot Canada, Extendicare, and Xerox Canada, a subtle barrier may still be in place in some firms. To compound the problem, some organizations have concentrated women and minority employees into certain occupations. These **glass walls** that segment employees deny them the opportunity to develop the variety of skills necessary for advancement.

There is some encouraging evidence that glass ceilings and walls may be less of a problem in some Canadian industry sectors than in their U.S. counterparts. A recent study prepared for Women in Capital Markets, a Toronto-based advocacy group for women in the investment banking industry, concluded that women working in the U.S. investment banking industry were "more likely than their Canadian counterparts to cite discriminatory policies and practices as the reasons for their lack of advancement."[10] To advance in their field, however, both Canadian and American women agreed that the key is to "exceed expectations. Be a star. Be perceived as a hard worker."[11]

Women and minorities also face disparities in their earning power. Statistics Canada census data from 2001 indicate that women earn 70 cents for every $1 men earn in full-time jobs, while male immigrants who had been in Canada one year earned 63 cents for every dollar earned by men born in Canada. Organizations must put into place policies and procedures to ensure that all workers are paid fairly for the contribution they make.

A survey conducted by Deloitte and Touche LLP found that women are evenly divided between being "fairly satisfied" and "not too satisfied" with the overall status of women in business today. By comparison, men perceive that there are higher satisfaction levels among women in general. Other findings of the poll include the following:

- More than two-thirds of the women believe that a woman needs more experience or more education than a man does to be considered for the same job.
- More than half of the females believe that women work harder than men.
- Men and women agree that the presence of women in the workforce has had positive effects on business. The effects most commonly cited by both men and women are "a greater importance placed on families" and "a greater awareness and acceptance of different styles and viewpoints."
- Both men and women see a male-dominated corporate culture as a major barrier to women succeeding and agree that women have a tendency to be excluded from the informal communications network.
- Women who work for smaller companies express higher levels of satisfaction and are more likely to be ahead of their own expectations for their career. The authors conclude that this may be because many smaller companies afford women the opportunity to affect decisions and take control of their own careers, better balance work and family life, and make a difference in the lives of others—all of which are important motivators for both genders.[12]

All employees will continue to need an effective combination of educational and job-related experiences to provide them with opportunities to develop their talents. Organizations will be expected to design programs to attract and develop women and minority employees, to ensure that they have access to a full range of career opportunities, and to ensure that they are paid fairly for the work they do.

Educational Preparation

Accompanying the changes in the racial and ethnic composition of the workforce are educational preparation factors that also will challenge supervisors in the future. More people than ever before have some postsecondary education. Nearly two-thirds of high school graduates go on to college or university. In 2000, 41 percent of Canadian adults aged 25 to 64 had a college or university education, the highest of all industrialized nations, ahead of 37 percent in the United States and 34 percent in Japan.

Some forecasters believe that we may soon encounter problems with an overeducated workforce. That is, more and more college- and university-educated employees will compete for jobs that do not necessarily require a post-secondary education to perform. The intense competition for jobs and the increase in lower-level service industry jobs may create underemployment. **Underemployment** occurs when employees bring a certain amount of skill, knowledge, and ability (**SKAs**) to the workplace and find that the job lacks meaning and/or the opportunity to fully utilize their SKAs. The challenge for supervisors will be to create a workplace environment that stimulates the under-employed. The current abundance of college and university graduates gives corporate recruiters a distinct advantage—the opportunity to pick the best.

Underemployment
Situation in which people are in jobs that do not utilize their skills, knowledge, and abilities (SKAs).

SKAs
Skills, knowledge, and abilities that a person has.

Yet we must keep in mind the other side of the coin: namely, that some young workers entering the workforce will not have completed a postsecondary education. The challenge will be for firms to provide employment and training opportunities for people whose specific skills are limited—despite their level of formal education—but who are motivated to work.

Competitive advantage
The ability to outperform competitors by increasing efficiency, quality, creativity, and responsiveness to customers and effectively utilizing employee talents.

An organization seeking to obtain a **competitive advantage** can do so by hiring the best employees and properly using their skills. This will require effective recruitment, retention, and training strategies to ensure that the organization is getting the most from its workforce.

Occupational and Industry Trends

Occupational and industry forecasts project that there will be a steady need for more people in business-related services such as computer services, retail trade, health care services, transportation, and banking and financial services well into the 21st century. Figure 1-7 lists the results of a 2003 Scotiabank study that identified the occupational sectors that are expected to display the highest growth through 2007.

All indications for the next 10 years are that the opportunities for those with managerial skills will greatly increase. There will be an acute need for skilled and experienced people with technology backgrounds to manage products, relationships, or people. Unfortunately, low-paying jobs will also be on the rise. Many new service workers—cashiering at the campus bookstore, washing dishes at a local restaurant, or providing homemaking services—are expected to be needed by 2005. The difference is that many entry-level positions in the service sector are low-paying jobs, averaging less than $10 per hour.

FIGURE 1-7   Canada's top employment prospects through 2007.

- Biotechnology.
- Business Services.
- Construction.
- Consulting.
- Consumer Services.
- Education.
- Energy-related fields.
- Engineering.
- Environment.
- Financial Planning.
- Health Care.
- Information Technology.
- Leisure and Recreation.
- Multimedia.
- Skilled Trades.

Source: Adrienne Warren, Scotiabank senior economist, as quoted by Steve Erwin, "Vital growth in high-skilled jobs forecast," *Toronto Star* (August 29, 2003), p. B4.

Some of Canada's large, high-profile corporations have eliminated thousands of jobs. One example of these reductions are the changes at Bombardier. In the period 2001–02, Bombardier announced a layoff of more than 3,800 workers in the aerospace group with the possibility of more to come.

While the popular press focuses on "Big Business," small businesses and mid-sized firms are expected to create most of the job growth in the foreseeable future. In 2001, small and medium-sized enterprises accounted for 77 percent of total employment. It is suggested that the biggest growth in management positions (and jobs in general) will be in smaller, rapidly growing organizations, especially technology companies. We believe that a strong small business provides a unique employment opportunity for the new graduate. Supervisors in small firms may be given the opportunity to gain broader and more diverse experience than those in larger firms.

Changing Technology and Business Conditions

Many business organizations have been completely revamped because of technological advances, computers, robotics, automation, changing markets, and other competitive influences that demand both internal and external adaptations.

Computer skills are a must for those seeking careers in management. Computers now give managers access to a tremendous amount of information—information that is necessary for making effective decisions. Information technology allows people to be no more than a few seconds away from anybody else in communication terms. This alters the traditional mode of face-to-face communication and the way things are done. The Computer Revolution will continue to be apparent throughout most organizations. Most supervisors have high-powered notebook-style computers and personal data assistants that allow them to access information and communicate virtually around the clock. Advances in hardware, software, and communication technology require supervisors to be computer literate as part of their day-to-day responsibilities.

A major problem that is likely to worsen is that of too much information. With the growth of communication capabilities, including e-mail, voice mail, instant messaging, and telephone and other devices, supervisors are being inundated by an estimated 200 or more messages sent and received every day. Many individuals have difficulty with the extra work generated by these messages, many of which waste time. The ability to properly manage information will be another of the many demanding responsibilities of supervisors both now and in the future.[13]

Since it is difficult to forecast specifically when and how technological change will affect a supervisor's position, every supervisor will have to continue to be broadly educated. Supervisors will have to prepare themselves and their employees, both technologically and psychologically, for anticipated changes. Those who keep up to date with change will unquestionably be more valuable to their organizations.

Global Challenges

Global challenges will continue to affect supervisors. Substantial investment has been made in Canadian firms by Americans, British, Germans, Swiss, Japanese, and others. Identifying the various cultural, value system, and work ethic differences is beyond the scope of this text. However, supervisors must recognize that management practices differ culturally and structurally in these firms compared with Canadian-owned and -operated firms. Within Canada, we even find significant cultural differences between the francophone and anglophone populations.

Low wages and other factors that provide a competitive advantage may entice Canadian firms to move their production facilities to locations such as Asia, Eastern Europe, Korea, South America, Africa, or Mexico. To be successful in foreign countries, Canadian firms must make a strong effort to understand the cultural customs in these environments. Over half of the world's population lives in Asia and a majority of that population is under the age of 25, which is dramatically different from the rest of the world.

To understand the potential of global competition, consider the case of General Motors (GM). GM has become Mexico's largest private employer with 75,000 employees. In Juarez, GM provides on-site education and volleyball courts, organizes Mother's Day parties, and sponsors a Mexican folk-dance troupe. The employees are provided free transportation and two meals a day. In return, management has been able to run the plants almost exactly as it wishes, with virtually no work rules. On the other hand, the impact of GM's relocation can be seen through the thousands of people unemployed, and vacant lots and buildings, in its previous locations in the United States and Canada.[14]

Work Scheduling and Employment Conditions

General working conditions are changing and will continue to evolve. Historically, approximately 60 percent of employed Canadians worked the traditional Monday through Friday workweek. In the future, fewer employees will be working the standard nine-to-five day because of the projected growth in jobs with evening, night, and weekend shifts.

Contingent worker
A part-time, temporary, or contract employee supplied on an "as needed" basis by an external agency for a specified period of time and for a fee.

Restructured companies will employ more part-time employees. The new contingent worker represents a quarter of the total employment base. **Contingent workers** are either temporary, part-time, or contract employees. This "interim" workforce consists of people who can be called in or sent home depending on the employer's needs. For a fee, agencies supply qualified employees to the firm. The firm does not incur recruiting costs, training costs, or other costs associated with long-term employment. But the per-hour cost of contract labour is usually higher than that of regular employees, largely due to the percentage paid to the employment agency. When a project is finished or business necessity dictates (e.g., orders decline), the contract employees leave.[15] More employers will expand the use of such workers in the future in their efforts to reduce wage and benefit costs associated with full-time employees. How will the supervisor motivate employees who consider themselves, at best, transient—that is, just working at the present firm until something better comes along? Numerous studies have indicated that lower productivity and increased accidents occur when employees are not fully committed to their jobs. Motivating employees who are not fully committed will be another supervisory challenge.

Two-tier wage system
Paying new employees at a lower rate than more senior employees.

Another thorny issue is that of the **two-tier wage system,** which is a company policy to pay inexperienced workers a lower wage than more experienced workers. An example of a two-tiered wage system is at the Detroit/Windsor Tunnel Corporation where new hires are paid a lower wage and never obtain more than 75 percent of current wage levels. In some situations, the supervisor will be challenged to motivate a workforce that includes employees who are compensated differently for doing essentially the same work.

Corporate Culture and Ethical Conduct

Although top-level management creates the overall vision and philosophy for the firm, **corporate culture** is the set of shared purposes, values, and beliefs that employees have about their organization. To provide a foundation for the type of corporate culture that is desired, many companies develop mission statements and ethical-conduct statements.

For example, when Hewlett-Packard was formed, David Packard and William R. Hewlett formulated a vision that was later stated in the Hewlett-Packard (HP) Statement of Corporate Objectives:

The achievements of an organization are the result of the combined efforts of each individual in the organization working toward common objectives. These objectives should be realistic, should be clearly understood by everyone in the organization, and should reflect the organization's basic character and personality.[16]

Bill Hewlett frequently described the "HP Way" as follows: "I feel that in general terms it is the policies and actions that flow from the belief that men and women want to do a good job, a creative job, and that if they are provided the proper environment they will do so."[17] This philosophy has been prominently communicated to every employee and as such has become a way of life at Hewlett-Packard. Today, Hewlett-Packard is headed by Chairman and Chief Executive Officer Carly S. Fiorina, who led the company through a highly publicized 2002 merger with Compaq Computer Corporation. The challenge for the "new HP" will be to ensure that the strong corporate culture that contributed to its earlier success can survive in the new corporate structure. Figure 1-8 further describes the strong corporate culture at Hewlett-Packard.

Figure 1-9 (page 18) is an example of a values and beliefs statement that was developed by the top management of the hospital described in Case 1-1 at the end of this chapter. As a new emergency room department supervisor in that case, Charlotte Kelly can use this type of values and beliefs statement as a reference point for many of the decisions that will confront her. Supervisors are major influencers in determining the direction of the corporate culture in their departments. Supervisors play a significant role in informing, educating, and setting examples for ethical behaviour. Although ethical behaviour and fair dealing have always been foundations for good management, it is clear that ethical conduct has become one of the most challenging issues confronting businesses today. The news is filled with stories about the misuse of business power and the contention that corrupt business practices are the primary way to earn profits. In the future, as never before, it will be important that ethical behaviour and fair dealing are at the forefront of good management practices, beginning at the supervisory level. A supervisor's personal ethics are also an important guide for making decisions when facing ethical problems in the workplace.

Other Governmental and Societal Issues

Other emerging governmental and societal issues will continue to complicate the supervisory management position in the future. For example, numerous environmental concerns remain as serious long-term problems for business, government, and the general public. Energy availability and costs may be determined by international and domestic political and economic changes. These types of issues and societal pressures often become part of business planning and operations.

FIGURE 1-8   The "HP Way!"

Stanford University classmates Bill Hewlett and Dave Packard founded HP in 1939. The company's first product, built in a Palo Alto, California, garage, was an audio oscillator—an electronic test instrument used by sound engineers. One of HP's first customers was Walt Disney Studios, which purchased eight oscillators to develop and test an innovative sound system for the movie *Fantasia*.

Hewlett-Packard's vigour comes in part from the management philosophy and values imparted over five decades by the founders. In Silicon Valley, where arrogance and braggadocio are common, HPers are generally known for being low-key, nice, earnest, and sincere. It's considered bad form at HP to trumpet one's personal achievements.

- Employees in the new HP share a passion for satisfying customers, an intense focus on teamwork, speed, and agility, and a commitment to trust and respect for all individuals.
- The typical senior manager began his or her HP career in a hands-on job.
- HP is structured into global, cross-functional teams that "own" their businesses and can react quickly to market changes. "Our profit-and-loss statement is like any other small company's," says Jim McDonnell, marketing manager for the network server division, which sells high-powered computers. In his slice of HP, he knows exactly what the costs are and where they come from—right down to the "tax" his division contributes for corporate overhead and HP's research and development.
- HP managers have an enviable degree of freedom. The company keeps experimenting with ways to extend autonomy to each employee. In the customer service centre where employees answer phones and respond to customers' questions, HP allows teams to pick their own supervisors. That gives employees a strong interest in seeing their manager succeed.
- The idea at HP is to lead by persuasion, not fiat; showing, not telling; pulling, not pushing. Integrity is key to the HP leadership style. Says Chairman and CEO Carly S. Fiorina, "I think leadership takes what I call a strong internal compass. And I use the term *compass* because what does a compass do? When the winds are howling, and the storms are raging, and sky is cloudy so you have nothing to navigate by, a compass tells you where true North is. And I think when a person is in a difficult situation, a lonely situation … you have to rely on that compass. Who am I? What do I believe? Do I believe we're doing the right things for the right reasons in the right ways? And sometimes that's all you have."
- Hewlett-Packard learned that while its managers resent being told what to do, they are not too proud to copycat good ideas. It's common practice to seek help from other divisions that have been conspicuously successful. "I've never seen someone say no if you ask for help," says Carolyn Ticknor, an HP employee.

Sources: Adapted from HP corporate website, www.hp.com; text of interview with Carly Fiorina found at www.hp.com/hpinfo/execteam/speeches/fiorina/churchill03.html (retrieved September 22, 2003); Stratford Smith, "How Tomorrow's Best Leaders Are Learning Their Stuff," *Fortune* (November 27, 1995), pp. 90–102; and Alan Deutschman, "How H-P Continues to Grow and Grow," *Fortune* (May 2, 1994), pp. 90–100.

FIGURE 1-9   A sample values and belief statement.

Every Pine Village Hospital employee is important. With mutual respect, trust, and open communication, we will work together to create an organization that consistently meets or exceeds the expectations of patients, visitors, physicians, employees, and other stakeholders.

Pine Village Hospital is dedicated to providing consistently superior services to all of our patients. We believe in fostering an environment that encourages superior service and performance.

We believe that superior service and performance result from

- A clear understanding of goals.
- Effective communication.
- Proper application of skills, knowledge, and ability.
- Wise use of resources.
- High standards of conduct.
- A safe and aesthetically pleasing work environment.
- Shared involvement in attaining goals.

A list of federal legislation that affects the supervisor's job is found in the Appendix at the end of this book. In addition, provincial and local governments have laws and regulations that affect businesses. The effect of such legislation can be quite costly, and organizations may be required to change their methods of operation in order to comply.

Supervisors are influenced both directly and indirectly by such governmental requirements, and they must continue to stay abreast of any legislation that may influence their operations. Furthermore, supervisors must be sensitive to pressures exerted by special-interest groups. Consumer groups, in particular, have demanded better products and services from business, labour, and government. Environmentalists seek to influence business decisions that may have an adverse environmental impact. Some parents of young children will demand that their employers provide day-care facilities so that they can better combine their family and job responsibilities. It seems likely that numerous other permanent and temporary special-interest groups will continue to place community and political demands on firms in ways that will affect how supervisors will operate in the future.

Workplace Incivility and Difficult People

Typical workers spend most of their waking hours in close contact with others in the workplace. Whenever people convene in one location, eight hours a day or more and often during trying economic times, their different personalities, expectations, and needs may clash from time to time. Many students can relate to the playground bully of their childhood. In some instances, the playground bully has grown up and now works alongside us. The dilemma for many employees is, "How can you expect me to get along with that troublemaker?" Two recent studies report that "rude behaviour is on the rise in the workplace and can undermine an organization's effectiveness."[18]

Almost everyone has been on the receiving end of a rude person's temper. Whether crude or impolite behaviour takes place behind closed doors or out in the open, it directly affects the recipient and lowers group morale. Who are these people? In his book, *Coping with Difficult People*, Robert M. Bramson writes:

They are the hostile customers or coworkers, the indecisive, vacillating bosses, and the overagreeable subordinates of the world who are constant headaches to work with. Although their numbers are small, their impact is large. They are responsible for absenteeism, significant losses in productivity, and lost customers or clients. They frustrate and demoralize those unlucky enough to have to work with them, and they are difficult to understand. Worst of all, they appear immune to all the usual methods of communication and persuasion designed to convince them or help them to change their ways.[19]

Various authors have given numerous titles to identify types of difficult people. Typically, employees arrive in an organization with little or no foundation in how to handle difficult people.

Empowerment and Employee Participation in Decision Making

Whether or not a labour union or employee association represents employees in an organization, many employees will want more from their jobs and will demand a voice in decisions that concern their employment. This should not be objectionable to a supervisor. In fact, once supervisors realize that their employees have something to contribute, they will welcome employee participation in decisions rather than fear it.

Empowerment | **Empowerment** means giving employees the authority and responsibility to
Giving employees the authority and responsibility to accomplish organizational objectives. | achieve objectives. Opportunities to make suggestions and participate in decisions affecting their jobs can and should be supported. However, some supervisors become worried when workers challenge what have traditionally been management rights, and they believe that certain areas should be beyond employee challenge. Many quality circles and other participatory management approaches of the last decade failed, in part, because managers failed to listen to the suggestions of employees, did not act on those suggestions in a timely fashion, or felt threatened by those suggestions. Nevertheless, there will continue to be pressure from employees, labour unions, and other groups for more influence in decisions pertaining to the workplace.

Participative management
Allowing employees to be involved in organizational decision making.

Many supervisors have become accustomed to the practice of **participative management,** which essentially means a willingness to permit employees to influence or share in managerial decisions. Learning to react to this in a positive way should improve supervisors' and their companies' performance.[20]

Although forecasts are always precarious, experienced supervisors will recognize that these trends have already begun. Supervisors must understand and plan for them. Empowerment and participative management will be discussed further in Chapter 6.

---

3 | THE PERSON IN THE MIDDLE

Summarize the challenges supervisors face in fulfilling managerial roles.

The supervisory position is a difficult and demanding role. Supervisors are "people in the middle"—the principal link between higher-level managers and employees. A supervisor is a first-level manager, that is, a manager in charge of entry-level and other departmental employees. Every organization, whether a retail store, manufacturing firm, hospital, or government agency, has someone who fills this role.

Throughout this text we use the terms *worker, employee,* and *subordinate* interchangeably to refer to individuals who report to supervisors or managers. An increasing number of companies are using the term *associate* or *team member* instead of *employee.* Regardless of the term used, employees may view their supervisor as the management of the organization; the supervisor is their primary contact with management. Employees expect a supervisor to be technically competent and to be a good leader who can show them how to get the job done.

But the supervisor also must be a competent subordinate to higher-level managers. In this role the supervisor must be a good follower. Moreover, the supervisor is expected to maintain satisfactory relationships with supervisors in other departments. Thus, a supervisor's relationship to other supervisors is that of a colleague who must cooperate and coordinate his or her department's efforts with those of others in order to reach the overall goals of the organization.

In general, the position of any supervisor has two main requirements. First, the supervisor must have a good working knowledge of the jobs to be performed. Second—and more significantly—the supervisor must be able to manage, that is, run, the department. It is the managerial competence of a supervisor that usually determines the effectiveness of his or her performance.

4	MANAGERIAL SKILLS MAKE THE DIFFERENCE

Explain why effective supervisors should possess a variety of skills.

Some supervisors appear to be under constant pressure and continuously do the same work their subordinates do. They are getting by, although they feel overburdened. These supervisors endure long hours, may be very devoted to their jobs, and are willing to do everything themselves. They want to be effective, although they seldom have enough time to actually supervise. Other supervisors appear to be on top of their jobs, and their departments function in a smooth and orderly manner. These supervisors find time to sit at their desks at least part of the day, and they are able to keep their paperwork up to date. What is the difference?

Of course, some supervisors are more capable than others, just as some mechanics are better than others. If we compare two maintenance supervisors who are equally good mechanics, have similar equipment under their care, and operate under approximately the same conditions, why might one be more effective than the other? The answer is that effective supervisors manage their departments in a manner that gets the job done through their people instead of doing the work themselves. The difference between a good supervisor and a poor one, assuming that their technical skills are similar, is the difference in their managerial skills.

The managerial aspects of the supervisor's position too often have been neglected in the selection and development of supervisors. Typically, people are selected for supervisory positions on the basis of their technical competence, their seniority or past performance, and their willingness to work hard. When appointed supervisors, they are expected to assume responsibilities of management, even though their previous job did not involve these skills. New supervisors must make a conscious effort to develop their managerial skills by learning from their own manager, through company training programs, or by any other avenues available to them.

We have grouped the managerial skills needed by supervisors into the following six major classifications:

1. **Technical skills:** the ability to perform the actual jobs within the supervisor's area of responsibility.
2. **Human relations skills:** the ability to work with and through people; includes the ability to motivate team members and the ability to remain open-minded.
3. **Administrative skills:** the ability to plan, organize, and coordinate the activities of a work group.
4. **Conceptual skills:** the ability to obtain, interpret, and apply the information needed to make sound decisions.
5. **Political skills:** the savvy to ascertain the hidden rules of the organizational game and to recognize the roles various people play in getting things done outside formal organizational channels.
6. **Emotional intelligence skills:** the "intelligent use of your emotions to help guide your behaviour and thinking in ways that enhance your results. You can maximize your emotional intelligence by developing good communication skills, interpersonal expertise, and mentoring abilities."[21]

Chess master Bruce Pandolfini stresses that there are two basic forms of intelligence: (1) the ability to read other people and (2) the ability to understand one's self.[22] The notion of knowing oneself is not new. Unfortunately, it was not too many years ago that people believed you could take "the best mechanics" or "the best salespeople," give them the title of "supervisor" or "manager," and success would automatically follow. Clearly, this is not the case. Hagberg Consulting Group's 12-year study of over 2,500 senior managers found that 25 percent of those on the rise in high-tech companies lacked "people skills" such as the ability to motivate teams or open-mindedness.[23] Apparently technical skills alone are not sufficient.

The Need for Technical Competence in Supervision

Nevertheless, a competent supervisor must thoroughly understand the specific, technical aspects of the department's operations. Perhaps the supervisor actually is the most skilled person within the department and is able to do a quicker, more efficient job than most of the subordinates. Yet the supervisor must learn to avoid stepping in and personally doing the employees' jobs except for the purpose of instruction or in short-handed or emergency situations. In some companies a union contract may restrict supervisors from performing employees' work. The responsibility of a supervisor as a manager is to see that the employees do their jobs properly. As a manager, the supervisor must plan, guide, and supervise.

In some organizations supervisors are considered to be "working supervisors," or "lead persons," whose responsibilities include performing certain jobs within their departments. Supervisors of very small departments, for example, often are expected to perform a share of the workload assigned to their units. Similarly, supervisors in retail stores and in many service occupations typically work along with their employees to accomplish the work. Nevertheless, whenever a supervisor is occupied with a job that could be performed by an employee, the supervisor's managerial functions necessarily are neglected.

At the other extreme, some departments are involved in varied and complex operations in which individual jobs may be quite diversified and even specialized. In these situations it would be impossible for a supervisor to comprehend the exact details of each job. However, it remains important for the supervisor to at least understand the broad technical aspects of each job under his or her supervision—and to know where to get help when needed.

Managerial Skills Can Be Learned and Developed

Many people believe that good managers, like good athletes, are born, not made. Much research has indicated that this belief is generally incorrect, even though it is true that people are born with different potential and that, to some degree, heredity does play a role in intelligence. An athlete who is not endowed with natural physical advantages is not likely to run 100 metres in record time. On the other hand, many individuals who are so-called "natural athletes" have not come close to that goal either.

Most superior athletes have developed their natural endowments into mature skills by practice, learning, effort, and experience. The same holds true for a good manager. The skills involved in managing are as learnable as the skills used in playing golf. It does take time, effort, and determination for a supervisor to develop managerial skills. Supervisors will make some mistakes, but people learn from mistakes as well as from successes. By applying the principles discussed in this text, the supervisor can develop the skills that make the supervisory job a challenging and satisfying career.

Throughout the text there are various activities designed to reinforce the concepts presented. Tips, suggestions, and cases will be available to allow you to practise the skills being presented. These tools do not guarantee supervisory success, however. For example, if you wanted to learn to play golf, you could take lessons from Butch Harmon, Tiger Woods' teacher.[24] But you would also need the proper tools (e.g., the right clubs) and time to practise, learn from your mistakes, and make corrections. There is one major difference between the beginning golfer and the newly appointed supervisor. Unlike beginning golfers, who can go to the driving range or the practice green to work on their games, newly appointed supervisors are on the job and have little opportunity for trial and error. To get the job done right, the supervisor must avoid some common mistakes. As you read this book, consider our suggestions and remember that the challenge for supervisors is to stay on the path of continuous improvement.

Benefits from Better Supervisory Management

You may recall from Figure 1-1 that there are many benefits accruing to the effective supervisor. A supervisor has daily opportunities to apply managerial principles on the job. Proper application of the principles will contribute to a smoother-functioning department in which the work gets done on time and the workers contribute toward stated objectives more willingly and enthusiastically. Thus, the supervisor will be on top of the job instead of being consumed by it. Supervisors who manage well are able to make suggestions to higher-level managers and to other supervisors. Effective supervisors become aware of the needs and objectives of other departments as well as the interrelationships between those other departments and their own. They seek to work in closer harmony with colleagues who supervise other departments. Briefly, better supervisory management means doing a more effective job with much less stress and strain.

In addition to direct benefits, there are indirect benefits to better supervisory management. The supervisor who manages well will become capable of handling larger and more complicated assignments, which could lead to more responsible and higher-paying positions within the managerial hierarchy. Managerial skills are applicable in any organization and at all managerial levels, regardless of where a supervisor's future career may lead.

5	**FUNCTIONS OF MANAGEMENT**

Define management and discuss how the primary managerial functions are interrelated.

Management
Getting objectives accomplished with and through people.

Enabler
The person who does the things necessary to enable employees to get the job done.

The term *management* has been defined in many ways. In general, **management** is the process of getting things accomplished with and through people by guiding and motivating their efforts toward common objectives.

Successful managers will assure you that their employees are their most important asset. Most successful managers recognize that they are only as good as the people they supervise. As illustrated in Figure 1-10, the supervisor should act as an **enabler**—someone who does what is necessary to enable employees to be the best they can be. In most endeavours, one person can accomplish relatively little. Therefore, individuals join forces with others to attain mutual goals. In a business, top-level managers are responsible for achieving the goals of the organization, but this requires the efforts of all subordinate managers and employees. Those who hold supervisory positions significantly influence the effectiveness with which people work together and use available resources to attain stated goals. The role of a supervisor is to make sure that assigned tasks are accomplished with and through the help of employees. Figure 1-11 (page 25) provides some supervisory tips that can assist the supervisor in fulfilling this role.

The Managerial Functions Are the Same in All Managerial Positions

The managerial functions of a supervisory position are similar, whether they involve supervision of a production line, sales force, laboratory, or small office. Moreover, the primary managerial functions are the same regardless of the level within the hierarchy of management. It does not matter whether one is a first-level supervisor, a middle-level manager, or part of top-level management. Managerial functions are the same whether the supervisor is working in a profit-making firm, a nonprofit organization, or a government office. Supervisors, as well as other managers, perform the same basic managerial functions in all organizations. In this textbook we classify these functions under the major categories of planning, organizing, staffing, leading, and controlling. The following description of these functions is general and brief since most of the book is devoted to discussing their application—particularly at the supervisory level.

Planning

Planning
Determining what should be done.

The initial managerial function—determining what should be done in the future—is called **planning.** It consists of setting goals, objectives, policies, procedures, and other plans needed to achieve the purposes of the organization. In planning, the manager chooses a course of action from various alternative courses that are available. Planning is primarily conceptual in nature. It means thinking before acting, looking ahead and preparing for the future, laying out in advance the road to be followed, and thinking about what and how the job should be done. It includes collecting and sorting information from numerous

FIGURE 1-10
The supervisor's multiple roles as an enabler.

sources and using it to make decisions. Not only does planning include deciding what, how, when, and by whom work is to be done, but also the development of "what if" scenarios.

Many supervisors find that they are constantly confronted with one crisis after another. The probable reason for this is that they neglect to plan; they do not look much beyond the day's events. It is every supervisor's responsibility to plan, and this cannot be delegated to someone else. Certain specialists, such as a budget officer, a production scheduler, or an engineer, may provide the supervisor with assistance in planning. But it is up to each supervisor, as the manager of a department, to make specific departmental plans that coincide with the general objectives established by higher-level management.

Planning is the managerial function that comes first, and, as the supervisor proceeds with other managerial functions, planning continues. Previous plans are revised and different alternatives are chosen as the need arises. This is particularly true as a supervisor evaluates the results of previous plans and adjusts future plans accordingly.

FIGURE 1-11　　Supervisory tips—The E-Z route for supervisory success.

- Above all, supervisors should do all of the things necessary to **enable** employees to be the best they can be at their assigned tasks.
- Supervisors must foster and sustain a commitment to **excellence**.
- Employees need to know what is **expected** in the way of performance.
- Supervisors should **establish** common goals and purpose.
- Employees must be **educated**, that is, acquire the requisite job skills through coaching and/or training.
- Employees must be **equipped**, that is, have the necessary tools, supplies, and equipment to do the job.
- Employees need to be **encouraged** to see things that need to be done and do them.
- Employees should be **empowered** so that they have the authority and responsibility to achieve objectives.
- Supervisors should nurture an **exciting** workplace where employees can find meaning and fulfillment of their individual needs.
- Employees should **experience** a variety of tasks and thus become experienced in many areas that use a variety of skills.
- Supervisors should **engage** their employees in two-way communication so that understanding takes place.
- Supervisors should keep their **emotions** under control.
- Supervisors should possess **empathy**, that is, understand their employees' feelings, needs, and concerns.
- Supervisors should **enthusiastically exalt** employees when the job is well done.

Organizing

Once plans have been made, the organizing function primarily answers the question, "How will the work be divided and accomplished?" This means that the supervisor defines the various job duties and groups these activities into distinct areas, sections, units, or teams. The supervisor must specify the duties required, assign them, and, at the same time, provide subordinates with the authority needed to carry out their tasks. **Organizing** means arranging and distributing work among members of the work group to accomplish the organization's goals.

Organizing
Arranging and distributing work among members of the work group to accomplish the organization's goals.

Staffing

The managerial tasks of recruiting, selecting, orienting, and training employees are grouped within the function called staffing. This function includes appraising the performance of employees, promoting employees where appropriate, and providing them with further opportunities for development. In addition, **staffing** includes devising an equitable compensation system and rates of pay. Some activities involved in the staffing function are handled by the human resources (or personnel) department in many companies. For example, the human resources department and top-level managers establish the compensation system. Supervisors generally do not perform this task. However, day-to-day responsibility for essential aspects of the staffing function remains with the supervisor.

Staffing
The tasks of recruiting, selecting, orienting, training, appraising, promoting, and compensating employees.

Leading means guiding employees toward accomplishing objectives. It is the day-to-day process around which all supervisory performance revolves.

Ryan McVay/Photodisc Red/Getty Images

Leading

Leading
The managerial function of guiding employees toward accomplishing organizational objectives.

Leading means guiding the activities of employees toward accomplishing objectives. The leading function of management involves guiding, teaching, and supervising subordinates. This includes developing the abilities of employees to their maximum potential by directing and coaching them effectively. It is not sufficient for a supervisor just to plan, organize, and have enough employees available. The supervisor must attempt to motivate employees as they go about their work. Leading is the day-to-day process around which all supervisory performance revolves. Leading is also known as directing, motivating, or influencing since it plays a major role in employee morale, job satisfaction, productivity, and communication. It is through this function that the supervisor seeks to create a climate that is conducive to employee satisfaction and at the same time achieves the objectives of the department. Finding ways to satisfy the needs of a diverse employee workforce is a significant challenge. In fact, probably most of a supervisor's time is spent on this function since it is the function around which departmental performance revolves.

Controlling

Controlling
Ensuring that actual performance is in line with intended performance and taking corrective action if necessary.

The managerial function of **controlling** involves ensuring that actual performance is in line with intended performance and taking corrective action as necessary. Here, too, the importance of planning as the first function of management should be obvious. It would not be possible for a supervisor to determine whether work was proceeding properly if there were no plans against which to check. If plans or standards are superficial or poorly conceived, the controlling function is limited. Thus, controlling means not only making sure that objectives are achieved, but also taking corrective action in case of failure to achieve planned objectives. It also means revising plans if circumstances require it.

The Continuous Flow of Managerial Functions

The five managerial functions can be viewed as a circular, continuous process. In Figure 1-12 we can see that the functions flow into each other and that each affects the performance of the others. At times there is no clear line to mark where one function ends and the other begins. Also, it is not possible for a supervisor to set aside a certain amount of time for one or another function since the effort spent in each function will vary as conditions and circumstances change. But there is no doubt that planning must come first. Without plans, the supervisor cannot organize, staff, lead, or control.

Managerial Functions Relative to Time and Position

The time and effort devoted to each of the managerial functions will usually vary depending on a person's level within the management hierarchy. Many studies have reported that top-level executives spend most of their time planning and controlling and less time organizing, staffing, and leading. Typically, supervisors spend more time leading and controlling and less time planning, organizing, and staffing (see Figure 1-13).

FIGURE 1-12
The circular concept illustrates the close and continuous relationship between the management functions.

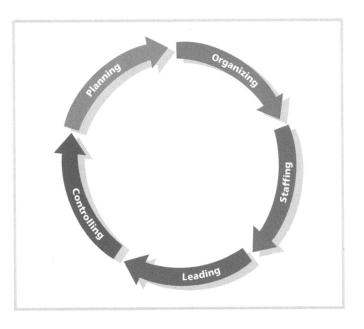

FIGURE 1-13
The time involved in
managerial functions
varies by a person's
position in the
management hierarchy.

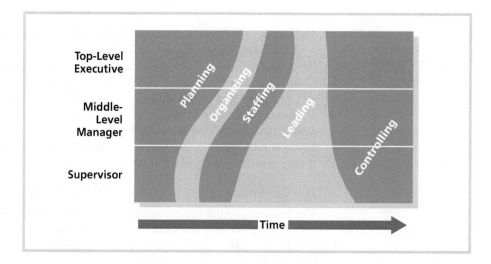

For example, first-line supervisors' plans will be more limited in span and magnitude than those of high-level managers. A top executive may plan to buy equipment involving millions of dollars and affecting the entire organization, perhaps for years to come. By comparison, the supervisor typically plans for using employees, equipment, and material for shorter periods of time involving restricted amounts of money and other resources. The top executive usually depends upon subordinate managers to carry out the organization's activities and thus spends a minimum of time in direct supervision. The first-line supervisor, however, is concerned with getting the job done each day and has to spend considerable time directing and leading the efforts of employees.

To summarize: all managers perform essentially the same managerial functions, regardless of the nature of the organization or their level in the hierarchy. The time and effort involved in each of these functions will vary depending on the rung of the management ladder the manager occupies. Of course, at times this may also depend on the scope and urgency of the situation at hand.

WHAT CALL DID YOU MAKE?

Every chapter in this text ends with a section called "What Call Did You Make?" This section refers back to the case problem posed in the section titled "You Make the Call" that appears at the beginning of each chapter. In this and other concluding sections, we will provide our analysis and recommendations, which you should first compare with your own before considering and discussing relevant areas of agreement and differences.

As Leslie McGuire, you are in the enviable position of having a job opportunity appear somewhat "out of the blue." Because you have been working part-time at Brant Coatings Ltd. you have some background information about the organization and its people. However, you need more information about the potential job opportunity and would be well advised to meet with the plant manager tomorrow to learn more.

Before your meeting, you should clarify your short- and longer-term career and personal goals. Many people simply "fall into" a job and are then surprised to find that it doesn't suit them. You do not seem to have formulated any specific career goals and your job search appears to have been unfocused. What kind of position are you looking for? What do you enjoy doing, and what strengths do you have? By engaging in a bit of self-analysis, you will be better able to decide whether the job at Brant Coatings is a good match for you.

Next, you need to clarify whether you are interested in supervisory management. Figure 1-1 described some of the "pluses" and "minuses" of the supervisory role. How do you feel about the rewards and stresses that you may encounter? Are you up for the challenge? Some people are excited about the possibility of leading a work group. Others would prefer to work independently and not be responsible for leading a team. Which statement best describes you? You seem to have a good rapport with your supervisor, Colleen Grenier. You may want to meet with Grenier or any other supervisors you may know to discuss their experiences in supervision and to learn more about what you could expect in this role.

Making the transition to supervisor can be particularly challenging when one is promoted from the front lines of the organization. It is particularly difficult to become the supervisor of people who were formerly your coworkers. This may or may not be an issue at Brant Coatings. The plant manager wants to talk to you about supervising on the night shift, and these would be employees that you have likely not worked closely with in the past. You will, however, be scrutinized closely by people who see you as the "new kid." There are likely some experienced production workers who may also be interested in the supervisory job. If you are promoted, you will need to ensure that you engage in some team building early in your mandate to ensure that these people are brought on side. If some of the front-line workers are "very set in their ways" you will have to be careful about how you go about implementing change, especially in the early days. Participatory management styles will be discussed later in the text. You may want to review strategies for ensuring that any changes you implement are fully supported by your team.

In addition to clarifying your career goals, you should also draft a list of specific questions that you would like to ask the plant manager. For example, you may want to know more about the specific areas of responsibility you would have, how much latitude you would have in implementing production efficiencies, and so on. Think about the specific information you need, and write your questions down.

The job of night shift supervisor may be an excellent way to gain some managerial experience. It was pointed out in this chapter's Contemporary Issue box that people generally do not expect "jobs for life" in the same organization. It is useful to realize that the skills that you can learn in supervisory management will certainly be transferable to other positions in other industries. If your goal is to own your own business some day, it is likely that you would have people working for you and supervisory skills would certainly be useful. Think about your longer-term career goals and decide how well this position is aligned with those goals.

You have an exciting job prospect in front of you. Engage in some self-analysis and gather as much information as you can to determine whether the job is a good match for you at this stage in your career.

SUMMARY

 Supervisors are the first tier of management. They manage entry-level and other departmental employees. New ways of managing employees will be the supervisor's challenge. In a rapidly changing business environment, the success of the supervisor will rest in his or her ability to balance the requirements for high work performance with the diverse needs of the workforce.

Supervisory management focuses primarily on the management of people. For many people, being a supervisor provides a variety of satisfying experiences. However, what one person sees as an opportunity and a reason for accepting the supervisory challenge, others may see as a negative. Among these are the challenge of getting diverse people to work together, the increased responsibility that comes with climbing the management hierarchy, and the unpredictable nature of the job. Being a supervisor is a demanding position that often places the supervisor in the middle of organizational pressures and conflict. A supervisor must endeavour to reconcile the needs of the organization with the needs of employees, which is often an elusive goal.

In addition, major environmental factors affect everything the organization does. These factors are not static; the whole world is changing rapidly, and some people do not want to deal with change.

 Many factors and trends in the workforce will have an impact on how most organizations operate. The workforce will grow at a somewhat faster rate than the overall population, and the age composition of the workforce will change. Women and minorities will continue to enter the workforce in increasing numbers, and they will be utilized more fully than in the past, including further advancement in supervisory and management positions. Substantial numbers of part-time employees and contract employees will be in the workplace. The more diverse workforce will create numerous challenges (e.g., multicultural and multilingual differences, family obligations versus job obligations). The workforce generally will consist of more college and university graduates, but many other people will not be prepared educationally to qualify for available employment opportunities.

Occupational and industry trends, changing technology and business conditions, and the competition from the global marketplace will be significant influences on supervisory management. Government laws and regulations will continue to have a major impact on the policies and activities of most organizations.

Because of increased incivility and even workplace violence, more firms will establish programs and procedures to help supervisors recognize the symptoms of problem employees.

Supervisors will have to be sensitive to existing and expected employee trends. For example, more employees than ever before will expect their jobs to have greater personal meaning to them as individuals. It is likely that supervisors will have to be somewhat flexible in their approaches to managing. Employees will continue to expect a greater voice in workplace decision making and to be empowered.

Supervisors are the "people in the middle." Employees see their supervisors as being management, but supervisors are subordinates to their own managers at higher levels. To supervisors of other departments, they are colleagues who must be able to work collaboratively. Supervisors must have good working knowledge of the jobs being performed in their department and the ability to manage.

 The effective supervisor needs to possess administrative, conceptual, human relations, technical, political, and emotional intelligence skills. The supervisor must understand the technical aspects of the work being performed. When attempting to manage job performance, understanding employee needs is essential. "People skills" help the supervisor accomplish objectives with and through people. It is equally important for the supervisor to possess an understanding of the dynamics of the organization and to recognize organizational politics.

The skills are important to all levels of management. Most supervisors come to the job equipped with at least some of these skills. Supervisors have daily opportunities to apply managerial skills and must continually strive to develop those skills. Effective application of the skills will contribute to the accomplishment of organizational objectives and will allow the supervisor to stay on top of the job. Supervisors who effectively apply these skills will be able to contribute suggestions to higher-level managers and will be able to work in harmony with their colleagues. In short, the skilled supervisor will be a candidate for advancement and additional job responsibilities.

 While there are numerous definitions of management, we have defined *management* as the process of getting things accomplished through people by guiding and motivating their efforts toward common objectives. Supervisors should look at themselves as enablers, that is, as clarifying expectations for employees and giving employees the right tools, training, and opportunities to succeed. In short, supervisors should do all those things that enable their employees to be the best they can be—while achieving organizational objectives.

The five major managerial functions are planning, organizing, staffing, leading, and controlling. The functions are viewed as a continuous flow—that is, the functions flow into each other, and each affects the performance of the others.

Planning is the first function of management, and the performance of all other managerial functions depends on it. The five managerial functions are universal, regardless of the job environment, the activity involved, or a person's position in the management hierarchy. Typically, supervisors spend most of their time leading and controlling. A supervisor's planning will cover a much shorter time and narrower focus than that of a top-level executive.

QUESTIONS FOR DISCUSSION

1. What are some of the advantages of being a supervisor? What are some of the disadvantages?
2. Of those factors or trends projected to reshape the workplace, which will create the greatest challenge for supervisors? Why do you think so?
3. What adjustments will you have to make in order to effectively lead a diverse group of people?
4. Based upon your experience, do you agree that employees want more from their jobs and demand a voice in decisions that concern their employment? Discuss specific examples from your own experience that either support or refute this statement.

5. Define participative management. What advantages can be gained by a supervisor who practises participative management techniques? Are there any potential disadvantages to this style of management?

6. Is it necessary that a supervisor be able to perform all of the job functions in his or her department? Discuss.

7. Define corporate culture. Is it possible for a supervisor to create a "departmental culture" in his or her own area that is distinct from the prevailing corporate culture? Is this advisable? Explain.

8. Identify the major managerial skills needed by every supervisor. Why are these important? Are emotional skills more or less important than the other skills? Explain.

9. How would you respond to someone who says, "I really get along well with everyone. I think I would be a good supervisor"?

10. We suggest that supervisors should view themselves as enablers. This suggests that the supervisor should clarify the objectives that must be attained, provide the training and tools needed to complete the task, and get out of the way. Should "management by getting out of the way" be an appropriate philosophy of management? Why or why not?

SKILLS APPLICATIONS

Skills Application 1-1: Creating Your Own Supervisory Credo

Most students have employment experience and have been supervised by one or more people in their past. Think back to the supervisors you have worked for. How effectively did these people carry out their supervisory responsibilities?

a. Thinking about these supervisors from your past, create two lists—one identifying the things you will definitely *not* do as a supervisor, and one identifying the behaviours and practices you *will* want to exhibit as an effective supervisor.

b. There is a risk that when you are in a supervisory position you will drift away from your "Will Do" list from above. Some supervisors find that, in the face of the day-to-day pressures of the job, they sometimes lose the vision of the type of supervisor they want to be. One way to avoid losing your focus is to write your own supervisory credo—a personal statement of your own supervisory values and beliefs that can be referred to whenever you feel you are not living up to your own expectations. Using the Internet, research the topic of management credos, then, referring to your list from part (a) above, draft your own supervisory credo.

Skills Application 1-2: Understanding the Workforce Profile in Your Community

Statistics Canada is a federal government agency that compiles and publishes a wide range of useful statistics about many aspects of Canadian life.

a. Go the Statistics Canada website at www.statcan.ca, and familiarize yourself with the information that is available there, including "The Daily" and the "Canadian Statistics" tabs.

b. From the www.statcan.ca homepage, click on the "Community Profile" tab, and type the name of your city or town to access specific census information for your community. You will be provided with a wealth of information about the demographic makeup of your geographic area. Analyze the information about labour force participation rates, age profiles, and ethnic diversity in your community. How does your community profile compare to the demographic trends discussed in this chapter? What are the specific areas of similarity or difference?

Skills Application 1-3: Classifying Supervisory Activities

In this chapter, you were introduced to the managerial functions of planning, organizing, staffing, leading, and controlling. Below are some common supervisory activities. For each activity, indicate the primary managerial function:

a. Reviewing last week's staff productivity reports.
b. Conducting an interview for a vacant position.
c. Meeting with staff to discuss their ideas for solving a quality assurance problem.
d. Completing the final draft of your department's budget for next quarter.
e. Meeting with a supervisor from another department to discuss a problem of work duplication between your two departments.
f. Conducting a performance review meeting with one of your employees.

CASES

CASE 1-1

From Shift Leader to Management: Can I Make the Transition?

Pine Village Hospital (PVH) is one of four hospitals in a metropolitan area of more than 400,000 people (see Figure 1-9 for PVH's values and belief statement). Upon graduating from nursing school some 30 years ago, Charlotte Kelly began as a cardiac-care nurse in Hope, British Columbia. There she met her husband and began a family. Kelly was a full-time mother while her two children were going through school. Shortly after her youngest child graduated from high school, Kelly's husband was killed in an automobile accident. She moved to Pine Village to be near her sister and because PVH was looking for someone to be the admitting department's evening shift team leader. As a shift team leader, Kelly had limited authority and was not considered to be part of PVH's management team. The hours were not convenient, but it was the best job opportunity available. Pat Rekus, the admitting department supervisor, was encouraging and supportive.

Even with the difficult work schedule, Kelly was able to take some distance learning courses that enabled her to receive a certificate in medical records technology and to pursue a diploma in supervision and organizational leadership. She also found time to attend a series of noncredit leadership courses at the local college. The classes were taught by experienced instructors with relevant work experience. Her favourite instructor was Agnello Monetti, a middle-aged supervisor at a local company who incorporated many anecdotes into his classes. Monetti usually started each class with a current problem or an issue that required students to interact and expand on their supervisory perspectives. Kelly enjoyed this "team" or "collaborative" approach to learning, because her fellow classmates brought a variety of experiences to the class, and learned from one another.

One afternoon, Rekus summoned Kelly to her office. To Kelly's surprise, Bob Murphy, vice president of administration, was also present. Murphy began the conversation. "Charlotte, we are very pleased with the job you've done as the team leader on the evening shift. You are an excellent role model and a good listener. You have a reputation as someone who expects the best from people and does the things necessary to enable them to be the best they can be. Effective Monday morning, we want you to become the Emergency Department supervisor. You've earned a promotion to management. While this is a big step, we know that you will be able to handle this assignment, even though you haven't worked in the Emergency Department before. This position reports to me, and

I'll be available to help you if any problems arise." Rekus added, "Charlotte, you've done such a good job of cross-training your people and delegating, we'd like you to recommend your replacement."

When Kelly returned to her department, she was both exhilarated and a bit sobered by this offer. "Wow," she thought to herself. "This will be hard. Pat Rekus has been a great mentor. I learned a lot from her, but I wonder if I've got the right stuff to be in a supervisory management position. Do I really want all the headaches, responsibilities, and pressures that the Emergency Department supervisor has to deal with? Come to think of it, they never gave me a chance to turn it down."

On her way home, Kelly reflected on what lay before her. She had learned that Amy Talmadge had been fired as Emergency Department supervisor. The Emergency Department had become the subject of many employee jokes, and turnover was extremely high. Kelly had heard that Talmadge had the reputation of being an autocratic, demanding, and insensitive person. She had expected her employees to do as she demanded, and at times she was known to have criticized and embarrassed people in public. The Emergency Department consisted of a very diverse group of employees, which apparently had contributed to Talmadge's inability to get them to work together. Kelly thought to herself as she pulled into her garage, "I know some things not to do, but I'm not certain that I can make the transition from team leader to supervisor."

Questions for Discussion

1. What are the greatest difficulties Kelly faces as she begins the new job?
2. List Kelly's strengths and weaknesses related to making this transition.
3. If you were Kelly, what would you do to prepare for Monday's new assignment?
4. How might Bob Murphy and Pat Rekus go about ensuring that Kelly succeeds in her new position?
5. Internet Activity: Find three or four programs or strategies that Kelly could implement to reduce the high turnover.

CASE 1-2

The Socializing Supervisor

Indra Shahir was promoted to a supervisory position in the Metro Insurance Company's Operations Division. She was chosen for the position by the manager of operations, Ronnie Callahan, who felt Shahir was the ideal candidate for the position. Shahir had been hired five years earlier as a general-purpose employee. Metro cross-trained all new employees so they were capable in a variety of functions. Two other employees had been in the division for at least 10 years, but they had consistently expressed their dislike for any leadership responsibilities. In addition, Shahir's job performance ratings were very good, her attendance was near perfect, and she seemed to be well liked by her colleagues and others who knew her well.

When Callahan told Shahir that she was to become supervisor of the accident claims department, she asked him how she should handle the problem that her fellow employees now would be her subordinates. Callahan told her not to be concerned about this and that her former associates would soon accept the transition. Callahan also told Shahir that the company would send her to a supervisory management training program sponsored by a local college as soon as time became available.

After several months, however, Callahan was getting the impression that Shahir was not making the adjustment to her new position. Callahan was particularly concerned that he had observed Shahir socializing with her employees during lunch breaks, coffee breaks, and the like. Callahan had received reports that Shahir often socialized with several of her employees after work, including going to bars and to parties arranged by these employees.

Furthermore, Callahan had received a number of reports from managers and team leaders of other departments that the work performed by the accident claims department was not being performed as it should be. Several managers in the company told Callahan that the department employees spent too much time away from their work on longer than normal breaks and lunch periods. One manager told Callahan, "Since Indra became supervisor, there is little discipline in the department, and it's just a big social group that reluctantly does a little work."

After reviewing various productivity reports, Callahan realized that Shahir had not made a good adjustment to supervising employees in her department. He wondered how much of this was attributable to her lack of experience as a supervisor and worried that her former colleagues might be taking advantage of her. At the same time, Callahan was concerned that Shahir perhaps did not have the desire to disassociate herself from socializing and being a "buddy" to her employees. Callahan wondered what his next step should be.

Questions for Discussion

1. Evaluate the decision to promote Indra Shahir to supervisor. Discuss the problems associated with promoting anyone to team leader or supervisor over his or her former fellow employees.
2. Besides sending Shahir to a supervisory training program, what other actions could Callahan and Shahir have taken to prepare Shahir for the transition to the supervisory role?
3. Why is it dangerous for a supervisor to socialize with direct-report employees? Why does this leave a team leader or supervisor open to criticism, as exemplified in this case?
4. What should Callahan do? Consider all alternatives.

APPENDIX: GETTING INTO SUPERVISION

Job hunting is not usually easy. For some people, opportunities appear when they least expect them. For others, the road appears to be steep. Many individuals get their first supervisory positions from nonsupervisory jobs in the same organization. It may be in the same department, or in another area. They may have formally applied for the position or, like Leslie McGuire in the "You Make the Call" feature, had a manager recommend them.

If you are employed while going to school, it can be tough to find the time to do an effective job search for a position outside your current firm. In addition, you will have the added burden of being discreet—many employers take a dim view of employees who are seeking employment elsewhere; their loyalty and commitment are questioned. Do not make or receive job search–related calls at work. Advise prospective employers to contact you at home or through the campus placement office. Schedule interviews before or after work, or on your days off. Most importantly, do not leave your job until you have a new one.

A former student told one of the authors that she had sent her résumé to a blind advertisement—neither the firm nor its address was listed. Her immediate supervisor informed her that he had received her résumé and was wondering why she was unhappy with her current position. She had applied for a job similar to the one she currently had, but the advertisement listed broader responsibilities and sounded challenging. She was at a loss for words. She later left the organization, not for a better job but because she felt the supervisor never gave her a chance after that.

Where to Look for Information

As a student, you have access to a variety of sources of information to assist in a job search. Attend on-campus career fairs. Contact your professors, and ask for their advice and information about their industry contacts. Visit your college or university career centre for government publications, industry data, and specific information about potential employers in your area.

Many students find that networking is a useful strategy. A recent study found that employee referrals were the single largest source—30 percent to 40 percent—of new hires. That is at least double the number of people hired through job listings.[25] Meet and talk with personal and professional colleagues and friends to help you identify potential opportunities. Talk to people you know through school, family, or other activities to gather information and referrals. "I'm finishing my diploma in April and am looking for career opportunities," you might say. "Your company has a reputation of being a good place to work. Do you know of any opportunities there?" Such an approach could be a good networking start. A visit to the library or the Internet will turn up lots of information about an organization, such as annual reports, trade magazines, and newspaper articles. This information will give you a good picture of the company's financial position, management style, and future prospects. Increasingly, employers are listing jobs online and describe their products and services on websites. Figure 1-14 contains a partial list of online services. You can submit your résumé to databases that employers consult for candidates. But remember, an online search should be only one of your many job search strategies.

Make Yourself More Valuable

In general, we believe that the best way to get a supervisory position is to find ways to make yourself more valuable. Always try to improve yourself. For example, if you are a student, make yourself available for internships and co-ops, or perhaps volunteer for some type of meaningful activity. Volunteer experiences in community groups can give you ideas and practical experiences and can help you become more comfortable working with and leading groups of diverse people. Get involved in one or more student organizations on your campus. The benefits of applying your expertise and using opportunities to enhance your communication and leadership skills are invaluable.

Remember, too, that continuing your educational preparation is an ongoing challenge. Finishing an academic degree or diploma is only a start; consider going further by enrolling in further credit and noncredit programs that may enhance your technical, managerial, or supervisory knowledge. Increasingly, colleges and universities are offering online programs that can be taken at home via computer.

Finally, evaluate your SKAs and your past experience. When applying for any position and particularly for a supervisory one, you must discover the specific needs of the hiring organization and show how your SKAs can add value to the firm. The message? Be assertive enough, bold enough, and knock on enough doors (see Figure 1-15 on page 38) and you will ultimately be successful.

FIGURE 1-14   Sources for online job searches.

Canada WorkInfoNet at *www.workinfonet.ca* is a national, provincial, and territorial partnership that provides access to over 2,000 Canadian websites. It describes its mandate as "helping Canadians connect to the resources they need in the areas of jobs, work and recruiting; learning, education and training; occupations and careers; labour market information and outlook; self-employment; workplace issues and supports; and financial help and issues." This collaborative venture developed by public, private, and not-for-profit sectors is a great place to start. There are valuable links to provincial and territorial partner sites.

Globecareers.com, combined with Workopolis, calls itself "Canada's biggest job site." This Canada-only database provides more than 7,000 available jobs and has a Career Alert feature that will e-mail listings to you that match your profile.

Human Resources and Skills Development Canada at *www.hrsdc.gc.ca* provides a variety of resources such as career counselling information and a national job bank. Its most unique feature is the Electronic Labour Exchange. A database of available jobs is compared to the candidate's skill profile. With a match, the profile is forwarded to the potential employer.

CACEE WorkWeb at *www.cacee.com* is dedicated to helping students and recent graduates find meaningful employment. Its WorkWeb (created by the Canadian Association of Career Educators and Employers) provides job-search advice, links to employers, and access to government and professional home pages. It even includes information about the rights of the job seeker.

Monster Board offers access to information on more than 50,000 jobs worldwide. It will find job listings that match your profile and e-mail them to you once a week. Although most of its jobs are aimed at experienced candidates, it also has plenty of entry-level positions. Its much smaller Canadian site at *www.monster.ca* offers the same features.

Source: Mary Ellen Guffey, Kathleen Rhodes, Patricia Rogin, *Business Communication: Process and Product, Brief Canadian Edition* (Scarborough: Nelson, 2003), p. 366.

FIGURE 1-15   Career Tips—Keep on Knocking!

1. Look for a job in the right places.
   - Networks.
   - Bulletin boards or websites.
   - Newspaper classifieds.
   - Job fairs.
   - Recruiting firms.
   - Temporary agencies.
   - Individual employers.
2. Think like an employer.
   - Ask yourself the following question: "If I were the one hiring for a position, what would I want to see in a résumé?"
   - Who are you?
   - What do you know?
   - What have you done?
   - What have you accomplished?
   - Who can give you a good recommendation?
3. Prepare for the interview.
   - Research the company.
   - Find the gatekeepers, those people who may be in touch with those doing the hiring.
4. Be proactive.
   - Ask questions about the job or the company (e.g., which qualifications are most important for this position, what are the expectations of the ideal person for this job?).
   - Sell yourself.
5. After the interview.
   - Write a thank-you note to the interviewer.
6. Continuously seek ways to "sharpen your saw."
   - Join professional or industry associations.
   - Attend seminars and conferences.
   - Seek volunteer positions that will build your skills.

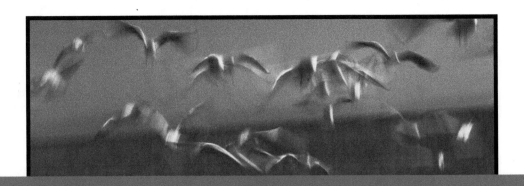

Chapter 2: Planning and Time Management

After studying this chapter you will be able to

1   Define planning and clarify why all management functions depend on planning.

2   Explain the concept of strategic planning.

3   Describe the supervisor's role in planning as related to other plans of the organization.

4   Discuss the need for well-defined organizational goals and objectives, particularly as they relate to the supervisor.

5   Explain management by objectives (MBO) and describe how it is applied.

6   Identify the major types of standing plans and explain how these are helpful in supervisory decision making.

7   Discuss the principal types of single-use plans in which supervisors play an important role.

8   Identify the benefits of supervisory planning.

9   Recognize the importance of planning for the unthinkable: crisis management.

10   Explain the role of planning in quality improvement.

11   Identify and describe two project scheduling and planning tools—Gantt charts and PERT.

12   Discuss the importance of time management, especially in reducing stress, and suggest techniques for supervisors to plan better use of their time.

You are Shannon O'Neill, transportation supervisor for the Middletown School Board. Your responsibilities include hiring, training, and evaluating all employees in the department; scheduling buses; purchasing all fuels and maintenance supplies; coordinating extracurricular activity transportation; and safely transporting 1,700 children to and from school each day. You are responsible for a fleet of 28 buses and a staff of 35 full- and part-time employees, including administrative staff, maintenance personnel, and school bus drivers.

When you became supervisor three years ago, you identified a need for better planning tools in the transportation department. The previous supervisor seemed to have a very short-term view of management, and you could find no evidence of any longer-term plans for improving the operations of the department. There were no forecasts to predict future busing requirements, and as a result you could not prepare far enough in advance for changes to the number of vehicles or people required to efficiently meet the department's goals. There was no overall maintenance plan for the bus fleet, and it appeared that too many problems were being allowed to develop instead of being predicted and prevented. Employees were not evaluated regularly, and there were no training plans in place for employee development.

In order to improve the transportation department's overall efficiency, you decided to focus first on ensuring that bus scheduling and maintenance plans were put in place. With the help of your staff, you developed a computerized planning system to schedule transportation requirements and preventive maintenance. Over the last three years, this system has allowed the Middletown School Board to reduce per-pupil transportation costs by 12 percent, and the Board was able to use the savings to provide enrichment experiences in the classroom. You are fre-

quently called upon to explain the benefits of your system to other school boards, and last year you were invited to address the annual meeting of the Canadian School Superintendents' Association.

You are highly regarded as a supervisor. Employee turnover is minimal, and the list of people wanting to work for you is long. Your department meets each Thursday afternoon to review progress, identify potential problem areas, and make recommendations for improvement. Your employees get together informally once each month to celebrate accomplishments.

The foundation of your supervisory style was inherited from your father, whose favourite saying was "Plan your work, then work your plan!" Each evening before you leave work, you develop your "Plan for Tomorrow." You list all the things to be done the next day in order of priority. You list the time of day that each task should be done and who is responsible for its accomplishment. Your employees follow the same procedure. Each workday begins with an employee meeting to recap the accomplishments of the previous day, list expectations for the current day, and discuss problems and issues in common. The process has worked very well.

A new superintendent of schools arrived this fall and announced a program of continuous improvement. At a meeting this morning, all supervisors were strongly encouraged to question their current supervisory practices and find ways to improve them. Each supervisor is to develop a list of three strategies for improvement in his or her area of responsibility and submit it within two weeks.

While you believe that your style works and that your system for continuous improvement is well in place, you know that there is always room for improvement. You wonder how you could go about gathering information to decide which areas still need to be improved in your department. How will you respond to the superintendent's request?

You make the call!

1 | MANAGEMENT FUNCTIONS BEGIN WITH PLANNING

Define planning and clarify why all management functions depend on planning.

Planning
Determining what should be done.

There is some disagreement among management scholars and practitioners concerning the number and designation of managerial functions. However, there is general consensus that the first and probably most crucial managerial function is **planning**.

Planning means deciding what is to be done in the future. It includes analyzing the situation, forecasting future events, establishing objectives, setting priorities, and deciding what actions are necessary to achieve those objectives. Planning logically precedes all other managerial functions since every manager must develop a framework and a course of action for the future before attempting to achieve desired results. For example, how could a supervisor organize the operations of a department without having a plan in mind? How could a supervisor effectively lead employees without first identifying a goal or target? How could a supervisor possibly evaluate the activities of employees without having standards and objectives for comparison? Thus, all of the other managerial functions depend on planning.

Planning is a managerial function that every supervisor must perform every day. It should not be a process used only occasionally or when the supervisor is not too engrossed in daily chores (see the accompanying Contemporary Issue box). By planning, the supervisor realistically anticipates future problems and opportunities, analyzes them, anticipates the probable effects of various alternatives, and decides on the course of action that should lead to the most desirable results. Of course, plans alone do not bring about desired results. But without good planning, activities become random, producing confusion, inefficiency, and frustration.

There is no substitute for regular planning.

Comstock IMAGES

CONTEMPORARY ISSUE
Make Plans, Not Excuses[1]

Supervisors who think they don't have time to plan need to take a closer look at their priorities—or risk the consequences. In 2003, supervisors at the Canadian Coast Guard "badly mismanaged" a project to link the organization's ship and shore facilities by computer. The system was designed to replace a variety of paper-based tracking tools throughout the Coast Guard, and was intended to save millions of dollars every year. But the project—originally estimated to cost $7.9 million—is already $5.4 million over budget and four years behind schedule. Supervisors came up with "incorrect technical requirements," made "incorrect training assumptions," and overall there was "insufficient project planning," according to a 2003 audit of the project. Most of the original supervisors involved in the project have "retired or moved to other positions" and the Coast Guard says it has improved procedures to avoid such problems in the future.[2]

The Canadian Coast Guard—and the Canadian taxpayer—paid a $5.4 million penalty for lack of planning. Dr. Robert D. Ramsey, a writer with extensive front-line supervisory experience, suggests that too many supervisors make excuses for their lack of planning. They manage "OK," but they don't lead. They don't have a plan. He acknowledges that "a lot of managers want to plan. Or, at least, think they want to plan. But they never get to it. They believe planning is what you do when the real work is done. For them, planning is a luxury. It's not reality. They're wrong. Today's plans are tomorrow's reality."

Dr. Ramsey outlines 10 good reasons supervisors have to be good planners:

1. Having a plan puts you back in control.
2. Planning is the only way things can get better.
3. Planning allows you to set priorities and allocate resources effectively.
4. A plan shows you (and others) how to spend your time.
5. Planning is the key to staying ahead of the curve and the competition.
6. A good plan motivates and inspires.
7. People follow the person with a plan.
8. The front office notices the manager with a plan.
9. Planning permits you to spend less energy on putting out other people's fires and start building some of your own.
10. Planning is fun.

Dr. Ramsey acknowledges that "making plans, great or small, takes time. But this is no reason not to do it." He recommends that all supervisors must "plan to plan. Plan first, not last. Put planning time on your to-do list, your daily planner, and your calendar. Incorporate planning as a regular part of your daily routine ... Effective planning won't happen as long as it is viewed as an add-on. Planning isn't extra. It's essential."

"Managers who don't plan have to settle for whatever comes along. You can do better than that."

Sources: (1) Dr. Robert D. Ramsey, "Make Plans, Not Excuses," *Supervision* (February 2003), p. 14; (2) Dean Beeby, "Coast Guard Botched Project, '03 Audit Shows; Ships-to-Shore Computer Link Will Be Four Years Late," *Daily News*, Halifax, N.S. (August 11, 2003), p. 8.

---

2 | THE STRATEGIC PLANNING PROCESS

Explain the concept of strategic planning.

Turbulent and rapid changes in economic conditions and technology, coupled with increasing domestic and international competition, have forced organizations to do a more thorough and systematic job of planning. As the first function of management, planning must start at the top level of management and permeate throughout all levels of the organization. For the organization as a whole, this means that top management must develop an outlook and plans for the future that will guide the organization as a whole. We will refer to this overall

Strategic planning
The process of establishing goals and making decisions that will enable an organization to achieve its long- and short-term objectives.

process as **strategic planning,** which means establishing goals and making decisions that will enable an organization to achieve its long- and short-term objectives.

For many years, noted management scholar Peter Drucker has stressed that every organization must think through its reasons for being and constantly ask the question, "What is our business?" Only by asking this question can a firm develop strategies, set goals and objectives, and make decisions that will lead to future success. Drucker emphasizes that this has to be done by that part of the organization that can see the entire business, balance all of the objectives and needs of today against the needs of tomorrow, and allocate resources to key results.[1]

In most organizations, top-level managers are primarily responsible for developing and executing the strategic or long-term plans. However, once the strategic goals and plans have been identified, middle managers and supervisors must be involved in the planning activities throughout the organization.[2] They must plan their work units' policies and activities toward achieving the organization's overall goals. A transportation supervisor such as Shannon O'Neill, in the "You Make the Call" section at the start of this chapter, will become involved in developing and carrying out certain overall strategic plans for the school board. O'Neill probably will not become part of curriculum and other academic classroom decisions; but she certainly will become involved in planning issues related directly to the operation of the transportation department, which contribute to carrying out the mission of the Middletown School Board.

Strategic planning principles are just as applicable to small business operations as they are to major corporations. The lack of strategic planning is often a serious obstacle for small business owners, since the strategic planning process in many small firms is nonexistent or quite informal. The benefits of strategic management in giving direction to the organization as a whole are just as important to small businesses as they are to large corporations. Regardless of the size or nature of the organization, managers need to be involved in strategy formulation because their participation in the strategic planning process is essential to gaining commitment for the chosen directions and strategies.[3]

Mission Statements

Mission statement
A statement of the organization's basic philosophy, purpose, and reason for being.

Effective strategic planning usually begins with the development of a **mission statement** that reflects the philosophy and purpose of the organization as defined by its top leadership. An organization's mission usually is understood to be the purpose or reason for the organization's existence. Figure 2-1 is an example of a mission statement used by a major supermarket chain; this statement is displayed in every store and office of this firm. The supermarket's entire management team is responsible for providing the leadership that sets the desired patterns of employees' behaviour. As such, the mission statement serves as a springboard or basis for assessing the company's performance and results.

While you can see that a mission statement is quite general and broad in its scope, it fulfills an important planning function. The mission statement sets the course for the organization as a whole. All other, more specific plans and strategies formulated throughout the organization should support the company's overall mission statement.

FIGURE 2-1   Corporate mission statement of a major supermarket chain.

MISSION STATEMENT

Nature of Business

We are committed to excellence as an innovative retailer of quality foods, drugs, consumable products, and services. We focus on providing value through quality, variety, service, competitive pricing, and friendliness.

Customers

Our customers are our most important asset and must receive our total effort toward their satisfaction.

Financial Objectives

We must achieve profits above the industry average to maintain leadership and provide for future growth.

Associates

We shall employ and promote only the best people available. We expect all associates to be competent and customer oriented. We will identify and recognize superior performance and will promote from within whenever practical.

Business Climate

We will conduct our business by treating all customers, associates, suppliers, and the community with honesty, fairness, respect, and integrity.

3   ALL MANAGERIAL LEVELS PERFORM THE PLANNING FUNCTION

Describe the supervisor's role in planning as related to other plans of the organization.

Planning is the responsibility of every manager, whether chairperson of the board, president, division manager, or supervisor. However, the magnitude of a manager's plans will depend on the level at which they are carried out. Planning at the top level is more far-reaching than it is at the supervisory level. The top-level executive is concerned with overall operations of the enterprise and long-range planning for new facilities and equipment, new products and services, new markets, and major investments. At the supervisory level, the scope is narrower and more detailed. The supervisor usually is concerned with day-to-day plans for accomplishing departmental tasks—for example, meeting production quotas for a particular day. Regardless of the level at which plans are being made, the guidelines in Figure 2-2 will help increase the probability of reaching the intended target.

In formulating plans, a supervisor may find that certain aspects of planning call for specialized help. For example, a supervisor may not have full expertise in implementing employment policies, computer and accounting procedures, or technical improvements to improve department efficiency. In such areas, the supervisor should consult with specialists within the organization to help carry out the required planning responsibilities. For example, a human resources staff specialist can offer useful advice concerning policies involving employees. A

FIGURE 2-2   How to reach your goal.

1. Develop a mission statement.
2. Involve others in setting SMART* goals and objectives:
   Stretching, yet attainable.
   Measurable; expressed in a quantity.
   Accountable by identifying the individual responsible for accomplishment.
   Realistic; set in light of past performance, organizational resources, states of nature, and the competitive environment.
   Time limited. This is often accomplished by expressing the objective in terms of the conditions or results to be achieved. What by when.
3. Communicate goals/objectives to all those who must know.
4. Develop plans/strategies for reaching the goal/objective.
5. Put the plan in writing.
6. Secure commitment to the plan.
7. Put the plan into action. Assign responsibility, accountability, and authority.
8. Establish feedback controls and monitor progress.
9. Make changes, if necessary.

Note: The authors would like to thank Mike Lynch and Harvey Lifton for introducing us to the notion of evaluating objectives by applying their SMART criteria. See *Training Clips: 150 Reproducible Handouts: Discussion Starters and Job Aids,* HRD Press (1998), p. 188.

supervisor should utilize all of the available help within the organization to accomplish thorough and specific planning. This also means consulting with employees for their suggestions on how to proceed in certain situations. Employees like to be consulted, and often have valuable insight into the day-to-day operations in their area. Their advice may help the supervisor develop better plans for running the department. In smaller firms, expertise may not be readily available, so the supervisor may want to draw on personal contacts outside the firm. In the final analysis, however, it is each supervisor's personal responsibility to plan.

Planning Periods

For how long a period should a manager plan? Usually a distinction is made between long-range and short-range planning. The definitions of long-range and short-range planning will depend on the manager's level in the organizational hierarchy, the type of enterprise, and the industry in which the organization is operating. Most managers define short-term planning as that which covers a period of less than one year. Long-term planning goes beyond a year and may involve a span of three, five, 10 years or even more. Figure 2-3 shows how the planning process might flow in a manufacturing firm from top-level management down through the supervisory level. Note how planning becomes more short-range and detailed as it progresses down the organization chart.

Strategic plans
Long-term plans developed by top management.

Although terminology is quite varied, some organizations identify or distinguish their planning time horizons as being "strategic," "tactical," or "operational" in nature. **Strategic plans** are developed by top or executive management

FIGURE 2-3   The planning flow.

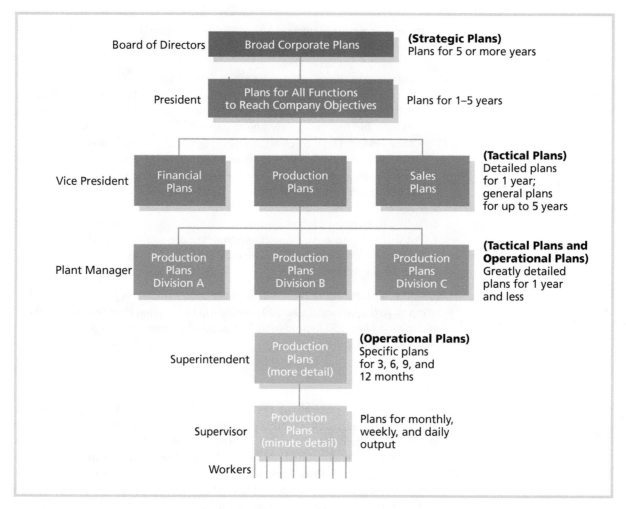

and stem from the vision and mission of the firm. Typically, strategic goals may be stated with five-year (or more) targets. **Tactical plans** are usually developed by middle and staff managers who identify annual objectives in regard to performance targets and other measures. In some organizations, tactical plans may be formulated for several years into the future and may be called *medium-range* or *intermediate plans*. **Operational plans** are usually the responsibility of first-line managers, supervisors, and department heads, who develop short-term objectives of a year or less to cover specific activities and areas of accountability.[4] Figure 2-4 lists some examples of strategic, tactical, and operational plans that may be found in a typical organization.

Of course, there is considerable overlap in the time horizons of strategic plans, tactical plans, and operational plans (see Figure 2-3). Regardless of terminology, however, plans must be supportive of each other at all management levels. As previously stated and for purposes of brevity in the discussion to follow, we will simply refer to "long-range" and "short-term" planning with the arbitrary dividing line between them being one year.

Tactical plans
Annual or intermediate-range plans developed by middle managers and staff specialists.

Operational plans
Short-range plans developed by supervisors to cover specific activities and areas of accountability.

FIGURE 2-4   Examples of strategic, tactical, and operational plans.

STRATEGIC PLANS DEVELOPED BY EXECUTIVE MANAGEMENT
- Acquisition plans to purchase a smaller competitor within the next five years to increase the company's market share and profitability.
- Plans to move the corporate head office within the next three years to be closer to the markets that the company serves.
- A plan to expand the company's product line from four to eight brands within the next five years.

TACTICAL PLANS DEVELOPED BY MIDDLE MANAGEMENT
- A planned investment of $500,000 over the next year in company-wide computer systems to improve efficiency and customer service.
- Plans to expand manufacturing capacity within the next year through the addition of an afternoon shift.
- An initiative that will introduce a division-wide employee incentive program during the next year.

OPERATIONAL PLANS DEVELOPED BY SUPERVISORS
- A department-wide plan for reducing customer waiting time by 10 percent.
- A production plan to produce 1,000 units of product by the end of the week.
- A training plan to ensure that all employees in the department learn a newly implemented computer software program.

Supervisory Role in Long- and Short-Term Planning

Supervisors occasionally are involved in long-range planning. As the need arises, middle-level managers may discuss with supervisors the part they are to play in planning for the future. For example, a company may be considering a major restructuring, or adapting a new technology to better compete in the marketplace. Supervisors may be asked to submit suggestions for long-range plans and to project the impact of long-term trends on their departmental operations. Supervisors may be required to develop longer-range plans for their own departments, which could include identifying long-term training needs, projecting the need for hiring or reassigning employees, or identifying new techniques that may be required to respond to changing market conditions. Thus, from time to time, every supervisor will participate in long-range planning.

Nevertheless, most of the time supervisors devote their attention to short-term planning. For example, very short-term planning would be required to schedule a production run in a manufacturing business or staff an end-of-summer sale in a department store. Many supervisors prefer to do this type of planning at the end of a day or at the end of a week. However, there are other activities, such as preventative maintenance, for which the supervisor can plan several months in advance. Regardless of the time horizon, however, the plans a supervisor makes should be integrated and coordinated with the long-range plans of upper management. Supervisors must be kept well informed about an organization's long-range plans so that they are in a better position to ensure that their departmental plans are aligned with the company's overall strategic direction.

4	## ORGANIZATIONAL GOALS AND OBJECTIVES

Discuss the need for well-defined organizational goals and objectives, particularly as they relate to the supervisor.

Earlier in this chapter, we discussed the role of a corporate mission statement and noted that the mission statement is, by nature, quite broad and general in its scope. When upper management is satisfied that the mission statement accurately reflects the organization's philosophy and reason for being, it is necessary to develop a general statement of goals and objectives that will identify the overall purpose and results toward which all plans and activities are directed. Setting overall goals is a function of top-level management, which must define and communicate to all managers the organization's priorities and primary targets. Figure 2-5 is an example of a company's statement of its corporate objectives.

While some firms make a distinction between the terms *goals* and *objectives*, we will use these terms interchangeably. Some firms define a *goal* as any long-term target—that is, one that will take more than a year to achieve—and an *objective* as a short-term target—that is, one that will take less than a year to achieve. Other firms reverse these definitions.

The goals formulated for an organization as a whole become the general framework for operations and lead to the formulation of more specific objectives for divisional and departmental managers and supervisors. Each division or department must clearly set forth its own objectives as guidelines for operations. These objectives must be within the general framework of the overall goals, and they must contribute to the achievement of the organization's overall purpose.

Objectives are usually stated in terms of what is to be accomplished and when. In general, a department's "what by when" statements are more specific

FIGURE 2-5   Statement of corporate objectives.

EDWARDS HOME CENTRE AND LUMBER COMPANY, INC.

Edwards Home Centre and Lumber Company, Inc. depends on the respect and support of four groups: (1) customers, (2) employees, (3) shareholders, and (4) the public, which includes the citizens of each community in which we do business. For us to have a satisfactory future, we must continuously earn the support, respect, and approval of all four groups. We believe in fostering an environment that encourages superior products, service, and performance. This requires each employee to clearly understand our corporate objectives.

Corporate Objectives

1. To achieve continuing long-term growth in earnings and a record of financial stability that attracts the capital required to support our growth.
2. To concentrate our efforts in business and product areas in which we can realistically expect to achieve a leadership position.
3. To have a working environment in which each individual is treated with fairness that encourages and rewards excellence and stimulates maximum growth of the individual.
4. To anticipate the needs of the future sufficiently well to develop the human talent necessary to remain an industry leader.
5. To be a responsible corporate citizen.

than the broadly stated objectives of the organization. While the higher-level goal may be to "provide quality maintenance services for the entire organization," the maintenance supervisor's objective might be to "reduce machine downtime by 12 percent by year-end." While the supervisory-level objectives are more specific than the broadly stated objectives of an organization, they are consistent with, and give direction to, efforts to achieve organizational objectives.

5	MANAGEMENT BY OBJECTIVES—A SYSTEM FOR PARTICIPATIVE MANAGEMENT

Explain management by objectives (MBO) and describe how it is applied.

Management by objectives (MBO)
A process in which the supervisor and employee jointly set the employee's objectives, and the employee receives rewards upon achieving those objectives.

Management by objectives (MBO) is a management approach in which managers and employees jointly set objectives against which performance is later evaluated. It is a management system—that is, a total approach to management—that involves participative management. MBO requires full commitment to organizational objectives, starting with top-level management and permeating throughout all levels.[5]

As Figure 2-6 shows, an effective MBO system has four major elements. The joint determination of specific, measurable, and verifiable objectives is the foundation. The other elements are the inputs, or the resources necessary for goal accomplishment; the activities and processes that must be carried out to accomplish the goal; and the results, which are evaluated against the objectives. While MBO emphasizes results rather than the techniques used to achieve them, an effective MBO system must be constructed in such a way that all of the aforementioned elements are integrated and support each other.

Why Use Management by Objectives?

There are numerous reasons many firms have adopted the management by objectives approach. The following are among the most important. First, MBO is results oriented. It requires thorough planning, organization, controls, communication, and dedication on the part of an organization. Properly implemented, MBO influences motivation and encourages commitment to results among all employees. It provides a sound means for appraising individuals' performance by

FIGURE 2-6
Elements of the MBO approach.

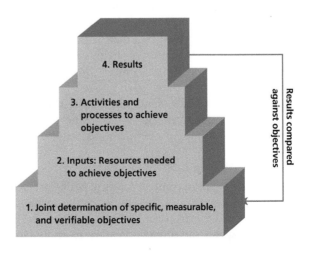

4. Results

3. Activities and processes to achieve objectives

2. Inputs: Resources needed to achieve objectives

1. Joint determination of specific, measurable, and verifiable objectives

Results compared against objectives

its emphasis on objective criteria rather than vague personality characteristics. Finally, MBO provides a rational basis for sharing the rewards of an organization, particularly compensation and promotion based on merit.

A Step-by-Step Model

Any management by objectives system must be developed to meet the unique purposes and character of the organization. There is no such thing as a "pure" model that fits all situations and all places. The following, however, is a suggested step-by-step model that would apply in most organizations.

Step 1: Jointly determine objectives

Top-level managers identify the broad objectives for the coming period in such areas as sales, production levels, costs, profitability, employee development, etc. Usually this is done at about the same time the annual budget is prepared. The more specific corporate objectives are, the more easily they can be communicated throughout the organization. Top-level managers develop these goals in consultation with managers at the next level of management. When finalized, there should be a consensus that the goals are challenging yet realistic and attainable within the established timeframe.

All managers, supervisors, and employees should review their job descriptions to be sure they understand their responsibilities and authority. A thorough review of the organizational structure will help to reveal grey areas where overlapping responsibilities need to be clarified.

Employees should specify their own objectives in relation to the broader organizational and departmental objectives. Each individual prepares a list of objectives—typically about six to ten—that cover key result areas (KRAs) in his or her areas of responsibility. Objectives must be stated in terms that are measurable and verifiable, that is, with a number, ratio, due date, or some other specific criterion of accomplishment. It is important for employees to develop not only routine objectives for their normal areas of responsibility but also objectives that involve some elements of creativity and personal growth.

A meeting must be arranged between each individual and his or her supervisor to discuss the employee's list of objectives. The final list of objectives should be negotiated to attain mutual agreement between supervisor and employee. Both parties should strive to agree on objectives that are challenging but realistic and attainable. Priorities must be established where appropriate.

Research results have shown that employees often stipulate more challenging objectives than their supervisors initially thought they were capable of attaining. When employees help create objectives that will affect them, they are more motivated to try to meet those objectives, because those objectives are "our goals" rather than "their goals." Pride in ownership is essential to gaining commitment to goals. Once the list of objectives is finalized, both the supervisor and the employee sign a copy, and this becomes the primary document on which the employee's performance will be judged.

Step 2: Assign resources

The second step in the MBO process is the resource-input stage. The supervisor must give the employee the resources necessary to accomplish the agreed-upon objectives. In Chapter 1, Figure 1-10 (page 24) stressed that supervisors must do all the things necessary to enable employees to be the best they can be. To this end, employees must be equipped with the necessary tools, supplies, and equipment. When resources are unavailable, objectives may have to be adjusted. The supervisor should ensure that all employees have the skills, ability, and information necessary to reach their goals and should provide support, encouragement, and help as needed. Once objectives are agreed upon, the supervisor must decide where to allocate resources.

Step 3: Develop plans of action

The third step in the MBO process is for employees to develop plans of action for achieving their objectives. Generally, employees should discuss their plans with their immediate supervisors and others affected by the plans. This provides a degree of accountability; everyone knows who is responsible for what. Objectives and plans should be communicated and recommunicated to everyone impacted by them. This may include supervisors and employees in other departments who might be affected by any changes.

Step 4: Review results

In Step 4 of the MBO process, employees and their supervisors periodically review the progress toward agreed-upon objectives. During such reviews, objectives may be adjusted upward or downward as appropriate.

Finally, results are compared with objectives at the end of the period, which is usually a year. Performance appraisals and appraisal meetings are discussed in greater depth in Chapter 9. A good approach is to have individuals do self-evaluations of performance in terms of their objectives. Some employees are more critical of their own performance than their supervisors are.

When the supervisor and employee meet to discuss the employee's performance, they should ask things like, "What was the employee's overall 'batting average'?" "Were objectives accomplished or not accomplished due to the employee's performance or because of circumstances beyond anyone's control?" "What does the performance-to-objectives relationship indicate about the employee's strengths and weaknesses?" It is important to build on each individual's strengths and to seek ways to improve areas of weakness. Step 4 starts the MBO process all over again, because setting the next period's objectives is a logical next step after analyzing the results of the previous period.

Most MBO advocates believe that salary adjustments should not take place during Step 4. Rather, the supervisor and employee should discuss salary adjustments several weeks after discussing performance results. At that time, those who have performed well should be rewarded, while those who fail to meet their objectives generally should not. When done properly, salary adjustments reinforce the MBO program as a means of rewarding most those who have contributed the most.

With or without MBO, effective high-level managers recognize the importance of delegating authority and responsibility to managers, supervisors, and employees if goals and objectives are to be achieved. The advantage of a formal MBO system is that it ties together many plans, establishes priorities, and coordinates activities that might otherwise be overlooked in the press of business operations. A sound MBO program encourages the contributions and commitment of people toward common goals and objectives.

| 6 | **TYPES OF PLANS** |

After setting major goals and objectives, all levels of management participate in the design and execution of additional plans for attaining desired objectives. In general, such plans can be broadly classified as (1) standing or repeat-use plans, which can be used over and over as the need arises, and (2) single-use plans, which focus on a single purpose or specific undertaking.

Standing Plans

Standing plans
Policies, procedures, and rules that can be applied to recurring situations.

Many of a supervisor's day-to-day activities and decisions are guided by the use of so-called **standing plans,** or repeat-use plans. Although terminology varies, these types of plans typically are known as policies, procedures, and rules. All of these should be designed to reinforce one another and should be directed toward the achievement of both organizational and work unit objectives. Top-level managers formulate company-wide standing plans, and supervisors formulate the necessary subsidiary standing plans for their work units.

Policies

Policy
A standing plan that serves as a guide to making decisions.

A **policy** is a general guide to thinking when making decisions. Corporate policies are usually statements that channel the thinking of managers and supervisors in specified directions and define the limits within which they must stay as they make decisions.

Effective policies promote consistency of decision making throughout an enterprise. Once policies are set, managers find it easier to delegate authority since the decisions a subordinate supervisor makes will be guided by policies. Policies enable supervisors to arrive at about the same decisions their managers would make or, at least, to be within acceptable parameters. Policies should be considered as guides for thinking. They do permit supervisors to use their own judgment in making decisions, as long as those decisions fall within the parameters of the policy.

For example, most companies have policies covering vacations with pay (see Figure 2-7 for an example). Depending on length of service with the company, an employee is entitled to one week, two weeks, three weeks, or more of vacation. All the supervisor has to do is ascertain an employee's years of service with the company in order to determine the length of that employee's vacation. However, the supervisor may have to develop a workable plan within the department concerning when each employee may take a vacation. The supervisor is likely to decide that the employee with the most seniority has first choice, the employee with the next highest seniority has second choice, and so on down the line. The supervisor may also limit the number of employees who can be on vacation at one time. In other words, the supervisor develops a departmental policy within the framework of the broader company policy. The supervisor's approval role is specifically included in the Figure 2-7 policy statement.

Major company-wide policies are originated by top-level managers since policy making is one of their important responsibilities. Top-level managers must develop and establish overall policies that guide the thinking of subordinate managers so that organizational objectives can be achieved. Broad policies become the guides for specific policies developed within divisions and departments.

FIGURE 2-7   Example of a policy statement.

VACATIONS

The following is a schedule of vacation time earned by you and paid for by the company:

1 through 5 years	2 full weeks
6 through 9 years	3 full weeks
10 years and over	4 full weeks

Vacation pay is 4 percent of regular earnings.
All vacation times must be approved by your supervisor and the Human Resource Manager.

Departmental policies established by supervisors must complement and coincide with the broader policies of the organization.

Smaller firms tend to have fewer policies than larger organizations.[6] On the one hand, the absence of policies gives the supervisor greater flexibility in dealing with situations as they occur. For example, many—if not most—small firms do not have policies for drug or alcohol use; they prefer to handle problems on an individual basis if and when such problems occur. The absence of policies, on the other hand, may cause inconsistent supervisory practice and lead to charges of unfairness or discrimination. All supervisors, but especially those working in smaller organizations, may encounter situations for which no policy exists. In such a case, the supervisor should consult with his or her manager in order to determine whether a policy should be drafted so that this and future occurrences can be dealt with consistently and fairly.

In addition to policies formulated by top-level managers, some policies are imposed on an organization by external forces such as government, labour unions, trade groups, and accrediting associations. The word *imposed* indicates compliance with an outside force that cannot be avoided. For example, government regulations concerning minimum wage, pay for overtime work, and hiring of people without regard to race, age, and gender automatically become part of an organization's policies.

Procedures

Procedure
A standing plan that defines the sequence of activities to be performed to achieve objectives.

A **procedure**, like a policy, is a standing plan for achieving objectives. Procedures are derived from policies but are more specific. Procedures essentially are guides to action, not guides to thinking. They define a chronological sequence of actions that will carry out the terms and objectives of a policy. They promote consistency by listing the steps to be taken and the sequence to be followed. Procedures at times are combined with or incorporated within policy statements. Figure 2-8 is an example of a firm's combined policy and procedure statement concerning educational tuition reimbursement.

Rules

A rule is different from a policy or procedure, although it is also a standing plan that has been devised in order to attain objectives. A rule is not the same as a policy because it does not provide a guide to thinking, nor does it leave

FIGURE 2-8   Example of a policy and procedure statement.

TOPIC: TUITION REIMBURSEMENT

The company intends to substantially support employees in pursuing training and education that will enhance the development of job-related skills and knowledge.

REQUIRED ATTENDANCE

A supervisor may require a subordinate to attend seminars, conferences, or classes, or to enroll in specific courses. All fees and related expenses shall be paid for by the company. Authorization and approval for reimbursement will be handled through normal disbursement procedures.

VOLUNTARY ATTENDANCE

1. All full-time employees, upon securing the necessary approval, may receive tuition reimbursement as follows:
    a. The company will pay 100 percent of the tuition fee for courses that are reasonably job related and/or are necessary to attain a job-related diploma or degree.
    b. The courses of study must be taken at an accredited institution.
2. Tuition will be paid provided:
    a. The employee submits *in advance* of attending classes a tuition reimbursement request form that identifies school, course(s) to be taken, reason for taking the course(s), amount of tuition, and starting and completion dates of course(s).
    b. The request has the written approval of both the employee's supervisor and a vice president or above.
    c. Evidence of a passing grade (C or better, or completion of course(s) if no grade is given).
    d. The individual is in the employ of the company upon completion of the course(s).
3. The company will not:
    a. Pay tuition in advance.
    b. Grant time off to attend classes or do research.
    c. Reimburse for books, travel expenses, meals, etc.

Rule
A directive that must be applied and enforced wherever applicable.

discretion to the parties involved. A rule is related to a procedure insofar as it is a guide to action and states what must or must not be done. However, it is not a procedure because it does not provide for a time sequence or set of steps. A **rule** is a directive that must be applied and enforced consistently. When a rule is a specific guide for the behaviour of employees in a department, the supervisor must follow it wherever it applies without deviating from it. For example, "No possession or consumption of alcoholic beverages on company premises" is commonly on the list of organizational rules. It means exactly what it says, and there are to be no exceptions. Rules that apply to the entire organization are made by upper-level managers, while specific departmental rules may be drafted by individual supervisors.

Example of a rule from which there should be no deviation.

Kevin Frayer/CP

7

Discuss the principal types of single-use plans in which supervisors play an important role.

Single-use plans
Plans developed to accomplish a specific objective or to cover only a designated time period.

Budget
A plan that expresses anticipated results in numerical—usually financial—terms for a stated period of time.

Single-Use Plans

As discussed in the preceding sections, policies, procedures, and rules are known as repeat-use or standing plans because they are followed each time a given situation is encountered. Unless they are changed or modified, repeat-use plans are used again and again. In contrast to repeat-use plans are plans that are no longer needed or are "used up" once the objective is accomplished or the time period of applicability is over. These are known as **single-use plans.** Single-use plans include budgets, programs, and projects. Major budgets, programs, and projects are usually the concern of higher-level managers, but supervisors also play a role in developing and implementing single-use plans at the departmental level.

Budgets

Although budgets are generally part of the managerial controlling function, a budget is first and foremost a plan. A **budget** is a plan that expresses anticipated results in numerical terms, such as dollars and cents, employee hours, sales figures, or units to be produced. It serves as a plan for a stated period of time, usually one year. All budgets eventually are translated into monetary terms, and an overall financial budget is developed for the entire firm. After the stated period is over, the budget expires. It has served its usefulness and is no longer valid. This is why a budget is a single-use plan.

As a statement of expected results, a budget is associated with control. However, the preparation of a budget is planning, and this again is part of every manager's responsibilities. Since a budget is expressed in numerical terms, it has the advantage of being specific rather than general. There is a considerable difference between just making general forecasts and attaching numerical values to specific plans. The figures that the supervisor finds in a budget are actual plans, which become standards to be achieved.

Programs and Projects

Program

A major single-use plan for a large undertaking related to accomplishing the organization's goals and objectives.

A **program** is a single-use set of plans for a major undertaking related to the organization's overall goals and objectives. A major program may have its own policies, procedures, and budgets and may take several years to accomplish. Examples of major programs are the expansion of a manufacturing plant or office and the addition of new facilities in a hospital. Such expansion programs usually involve plans for architectural design, new equipment or technology, financing, recruitment of employees, and publicity, all of which are part of the overall program. Once the expansion program is completed, its plans will not be used again. Thus, a program is a single-use plan.

Project

A single-use plan for accomplishing a specific nonrecurring activity.

Supervisors are typically more involved in planning projects. While a **project** may be part of an overall program, it is an undertaking that can be planned and fulfilled as a distinct entity, usually within a relatively short period of time. For example, the preparation of a publicity brochure by the public relations department to acquaint the public with new facilities as part of a hospital expansion program would be called a project. Arranging the necessary construction financing for the building expansion would be another project. Although connected with a major program, these projects can be handled separately by individuals designated to implement them.

An example of a project at the supervisory level is the design of a new inventory control system by a warehouse supervisor. Another example is a research project conducted by a marketing department supervisor to determine the effectiveness of a series of television commercials. Projects such as these are a constant part of the ongoing activities at the departmental level. The ability to plan and carry out projects is another component of every supervisor's managerial effectiveness.

8 SUPERVISORY PLANNING FOR RESOURCE USE

Identify the benefits of supervisory planning.

Supervisors are especially concerned with day-to-day planning for the best use of the physical and human resources available to them. Planning promotes efficiency and reduces waste and costs. Through effective planning, haphazard approaches can be minimized and duplication can be avoided. Even in a small department or small firm, the total investment in physical and human resources may be substantial. Figure 2-9 highlights some of the specific day-to-day planning that a supervisor may undertake in an effort to ensure that all resources are being used to their fullest potential. See our website (www.supervision2e.nelson.com) for further information on day-to-day supervisory planning for resource use.

9 CRISIS MANAGEMENT: PLANNING REQUIRED

Recognize the importance of planning for the unthinkable: crisis management.

Crisis planning has become integral to every organization's long- and short-term planning. Crises appear suddenly: a robber brandishing a gun enters a bank; a ladle of molten steel falls on workers; a bookkeeper steals from a church; an unsafe product is designed, produced, and distributed. Such crises must be addressed in a timely fashion. Clearly, the unthinkable will continue to take place in our society, and organizations must prepare and develop action plans should a crisis occur.

FIGURE 2-9 Examples of supervisory plans for efficient use of resources.

TYPE OF PLAN	EXAMPLES OF SUPERVISOR'S RESPONSIBILITIES
Plans for efficient use of space.	• Creation of floor layout charts to ensure space is being utilized to its best potential. • Analyzing current use of space and, when appropriate, making a business case to upper management for increasing departmental space allocations.
Plans for use of other major physical resources.	• Ensuring that physical resources such as tools, machinery, computers, and various types of equipment and furniture are adequate and efficient. • Working closely with the maintenance department to ensure that these resources are properly maintained. • Researching new equipment alternatives and making recommendations to upper management about new equipment purchases.
Plans for use and security of materials, supplies, merchandise, and data.	• Ensuring that materials and supplies are used appropriately and economically. • Taking measures to ensure that loss and theft of materials, supplies, inventory, and other company property is minimized. • Working with information technology specialists to ensure that department employees have appropriate levels of access to confidential data and that computer files are resistant to tampering, viruses, and theft.
Plans for a safe work environment.	• Ensuring that all employees are aware of their rights and responsibilities under provincial health and safety legislation. • Ensuring that all department activities are carried out in a safe manner. • Participating in meetings with health and safety representatives or committees to improve departmental safety.
Plans for full use of human resources.	• Drafting plans for recruiting, selecting, and training employees. • Appraising performance of employees and recognizing achievement. • Ensuring that employees are adequately compensated and rewarded. • Taking just and fair disciplinary action when required.
Planning employee work schedules.	• Ensuring that enough employees are available to accomplish the work of the department without undue reliance on overtime. • Planning for anticipated absences due to vacations, temporary layoffs, turnover, and other types of leaves. • Administering alternative work schedules such as flextime or telecommuting arrangements. • Planning for the use of part-time or contract employees as appropriate.
Planning improvements in work procedures and methods.	• Periodically analyzing departmental operations to ensure that work procedures and methods are up to date. • Working with an industrial engineer or systems analyst to identify areas of work that can be done more efficiently.
Planning inventory.	• Analyzing the levels of materials and supplies to ensure that inventory levels are not excessive. • Implementing just-in-time inventory principles to streamline operations of the department.

The most recognizable example of how to effectively deal with a crisis is Johnson & Johnson's (J&J) Tylenol crisis of the 1980s. The unthinkable occurred when someone injected cyanide into Extra-Strength Tylenol™ capsules. In all, eight deaths in the United States were linked directly to cyanide-laced Tylenol capsules. The company recalled over 30 million bottles of the product, with an estimated retail value of over $100 million. This unforced recall was the first example of a corporation voluntarily assuming responsibility for its products. Because J&J's credo taught managers to focus on the company's responsibility to the public and to the consumer, the decision to recall was easy; the corporation's values were clear. J&J survived the crisis with its reputation enhanced.[7]

Every company risks crisis of one kind or another. Regardless of the size or nature of the organization, supervisors must be involved in crisis-management planning. Every member of the management team, utilizing concepts suggested in Figure 2-10, should plan for the unthinkable. While it is not possible for every possible crisis to be anticipated, each organization should analyze its most significant risks and involve all levels of management in the development of action plans that can be automatically put into place should the unthinkable occur.

10   PLANNING FOR QUALITY IMPROVEMENT

Explain the role of planning in quality improvement.

Total quality management (TQM)
An organizational approach involving all employees in the effort to satisfy customers by continual improvement of goods and services.

In recent decades, successful firms have shown an emerging commitment to quality. Many firms have turned to total quality management (TQM) and continuous improvement. In manufacturing firms, quality control traditionally meant inspecting the product at the end of the production process. Today, the notion of **total quality management** means that the total organization is committed to quality—everyone is responsible for doing the job right the first time. TQM means a total effort toward meeting customer needs by planning for quality, preventing defects, correcting defects, and continuously building increased quality into goods and services as far as economically and competitively feasible.[8]

If it is to succeed, TQM requires planning and commitment at every level of the organization.

The increased emphasis on achieving higher product quality has led many firms to follow guidelines or criteria developed by others. The process of identifying and improving on the best practices of the leaders in the industry or related fields is called **benchmarking.** Some executives even advocate benchmarking using "best in the world" comparisons.[9] All of us have used benchmarking. When we evaluate the performance of our favourite sports team, we look to see how well it is doing in comparison with the team on top. We analyze the attributes of the players of the top team, the coaching styles, and so forth and conclude that our team could be just as good—if not better—if the owners/managers would make the necessary changes and copy the successful practices of the leaders of the top team.

Benchmarking
The process of identifying and improving on the practices of the leaders.

ISO 9000
A rigorous series of manufacturing quality standards created by the International Organization for Standardization.

In recent years, many firms have given serious attention to ways of achieving quality improvements. Adherence to the quality standards established by **ISO 9000** is an option available to firms that wish to compare themselves to the best. ISO 9000 is a series of quality management and assurance standards that were originally developed for the manufacturing sector, although they can also be applied to service organizations.[10] ISO 9000 was created in 1987 by the

FIGURE 2-10 Crisis management planning.

1. **Identify the unthinkables.** What are your areas of vulnerability? What has been happening to or in other organizations? Become a learning organization, and learn from the experiences of others. It must be made clear that every employee is responsible for reporting potential areas of concern and doing so promptly.

2. **Develop a plan for dealing with the unthinkables.** Ask "What if?" questions. For example, "If this happens, what should be done?" "Who should do it?" Learn from the mistakes of others. They are good indications of what not to do. Plans should include who will be the company's spokesperson in the event a crisis occurs. Speak with one voice to ensure consistent and uniform information.

3. **Develop contingency plans.** If Plan A does not work, then what should be done?

4. **Form crisis teams.** Have a team of qualified, well-trained individuals ready to go at a moment's notice. The events of 9/11 pointed out the need to have several backup teams ready to go.

5. **Simulate crisis drills.** When you were a youngster, your school probably had fire drills. Why? The school probably had never experienced a fire, but the potential existed. The exercise was repeated so that all knew what to do if the crisis occurred.

6. **Respond immediately, if not sooner.** Create a culture in your organization that empowers employees rather than compels them to send memos or e-mails and to await approval. Many companies have retreated when unthinkable situations arose. Supervisors must share all they know as soon as they know it. Management professor James O'Toole contends, "You can't get into trouble by admitting what you don't know or by giving people too much information."

7. **Do not be afraid to apologize.** Think about how you would like to be treated if something unthinkable happened to you. What would make it right? In many situations, nothing will make it right, but the right step is to apologize sincerely and to offer to make amends. As professor Gerald Meyers says, "If you win public opinion, the company can move forward and get through it."

8. **Learn from experience.** Learn from your own mistakes and those of others. Ask what you have learned from past crises and how you can integrate that knowledge into the planning process.

9. **There is no "rewind" button when a crisis occurs.** Plan now!

Sources: Adapted from Carol Hymowitz, "Managing in a Crisis Can Bring Better Ways to Conduct Business," *The Wall Street Journal* (October 23, 2001), p. B1; Howard Paster, "Be Prepared," *The Wall Street Journal* (September 24, 2001), p. A24; Elizabeth Hlotyak, "Crisis Communications," *Westchester County Business Journal* (September 25, 2000), pp. 13–14; Norman Augustine, "Managing the Crisis you Tried to Prevent," *Harvard Business Review* (November–December 1995), pp. 147–58; John A. Byrne, "Here's What to Do Next, Dow Corning," *BusinessWeek* (February 24, 1992), p. 33; and "How Companies Are Learning to Prepare for the Worst," *BusinessWeek* (December 23, 1985), pp. 74+.

International Organization for Standardization, in Geneva, Switzerland. In order to obtain ISO 9000 certification, a business must demonstrate that its quality management system meets a stringent set of standardized requirements. For more information about ISO standards, visit the organization's website at www.iso.org.

11 TOOLS FOR PROJECT PLANNING AND SCHEDULING

Identify and describe two project scheduling and planning tools—Gantt charts and PERT.

Scheduling
The process of developing a detailed list of activities, their sequence, and the required resources.

Gantt chart
A graphic scheduling technique that shows the activity to be scheduled on the vertical axis and necessary completion dates on the horizontal axis.

Much supervisory time is spent planning various projects. Supervisors need to consider what needs to be accomplished, the necessary activities, the order in which they are to be done, who is to do each, and when they are to be completed. This process of planning activities and their sequence is called **scheduling**. Two well-known project planning and scheduling tools are Gantt charts and PERT.

Gantt Charts

A **Gantt chart** is a graphic scheduling technique that shows the relationship between work planned and necessary completion dates.[11] Figure 2-11 depicts a simplified Gantt chart developed by a student for completing a college or university admission process. The student needs to decide what activities must be done to get admitted, the order in which they must be done, and the time that must be allocated to each activity. The project is broken down into separate major activities, and these are listed on the vertical axis. The timeframe is indi-

FIGURE 2-11 Example of a Gantt chart.

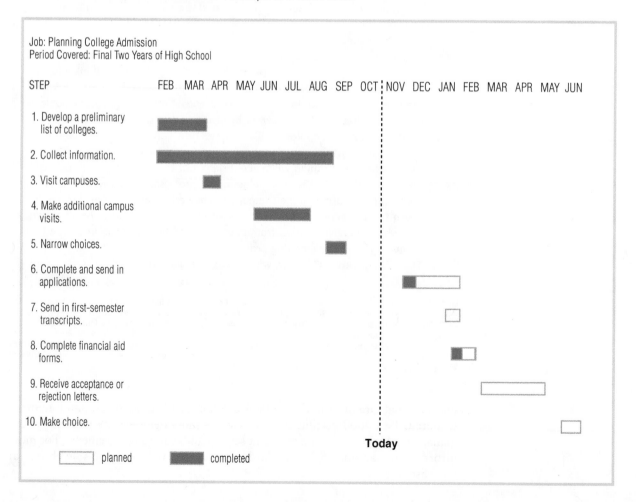

cated on the horizontal axis. The bars show the duration and sequence of each activity. Each bar is shaded to indicate the actual progress. Thus, it is possible to assess progress at a glance.

Gantt charts are helpful in projects in which the activities are independent of each other. However, if a large project such as a complex quality improvement program needs to be planned, PERT is more likely to be applicable.

Program Evaluation and Review Technique (PERT)

PERT
A flowchart for managing large programs and projects showing the necessary activities with estimates of the time needed to complete each activity and the sequential relationship among them.

Successfully used in many major production and construction undertakings, **PERT** is a flowchart-like diagram showing the sequence of activities needed to complete a project and the time associated with each. PERT goes beyond Gantt charts by clarifying the interrelatedness of the various activities.

PERT helps a supervisor think strategically. A clear statement of goals serves as the basis for the entire planning process. PERT begins with the supervisor defining the project not only in terms of the desired goal but also all the intermediate ones upon which the ultimate goal depends. The construction of a PERT network includes the following steps:

PERT event
The beginning and/or ending of an activity.

PERT activity
A specific task to be accomplished.

Critical path
The path of activities in the PERT network that will take the longest time to complete.

Step 1: Determine the goal. For example, a firm may want to improve its customer service by improving delivery times.

Step 2: Clarify events. A **PERT event** is the beginning and/or ending of an activity. Receiving an order from a customer is an event. Thus, an event is a particular point in time.

Step 3: Identify all activities that must be accomplished for the project and the sequence in which these activities should be performed. A **PERT activity** is a specific task to be accomplished. Contacting the customer, demonstrating how a product can provide a solution to a specific problem, and motivating the customer to action are activities. Activities require a certain amount of time to complete.

Step 4: Determine time estimates for the completion of each activity.

Step 5: Develop a network diagram that includes all the information in the previous steps.

Step 6: Identify the **critical path,** which is the sequence of activities requiring the longest period of time to complete.

Step 7: Allocate necessary resources.

Step 8: Record actual activity time and compare with estimates.

Step 9: Make necessary revisions or adjustments to the schedule.[12]

Suppose that the organization decides to implement a program to improve the quality of customer service. The supervisor identifies the PERT events, lists all activities that must be accomplished, and determines which activities must precede others. The data are then presented on a flowchart or network, which is a visual portrayal of the sequence and interrelationships among all the activities necessary for achieving improved customer service. A simple PERT network is shown in Figure 2-12. In the PERT network, events are represented by circles. Activities to be accomplished are represented by an arrow. Figure 2-12 illustrates that after "Complete Quality Audit" (Event A) has happened, certain activities represented by arrows must be performed before "Implement Quality Program" (Event G), represented by another circle, can happen. In developing the network, the supervisor provides realistic estimates of how much time it will take to complete certain stages of the work and what the costs will be.

FIGURE 2-12
Example of a PERT
network for quality
improvement.

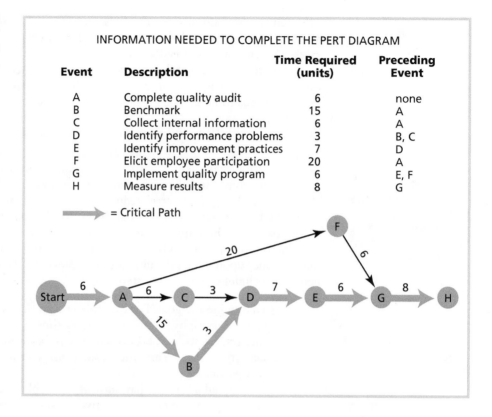

INFORMATION NEEDED TO COMPLETE THE PERT DIAGRAM

Event	Description	Time Required (units)	Preceding Event
A	Complete quality audit	6	none
B	Benchmark	15	A
C	Collect internal information	6	A
D	Identify performance problems	3	B, C
E	Identify improvement practices	7	D
F	Elicit employee participation	20	A
G	Implement quality program	6	E, F
H	Measure results	8	G

= Critical Path

PERT is a helpful planning tool because it requires systematic thinking and planning for large, nonroutine projects. The development of PERT networks by hand is time consuming; however, the use of Gantt charts and PERT is likely to increase because of the proliferation of commercially available computer software packages that can assist supervisors in planning, decision making, and controlling. Effective supervisors will become familiar with the various planning tools and apply them as the situation warrants.

12 TIME MANAGEMENT

Discuss the importance of time management, especially in reducing stress, and suggest techniques for supervisors to plan better use of their time.

To this point, we have emphasized the need for thorough planning as a key to effective supervisory management. Another important resource that affects all other resources is the supervisor's own time. The old saying that "time is money" applies with equal relevance to both the supervisor's and employees' time. A supervisor's time is a major resource that must be expended carefully. Many supervisors experience days that are so full of demands that they feel as though they can never take care of all the matters that need attention. The days and weeks are too short; they would like to "buy" additional time somewhere. However, the supply of time is inflexible, and it cannot be renewed or stored. If supervisors want more time, they must make it themselves.[13]

Most supervisors would welcome even a modest increase in their effectiveness. Given the many demands on them, supervisors who have a system for managing their time are far more likely to be effective than those who approach each day haphazardly. Although some supervisors insist that they need more time, what they really need is better use of the time they already have. As a starting point, this means preparing each day for the day at hand.

Some supervisors put in extremely long days, but they are not on top of their jobs. These supervisors equate long hours with devotion and effectiveness. Many times just the reverse is true. Such supervisors need to examine what effort is put into the hours worked and with what results, rather than looking only at the number of hours they have worked as a sign of their dedication. The key is to gain control over the workday rather than to be controlled by it. Time management, too, starts with careful planning.

Managing Time Means Reducing Stress

Stress
A person's nonspecific bodily reactions to demands and conditions that he or she encounters.

Many supervisors constantly complain that they do not have enough time to do all the things that must be done. Although some supervisors do work better under pressure, many others become less efficient under such conditions. **Stress** can be defined as a person's nonspecific bodily reactions to demands and conditions that he or she encounters.[14] Typical symptoms of stress include fatigue, headaches, irritability, and tension. Excessive levels of stress have been tied to lower productivity, increased accidents, higher absenteeism, and alcohol and drug abuse. Although a reasonable amount of stress can motivate people toward greater achievement, Canadian workers report that their overall negative stress levels over the last 10 years have been on the rise (see Contemporary Issue box on page 64). While it is beyond the scope of this text to give broad coverage to techniques for managing stress, supervisors should understand that much of what is attributed to stress is directly related to the ability to cope with various time pressures and other factors.

External stressors
Causes of stress that arise from outside the individual, such as job pressures, responsibilities, and work itself.

External stressors are causes of stress that come from outside the person, such as pressures of the job, the family, and environmental conditions. The supervisory position by its very nature is pressure-prone since supervisors are barraged by many demands from managers, employees, and fellow supervisors. Interpersonal conflicts with others on the job are often more difficult to cope with than pressures of difficult tasks and deadlines. At the same time, supervisors have to deal with their own **internal stressors**; these are pressures that people put on themselves—for example, by being ambitious, diligent, competitive, and aggressive.

Internal stressors
Pressures that people put on themselves, such as feeling a need to be outstanding in everything.

Many articles and seminars teach people ways of coping with the pressures that induce stress. Some recommended stress-control techniques are exercise, meditation, biofeedback training, and progressive relaxation. Typically, however, the suggested remedy is better time management, or as one author succinctly stated, "Managing stress means managing time. The two are so intertwined that controlling one can only help the other."[15] By employing better time management procedures, supervisors learn to prioritize duties and tasks, which, in turn, enables them to accomplish more of what they really need to get done. Virtually by definition, better time management means increased accomplishment and reduced stress and frustration.

Classifying Duties with a Time-Use Chart

A first step toward better time management is for supervisors to analyze how they currently use time. A time-use chart, or time inventory, is an excellent tool to help supervisors examine how and where they currently are spending their time. Then they can begin to attack pockets of inefficiency.

CONTEMPORARY ISSUE
Yes, Your Job Is Killing You: So Much for "Putting People First" as Stress Soars, Satisfaction Plummets

Stress on the job doubled in the past decade as workloads rose and job satisfaction plummeted, according to a study that tracked thousands of Canadian workers between 1991 and 2001. The study, called "Work-Life Balance in the New Millennium," concludes that many people are losing the battle to balance the work and personal demands that are being placed on them. The study's authors, Linda Duxbury of Carleton University's Sprott School of Business and Chris Higgins of the Richard Ivey School of Business at the University of Western Ontario, conclude that "while the rhetoric of management throughout the 1990s was one of 'putting people first' ... management's practices throughout the decade tended to move in the opposite direction."

The study found, for example, that the average employee spent 45 hours per week in paid employment in 2001, up from 42 hours in 1991. Much of the increase arose because 52 percent of all employees said they took work home at night or on their days off. Only 31 percent reported taking work home in 1991.

The number of hours spent in the office or workplace also rose, to 43 hours per week in 2001 from 40.8 hours per week a decade earlier. Those increased hours and other factors, such as technology that connects people to their jobs 24 hours a day, contributed to growing problems and a sense that people feel pushed "to the limit" by demands inside and outside work, Duxbury says.

Other key findings of the report include:

- Twice as many people reported high levels of job stress in 2001 as did 10 years earlier. The figure was 27 percent in 2001 versus 13 percent in 1991.
- Job satisfaction plummeted from 62 percent who were highly satisfied in 1991 to only 45 percent in 2001.
- The number of work days missed due to health problems increased in 2001. Among employees who met the study's definition of having "high work-life conflict," absenteeism was three times that of those with low work-life conflict.

This report (available in its entirety at www.cprn.org) has significant implications for Canadian supervisors and their upper-level managers. Clearly, workers are struggling with the often conflicting demands of work and home life. They are feeling increased pressure and role overload. The report suggests that organizations must develop better management policies with a focus on giving employees more flexibility and control. Supervisors themselves must attempt to balance the time pressures and stresses that are inherent to the supervisory position, but must recognize that employees are also struggling with the same issues. Flextime arrangements, telecommuting alternatives, and increased sensitivity to the conflicts between work and family pressures are just some of the ways that organizations can address the report's troubling findings.

Source: Adapted from Kristin Goff, "Yes, your job is killing you: So much for 'putting people first' as stress soars, satisfaction plummets," *The Ottawa Citizen*, October 23, 2001, p. C1.

Routine duties
Minor tasks, done daily, that make a minor contribution to achievement of objectives.

Regular duties
The essential components of a supervisor's job, such as giving directives and checking performance.

Prior to constructing such a chart, supervisors should identify their primary job duties and daily activities and classify them as (1) routine duties, (2) regular duties, (3) special duties, or (4) innovative duties. Supervisors may wish to add another classification to cover time spent handling emergencies, although it is difficult to predict an emergency or the time needed to correct a crisis situation.

Routine duties are minor tasks that are done daily but make a limited contribution to the objectives of the department. Such work includes answering the telephone, reviewing the mail, chatting informally with others, cleaning up, etc. Some of these tasks can be assigned to subordinates. **Regular duties** constitute the supervisory work most directly related to accomplishing the objectives of the department. Regular duties primarily involve the day-to-day activities that a supervisor must do personally and that are the essential components of the supervisor's responsibilities. Examples of these are giving directives, checking performance, writing reports, counselling employees, updating job descriptions, training new employees, and reviewing departmental operating procedures. **Special duties** consist of meetings, committee work, and special projects that are not directly related to core tasks of the department. **Innovative duties** are creative-thinking and improvement-oriented activities—for example, looking at new or improved work methods or finding better ways to communicate with employees.

Special duties
Tasks not directly related to the core tasks of the department, such as meetings and committee work.

Innovative duties
Creative activities aimed at finding a better way to do something.

Supervisors who are effective at managing their time do find time for innovative duties. Indeed, it is the innovative supervisor who usually stands out and is most often noticed by higher-level managers. This, of course, should not imply that a supervisor ought to work on innovative duties to the exclusion of other duties. The amount of supervisory time spent on various duties will vary. Supervisors themselves must judge what time allocations are appropriate for their particular situations. One thing is clear, however: if a supervisor does not plan carefully, routine and special duties have a way of crowding out the time needed for regular and innovative duties.

A time-use chart is a useful technique for gathering information about how a supervisor is currently spending time. The supervisor can start by constructing a time-use chart similar to the one shown in Figure 2-13. Duties should be classified as routine, regular, special, or innovative. Then the supervisor should decide what amount of time should normally be allocated to duties under each category and correspondingly set goals for each day. Once these steps are taken, the supervisor should keep an ongoing record of the time that actually was spent on various duties. After a week or two of recording daily how time is actually spent, the supervisor should bring together the time-use sheets and total the amount of time spent in each of the categories. These totals should be compared with the original estimates or goals. The supervisor is then in a position to evaluate his or her use of time. With rare exceptions, the supervisor will be in for some surprises!

By analyzing the actual times versus the goals or estimates, the supervisor can determine whether appropriate amounts of time are being spent on various duties. For example, are some regular duties not getting done because too much time is devoted to routine duties or special projects? Could some tasks be eliminated altogether? Is there sufficient time for innovative work and planning? Answers to these and similar questions give the supervisor a better feel for what she or he ought to be working on, rather than simply tackling the problems that happen to come up first or the tasks that seem most pleasant to work on at the moment.

Overcoming Time Wasters by Setting Priorities

Invariably, supervisors discover time wasters that have hampered their ability to work on important things in their department. Such time wasters as random activities, too much time on the telephone, too much time visiting or being visited, procrastination, unnecessary meetings, and lack of delegation may be revealed by a time inventory. The discovery and recognition of time wasters represent only one step. The supervisor must begin immediately to attack these old habits and build desirable ones.

FIGURE 2-13   Time-use chart.

Goals for the Day	Estimated Time (in hours and fractions of hours)	Percentage (calculate)
Routine		
Regular		
Special		
Innovative		

Actual Time Use	Routine	Regular	Special	Innovative
		(Record the time spent in hours and fractions of hours)		
6:00–7:00				
7:01–8:00				
8:01–9:00				
9:01–10:00				
10:01–11:00				
11:01–12:00				
12:01–1:00				
1:01–2:00				
2:01–3:00				
3:01–4:00				
4:01–5:00				
5:01–6:00				
Totals				
Calculated Percentages				

Evaluation of Effectiveness

Supervisory problems crop up continually, often without an apparent sequence of priority. Therefore, supervisors must discipline themselves to decide between matters that they must handle personally and those that can be assigned to someone else. For every task delegated—particularly routine duties—a supervisor gains time for more important matters such as regular and innovative duties. Delegating may be worthwhile even if the supervisor has to spend extra time training an employee in a particular task. The supervisor then should plan the remaining available time so that it is allocated properly among the duties that he or she alone must perform. These duties must be classified according to which are the most and the least urgent.

The "Pareto Principle," named after a 19th-century Italian economist, holds that many people, because they fail to set priorities, spend most of their time on minor, unimportant tasks. It has been estimated that some supervisors spend 80 percent of their time on duties that contribute to only 20 percent of the total job results. A supervisor who does not prioritize duties is inclined to pay equal attention to all matters at hand. This type of supervisor tends to handle each problem in the order it happens and, consequently, the most important matters may not receive the attention they deserve. When priorities are established, time is planned so that the most important things have sufficient space on the schedule. However, supervisors should leave some flexibility in their schedules because not every event that occurs can be anticipated. Emergencies and changing priorities do occur, and supervisors must attend to them. Flexibility permits supervisors to take care of unanticipated problems without significantly disrupting their schedule of priorities.

Tools of Time Management

Effective time utilization requires mental discipline. This means that supervisors should assign priorities to duties and stop trying to do everything brought to their attention. Once such a mental attitude is fixed, supervisors can better use a number of common tools as aids in managing their time.

Every supervisor should use a pocket or electronic calendar every day to note activities that need major attention, such as appointments, meetings, reports, and discussions. By scheduling such activities as far in advance as practicable and noting them on their calendars, supervisors are less likely to overlook them.

Another tool for effective time utilization is the weekly planning sheet (or, if preferred, a monthly planning sheet). Typically, a planning sheet for a week is prepared at the end of the previous week. The planning sheet shows the days of the week divided into mornings and afternoons and lists the items to be accomplished (see Figure 2-14). At a glance the supervisor can check what is planned for each morning and afternoon. As each task is accomplished, it is circled. Tasks that have been delayed must be rescheduled for another time. Tasks that are planned but not accomplished during the week remain uncircled and should be rescheduled for the following week. This record indicates how much of the original plan was carried out, and it provides information concerning how the supervisor's time was spent.

Still another technique that many supervisors find helpful is the "to-do" list, which can be used in conjunction with a calendar or weekly planning sheet. This is essentially an ongoing listing of things to do—both major and minor—to which a supervisor can refer as each day progresses. As an item is accomplished, it is crossed off the list. The supervisor must prioritize all items on the list and schedule and perform important tasks before attending to the minor items. Many supervisors find that the best time to review and reprioritize their to-do lists is at the beginning of the workday or at the end of the day before they leave.

FIGURE 2-14   The weekly planning sheet.

Sunday 9/19	Monday 9/20	Tuesday 9/21	Wednesday 9/22	Thursday 9/23	Friday 9/24	Saturday 9/25
A.M.	A.M. 7:30 (Staff Mtg.) Monthly safety committee meeting	A.M. (Discuss with human resources director interpretation of changes in policy)	A.M. (Turn in scrap report) 11 A.M. (Staff Mtg.)	A.M. Talk to engineering about preventive maintenance plan	A.M. Attend management seminar	A.M.
P.M.	P.M. (Discuss direct labour cost figures with controller)	P.M. Work on next year's departmental budget	P.M.	P.M. Check absentee, turnover, and accident rates	P.M. (Meeting with union grievance committee to discuss unresolved grievances)	P.M.

WHAT CALL DID YOU MAKE?

As Shannon O'Neill, you have a well-defined planning process in place. Your system is forward looking, involves employees in the process, and provides for immediate feedback on performance. Total quality management improves quality of service by involving everyone in the process. You do not appear to have a system to evaluate the students' or their parents' perceptions of quality so you may want to solicit input from them regarding their perceptions of the service provided.

However, before you spend too much time trying to determine what, exactly, the new superintendent wants, you should talk to your immediate supervisor. Before the various management levels can begin working on their plans for continuous improvement, the superintendent needs to share his or her vision for the school board.

There is no right or wrong answer for this scenario. Every process, procedure, and activity can be improved. The purpose of this "You Make the Call" section is to have you think of ways that you can get ideas for improvement. While you travel around the country sharing your computerized transportation scheduling with others, you can probably get some ideas on things that other districts do better than you do.

Employee involvement is the key to a system of total quality management and continuous improvement. Ask your employees to help you create a vision for their department, areas of responsibility, and so forth. Ask them questions such as the following: What will the taxpayers expect of the Middletown School Board's transportation department three to five years from now? What will they be willing to pay for those services? What essential services will we be expected to provide at that time? The answers to these questions will help guide your continuous improvement efforts.

In addition, look at the policies, procedures, and methods currently in place. Are they needed? Should some be refined or discarded? You may want to use

(continued)

Gantt charts, PERT, and other planning techniques to improve maintenance scheduling. A review of inventory levels might reveal that the inventory of spare parts is too high or that a modification to a just-in-time system for supplies and parts could be implemented.

Remember that whatever continuous improvement plan you and your department develop, it must complement the vision and strategic plans of the Middletown School Board.

SUMMARY

1 Planning is the managerial function that determines what is to be done in the future. It includes analyzing the situation, forecasting future events, establishing objectives, setting priorities, and deciding what actions are necessary to achieve objectives. It is a function of every manager from the top-level executive to the supervisor. Without planning, there is no direction to the activities of the organization.

2 Strategic planning involves making decisions that will enable the organization to achieve its short- and long-term objectives. It may involve developing a mission statement that identifies the philosophy and purpose of the organization. Strategic planning is typically the responsibility of upper-level management, although the input of people from all levels of the organization may be sought. Strategic planning typically results in the development of a three to five year plan that sets the course for the entire organization.

3 Planning is the responsibility of every manager. Often, the supervisor needs to consult with others to develop departmental plans that are consistent with those of upper-level management. Supervisors devote most of their attention to short-term (operational) planning. The supervisor's short-term plans should be integrated and coordinated with the longer-term plans (strategic and tactical) of upper-level management. Supervisors need to communicate to employees in a timely fashion what is being planned.

4 Setting objectives is the first step in planning. Although the overall goals and objectives are determined by top-level management, supervisors formulate their departmental objectives, which must be consistent with and direct employee efforts toward achieving organizational goals and objectives. Objectives should state what should be done and when.

5 Management by objectives (MBO) is an approach based on organizational objectives. The effective MBO system has four major elements. The development of specific measurable and verifiable objectives serves as the foundation for determining the necessary resources, the activities that must be carried out, and the results, which are evaluated against the objectives. MBO ties together planning, establishes priorities, and provides coordination of effort.

In practice, specific objectives are mutually agreed upon by employees and their supervisor. Periodic reviews are conducted to make sure that progress is being made. At the end of the appraisal period, results are evaluated against objectives, and rewards are based on this evaluation. Objectives for the next period are then set, and the process begins again.

6 In order to attain objectives, standing plans must be devised. Top-level managers typically develop company-wide policies, procedures, and rules, and each supervisor formulates the necessary subsidiary standing plans for his or her work unit.

Policies are guides to thinking for decision making, and many of them originate with higher-level management. The supervisor's primary concern with policies is one of interpreting, applying, and staying within them when making decisions for the department. Policies are more likely to be followed consistently if they are written.

Procedures, like policies, are standing plans for achieving objectives. They specify a sequence of actions that will guide employees toward objectives. The supervisor often develops procedures to determine how work is to be done. The advantages of procedures are that they require analysis of what needs to be done, promote uniformity of action, and provide a means of appraising the work of employees.

In addition, the supervisor will be called on to design and follow rules. A rule is a directive that must be applied and enforced wherever applicable. Rules serve as guides for action.

7 Supervisors should participate in establishing budgets, which are single-use plans expressed in numerical terms. A budget serves as a control device that enables the supervisor to compare results achieved during the budget period against the budget plan. Supervisors often play a role in organizational programs and projects, which are single-use plans designed to accomplish specific undertakings.

8 Planning facilitates the use of human and physical resources to their fullest potential. Planning how best to utilize the material, capital, and human resources of the firm is essential for effective completion of any activity. Planning promotes efficiency.

9 Crisis management has become a necessity for every organization. Being prepared for the unthinkable, especially in today's uncertain and chaotic world, requires that the supervisor identify potential crisis situations and develop plans for responding to the threats. Supervisors must use their information-gathering and information-giving skills to help employees prepare for and address crises.

10 Not surprisingly, various quality improvement concepts relate directly to planning. Total quality management (TQM) means planning for quality, preventing defects, correcting defects, and continuously improving quality and customer satisfaction. Benchmarking—the process of identifying and improving on the best practices of others—precedes the development of plans. Organizations that want to be as good as or better than the "best in the world" will aim to conform to quality standards established in ISO 9000.

11 Gantt charts and PERT networks are graphic tools to aid supervisors in planning, organizing, and controlling operations, particularly in the context of managing a unique project. Gantt charts require supervisors to identify various activities, determine their sequence, and specify the time spent on each activity. A visual check shows the progress of various activities. If the project is behind schedule, supervisors must develop plans for getting it back on schedule.

Program evaluation and review technique (PERT) is especially applicable for scheduling and sequencing large, complex projects. PERT aids in planning because it forces the supervisor to estimate the time the project will take to complete. Computer software packages are available to reduce the time required to develop PERT networks.

12 Time is one of the supervisor's most valuable resources; therefore, supervisors must plan and manage their own time if they are to be effective. Better time management can result in reduced stress.

Supervisors need to analyze and plan their schedules so as to maximize their time on regular and innovative duties and, by delegating and setting priorities, minimize the time they spend on routine and other low-priority tasks.

Since supervisors never seem to have enough time to do all the things that must be done, they must screen their time-use charts to identify the time wasters that "steal" time from them. Some of the basic tools are calendars, weekly or monthly planning sheets, and to-do lists. Establishing priorities, developing a plan, and working the plan are essential to better use of time.

QUESTIONS FOR DISCUSSION

1. Define planning. How would you respond to a supervisor who reports that he or she is too busy to engage in planning?
2. Distinguish between long-range planning and short-range planning. Relate these concepts to the planning period for top-level managers as compared with the planning period for first-line supervisors. Does a supervisor ever engage in long-range planning? Discuss.
3. Why should a first-line supervisor understand the organization's objectives? Why is this knowledge important to planning at the supervisory level?
4. Identify the four steps in the model for management by objectives presented in the text. Explain the most significant ways that MBO varies from traditional methods of assigning and evaluating work.
5. Distinguish among and provide an example of each of the following:
   a. Policy.
   b. Procedure.
   c. Rule.
6. Distinguish between standing and single-use plans, and provide two examples of each.
7. If you were a supervisor in a small firm that had few policies and you believed that several employees were using illegal drugs, how would you go about developing a plan to handle the situation?
8. Gantt charts and PERT are both planning tools. Identify the most important similarities and differences between these two tools. Under what conditions would each tool be most useful?
9. Discuss each of the following types of supervisory duties in connection with a time-use chart:
   a. Routine duties.
   b. Regular duties.
   c. Special duties.
   d. Innovative duties.

SKILLS APPLICATIONS

Skills Application 2-1: Planning Comparison

1. Interview two supervisors from different areas (e.g., production, banking, health care, retail, etc.). Ask them the following questions:
   a. To what extent do you use planning in your daily work?
   b. What advantages do you gain from planning?
   c. What problems do you have in fulfilling your plans?
   d. What one tip can you give me as a prospective supervisor that would enable me to do a better job of planning?
2. Compare the answers of the two supervisors. What items are similar? Dissimilar?
3. Compare your tips for better planning with those of other students.
4. Make a composite list of tips. Which of those do you currently use in your planning process? Which should you add to your own toolbox of skills?

Skills Application 2-2: Developing a Personal Time Budget

1. Take one hour on Sunday evening as your personal weekly planning period. Develop a time plan for the forthcoming week. List all of the routine, regular, special, and innovative duties that need to be done and estimate the time required for each.
2. Keep a time-use chart for the week, listing all activities and the time spent on each. Compare your time plan with the chart. How well did you plan? Identify the activities (time wasters) that impeded your schedule. Which category of duty consumed most of your time?

Skills Application 2-3: Stress in the Workplace

1. The Contemporary Issue box on page 64 summarizes the results of a study entitled "Work-Life Balance in the New Millennium." Go to the website for the Canadian Policy Research Network at www.cprn.org. Use the browser to type in the name of one of the study's authors (Duxbury) as a quick way to access the report. Download the free report.
2. Review the results of the report, particularly Section 5.5, "Why Should We Worry about Work-Life Conflict?" and Section 6, "What Can Be Done to Reduce Work-Life Conflict?" As a supervisor, what specific strategies can you put in place to ensure that you and your employees can better manage work and life stresses?
3. From your past experience, how well have you handled internal and external stressors? Do you fit the profile of someone with high work-life stress?
4. Identify the top external and internal stressors that you are likely to face this year. Develop a specific action plan to manage that stress. What specific action can you take now and over the course of the next year that will help to ensure that stress is a positive force that motivates you, as opposed to a destructive force that paralyzes you?

SKILLS DEVELOPMENT

Skills Development Module 2-1: Planning and Time Management

This video segment focuses on Janet Ferrell, store operations supervisor for McElvey Department Store, and her planning and time management skills.

Questions for Discussion: The Ineffective Version

1. Identify what Janet Ferrell does well.
2. Discuss Janet Ferrell's planning and time-management techniques.

3. What specific planning and time-management tips would you give Janet Ferrell to help her become more effective?

Questions for Discussion: The More Effective Version

1. Discuss Janet Ferrell's planning and time-management techniques.
2. What else can Janet Ferrell do to be a more effective supervisor?
3. Explain the statement, "Effective planning by Janet Ferrell does not create emergencies for her subordinates."

CASES

CASE 2-1

A Shortage of Policies

The Montclair Manufacturing Company produced a wide array of electronic gauges, and employed about 250 people. Hardeep Parmar, the factory superintendent, was eating his lunch in the company cafeteria with Stan Stefaniuk and Gerry Parker, two supervisors on the assembly line; Mitra Stoebeck, the purchasing agent; and Werner Koff, one of the district sales managers. Their conversation centred around a common complaint—namely, that the company had few written policies or guidelines and that this caused supervisors unnecessary discomfort when they had to make decisions. Parmar deplored the fact that some employees ate their lunches at their work stations, and he also felt that there should be a policy on granting employees leaves of absence. Stoebeck stated that she needed a clear policy specifying how to obtain bids from prospective suppliers. Koff was concerned that top-level management had not bothered to issue a policy regarding a dress code for salespeople when calling on prospective customers. In addition to these specific concerns, there were numerous other complaints that reflected a general feeling of dissatisfaction among the company's managers.

The group concluded that the best way to attack this problem would be to confront Jay Montclair, the president of the company, with their questions and ask him to define policies in these and other areas. While they were deliberating this, May Chiarelli, the assistant to the president, joined them at lunch and listened to much of the conversation. Chiarelli asked, "Are these really matters for the president to decide, or should you supervisors be making these types of decisions for your own departments?"

Questions for Discussion

1. Analyze each of the individual problem situations mentioned in the case. For which areas should policies come from top-level management, and for which areas should policies be made by departmental supervisors?
2. Is there an appropriate dividing line between policies to be made by top-level management and policies that must be made at the departmental level? Discuss.
3. Should the group of supervisors confront the president of the company with a request for more clearly defined policies? What strategies might be suggested for the supervisors to bring their concerns to the company president?
4. Is it beneficial for a company to minimize the number of policies it has in order to permit flexibility in dealing with individual situations? Discuss.

CASE 2-2

The Busy Manager

Wafa Jackson, president of the Laclede Manufacturing Company, arrived at her desk and found a stack of papers on it, although she remembered that she had cleared everything away before she left at eight o'clock the previous night. She asked her assistant what these papers contained. Jackson was informed that they had arrived in the mail late yesterday afternoon and that they were requisitions and letters for authorization from the Oshawa plant. Since she had read them, Jackson asked her assistant to tell her briefly what each request contained. Jackson thought she could save time by doing this. The discussion went as follows:

Assistant:	Request for approval for the purchase of five hectares of land adjoining the Oshawa plant amounting to $195,000, as discussed while you were in Oshawa the last time.
Jackson:	Okay, I'll sign it.
Assistant:	Request for approval to purchase an additional computer and printer for word processing, $4,000.
Jackson:	I know nothing about this. Please inquire why it is needed and who is supposed to get it.
Assistant:	Requisition for a new sign at the entrance of the plant costing $900.
Jackson:	Okay, I'll sign it.
Assistant:	Request for approval to place an ad amounting to $100 as a contribution to the local Police Circus.
Jackson:	Why not? I'll approve.
Assistant:	Requisition to contribute $1,000 to the company's bowling league expenses.
Jackson:	Absolutely not. Get some more information on this.
Assistant:	This needs your approval, also. Some of the offices need painting, and the contractor's estimate is $2,800. (Jackson didn't answer, but put her signature on this paper.)
Assistant:	Request for approval of the purchase of stationery and factory work tickets, totalling $650. (Again, Jackson signed the paper without comment.)

On and on it went. After more than an hour, Jackson was finished with these requisitions, and all the other incoming mail from the morning was placed on her desk. As she started to read, she received numerous telephone calls. While she was still reading the mail, her assistant informed her that the plant superintendent had an important problem on the factory floor and asked that she come to the plant at once. Jackson immediately left her desk and returned after half an hour, wondering to herself why the superintendent could not have solved the problem on his own. All day things piled up regardless of how many decisions she made and how many problems she solved.

On her way home late in the afternoon, Jackson asked herself, "Why do I seem to be so terribly busy and yet, when the day is over, I don't know where all the hours have gone? The day passes all too quickly, and too little is accomplished. And there are so many people who think that being the president of a company is a soft job."

Questions for Discussion

1. What is the major problem in this case? Why?
2. What would you recommend to Jackson to help her to manage her time? Discuss.
3. How can a subordinate help his or her manager allocate time more effectively?

Chapter 3: Problem Solving and Decision Making

After studying this chapter you will be able to

1 Explain the importance of decision-making skills in supervisory management.

2 Describe the types of decisions made in organizations.

3 Describe and apply the basic steps of the decision-making process.

4 Explain why a supervisor should not make hasty decisions.

You are Tom Leeming, supervisor of the shipping department of Zeltin Corporation. You supervise a team of eight employees, and are responsible for ensuring efficient outbound shipments of all the company's finished product.

Zeltin Corporation manufactures electronic components used in the telecommunication industry. At its peak three years ago, the company employed a total of 450 employees at two separate production facilities. Since then, the entire industry has been suffering from drastically reduced sales and profits. Competition in the industry is intense. Last year, Zeltin closed one production facility, and now employs just over 200 workers. All departments have been required to "tighten up" their budgets in order to comply with the president's objective to reduce spending by 20 percent compared to last year. The only hope for Zeltin's long-term survival, the president says, is to cut costs and aggressively promote its products in new market areas.

In keeping with the 20 percent budget reduction mandate, you and other company supervisors have been given strict instructions to absolutely minimize any overtime expenses. In previous years, department supervisors could authorize employees to work overtime at time-and-a-half rates whenever those supervisors considered it necessary. In the past, supervisors scheduled overtime only occasionally. The president recently issued a memo stating that all overtime now must be authorized by the plant manager. In the plant manager's absence, the president's authorization would be required.

You have been experiencing a significantly increased workload in the last six months and have been putting in long hours. Due to unexpected employee absences, the last week has been particularly difficult and the shipping department is several days late in sending out a number of important orders. You worry that these orders might be cancelled by the customers if they are not shipped before the week is over. Because you are convinced that overtime work would help alleviate this situation, you tried to contact the plant manager. However, the plant manager is out of town at an industry trade show and your attempts to reach him have been unsuccessful. You have asked about contacting the president of the company, but were told that he is also out of town and cannot be reached.

Your decision is complicated by a rumour you have heard about a similar situation that occurred in the maintenance department last month. The supervisor in charge had apparently authorized overtime without the plant manager's permission. Although the maintenance supervisor claimed that waiting for the plant manager's return the next day would have made the repair job much more difficult and costly, rumour has it that he was disciplined for his actions.

You are confused about what to do. If you authorize overtime, you might be stepping outside your area of authority. If you do not, some orders will likely fail to ship in time and will likely be cancelled. It is now mid-afternoon on Thursday, and you must decide what to do.

You make the call!

| 1 | THE IMPORTANCE OF DECISION-MAKING SKILLS TO SUPERVISORS |

Explain the importance of decision-making skills in supervisory management.

All human activities involve decision making. Everyone has problems at home, at work, and in social groups for which decisions must be made. Decision making is a normal human requirement that begins in childhood and continues throughout life.

In work settings, when asked to define their major responsibilities, many supervisors respond that "solving problems" and "making decisions" are the most important components of what they do on a daily basis and throughout their ongoing supervisory management tasks. **Decision making** is the process of defining problems and choosing a course of action from among alternatives. The term *decision making* often is associated with the term *problem solving*, since many supervisory decisions focus on solving problems that have occurred or are anticipated. However, the term *problem solving* should not be construed as being limited only to making decisions about problem areas. Problem solving also includes making decisions about realistic opportunities that are present or available if planned for appropriately. Therefore, throughout this chapter, we will use these terms interchangeably. While decision making is an integral part of all the managerial functions, it is particularly at the core of the planning function of management.

Decision making
Defining problems and choosing a course of action from among alternatives.

Many of the problems that confront supervisors in their daily activities are recurring and familiar; for these problems, most supervisors have developed routine answers. But when supervisors encounter new and unfamiliar problems, many find it difficult to decide on a course of action.

Managers and supervisors at all levels are constantly required to find solutions to problems caused by changing situations and unusual circumstances. Regardless of their level, all managers should use a similar, logical, and systematic process of decision making. Although decisions made at the executive level usually are of a wider scope and magnitude than decisions made at the supervisory level, the decision-making process should be fundamentally the same throughout the entire management hierarchy.

Of course, once a decision has been made, effective action is necessary; a good decision that no one implements is of little value. However, in this chapter we are not concerned with the problem of getting effective action. Rather, we discuss the process that should lead to the "best" decision or solution before action is taken.

A decision maker often is depicted as an executive bent over some papers, pen in hand, contemplating whether or not to sign on the dotted line. Or the image may be that of a manager in a meeting, raising an arm to vote a certain way. Both of these images have one thing in common: they portray decision makers as people at the moment of choice, ready to choose an alternative that leads them from the crossroads. Often, a supervisor would like to know in which direction to go, but has not given a lot of thought to the end result. Supervisors need to understand that information gathering, analysis, and other processes must precede the final moment of selecting one alternative over the others.

Decision making is an important skill for supervisors. It is a skill that can be developed—just as the skills involved in playing golf are developed—by learning the steps, practising, and exerting effort. By doing this, supervisors can learn how to make more thoughtful decisions and improve the quality of their decisions.

At the same time, supervisors should ensure that their employees learn to make their own decisions more effectively because a supervisor cannot make all the decisions necessary to run a department. For example, what materials to use, how a job is to be done, when it is to be done, and how to achieve coordination with other departments are decisions that employees often have to make without their supervisor. As evidenced by the Contemporary Issue box on page 80, companies are giving employees a more active role in decision making.[1] Therefore, training subordinates in the process of making decisions should be a high priority for all supervisors.

2	**TYPES OF DECISIONS**

Describe the types of decisions made in organizations.

Management decision-making theorists often classify managerial decisions as being either programmed or nonprogrammed, with many decisions falling somewhere between these two extremes.[2]

Programmed decisions

Solutions to repetitive and routine problems provided by existing policies, procedures, rules, and so on.

Programmed decisions are solutions to problems that are repetitive, well structured, and routine. The term *programmed* is used in the same sense that it is used in computer programming; there is a specific procedure, or program, that can be applied to the problem at hand. Many daily problems that confront supervisors are not difficult to solve because a more or less "pat" answer is available. These problems usually are routine or repetitive, and fixed answers, methods, procedures, rules, and the like exist. Supervisors can delegate these kinds of decisions to subordinates and be confident that the decisions will be made in an acceptable and timely manner.

Nonprogrammed decisions

Solutions to unique problems that require judgment, intuition, and creativity.

Nonprogrammed decisions occur when supervisors are confronted with new or unusual problems for which they must use their intelligent, adaptive problem-solving behaviour. Such problems may be rare, unstructured, or unique, and they are typically one-time occurrences. There are no "pat" answers or guidelines for decision making in these situations. Nonprogrammed decisions tend to be more important, demanding, and strategic than programmed decisions. In nonprogrammed decision making, supervisors are called on to use good judgment, intuition, and creativity in attempting to solve problems. In these situations they should apply a decision-making process by which they can approach the problems in a consistent and logical, but adaptable, manner.[3] The remainder of this chapter will refer primarily to nonprogrammed decision making.

3	**THE DECISION-MAKING PROCESS**

Describe and apply the basic steps of the decision-making process.

In making nonprogrammed managerial decisions, supervisors should follow the steps of the **decision-making process** (see Figure 3-1 on page 81). First, supervisors must define the problem. Second, they must analyze the problem using available information. Third, they need to establish decision criteria—factors that will be used to evaluate the alternatives. Fourth, after thorough analysis, they should develop alternative solutions. After these steps have been taken, supervisors should carefully evaluate the alternatives and select the solution that appears to be the best or most feasible under the circumstances. The concluding step in this process is follow-up and appraisal of the consequences of the decision.

Decision-making process

A systematic, step-by-step process to aid in choosing the "best" alternative.

CONTEMPORARY ISSUE
Burn the Suggestion Box! Strategies for Improving Creative Problem Solving and Decision Making

Businesses have known for centuries that it makes sense to encourage all employees to develop creative solutions to organizational problems. The first use of suggestion boxes can be traced to 14th-century shipbuilding companies in medieval Venice.[1] But Alan Robinson, co-author of "Corporate Creativity: How Innovation and Improvement Actually Happen" says that organizations that rely on suggestion programs are missing the boat when it comes to realizing the creative potential of their employees. "That's the most outmoded way to think of asking your employees for input ... When I walk into a company and see a suggestion box on the wall, I know the place is dead creatively."[2]

Some businesses try to show their commitment to creative problem solving by paying their employees for solutions that result in direct cost savings to the company. This "share the wealth" strategy is designed to motivate employees to think creatively and solve problems rather than just letting problems smolder in the organization. But Robinson claims that, like suggestion boxes, incentive programs are a "definite no-no ... If I offer you a special reward, then I'm sending the signal that I don't expect you to be creative as a normal part of your work. That's the opposite of what we're trying to encourage ... The more you pay for ideas, the fewer you'll get."[3]

So if incentive programs and suggestion boxes don't work, what *can* organizations do to improve the creative decision-making process in the organization? Some companies hire outside "creativity consultants" to try to stir up the collective creative juices of the organization. Lola Rasminsky, director of Toronto's Avenue Road Arts School, developed a program called "Beyond the Box" designed to encourage corporate creative thinking and problem solving. Using music, arts and crafts materials, and drama exercises, Rasminsky challenges corporate executives to role-play and to "find ways of thinking and responding that [they] might not have considered in the past."[4] Paddy Stewart, an ex–high school teacher in Ottawa, has made a business of running what he calls "The Team Humour Experience." Teams of employees come together for a day of interactive initiative games. One game is called "Bedlam Ball Tag," in which 20 balls are dumped on the floor. Employees throw balls at one another and, if hit, must fall to their knees and can't rejoin the game until a ball comes close enough for them to reach.

Arts and crafts, ball games, and role-playing all sound like a fun day away from the usual "desk job," but why do companies such as Bell Canada, the Bank of Montreal, and Alliance Atlantis Communications pay up to $500 per day per person to have their executives attend creativity workshops? Will throwing balls at one another really filter back to better organizational decision making?

Experts in corporate creativity seem to think so. Fred Rosenzveig, a professor at the McGill Management Institute in Montreal, says that anyone can be taught to think and solve problems creatively. He encourages participants at his creativity seminars to "think outside the rules and abandon traditional, 'vertical' thinking."[5] Rosenzveig says that "creative thinking is trained out of us by the school system ... Schools teach us to follow the rules and be right, so we're terrified of being wrong. Most creative people have been thought to be wrong at some point in their lives. To be creative, you have to take risks."[6]

Creativity takes practice, but the results are worth the effort for organizations that want to harness the creative potential of their employees. And it's not just top executives that should be encouraged to use creativity when solving problems and making decisions. Alan Robinson says that "most ideas come from the bottom of organizations. ... most creativity is unexpected and occurring at a real low level [of the organizational ladder]."[7] Employees at all levels need to be encouraged to bring forward creative new ideas, even if those ideas are for small, incremental changes in the way the organization operates. Robinson points out that small ideas, if supported, can "add up and be leveraged, often in unexpected ways. And the "big stuff" is more likely to happen if employees are accustomed to offering up their observations and suggestions and having them acted on. Unless you manage the little stuff, you're not going to get the big innovations, the home-run ideas."[8]

(continued)

Encouraging innovative problem solving and decision making requires a corporate-wide commitment. Some companies have set up entire divisions to handle employee input. Others have established "creativity rooms" or "talk rooms" where employees can go to explore their ideas with others. Whatever the physical structure, there must be a corporate commitment to creative problem solving, including acceptance of the failures that might accompany the successes. Edmonton-based innovation consultant Ernie Zelinski points out that "to double your success rate is also to double your failure rate. If you only reward success, people are afraid to fail. If you are afraid to fail, you are afraid to try anything."[9]

We all know people who claim that they just aren't creative. But these people are taking a limited view of creativity—thinking of it in terms of art, music, or drama. Creativity is a skill that can be learned, like riding a bike or adding and subtracting. Employees at all levels of the organization need to feel comfortable practising these skills, and applying creative thinking to everyday problems in the workplace. Organizations that set up an environment where creative problem solving is respected and encouraged will reap the benefits of better decisions and more engaged workers.

Sources: (1) Alan Robinson as quoted by Barbara Aarsteinsen, "'Little stuff' can add up in often unexpected ways: Good ideas also come from ladder's lower levels," *The Vancouver Sun* (September 8, 1998), p. F1; (2) Ibid., p. F1; (3) Ibid., p. F1; (4) Helen Buttery, "Portrait of artist as free-form exec: In this arts-based program, executives are encouraged to think beyond their routine and daily mental box," *Financial Post* (November 21, 2000), p. C7; (5) Fred Rosenzveig as quoted by Laura Eggertson, "Creativity takes terror out of risk-taking," *The Ottawa Citizen* (August 25, 1986), p. A13; (6) Ibid., p. A13; (7) Robinson as quoted by Aarsteinsen, p. F1; (8) Ibid., p. F1; (9) Ernie Zelinski as quoted by Laura Ramsay, "Rewarding failure the key to creativity," *Financial Post* (August 28, 1991), p. 35. See also Bruce Deachman, "Finding strength in humour: High-tech team-building exercises are a real workout for the funny bone," *The Ottawa Citizen* (December 18, 2000), p. B10; Alan R. Procter, "Creativity and innovation: a culture and not something that is turned on in a crisis," *Pulp & Paper Canada* (March 1, 2002), p. 9.; William Cottringer, "Challenge Your Own Best Thinking," *Supervision* (August 2003), p. 7.

FIGURE 3-1
Effective supervisors follow the decision-making process.

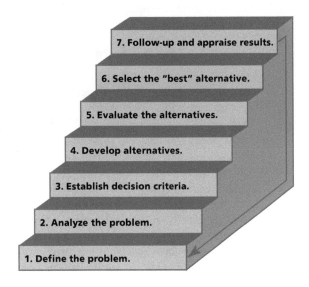

Step 1: Define the Problem

Before seeking answers, the supervisor first should identify the real problem. Nothing is as useless as the right answer to the wrong question. Defining the problem is not an easy task. What appears to be the problem might be merely a symptom that shows on the surface. It usually is necessary to delve deeper to locate the real problem and define it.

Consider the following scenario. Kevin Engle, an office supervisor, believes that a problem of conflicting personalities exists within the department. Two employees, Diana and Stuart, are continually bickering and cannot get along. Because of this lack of cooperation, the job is not being done in a timely manner. Engle needs to develop a clear, accurate problem statement. The problem statement should be brief, specific, and easily understood by others. A good problem statement should address the following key questions:

- What is the problem?
- How do you know there is a problem?
- Where has the problem occurred?
- When has the problem occurred?
- Who is involved in or affected by the problem?

Expressing a problem through a problem statement can help the supervisor understand it. A careful review of answers to the key questions can lead to a problem statement such as that shown in Figure 3-2, which reveals that the major problem is that the work is not getting done in a timely manner. When considering this situation, Engle should focus on why the work is not getting done.

Defining a problem often can become a time-consuming task, but it is time well spent. A supervisor should not go any further in the decision-making process until the problem relevant to the situation has been specifically determined. Remember, a problem exists when there is a difference between the way things are and the way they should be. The effective supervisor will use problem solving not only to take corrective action but also as a means to make improvements in the organization.

Step 2: Analyze the Problem: Gather Facts and Information

After the problem—not just the symptoms—has been defined, the next step is to analyze the problem. The supervisor begins by assembling facts and other pertinent information. This is sometimes viewed as being the first step in decision making, but until the real problem has been defined, the supervisor does not know what information is needed. Only after gaining a clear understanding of the problem can the supervisor decide how important certain data are and what additional information to seek.

Kevin Engle, the office supervisor in the earlier scenario, needs to find out why the work is not getting done. When he gathers information, he finds out that he never clearly outlined the expectations for each employee—where their duties begin and where they end. What appeared on the surface to be a problem of personality conflict was actually a problem caused by the supervisor. The chances are good that once the activities and responsibilities of the two employees are

FIGURE 3-2   Example of a problem statement.

The bickering between Diana and Stuart detracts from the completion of work assignments. Last Monday and Tuesday, neither of them completed assigned customer callbacks. Customers, other department employees, and the shipping department are all affected.

A supervisor rarely makes a decision that pleases everyone.

Getty Images/Photodisc Collection

clarified, the friction will end. Engle needs to monitor the situation closely to ensure that the work is being completed on time.

Being only human, a supervisor will find that personal opinion is likely to creep into decision making. This is particularly true when employees are involved in the problem. For example, if a problem involves an employee who performs well, the supervisor may be inclined to show this person greater consideration than would be accorded a poor performer. Therefore, the supervisor should try to be as objective as possible in gathering and examining information.

Sometimes the supervisor does not know how far to go in searching for additional facts. A good practice is to observe reasonable time and cost limitations. This means gathering all the information that can be obtained without undue delay and without excessive costs.

In the process of analysis, the supervisor should try to think of intangible factors that play a significant role. Some intangible factors are reputation, morale, discipline, and personal biases. While specific intangible factors will vary from situation to situation, they should be considered in the analysis of a problem. As a general rule, written and objective information is more reliable than opinions and hearsay.

Step 3: Establish Decision Criteria

Decision criteria

Standards or measures to use in evaluating alternatives.

Decision criteria are standards or measures used when evaluating alternatives; they are typically statements of what the supervisor wants to accomplish with the decision. Such criteria can also be used to determine how well the implementation phase of the process is going—that is, whether the solution is doing what it was intended to do. To illustrate, suppose that Engle's initial actions do not remedy the situation. It will be appropriate to establish decision criteria. Figure 3-3 provides examples of the decision criteria Engle could use for evaluating alternate courses of action.

FIGURE 3-3 Sample decision criteria.

THE SOLUTION:
- Should result in the work assignments being completed on time.
- Should incur no financial cost to implement.
- Must not impede quality of service to the customer.
- Should put neither Diana's nor Stuart's job in jeopardy.
- Should not have a negative impact on other employees.
- Must alleviate the problem within one week.

Once the decision criteria are established, the supervisor must determine which criteria are absolutely necessary and their order of priority. Because it is likely that no alternative will meet all the criteria, the supervisor needs to know which criteria are most important so that alternatives can be judged by how many of the important criteria they meet. The supervisor may want to consult with upper-level managers, peers, or employees to assist in prioritizing the criteria.

Step 4: Develop Alternatives

After the supervisor has defined and analyzed the problem and established decision criteria, the next step is to develop various alternative solutions. The supervisor should consider as many possible solutions as can reasonably be developed. By formulating many alternatives, the supervisor is less apt to overlook the best course of action. A decision can be only as good as the best alternative that has been developed.

Almost all problem situations have a number of alternatives. The full range of choices may not always be obvious, but supervisors must search for them. If supervisors do not do this, they are likely to fall into "either/or" type of thinking, examining only a limited number of options. It is not enough for supervisors just to decide from among alternatives that employees have suggested, because there may be other alternatives to consider. Supervisors must stretch their minds to develop additional alternatives, even in the most discouraging situations. None of the alternatives might be desirable, but at least the supervisor can strive to find one that is least undesirable.

Suppose that an office supervisor has been ordered to make a 20 percent reduction in employment because the firm is experiencing financial problems. After careful study, the supervisor develops the following feasible alternatives:

1. Lay off employees who have the least seniority, regardless of their job classification or performance, until the overall 20 percent reduction is reached.
2. Lay off employees who have the lowest performance ratings until the overall 20 percent reduction is reached.
3. Analyze department duties and decide which jobs are essential. Keep the employees who are best qualified to perform those jobs.
4. Without laying off anyone, develop a schedule of reduced work hours for every employee that would be equivalent to a 20 percent reduction.
5. Develop proactive alternatives to increase the firm's revenues so that no employee has to be laid off.

While alternative five is most attractive, it is not realistic, given the current economic situation. Although none of the other alternatives may be an ideal solution to this unpleasant problem, at least the office supervisor has considered several alternatives before making a decision. While these may be "no-win" situations, the illustration does portray the realities of organizational life and the difficult decisions that supervisors must sometimes make.

Brainstorming and Creative Problem Solving

When enough time is available, a supervisor should assemble a group of other supervisors or employees to brainstorm solution alternatives to a perplexing problem. **Brainstorming** is a free flow of ideas within a group, with judgment suspended, in order to come up with as many alternatives as possible. Using this technique, the supervisor presents the problem and the participants offer as many alternative solutions as they can develop in the time available. It is understood that any idea is acceptable at this point—even those that may at first appear to be wild or unusual. Evaluation of ideas is suspended so that participants can give free rein to their creativity.

Brainstorming requires an atmosphere that encourages creativity. When supervisors are unwilling to devote sufficient time to brainstorming, or when supervisors try to dominate the process with their own opinions and solutions, the brainstorming effort is likely to fail.[4]

Alex Osborn, an authority on creativity and the brainstorming approach, has suggested the following four guidelines for effective brainstorming:

1. Defer all judgment of ideas. During the brainstorming period, allow no criticism by anyone in the group. It is natural for people to suppress new ideas both consciously and unconsciously, and this tendency must be avoided. Even if an idea seems impractical and useless at first, it should not be rejected

Brainstorming
A free flow of ideas within a group, while suspending judgment, aimed at developing many alternative solutions to a problem.

Using brainstorming, the supervisor presents the problem and the participants offer as many solutions as they can in the time available.

Ryan McVay/Photodisc Red/Getty Images

by quick initial judgments because such rejection could inhibit the free flow of more ideas.

2. Seek quantity of ideas. Idea fluency is the key to creative problem solving, and fluency means quantity. The greater the number of ideas, the greater the likelihood that some of them will be viable solutions.

3. Encourage "freewheeling." Being creative calls for a free-flowing mental process in which all ideas, no matter how extreme, are welcome. Even the wildest idea may, on further analysis, have some usefulness.

4. "Hitchhike" on existing ideas. Combining, adding to, and rearranging ideas often can produce new approaches that are superior to the original ideas. When creative thought processes slow or stop, review some of the ideas already produced and attempt to hitchhike on them with additions or revisions.[5]

The preceding guidelines are applicable to brainstorming both on an individual and group basis. When it involves a large group of people, an unstructured brainstorming session can become rather long, tedious, and unproductive because many of the ideas are simply not feasible and because conflicts may develop within the group due to individual biases. For this reason, the **nominal group technique (NGT)**, which provides a means to enable group members to generate ideas more efficiently, is advocated. Typically, NGT first involves having individual members of the group develop and write down their own list of ideas and alternatives to solve the problem at hand. Then there is a sharing of ideas among group members with ensuing discussion, evaluation, and refinements. The group's final choice(s) may be made by a series of confidential votes in which the list of ideas is narrowed until a consensus is attained.[6]

Creative approaches and brainstorming meetings are particularly adaptable to nonprogrammed decisions, especially if the problem is new, important, or strategic in nature. Even the supervisor who takes time to mentally brainstorm a problem alone is likely to develop more alternatives for solving the problem than one who does not brainstorm.[7]

Nominal group technique (NGT)

A group brainstorming and decision-making process by which individual members first identify alternative solutions privately and then share, evaluate, and decide on them as a group.

Ethical Considerations

Both in the development and the evaluation of alternatives, a supervisor should consider only those that are lawful and acceptable within the organization's ethical guidelines. In recent years, many firms have required that their managers, supervisors, and employees make ethical decisions because they recognize that, in the long term, good ethics is good business.[8] Consequently, many firms have developed handbooks, policies, and official statements that specify the ethical standards and practices expected from their employees.[9]

The following list of guidelines, or **ethical "tests"** for ethical decision making, is not totally comprehensive, but these considerations are relevant in addressing the ethical aspects of most problem situations.

Ethical "tests"

Considerations or guidelines to be addressed in developing and evaluating ethical aspects of decision alternatives.

> *Legal/compliance test:* Laws, regulations, and policies are to be followed, not broken or ignored. The rationale and explanation that "everybody's doing it" and "everybody's getting away with it" are poor excuses for violating a law, policy, or regulation. If in doubt, ask someone who knows the law or regulation for proper guidance. However, legal compliance should be only a starting point in most ethical decision making.

Public-knowledge test: What would be the consequences if the outcome of a particular alternative decision became known to the public, one's family, the media, or a government agency?

Long-term-consequences test: What would be the long-term versus short-term outcomes? Weigh these against each other.

Examine-your-motives test: Do the motives for a proposed decision benefit the company and others? Or are they primarily selfish in nature and designed to harm other people and their interests?

Inner-voice test: This is the test of conscience and moral values that have been instilled in most of us since childhood. If something inside you says that the choice being contemplated may be wrong, it usually is. It is prudent then to look for a different and better alternative.

It cannot be stressed enough that if a supervisor believes that a particular alternative is questionable or might not be acceptable within the firm's ethical policies, the supervisor should consult with his or her manager or with a staff specialist who is knowledgeable in the area for guidance in how to proceed.

Step 5: Evaluate the Alternatives

The ultimate purpose of decision making is to choose the specific course of action that will provide the greatest number of wanted and the smallest number of unwanted consequences. After developing alternatives, supervisors can mentally test each of them by imagining that each has already been put into effect. Supervisors should try to foresee the probable desirable and undesirable consequences of each alternative. By thinking the alternatives through and appraising their consequences, supervisors will be in a position to compare the desirability of the various choices.

The usual way to begin is to eliminate alternatives that do not meet the supervisor's previously established decision criteria and ethical standards. The supervisor should evaluate how many of the most important criteria are met by each remaining alternative. The successful alternative is the one that satisfies or meets the most criteria at the highest priority levels.

Nonprogrammed decisions usually require the decision maker to choose a course of action without complete information about the situation. Because of this uncertainty, the chosen alternative may not yield the intended results. Thus, there is risk involved. Some supervisors will consider the degree of risk and uncertainty associated with each course of action. There is no such thing as a riskless decision; one alternative may simply involve less risk than the others.[10]

The issue of time may make one alternative preferable to all others. This is especially true if there is some urgency to the decision and one alternative clearly will take less time to implement than the available alternatives. The supervisor should also consider the facilities, records, tools, and other resources available. It is critically important to judge different alternatives in terms of economy of effort and resources. In other words, which action will give the greatest benefits and results for the least cost and effort?

When one alternative clearly appears to provide a greater number of desirable consequences and fewer unwanted consequences than any other alternative, the decision is fairly easy. More often than not, however, there is no clear choice. At times, two or more alternatives may seem equally desirable. Here the choice may become a matter of personal preference. It is also possible that the supervisor may believe that no single alternative is significantly stronger than any other. In this case, it might be possible to combine the positive aspects of the better alternatives into one composite solution.

Sometimes none of the alternatives is satisfactory; all of them have too many undesirable effects, or none will bring about the desired results. In such a case, the supervisor should begin to think of new alternative solutions or perhaps even start all over again by attempting to redefine the problem.

A situation might arise in which the undesirable consequences of all the alternatives appear to be so overwhelmingly unfavourable that the supervisor feels that the "best" available solution is to take no action at all. However, this may be self-deceiving, since taking no action will not solve the problem. Taking no action is as much a decision as is taking a specific action, even though the supervisor may believe that an unpleasant choice has been avoided. The supervisor should visualize the consequences that are likely to result from taking no action. Only if the consequences of taking no action are the most desirable should it be selected as the appropriate course.

Step 6: Select the "Best" Alternative

Optimizing
Selecting the "best" alternative.

Satisficing
Selecting the alternative that minimally meets the decision criteria.

Selecting the alternative that seems to be the "best" is known as **optimizing**. However, sometimes the supervisor makes a **satisficing** decision by selecting an alternative that minimally meets the decision criteria. A famous management theorist, Herbert Simon, once likened the difference to the comparison between finding a needle in a haystack (satisficing) and finding the biggest, sharpest needle in the haystack (optimizing).[11] Nevertheless, after developing and evaluating alternatives, the supervisor needs to make a choice.

Among the most prominent bases for choosing the "best" alternative are experience, intuition, advice from others, experimentation, and statistical and quantitative decision making. Regardless of the process used, a supervisor will rarely make a decision that is equally pleasing to everyone.

Experience

In making a selection from among various alternatives, the supervisor should be guided by experience. Chances are that certain situations will recur, and the old saying that "experience is the best teacher" does apply to a certain extent. A supervisor often can decide wisely based on personal experience or the experience of some other manager. Knowledge gained from experience is a helpful guide, and its importance should not be underestimated. On the other hand, it is dangerous to follow experience blindly.

When looking to experience as a basis for choosing among alternatives, the supervisor should examine the situation and the conditions that prevailed at the time of the earlier decision. It may be that conditions still are nearly identical to those that prevailed on the previous occasion and that the decision should be similar to the one made then. More often than not, however, conditions have changed considerably and the underlying assumptions are no longer the same. Therefore, the new decision probably should not be identical to the earlier one.

Experience can be helpful in the event that the supervisor is called on to substantiate his or her reasons for making a particular decision. In part this may be a defensive approach, but there is no excuse for following experience in and of itself. Experience must always be viewed with the future in mind. The underlying circumstances of the past, the present, and the future must be considered realistically if experience is to help supervisors select from among alternatives.

Intuition

Supervisors admit that at times they base their decisions on intuition. Some supervisors even appear to have an unusual ability to solve problems satisfactorily by subjective means.[12] However, a deeper search usually will disclose that the so-called "intuition" on which the supervisor appeared to have based a decision was really experience or knowledge that had been stored in the supervisor's memory. By recalling similar situations that occurred in the past, supervisors may reach a better decision even though they label it as "having a hunch."

Intuition may be particularly helpful in situations in which other alternatives have been tried previously with poor results. If the risks are not too great, a supervisor may choose a new alternative because of an intuitive feeling that a fresh approach might bring positive results. Even if the hunch does not work out well, the supervisor has tried something different. The supervisor will remember this as part of his or her experience and can draw upon it in reaching future decisions.

Advice from Others

Although a supervisor cannot shift personal responsibility for making decisions in the department, the burden of decision making often can be eased by seeking the advice of others. The ideas and suggestions of employees, other supervisors, staff experts, technical authorities, and the supervisor's own manager can be of great help in weighing facts and information. Seeking advice does not mean avoiding a decision, since the supervisor still must decide whether or not to accept the advice of others.

Many believe that two heads are better than one and that input from others will improve the decision process.[13] The following four guidelines can help the supervisor decide whether groups should be included in the decision-making process:

1. If additional information would increase the quality of the decision, involve those who can provide that information. Quality is the degree to which a decision solves the problem and meets the decision criteria.
2. If acceptance of the decision is critical, involve those whose acceptance is important.
3. If people's skills can be developed through participation, involve those who need the development opportunity.
4. If the situation is not life threatening and does not require immediate action, involve others in the process, as this builds commitment to ensuring successful implementation.[14]

Generally, the varied perspectives and experiences of others will add to the decision-making process.

Experimentation

In the scientific world, where many conclusions are based on tests in laboratories, experimentation is essential and accepted. In supervision, however, experimentation to see what happens is often too costly in terms of people, time, and money. Nevertheless, there are some instances in which a limited amount of testing and experimenting is advisable. For example, a supervisor may find it worthwhile to try several different locations for a new copy machine in the department to see which location employees prefer and which is most convenient for the work flow. There are also some instances in which a certain amount of testing is advisable in order to provide employees with an opportunity to try out new ideas or approaches, perhaps of their own design. While experimentation may be valid from a motivational standpoint, it can be a slow and relatively expensive method of reaching a decision.

Quantitative Decision Making

Numerous techniques and models of quantitative decision making have received much attention in management literature and practice. Included among these techniques are linear programming, operations research, and probability and simulation models. These tend to be sophisticated statistical and mathematical approaches, often used in connection with computers.[15] They require the decision maker to quantify most of the information that is relevant to a particular decision. For many supervisors, these quantitative decision-making techniques are rather remote. Yet many large firms have management decision support systems that assist supervisors in making nonprogrammed decisions. One desirable feature of quantitative decision making is the ability of the user to perform "what if" scenarios—the simulation of a business situation over and over again using different data in each case for selected decision areas.

With the increasing use of computer networks, many firms are able to develop programs and information storage and retrieval systems that supervisors can use relatively easily for certain types of decisions, especially when historical and statistical databases are involved. For some types of problems, supervisors may be able to seek the help of mathematicians, engineers, statisticians, systems analysts, and computer specialists who can bring their tools to bear on relevant problems. This can be an involved and costly procedure, however, and decisions such as those facing Tom Leeming in the "You Make the Call" section generally cannot be made from statistical or quantitative models.

Step 7: Follow Up and Appraise the Results

After a decision has been made, specific actions are necessary to carry it out. Follow-up and appraisal of the outcome of a decision are actually part of the process of decision making.

Follow-up and appraisal of a decision can take many forms, depending on the nature of the decision, timing, costs, standards expected, personnel, and other factors. For example, a minor production scheduling decision could easily be evaluated on the basis of a short written report or perhaps even by the supervisor's observation or a discussion with employees. However, a major decision involving the installation of complex new equipment will require close and time-consuming follow-up by the supervisor, technical employees, and higher-level managers. This type of decision usually requires the supervisor to prepare numerous detailed written reports of equipment performance under varying conditions, which are compared closely with plans or expected standards for the equipment.

The important point to recognize is that the task of decision making is incomplete without some form of follow-up and appraisal of the actions taken. Part of the evaluation process is to establish periodic checkpoints that cause the supervisor to review the outcomes. If the supervisor has established decision criteria or specific objectives that the decision should accomplish, it will be easier to evaluate the effects of the decision. If the consequences have turned out well, the supervisor can feel reasonably confident that the decision was sound.

If the follow-up and appraisal indicate that something has gone wrong or that the results have not been as anticipated, then the supervisor's decision-making process must begin all over again. This may even mean going back over each of the various steps of the decision-making process in detail. The supervisor's definition and analysis of the problem and the development of alternatives may have to be completely revised in view of new circumstances surrounding the problem. In other words, when follow-up and appraisal indicate that the problem has not been resolved satisfactorily, the supervisor will find it advisable to treat the situation as a brand-new problem and go through the decision-making process from a completely fresh perspective. See Figure 3-4 for a review of specific suggestions for improving the decision-making process.

| 4 | **TIME AFFECTS THE DECISION-MAKING PROCESS** |

Explain why a supervisor should not make hasty decisions.

In some situations, supervisors may believe they do not have enough time to go through the decision-making process outlined here. Frequently, a manager, a co-worker, or an employee approaches the supervisor, says "Here's the problem," and looks to the supervisor for an immediate answer. However, supervisors cannot afford to make a decision without considering the steps of the process. Most problems do not require an immediate answer.

When an employee brings up a problem, the supervisor should ask questions such as the following:

1. How extensive is the problem? Does it need an immediate response?
2. Who else is affected by the problem? Should they be involved in this discussion?

FIGURE 3-4   Some suggestions for improving problem solving and decision making.

1. Take enough time to state the problem accurately and concisely and to identify the objectives you want to accomplish with your decision.
2. Whenever appropriate, seek opinions and suggestions from others who can contribute their ideas toward solving the problem.
3. Before deciding what to do, gather ample facts and information that will help define/clarify the problem and suggest solutions.
4. Stretch your mind to develop numerous alternative solutions; brainstorm with others when practicable.
5. Make your decision based on objective criteria; avoid letting personal biases and organizational political considerations direct your choice.
6. When implementing and following up your decision, do not hesitate to admit and rectify errors in the decision, even if doing so causes some personal embarrassment. (Admitting mistakes early is prudent and builds your integrity with others.)

3. Have you (the employee) thought through the problem, and do you have an idea of what the end result should be?
4. What do you recommend? Why?

This approach is a form of participative supervision and can help to develop the employee's analytic skills. The supervisor can then better think through the problem, apply the decision-making steps, and make a decision.

Many supervisors get themselves into trouble by making hasty decisions without following all of the steps outlined in the decision-making process. A word of caution here: if supervisors tell other people that they "will get back to them," the supervisors should state a specific time. If a supervisor fails to make a decision or give feedback to the other people by the specified time, he or she may incur a serious breach of trust.

WHAT CALL DID YOU MAKE?

As Tom Leeming, you are in a difficult situation that requires you to make a decision. You are under strict orders not to schedule departmental overtime without authorization from higher management, and you have been unable to obtain that authorization. You are convinced that unless your employees work overtime, certain orders will not ship on time and may be cancelled, probably to the detriment of Zeltin Corporation.

Certainly, top managers are at fault for failing to clarify their overtime directive. There has been no indication of any alternative method for supervisory decision making when top managers are not present. The original, strict directive was bound to cause difficulties. However, Leeming and other supervisors should have questioned the directive before problems arose. They are also to blame for leaving the directive as a "policy" with unclear application. Situations like the one in this case can be prevented when supervisors and managers discuss policies and directives in meetings and resolve ambiguities or possible conflicts. Asking "what if?" in regard to applications of a policy or directive can often bring about the clarification that avoids these types of situations.

At this point, as Leeming, you must decide what to do. If you believe that your primary responsibility is to meet the important goal of customer satisfaction, you will authorize the overtime and you will risk being disciplined accordingly.

If, however, you believe the important short-term objective of the company is to reduce costs, even at the expense of losing customers, you should not go beyond your authority by authorizing the overtime. That is, if you believe your first obligation is to comply with a management directive while being on the safe side with regard to your authority, you will schedule no overtime and you will hope the adverse consequences will not be too great.

Before you decide what to do, review the steps of the decision-making model described in this chapter. In particular, consider what other alternatives could enable you to "harmonize" what appears to be a "no-win" situation. A number of alternatives might be suggested here, including shifting delivery priorities, contacting affected customers, and borrowing workers from other departments. You may want to consult with other supervisors or your employees to seek other approaches to solving the problem.

At times like this, supervisory decision making requires a certain amount of thoughtful problem solving, perhaps using some of the principles of creative problem solving discussed in this chapter.

SUMMARY

 All supervisory activities involve decision making. Supervisors must find solutions for problems that are caused by changing situations and unusual circumstances. Decision making based on careful study of information and analysis of the various courses of action available is still the most generally approved avenue of selection from among alternatives. Decision making is a choice between two or more alternatives, and the decisions made by supervisors significantly affect departmental results.

Decision making is a skill that can be learned. Organizations are giving employees a more active role in decision making today than they did in the past.

 Supervisors confront many decision situations, which can vary from the programmed type at one extreme to the nonprogrammed type at the other. Decisions for routine, repetitive-type problems are usually made more easily with the use of policies, procedures, standard practices, and the like. However, nonprogrammed decisions are usually one-time, unusual, or unique problems that require sound judgment and systematic thinking.

 Better decisions are more likely to occur when supervisors follow the steps of the decision-making process:

1. Define the problem.
2. Analyze the problem; gather facts and information.
3. Establish decision criteria.
4. Develop a sufficient number of alternatives.
5. Evaluate alternatives by using the decision criteria or by thinking of them as if they had already been placed into action and considering their consequences.
6. Select the alternative that has the greatest number of wanted and least number of unwanted consequences.
7. Implement, follow up, and appraise the results. It may be necessary to take corrective action if the decision is not achieving the desired objective.

The supervisor should develop a problem statement that answers the questions of what, how, where, when, and who. Proper problem definition clarifies the difference between the way things are and the way they should be.

After defining the problem, the supervisor must gather information. Decision criteria, which are measures or standards of what the supervisor wants to accomplish with the decision, should be specified. In developing alternatives, supervisors can use brainstorming and creative thinking techniques.

Only alternatives that are legal and ethical within the organization's guidelines should be considered. In the process of evaluation and choice, a supervisor can be aided by ethical guidelines, personal experience, intuition, advice from others, experimentation, and quantitative methods.

Once the decision has been made, specific actions are necessary to carry it out. Follow-up and appraisal are essential.

 Supervisors run the risk of getting themselves into trouble unless they follow the steps of the decision-making process. The process is time consuming but most problems do not require an immediate answer. It is often valuable to allow subordinates to assist in the decision-making process. They may see the problem from a different perspective, and they may have information that bears on the problem.

QUESTIONS FOR DISCUSSION

1. Think of a major decision you have made in your life. For example, why did you decide to go to college or university? Why did you decide on the school you selected? How did you decide on your major? Explain how you applied the decision-making steps identified in this chapter. Are there any other factors you should have considered when making your decision?

2. Define decision making. Does the decision-making process vary depending on where a manager or supervisor is located in the managerial hierarchy? Discuss.

3. Distinguish between programmed and nonprogrammed types of decisions. Identify a relatively significant decision and a relatively insignificant decision for each type.

4. Why should supervisors write a problem statement to assist them in defining the problem?

5. Review the steps of the decision-making process in their proper sequence. What pitfalls should the supervisor avoid at each step?

6. Identify the major elements of the brainstorming approach.

7. Describe a situation in which you would prefer to solve the problem in a group rather than by yourself. Why? What are the advantages of each approach? The limitations?

8. Define and discuss the factors that a supervisor should consider in developing and evaluating alternatives in the decision-making process. To what degree should ethical issues be a consideration? Identify and discuss five ethical "tests" in this process.

9. Is it ever appropriate to use "no decision" as your approach to solving a problem? Discuss.

10. When deciding on a course of action, do you tend to rely more on past experiences or on the need to be creative? Provide an example from your past to support your answer.

11. Do you believe that creative problem solving can be encouraged in an organizational setting? Why or why not? Have you ever worked in an environment that fostered creative problem solving? If so, what specific strategies did the organization use to encourage its employees to use creative problem solving?

SKILLS APPLICATIONS

Skills Application 3-1: Assess Your Creative Problem-Solving Skills

Although simple quizzes and tests cannot assess with certainty an individual's ability in any area, they can be a fun way to learn more about ourselves. The Internet provides access to a wide variety of personality tests and quizzes. Queendom.com describes itself as "an internet magazine with a difference: We provide an interactive avenue for self-exploration with a healthy dose of fun."

Go to www.queendom.com/tests/career/create_ps_access.html and take the free creative problem-solving test. There is no need to register or provide any personal information about yourself. After completing the 30-question quiz, submit your results and you will be provided with a brief assessment of your current level of creative problem-solving ability.

1. Do you generally agree or disagree with the assessment of your creative problem-solving ability provided by this quiz tool? Explain.

2. Visit the site http://riri.essortment.com/creativityprobl_rcch.htm and read the brief article entitled "How to Improve Your Creativity and Problem Solving" by Sally Nulph. Think of a complex problem you were faced with in the past. Which strategies described in this article may have helped you solve this problem more creatively?

Skills Application 3-2: Mastering the Registration Process

The notion of continuous improvement assumes that every process can be improved. Think back to the registration process at your college or university. Were you able to complete the registration process with a minimum of effort, or was the process cumbersome and inefficient?

1. Break into groups of seven or more people. Each student should consider the registration process from one of the following perspectives:
   a. The registrar (responsible for scheduling classes and rooms).
   b. The cashier's office (responsible for collecting fees).
   c. The president of the college or university.
   d. The bookstore manager.
   e. A faculty member (responsible for teaching a variety of courses at various times).
   f. Student (one or more).
2. As a group, formulate a clear problem statement.
3. Make a list of the information you believe you will need in order to solve the problem. Where will you get the information?
4. List the decision criteria that any solution must meet.
5. Brainstorm alternative solutions.
6. Suppose the college or university president says that the registrar has the responsibility for making the final decision. If the registrar solves the problem from his or her own perspective, does that person run the risk of creating greater problems for others? Explain.

Skills Application 3-3: An Exercise in Brainstorming

A long-term customer tells you that your competitor can provide the same service that you offer but at a significantly lower price. The customer wants to know whether you can meet or beat the price. You have the authority to reduce prices, but not to the extent the customer implies. The competitor's price is less than your breakeven point. You promise to give the matter some thought, check with others, and respond with an answer tomorrow afternoon.

1. Working alone, take a few minutes to make a list of at least three possible solutions to the problem.
2. Get together with three other people and brainstorm as many options as you can (other than cutting price) that might meet the customer's needs.
3. Analyze the brainstorming activity. Did the process take more time than working alone? Did the process enable you to see a variety of options? Did the group generate several options that you would not have thought of?
4. What do you conclude from this exercise about the benefits and limitations of brainstorming?

SKILLS DEVELOPMENT

Skill Development Module 3-1: Decision Making

VIDEO

This video segment shows McElvey Department Store's operations supervisor, Janet Ferrell, as she tries to prepare for the biggest sale of the year.

Questions for Discussion: The Ineffective Version

1. What does Janet Ferrell do well?
2. Discuss what Janet Ferrell should do to be a more effective supervisor.
3. After observing the video, list as many situations as you can that require a decision.
4. Decide which problem confronting Janet Ferrell is most urgent. Following the steps in the decision-making process identified in Figure 3-1 (page 81), solve the problem.

Questions for Discussion: The More Effective Version

1. Discuss how Janet Ferrell used the decision-making process to solve the store's problem.
2. What could Janet Ferrell have done to be even more effective as a supervisor?
3. Explain why supervisors often involve subordinates in the decision process.
4. Would Janet Ferrell be more effective if she delegated the decisions to others? Why or why not?

CASES

CASE 3-1

The Little Things Add Up!

Lynda Lamarche had worked for Economy Parcel Service (EPS), a regional courier service, for the past 22 years. She knew that pleasing the customer was the key to operating a successful business. She was extremely proud of the "Employee of the Month" awards she had received. Several times before, Lamarche had been offered various supervisory positions but had always turned them down because she did not feel she wanted the extra duties and responsibilities that came with the advancement. Management considers her the "ideal employee." She rarely needed to be told what to do and never missed work. Her work was always done the right way the first time. Operations manager Shaquan Brown had been overheard to remark, "I wish we could figure out a way to clone Lynda. She's by far the best employee we've got."

Lamarche worked the 11 P.M. to 7:30 A.M. shift. Her position was vital because she sorted packages on both sides of the master conveyor belt and directed them onto assorted belts where others loaded them into bins and then into delivery vehicles. EPS has been experiencing some ups and downs in business over the last year. Larger, national courier services have been cutting prices, and EPS has struggled to remain competitive. Employees were being asked to do more with less, increase productivity, tighten delivery schedules, and have been told to expect no pay raises. The last item was especially difficult for Lamarche because she is principal caregiver for her elderly mother, and the household budget is tight. "The harder I work, the more behind I get," Lamarche lamented.

Lamarche came into work promptly one evening, as always, and told her immediate supervisor, Tony Barrett, that she had to leave by 6:30 A.M., one hour early, because her mother had an 8:00 A.M. appointment at the hospital. Barrett responded, "Fine. Just remind me later." Barrett had been Lamarche's immediate supervisor for the past seven months, but they have known each other for about 15 years. Lamarche's previous supervisor had been downsized, and Barrett's duties had been expanded to cover several additional areas, including the one that Lamarche worked in. Unlike Lamarche's previous supervisor, Barrett failed to tell employees what he expected and rarely gave them any feedback.

At 5:30 A.M., Larmarche reminded Barrett about the appointment. Barrett asked the operations manager if he had an employee to cover the hour after Lamarche had to leave. The operations manager's response was, "No, I don't have anyone. In fact, we're so short of people right now that I don't know if we'll meet the delivery schedule. If I would have known sooner, I might have been able to find coverage for you."

When Barrett told her she would be unable to leave early, Lamarche immediately began to fume. "So this is the way they treat dedicated and loyal employees. After all, I asked my supervisor at the beginning of the shift if I could leave early—just like the handbook says," Larmarche complained to anyone willing to listen. She stayed until her regular quitting time, but her full attention was not on her work. As a result, several missorts occurred.

After punching out, Lamarche rushed home, hustled her mother into the car, and left for the hospital. While waiting for her mother to have her tests done, Lamarche replayed the night's events over and over in her mind. "I don't ask this company for much and I bend over backward to get the job done. I'll show them: I'll call in sick tomorrow and see how they appreciate the inconvenience."

About 15 minutes before her assigned shift the next day, Lamarche called her supervisor and said, "I'm not feeling well this evening. I think it might be that new strain of flu, and I'd hate to spread it to anyone else. I'll call you tomorrow and let you know how I'm feeling, because I'm scheduled to work tomorrow evening as well." Lamarche had several sick days left, and company policy required employees to report their sicknesses at least 15 minutes before the start of their shifts.

The employee assigned to Lamarche's duties lacked the skill and knowledge to do the job in a correct and timely fashion. Additionally, that employee feared making mistakes, so every package was checked and double-checked to ensure it got onto the right conveyor. Work in progress backed up, and many trucks did not get loaded until mid-morning. Many customers received their packages late.

Questions for Discussion

1. What problems must be addressed at EPS?
2. What could Barrett have done to prevent or minimize those problems?
3. Why did Lamarche behave the way she did?
4. What can Barrett do to change Lamarche's current outlook about her job?
5. Everyone must learn from their mistakes. How can EPS use this situation as a case study for the entire organization?

CASE 3-2

Break Time Is My Time

Sonic Boom Inc. is a year-old division of Great Audio Dynamite (GAD), the market leader in compact disc recording machines. Being a young company, Sonic has not yet completed its employee handbook, so in an effort to proceed with daily operations, Sonic implemented the employee handbook of its parent company, GAD, on an interim basis.

Sonic operated on the outskirts of a major city. During its start-up year, GAD promoted some of its best younger personnel into managerial roles at Sonic. Hiring quality workers to meet production demands became a formidable task as neighbouring area companies had excellent wages and benefits to offer. In an effort to attract good workers to the company, Sonic advertised and promoted the advantages of a nonunion work environment and its generous packages of wages, benefits, and flexible work hours. Even applicants with marginal skills were hired in an effort to staff the busy production line. This did not seem to pose major problems, however, since Sonic implemented GAD's well-established employee training programs to bring new employees "up to speed" as soon as possible.

During the hiring process, close relatives, including siblings and spouses, were hired due to the competitive circumstances. Sid and Nancy Hendrix were both employed by Sonic. Nancy was hired as a draftsperson based on previous job experience, while Sid was offered an interview and, subsequently, a job following a chance meeting with Tim Armstrong, production supervisor, at a local restaurant.

Both Sid and Nancy Hendrix were model employees. Sid was hired to work on the production floor operating industrial machines. He had completed his operator and teamwork training at a local college, and he graduated from the program at the top of his class. Sonic management saw Sid as being "highly promotable" and assigned him as a team leader on the first-shift production crew. Team leaders were still hourly employees, but were given some added responsibilities for ensuring that work teams accomplished their production targets. The understanding was that if Sid excelled as a team leader, he would soon be offered the chance to move into management as a front-line supervisor. Nancy worked in the drafting office, which was just steps from the production floor. Nancy's job involved completing production drawings for use in the shop. Like Sid, Nancy had also taken courses at the local college, and had received high marks in her courses. Based on her performance, Nancy was being considered for a possible supervisory position next fall.

However, Armstrong was not at all happy with what he frequently had observed. Armstrong noticed that during production-floor break periods, Sid Hendrix usually made his way into the office to spend his 15-minute break allotments with Nancy. Nancy's department did not have formal break periods, and staff there could take breaks as needed. Sid and Nancy Hendrix usually spent this time discussing family matters, and they did not interfere with the work of other employees.

Since Sid Hendrix had recently been promoted to team leader, Armstrong believed that Sid should use production-floor break time to establish and improve relationships important to his production team. From his own experience, Armstrong had found that break periods were an opportune time to get closer with his people on an informal level and to open lines of communication for work-related activities.

After explaining his point of view to Sid Hendrix on several occasions, Armstrong became discouraged when Sid refused to change his ways. Sid stood firm in his response that "break time is my time!" Sid also went so far as to say, "If you don't like it, fire me!" Armstrong contemplated the situation at hand and was struggling with how to resolve the issue with Sid.

Questions for Discussion

1. Evaluate Armstrong's situation with Sid Hendrix. Do you agree that Armstrong should try to enforce his "break time is for team building" concept? Discuss.

2. Should Armstrong consult with anyone prior to resolving this issue? If so, whom?

3. Develop a list of decision criteria that Armstrong should consider when solving this problem.
4. What alternatives are available to Armstrong in this case? Evaluate how well each alternative satisfies the decision criteria you established in Question 3.
5. If you were Armstrong, what would you do?

Chapter 4: Supervisory Organizing at the Department Level

After studying this chapter you will be able to

1 Identify the organizing function of management.

2 Discuss the impact of the informal organization and informal group leaders and how supervisors should deal with them.

3 Explain the unity of command principle and its applications.

4 Define the span of management principle and the factors that influence its application.

5 Describe departmentation and alternative approaches for grouping activities and assigning work.

6 Explain the meaning of line and staff authority and how these influence organizational structures and supervisory relationships.

7 Describe how functional authority may be granted to specialized staff for certain purposes.

8 Explain the advantages of the matrix (project management) organizational structure.

9 Define and discuss organizational tools that are useful in supervisory organizing efforts.

10 Define downsizing (restructuring) and its implications for organizational principles.

YOU MAKE THE CALL

You are Alice Austin, supervisor of the information services department of Gatewood Community College. You supervise about 15 employees involved in desktop publishing and administrative service. You report directly to the vice president of administration, who in turn reports to the president of the college. Your department provides services for faculty as well as for other administrative, operations, and communications departments.

Several problems facing you have grown in recent months. Although all work orders and requests are supposed to come directly through you, faculty members, supervisors, administrators, and others are bringing their work requests directly to individual employees in the department. The vice president of administration and the college president or their assistants have bypassed you on occasion by making direct work requests or demanding expedited services from selected employees. Several employees have told you that these requests or demands were impossible to meet, or that they required shifting other job requests or priorities that you had established. The matter came to a head this morning. While you were temporarily out of the office, two faculty members from the business division came into your office and gave instructions to two employees to have a major report processed by the next day. When your employees protested, the faculty members became vocal and angry and criticized them in front of other employees in the department. Hearing this report, you know that you will have to do something to remedy these problems.

You make the call!

1 ORGANIZING AS AN ESSENTIAL MANAGERIAL FUNCTION

Identify the organizing function of management.

As one of the five major functions of management, the organizing function requires that every manager be concerned with building, developing, and maintaining working relationships that will help achieve the organization's objectives. Even the smallest companies have some level of organizational structure—someone has made decisions regarding who does what, how work is divided, and who reports to whom. In larger companies, the organizing function is even more crucial. Without well thought out organizing decisions, the company will struggle with duplication of work or, conversely, will have some important activities overlooked. There will be unclear areas of responsibility and frequent misunderstandings about authority relationships among individuals and departments. Large or small, every business must give thought to the fundamental principles of organizing to ensure smooth and efficient operations.

Organizing
Designing a structure by grouping activities, assigning them to specific work units, and establishing authority and responsibility relationships.

A manager's **organizing** function consists of designing a structure—that is, grouping activities and assigning them to specific work units (e.g., departments, teams) to carry out as planned. Organizing includes establishment of formal authority and responsibility relationships among activities and departments. In order to make such a structure possible, management must delegate authority throughout the organization and establish and clarify authority relationships among the departments. We will use the term **organization** to refer to any type of group structured by management to carry out designated functions and accomplish certain objectives.

Organization
Group structured by management to carry out designated functions and accomplish certain objectives.

Some people incorrectly assume that the organizing function consists solely of drawing and distributing a corporate organizational chart. While organizational charts are important, organizing encompasses a much wider range of activities.

Organizing requires that management design a structure and establish authority relationships based on sound principles and organizational concepts, such as delegation of authority, unity of command, span of supervision, division of work, and departmentation.

Organizing the overall activities of the enterprise is the responsibility of the chief executive. However, eventually it becomes the responsibility of supervisors to organize their departments. Therefore, supervisors must understand what it means to organize. Although the range and magnitude of problems associated with the organizing function are broader at higher managerial levels than for supervisors, the principles to be applied are the same.

Organizations Are People

Throughout this chapter's discussions of the concepts and principles of organizing, it is important not to forget that people are the substance and essence of any organization, regardless of how the enterprise is structured. Managers and supervisors must never become so preoccupied with developing and monitoring the formal structure that they neglect the far more important aspects of relationships with and among their people. Organizational success is more likely to happen when employees are truly given top priority attention by their managers and supervisors.[1] Our focus in this chapter is on building the sound organizational structures that can be the foundations to support the mutual goals of effective work performance and high job satisfaction.

2	THE INFORMAL ORGANIZATION

Discuss the impact of the informal organization and informal group leaders and how supervisors should deal with them.

Informal organization
Informal gatherings of people, apart from the formal organizational structure, that satisfy members' social and other needs.

Grapevine
The informal, unofficial communication channel.

Every enterprise is affected by a social subsystem known as the **informal organization,** sometimes called the "invisible organization." The informal organization reflects the spontaneous efforts of individuals and groups to influence their environment. Whenever people work together, social relationships and informal work groups inevitably arise. The informal organization develops when people are in frequent contact, but their relationships are not necessarily a part of formal organizational arrangements. Their contacts may be part of or incidental to their jobs, or they may stem primarily from the desire to be accepted as a group member.

At the heart of the informal organization are people and their relationships, whereas the formal organization primarily represents the organization's structure and the flow of authority. Supervisors can create and rescind formal organizations they have designed; they cannot eliminate an informal organization because they did not establish it.

Informal groups arise to satisfy the needs and desires of their members that the formal organization does not satisfy. Informal organization particularly satisfies members' social needs by providing recognition, personal contacts, status, and companionship. Groups also offer their members other benefits, including protection, security, and support. They also provide convenient access to the informal communication network, or **grapevine.** The grapevine provides a communication channel and satisfies members' desires to know what is going on. The informal organization also influences the behaviour of individuals in the group. For example, an informal group may pressure individuals to conform to the performance standards to which most group members subscribe. This phenomenon may occur in any department and at any level in the organization.[2]

The Informal Organization and the Supervisor

At different times, the informal organization makes the supervisor's job easier or more difficult. Supervisors must be aware that informal groups can be very strong and can shape employee behaviour, either positively or negatively. Numerous research studies have demonstrated that informal groups can influence employees to strive for high work performance targets or to restrict production, to cooperate with or work against supervisors.

To influence the informal organization to play a positive role, the supervisor first must accept and understand it. The supervisor should group employees so that those most likely to compose harmonious teams work on the same assignments. The supervisor should avoid activities that would unnecessarily disrupt those informal groups whose interests and behaviour patterns support the department's overall objectives. Conversely, if an informal group is threatening the smooth operation of the department, a supervisor may have to do such things as redistribute work assignments or adjust work schedules.

Supervising and Informal Work Group Leaders

Most informal work groups develop their own leadership. An informal leader may be chosen by the group or may assume leadership by being a spokesperson for the group.[3] Work group leaders play significant roles in both formal and informal organizations. Without their cooperation, the supervisor may have difficulty maximizing the performance of the department. A sensitive supervisor will

Informal work groups can constructively or negatively influence a department's operations and accomplishments.

Stockbyte Fotosearch Stock photography

make every effort to gain the cooperation and goodwill of informal leaders and will solicit their cooperation in meeting the department's goals. When approached properly, informal leaders can help the supervisor, especially as channels of communication. Informal leaders may even be viable candidates for the role of supervisory understudy.

Instead of viewing informal leaders as "ringleaders," supervisors should consider them to be employees who have influence and are "in the know" and then try to work with them. For example, to try to build good relationships with informal leaders, a supervisor may periodically give them information before anyone else or ask their advice on certain problems. The supervisor should look for subtle approaches to encourage informal groups and their leaders to match their special interests with the department's activities and objectives. We discuss this and other aspects of managing effective work groups in Chapter 11.

3	UNITY OF COMMAND AND AUTHORITY RELATIONSHIPS

Explain the unity of command principle and its applications.

The chief executive groups the activities of the organization into divisions, departments, services, teams, or units and assigns duties accordingly. Upper-level management places managers and supervisors in charge of divisions and departments and defines their authority relationships. Supervisors must know exactly who their managers are and who their subordinates are. To arrange authority relationships in this fashion, management normally follows the principle of unity of command. Unity of command means that each employee has only one immediate supervisor—that is, only one person to whom the employee is directly accountable.

Unity of command principle
Principle that each employee should report to only one immediate supervisor.

When the **unity of command principle** is violated, conflicts or confusion usually result. As illustrated by this chapter's "You Make the Call" feature, employees can become uncertain about their work assignments and priorities when more than one person is assigning work to them. Therefore, a supervisor should make certain that, unless there is a valid reason for an exception, each employee reports to only one supervisor. That one supervisor can ensure that employees' work priorities are clear, that each employee has an appropriate work load, and that employees are receiving clear communication about what is expected of them.

Formal communications normally flow upward and downward through the chain of command. There are times, however, when management will intentionally cause the unity of command principle to be violated. The use of functional authority and the matrix organizational structure, which are discussed later in this chapter, may result in some people "serving two masters." Similarly, having employees participate in task forces, project groups, and special committees may temporarily blur the unity of command concept.

4	THE SPAN OF MANAGEMENT PRINCIPLE

Define the span of management principle and the factors that influence its application.

The establishment of departments and the creation of several managerial levels are not ends in themselves; actually, they can be the source of numerous difficulties. Departments are expensive because they must be staffed by supervisors and employees. Moreover, as more departments and levels are created, communication and coordination problems arise. Therefore, there must be valid reasons for

Span of management principle
Principle that there is an upper limit to the number of subordinates a supervisor can manage effectively.

creating levels and departments. The reasons are associated with the **span of management principle.** The upper limit of the number of employees a supervisor can effectively manage is considered the "supervisor's span of management." This principle is often called "span of supervision," "span of managerial responsibility," "span of authority," or "span of control."

Because no one can manage an unlimited number of people, top-level managers must organize divisions and departments as separate operating units and place middle-level managers and supervisors in charge. Top-level managers then delegate authority to the middle-level managers who, in turn, redelegate authority to supervisors who, in turn, supervise the front-line employees. If a manager could supervise 100 or more employees effectively, each of the 100 would report directly to that manager and their different activities would not have to be grouped into departments. Of course, such a wide span of management is often not practical.

The principle that a manager can effectively supervise a limited number of employees is an ancient managerial theory. However, it is not possible to state a definite figure as to how many subordinates a manager should have. It is correct only to say that there is some upper limit to this number. In many industrial firms, the top-level executive will have from three to eight subordinate managers. But the span of management usually increases the farther down a person is within the managerial hierarchy. It is not unusual to find a span of management of between 15 and 25 employees at the first level of supervision.

Factors Influencing the Span of Management

The number of employees that one person can effectively supervise depends on a number of factors, such as the abilities of the supervisor, the type and amount of staff assistance available, the employees' capabilities, the location of employees, the kinds of activities performed, and the degree to which objective performance standards are in place.

Supervisory Competence

Among the most significant factors that influence the span of management are the training, experience, and know-how that the supervisor possesses—in other words, the supervisor's competence. Some supervisors are capable of handling more employees than others. Some are better acquainted with good management principles, have had more experience, and are better managers overall. For example, a supervisor's ability to manage his or her use of time is very important. The supervisor who must make individual decisions on every departmental problem takes more time than does the supervisor who has established policies, procedures, and rules that simplify decision making on routine problems. Comprehensive planning can reduce the number of decisions the supervisor has to make and hence can increase the potential span of management. Thus, the number of employees a supervisor can oversee effectively depends to some degree on the supervisor's managerial capabilities.

Specialized Staff Assistance

Another factor that influences the span of management is the availability of help from specialists within the organization. If numerous staff experts are available to provide specialized advice and service, then the span of management can be wider. For example, when a human resources department assists supervisors in recruiting, selecting, and training employees, supervisors have more time and energy available for their departments. But if supervisors themselves are obligated to do all or most of these activities, then they cannot devote that portion of time to otherwise managing their departments. Therefore, the amount and quality of staff assistance available can significantly influence the span of management.

Employee Abilities

A supervisor's span of management is influenced by the abilities and knowledge of employees in the department. The greater the employees' capacity for self-direction, the broader the feasible span. Here, of course, the employees' training and experience are important. For example, the span of management could be greater with fully qualified mechanics than with inexperienced mechanics. However, the factor of employee competence may be offset to some degree by the location of the employees and by the nature of the activities being performed.

Location of Employees

The location and proximity of employees to a supervisor can influence the span of management. When departmental employees are all located in close proximity to each other and to the supervisor—such as being in the same office or same part of a building—a supervisor generally can supervise more employees because observation and communication are relatively easy. However, if the employees are widely dispersed—such as being located in different stores, working in their homes, or working as separate outdoor crews throughout a metropolitan area—the span of management may be somewhat limited because of communication and coordination difficulties.[4]

Nature and Complexity of Activities

The nature, complexity, and predictability of activities in a department influence the span of management. The simpler, more routine, and more uniform the work activities, the greater the number of people a supervisor can manage. If the tasks are repetitive, the span may be as broad as 50 or more employees. If the activi-

When employees are close to each other and to the supervisor, the supervisor can observe and communicate with them easily.

Corel Corporation

ties are varied or interdependent, or if errors would have serious consequences, the span might have to be as small as three to five. In departments engaged in relatively unpredictable activities—for example, nurses in an intensive care unit in a hospital—the span will tend to be narrow. In departments concerned with fairly stable activities—such as an assembly line or a customer service call centre—the span can be broader.

Objective Performance Standards

Span of management is influenced by the degree to which a department has ample objective standards for guiding and measuring employee performance. If each employee knows exactly what standards are expected, the supervisor will not need to have frequent discussions with employees to clarify performance targets. If employees know, for example, that they are expected to produce a specific number of units each shift, they will not be looking to the supervisor for constant guidance about what is expected of them. Thus, performance standards that are objective and clearly communicated support a broader span of management.

Weighing the Factors

The principle of span of management indicates only that an upper limit exists for the number of employees a supervisor can manage effectively. In most situations, there must be a weighing or balancing of the factors discussed above to arrive at an appropriate span of management for each supervisor. Such weighing of factors is, for the most part, the responsibility of higher-level management. Supervisors should, however, be asked to express their opinions concerning what they believe is an appropriate span of management for their departments.

How Managerial Levels and Span of Management Are Related

If a higher-level manager concludes that the span of management for a certain activity or department is too broad, he or she may decide to divide the span into two or three groups and place someone in charge of each group. By narrowing the span to a smaller number of employees, the manager creates another organizational level because a supervisor or "lead person" has to be placed over each of the smaller groups. A **lead person**, sometimes called a "working supervisor," is usually not considered to be part of management, especially in unionized firms. Nevertheless, these individuals perform most of the managerial functions, although their authority is somewhat limited, particularly when it comes to making disciplinary decisions.

Lead person
Employee placed in charge of other employees who performs limited managerial functions but is not considered to be part of management.

Other things being equal, the narrower the span of management becomes, the more managerial levels have to be introduced into organizational design. Stated another way, organizational structures will tend to be taller when spans of management are narrower, and structures will tend to be flatter when spans of management are wider, especially at the supervisory level. Of course, this is a generalization that may vary because of other organizational considerations. Adding or reducing levels of management may or may not be desirable. For example, adding levels can be costly and can complicate communication and decision making. On the other hand, reducing levels may widen the spans of management to the extent that supervisors become overburdened and cannot maintain adequate control of employees and activities of the department.

FIGURE 4-1   The relationship between span of management and organizational levels.

One level of management and one manager

Two levels of management and four managers

Three levels of management and thirteen managers

Thus, there is a tradeoff between the width of the span and the number of levels (see Figure 4-1). The managerial problem is, which is best—a broad span with few levels, or a narrower span with more levels? Higher management, not a first-line supervisor, normally confronts this question, but supervisors should understand how it influences the design and structure of their organizations.

5	DEPARTMENTATION

Describe departmentation and alternative approaches for grouping activities and assigning work.

Division of work (specialization)
Dividing work into smaller components and specialized tasks to improve efficiency and output.

Organizational structure is largely influenced by the principle of **division of work** or **specialization.** This principle holds that jobs can be divided into smaller components and specialized tasks to achieve greater efficiency and output. Technological advances and increasing job complexity make it very difficult for employees to keep up with everything about their work or specialty, and dividing the work into smaller tasks allows employees to specialize in narrower areas within their fields. Employees can then master these smaller tasks and produce more efficiently. For example, as cars become more complex and diverse, it becomes more difficult for a mechanic to know how to fix everything on every type of car. Thus, specialty repair shops such as muffler shops, oil-change services, and foreign car specialists have emerged. Even within shops that do many types of repairs, mechanics often specialize in particular areas. By specializing, employees can become expert enough in their areas to produce efficiently.

Departmentation is the process of grouping activities and people into distinct organizational units, usually known as departments. A **department** is a designated set of activities and people over which a manager or supervisor has responsibility and authority. Terminology used by organizations is quite varied. A department in one company may be called a division, an office, a service, or a unit in another. Most organizations have departments of some sort, since division of work and specialization contribute to efficiency and better results.

Departmentation
The process of grouping activities and people into distinct organizational units.

Department
An organizational unit for which a supervisor has responsibility and authority.

Approaches to Departmentation

Whereas major departments of an organization are established by top-level managers, supervisors primarily are concerned with activities within their own areas. Nevertheless, from time to time supervisors will be confronted with the need to departmentalize within their areas, and they should be familiar with the alternatives available for grouping activities. These are the same options available to top-level managers when they define the major departments. Figure 4-2 summarizes the most common approaches to departmentation. See our website for further discussion and illustration of design alternatives (www.supervision2e.nelson.com).

Work Assignments and Organizational Stability

One of the supervisor's most important responsibilities is to assign work so that everyone has a fair share and all employees do their parts equitably and satisfactorily. The problem of how and to whom to assign work confronts a supervisor much more frequently than does the problem of how to organize departments. This problem always involves differences of opinion. Nevertheless, the assignment of work should be justifiable and explainable on the basis of good management, rather than on personal likes and dislikes or hunches and intuition. The supervisor is subject to pressures from different directions when assigning workloads. Some employees are motivated and want to assume more work, while others believe that they should not be burdened with additional duties.

A supervisor's task of assigning departmental work will ultimately be easier if the supervisor consistently utilizes the strengths and experience of all employees. However, some supervisors are inclined to assign difficult and more complex tasks to the capable employees who are most experienced. Over the long term, however, it is advantageous to train and develop the less experienced employees so that they, too, can perform the difficult jobs. These employees may initially require more time and attention from the supervisor while completing the work but, in the long run, these employees will have better skills and will contribute more to the department.

If work is distributed inequitably, supervisors will rely too much on one person or a few people, and a department will be weakened if the top performers are absent, promoted, or leave the enterprise. The **principle of organizational stability** advocates that no organization should become overly dependent on one or several "indispensable" individuals whose absence or departure would seriously disrupt the organization. Organizations need a sufficient number of employees who have been trained well and have flexible skills. One way to develop a flexible workforce is to assign certain employees to different jobs within the department on a

Principle of organizational stability
Principle that holds that no organization should become overly dependent upon one or several "indispensable" individuals.

FIGURE 4-2 Common approaches to departmentation.

FUNCTIONAL DEPARTMENTATION
- The most widely used approach; similar activities are placed together in one department (e.g., marketing department, accounting department, etc.).

PRODUCT OR SERVICE DEPARTMENTATION
- A relatively independent unit is established within the enterprise for each major product (e.g., a food-products company divides its operations into a frozen-food department, a dairy-products department, a produce department, and the like).

GEOGRAPHIC DEPARTMENTATION
- Separate divisions for major geographical areas in which the enterprise does business; may be organized by city, region, province, country, etc.

CUSTOMER DEPARTMENTATION
- Departments are organized according to major customer grouping (e.g., a supplier of building materials with separate divisions to cater to retail customers versus trade contractors).

PROCESS AND EQUIPMENT DEPARTMENTATION
- Activities that involve the use of specialized equipment are grouped into separate departments (e.g., CAT scan, X-ray, and ultrasound departments of a hospital).

TIME DEPARTMENTATION
- Activities are departmentalized by the period of time during which the work is performed (e.g., day, afternoon, night shift).

MIXED DEPARTMENTATION
- Several types of departmentation are applied at the same time in order to achieve an effective structure (e.g., inventory control clerk on the third floor during the night shift; involves functional, geographic and time departmentation).

temporary basis as, for example, during vacation periods or employee absences. In this way there will usually be someone available to take over any job if the need arises.

6

Explain the meaning of line and staff authority and how these influence organizational structures and supervisory relationships.

AUTHORITY RELATIONSHIPS AND ORGANIZATIONAL STRUCTURES

Once management establishes departments, it must then establish and clarify relationships among and within the departments. In order for the organization to operate efficiently, it is essential that everyone have a clear understanding of who

Authority
The legitimate right to direct and lead others.

is responsible for what and who has **authority** over whom. The following discussion serves as a basis for discussing how management establishes authority and responsibility relationships in organizational structures.

Line Organizational Structure

Line authority
The right to direct others and to require them to conform to decisions, policies, rules, and objectives.

In every organization there is a vertical, direct line of authority, which can be traced from the chief executive to the departmental employee level. **Line authority** (also referred to as "scalar authority") provides the right to direct others and require them to conform to decisions, policies, rules, and objectives. Line authority establishes who can direct whom throughout the organization. A primary purpose of line authority is to make the organization work smoothly.

Line organizational structure
A structure that consists entirely of line authority arrangements with a direct chain of authority relationships.

Some organizations consist entirely of line authority arrangements (see Figure 4-3). Usually these organizations are fairly small, both in operations and in number of employees. A **line organizational structure** enables managers to know exactly to whom they can give directives and whose orders they have to carry out. Throughout, there is unity of command, which can be traced in a direct line (or chain) of authority relationships. Because authority relationships are very clear in a line organizational structure, decisions can usually be made and carried out more quickly as compared with other structures.

Many small companies essentially are line-type organizations, built around one or several key people who also may own the firm. These owner/managers usually are quite versatile, and they make most of the decisions necessary to carry out business operations. When they need special assistance, they often go outside the firm to pay consultants or others for services. Many small companies are built around one or two key individuals, who must have knowledge in a wide range of business areas. These types of enterprises can be successful as long as the business remains relatively small and operations focus on a limited range of activities. As a

FIGURE 4-3
Line organizational structure.

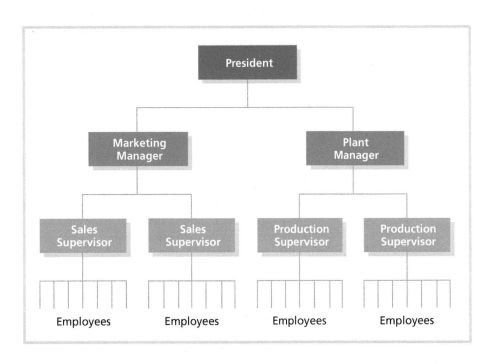

small business grows, it can outgrow its owner/manager's expertise, resulting in a need to hire specialists into the company to fill these knowledge gaps.

Line and Staff Organizational Structure

With organizational growth, activities tend to become more specialized and complicated. As the business becomes more complex, managers cannot be expected to direct subordinates adequately and expertly in all phases of operations without some assistance. Managers of **line departments** (those directly involved in making, selling, or distributing the company's product or service) need the assistance of specialists who have expert knowledge. As a business grows, additional departments are typically established to provide advice and support to line managers regarding policies, procedures, technical issues, and problems that the line managers may be dealing with. The departments that provide this advice and support to line managers are known as **staff departments.** The most common staff departments are established to provide expertise in the areas of human resources, legal issues, and accounting and budgeting matters. When staff departments are introduced, the organization is said to be using a **line and staff organizational structure**.

Based on their specialized knowledge, managers who work in staff departments are granted **staff authority**—the right and duty to provide counsel, advice, support, and service in specific areas of expertise. People who hold staff positions do not issue orders or directives except within their own departments. Rather, staff people assist other members of the organization whenever the need arises for specialized help. For example, human resources specialists, not the line managers, often screen applicants for jobs and recommend only the most qualified candidates for line managers to interview. Although line managers maintain the authority to make the ultimate hiring decision, they may seek advice and support from the staff specialists in the human resources department. While the human resources managers can direct the work of employees within their own department (line authority), they can advise managers in other departments only about human resources matters (staff authority). Staff authority is not inferior to line authority; it is different. The objectives of staff groups ultimately are the same as those of the line departments—namely, the achievement of overall organizational objectives.

Staff supervisors primarily provide guidance, counsel, advice, and service in their specialty to those who request it. Typically they also have the responsibility to see that certain policies and procedures are being carried out by line departments. However, staff supervisors do not have the direct authority to order line people to conform to policies and procedures; they can only persuade, counsel, and advise. Line supervisors can accept the staff person's advice, alter it, or reject it; but since the staff person is usually the expert in the field, line supervisors usually accept and even welcome the advice of the staff specialist.

All supervisors should know whether they are part of the organization in a line or staff capacity, and what these words imply in terms of their relationships to other departments. Supervisors should consult their job descriptions or organizational manuals. If necessary, they should ask higher-level managers for clarification, because it is top-level management that grants line or staff authority in a department. In the end, however, regardless of whether the supervisor's department acts in a line or staff capacity in the organization, the supervisor's responsibilities for leading and managing his or her department are universal.

Line department
Department whose responsibilities are directly related to making, selling, or distributing the company's product or service.

Staff department
Specialized department responsible for supporting line departments and providing specialized advice and services.

Line and staff organizational structure
Structure that combines line and staff departments.

Staff authority
The right to provide counsel, advice, support, and service in a person's areas of expertise.

FIGURE 4-4   Line and staff organizational structure.

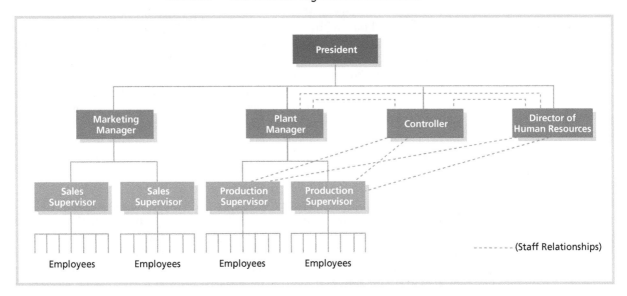

Figure 4-4 illustrates a typical line and staff organizational structure. Note that the controller and director of human resources are staff managers. These staff relationships are illustrated with dashed lines. However, these positions and departments are not always staff. Line and staff are characteristics of authority relationships and not necessarily of functions. Nor does a person's title indicate whether he or she is a line or staff manager. For example, in manufacturing organizations it is common to find vice presidents in line areas (e.g., production, sales) as well as vice presidents in staff areas (e.g., human resources, legal). Merely looking at an organizational chart may not be sufficient to identify authority relationships.

| 7 | **THE ROLE OF FUNCTIONAL AUTHORITY** |

Describe how functional authority may be granted to specialized staff for certain purposes.

Principle of compulsory staff advice (service)

Situation in which supervisors are required by policy to consult with specialized staff before making certain types of decisions.

Generally, in a line and staff organization, staff managers provide counsel and advice to line managers but do not have the right to give them direct orders. This arrangement maintains the principle of unity of command. However, there are exceptions to this generalization. For example, if an organizational policy requires a supervisor to consult with a staff person before making a certain type of decision, this is known as following the **principle of compulsory staff advice** (or **compulsory staff service**). Having obtained advice from the staff person, it is up to the supervisor to decide whether to accept or reject that advice. The supervisor retains the ultimate responsibility for the decision.

In some organizations, supervisors are required to consult with a staff person before making certain types of decisions, and the staff person has functional authority to make the ultimate decision.

Functional authority
The right granted to specialized staff people to give directives concerning matters within their expertise.

Functional authority (or "functional staff authority") is a special right given by higher-level management to certain staff people to direct other members of the organization about matters within the staff person's specialized field. For example, assume that a company president wants to be sure that the grievance procedures in the labour agreement are interpreted uniformly. Therefore, the president decides to confer sole authority to the labour relations director for the final settlement of grievances—a function that otherwise might belong to line managers. The labour relations director is part of the human resources department, which is a staff department. By giving sole authority for the final adjustment of grievances to the labour relations director, the company president confers authority for this function on someone who ordinarily would be acting in only an advisory capacity. Now the labour relations director has this authority, and it no longer belongs to the line supervisors.

Another example of functional authority is the common case in which a human resources department is given full authority to maintain legal compliance with wage and hour laws, human rights legislation, and the like.[5] The decisions of line supervisors in these matters must conform to the stipulations of the human resources department. (In a large company, the human resources department itself may rely on advice it receives from the company's legal department or from an outside legal firm.)

The use of functional authority violates the principle of unity of command since it introduces a second source of authority for certain decisions. Not only are supervisors accountable to their own managers, but also must take direction from a staff expert when making certain types of decisions. Despite the confusion and uncertainty that can arise when the unity of command principle is violated, some organizations find that functional authority is advantageous because it facilitates a more effective use of staff specialists. It is up to top-level management to weigh the advantages and disadvantages of granting functional authority to staff specialists before conferring it.

CONTEMPORARY ISSUE
Cutting the Fat—Canadian Manufacturers Go Lean

Canadian manufacturers are on a diet—cutting the fat and going lean—in an effort to eliminate inefficiencies and cut costs. Lean manufacturing is the hottest trend in manufacturing today, and companies that ignore the revolution risk being left behind by competitors who harness the power of lean thinking and implement lean principles throughout the organization.

Lean manufacturing is a fundamental philosophy about doing business that aims to identify and eliminate inefficiencies (or, as the Japanese call it "muda") from every aspect of a company's operations. For employees who have come through years of "slash and burn" downsizings, the lean concept may evoke fears of job losses and memories of the tired mantra that they must "do more with less." But lean is not about downsizing per se. It's built on the philosophy that, with the right tools, everyone in the organization can "minimize waste and strive for perfection through continuous learning, creativity, and teamwork."[1] Lean production "is aimed at the elimination of waste in every area of production, including customer relations, product design, supplier networks, and factory management. Its goal is to incorporate less human effort, less inventory, less time to develop products, and less space to become highly responsive to customer demand."[2] Specifically, lean manufacturers share the following attributes:[3]

(continued)

- They use just-in-time techniques to eliminate virtually all inventory.
- They build systems that help employees produce a perfect part every time.
- They reduce space requirements by minimizing the distance a part travels.
- They develop close relationships with suppliers, helping suppliers to understand the manufacturer's needs and its customers' needs.
- They educate suppliers to accept responsibility for helping meet customer needs.
- They strive for continually declining costs by eliminating all but value-added activities. Material handling, inspection, inventory, and rework jobs are among the likely targets because these do not add value to the product.
- They develop the workforce. They constantly improve job design, training, employee participation and commitment, and teamwork.
- They make jobs more challenging, pushing responsibility to the lowest level possible.
- They reduce the number of job classes and build worker flexibility.

To become truly lean, an organization must adopt a structure that supports lean initiatives at all levels. It doesn't work to simply set up a "lean team" whose mandate is to implement a quick fix. Lean manufacturing must permeate through all levels of management, right down to the front lines of the business, and requires a "company-wide cultural transformation"[4] in order to succeed. A traditional line structure often doesn't support the shared authority and decentralized decision making that lean manufacturing initiatives require. Rather, "the lean enterprise has a flat, team-based structure, with a high degree of work autonomy. A lean organization breaks down organizational barriers."[5]

Many Canadian companies are well on their way on their "lean journey." In October 2003, Cutler-Hammer Canada was awarded one of three innovation awards by Canadian Manufacturers and Exporters at a Toronto conference on lean manufacturing. The Cutler-Hammer Canada plant is located in Milton, Ontario, and is a division of Cleveland-based Eaton Corporation. Cutler-Hammer produces four product lines for the electrical and semi-conductor industries. By revamping all aspects of its production on the basis of lean principles, Cutler-Hammer was able to free up 1,700 square metres of space and chop its cycle time (the time to get the product from order to customer) by 30 percent. The company estimates inventory reductions alone will save over $500,000 annually. Clayton Tychkowsky, general manager of the company's Canadian operations, says, "You wouldn't even recognize the two (before and after) operations. It's completely different."[6]

Lean manufacturing is a process that can take many years to fully implement. While the basic tenants of lean are simple enough, achieving the organizational commitment to really "pull it off" and sustain the lean efforts can be quite difficult. Many organizations find that accomplishing lean status results in many months or even years of organizational discomfort. But for many, there is no alternative as customers demand better products, better quality, faster delivery—all for a better price. It's a matter of going lean or getting driven out of the market by those who do.

For more information on lean manufacturing, see the website of *Advanced Manufacturing* at www.advancedmanufacturing.com, which contains many links and articles about lean manufacturing principles.

Sources: (1) Jay Heizer and Barry Render, *Operations Management,* 6th ed. (Upper Saddle River, NJ: Prentice-Hall, Inc. 2001), p. 529; (2) From the Production System Design Laboratory (PSD), Massachusetts Institute of Technology (MIT) as quoted by Todd Phillips, "Building the Lean Machine," *Advanced Manufacturing* (January 2000), pp. 21–26; (3) Heizer and Render, p. 530; (4) Phillips, p. 23; (5) Phillips, p. 24; (6) Mike Pettapiece, "Electronics plant cut the fat and won a prize," *The Hamilton Spectator* (October 17, 2003), p. A22.

8 | THE MATRIX ORGANIZATIONAL STRUCTURE

Explain the advantages of the matrix (project management) organizational structure.

Matrix organizational structure

A hybrid structure in which regular functional departments co-exist with project teams comprising people from different departments.

In many organizations the need to coordinate activities across department lines has contributed to the development of the **matrix organizational structure.** The matrix form of organization is also called "project structure," "product management structure," or "grid." The matrix arrangement, which is superimposed on the line and staff organization, adds horizontal dimensions to the normally vertical (top-down) orientation of the organizational structure. It is a hybrid arrangement in which regular line and staff departments co-exist with project teams or group assignments across departmental lines.

Many high-tech firms and companies implementing lean manufacturing (see Contemporary Issue box on pp. 114–15) employ matrix or project structures in order to focus special talents from different departments on specific projects for certain periods. Matrix structure enables managers to undertake several projects simultaneously, some of which may be of relatively short duration. Each project is assigned to a project manager, who manages the project from inception to completion. Employees from different functional departments are assigned to work on each project as needed, either part time or full time.

Although the complexity of matrix structure varies, a basic matrix form might resemble the chart shown in Figure 4-5. This chart illustrates how some managers have been given responsibility for specific projects within the firm, while departmental supervisors primarily have the responsibility for supervising employees within their regular departments. The type of arrangement shown in Figure 4-5 might apply to an engineering or architectural firm. The project managers (A and B) are responsible for coordinating activities on their designated projects. However, the project managers must work closely with the departmental supervisors of functions X, Y, and Z. The employees who work in these

FIGURE 4-5
Matrix organizational structure.

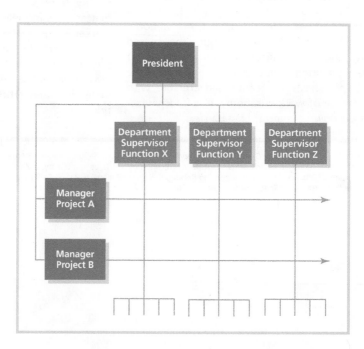

departments report directly (functionally) to the departmental supervisors, but their services are utilized under the authority and responsibility of the project managers to whom they are assigned for various periods of time.

There are several problems associated with the matrix organizational structure. The most frequent problem is the question of direct accountability. Like functional authority, the matrix structure violates the principle of unity of command, since departmental employees are accountable to both a departmental supervisor and one or more project managers. Other problems involve priorities of scheduling for individual employees who are assigned to work on several projects. Employees may be given conflicting information from each of the project managers for whom they work, as each project manager attempts to monopolize the employees' time. These problems can be avoided, or at least minimized, by proper planning and clarification of authority relationships by the top-level manager prior to the start of a project.

Despite such problems, the matrix structure is widely used because organizations find it advantageous. The success of a matrix arrangement depends primarily on the willingness of both the project managers and the departmental supervisors and their employees to coordinate various activities and responsibilities in working toward completion of each project. Such coordination is vital in the scheduling of work, and it is imperative in the performance appraisal of employees. Employees must recognize that they remain directly accountable to their departmental supervisor, who will rely to a great extent on the project managers' evaluations of the employees' work when conducting performance appraisals and salary reviews.

9 | ORGANIZATIONAL TOOLS AND THEIR APPLICATIONS

Define and discuss organizational tools that are useful in supervisory organizing efforts.

Some managers, supervisors, and employees do not understand how their positions and responsibilities relate to the positions and responsibilities of other employees. Organization charts and manuals, job descriptions, and job specifications can reduce this confusion. These tools clarify the organization's structure and help supervisors understand their positions and the relationships between various departments of the enterprise. The obligation to prepare a firm's overall organizational chart and manual rests with top-level management. However, supervisors usually develop and maintain these tools for their departments.

Departmental Organization Charts

Organization chart
Graphic portrayal of a company's authority and responsibility relationships.

In planning their organizational structures, many firms develop **organization charts** for all or part of their operations. An organization chart is a graphic portrayal of organizational authority and responsibility relationships using boxes or other depictions. Each box normally represents one position category, although several or more employees may be included in a position category. For example, Figure 4-6 shows a position called "nurses." This is one position, but there may be many nurses. By studying the vertical relationships of categories, anyone can readily determine who reports to whom. Although different types of organization charts are used, most are constructed vertically and show levels of organization arranged in some type of pyramid.

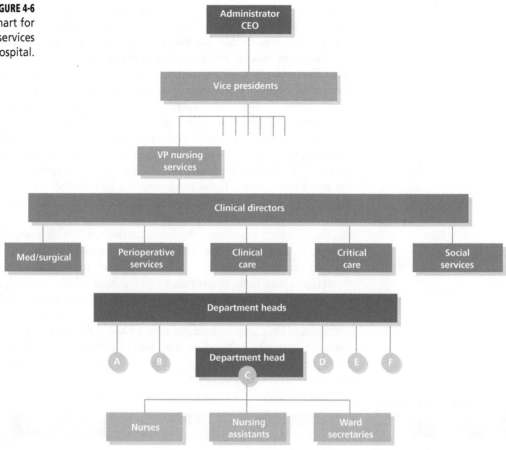

FIGURE 4-6
Organization chart for the nursing services department of a hospital.

A supervisor gains a number of advantages from establishing and maintaining a departmental organization chart. First, it requires careful study and analysis of departmental structure. When preparing the chart, the supervisor might identify duplicate efforts or inconsistencies in certain functions or activities. A chart might enable the supervisor to identify where dual-reporting relationships exist (that is, where one employee is reporting to two supervisors) or where positions overlap. The chart may also suggest whether the span of management is too wide or too narrow.

An organization chart is a convenient way to acquaint new employees with the structure of the department and the enterprise. Most employees want to know where they stand and where their supervisor stands relative to higher-level managers. Organization charts show formal authority and responsibility relationships; they do not reflect the informal organization discussed earlier in this chapter. Of course, organization charts are limited, especially if they are not kept up to date. All changes in organization structure should be recorded promptly.

Organization Manuals

Organization manual
Written description of the authority and responsibilities of managerial and supervisory positions, as well as formal channels, major objectives, and policies and procedures.

The **organization manual** is another helpful tool, because it provides, in comprehensive, written form, the decisions about a company's organizational structure. Not every company has an organization manual, but most firms of appreciable size do. These manuals are referred to by a variety of names, but whatever the label, the organization manual defines and describes the scope of authority and the responsibilities of managerial and supervisory positions. Organization manuals also describe the formal channels for obtaining information and assistance from various departments or individuals. The manual usually specifies the responsibilities of supervisory positions and how each position relates to other positions in the organization. The manual may outline the functions of each department and explain how relationships in the organization contribute to objectives. The manual may also contain major policies and procedures, particularly those relating to human resource issues. Every supervisor should be thoroughly familiar with the contents of the organization manual, especially those sections that most affect their departments.

Job Descriptions and Job Specifications

Job descriptions are often included in an organization manual, or they can be obtained from the human resources department. A **job description,** sometimes called a "position description," identifies the principal elements, duties, scope of authority, and responsibility of a job. Some job descriptions are brief; others are lengthy. Job descriptions are often based on information obtained both from employees who perform the jobs and from those employees' supervisors. Some firms include certain expectations in job descriptions, such as the availability to work evenings or to travel. Some even indicate specific productivity or quality performance standards that must be attained after a training period.[6]

In practice, there is some overlap in the terms job description and **job specification.** Generally speaking, a job description describes the major duties of a position, whereas a job specification refers to the skills, capacities, and qualities—personal qualifications—that are needed to perform the job successfully. Many organization manuals include the job specification as part of each job description. Figure 4-7 is a combined job description and specification. Note that the requirements to fill the job are called "placement criteria" on this form.

Job description
Written description of the principal duties and responsibilities of a job.

Job specification
Written description of the personal qualifications needed to perform a job adequately.

FIGURE 4-7 Job description and specification for a registered nurse at Pine Village Hospital.

JOB TITLE	JOB CODE	POSITION	STATUS
Registered Nurse (RN)	G-45-XXX	Exempt	Nonexempt

Organizational Unit _____ Location _____

Position Definition (A brief statement of the purpose of this position)

The registered nurse uses the nursing process to deliver compassionate, individualized, holistic care for the patient throughout the stages of the life span in accordance with PVH's mission.

Responsible to _____

Placement Criteria (Minimum educational, skill, and/or experience as of September 15, 2002.)

 1. Education
     a. Degree from an accredited school of nursing.
     b. Current professional registration. Copies filed in HR and with department head.
 2. Orientation

(continued)

FIGURE 4-7   *(continued)*

  a. Satisfactory completion of PVH's general orientation.
  b. Satisfactory completion of nurse orientation.
  c. Satisfactory completion of unit orientation supervised by department head.
3. Personal Qualities
  a. Displays mature, professional conduct through action, attitude, and behaviour.
  b. Demonstrates leadership qualities and ability to act independently.
  c. Relates to others constructively.
  d. Demonstrates leadership qualities by making appropriate decisions and initiating necessary action.
  e. Possesses the ability to function calmly, efficiently, and effectively in stressful situations.
4. Physical Qualities
  a. Satisfactory health evaluation according to PVH's policy.
  b. Maintains physical and emotional health sufficient to meet the demands of the position.
5. Physical Demands of Work
  a. Classification of biohazard exposure: Performs tasks that involve exposure to blood, body fluids, or body tissue. Limited risk of exposure to hazardous materials. Possible risk of radiation exposure.
  b. Physical Demands
    i.   Level V, medium: Lift/carry 22 kilograms; push, pull, or roll 45 kilograms (twice stated weight if wheelchair).
    ii. Prolonged, extensive, or considerable standing/walking.
    iii. Frequent reaching, stooping, bending, kneeling, and crouching.
    iv. Must be able to see and hear well enough to perform all nursing-care activities.
  c. Emotional Demands
    i.   Subject to varying and unpredictable situations.
    ii. Handles emergency or crisis situations.
    iii. Subject to many interruptions.
    iv. Occasionally subjected to irregular hours.

JOB RELATIONSHIPS
1. Works well with other staff members.
2. Responsible to department head or designee.
3. Follows chain of command appropriately to address concerns and conflicts in a timely manner.
4. Works with members of other clinical disciplines to provide holistic health care and promote patient self-sufficiency.
5. Helps physicians, staff, and family members deliver holistic health care.

GENERAL PERFORMANCE STANDARDS—PRODUCTIVITY
1. Meets attendance and punctuality standards.
2. Demonstrates dependability, flexibility, and initiative.
3. Adapts to changes in hospital functions and patient care/department needs.

(continued)

FIGURE 4-7 *(continued)*

4. Uses resources efficiently.
5. Sets priorities and completes job responsibilities in a timely manner.
6. Demonstrates effective organizational skills.
7. Demonstrates knowledge of department infection-control procedures.
8. Participates continuously in performance-improvement activities.
9. Looks for and shares with supervisor(s) ways to improve work practices.
10. Participates in departmental meetings and committees.

GENERAL PERFORMANCE STANDARDS—PROFESSIONALISM

1. Demonstrates effective working relationships through tact, sensitivity, sound judgment, and a positive attitude when relating to coworkers, patients, family, all hospital staff, and physicians.
2. Offers assistance and addresses the concerns of visitors, patients, physicians, and families courteously and positively.
3. Supports PVH's mission, beliefs, objectives, policies, and procedures.
4. Demonstrates effective communication skills.
5. Seeks appropriate assistance from supervisors and peers.
6. Uses the telephone courteously.
7. Maintains the confidentiality of clinical, financial, patient, public, and/or employee information via written or computerized records, documents, ledgers, internal correspondence, conversation, and/or discussion.
8. Presents a professional appearance.
9. Follows the chain of command appropriately to address concerns and conflicts in a timely manner.
10. Offers assistance to coworkers.
11. Keeps informed of new policies and procedures.
12. Assumes responsibility for professional growth/continued learning.

ESSENTIAL JOB FUNCTIONS

1. Demonstrates the knowledge and skills needed to provide age-appropriate care throughout the life span, from infancy through adulthood, using the principles of growth and development.
2. Documents patient care legibly, completely, clearly, and concisely.
3. Collaborates with other health-team members to develop and deliver a patient-oriented, continuous plan of care.
4. Demonstrates appropriate critical-thinking and delegation skills.
5. Accepts and completes assignments according to experience, skill level, and demonstrated knowledge. Clinical and technical skills assigned should comply with and be acceptable within the clinical practice guidelines of PVH's Nursing Services Division.
6. Provides patient/family teaching based on patient needs.
7. Proactively and concurrently participates in the monitoring, identifying, and reporting of safety-related issues. This includes, but is not limited to, patient safety, family/visitor safety, and employee safety.
8. Demonstrates appropriate follow-up skills.
9. Completes applicable competencies and mandatory requirements; CPR required. Additional unit-specific requirements may apply.
10. Performs all duties and tasks as assigned (e.g., preceptorship), specific to department requirements.

When a department lacks job descriptions or job specifications, or when new jobs are created, the supervisor should ensure such documents are produced. If help with this task is needed, the supervisor should seek help from the human resources department, which has the experience and knowledge to facilitate this task. We will discuss the development of job descriptions and job specifications further in Chapter 5.

10	## ORGANIZATIONAL PRINCIPLES IN AN ERA OF CORPORATE DOWNSIZING

Define downsizing (restructuring) and its implications for organizational principles.

Downsizing (restructuring, right-sizing)
Large-scale reduction and elimination of jobs in a company that usually results in reduction of middle-level managers, removal of organizational levels, and a widened span of management for remaining supervisors.

Among the most publicized aspects of business during recent years has been the permanent elimination of thousands of job positions in many major companies. This has been accomplished by plant and office closings, sales of divisions, extensive employee layoffs, attrition, early retirements, and the like. As a result, many companies have eliminated large segments of their workforce; this has been referred to as **downsizing, restructuring,** or **right-sizing**.

Typically, management downsizes to reduce costs, streamline operations, and become more efficient and competitive. Downsizing often results in a reduction in the number of middle-level managers and the removal of a layer or more of organizational levels. The span of management is usually widened for first-line supervisors and other managers who survive the downsizing. Many supervisors are stretched by being required to add unfamiliar departments or functions to their previous departmental operation.[7]

Studies of the pros and cons of downsizing have revealed a mixed pattern of results. The economic benefits that are achieved from reducing the size of the workforce are often not as significant as expected. The impact on organizational morale and productivity often is negative or detrimental to efficiency efforts. However, the firms that have downsized most effectively appear to be those that have planned for it systematically and have tried to harmonize (insofar as possible) the previous organizational structures and operations with the newer realities in a way that is compatible and acceptable to those who remain. Typically, ideas about authority and the use of authority must be reshaped to give supervisors and employees greater decision-making responsibility.[8] Even with a lessening of organizational structure, most individuals still need to have clear lines of accountability for their performance to be evaluated. This, in turn, is vital if reward systems are to be meaningful and motivational.[9]

Some organizational theorists predict that downsizing will continue indefinitely, and that in some firms there will be a "radical restructuring." This could result in organizational structures and practices that conflict with time-honoured organizational principles. Proponents of downsizing and restructuring have typically advocated employee empowerment. Empowerment, as identified in Chapter 1, essentially means delegating sufficient authority to employees to allow those employees to make decisions and become more involved in achieving organizational goals. Employee groups that are given wide latitude and considerable authority to make job-related decisions are often referred to as **self-directed (self-managed) work teams (SDWTs)**. We discuss team concepts further in Chapter 11.

Self-directed (self-managed) work teams (SDWTs)
Employee groups who are given wide latitude and considerable authority to make many of their own job-related decisions.

Re-engineering
Concept of restructuring a firm on the basis of processes and customer needs and services, rather than by departments and functions.

Some firms have tried **re-engineering,** whereby they restructure more on the basis of processes (e.g., meeting customer orders and requirements) than on the basis of departments or functions (e.g., sales and production). Such an approach requires supervisors and employees to directly focus on customer needs and services rather than on their own functions and specialties. Focusing on the customer may enhance a firm's efforts to be more efficient and competitive in the marketplace, but it also can mean a blurring of line and staff functions and roles. Some authorities have suggested that re-engineering will require an emergence of "process managers" who will manage key processes and whose broadened responsibilities will cut across line and staff functions and levels of an organization.[10] A number of major corporations already have restructured parts of their organizations along customer–process dimensions. If carried out throughout a firm, re-engineering could create what has been referred to as the **horizontal corporation,** in which organizational structures become quite flattened and managerial authority relationships are minimal.[11]

Horizontal corporation
A very flat firm resulting from restructuring by customer process.

Perhaps the most extreme forecast about the corporate organization of the future been called the **virtual corporation.** Companies presumably could join as temporary partners or networks and share skills, employees, and access to each other's markets to exploit various opportunities. A virtual corporation would have no organization chart or hierarchy, and it could be considered as the "ultimate" project-type of organization. At the end of the collaboration in a project or market opportunity, the various partners would separate and have no continuing permanent relationship. Of course, a virtual corporation would require member companies to share a high level of trust and collaboration. Even with this, a concern would be that individual firms might lose control over their own operations. Although a number of companies have moved in this direction in certain types of joint ventures, the virtual corporation is currently more a theory than a reality.[12]

Virtual corporation
Companies linked temporarily to take advantage of marketplace opportunities.

Whether or not radical restructurings will become commonplace in the future is speculative. What does seem likely, however, is that the application of organizational principles will always be part of the supervisory position, and that any types of organizational change will require that supervisors understand how to apply and adapt certain organizational principles to their situations.[13]

WHAT CALL DID YOU MAKE?

As Alice Austin in the chapter-opening vignette, you should review and apply the basic organizational principles that were discussed in this chapter. Probably the most important is to take steps to restore the unity of command principle in your department. All direct work requests must be communicated through you, and you must not be bypassed if you are going to retain work control. It may be that your span of supervision is too wide. Perhaps you need to identify one or two lead persons who can serve in your absence in order to have a proper chain of command.

Although there are several approaches that you can take, you probably should first discuss this with your manager, the vice president of administration, in order to get support to rectify the situation. You need to review the organizational structure and to clarify the various types of line and staff authority that affect your position. Then, all parties who use your department's services need to be informed again of the proper workflow procedures. Further, you need to instruct your employees that they are to accept no direct work requests unless they have your approval to do so or the approval of a lead person if you decide to appoint such an individual.

You also must remind your employees that their jobs require a customer point of view as well as just carrying out work requests. You should solicit their ideas concerning how departmental procedures and organization structure can be improved.

SUMMARY

1 The organizing function of management is to design a structural framework—that is, to group and assign activities to specific work areas so as to achieve the desired objectives. Organizing includes establishing authority relationships among managers, supervisors, and departments.

2 The informal organization interacts with, yet is apart from, the formal organization structure. It can constructively or negatively influence departmental work performance. To use the informal organization positively, supervisors should become familiar with informal groups and their leaders and determine how to enlist their cooperation in achieving departmental objectives.

3 An organization should normally adhere to the principle of unity of command. This principle requires that everyone be directly accountable to only one supervisor and that formal communications should normally flow through the chain of command.

4 In assigning the number of employees reporting to one supervisor, the principle of span of management should be observed. Also known as the span of supervision or span of control, this principle recognizes that there is an upper limit to the number of individuals a supervisor can manage effectively. The span of management is determined by factors such as the competence of the supervisor, the previous training and experience of employees, their work locations, and the amount and nature of work to be performed. Other things being equal, the smaller the span of management, the more levels of management will be needed; the broader the span of management, the fewer levels will be required.

5 Departmentation is the process of grouping activities and people into distinct organizational units. Departmentation is most often done according to function, but activities can also be grouped along geographic lines, by product or service, by customer, by process and equipment, or by time. Rather than designing new departments, supervisors most often will be faced with the task of assigning activities and employees within an existing department to achieve efficiency and stability.

6 Supervisors are attached to an organization in either a line or a staff capacity. Within their own departments, supervisors are line managers with line authority to direct their employees. If a person is in a staff authority position, his or her normal role is to provide guidance, advice, and service in a specialized field.

A line organizational structure has only line authority relationships in a direct chain-of-command arrangement. This is commonplace in very small firms. As organizations increase in size, they usually adopt a line and staff type of structure. This enables the use of staff people whose specialized knowledge and skills support line managers and others throughout the organization. In a line and staff structure, a line supervisor usually has the discretion to accept or reject the staff person's advice. The human resources department is typically a staff department whose services and advice are generally utilized by line supervisors.

When higher-level management grants functional authority to a specialized staff person, this person has the right to issue directives about certain matters within his or her area of expertise. When a staff person has been granted functional authority over a specialized area, line supervisors are not free to reject the advice or directives that this person may give.

A matrix (project management) type of organizational structure places certain managers in charge of project teams whose members are drawn from different departments. At the same time, line supervisors manage the employees in regular departments.

This structure facilitates more efficient use of employees on multiple projects without disrupting the regular departmental arrangements. However, a matrix structure may create problems of priority scheduling and accountability since employees report both to a departmental supervisor and to a project manager.

A departmental organization chart is a picture of authority and responsibility relationships. Organization manuals contain statements of objectives, policies, and procedures; identify the authority and responsibilities of managerial and supervisory positions; and describe formal channels for obtaining information and assistance. Such manuals may also contain job descriptions that identify the major elements of a job and job specifications that identify the requirements for qualifying for or performing a job.

Downsizing usually involves the elimination of job positions and levels of management. Supervisors who survive a downsizing have to adapt organizational principles to the changes that have occurred. This usually includes a widened span of management and the need to provide more opportunity for employees to share in decision making. To empower employees, supervisors should structure their departments to allow for more employee participation. Various changes, such as restructuring, SDWTs, and horizontal and virtual organization structures, can help companies reduce costs and be more responsive to customer demands.

QUESTIONS FOR DISCUSSION

1. Define the managerial organizing function, unity of command, and the span of management principle and explain how these concepts relate to one another.
2. What is the informal organization? How does the informal organization affect a supervisor? Discuss the approaches a supervisor can take to foster cooperation with informal groups and their leaders.
3. Explain the tradeoff between the number of levels of management and the span of management. How does this problem typically affect a supervisor?
4. Explain how the fair assignment of work activities contributes to achieving stability of a department's operation.
5. Define line authority and staff authority. What is the difference between a line type of organization and a line and staff type of organization?
6. Does the relationship between a line supervisor and a staff person (from whom the line supervisor seeks advice or counsel) violate the concept of unity of command? Why or why not?
7. Discuss the nature of supervisory relationships with staff personnel in a human resources department. In what specific areas can the human resources staff assist the supervisor?

8. Discuss the concept of functional authority. Give several examples of how organizations have used this concept. Does the use of functional authority (or functional staff authority) violate the principle of unity of command? Discuss.

9. Describe the matrix organization. What are the primary strengths and weaknesses of a matrix organization? How can supervisors minimize the potential problems that a matrix structure might present?

10. Define the following organizational tools and explain the usefulness of each tool to the supervisor:
   a. Organization chart.
   b. Organization manual.
   c. Job descriptions.
   d. Job specifications.

SKILLS APPLICATIONS

Skills Application 4-1: Organization Chart Analysis

Obtain the organization charts from two medium to large organizations that you are interested in learning more about. To do this, go to a popular search engine on the Internet (e.g., www.google.ca) and search for "organization chart" on Canadian websites. You will be provided with an extensive list of Canadian entities that have made their organization charts available on their websites. Review the organization charts and answer the following questions:

1. Identify the departmentation options that appear in each chart that you have selected. Are the organizations using functional, geographic, customer, process and equipment, time, or some other form of departmentation?

2. Does it appear that the organization is primarily oriented around a line, line and staff, or matrix structure? What leads you to this conclusion?

3. Imagine you were seeking a job in one of these organizations. What information is contained on the chart that might help you prepare for an interview with this organization?

Skills Application 4-2: Understanding the "Virtual Corporation"

Using a Canadian-based search engine (e.g., www.google.ca), perform a search for the term "virtual corporation" to find websites of virtual corporations. Visit at least five of these sites and answer the following questions:

1. Based on your research, what distinguishes a "virtual corporation" from more traditional business partnerships that have always existed among Canadian businesses?

2. Is the term *virtual corporation* simply a new label for an old idea, or does it define a unique organizational approach to doing business in a demanding marketplace? Discuss.

CASES

CASE 4-1

Problems with the Project

Jordan White is supervisor of shipping and receiving at Canadian Modular Homes Inc. (CMH). CMH is a 15-year-old Canadian company that designs and partially constructs homes that are sold as "kits." The advantage of these homes is that they are partially constructed in an indoor environment and therefore quality tends to be very consistent. The company also takes advantage of production efficiencies because multiple units of the same model can be constructed at the same time. The kits have been very successful in the Canadian market, with

75 percent of the company's sales occurring in the cottage or vacation home market. Purchasers buy the kit and construct it on their cottage site themselves or with the assistance of a local contractor. Total construction time is vastly reduced from traditional construction, since much of the work is done at CMH's factory before the kit is shipped.

White supervises a group of 12 employees in the shipping and receiving department. This area of the company is particularly crucial to the firm's success, since the department is responsible for ensuring that all components of the kit are gathered accurately and shipped together. Customers have little tolerance for shipping errors, as a missing item or component can delay the entire construction project. Having to "rush" even a small component to the customer due to mistakes by the shipping department can cost CMH more than the original cost of shipping the entire kit.

Three months ago, White attended a meeting called by the president of the company, Ted Schaeffer. At the meeting, Schaeffer reported that the marketing department had identified a potentially lucrative new market for the company's modular kits. Apparently, market research indicates that the Japanese are very interested in homes based on "kit" construction. Due to the high cost of building materials in Japan, it appears that even with the cost of shipping from Canada, CMH's kits would represent a good value to Japanese consumers. This market has the potential to more than double the company's annual sales volume, and the president urged everyone at the meeting to gear up quickly to take advantage of this opportunity, as a U.S. company may be close to entering the Japanese market. Schaeffer reported that a project team would be assembled that would research and plan for entry into the Japanese market. Managers were asked to cooperate fully with the project team to ensure that it could bring the company into the Japanese market as quickly as possible.

Shortly after the meeting, Linh Sho was appointed as the leader of the "Enter Japan" project team. Sho called and asked White to identify a senior person from his area to work on the project. She indicated that she required approximately 10 hours per week from someone who could research the shipping issues that would be involved in getting the company's kits to Japan. White struggled with the decision about whom to appoint to the team. The shipping department is constantly under time pressure, and he believed that he really couldn't afford to lose anyone, even for 10 hours a week. He also worried about the impact of appointing a very high performer to the project. Could he really afford to lose his best person? Would it be better to assign someone who was not as good a worker, since his or her loss wouldn't have as much of an impact on the department's operations?

After much internal debate, White decided to appoint Gail Simpson, his most senior and productive employee. White decided that the importance of the "Enter Japan" project required that he choose a high-performing employee. He would make up for Simpson's reduced contribution to the department somehow. White forwarded Simpson's name to Sho, and asked Sho to contact him if she needed any further information.

Simpson has now been working on the "Enter Japan" project for the better part of two months and White has noticed that she seems quite stressed. Simpson told White at the beginning of the project that she wasn't sure that she was the right person to be working on the project, as it was so different from anything she had ever been involved in. White reassured her that he was confident in her abilities, but she still seemed apprehensive. Today she was visibly upset when she came into White's office. "I've had it with this "Enter Japan" project, Jordan. It's gotten to the point that I hate coming to work. Not only am I up to my ears with my regular job, but I'm constantly being harassed by Linh. I'm supposed to be working 10 hours a week for her, and even after 20 hours I'm nowhere near finished what she wants me to have done. She's setting unrealistic deadlines and I've been coming in on weekends just to keep up. I've tried telling her that I still have my regular job to do, but she says what she needs is more important. I just can't take it anymore." With that, Simpson stormed out of White's office, slamming the door behind her.

Questions for Discussion

1. Using the concept of unity of command, evaluate the cause of Simpson's angry outburst.
2. What could White have done differently when he first was asked to appoint someone from his department to the team? What could he have done to ensure that Simpson's work load was more manageable?
3. When project teams are assembled, how should the members be chosen? Was Gail Simpson the right choice for this project team? Why or why not?
4. Evaluate White's communication with Simpson and Sho. What did he do well? What could he have done differently?
5. What should White do now to address the situation? Be specific.

| CASE 4-2 |

A Shortage of Supervisors

David Simms is store manager of a local restaurant that is part of a nationwide chain of popular family restaurants. While Simms has overall responsibility for all aspects of his store's operations, he relies heavily on four shift supervisors who are "on the floor" coordinating the restaurant's kitchen and serving staff.

According to company policy, all supervisors and managers are to be promoted from within the corporation. Simms knows of a few situations in which individual restaurants went outside to find qualified supervisors, but this practice is generally frowned upon because upper management believes in promoting from within and encouraging people to "work their way up" in the organization. Simms has always prided himself on his dedication to this policy. Many of his employees attained supervisory positions in other restaurants within the chain; several went on to become managers of their own stores. Simms is also proud of his abilities as a manager. The restaurant he manages has a reputation for being profitable, stable, and relatively problem-free. His employees and supervisors get along quite well, and employee turnover is the lowest in the area. However, during the past week Simms faced a perplexing problem.

Last week, Natalka Katzenbach, the weeknight shift supervisor, notified Simms that in two weeks her husband is being promoted and transferred to another province. Katzenbach apologized for the short notice, and she explained that she and her husband had no choice but to accept this "once in a lifetime" offer. Therefore, Katzenbach will be supervising her last shift in about a week. Simms never expected, and has done little to prepare for, such an occurrence. Katzenbach always joked that she loved her job so much that she'd work until she was 80 if the company would let her.

In the past couple of days, Simms has tried to find someone who could fill Katzenbach's position, but he has reached only dead ends. Simms contacted his regional manager and explained the situation. She informed Simms that there was not a store in the area that could spare a supervisor or a supervisory trainee. Because the labour market is very tight, Simms expected such an answer. The only other option he can think of is to promote an employee named Margo James, who is a great server and who has helped him occasionally when supervisors were sick or on vacations. However, Simms has heard that while James is a well-liked server, front-line staff were not at all happy with her performance as a temporary supervisor. James's coworkers complained that she was a "control freak" and extremely autocratic whenever she filled in for a supervisor. Simms is not sure that promoting James is the best alternative, but he also knows that he is supposed to promote from within, so he has a difficult set of decisions to make.

Questions for Discussion

1. As Simms, how important is it that you follow upper management's "promote from within" policy?
2. What organizational changes could Simms have made to minimize the risk of finding himself in this situation?
3. Is it possible to promote James and maintain employee morale and stability? Discuss.
4. What should Simms do now, both to fill the vacant position and to prevent a similar problem from occurring in the future?

Chapter 5: Staffing

After studying this chapter you will be able to

1 Discuss the staffing function and describe the roles of the human resources staff and supervisors.

2 Explain how the supervisor prepares to fill job openings and why job descriptions and job specifications are critical to this task.

3 Discuss the selection process and the use of directive and nondirective interviewing in the process.

4 Describe how the supervisor should prepare for and conduct an effective selection interview.

5 Explain the hiring decision and the importance of documentation.

6 Identify the characteristics of an effective orientation program.

7 Explain approaches to training and the supervisor's role in employee development.

You are Emma Winger, manager of accounting and financial services for Western Diagnostic Laboratories, a Canadian company that operates over 40 medical laboratories in three provinces. The company's head office is located in Winnipeg and is home to the company's human resources, accounting, and other management and administrative staff.

Due to rapid corporate expansion, you been involved in more hiring decisions over the last year than you have ever experienced in your five years as supervisor. Workload in the accounting department is increasing at an unexpected rate, and you have filled quite a number of job openings. Although you are becoming more comfortable with the selection process, you still find that conducting interviews is not your favourite part of your job. You are not certain that you are always asking the right questions to make the best hiring decision possible. While the people you have hired have generally proven to be good employees, you wonder if you have always hired the very best people.

A little over a year ago, you hired a senior accounting assistant named Carrie Webster. The knowledge and skills required for the position indicated that the applicant should have at least three years of job-related experience and a college diploma in accounting. Webster has been a reliable member of the department, and her most recent employee performance form indicates that she is an above-average employee who learns very quickly.

This morning you had a disturbing encounter with Bob Trotter, another of your employees in the accounting department. Bob Trotter has worked for you for four years and has held a relatively junior position during that time. When the senior accounting assistant position became available last year, Trotter applied for it. He was passed over in favour of Webster, however, because he did not have an accounting diploma. Several years ago, Trotter had been working toward his diploma through online and night school courses, but had abandoned the effort when family demands became too stressful. After being passed over last year, Trotter resumed his education and has been attending night classes once again. Trotter stormed into your office this morning complaining that a new night school class had started last night and that he was shocked to see that Webster was enrolled in his class. Trotter contends that Webster is attending school at night to get the diploma she claimed to have already held when she was hired. You told Trotter that you would look into the situation and asked him to avoid spreading unfounded rumours until you got all of the facts.

You review the job file and recall that the competition for the position of senior accounting assistant was keen. You interviewed six candidates—four outsiders and two internal candidates. The post-interview evaluation forms indicate that the two internal applicants (including Trotter) were eliminated from consideration because they did not possess the required diploma. Further, under educational attainment, Webster cited a diploma in business administration, with a concentration in accounting, from Concord College. However, on both her application and on her résumé, Webster did not mention a specific completion date.

Before Webster was offered employment, the human resources department verified her employment record and found it to be very good. Apparently, no one had checked Webster's educational background. Upon further investigation, you discover that Webster does not have a college diploma. She is currently enrolled in two courses, and her diploma completion is approximately one year away.

You know that if Webster is dismissed, it will take several months before a replacement can perform at her level. You wonder what you should do now.

You make the call!

1

THE STAFFING FUNCTION AND THE HUMAN RESOURCES DEPARTMENT

Discuss the staffing function and describe the roles of the human resources staff and supervisors.

The management of human resources is the supervisor's most important activity, and it begins with staffing. As it was defined in Chapter 1, staffing is the recruitment, selection, placement, orientation, and training of employees. These activities are part of every supervisor's responsibilities, although in large organizations staff specialists provide help and support. The supervisory staffing function also includes the evaluation of employee performance and input into how employees are to be rewarded based on their performance.

Human resources management (HRM)
Organizational philosophies, policies, procedures, and practices that strive for the effective use of employees.

In a broad sense, **human resources management (HRM)** is the philosophy, policies, procedures, and practices related to the management of people in an organization. To perform the activities necessary to accomplish its goals, every organization must have human resources and use them effectively. To facilitate this, many firms have a human resources department with a director of human resources and other personnel.

Human resources (HR) department
Department that provides advice and service to other departments on human resource matters.

In most organizations, the director of human resources and the human resources department operate in a staff capacity. The **human resources (HR) department,** which may be called the "personnel department," "the industrial relations division," or some other name, usually exists to provide advice and service to all departments concerning such employment matters as applicant recruiting, screening, and testing; maintenance of personnel records; wage and salary administration; discipline and fair employment practices; and other services and assistance.

Not every organization has an HR department. Very small firms, for example, usually do not need or cannot afford to have specialized staff personnel. In these firms, supervisors, in consultation with their managers, may carry out certain employment-related tasks, or the firm may designate someone to share hiring and record-keeping duties with other managerial personnel. However, when an organization grows, at some point top-level managers will likely hire an HR director and staff specialists to help carry out human resources functions. For most organizations, the role and size of the typical HR department have expanded considerably in recent years. Because of expanded needs, some organizations have found it cost effective to contract out, or "outsource," some HR activities.

HR Advice and Supervisory Decisions

Regardless of its official name, the usefulness and effectiveness of any HR department depends on its ability to develop close working relationships with managers and supervisors. The quality of these line–staff relationships, in turn, depends on how clearly top-level managers have defined the scope of activities and authority of the HR department.[1]

The HR department is often given primary responsibility for some decisions that supervisors must abide by. For example, certain policies and practices regarding compliance with human rights legislation, labour relations, and wage rates are typically formulated and directed by the HR department. There are, however, many other areas in which supervisors must use their own discretion in making decisions about employee matters. Even in these instances, however, supervisors often consult with HR department staff for assistance, information, and advice. HR staff usually begin by offering suggestions to line supervisors who, in turn, must decide whether to accept, alter, or reject those suggestions or recommendations. When supervisors believe a recommendation of the HR staff is not feasible, those supervisors should make their own decisions. For the most part, though, line supervisors will accept the recommendations of HR staff, because the HR staff are experts in employee relations matters and usually have a good understanding of the organizational dynamics.

Some supervisors readily welcome the HR staff's willingness to make certain decisions for them so that they will not have to solve difficult employee problems in their own departments. These supervisors reason that their own departmental tasks are more important than dealing with issues the HR staff can handle just as well or better than they can. Other supervisors may accept the staff's advice based on the premise that if the decision later proves to be wrong or dubious (e.g., in disciplinary cases), they can say, "It wasn't my choice; HR made the decision—not me!" For them, it is a relief to rely on the staff's advice and consider it a decision. In so doing, these supervisors defer to the HR department in the hope they will not be held accountable for the decision. However, even when supervisors follow the HR staff's advice, they are still accountable for the ultimate decisions.

While it is easy to understand why some supervisors are reluctant to reject an HR staff person's advice, those supervisors should recognize that the staff person may see only part of the picture. The director of HR is not responsible for the performance of a supervisor's department. Quite often, many unique factors are better understood by each departmental supervisor than by anyone else.

2   PREPARING TO MEET STAFFING NEEDS

Explain how the supervisor prepares to fill job openings and why job descriptions and job specifications are critical to this task.

The staffing function is an ongoing process for the supervisor; it is not something that is done only when a department is first established. It is more realistic to discuss staffing in the typical situation in which a supervisor is placed in charge of an existing department. Although it has a nucleus of employees, changes in the department take place due to employee separations from the workforce, changes in operations, growth, or other reasons. Since supervisors depend on employees for results, they must make certain that there are enough well-trained employees available to fill all positions.

Determining the Need for Employees

A continuous aspect of the supervisory staffing function is that of determining the department's need for employees, both in number and job positions. Supervisors should become familiar with departmental jobs and functions and consult the organization chart or manual if one is available. For example, the supervisor of a maintenance department may be responsible for employees who are painters, electricians, and carpenters, each with different skills. The supervisor should study each of these job categories to determine how many positions are needed to get the work done and how employees should work together. The supervisor may have to compromise by adjusting a preferred arrangement to existing realities or by combining several positions into one if there is not enough work for one employee to perform a single function. By carefully studying the organization of the department, the supervisor can reasonably determine how many employees and what skills are needed to accomplish the various work assignments.

Developing Job Descriptions and Job Specifications

After determining the number of positions and types of skills needed, the supervisor's next step is to match the jobs available with individuals to perform them. This usually is done with the aid of job descriptions, which, as described in Chapter 4, indicate the duties and responsibilities involved in each job. A supervisor may have access to existing job descriptions. If such descriptions are not available, they can be developed with the assistance of higher-level managers or the HR staff. Similarly, if a new job is created, the supervisor should determine its duties and responsibilities and develop an appropriate job description.

The supervisor may find it helpful to ask departmental employees to list the tasks they perform during a given time period—say, a day or a week. This will provide the supervisor with considerable information from which to develop a job description. Although the final form of the job description may be written by an HR staff person, it is the supervisor's responsibility to determine what actually goes into it.[2] Figure 5-1 shows a step-by-step approach to developing a job description (this one for the position of housekeeper in a hospital) that would be adaptable to many other types of jobs.

FIGURE 5-1   Example of how to develop a job description.

The following steps were developed for the preparation of a job description for the position of housekeeper in a hospital:

1. Prepare a questionnaire to be sent to housekeeping employees and their supervisors, asking them to list what they believe are the major functions and subfunctions that must be performed to do their job effectively.
2. Have several higher-level managers who are interested in housekeeping list what functions they believe should and should not be performed by housekeepers.
3. Find out from others in the organization what they believe should be and should not be the functions of a housekeeper.
4. Tabulate the results of each of the three steps above.
5. Reconcile the differences of the above three viewpoints with the objectives of your organization, and prepare a detailed list of activities to be performed.
6. Classify activities as major or minor activities.
7. Determine what each housekeeper needs to know, what qualifications are necessary to perform designated activities, and specifically why each activity is to be performed.
8. Submit the results of Steps 5 to 7 to a committee of housekeepers and supervisors for their discussion and recommendations. For example, you may find that you have been asking housekeepers to do more than could possibly be accomplished reasonably. Revise and finalize the job description and job specification as appropriate.
9. Periodically—at least annually—review and revise the job description, following the eight steps listed above. Update and revise the job description whenever you believe that changes in products, equipment, the economic climate, or service demands necessitate a change in the job to be performed.

A supervisor should periodically (at least annually) compare each job description with what each employee does. As jobs change over time, the job descriptions may become outdated and should be updated. The supervisor may find that some of the duties assigned to a job no longer belong to it and should be deleted or assigned elsewhere. Supervisors should not take the preparation of job descriptions lightly because they can be used to explain to applicants the duties and responsibilities of a particular job. Job descriptions that describe the jobs accurately are useful in providing a realistic job preview, developing performance standards, conducting performance appraisals, and performing other staffing functions.

When the content of each job has been determined or re-evaluated, a supervisor next should identify the knowledge and skills that are required of employees who will perform the job. As defined in Chapter 4, a written statement of required knowledge, skills, and abilities is referred to as a job specification. The approach for determining what an employee needs to know is found in Figure 5-1, Step 7. Typically, the job description and job specification are combined into one document.

Determining How Many Employees to Hire

Supervisors are not frequently confronted with a situation in which large numbers of employees have to be hired at the same time. This situation occurs when a new department is created or when a major expansion takes place. The more usual pattern is to hire one or a few employees as the need arises. Of course, some supervisors constantly request additional employees because they feel pressured to get their work done on time. In many cases, however, a supervisor's problems are not solved by getting more help. In fact, the situation may become worse. Instead of problems being reduced, new problems may arise due to inefficiencies that accompany overstaffing.

Normally, a supervisor will need to hire a replacement when a regular employee leaves the department due to promotion, transfer, resignation, dismissal, retirement, or for some other reason. There is little question then that the job must be filled. However, if major technological changes or a downsizing are anticipated, a replacement may not be needed. There are other situations in which additional employees have to be hired. For example, if new functions are to be added to the department and no one in the department possesses the required knowledge and skills, it may be necessary to go into the labour market and recruit new employees. Sometimes a supervisor will ask for additional help because the workload has increased substantially and the department is under extreme pressure. Before requesting additional help, the supervisor should make certain that the employees currently in the department are being utilized fully and that any additional help is absolutely necessary and within the budget.

Assisting in Recruitment

When supervisors have positions open in their departments, they normally ask the HR department to recruit qualified applicants. Whether a particular job vacancy will be filled by someone from within the organization or someone from outside, the HR department usually knows where to look to find qualified applicants. Most organizations try to fill job openings above entry-level positions through promotions and transfers. Promotions reward employees for past accomplishments, and transfers can protect them from layoff or broaden their job knowledge. Internal applicants already know the organization, and the costs of recruitment, orientation, and training are usually less than those for an external applicant.

Generally, internal applicants can be found through the use of computerized skills inventories or job posting and bidding. Information about every employee's skills, educational background, work history, and other pertinent data can be stored in a database that can be reviewed to quickly determine whether any existing employees qualify for a particular job opening. This procedure helps ensure that every employee who has the necessary qualifications is identified and considered. Most organizations communicate information about job openings electronically, by posting vacancy notices on bulletin boards, or in newsletters. Interested employees apply or "bid" for the vacant position by submitting applications to the HR office with a copy to their current supervisor. Job posting creates a greater openness in the organization by making all employees aware of job opportunities.

The outside sources of job applicants will vary depending on the type of job to be filled. In all likelihood, a data entry clerk will not be recruited from the same source as a medical technologist. Advertising, public or private employment agencies, educational institutions, employee referrals, walk-ins, Internet job sites, and contract or temporary help agencies are some of the sources that may be used.[3]

To screen the applicants, usually the HR department has candidates complete employment application forms and conducts preliminary interviews to determine whether the applicants' qualifications match the requirements for the positions available. The HR department also makes reference checks of the applicants' previous employment and background. For certain positions, the department may administer one or more tests to determine whether applicants have the necessary skills and aptitudes. This may mean conducting statistical studies of tests that are used to determine whether they validly predict how an employee will perform on the job.[4] Eventually, applicants who do not have the required qualifications are screened out. Those who do have appropriate qualifications are referred to the supervisor of the department where the job is open.

3	THE SELECTION PROCESS

Discuss the selection process and the use of directive and nondirective interviewing in the process.

Selection is the process of screening applicants to choose the best person for a particular job. Once job applicants have been recruited, the next step is to gather information that will determine who should be hired. While the department supervisor may be assisted by staff from the HR department, the ultimate responsibility for the selection decision should rest with the supervisor. The supervisor is in the best position to evaluate how well a candidate would meet the demands of the available job and fit into the existing department.

Selection
The process of choosing the best applicants to fill open positions.

Selection criteria
Factors used to choose among applicants who apply for a job.

Regardless of who makes the final hiring decision, selection criteria must be developed as the first step of the selection process. **Selection criteria** are the factors that will be used to differentiate among the various applicants. Education, knowledge, previous experience, test scores, and interpersonal skills often serve as selection criteria. It is important that anyone who will be involved in the selection process has a very clear understanding of the selection criteria and the significance or weighting that the various criteria will have in the hiring decision. Without well-defined selection criteria, there is an inceased risk that the hiring decision will be swayed by irrelevant, non–job related factors or by individual biases.

Supervisors should not make staffing decisions without considering the legal ramifications of their decisions. It is easy to understand why supervisors are confused by the numerous laws, orders-in-council, regulations, and guidelines they may have heard or read about (see Appendix I for an overview of federal employment legislation). For example, the Human Rights Code prohibits employment practices that discriminate on the basis of race, gender, colour, religion, and national origin. Under employment equity programs, employers make good-faith efforts to recruit, hire, and promote designated groups. While it is difficult to be current on all aspects of the law, effective supervisors should acquaint themselves with the applicable provincial or federal legislation and, if needed, seek clarification from the HR or legal departments.

The Employee Selection Interview

For supervisors, the most frequently used selection criterion—and often the most important part of the selection process—is the employee selection interview. Even expert interviewers contend, however, that it is often difficult to make an accurate appraisal of a person's strengths and potential from a brief interview. If there are several applicants for a position, the supervisor must ascertain which one is most qualified. This means trying to determine which applicant is most likely to perform best on the job and to stay with the company for the long term.

The employment interview plays a very important role in the selection process. Depending on the type of job, the applicant may be interviewed by one person or by a selection committee. It is important to remember that the applicant is also interviewing the organization (see Figure 5-2). The supervisor and/or committee members must properly prepare for the interview and remember that they are "selling" the organization. Interviewing is much more than a technique;

FIGURE 5-2   Goals of the employment interview.

GOALS OF THE APPLICANT

1. Obtain information about the job.
2. Obtain information about the organization.
3. Determine whether the job matches his or her needs.
4. Determine whether he or she wants the job.
5. Communicate important information about him- or herself.
6. Favourably impress the employer (the interviewer).

GOALS OF THE EMPLOYER (THE INTERVIEWER)

1. Promote the organization.
2. Attract the best possible applicant.
3. Gather information about the applicant.
4. Assess how well the applicant's qualifications match the job requirements.
5. Determine whether the applicant will fit in with the organization and other employees.

Source: Northeastern University's Career Services' "Successful Interviewing" website provided the foundation for this figure. Students may wish to visit www.dac.neu.edu/coop.careerservices/interview.html to obtain a copy of the "Successful Interviewing" handout.

it is an art that every supervisor must learn. Although our focus in this chapter is on the employee selection interview, over time every supervisor will conduct or be involved in other types of interviews that occur during the normal course of events. Among these are appraisal and counselling interviews, interviews regarding complaints and grievances, interviews regarding disciplinary measures or discharge, and exit interviews when employees quit voluntarily. The basic techniques, however, are generally common to all interviewing situations.

Basic Approaches to Interviewing

There are two basic approaches to interviewing: (1) directive and (2) nondirective. These approaches are classified primarily according to the amount of structure imposed on the interview by the interviewer.

Directive Interview

Directive interview
Interview approach in which the interviewer guides the discussion along a predetermined course.

In a **directive interview,** the interviewer guides the course of the discussion with a predetermined outline and objectives in mind. This approach is sometimes called a "patterned" or "structured" interview. Using an outline helps the interviewer ask specific questions to cover each topic for which information is being sought. Although the outline of the interview is predetermined, the interviewer does have the ability to question and expand on related areas. For example, if a supervisor asks about the applicant's previous work experience, this may lead to questions about what the applicant liked and did not like about previous jobs. The supervisor guides and controls the interview but does not make it a rigid, impersonal experience. As a result of human rights requirements, organizations are increasingly asking all applicants the same questions to ensure that all applicants are fairly considered. This approach makes it easier to compare applicants since all have responded to the same questions.

Nondirective Interview

Nondirective interview
Interview approach in which the interviewer asks open-ended questions that allow the applicant greater latitude in responding.

The purpose of a **nondirective interview** is to encourage interviewees to talk freely and in depth. The applicant has maximum freedom in determining the course of the discussion. Rather than asking specific questions, the interviewer may stimulate the discussion by asking broad, open-ended questions such as, "Tell me about your work in the computer field." Generally, the interviewer will develop a list of possible topics to cover and, depending on how the interview proceeds, may or may not ask them. This unstructured approach to interviewing allows for great flexibility, but is generally more difficult and time consuming than directive interviewing. There is also a concern that, because a common set of questions is not being asked of all applicants, there is more room for interviewer bias to enter into the selection decision. For example, if a great deal of the conversation happened to be spent discussing a candidate's hobby that the interviewer happens to share, the interviewer may be biased in favour of the candidate for reasons that have nothing to do with the candidate's ability to do the job. For these reasons, the nondirective technique is rarely used in its pure form.

Blending Directive and Nondirective Approaches

Ultimately, the purpose of any interview is to promote mutual understanding—to help the interviewer and interviewee understand each other better through open and full communication. In employee selection interviews, the directive approach is used most often since supervisors find it convenient to obtain infor-

Interviewing is much more than a technique; it is an art that every supervisor must learn.

Getty Images/Photodisc Collection

Situational interview questions

Questions that ask a job applicant to describe what the applicant thinks he or she might do in a given hypothetical situation.

Behaviourally based interview questions

Questions that ask a job applicant to describe his or her performance in a past situation.

mation by asking the same direct questions of all applicants. At times, however, supervisors should strive to blend both directive and nondirective techniques to obtain additional information that might be helpful in reaching a decision. For example, the use of **situational interview questions** asks the applicant to describe what he or she would do in a certain situation. All applicants are given a specific situation to respond to. For example, the question "How would you assign daily work when two employees are absent?" allows the applicants to organize and express their thoughts about a realistic work situation. The supervisor may gain deeper insights about applicants' abilities to think and solve problems that could make the difference in choosing which applicant to hire.

Another technique that blends the use of directive and nondirective questions is the use of **behaviourally based interview questions**. A behaviourally based question asks the candidate to describe an actual situation from past experience and relay how he or she handled that situation. Since it is widely recognized that the best predictor of future behaviour is actual past behaviour, the use of behaviourally based interview questions may allow an interviewer to get a better sense of how an applicant actually performs in specific situations.

Regardless of the approach used, development of relevant job-related questions is essential. For example, questions such as "Explain how you trained other employees in the use of the new equipment" or "What are the steps involved in backing up a computer hard drive?" allow the applicants to reveal their knowledge and skills more clearly than could be ascertained from other sources. The supervisor should avoid using judgmental questions such as, "I believe that unions are unnecessary. What do you think?" Also, answers to questions that require a yes or no response, such as "Do you like to work with numbers?" reveal very little about the applicant's ability to perform a particular job. The supervisor will gather more valuable information by asking why the applicant does or does not like to work with numbers.

| **4** | **PREPARING FOR A SELECTION INTERVIEW** |

Describe how the supervisor should prepare for and conduct an effective selection interview.

Since the purpose of an employee selection interview is to collect information and arrive at a decision concerning a job applicant, the supervisor should prepare carefully for the interview. The supervisor must know what information is needed from the applicant, how to get this information, and how to interpret it. Figure 5-3 provides guidelines for planning and conducting the employee interview. These guidelines are elaborated upon in the following sections.

As stated earlier, the directive interview is the most common approach used in selecting employees. Although most supervisors develop their own questions, some organizations have forms and procedures to guide supervisors in selection interviewing. For example, some firms require supervisors to complete a detailed form on all applicants who are interviewed. Others use a standard interview form that more or less limits supervisors to asking only the questions that are included on the form. These interview forms sometimes are used to prevent supervisors

FIGURE 5-3   Guidelines for conducting a selection interview.

1. Carefully review the application, the applicant's résumé, and other background information about the job candidate.
2. Determine the objectives and the form of interview to be conducted (i.e., directive and/or nondirective); develop specific questions to ask.
3. Find a quiet, private place to hold the interview where interruptions will not occur.
4. After a cordial "warm-up," explain the nature of the job and its requirements; do not attempt to oversell the job or what is needed.
5. Ask directive questions to verify information and qualifications on the application and also to fill in any gaps that may be significant to the hiring decision.
6. Ask the candidate to state what he or she could most contribute to the job; ask the applicant to provide examples of previous job situations that might be relevant.
7. Encourage the candidate to speak freely and to ask as many questions as necessary.
8. Take notes of the candidate's statements and comments that are most pertinent to meeting the requirements of the job.
9. Avoid judging the candidate's suitability until the interview is completed; avoid possible biases or stereotypes that could unfairly influence the hiring decision.
10. Close the interview positively by thanking the candidate and indicating when a hiring decision will be made.

from asking questions that might be considered discriminatory. Therefore, in preparing for an employee selection interview, the supervisor must know what can be and what should not be asked of job applicants during the interview.

Understanding the Influence of Human Rights Legislation

Under the Canadian Human Rights Act (see http://laws.justice.gc.ca/en/H-6/index.html), it is unlawful to discriminate on the basis of race, national or ethnic origin, colour, religion, age, sex, sexual orientation, marital status, family status, disability, or conviction for an offence for which a pardon has been granted. Each province and territory in Canada has established human rights commissions to investigate complaints of discrimination and harassment and to make efforts to settle complaints between parties. For links to websites maintained by the human rights commissions in each province and territory, visit www.ohrc.on.ca/english/commission-links.shtml.

In order to comply with human rights legislation, it is important that interview questions not be asked that seek information about any prohibited area of inquiry. The overriding principle to follow in employee selection interviews is to ask job-related questions. Questions about topics not related to a person's ability to perform the job should be avoided. For example, asking an applicant for a data-entry clerical position about keyboarding experience is valid. However, asking this applicant "Who cares for your children?" would not be acceptable, since family status is an area that the employer cannot base a decision upon. Figure 5-4 lists some of the most common areas of inappropriate and potentially illegal inquiry. The guidelines in Figure 5-4 apply to all phases and criteria used in the selection process, including application forms and selection interviews.

Application forms, tests, interviews, reference checks, and physical examinations must all be nondiscriminatory and focus on job-related requirements. To determine whether or not a selection criterion is appropriate and complies with the law, one consulting firm has suggested the "OUCH" test.[5] OUCH is a four-letter acronym that represents the following:

O—Objective.
U—Uniform in application.
C—Consistent in effect.
H—Has job relatedness.

A selection criterion is *objective* if it systematically measures an attribute without being distorted by personal feelings. Examples of objective criteria include typing-test scores, number of years of education, degrees, and length of service in previous positions. Examples of subjective criteria include a supervisor's general impression about a person's interest in a job or feelings that a person is "sharp."

A selection criterion is *uniform in application* if it is applied consistently to all job candidates. Asking different interview questions of male and female applicants would not be uniform in application.

A selection criterion is *consistent in effect* if it has the same proportional impact on all candidates. For example, criteria such as possessing a high school diploma or living in a certain area of town may be objective and uniformly applied to all job candidates, but they could screen out proportionately more members of minority groups. Similarly, requiring that a candidate meet a

FIGURE 5-4   Areas of unlawful or potentially unlawful questions in applications and employment interviews.

SUBJECT OF INQUIRY	UNLAWFUL OR POTENTIALLY UNLAWFUL QUESTIONS AND PRACTICES
Applicant's Name	Maiden name Original name (if legally changed)
Family Status	Marital status Number and ages of applicant's children Information about spouse
Age	Prior to hiring: requests for birth certificate, baptismal records, or valid driver's licence (unless job requires operation of a vehicle)
Birthplace	Birthplace of applicant, applicant's spouse, and applicant's parents Native tongue or how foreign language skills were acquired
Race and Colour	Any inquiries relating to race and colour, questions about physical characteristics such as eye colour, hair, height, and weight Requiring a photo to be submitted with an application
Citizenship	Inquiries about being a Canadian citizen, landed immigrant, permanent resident, or the date that citizenship was received
Religion and Creed	Inquiries about religious affiliations, churches attended, religious holidays, etc.
Record of Offences	Inquiries about non-job-related offences
Education	Nationality, race, or religious affiliation of schools attended
Memberships in Organizations	Membership in any association other than a union and/or a professional or trade organization unless such affiliations are pertinent to the nature of the employment
Disability	Pre-employment physical examinations, questions about applicant's physical and mental conditions, learning disabilities, etc., which are not directly related to performing the essential duties of the job

minimum height requirement might potentially screen out more women than men. When a selection criterion is not consistent in effect, the burden of proof is on the employer to demonstrate that it is job related.

A selection criterion *has job relatedness* if it can be demonstrated that it is necessary to perform the job. For example, in most cases it would be extremely difficult to prove that a selection criterion such as marital status is job related. Job-related criteria should stress skills required to perform the job.

Supervisors may not always understand the reasons for some of the restrictions imposed on them by the employment equity policies of their organizations. They should not hesitate to consult with specialists in the HR department for explanations and guidance in this regard.

Reviewing the Applicant's Background

Before interviewing a job applicant, the supervisor should review all available background information that has been gathered by the HR department. By studying whatever is available, the supervisor can review, in advance, the general qualifications of the job applicant. The application form will supply information concerning the applicant's schooling, experience, and other items that may be relevant.

When studying the completed application form, the supervisor should always keep in mind the job for which the applicant will be interviewed. If questions come to mind, the supervisor should write them down. For example, if an applicant shows a gap of a year in employment history, the supervisor should plan to ask the applicant about this gap and why it occurred.

A supervisor should also review the results of any employment tests that were taken by the applicant.[6] More and more organizations are administering job performance, integrity, honesty, and drug tests prior to the interview stage. Tests should be validated before they are actually used to assist in making hiring decisions. HR departments often administer job performance tests that measure skill and aptitude for a particular job as part of their normal procedures to screen out unqualified applicants. The HR department must be able to document that these tests are valid, job related, and nondiscriminatory. This typically involves studies and statistical analyses by staff specialists—procedures that normally are beyond the scope of a supervisor's concern. Applicants whose test scores and other credentials appear to be acceptable are referred to the departmental supervisor for further interviewing. It is essential for the supervisor to understand what a test score represents and how meaningful it is in predicting an applicant's job performance. By consulting the HR department staff, the supervisor can become more familiar with the tests that are used and learn to interpret the test scores.

An additional source of information is the personal or employment reference. For the most part, information obtained from personal sources such as friends or character references will be positively slanted because applicants tend to list only people who will give them good references. Information from previous supervisors who were in a position to evaluate the applicant's work performance are best. However, because of emerging personal privacy regulations and potential lawsuits, an employment background investigation is best conducted by HR department specialists. If possible, job references should be obtained in writing, should deal with job-related areas, and should be gathered with the knowledge and permission of the applicant. After reviewing all available background information, the supervisor should be able to identify areas in which little or no information is available and areas that require expansion or clarification.

Because of privacy and other legal concerns, many former employers of a job applicant will provide only minimal information when asked to provide a reference. Some former employers will respond to an inquiry only with a statement such as "John Jones worked here from 2001 to 2003" and will supply very little other detail. So, is background checking fruitless? Consultant and author Bradford Smart recommends using a threat of reference check. He suggests using the question, "If I were to ask you to arrange an interview with your last boss, and the boss were very candid with me, what's your best guess as to what he or she would say were your strengths, weaker points, and overall performance?" The interviewer may then gain insight into how this applicant is apt to perform on the job.[7]

The importance of verifying reference or application form data cannot be overemphasized. Various organizations have been charged with negligently hiring employees who later commit crimes. Typically, the lawsuits charge that the organization failed to adequately check references, criminal records, or general background information that would have shown the employee's propensity for deviant behaviour. The rulings in these cases, which range from theft to homicide, should make employers more aware of the need to check references thoroughly. It is suggested that the organization include on the job application a statement to be signed by the applicant stating that all information presented during the entire selection process is truthful and accurate. The statement generally notes that any falsehood is grounds for refusal to hire or for termination.[8]

Preparing Key Questions

In preparing for the interview, the supervisor should develop a list of questions, which may include both directive and nondirective components.[9] Preferably, the supervisor should develop a list of key questions—perhaps six to 10—that are vital to the selection decision and are job related. It is important that all applicants be asked the same core set of key questions so that responses can be compared and evaluated. For example, the supervisor may want to know technical information about an applicant's previous work experience, why the applicant left a previous employer, and whether the applicant can work alternative shift schedules and overtime without difficulty. By planning such questions in advance, the supervisor can devote more attention during the interview to listening to and observing the applicant, instead of having to think about what else should be asked. A thorough plan for the employment interview is well worth the time spent preparing it.

Establishing a Conducive Physical Setting

Privacy and some degree of comfort are important components of a good interview setting. If a private room is not available to conduct an interview, then the supervisor should at least create an atmosphere of semiprivacy by speaking to the applicant in a place where other employees are not within hearing distance.

Conducting the Selection Interview

The employee selection interview is not just a one-way questioning process, since the applicant also will want to know more about the company and the potential job. The interview should enable the job seeker to learn enough to help him or her decide whether or not to accept the position if it is offered. The supervisor must conduct the interview professionally by opening the interview effectively, explaining the job requirements, and using good questioning and note-taking techniques.

Opening the Interview

The experience of applying for a job is often filled with tension for an applicant. It is to the supervisor's advantage to relieve this tension. Some supervisors try to create a feeling of informality by starting the interview with social conversation about the weather, the heavy city traffic, the Stanley Cup, or some other topic of broad interest. The supervisor may offer a cup of coffee or make some other appropriate social gesture. An informal opening can be helpful in reducing an applicant's tensions; however, it should be brief, and the discussion should move quickly to job-related matters.

Many supervisors begin the employee selection interview with a question that is nonthreatening and is easily answered by the applicant, but also contains job-related information that the supervisor might need. An example is "How did you learn about this job opening?"

The supervisor should avoid excessive informal conversation because studies of employee selection interviews have revealed that frequently an interviewer makes a favourable or unfavourable decision after the first five minutes of the interview. If the first 10 minutes are spent discussing items not related to the job, then the supervisor may be basing the selection decision primarily on irrelevant information.

Explaining the Job

Realistic organizational preview (ROP)
Sharing of information by an interviewer with a job applicant concerning the mission, values, and future direction of the organization.

Realistic job preview (RJP)
Information given by an interviewer to a job applicant that provides an honest view of both the positive and the negative aspects of the job.

During the interview, the supervisor should discuss details of the job, working conditions, wages, benefits, and other relevant factors in a realistic way. A **realistic organizational preview (ROP)** includes sharing complete information about the organization: its mission, philosophy, opportunities for the future, and other information that gives applicants a good idea of where the job under consideration will fit in and its importance. In discussing the job itself, a **realistic job preview (RJP)** informs applicants about the desirable as well as the undesirable aspects of the job. Because of eagerness to attract a top-notch candidate, the supervisor may be tempted to describe a job in terms that make it more attractive than it actually is. For example, a supervisor might "oversell" a job by describing in glowing terms what actually is available only for exceptional employees. If the applicant is hired and turns out to be an average worker, this could lead to disappointment and frustration. Applicants who are given realistic information are more likely to remain on the job because they will encounter few unpleasant surprises.[10]

Asking Effective Questions

Even though the supervisor will have some knowledge of the applicant's background from the completed application form and from information that the applicant volunteers, he or she still needs to determine the applicant's specific qualifications for the job opening. The supervisor should not ask the applicant to repeat information already provided on the application form. Instead, questions should be rephrased to probe for additional details. For example, the question "What was your last job?" is likely to be answered on the application form. This question could be expanded as follows: "As a computer help-desk adviser at Omega, what types of computer problems did you solve?"

Some questions that may not appear to be directly job related nevertheless may be appropriate (see Contemporary Issue box on page 146). For example, it may be important to know what an individual considers to be an acceptable income level. The salary limits of a position for which an applicant is interested may make it impossible for that person to meet existing financial obligations. This could force the individual to seek an additional part-time job to supplement income, thereby taking away some energy from the primary job. Or, in order to meet immediate financial needs, the applicant might accept a low-paying position as a temporary solution and continue to look for a higher-paying position with

CONTEMPORARY ISSUE
Interview Brainteasers

Think back to the preparation you did before your last job interview. As a candidate, you probably tried to prepare answers for some of the generic interview questions like "Tell me about yourself" and "What are your strengths and weaknesses?" But did you consider questions such as "How many piano tuners are there in the world" or "How many quarters would you need to stack to reach the height of the CN Tower?" If these sound completely "off the wall," think again.

Known as "interview brainteasers," these seemingly unanswerable questions can be traced to interviewing practices at high-tech giant Microsoft, which uses these riddles to find the "best and brightest" programmers in a competitive hiring market. But other companies, from Hewlett-Packard to Bay Street investment banks, are also finding that brainteasers can offer valuable insights into an applicant's thought processes and ability to think analytically. While it may not be readily apparent why it might be useful to ask a candidate "How many Ping-Pong balls can you stuff into a 747?" advocates of brainteasers insist that these questions can really allow high-potential candidates to shine in an interview.[1] The interviewer probably doesn't know the answer to the question, nor does he or she care whether the candidate does. It's all about examining how a candidate thinks.

William Poundstone, author of "How Would You Move Mount Fuji?" studied the phenomenon of interview brainteasers at Microsoft and offers tips to candidates about what the interviewer is really looking for. Poundstone claims that interviewers are really trying to probe the candidate's thought processes. Does this candidate have the ability to cre-atively tackle a difficult problem and work his or way through a chain of analysis that will result in a plausible answer to the question? It's not the candidate who comes closest to the "right" answer who will get the job—it's the one who demonstrates a solid thought process who will stand out.[2]

So can you prepare for an interview brainteaser? Should you get out your rolls of quarters and start stacking them or stuff Ping-Pong balls into your suitcase the next time you take a flight? Poundstone emphasizes that there will always be new brainteasers that companies can develop, so it is completely fruitless to try to "study" for specific questions. Instead, think in advance about how you will handle this type of question. For example, Poundstone recommends that you assume that the first answer you think of will almost always be wrong. If there appears to be an obvious answer to the problem, reject that answer. Think deeper. A better approach is to start thinking out loud, and provide the interviewer with a running commentary about how you are breaking down the problem. Talk out loud, don't get discouraged, and look for novel approaches that the interviewer probably hasn't heard before. Even if your answer is wrong, you'll get points for creativity. It also doesn't hurt to know some basic information such as the approximate population of your city, Canada, and the world. These numbers might help you make some beginning assumptions that can get your analysis started.[3]

So next time you're crossing the street, you might want to ask yourself "Why is a sewer cover round?" You never know when you might be asked that question.

Sources: (1), (2), (3) William Poundstone, "How many interviewers fit around a water cooler? Thought processes probed in today's tough talent search," *Financial Post/National Post* (August 25, 2003), p. FE3. See also Ellen McCarty, "Close encounters of the brain-baffling kind: how to survive a programming job interview," *Financial Post/National Post* (August 4, 2000), p. C7; Mark Gimein, "Smart Is Not Enough," *Fortune* (January 8, 2001), p. 124; Daniel McGinn, "Testing, Testing, The New Job Search," *Newsweek* (September 6, 2003), p. 36.

another firm. Problems of this nature, although not directly connected with job requirements, are relevant to the work situation and may be part of a selection decision.

A supervisor must use judgment and tact when questioning applicants. The supervisor should avoid leading questions such as "Do you daydream frequently?" or "Do you have difficulty getting along with other people?"

Questions such as these are sometimes used by interviewers to see how an applicant responds to difficult personal questions. However, these questions may antagonize the applicant. By no means should the supervisor pry into personal affairs that are irrelevant or removed from the work situation.

Taking Notes

In their efforts to make better selection decisions, many supervisors take notes during or immediately after the interview. Having written information is especially important if a supervisor interviews a number of applicants. Trying to remember what several applicants said during their interviews, and exactly who said what, is virtually impossible.

The supervisor should avoid writing while an applicant is answering a question. Instead, the supervisor should jot down brief summaries of responses after the applicant has finished talking. Although the supervisor does not have to take notes about everything said in the interview, key facts that might aid in choosing one applicant over the others should be noted.

Avoiding Pitfalls in Interviewing and Evaluation

The main problem in employee selection usually lies in interpreting the applicant's background, personal history, and other pertinent information. As normal human beings, supervisors are unable to completely eliminate their personal preferences and prejudices, but they should face up to their biases and make efforts to avoid or control them. Supervisors should particularly avoid making judgments too quickly during interviews with job applicants. Although it is difficult not to form an early impression, the supervisor should complete the interview before making any decision and should strive to apply the OUCH test to avoid the numerous pitfalls that can occur both during and after an interview.

Supervisors should avoid generalizations. The situation in which a supervisor generalizes from one aspect of a person's behaviour to all aspects of the person's behaviour is known as the "halo" or "horns" effect. In practice, this means basing one's overall impression of an individual on only partial information and using this limited impression as a primary influence in rating all other factors. This may work either favourably (the **halo effect**) or unfavourably (the **horns effect**), but in either case it is improper. For example, the halo effect occurs when a supervisor assumes that if an applicant has superior interpersonal skills, he or she will also be good at keyboarding, making decisions, and so forth. On the other hand, if a supervisor judges an applicant with a hearing impairment as being low on communication skills and allows this to serve as a basis for low ratings on other dimensions, the horns effect prevails. The process we have suggested does not guarantee that the supervisor will not form erroneous opinions. However, objectivity minimizes the chances of making the wrong choice.

Halo effect
The tendency to allow one favourable aspect of a person's behaviour to positively influence judgment on all other aspects.

Horns effect
The tendency to allow one negative aspect of a person's behaviour to negatively influence judgment on all other aspects.

Closing the Interview

At the conclusion of the employee selection interview, the supervisor likely will have a choice among several alternatives, ranging from hiring the applicant, deferring the decision until later, or rejecting the applicant. What the supervisor decides will be guided by the policies and procedures of the organization. Some supervisors have the authority to make selection decisions independently; others are required to check with either their managers or the HR department. Still others may have the authority only to recommend which applicant should be hired. For purposes of brevity, we assume in the following discussion that the supervisor has the authority to make the final selection decision. Under these circumstances, the supervisor can decide to hire an applicant on the spot. All the supervisor has to do is tell the applicant when to report for work and provide any additional instructions that are pertinent.

If the supervisor wishes to defer the decision until several other candidates for the job have been interviewed, the applicant should be informed that he or she will be notified later. The supervisor should indicate a time frame within which the decision will be made. However, it is unfair to use this tactic to avoid the unpleasant task of telling an applicant that he or she will not be hired. By telling the applicant that a decision is being deferred, the supervisor gives the applicant false hope. While waiting for the supervisor's decision, the applicant might not apply for other jobs, thereby letting opportunities slip by. Therefore, if a supervisor has made the decision not to hire an applicant, the supervisor should tell the applicant tactfully. Some supervisors deem it best to turn down the job seeker in a general way without stating specific reasons. This is often accomplished by merely saying that there was not a sufficient "match" between the needs of the job and the qualifications of the applicant.

The supervisor should keep in mind that an employment interview is an excellent opportunity to build a good reputation for the employer. The applicant realizes that other candidates probably have applied for the job and that not everyone can be selected. The last contact an applicant may ever have with the organization is with the supervisor during the employment interview. Therefore, even if the applicant does not get the job, the supervisor should recognize that the way the interview was handled will make either a positive or a negative impression, sometimes a permanent one. Regardless of the outcome, an applicant should leave the interview feeling that he or she has been treated fairly and courteously. It is every supervisor's managerial duty to build as much goodwill as possible since it is in the organization's self-interest to maintain a good image.

Completing the Post-Interview Evaluation Form

Some organizations have the supervisor and other members of the interview team complete an evaluation form shortly after the interview—while the information is still fresh in their minds. Figure 5-5 is an adaptation of a form used by a retail store. This approach increases the likelihood that the same selection criteria are applied to each applicant. Other firms may require that supervisors submit a written evaluation that summarizes their impression and recommendation concerning each job candidate.

5

Explain the hiring decision and the importance of documentation.

MAKING THE HIRING DECISION

The decision to hire can be challenging when the supervisor has interviewed several applicants and all of them appear to be qualified for the job. There are no definite guidelines that a supervisor can always utilize to select the best-suited individual. At times, information from the application forms, tests, and interviews will indicate which of the applicants should be hired.[11] However, there will be other times when available information is not convincing or perhaps is even conflicting. For example, an applicant's aptitude test score for a sales job may be relatively low, but the person has favourably impressed the supervisor in the interview by showing an enthusiastic interest in the job.

FIGURE 5-5   Example of a postinterview evaluation form.

POSTINTERVIEW EVALUATION FORM			
Position	**Major Job Requirements**		
	(List major job requirements here.)		
Applicant's Name:	(Evaluate SKAs here.)		
			(Total)
Strengths: **Weaknesses:**			
Applicant's Name:	(Evaluate SKAs here.)		
			(Total)
Strengths: **Weaknesses:**			
Applicant's Name:	(Evaluate SKAs here.)		
			(Total)
Strengths: **Weaknesses:**			

Instructions to Interviewers

1. The interviewer(s) may decide that some job requirements are more important than others. Therefore, it may be appropriate to assign weights to those requirements to illustrate their relative importance.
2. Evaluate each applicant's skills, knowledge, or abilities (SKAs) for each of the major job requirements:

    1 = Unacceptable   2 = Moderately acceptable
    3 = Acceptable   4 = Strongly acceptable

3. Total the rating for each applicant. (By totalling the ratings, the interviewer[s] will have a system by which to make a more objective choice.)
4. Record each applicant's strengths and weaknesses.
5. Retain the form as documentation.

This is where supervisory judgment and experience come into play. The supervisor must select employees who are most likely to contribute to good departmental performance. The supervisor may consult with the HR staff for their evaluations, but in the final analysis it should be the supervisor's responsibility to choose. Before the final decision is made, the supervisor should evaluate each applicant against the selection criteria. By carefully analyzing all of the information available and keeping in mind previous successes and failures in selecting employees, the supervisor should be able to select applicants who are most likely to succeed.

Of course, hiring decisions always involve uncertainties. There are no exact ways to predict how individuals will perform until they actually are placed on the job. However, a supervisor who approaches the hiring decision in a thorough, careful, and professional manner is likely to consistently select applicants who will become excellent employees.

Employee Involvement in the Hiring Decision

The degree to which employees are involved in the selection process varies among organizations. In some organizations, subordinates, peers, or work-team members meet with the applicant and give their impression to the ultimate decision maker. Members of employee work teams, for example, are generally most knowledgeable about particular job responsibilities and challenges. They can offer valuable insight into the employee selection process. Even without formal teams, some organizations allow employees to fulfill various roles, from assisting with the definition of job responsibilities to having a direct say in the final hiring decision.[12]

Documenting the Hiring Decision

In recent years, many supervisors have been asked by higher-level managers and the HR staff to document the reasons for their decisions to hire particular individuals from among the applicants interviewed. Documentation is necessary to ensure that a supervisor's decision to accept or reject an applicant is based on job-related factors and is not discriminatory. At times, a supervisor's hiring decision will be challenged; the supervisor must be able to justify that decision or risk it being reversed by higher-level managers. In general, however, if supervisors follow the approaches suggested in this chapter, they should be able to distinguish the most qualified people from among the applicants and also be prepared to justify their employment selections.

| 6 | **ORIENTATION OF NEW EMPLOYEES** |

Identify the characteristics of an effective orientation program.

Orientation
The process of smoothing the transition of new employees into the organization.

When new employees report for their first day of work, the manner in which the supervisor welcomes them and introduces them to other employees in the department may have a lasting effect on their future performance. For most new employees the first days on the job can be stressful. New employees typically feel like strangers in new surroundings. It is the supervisor's responsibility to make the transition as smooth as possible and to lead new employees in the desired directions. This initial phase is called orientation.[13] **Orientation** is a process designed to help new employees become acquainted with the organization and understand the expectations the organization has for them. In short, orientation helps the employee to develop a sense of belonging to the organization and to become productive as soon as possible.

There are several approaches that a supervisor can use in departmental orientation of new employees. The supervisor may choose to personally escort the new employees around the department, showing them equipment and facilities and introducing them to other employees. Alternately, the supervisor may prefer to assign new employees to an experienced, capable employee and have this person do all of the orienting, perhaps including instructing all new employees on how to perform their jobs.

Using a Checklist

A useful technique to ensure that new employees are well oriented is to use a checklist. When developing an orientation checklist, the supervisor should strive to identify all the things that a new employee ought to know. Without some type of checklist, the supervisor is apt to skip some important item. Figure 5-6 shows an orientation checklist prepared by the HR department of an insurance company for use by supervisors.

Discussing the Organization

It usually is a good idea for the supervisor to sit down with new employees on the first day in some quiet area to discuss the department, the organization, and its policies and regulations. In some firms, the HR department provides booklets that give general information about the firm, including benefits, policies, and procedures. There may even be a formal class that provides this type of information to employees and takes them on a tour of the firm's facilities. In small firms, it may be appropriate to introduce new employees to the owner or top-level managers. In larger firms, this may not be practical, so sometimes these firms videotape an interview with the chief executive officer or other members of top-level management. In these videotapes, managers present the vision for the future, corporate philosophy, market and product development, etc. Employees should receive an explanation of what they can expect from the organization. As discussed earlier in this chapter, realistic organization and job previews should clarify employee expectations. The information must be accurate, and all employees must receive the same information.

A common mistake made by some supervisors when orienting new employees is to give them too much information on the first day. Presenting too many items in a very short time may result in information overload. A new employee is not likely to remember many details if they are all presented in the first two hours of the first day. Consequently, the supervisor should spread different aspects of orientation over a new employee's first few days or weeks. Also, the supervisor should schedule a review session several days or weeks later to discuss any problems or questions the new employee might have.

Being Supportive

More important than the actual techniques used in orienting new employees are the attitudes and behaviour of the supervisor. If a supervisor conveys sincerity in trying to make the transition period a positive experience and tells new employees that they should not hesitate to ask questions, this in itself will smooth their early days on the job. Even when the HR department provides formal orientation, it remains the supervisor's responsibility to assist each new person to

FIGURE 5-6   Orientation checklist of an insurance company.

WELCOME THE NEW EMPLOYEE.
Meet the new employee at the door. Take the new employee to the reception area and try to make him or her feel at ease.

SHOW THE WORKPLACE.
Briefly describe the group's work and where his or her job fits in the group.

INTRODUCE THE NEW EMPLOYEE TO COWORKERS.
It is important to create a sense of belonging right away.

GIVE A TOUR OF THE COMPANY.
This can be done by one of your experienced employees. Show the coat closet, cafeteria, time clock, restroom facilities, areas where announcements are posted, and the other departments that will be pertinent to the new employee's job. Schedule the "President's Perspective" video and the vice president's chat.

ILLUSTRATE OUTSTANDING CUSTOMER SERVICE.
Schedule with the employee a time to show the customer-service video and group discussion.

TAKE THE NEW EMPLOYEE TO THE HR DEPARTMENT.
After a tour of the company, take the new employee to the HR department to complete the necessary employment papers.

EXPLAIN THE TELEPHONE SYSTEM.
Take the new employee to the reception area, where a switchboard operator will explain the telephone system.

EXPLAIN THE COMPUTER SYSTEM.
Take the new employee to the data-processing area, where a staff member will instruct the employee in the procedures for computer usage, that is, password, logon, and other shortcuts. (The introductory two-hour session will be scheduled the first afternoon.)

MAKE SURE THE NEW EMPLOYEE UNDERSTANDS THE FOLLOWING:
- Use of the time clock and sign-out procedures.
- Starting and stopping times.
- Proper work clothes.
- Parking facilities.
- Identification requirements.
- Lunch and break periods.
- Restrictions on leaving the building during work hours.
- No-smoking policy.
- Rate of pay and how it is determined.
- Overtime pay.

(continued)

FIGURE 5-6   *(continued)*

- Pay deductions.
- What to do about paycheque errors.
- Probation period of 30 days.
- Performance evaluation. Discuss reward programs and career-development opportunities.
- Reporting of absences.

CLARIFY JOB RESPONSIBILITIES.

Set performance standards and clarify expectations. This is the first step in setting the stage so the new employee can get up to speed as quickly as possible.

ASSIGN THE NEW EMPLOYEE TO A "STAR" EMPLOYEE.

The star employee will serve as the new employee's shepherd to help get the new employee off to a good start.

REMIND THE NEW EMPLOYEE TO COME TO YOU FOR INFORMATION AND ASSISTANCE.

quickly become an accepted member of the departmental work team and a contributing, productive employee.

Setting the Stage

Supervisory responsibility goes beyond passing out the employee handbook and distributing department work rules. The supervisor should inform the other employees that someone new is joining the group and let them know something positive about the new person. Imagine how difficult it would be for a person to be received into the work group if the employees had been told "we had to hire this person." The supervisor needs to set the stage for the new employee's arrival so that he or she is properly socialized into the work group.

Organizations that use work teams believe in pushing authority, responsibility, and accountability downward throughout the organization. For many employees, this has meant learning to work more closely with others as team members and to depend on each other for the completion of assigned tasks. Over a period of time, effective teams develop openness in communication and relationships. New employees need to understand the purpose of the work group, its goals, why the job is important, where it fits in the organization, and so forth. They also need to understand the roles that various members fulfill. Supervisors must make certain that members of the work team understand it is their responsibility to communicate and contribute to this understanding.

Part of the orientation process is to shape the new employee's behaviour in a positive manner. Since people observe and imitate the behaviour of others, it is not enough for a supervisor to simply state what is expected of the employee. People tend to act—both productively and counterproductively—like those with whom they closely identify. Effective work-team members will model positive norms for the new employee. An effective technique is to place the new employee with an outstanding performer who acts as a coach or mentor to perpetuate excellent performance. Finally, all employees need positive feedback on performance, and an effective supervisor reinforces the new employee's early successes by giving sincere praise.

Mentoring

Mentoring
The guiding of a newer employee by an experienced employee in areas concerning job and career.

Since the publication of the 1978 classic *Harvard Business Review* article "Everyone Who Makes It Has a Mentor," research during the past two decades has explored the role that mentors or sponsors play in an employee's development.[14] **Mentoring,** the process of having a more experienced person provide guidance, coaching, or counselling to a less experienced person, is deeply rooted in history, as illustrated by the story of Odysseus turning over the care and development of his young son, Telemachus, to Mentor. In the Middle Ages, guild masters were responsible for their protégés' social, religious, personal, and professional skills. Broadly defined, the mentor teaches "the tricks of the trade," gives the protégé all the responsibility he or she can handle, thrusts the protégé into new areas, directs and shapes the protégé's performance, suggests how things are to be done, and provides protection.[15]

Mentoring should be looked upon as one way to smooth the transition of new employees into the organization and develop them into productive employees. New employees can build a network of people who can collectively provide the many benefits of a mentor. The supervisor can also fulfill this role by delegating appropriately challenging tasks that help build the new employees' knowledge and skill base.

7   TRAINING AND DEVELOPING EMPLOYEES

Explain approaches to training and the supervisor's role in employee development.

In most job situations, new employees require both general and specific training. If skilled workers are hired, the primary training need may be in the area of company and departmental methods and procedures. If unskilled or semiskilled workers are hired, they will have to be taught specific job skills to make them productive within a short period of time. Methods of formal training vary among organizations and depend on the unique circumstances involved in each situation. At the departmental level, helping employees improve their skills, knowledge, and abilities (SKAs) to perform both current and future jobs is an ongoing responsibility of the supervisor.[16]

Providing On-the-Job Training

Most training at the departmental level takes the form of on-the-job training. The supervisor may prefer to do as much of the training personally as time will permit. This has the advantage of helping the supervisor get to know the new employees while they are being trained in the proper methods and standards of performing the job. It also ensures uniform training since the same person is training everyone. If the supervisor does not have the time or the technical skills to do the training, then the training should be performed by one of the best current employees. The supervisor should give the training task only to experienced employees who enjoy this additional assignment and are qualified to do it. The supervisor should make periodic follow-up visits to see how each new employee is progressing.

When a supervisor does on-the-job training personally, he or she is given the opportunity to get to know the new employee.

Corel Corporation

Off-the-Job Training

Many training programs for new as well as existing employees are conducted outside the immediate work area. Some of these may be coordinated or taught by HR staff or training departments. For skilled trades involving, for example, electricians, machinists, or toolmakers, a formal apprenticeship training program may be established. Usually this requires the employee to be away from work periodically in order to attend formal schooling.

Increasingly, companies are using college-based programs for training their employees. Generally, college representatives and the firm's supervisors work together to develop a curriculum for employees. Employees attend classes at the college during nonworking hours. Tuition is paid by the firm, and employees receive credit for taking classes related specifically to their jobs. One example is an apprentice training program developed by representatives of a steel company and a community college. Employees are divided into two groups, each of which receives 640 hours of college lecture and laboratory training pertinent to their trade. The groups alternate every four weeks, with one group assigned to the plant for hands-on experience while the other group receives classroom training. A continual process of curriculum review and assessment of employee on-the-job performance ensures that the program meets the firm's needs.

There also may be programs offered within the firm during or outside working hours. For example, safety training meetings and seminars are commonly scheduled during working hours for supervisors and employees alike.

Ensuring Ongoing Employee Development

Supervisors should assess the skills and potential of employees and provide opportunities for ongoing development of their skills so that these employees can perform better both now and in the future. If a supervisor believes that training is needed that cannot be provided at the departmental level, the supervisor should go to a higher-level manager or to the HR department to see whether there are existing courses outside the organization that can meet training needs.

Many organizations have tuition-aid programs to help employees further their education. A supervisor should be aware of available course offerings at nearby educational institutions and encourage employees to take advantage of all the educational avenues open to them. These learning experiences can help employees develop skills, knowledge, and abilities that improve their performance and prepare them for more demanding responsibilities.[17]

The Supervisory Role in Employee Development

The impetus for a training program can come from many directions. Generally, operating problems and failure to meet organizational objectives may highlight the need for training. The entire training activity must be based on the identification of the combined needs of the organization and the employees.

Training must be viewed as an ongoing developmental process, not a simple bandage for a short-term problem. Therefore, training must be relevant, informative, interesting, applicable to the job, and actively involve the trainee in the process. As Confucius put it:

> *I hear and I forget*
> *I see and I remember*
> *I do and I understand.*

Skills that employees need in order to perform the essential departmental tasks should be the initial training focus. However, in the current business environment, cross-training is becoming essential. Corporate downsizing and consolidation of job duties suggest that supervisors will need to identify jobs that are important to the ongoing performance of their departments and that can be learned by other employees. Employees will need to learn new skills that will make them more valuable to their organizations. Cross-trained employees will be called on to assume additional responsibilities.

In formulating an employee development program, supervisors should seek answers to the following questions:

1. Who, if anyone, needs training?
2. What training do they need?
3. What are the purposes of the training?
4. What are the instructional objectives that need to be incorporated into the training program? (Instructional objectives comprise what the employee will know or be able to do upon completion of the training.)
5. What training and development programs best meet the instructional objectives?
6. What are the anticipated benefits to be derived from the training?
7. What will the program cost?
8. When and where will the training take place?
9. Who will conduct the training?
10. How will the training effort be evaluated?

Efficient and effective training should contribute to the achievement of organizational objectives. Development of instructional objectives is essential to the formulation of an evaluation plan. Training and development expert Donald Kirkpatrick formulated four levels of evaluation that can be used to measure the benefits of training: (1) employees' reactions to the training program, (2) their learning, (3) their application of learning to the job, and (4) the training's business results.[18]

Making Yourself More Valuable

The need for training and development is not limited to departmental employees. Supervisors also need training and development to avoid obsolescence or status-quo thinking. By expanding their own perspectives, supervisors are more likely to encourage employees to improve their knowledge and abilities and to keep up to date.

Most supervisors will probably attend a number of supervisory management training and development programs, as well as courses in technical aspects of company and departmental operations. Supervisors may want to belong to one or more professional or technical associations whose members meet periodically to discuss topics of current interest and share common experiences. In addition, they should subscribe to technical and managerial publications and read articles of professional interest.

Supervisors also should give some thought to their own long-term career development. The ambitious supervisor will find it helpful to formulate a career plan, writing down definite goals he or she would like to achieve during the next five to 10 years. Such a plan includes both a preferred pattern of future assignments and job positions and a listing of educational and training activities that will be needed as part of the desired career progression.[19]

Some companies expect their supervisors to periodically indicate their personal training and development needs and objectives on an official company form. This is particularly true if the company uses management by objectives (MBO).

WHAT CALL DID YOU MAKE?

It is vital for supervisors to verify references and confirm the accuracy of applicant information. Generally, HR departments do this for organizations. The reluctance of firms to take the time to do full reference checks has, however, fuelled applicant dishonesty. Many applicants seem to feel that the chances of getting caught are minimal, and that falsifying their application is worth the risk if it provides them with an advantage over other applicants.

The fact that Webster is an above-average performer and is excelling in this position may indicate that a college diploma is not really a job requirement. Despite her favourable job performance, however, Webster did convey misleading information when she applied for her position. While this omission or falsification is not as bad as some possibilities (e.g., a hospital hiring a surgeon who was found to be an imposter with no medical degree whatsoever), Webster did falsify her application to get the job and this raises some concerns, particularly when other candidates were told that having the diploma was a job requirement.

What should you do? In practice, each supervisor will apply his or her own set of experiences and values to make the decision. Some supervisors will take the comfortable route; Carrie is doing a good job, and the time and cost involved in replacing her are not worth the effort. Others may rationalize that "everyone is doing it," while still others believe that if a person is dishonest in one aspect of the job, this behaviour will spill over into other aspects of the person's job. You should consult with the HR department to determine whether there is a company-wide policy that you must abide by in this case. Some companies have well-publicized policies that clearly state

(continued)

that falsifying a job application is grounds for immediate dismissal. If such a policy exists, you will be bound by it. In the absence of such a policy, the decision must be based on your own judgment. You may want to consult with the HR department to get advice about this delicate matter.

Regardless of what you decide to do about Webster, you should develop safeguards to prevent the situation from recurring. You should begin by developing a cooperative arrangement with the HR department. Clarify who is responsible for background checks, and how extensive those checks will be. Review the job descriptions and job specifications for all of your positions. Ensure that the necessary background checks are made. Require written verification of work and educational experiences.

Try to recall the selection interview that you had with Webster to ascertain the types of questions you

asked. (If you took notes, this task will be easier.) It is often easy for people to place the blame on others, but you had the responsibility for conducting the employment interview. Did you ask the kinds of questions that would have enabled you to detect the omissions or falsifications? If you are concerned about your ability to conduct effective interviews, you may want to have an experienced interviewer sit in on some interviews to provide you with advice and suggestions to improve your skills in this area.

Finally, whatever your decision about Webster, do not ignore the fact that this situation also affects Trotter and the other internal candidate who was denied the position because of lack of educational qualifications. Your decision should include a plan to acknowledge the impact of this situation on them and minimize the negative feelings that might be emerging in the department.

SUMMARY

Managing human resources is the supervisor's most important activity. In fulfilling responsibilities for staffing, the supervisor can be substantially aided by the HR department.

There must be a balance of authority between line supervisors and HR staff in staffing policies and decisions. Usually, the HR department aids in recruitment—advertising the opening, recruiting a pool of applicants, screening, testing, checking background, etc. The departmental supervisor then interviews applicants and either makes or has most of the say in the final hiring decision.

The HR staff typically assumes much of the responsibility for ensuring that an organization's employment policies and practices comply with human rights legislation. Sometimes HR departments take primary responsibility for hiring, interpreting policy, determining selection criteria, writing job descriptions and specifications, testing applicants, and the like. Supervisors should not release these staffing areas totally to HR, although at times it might seem expedient to do so. A supervisor remains accountable for decisions even when relying on the advice of the HR staff.

An ongoing process of the staffing function is determining how many employees and what skills are needed to accomplish various work assignments. Job descriptions indicate the duties and responsibilities of the job and must be reviewed periodically. Job descriptions that accurately describe the job are useful in providing a realistic job preview, developing performance standards, conducting performance appraisals, and other staffing functions.

Job specifications detail the knowledge, skills, and abilities an employee should have to perform a job adequately. Applicants are recruited and screened based on the job description and job specification.

Supervisors need to ascertain how current employees are being utilized before they make requests for additional help. If new functions are added to the department or the workload increases substantially, supervisors need to determine the number and types of employees needed.

3 Selection is the process of choosing the best applicant to fill a particular job. After job applicants are located, information must be gathered to help in determining who should be hired.

Supervisors are most likely to be involved in employee selection interviews. Two basic approaches are the directive interview and the nondirective interview. The directive interview is highly structured; the supervisor asks specific questions of each applicant and guides the course of the discussion. In the nondirective interview, the supervisor allows the applicant much freedom in determining the course of the discussion.

4 Regardless of the interview approach used, supervisors must develop job-related questions. Situational questions may be used to assess how the applicant would act in a given situation. Judgmental questions and questions that can be answered with a simple yes or no should be avoided.

It is vital for a supervisor to thoroughly prepare for the selection interview. A supervisor should be aware of human rights guidelines. Job-related questions that foster nondiscriminatory treatment should be used. Selection criteria should be objective, uniform in application, consistent in effect, and job related (following the OUCH test). Before conducting the interview, the supervisor should review the applicant's application form, test scores, and other available background materials. By having a list of key questions to ask, the supervisor should be able to cover the most important areas in which more information is needed.

The supervisor may open the employee selection interview by using an approach that reduces tension, such as asking a question that is easily answered. The supervisor should explain the job, use effective questioning techniques, and take appropriate notes.

When evaluating an applicant, the supervisor should avoid such common pitfalls as making hasty judgments, being influenced by generalizations such as the halo effect or the horns effect, or forming impressions based on his or her own personal bias and preferences. Application of the OUCH test will help the supervisor minimize judgmental errors.

At the conclusion of the interview, the supervisor should remember that the applicant is entitled to a decision as soon as possible. The supervisor should strive to have the applicant leave with an impression of fair and courteous treatment.

5 The supervisor wants to select employees who will contribute to excellent department performance. A review of the selection criteria is critical in determining the best applicant. In some organizations, subordinates, peers, or team members may have a say in determining who is ultimately hired. This involvement ranges from assisting in defining job duties all the way to having a say in the final decision.

Documentation of the selection process is critical in helping to demonstrate that the process is based on job-related factors and is not discriminatory.

6 Effective orientation of new employees is a top supervisory responsibility. Orientation means helping new employees become acquainted with the organization and understand what is expected in the way of job duties. An orientation checklist can ensure that each new employee receives the same information. In most large organizations, the HR department helps the supervisor with orientation. Effective orientation programs avoid information overload and generally look at orientation as a process rather than just the first day on the job. The supervisor's supportive attitude and the involvement of other employees is critical. Effective orientation shapes the new employee's behaviour in a positive manner. Positive role models, coaches, or mentors should be used to perpetuate excellent performance standards.

7 On-the-job training is one of the supervisor's major responsibilities. When a supervisor lacks the time or technical skills to do the training personally, he or she can delegate the task to an experienced employee with excellent job performance. Off-the-job training programs can also help employees improve their performance. Training and development is a continuous process, not just a one-time effort.

Supervisors need to determine the skills employees need to do their jobs better. Factors such as failure to meet organizational objectives, operating problems, introduction of new machines and equipment, or addition of new job responsibilities to a position can help the supervisor pinpoint training needs. The supervisor should constantly monitor who needs training and what the training requirements are. Development of instructional objectives and a procedure for evaluating the effectiveness of training are critical.

Also, supervisors must recognize the need for their own training and development, and they should utilize whatever opportunities for career development are available to them. Supervisors should also consider having career plans to help them chart and monitor their own long-term career progression.

QUESTIONS FOR DISCUSSION

1. What are some of the major activities of the HR department that can assist the line supervisor in the staffing function? What should be the primary responsibility of HR staff and of line supervisors for various employment and other staffing activities? Is there a clear dividing line of responsibility? Discuss.

2. Why have many organizations made the HR department primarily responsible for making sure that their employment policies and practices are in compliance with government legislation?

3. Discuss the differences between a directive interview and a nondirective interview. Does the employee selection interview tend to be directive or nondirective in nature or both? Why?

4. Discuss how adequate supervisory preparation for an employee selection interview can be crucial to the interview's success. What specifically should a supervisor do before interviewing a candidate?

5. Discuss each of the following aspects of conducting an employee selection interview:
   a. Opening the interview.
   b. Explaining the job.
   c. Using effective questioning techniques.
   d. Taking notes.
   e. Concluding the interview.

6. Explain the difference between situational and behaviourally based interview questions. Provide an example of each type of interview question.
7. Why are supervisors and many employers now required to document why they did or did not hire applicants they have interviewed?
8. How is orientation of a new employee related to future performance? Discuss approaches that a supervisor may take in orienting a new employee.
9. What is mentoring? Discuss the advantages and disadvantages from the perspective of the person being mentored.
10. Why is on-the-job training most likely to be the type of training utilized at the department level? Enumerate other approaches for training and development that may be available.
11. Why should training programs be evaluated?

SKILLS APPLICATIONS

Skills Application 5-1: Developing Interview Questions

Go back and review Figure 4-7 on pages 119–21, which presents the job description and job specification for the position of nurse at Pine Village Hospital. Suppose you are hiring someone to hire a vacant nursing position at the hospital.

1. Using the strategies recommended in this chapter, develop a list of 10 questions that you would ask any applicant for this position.
2. Meet with another student and review your questions. Find examples of directive and nondirective questions in your lists. Did you include any situational or behaviourally based questions?
3. In addition to the interview, what other employment screening tools would you recommend be used?
4. Suppose the successful candidate would be working on the cardiac care floor of the hospital. Identify the advantages and disadvantages that might be associated with having other nurses from the cardiac care floor take part in the interview. Should coworkers be involved in hiring the people with whom they will be working, or should this responsibility rest with the supervisor? Discuss.

Skills Application 5-2: Illegal Interview Questions

Employment equity legislation has placed restrictions on questions employers may ask job applicants. Whether you are a person seeking a job or an interviewer hiring a candidate, it is important that you recognize the types of questions that are not permissible by law. Some interviewers may quite innocently ask questions that are, technically, not legal.

1. Go to www.google.ca and type in the search "illegal interview questions." Be sure to click the "pages from Canada" button to return information that is applicable to Canadian legislation. Review at least three sites that discuss the topic of illegal interview questions.
2. Based upon your research, evaluate each of the following interview questions. Discuss whether the question is absolutely not legal, absolutely legal, or whether it may be legal depending upon the requirements of the job.
   a. What is your first language?
   b. What languages are you able to speak and write fluently?
   c. How tall are you? How much do you weigh?
   d. Are you able to carry a 20 kg weight up five flights of stairs in under two minutes?
   e. Do you currently have or plan to have children in the near future?
   f. This job requires a great deal of travel. Will your family commitments allow you to do this?

3. What options are open to a candidate who is asked an illegal question? Should the candidate answer? What do you believe is the best way to handle this situation?

Skills Application 5-3: The First Day on the Job

1. Reflect upon the first day you spent in your most recent job. Meet with another student and compare your experiences.
2. How were your respective orientations conducted? Were they effective? Why or why not?
3. Were the job expectations clearly stated? Did they accurately reflect what was expected of you in the job?
4. What should have been done to provide a more useful orientation experience for each of you? Be specific.
5. Think back to your orientation as a new college or university student. What recommendations would you make for the orientation of new students at your school?
6. (Optional Application Project) Send your list of recommendations for new student orientation to the dean of students or other appropriate official. What was the administration's reaction to your recommendations?

SKILLS DEVELOPMENT

Skills Development Module 5-1: Employee Selection and Interviewing Protocol

This video segment shows Tony Roberts, accounting department supervisor at Lexicon Dynamics, who is faced with the challenge of finding someone to replace an employee who was recently promoted to another division within the company.

Questions for Discussion: The Ineffective Version

1. Discuss all the employee selection mistakes Tony Roberts made.
2. Explain what procedures you'd recommend for finding someone for the staff accountant position.
3. Identify various reasons for not hiring a relative or a close friend for a subordinate position.
4. If you were Roberts, what kinds of questions would you ask?

Questions for Discussion: The More Effective Version

1. Discuss the procedure that Roberts followed in the selection and interview process.
2. What other questions should Roberts ask the applicants to ascertain their suitability for the job?
3. What else could Roberts do to more effectively select the staff accountant?
4. Based on the conclusions you drew from watching the video, what might be reasons for hiring or not hiring Perry? Joann? Renee?

CASES

CASE 5-1

The Stress Interview Approach

Bradley Distributors, Inc. employed 500 employees in its warehouse and retail outlets. Sterling Durbin, the director of HR, had held this position for the past 17 years. He prided himself on his ability to conduct interviews effectively. When Jugnu Kanwar was hired as a new assistant HR manager, Durbin took great pleasure in "breaking in" this recent university graduate on the practical aspects of effective interviewing.

"I can size up anyone in 10 minutes or less in an interview. My record shows how good I am at this, and I'll give you a few tips," Durbin told his new assistant. "We don't use written tests anymore because of hassles with them. It's just as well, because I didn't put much faith in what those tests showed anyway. As for personal interviews, we use several interviewers for important positions to get the effect of a group interview. All of the interviewers ask the questions that they feel are important, and they report to me anything outstanding or particularly negative that turns up. My interview with a prospective employee is the one that usually counts the most, though. I'm looking for 'hard drivers' and people who I think will succeed around here. In just a few minutes, I can tell by the way they look at me, the kind of clothes they wear, and their general confidence in themselves whether or not they're likely to be good employees. Also, I put a lot of stock in whether or not the applicants have finished the education they began, whether it's high school, college, or university. It shows that they can finish what they start."

Durbin continued, "The best technique I've found to separate the poor applicants from those with real promise is to ask them how they would handle the following situation. I give them two alternatives to stop employees from arguing constantly with each other. First, the employees could be told either to work it out among themselves or to get a transfer out of the department. Second, the supervisor could sit down with the employees and work out the difficulties together. Whichever approach the applicant picks, I tell them that they are wrong. If they select the first method, I tell them that their job is to develop and help employees to perform better. If they select the second, I tell them they have more important things to do than to work out personal problems between employees. By doing this, I see how applicants handle stress and find out what they're made of. Good potential employees will stick to their guns and give me some good reasons why their approach should be followed. With all this information, I can usually make a good decision in a pretty short time. I've found that I am seldom wrong."

Questions for Discussion

1. Evaluate Durbin's interview techniques. What are the strengths and weaknesses of his system?
2. Is it possible to do an adequate job of interviewing in so short a time? Discuss.
3. How valid is the stress aspect of the interview? By putting candidates under stress and seeing whether they will defend their positions, is Durbin increasing the chance that he will hire the right person for the job? Discuss.
4. What recommendations would you make to Kanwar, concerning how she should respond to Durbin's comments?

CASE 5-2

Sanders Supermarkets Store #21: Orientation of a New Employee

Max Brown was one of the most promising young applicants Suhana Gupta had interviewed and hired in months. As the employment manager of Sanders Supermarkets, she had instructed Brown on company policies, dress codes, pay periods, rate of pay, and so forth, and had given him information about the union. He then left with his referral slip to report to Store #21, located in a suburban shopping centre.

Before Brown went to his new job, he stopped at his favourite clothing store and bought new white shirts to conform with the company dress code. In response to Gupta's suggestion that employees must be "clean cut," he then went to the barber shop for a haircut, his first since graduating from high school several months ago.

Upon arriving at Store #21, Brown introduced himself to Carl Dressel, the store supervisor. Dressel then told Brown to go over to aisle three and tell Sean Kelly, the head stock clerk, that he was to work with him. Brown walked into aisle three, but no one was there. Not knowing what to do next, he just waited for someone to show up. About 20 minutes later, Kelly came into the aisle with a stock truck full of cases. Brown introduced himself and said, "Mr. Dressel told me to come and work with Sean Kelly. Is that you?"

"Yeah," said Kelly, "I was just going to lunch. Here's my case cutter and stock list. You can figure it out. I'll see you in 30 minutes or so."

Kelly then left Max Brown standing there, rather confused. "Some training program," he thought to himself. Suhana Gupta had said that there would be lockers in the store for his personal items, but he wondered where they were. Gupta had also told him about punching a time card, and he wondered where the time cards were. Since Kelly had an apron on to protect his clothes, Brown tried to figure out where he could get one, too. He thought he might look in the back room to see whether the answers to some of his questions might be back there. Walking into the back room, he introduced himself to a young woman who said that she was Evita Chavez, one of the store's produce department clerks. Brown asked her whether she knew where he could hang his coat, get a time card, and find an apron. Chavez responded, "For the most part, we just throw our coats on top of the overstock; the aprons are in the office, and so are the time cards."

"At last," thought Brown. "Now I'm getting someplace." On his way to the office, he saw several stock clerks working in aisle one. He had seen four stock clerks so far, and only one wore a tie. Two had on plaid shirts, and the other had hair at least three inches below the collar. "I don't understand why Suhana Gupta was worried about the way I looked," he thought.

Finally, Brown found an apron and a time card. To find the time clock, he went toward the back room again and asked one of the meat cutters where the time clock was. He was given directions to go through the meat department to the other side of the store. He went through the door he was told to go through, which had a sign on it saying "Authorized Personnel Only." He was worried that he might not be an "authorized" person. He finally found the time clock, and, with a little difficulty, he figured out how to clock in. This done, he hurried back to aisle three, where Carl Dressel stood waiting for him. "Where have you been?" asked Dressel. "And where is Kelly?"

Brown explained that Kelly had gone to lunch and that he himself had been looking for an apron, the time clock, and a place to hang his coat. "You might as well learn right away that your job is putting up the loads of stock—and fast! I don't want to hear any more excuses. Now get to work," said Dressel.

As Brown started to open the top of the first box, he thought to himself, "The only thing I know for sure right now is that Suhana Gupta has never worked in this store!"

Questions for Discussion

1. Identify and discuss several areas in which Brown's experiences in Store #21 could have been improved by proper orientation.
2. Although Dressel's approach is certainly lacking, could some of the blame for Brown's poor orientation be attributed to Suhana Gupta? Why or why not? Discuss.
3. Outline a checklist or approach for orienting new employees in this type of work environment.

Chapter 6: Motivational Principles as Applied to Supervision

After studying this chapter you will be able to

1 Discuss reasons people behave the way they do.

2 Compare various motivation theories and explain their importance for understanding employee behaviour.

3 Explain the ABCs of shaping behaviour.

4 Compare the assumptions and applications of Theory X and Theory Y in supervision.

5 Discuss supervisory approaches for stimulating employee motivation—especially job redesign, broadened job tasks, and participative management.

You are Don Davis, director of reloading operations for Economy Moving and Storage, a large shipping company. Due to a corporate reorganization, you were recently transferred and promoted to the Halifax, Nova Scotia, centre, where you are in charge of five front-line supervisors who oversee the reloading operations of 80 employees. You were looking forward to the challenge and responsibility of your new position, but you knew you would miss your old network of friends. Maintaining contact via e-mail would be no substitute for working alongside such a great group of people.

In your first week on the job, it became obvious that the Halifax centre had some serious problems that had to be corrected quickly. Recently, customers had begun to complain that packages shipped from the Halifax centre arrived at their destinations late and in poor condition. For a company that prides itself on quality customer service and timely delivery, these conditions are unacceptable, and it is your responsibility to correct the situation.

Upon learning of these problems, the first thing you did was to gather information regarding the customer complaints. Then you checked with Holly Henderson, the human resources supervisor, to gather information on various employment statistics at the Halifax centre. You discovered that your centre had the company's highest employee turnover and lost-time injury rates. Absenteeism and tardiness were running rampant, and the number of employee grievances had been increasing over the past six months. Realizing that poor performance equals poor customer service, you decided to meet with the five reloading supervisors in an attempt to understand why the employees were performing below expectations.

During the meeting, you illustrated with charts and graphs the current month's performance results to Amy, Steve, Khan, Katya, and Ryan and asked for their input. Amy, the supervisor with greatest seniority, pointed out that the conditions in which the employees worked were terrible. "We had record cold temperatures every day last week and the heating system just isn't adequate," she said. "Two days ago it was below 10 degrees in here. How can you expect people to perform under those conditions?"

Khan, the newest of the supervisors, added, "Most workers are part time. Many have other jobs or are working here while they attend school. They come in here tired and with other things on their minds. They're here just for the paycheque. Most of the injuries I see are related to a lack of concentration. They are just stupid mistakes. Even during our safety meetings, workers seem bored and do not seem to pay attention."

Steve claimed, "The job the employees perform is very repetitious. They seem bored and lack enthusiasm. In fact, on several occasions employees have pointed out that their work is mindless and never changes. If you ask me, boredom is the main problem with employee performance."

Ryan continued, "I think the performance of our employees is affected by a few 'bad apples.' Overall, most of our employees are good people. They want to do a good job. I've seen them get frustrated because of a poorly performing coworker who should be reprimanded. I can't do anything about it; we're short staffed, and if I discipline someone, they will probably quit. That's what happened a week ago when I leaned on Rueben to improve his performance. He quit. Our employees know what to do, but sometimes they just don't or won't do it. Even when I plead with them to improve or threaten to write them up, it doesn't work. If I could only get the bad workers motivated, I think the rest would fall in line and improve their performance."

Last, Katya chimed in, "I'm having trouble motivating my workers. Just yesterday, one of my best workers left with a back injury and the rest failed to pick up the slack. I explained how important it was that we get our shipments out on time, but no one seemed to listen. If we don't find a way to motivate these people, none of us will have a job."

The real question is "How do you go about motivating employees to perform better?" A corporate pay freeze prevents you from tempting them with pay increases. You know you will have to do something, and quickly. What will you do?

You make the call!

<table>
<tr><td>

1

Discuss reasons why people behave the way they do.

</td><td>

DETERMINANTS OF HUMAN BEHAVIOUR

</td></tr>
</table>

In Chapter 1, we defined *management* as getting things accomplished with and through people by guiding and motivating their efforts toward common objectives. To manage effectively, as this definition suggests, supervisors must understand employee motivation and develop approaches that encourage employees to work to the full extent of their capabilities.

Human beings constitute a resource that is quite different from any other resource the supervisor is asked to manage. People have values, attitudes, needs, and expectations that significantly influence their behaviour on the job. The feelings people have toward their supervisors, their job environment, their personal problems, and numerous other factors are often difficult to ascertain. Yet these feelings have a tremendous impact on employee motivation and work performance.

What causes employees to behave the way they do? This question is difficult to answer because each individual is unique. The behaviour of people as individuals and in groups at work is often rational, consistent, and predictable. However, at times, people's behaviour may seem irrational, inconsistent, and unpredictable. When an employee's behaviour is not consistent with the organization's expectations, problems arise for the supervisor. Because behaviour is influenced by many forces, it is often difficult for the supervisor to formulate simple strategies that apply to every situation.

The forces that stimulate human behaviour come from within individuals and from their environment. Every day, employees confront issues that were unheard of a decade or two ago. "People are working longer hours, increasing numbers are having to deal with heavy workloads, and work pressures are increasingly having a negative effect on organizations, families and people."[1] The typical employee now spends more of his or her waking hours going to, being at, and coming home from work. Yet with the explosion of two-income households, employees find less time to spend with growing children and aging parents, or on taking vacations and pursuing other leisure activities. Some employees find themselves in intolerable or soured personal relationships. Many experienced managers speak about supervising a star performer, only to see that person's performance decline dramatically due to off-the-job pressures. Understanding the "baggage" that affects employee performance is critical to the supervisor's success in dealing with people.

Determinants of Personality[2]

Personality
The knowledge, attitudes, and attributes that combine to make up the unique human being.

Every individual is the product of many factors, and it is the unique combination of these factors that results in an individual human personality. **Personality** is the complex mix of knowledge, attitudes, and attributes that distinguish one person from all others.

Many people use the word *personality* to describe what they observe in another person. However, the real substance of human personality goes far beyond external behaviour. The essence of an individual's personality includes his or her attitudes, values, and ways of interpreting the environment, as well as many internal and external influences that contribute to his or her behaviour patterns. There are several major schools of personality study that can help us comprehend the complexity of human beings. We will first discuss the primary determinants of personality and then describe how some major theories relate these factors to employee motivation.

Physiological (Biological) Factors

One major influence on human personality is a person's physiological (or biological) makeup. Such factors as sex, age, race, height, weight, and physique can affect how a person sees the world. Intelligence, which is at least partially inherited, is another factor. Most biological characteristics are apparent to others, and they may affect the way in which a person is perceived. For example, a person who is tall is sometimes considered to possess more leadership ability than a shorter person. One research study showed that tall male job applicants usually were offered higher starting salaries than were shorter male applicants. While physiological characteristics should not be the basis for evaluating an employee's capabilities, they do exert considerable influence on an individual's personality as well as define certain physical abilities and limitations.

Early Childhood Influences

Many psychologists believe that the very early years of a person's life are crucial in that individual's development. The manner in which a child is taught, shown affection, and disciplined will have a lifelong influence. When parents encourage autonomy, independence, exploration, the ability to deal with risk, and a willingness to work with others, the child learns valuable lessons. Author and consultant Sandra A. Crowe says, "Our history creates our present. So, people's backgrounds affect the way they are—and the way they act at work. Problems with a critical parent in younger years, for instance, may lead to insecurity in adult life. Such folks end up humiliating others, blaming them for their shortcomings, and taking credit for others' work."[3] Various biographies illustrate that an individual's ability to cope with problems and work in harmony with others may be determined partly through early childhood influences.

Environmental (Situational) Factors

Sociologists and social psychologists emphasize the immediate situation or environment as being the most important determinant of adult personality. Factors such as education, income, employment, and many other experiences that confront an individual throughout life will influence that person's personality.

Every day's experiences contribute to an individual's makeup. This is particularly true in terms of the immediate working environment. For example, the personality of a worker whose job consists exclusively of repetitive, routine tasks will be affected differently than if that same worker was required to apply creative solutions to unique problems every day. In addition, what a supervisor does in a work situation affects certain aspects of the personalities of the people being supervised. For example, employees who work for a supervisor who is critical and harsh will, over time, display different personality characteristics than employees who work for a supportive and encouraging supervisor.

Cultural (Societal) Values

The broader culture also influences personality. In North America such values as competition, rewards for accomplishment, and equal opportunities are part of a democratic society. Individuals are educated, trained, and encouraged to think for themselves and to strive for the achievement of worthwhile goals. However, some cultural values are changing. In recent decades the workforce has become increasingly diversified, reflecting many different subcultures and subgroups. As the diversity of the workforce has increased, so has the effect of different cultural norms and values on the workplace. In particular, the values of certain ethnic, age, and other minority groups may be quite different from the values of the majority. By recognizing and respecting different cultural values, supervisors should become more adept in dealing effectively with all employees.

Recognizing Human Differences and Similarities

The many complexities of human personality have been discussed here only briefly because there are an infinite number of factors that cause personality to adapt and change over time. Ideally, supervisors should get to know their employees so well that they can tailor their supervisory approaches to the uniqueness of each individual's personality. Realistically, however, it is impossible to understand all the unique characteristics of a person's personality.

Fortunately, behavioural studies have demonstrated that people tend to be more alike than different in their basic motivational needs and their reasons for behaving the way they do. Supervisors can implement managerial techniques that emphasize the similarities rather than the differences among people. This does not mean that unique differences in people should be overlooked; supervisors can understand the unique needs and personality makeup of individual employees enough to adapt general approaches to individuals to some extent. But a consistent supervisory approach based on similarities rather than differences is a practical way to lead a group of employees toward achieving company goals.

Supervisors should look to the "best practices" of leading companies for tips about what employees want from their employers. Regardless of the industry, size of the workforce, or personality mix of the employees, there are common things that employees seem to value in their jobs. Many of the things on the employees' "wish list" are often within the supervisor's direct area of responsibility. *Canada's Top 100 Employers* by Richard Yerema provides some valuable information about the common characteristics of Canadian companies that are rated as the best places to work (see Contemporary Issue box on the next page).

| 2 | **UNDERSTANDING MOTIVATION AND HUMAN BEHAVIOUR** |

Compare various motivation theories and explain their importance for understanding employee behaviour.

Too often, motivation is viewed as something that one person can give to or do for another. Supervisors sometimes talk in terms of giving a worker a "shot" of motivation or of having to "motivate employees." However, motivating employees is not that easily accomplished, since the concept of human motivation really refers to an inner drive or an impulse. Motivation cannot be poured down another's throat or injected intravenously! In the final analysis, it comes from within a person. **Motivation** is a willingness to exert effort toward achieving a goal stimulated by the effort's ability to fulfill an individual need. In other words, employees are more willing to do what the organization wants if they

Motivation
A willingness to exert effort toward achieving a goal, stimulated by the effort's ability to fulfill an individual need.

CONTEMPORARY ISSUE
Canada's Best Employers

At first glance, it's not immediately obvious that Hamilton-based steel maker Dofasco Inc., furniture retailer Ikea Canada, and the Toronto Transit Commission have much of anything in common. But all three companies are celebrating a significant achievement—each has been profiled in the 2004 edition of Richard Yerema's book *Canada's Top 100 Employers*. The book showcases an extremely diverse group of Canadian companies, large and small, that are doing the most interesting things to attract and motivate their employees.

So what does it take to be considered one of the best places to work in Canada? Yerema started by reviewing the recruitment history of over 51,000 employers across Canada. From this group, 6,000 of the fastest-growing employers were invited to complete an extensive application process to uncover "the really interesting and novel things employers are doing"[1] to attract and retain quality employees.

Companies were rated according to how well they meet the needs of their employees in seven key areas: (1) Physical Workplace; (2) Work Atmosphere & Social; (3) Health, Financial, & Family Benefits; (4) Vacation & Time Off; (5) Employee Communications; (6) Performance Management; and (7) Training & Skills Development. "The grading system lets readers quickly identify what's really remarkable about each employer—and where there's room for improvement."[2] Each company's community involvement and charitable efforts were also assessed because, according to the author, "a strong correlation was observed between charitable work and how an employer treats its own employees. Employers who take a broader view of their responsibilities to the community, it turns out, are almost always better places to work."[3]

The list is a revealing look at the best practices that companies are using to try to retain and motivate employees (see the full list at www.macleans .ca/pdf/top100list.pdf). While financial incentives are certainly part of the overall evaluation, the "top 100 companies" offer far more than just a paycheque. "More than ever, employers across Canada are competing for quality employees—not only with attrac-tive salaries but also with vastly improved working conditions and innovative employee benefits,"[4] says author Richard Yerema. These organizations make the list because they are responsive to the needs of their employees, find innovative ways to show their appreciation for employees' efforts, and look for ways to contribute to the community.

It's not a surprise that employees at the "top 100 companies" have good things to say about their employers. Animation and graphics software developer Alias Systems employs about 350 people in Toronto and won a technical Oscar award in 2003 for its Maya animation and effects package. Mark Charlesworth, director of product management for new products at Alias Systems says that "Alias is a mix of fun and hard work. Everyone is incredibly smart, energetic, talented, skilled, passionate and creative. They're very dedicated but also full of good humour. All the people here have core values of respect for each other, fairness and integrity. There's a lot of laughter and camaraderie."[5]

Tonya Frizzell is a communications specialist at Vancouver City Savings Credit Union. From March 2001 to March 2002, she was on leave from VanCity, working as a volunteer in Albania. Of the five individuals who arrived with Frizzell in Elbasan, Albania's second largest city, she was the only one with a job back home—the others had had to quit because their employers wouldn't hold their positions for them. "Companies should be more open to this," Frizzell says. "I brought back skills and, after a good, long break, a fresh perspective. It's important to shake things up and not get too comfortable."[6]

While companies on the list are celebrating, those that didn't make the list are taking notice. Yerema reports that "one of the interesting things we noticed this year is that some of the organizations we studied recently implemented excellent new benefits and other perks 'borrowed' from the employers that were featured in our last edition."[7] In addition to being a reference for job-seekers, author Richard Yerema hopes the new book will encourage other employers to create better workplaces for their employees.

Sources: (1), (2), and (3) www.canadastop100.com/research.html (retrieved November 6, 2003); (4) Richard Yerema as quoted by Jay Robb, "Some of nation's top 100 employers are right here," *The Hamilton Spectator*, February 17, 2003, p. D11; (5) www.macleans.ca/webspecials/article .jsp?content=20031020_67475_67475 (retrieved November 6, 2003); (6) www.macleans.ca/webspecials/article.jsp?content=20031020_67488_67488 (retrieved November 6, 2003); (7) www.co-operativetrust.ca/press_conf/national.asp (retrieved November 6, 2003).

believe that doing so will result in a meaningful reward. The supervisor's challenge is to stimulate that willingness by ensuring that achievement of organizational goals results in rewards that employees want. The rewards need not always be monetary; they can be anything employees value. For example, praise and recognition can be powerful motivators.

Since employee motivation is crucial to organizational success, it is a subject about which there has been much research. The theories presented in this chapter are fundamental, and much more has been written elsewhere. However, most theories emphasize the similarities rather than differences in the needs of human beings.

The Hierarchy of Needs (Maslow)

Most psychologists who study human behaviour and personality generally are convinced that all behaviour is caused, goal oriented, and motivated. Stating this another way, there is a reason for everything that a person does, assuming that the person is rational, sane, and not out of control (e.g., not under the influence of drugs or alcohol). People constantly are striving to attain something that has meaning to them in terms of their own particular needs and in relation to how they see themselves and the environment in which they live. Often we may not be aware of why we behave in a certain manner, but we all have subconscious motives that govern the way we behave in different situations.

One of the most widely accepted theories of human behaviour is that people are motivated to satisfy certain well-defined and more or less predictable needs. Psychologist Abraham H. Maslow formulated the concept of a **hierarchy** (or priority) **of needs.**[4] He maintained that these needs range from lower-level needs to higher-level needs in an ascending priority (see Figure 6-1). These needs overlap and are interrelated, and it may be preferable to consider them as existing along a continuum rather than as being separate and distinct from one another.

Maslow's theory of a hierarchy of human needs implies that people attempt to satisfy these needs in the order in which they are arranged in the hierarchy. Until the lowest-level or most basic needs are reasonably satisfied, a person will not be motivated strongly by the other levels. As one level of needs is satisfied to some extent, the individual focuses on the next level, which then becomes the stronger motivator of behaviour. Maslow even suggested that once a lower level of needs was reasonably satisfied, it no longer would motivate behaviour, at least in the short term.

Biological (Physiological) Needs

At the first level are the **biological** (or physiological) **needs.** These are needs that everyone has for food, shelter, rest, recreation, and other physical necessities. Virtually every employee views work as being a means for taking care of these fundamental needs. A paycheque enables a person to purchase the necessities vital to survival as well as some of the comforts of life.

Security (Safety) Needs

Once a person's physiological needs are reasonably satisfied, other needs become important. The **security** (or safety) **needs** include the need to protect ourselves against danger and to guard against the uncertainties of life. Most employees want some sense of security or control over their future. In order to satisfy such

Hierarchy of needs
Maslow's theory of motivation, which suggests that an individual's needs are arranged in priority order such that lower-order needs must be satisfied before higher-order needs become motivating.

Biological needs
The basic physical needs, such as food, rest, shelter, and recreation.

Security needs
Desire for protection against danger and life's uncertainties.

FIGURE 6-1
Hierarchy of needs.

SELF - FULFILLMENT

SELF - RESPECT   (ESTEEM)

SOCIAL   (BELONGING)

SECURITY   (SAFETY)

BIOLOGICAL   (PHYSIOLOGICAL)

expectations, many employers offer a variety of supplementary benefits. For example, medical, retirement, hospitalization, disability, and life insurance plans are designed to protect employees against various uncertainties and their possible serious consequences. Wage and benefit packages are designed to satisfy employees' physiological and safety needs. By fulfilling these basic needs, organizations hope to attract and retain competent personnel.

Social (Belonging) Needs

Social needs

Desire for love, affection, and affiliation with something worthwhile.

Some supervisors believe that good wages and ample benefits are sufficient to motivate employees. These supervisors do not understand the importance of the higher-level needs of human beings, beginning with social (or belonging) needs. **Social needs** are those that people have for attention, for being part of a group, for being accepted by their peers, and for love. Many studies have shown that group motivation can be a powerful influence on employee behaviour at work in either a negative or a positive direction. For example, some employees may deliberately perform in a manner contrary to organizational goals in order to feel that they are an accepted part of an informal group. On the other hand, if informal group goals are in line with organizational goals, the group can influence individuals toward exceptional performance. Some employers provide off-the-job social and athletic opportunities for their employees as a means of helping them satisfy their social needs and to build loyalty to the organization as a whole.

Self-Respect (Esteem) Needs

Self-respect needs

Desire for recognition, achievement, status, and a sense of accomplishment.

Closely related to social needs are **self-respect** (or esteem or ego) **needs.** These are needs that everyone has for recognition, achievement, status, and a sense of accomplishment. Self-respect needs are very powerful because they relate to personal feelings of self-worth and importance. Supervisors should look for ways by which these internal needs may be satisfied, such as providing variety and challenge in work tasks and recognizing good performance. Something as simple as saying "good job" to someone can keep that person doing good work.

Self-Fulfillment Needs

At the highest level of human needs are **self-fulfillment** (or self-realization) needs—the desire to use one's capabilities to the fullest. People want to be creative and to achieve to the full extent of their capacities. These highest-level needs are not satisfied until a person reaches his or her own full potential. As such, they persist throughout the person's life and probably can never be completely satisfied. Many jobs frustrate rather than fulfill this level of human needs. For example, many factory and office jobs are routine and monotonous, and workers must seek self-fulfillment in pursuits off the job and in family relationships. However, supervisors can provide opportunities for self-fulfillment on the job by assigning tasks that challenge employees to use their abilities more fully and creatively.

Applying the Needs Theory to Supervisory Management

Supervisors can use the model of a hierarchy of human needs as a framework to visualize the kinds of needs that people have and to assess their relative importance in motivating individuals in the work group. The supervisor's challenge is to make individual fulfillment a result of doing a good job. For example, if the supervisor senses that an employee's most influential motivator at the time is social needs, then the employee is most likely to do a good job if he or she is assigned to work with a group and the whole group is rewarded for doing the job well. If an employee seems to be seeking self-respect, then to influence this employee toward good performance the supervisor might provide visible signs of recognition, such offering praise in front of the employee's peers at a departmental meeting. The key for the supervisor is to recognize where each employee is in the hierarchy so that the supervisor can determine what needs are currently driving the employee.

It is normal for employees to expect good wages, generous benefit plans, and job security. But realistically, the notion that an employee will spend his or her lifetime in the same firm is essentially gone forever. As downsizing continues, individuals' loyalty to the company may lessen. Managers who are asked to develop effective work teams may find it increasingly difficult as employees become less enthusiastic about "winning one for the team." Further, the lack of trust and low job security may create a strong individual orientation that encourages people to look out for themselves as opposed to always working in the best interest of the organization.

The key to longer-term, positive motivation of employees resides in better satisfying their higher-level needs (social, self-respect, and self-fulfillment). Supervisors should recognize that just giving employees more money, better benefits, and better working conditions will not bring about excellent work performance. For many employees, these items may play a secondary role in day-to-day motivation. Supervisors who want to obtain better performance from all employees must be flexible in helping their employees fulfill their personal needs.

Negative Employee Motivation and Frustration

Conditions that do not bring about the fulfillment of a person's needs will ultimately result in dissatisfaction and frustration. Thus, when their needs are not satisfied on the job, many employees resort to behaviour patterns that are detrimental to their job performance and to the organization. A typical approach for frustrated employees is to resign themselves to just getting by on the job. This means that they simply go through the motions and put in time without trying to perform in anything other than an average or marginal manner. They look for personal satisfaction off the job and are content to do just enough at work to draw a paycheque.

Some employees constantly find things that distract them from doing the job, and at times they even try to beat the system. They often are absent or tardy, or they break the rules as a way of rebelling against situations they find frustrating.

Still other employees who are dissatisfied adopt aggressive behaviour, which ultimately may cause them to leave the job. Examples of aggressive behaviour are poor attitudes, vandalism, theft, fighting, and temper outbursts. When the situation becomes intolerable, they quit or almost force their supervisors to fire them.

These types of reactions to job situations are undesirable and should be prevented. Costs of employee turnover, absenteeism, tardiness, poor performance, and other unsatisfactory conduct on the job can be extremely high to an organization. These behaviours affect all other employees directly or indirectly and will be reflected in generally poor morale and subsequent lowered productivity. Rather than just accepting an employee's behaviour, a supervisor should endeavour to relieve frustration by providing more opportunities for need fulfillment.

Motivation-Hygiene Theory

Motivation-hygiene theory
Herzberg's theory that factors in the work environment only influence the degree of job dissatisfaction, while intrinsic job-content factors influence the amount of job satisfaction.

Another theory of motivation is the **motivation-hygiene theory,** sometimes called the two-factor theory or the dual-factor theory, developed by Frederick Herzberg.[5] Herzberg's research has demonstrated that some factors in the work environment that traditionally were believed to motivate people actually serve primarily to reduce their dissatisfaction rather than motivate them positively.

Herzberg and others have conducted numerous studies in which people were asked to describe events that made them feel particularly good or bad about their jobs. Other questions were designed to determine the depth of their feelings, the duration for which these feelings persisted, and the types of situations that made employees feel motivated or frustrated. These studies were conducted with employees in various organizations and industries, including personnel at all levels and from different technical and job specialties. Interestingly, the general pattern of results was fairly consistent. It revealed a clear distinction between factors that tend to motivate employees (motivation factors) and those that, while expected by workers, are not likely to motivate them (hygiene factors).

Motivation Factors

Motivation factors
Elements intrinsic in the job that promote job performance.

Herzberg identified the **motivation factors** as elements intrinsic in the job that promote job performance and satisfaction. Among the most frequently identified factors that can positively motivate employees are the following:

- Opportunity for growth and advancement.
- Achievement or accomplishment.
- Recognition for accomplishments.
- Challenging or interesting work.
- Responsibility for work.

Job factors that tend to motivate people positively are primarily related to their higher-level needs and aspirations. These factors are all related to outcomes associated with the content of the job being performed. Opportunity for advance-

A bit of genuine praise goes a long way.

Ryan McVay/Photodisc Red/Getty Images

ment, greater responsibility, recognition, growth, achievement, and interesting work are consistently identified as the major factors that make work motivating and meaningful. The absence of these factors can be frustrating and lead to reduced job satisfaction and performance. These motivation factors are not easily measured, and they may be difficult to find in certain types of jobs.

Hygiene Factors

Hygiene factors

Elements in the work environment that, if positive, reduce dissatisfaction but do not tend to motivate.

Also referred to as the "dissatisfiers," **hygiene factors** are elements in the work environment that, if positive, reduce dissatisfaction but do not tend to motivate. Herzberg identified the following hygiene factors:

- Working conditions.
- Money, status, and security.
- Interpersonal relationships.
- Supervision.
- Company policies and administration.

In recent years, the conflict between work demands and personal life has been identified as another hygiene factor.

Where hygiene factors are negative or inadequate, employees will be unhappy. However, where these factors are adequate or even excellent, they do not, by themselves, promote better job performance. This does not mean that hygiene factors are insignificant; they are very important but they serve primarily to maintain a reasonable level of job motivation, not to increase it.

Applying Herzberg's Theory to Supervision

Herzberg's theory suggests that, to obtain better performance, the supervisor should implement strategies that target the motivation factors—that is, those that contribute to the satisfaction of employees' social, self-respect, and self-fulfillment needs. One of the supervisor's strategies should be to "catch people doing something right" and "give them credit when credit is due." A note of caution: praise and other forms of recognition must be highly individualized and genuinely deserved in order to be effective. A key element in effective supervision is to give employees an opportunity to fulfill their needs as a result of good job performance.

Employees often take hygiene factors for granted, especially when job opportunities are plentiful. Even if wages and benefits are extremely generous, employees will tend not to be motivated unless the motivating factors (such as recognition, challenging work, opportunity for growth, etc.) are present. Positive employee motivation is more related to people's higher-level needs.

Expectancy Theory

Expectancy theory

Theory of motivation that holds that employees perform better if they believe such efforts will lead to desired rewards.

Another interesting and practical way of looking at employee motivation is provided by expectancy theory.[6] **Expectancy theory** is based on workers' perceptions of the relationships among effort, performance, and reward. According to expectancy theory, workers will be motivated to work harder if they believe that their greater efforts will actually result in improved performance and that such improved performance will then lead to rewards they desire. The expectancy theory model is illustrated in Figure 6-2.

Expectancy theory is based on worker perceptions and on relationships referred to as linkages. Employee motivation is dependent on workers being able to perceive an effort–performance linkage as well as a performance–reward linkage. If an employee cannot recognize that such linkages clearly exist, he or she will not be highly motivated.

FIGURE 6-2   Expectancy theory.

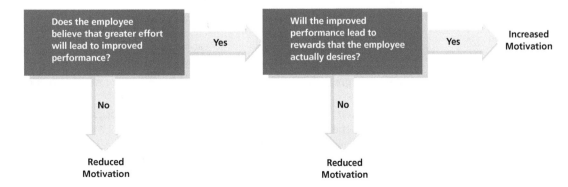

For example, if computer operators have not received adequate training, they will probably not be able to perceive a relationship between their effort and performance. Instead they will conclude that no matter how much effort they expend, there will be no significant improvement in their job performance. Similarly, if nurses' aides in a hospital perceive that high-performers are not being rewarded any more than the average or even substandard performers, they will not believe that there is a performance–reward relationship, so they will not be motivated toward good performance.

Supervisors may believe that their organization rewards high-quality work. However, such a belief may be based on management's perception of the reward system. Supervisors should try to verify whether the workers perceive the linkages. Supervisors and employees often do not view reward systems in the same way. For example, on his last day on the job, an assembly-line employee in a manufacturing plant participated in an exit interview. When the interviewer asked him why he was leaving, the worker said that he had become extremely frustrated waiting for work to come to his workstation. The worker said that he became fed up with coming to work every day knowing that no matter how hard he was willing to work, his efforts would not be reflected on the production chart.

It does not matter how clearly supervisors view the linkages among effort, performance, and rewards. If the workers cannot see them, the linkages might just as well not be there. Supervisors should strive to show employees that increased effort will lead to improved work performance, which in turn will result in increased rewards. Rewards may be extrinsic, in the form of additional pay or some type of praise or recognition, or intrinsic, such as a sense of accomplishment. Probably the most important characteristic of a reward is that it is something the person desires and values.

A supervisor may have limited control over the rewards that are available. Union–management agreements and other pay and promotional systems typically are tied to seniority. Supervisors often complain that many employee wage increases are automatic, and not related to merit or job performance. Even in these types of situations, however, there are approaches available to supervisors that can yield motivational results.

3   USING THE ABCs TO SHAPE EMPLOYEE BEHAVIOUR

Explain the ABCs of shaping behaviour.

Organizational behaviour researchers have studied extensively the influence of job satisfaction on performance. It is generally believed that employees who experience high levels of job satisfaction are more likely to engage in positive behaviours that influence organizational efficiency and productivity.

Performance management expert Aubrey Daniels developed a practical guide for shaping employee behaviour.[7] According to Daniels, "behaviour (the "B") cannot be separated from the antecedents (the "A") that come before it and the consequences (the "C") after it."[8] See Figure 6-3 for suggestions on how to use the ABCs.

Common sense dictates that if supervisors expect good performance, they must set the stage so that the expected performance occurs. First, supervisors should clearly identify what they want the employee to do. Then, the employee must know what the job entails and what is expected in the way of performance.

FIGURE 6-3   Steps in ABC analysis.

- Regularly monitor employee performance to uncover areas of low productivity and to identify the behaviour leading to undesirable performance.
- Describe the performance you don't want and who is doing it.
- Record the specific behaviour that needs to be changed.
- Determine all possible links between the antecedents, the undesirable behaviour, and its consequences.
- Tell the employee what is expected in the way of performance (i.e., set specific goals).
- Set the stage for good performance (i.e., arrange antecedents so the employee can achieve the desired behaviour).
- Eliminate any consequence that is irrelevant to the employee.
- Ensure an appropriate linkage between desired behaviour and consequences the employee values.
- Monitor performance.
- Provide support and feedback on performance.
- Reinforce the positive aspects of the employee's performance with consequences the employee values.
- Ensure consequences are positive, immediate, and certain.
- Evaluate results and continue to reinforce desired behaviour with desirable consequences.
- Experiment to find the most effective forms of reinforcement and rate of reinforcement.

Remember:

- You cannot change people; you can change only their behaviours.
- You will get the behaviours you consistently expect and reinforce. Therefore, expect only the best from your employees.
- Employees need to know exactly what behaviours will be reinforced and precisely what they are doing that is right or wrong.

Source: Based, in part, on Aubrey C. Daniels, Ph.D., *Performance Management,* 3rd ed. (Atlanta: Performance Management Publications, Inc., 1989).

Ask someone you know to think back to his or her first day on the job. How did the employee know what was expected? Many respondents will say it was a process of "trial and error"—that the supervisor never clearly explained what was expected. The supervisor either does not sense the importance of, or is too busy to explain, expectations. In Chapter 1, we discussed the supervisor's role as enabler. The enabler ensures that employees have all they need to do their jobs correctly the first time. This includes appropriate instruction, training, tools, materials, and the like. Unfortunately, this is often not the way it works. If the supervisor does not set the stage by providing the proper antecedents, employee performance is likely to be unsatisfactory.

Consequences can affect behaviour in one of two ways. Thorndike's **law of effect** postulates that "behaviour with favourable consequences tends to be repeated, while behaviour with unfavourable consequences tends to disappear."[9] Unfortunately, some supervisors incorrectly assume that what would be a

Law of effect
Theory that behaviour with favourable consequences is repeated; behaviour with unfavourable consequences tends to disappear.

favourable consequence for them would also be a desirable consequence for others. Consider the following:

Question 1: *When you do your job exceptionally well and your immediate supervisor knows you do your job exceptionally well, what happens?*

Answer 1: *"Nothing—absolutely nothing. My immediate supervisor takes good performance for granted."*

Implication: When good performance is ignored or goes unrecognized, what happens? Clearly, the lack of feedback and recognition for good performance can cause employee discontent. Also, the good performance is weakened because it is not reinforced. This process is called **extinction.**

Answer 2: *"Here's some more work to do."*

Implication: If the employee perceives that the additional work will require a variety of skills or fulfill higher-order needs, then the consequence is desirable. This is called **positive reinforcement.** Linking something the employee values or sees as pleasing to good performance strengthens behaviour. As a result, good performance is likely to repeat itself. On the other hand, if the employee perceives the extra work to be boring, monotonous, or mundane, then the consequence of good performance is perceived to be **punishment.** The employee got something unwanted—an unfavourable consequence. The result is that the employee's good performance will decrease. Chapter 10 discusses punishment and discipline in greater detail.

Answer 3: *"We really appreciate the good job you did. I've recommended moving you from the six-person cubicle into your own office."*

Implications: This response illustrates the importance of ensuring that the supervisor clearly understands what constitutes a reward in the eyes of the employee. For some employees, the move from a six-person shared cubicle to a private office would actually be seen as a punishment. Suppose the employee really enjoyed the social aspects of working in a cubicle with other people. That employee would feel isolated in a private office and the move might actually result in reduced future work performance.

Other employees would consider the move to a private office a welcome change. For these people, going from a noisy and crowded work environment to a private office would reinforce good performance. This is an example of **negative reinforcement,** which means that the employee is rewarded when the supervisor removes a consequence that is unpleasant or undesirable. A behaviour that is desired (in this case, good work performance) is encouraged because it results in the removal of an unpleasant or undesirable situation (the noisy cubicle).

Question 2: *What happens when a coworker, Charlie, fails to show up for work regularly?*

Answer 1: *"Nothing ever happens."*

Implications: The chronically tardy employee continues to be tardy regularly. Ignoring bad performance tends to strengthen the behaviour. Unintentionally, management sends a message to employees that "it's okay to show up late for work." When management ignores poor performance in one employee, that employee usually has a negative impact throughout the entire work group. Others might assume, and rightfully so, that management has sanctioned showing up for work late.

Answer 2: *"The employee was given an unpleasant task or made to stay late and complete necessary work."*

Extinction
Good behaviour occurs less frequently or disappears because it is not recognized.

Positive reinforcement
Making a behaviour occur more often because it is linked to a positive consequence.

Punishment
Making behaviour occur less frequently because it is linked to an undesirable consequence.

Negative reinforcement
Making behaviour occur more frequently by removing an undesirable consequence.

Implication: The tardy employee perceives staying late as an undesirable consequence. Because of the punishment, the employee may make special efforts to get to work on time. Other employees will also see the linkage that by arriving on time they are able to avoid the undesirable consequence of having to stay late. Remember that the process of removing undesirable consequences when an employee's behaviour improves is called negative reinforcement.

Supervisors must continually be alert for what their employees perceive to be important, and, like so many things in life, timing is critical. Aubrey Daniels contends "that an intelligently timed consequence has much more influence than a random one."[10] Immediate feedback on performance and positive reinforcement are essential if the supervisor wants to shape employee behaviour positively.

| **4** | **COMPARING McGREGOR'S THEORY X AND THEORY Y** |

Compare the assumptions and applications of Theory X and Theory Y in supervision.

A continuous (and unresolved) question that often confronts supervisors is what general approach, or style, will best contribute to positive employee motivation. This age-old dilemma typically focuses on the degree to which supervisory approaches should be based on satisfying employees' lower-level and higher-level needs. This often becomes an issue of the degree to which supervisors should rely on their authority and position as compared with trying to utilize human relations practices that may provide greater opportunities for employee motivation.

In his book *The Human Side of Enterprise,* Douglas McGregor noted that individual supervisory approaches usually relate to each supervisor's perceptions concerning what people are all about. That is, each supervisor manages employees according to his or her own attitudes and ideas about people's needs and motivations. For purposes of comparison, McGregor stated that the extremes in attitudes among managers could be classified as Theory X and Theory Y.

The basic assumptions of Theory X and Theory Y as stated by McGregor are as follows:[11]

Theory X
Assumption that employees dislike work, avoid responsibility, and must be coerced to do the job.

Theory Y
Assumption that employees enjoy work, seek responsibility, and are capable of self-direction.

Theory X: The assumption that employees dislike work, avoid responsibility, and must be coerced to work hard.

Theory Y: The assumption that employees enjoy work, seek responsibility, and are capable of self-direction.

Supervisors who are Theory X oriented have a limited view of employees' capabilities and motivation. They believe that employees must be strictly controlled and closely supervised. Theory X supervisors believe that employees are motivated on the basis of money, discipline, and authority. These supervisors believe that the key to motivation is in the proper implementation of approaches designed to satisfy employees' lower-level needs.

Theory Y supervisors have a much higher opinion of employees' capabilities. They believe that if the proper approaches and conditions can be implemented, employees will exercise self-direction and self-control toward the accomplishment of worthwhile objectives. According to this view, management's objectives should fit into the scheme of each employee's particular set of needs. Therefore, Theory Y managers believe that the higher-level needs of employees are more important in terms of each employee's own personality and self-development.

The two approaches described by McGregor represent extremes in supervisory styles. Figure 6-4 summarizes some of the overriding beliefs about human nature that would be held by an extremely Theory X versus an extremely Theory Y manager. Realistically, most supervisors are somewhere between Theory X and Theory Y. Neither of these approaches is right or wrong in and of itself, for the appropriateness of a given approach will depend on the needs of the individuals involved and the demands of the situation. In practice, supervisors may occasionally take an approach that is contrary to their preferred one. For example, even the strongest Theory Y supervisor may revert to Theory X in a time of crisis, such as when the department is shorthanded, when there is an equipment failure, when a serious disciplinary problem has occurred, or when a few employees need firm direction.

Advantages and Limitations of Theory X

Supervisors who adopt the Theory X style typically find that, in the short term, a job is accomplished faster. Since the questioning of orders is not encouraged, it may appear that the workers are competent and knowledgeable and that work groups are well organized, efficient, and disciplined.

A major disadvantage of the Theory X approach is that there is little opportunity for employees' personal growth. Since supervision is close and constant, employees are unlikely to develop initiative and independence. Moreover, most workers resent Theory X supervision, and this may breed negative motivation. Traditionally, supervisors who advocated the Theory X approach could get employees to do what they wanted by using the "carrot-and-stick" approach ("Do what I want you to do and you will be rewarded!"). Punishments were applied when the job was not done. This approach is still used by many. However, employees may rebel when confronted with the "stick," and supervisors may not have sufficient rewards to get employees to subject themselves to this tight control over the long term.

FIGURE 6-4   Comparison of beliefs held by Theory X versus Theory Y managers.

TYPICAL BELIEFS HELD BY A THEORY X MANAGER
- People are generally lazy and will avoid work whenever they can.
- Employees will not achieve work objectives unless they are closely controlled and monitored.
- People will generally need to be threatened with punishment in order to coerce them to work hard.
- The average person likes to be directed and dislikes responsibility.

TYPICAL BELIEFS HELD BY A THEORY Y MANAGER
- People generally enjoy work. Work is as natural as play or rest.
- People will direct themselves toward the accomplishment of work objectives if they are committed to the aims of the organization.
- The average person, under proper conditions, will accept and even seek responsibility.

Theory Y supervisors see their employees as responsible and capable of self-direction.

Advantages and Limitations of Theory Y

An overriding advantage of Theory Y supervision is that it promotes individual growth. Since workers are given opportunities to assume some responsibility on their own and are encouraged to contribute their ideas in accomplishing their tasks, it is possible for them to partially satisfy their higher-level needs on the job.

Although the Theory Y approach is often viewed as a more desirable approach to supervision, it is not without some disadvantages. Theory Y can be time consuming in practice, especially in the short term. Since personal development is emphasized, supervisors must become instructors and coaches if they are to help their employees move toward the simultaneous attainment of organizational and personal goals. Some supervisors find the extreme application of Theory Y to be more idealistic than practical since some employees expect (and some situations require) firm direction from the supervisor.

5 | SUPERVISORY APPROACHES FOR ATTAINING POSITIVE EMPLOYEE MOTIVATION

Discuss supervisory approaches for stimulating employee motivation—especially job redesign, broadened job tasks, and participative management.

Having reviewed several prominent theories of employee motivation, the next question is, "How can these be applied in the most meaningful ways?" While there are some general guidelines that a supervisor can follow to encourage positive motivation (see Figure 6-5), there is no simple set of do's and don'ts that a supervisor can always implement to achieve high motivation and excellent performance. Human beings are much too complex for that. Although supervisory skills can be learned and developed, no single formula will apply in all situations and with all people.

FIGURE 6-5   Guidelines for encouraging positive motivation.

- People need to know what is expected in the way of performance. Therefore, clearly define expectations.
- People want to know how they are doing. Therefore, provide immediate feedback on performance.
- People want recognition for a job well done. Therefore, when employees do their jobs well, reinforce their behaviour with the consequences they desire and value.
- People need to know that it is okay to make mistakes. Therefore, create a learning organization that says to all employees, "We'll learn what not to do from the mistakes we make." The supervisor can say, "Everything I've learned, I learned from either the mistakes I've made or the mistakes of others."
- People will do their best work for those they trust and respect. Therefore, treat your employees as you want to be treated.
- People need support and encouragement. Therefore, be an enabler. Do the things that enable others to be the best they can be.

Job Redesign

It is generally believed that well-designed jobs lead to increased motivation, higher-quality performance, higher satisfaction, and lower absenteeism and turnover. These desirable outcomes occur when employees experience three critical psychological states:

1. They believe that they are doing something meaningful because their work is important to other people.
2. They feel personally responsible for how the work turns out.
3. They learn how well they performed their jobs.

Job redesign
The process of changing the structure of a job in order to improve employee motivation.

Many **job redesign** programs are based on the model developed by professors Hackman and Oldham (see Figure 6-6). Their model says that the greater the experienced meaningfulness of work, responsibility for the work performed, and knowledge of the results, the more positive the work-related benefits will be. According to this model, any job can be described in terms of the following five core job dimensions:

1. **Skill variety:** the degree to which an employee has an opportunity to do various tasks and to use a number of different skills and abilities.
2. **Task identity:** the completion of a whole, identifiable piece of work.
3. **Task significance:** the degree to which the job impacts the lives or work of others.
4. **Autonomy:** the amount of independence, freedom, and discretion that an employee has in making decisions about the work to be done.
5. **Feedback:** the amount of information an employee receives on job performance.[12]

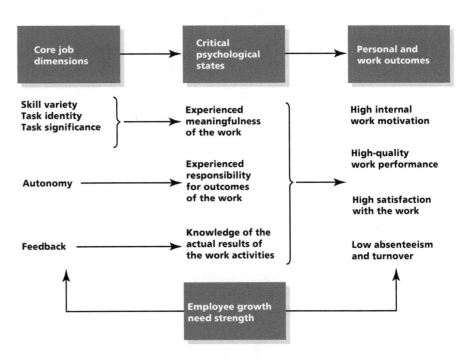

Source: J. Richard Hackman and Greg R. Oldham, *Work Redesign* (adapted from Figure 4.6), ©1980 by Addison-Wesley Publishing Company, Inc. Reprinted by permission of Addison-Wesley Longman, Inc.

The questionnaire contained in Skills Application 6-2 at the end of this chapter can be used to evaluate your own job to determine the extent to which each of these characteristics is present. Using this questionnaire it is possible to calculate a "motivating potential score" (MPS) for a specific job. Low scores indicate that the individual will not experience high internal motivation from the job. Such a job is a prime candidate for job redesign. For example, suppose that close examination reveals that the task significance score for a particular job is relatively low. This indicates that the employees who perform that job do not believe that their work has an impact on anyone else and will therefore experience reduced motivation. To improve task significance, the supervisor could, for example, assign workers in a data-entry group to specific departments as opposed to letting the group serve the company as a whole. This approach could increase task significance scores because the workers would be located within the department they serve and would have more contact with and feedback from the people for whom they work. This would increase the job's motivating potential.[13]

On the other hand, high scores indicate that the job is currently stimulating high internal motivation. According to Hackman and Oldham's theory, internal motivation occurs because the employee is "turned on to [his or her] work because of the positive internal feelings that are generated by doing well, rather than being dependent on external factors (such as incentive pay, job security, or praise from the supervisor) for the motivation to work effectively."[14]

Broadening the Scope and Importance of Each Job

There are ways to give employees new tasks and new work experiences by broadening the scope and importance of what the employees do. Variety and challenge can keep jobs from becoming monotonous and can fulfill employee needs. If jobs are currently repetitive and routine, the supervisor should consider job rotation, job enlargement, and job enrichment as possible ways to improve employee motivation.

Job Rotation

Job rotation
The process of switching job tasks among employees in the work group.

Switching job tasks among employees in the work group on a scheduled basis is known as **job rotation.** This is a process that most supervisors can implement, and it often is accompanied by higher levels of job performance and increased employee interest. Job rotation not only helps to relieve employees' boredom, but also enhances their job knowledge. Although the different tasks may require the same skill level, learning different jobs may prepare employees for promotion in the future. A major side benefit to the supervisor is that job rotation results in a more flexible workforce, which can be advantageous during periods of employee absence. Job rotation should mean that employees share both pleasant and unpopular tasks so work assignments are perceived as fair.

Job Enlargement

Job enlargement
Increasing the number of tasks an individual performs.

Another motivational strategy is **job enlargement,** which means expanding an employee's job with a greater variety of tasks to perform. For example, tasks that previously were handled by several employees may be combined or consolidated within one or two enlarged jobs.

Some employees respond positively to job enlargement, and this is reflected in their performance and in increased job satisfaction. In one furniture factory, for example, a number of routine jobs were changed so that each job required five or six operations rather than just one constantly repeated operation. Employees were supportive of the change. Such comments as, "My job seems more important now" and "My work is less monotonous now" were common reactions.

There can be problems in implementing job enlargement. Union work rules and job jurisdictional lines may limit the supervisor's authority to change job assignments. Attitudes toward the idea of job enlargement may also present significant difficulties. Some employees, for example, may object to the idea of being given expanded duties because they are content with their present jobs and pay. Usually they will not object if at least a small increase in pay comes with the enlarged job.

Job Enrichment

Job enrichment
Job design strategy that helps fulfill employees' higher-level needs by giving them more challenging tasks and more decision-making responsibility for their jobs.

A motivational approach that is increasingly advocated is **job enrichment,** which means assigning more challenging tasks and giving employees more decision-making responsibility for their jobs. Job enrichment goes beyond job rotation and job enlargement in an effort to appeal to the higher-level needs of employees. To enrich jobs, the supervisor should assign everyone in a department a fair share of the challenging as well as the routine jobs and give employees more autonomy in accomplishing the tasks. Unfortunately, many supervisors prefer to assign the difficult, challenging jobs only to their best employees and the dull jobs to the weaker employees. This can be counterproductive in the long term. The supervisor should provide opportunities for all employees to find challenging and interesting work experiences within the realistic framework of the department's operations. Sometimes job enrichment can be accomplished by assigning employees to special projects, problem-solving teams, or other unusual job experiences that go beyond the routine performance of day-to-day work. In its most developed form, job enrichment may involve restructuring jobs in such a way that employees are given direct control and responsibility for what they do.

Supervisors may be uncomfortable with job enrichment at first. It may require them to relinquish some control and delegate some planning and decision-making authority. But if job enrichment is practised sincerely, subordinates will, over time, usually assume an active role in making or participating in decisions about their jobs. The result can be better decisions and a more satisfied and motivated workforce. For example, one supervisor enriched the jobs of machine operators by giving them a greater role in scheduling work and devising their own work rules for the group. The result was a schedule that better met their needs and rules that they were willing to follow since they helped create them.

In a sense, job enrichment involves the employees' assumption of some of the supervisor's everyday responsibilities. The supervisor remains accountable, however, for the satisfactory fulfillment of these obligations. Therein lies a major risk inherent in job enrichment; yet, despite the risk, many supervisors endorse job enrichment because it works.

Comparing the Approaches to Job Enhancement

The differences among job rotation, job enlargement, and job enrichment are a matter of degree. Each is an attempt to diversify work and make it more meaningful to employees. Job enrichment adds a vertical dimension, or greater depth, to the task so that employees can satisfy their higher-level needs through their work. Job enlargement emphasizes the horizontal dimension of the task since it gives employees more duties. Job rotation moves an employee from one job to another on a periodic basis with the intent of reducing boredom and increasing employee interest and breadth of knowledge. These three job design strategies are similar in the sense that each attempts to increase employee performance by improving job satisfaction.

Participative Management

In his best-selling book *A Great Place to Work,* Robert Levering postulates that the high morale of great workplaces consists of pride in what you do (the job itself), enjoying the people you're working with (the work group), and trusting the people you work for (management practices and economic rewards).[15] As mentioned in Chapter 1 of this text, *empowerment* refers to giving employees the authority and responsibility to accomplish organizational objectives. Providing opportunities to make suggestions and participate in decisions affecting their jobs is one of the most effective ways to build a sense of employee pride, teamwork, and motivation. This supervisory approach, in which employees have an active role in decision making, has historically been referred to as **participative management.**

Participative management
Supervisory approach that gives employees an active role in making decisions about their jobs.

Delegation (which will be discussed in more detail in Chapter 7) is important to building positive motivation among employees. This does not mean turning over all decisions to employees, nor does it mean just making employees believe that they are participating in decisions. Rather, it means that the supervisor should earnestly seek employees' opinions whenever possible and be willing to be influenced by their suggestions and even by their criticisms. When employees believe that they are part of a team and that they can have an influence on the decisions that affect them, they are more likely to accept the decisions and seek new solutions to future problems.

However, if supervisors want employees to be increasingly responsible for business results, they must teach them how the business works. Noted author Ken Blanchard asserts that "management must start by sharing information about its financial performance, its market share, its profitability, its costs—everything managers use to make informed decisions. Sharing information that tells it like it really is creates a sense of ownership in employees."[16] Supervisors who practise participative management properly are aware of the importance of their information-giving and information-getting skills. They also know that it is vital to respond fully to subordinates' suggestions as soon as they have had sufficient time to consider them.

The major advantages of participative management are that decisions tend to be of higher quality and that employees are more willing to accept them. One disadvantage is that this approach can be time consuming. Also, open participation makes it easier for employees to criticize, which some supervisors find threatening. On balance, however, participative management is widely recognized as an effective motivational strategy; its advantages outweigh its disadvantages.

Employee Suggestion Programs

Some organizations have found that formal employee suggestion systems are helpful.[17] While most suggestion systems provide monetary rewards to employees for suggestions that are received and accepted, the monetary reward is only part of the overall benefit to the employee. Employees like to have their suggestions heard and answered. To some employees, the fact that a suggestion has been accepted may mean more than the monetary reward.

Proponents of employee suggestion programs claim that they are cost effective and can result in increased employee recognition and motivation. Even if an individual employee's suggestion is ultimately not adopted, the process results in increased dialogue among employees and supervisors. The employee also may develop an increased understanding of the business and the industry in which the company operates.

As illustrated in Chapter 3's Contemporary Issue box on pages 80–81, some people believe that paying people to think creatively sends the wrong message. They assert that employees should be encouraged to develop ideas and offer suggestions as an integral part of their jobs, rather than as part of a special program that individuals may or may not participate in.

If the decision is made to use a formal suggestion program, supervisors must ensure that their actions indicate full support of the program. For example, each suggestion must be responded to quickly. Employees will stop contributing to the program if they perceive that their ideas are not acted upon quickly. Suggestions should be published throughout the organization to show other employees the value of their coworkers' ideas. Finally, supervisors should evaluate the suggestion program regularly to ensure that valid employee suggestions are actually being implemented. Having a suggestion program that is not actively supported is far worse than having no program at all.

Employee Involvement Programs

During the past two decades, most organizations have adopted various forms of participative management programs. These types of programs often are known by other labels, such as employee involvement programs, problem-solving teams, quality circles, and semi-autonomous or self-directed work teams. These programs are based on the belief that employees want to contribute to the long-term success of the organization. In order to succeed, these initiatives require that managers at all levels have a strong commitment to participative management as a way of organizational life.

WHAT CALL DID YOU MAKE?

Improving employee motivation is central to the challenge facing Don Davis. Currently, the goals of the employees are inconsistent with organizational expectations.

As Davis, you must cultivate motivation through supportive actions. You are to be applauded for acting immediately. Based on the information you uncovered, it is apparent that there are major problems in your work unit. Absenteeism, turnover, grievances, injuries, and customer complaints are all on the rise. You recognize the need to understand your employees and their needs. However, each of your direct reports perceives the causes differently. Because each employee is unique, the next time you discuss productivity issues with your supervisory team, do it individually. You might learn more about their personal values, attitudes, needs, and expectations.

You should not try to motivate all 80 employees, but instead teach your supervisors how to do it themselves. Job satisfaction needs must be met. The costs of not dealing with employee needs and concerns are high—witness the unacceptable productivity level. You will need to establish and clarify desired behaviour patterns for each of your supervisors so those supervisors can model the desired behaviour. Ask your supervisors these questions: "What happens when employees do the job right?" "Are they being appropriately recognized for achievement?"

You will need to develop a reward system for reinforcing employee accomplishments. The reward system for performing the job well must be consistent with employees' needs. You should ascertain what employees consider undesirable about the work, the working conditions, and the work environment. Review the section of this chapter on the ABCs and ascertain that your supervisory team has set the stage for employee success. Clearly, it is up to you to find out what motivates your direct reports and, in turn, to emphasize their responsibility to find out what motivates their subordinates. Your supervisory team must understand that employees are motivated by different things. Praise, recognition, openness, and honesty may motivate most employees, but unless the employees desire these things, they are not motivators. Ultimately, it comes down to supervisors building healthy relationships with their workers to find out how to motivate those employees.

Good communication is essential to your success. You must listen and observe to assess your employees' needs, and you must communicate your expectations. Quality customer service and timely delivery are among the most important accomplishments of an organization. Therefore, you must constantly stress their importance. You might consider allowing small groups of employees to meet with their immediate supervisors and you to fully understand and appreciate the importance of doing the job right the first time. This would elevate the task significance aspect of their jobs.

The fact that grievances are on the rise suggests that employees believe their problems and concerns are not being addressed. Identify working conditions that the employees find unacceptable or current policies and practices that the employees may think are unfair. Work with your supervisory team to address these issues. You may be surprised at how easily some of the employees' "pet peeves" can be addressed and changed. Acting on employee problems is a good way to build trust with your employees. When employees see that their suggestions are acted upon promptly and that management is listening to them, performance often improves very quickly.

Often, employees perform below standards because they lack the skills or confidence to do their

(continued)

jobs. Placing workers in jobs that best suit their talents may help to improve worker productivity. There are other strategies you might use to increase the meaningfulness of employees' jobs. The self-reporting questionnaires in Skills Applications 6-1 and 6-2 could be used to assess employee needs and to identify the motivating potential of these jobs. If scores are low, you can attempt to discover which of the core job characteristics is causing the problem. If the scores are high, you will need to look for other factors that are causing the dissatisfaction.

The nature of the employees' jobs may be contributing to the lack of performance. Review the information in this chapter on job design and consider whether job rotation, job enlargement, or job enrichment strategies might improve morale and motivation.

It may be appropriate to use an employee participation program as described in this chapter. However, if the comments by your direct reports reflect the feelings of the majority, you will have to deal with the feelings of inequity and frustration before you can begin an employee participation program. You will need to gain the trust of the workers before they will actively support a participative approach.

The vast majority of people want to do a good job when they are at work. Under the right conditions, they will take pride in what they do and work hard toward goals that are meaningful to them. While discipline may be appropriate if performance does not improve, the open and collaborative approach described above should help to encourage better performance. Ultimately, if quality does not improve substantially, Economy Moving and Storage may lose customers, and many employees may lose their jobs.

SUMMARY

Behaviour is influenced by many factors within both the individual and the environment. Personality is the complex mix of knowledge, attitudes, and attributes that distinguish one person from another.

Prominent factors that interact to form the personality of each individual include physiological makeup, early childhood experiences, the immediate and continuing environment through life, and cultural values. The working environment is one of the almost unlimited influences that become part of an employee's personality.

Although supervisors need to be sensitive to individual differences, a consistent supervisory approach based on similarities is a practical way to lead employees.

Motivation is a willingness to exert effort toward achieving a goal, stimulated by the effort's ability to fulfill an individual need. According to Maslow, needs in ascending order of importance are biological, security, social, self-respect, and self-fulfillment. When a lower-level need is fulfilled, higher-level needs emerge that influence one's motivation.

It is important for supervisors to recognize the different need levels. Supervisors can influence employee motivation in a positive way if they rely on supervisory approaches that promote higher-level need fulfillment. When employee needs are not satisfied on the job, job performance usually suffers. Some employees express their dissatisfaction through absenteeism; others may display aggressive and disruptive behaviour; still others quit. The result is that the organization suffers from a decrease in production and a loss of quality.

Herzberg's motivation-hygiene research studies indicate that hygiene factors such as money, management policies, working conditions, and certain aspects of supervision must be adequate to maintain a reasonable level of motivation. Forces that stimulate good performance, called motivation factors, are intrinsic to the job—for example, the employees' needs for achievement, opportunity for advancement, challenging work, promotion, growth, and recognition. Effective supervisors implement strategies that target motivation factors to promote good job performance. It is not enough to rely on hygiene factors alone to stimulate employee performance.

Expectancy theory suggests that employees will be motivated if they perceive links between their efforts and performance, and between their performance and rewards. Supervisors must clarify such relationships for the workers or strive to develop them.

The ABC model of behaviour is built on the notion that antecedents (those things that precede behaviour) and consequences (the results of behaviour) can be used by the supervisor to encourage desirable behaviour or to extinguish undesirable behaviour. The use of extinction, positive reinforcement, punishment, and negative reinforcement can be used to make specific behaviour occur more or less often. Feedback and positive reinforcement should be used regularly to shape employee behaviour in the desired direction.

Theory X and Theory Y are two approaches to supervision that were described by Douglas McGregor. Theory X and Theory Y supervisors use different supervisory approaches based on their underlying assumptions about human nature. The Theory X (authority–obedience) supervisor believes primarily in autocratic techniques that relate to the lower-level human needs. The Theory X approach implies the use of a "carrot-and-stick" approach to fulfill the most basic needs. The Theory Y (team) supervisor prefers to build motivation by appealing to employees' higher-level needs.

The job characteristics model has been used to guide job redesign efforts. The major approaches to job redesign include job rotation, job enlargement, and job enrichment.

The advantages of participative management include decisions that tend to be higher quality and employees who are more willing to accept decisions. Employee participation programs are widely used and varied in application. Delegation strategies, suggestion programs, and self-directed work teams are approaches that emphasize employee involvement.

Getting people at all levels of the organization involved in setting objectives and problem solving, rearranging duties and responsibilities, and creating ways to reward people for their accomplishments are the essence of the approaches to motivate employee performance. The supervisor must learn to implement different supervisory approaches as appropriate to different people and settings.

QUESTIONS FOR DISCUSSION

1. Discuss four determinants of human personality. Which of these can be influenced or controlled to the greatest degree by the supervisor?
2. From the aspect of practical application, what are the benefits of each of the following motivational theories:

    a. Maslow's hierarchy of needs.

    b. Herzberg's motivation-hygiene theory.

3. What are the basic elements of Theory X and Theory Y? Can you think of any reasons Theory Y would not be appropriate for every supervisor in all situations?

4. Using examples, explain the differences among job rotation, job enlargement, and job enrichment.

5. Why might an employee not respond positively to the supervisor's efforts to enrich his or her job?

6. Some people believe that employee suggestion programs that offer monetary rewards should not be required in a truly participative work environment. They argue that if the company has to pay employees to put forward good ideas, then true participative management has not been achieved. Other people think that employee suggestion programs are an effective way to encourage and reward innovative thinking. Which statement best describes your beliefs about employee suggestion programs? Why?

7. How does the concept of employee empowerment change the role of the supervisor?

SKILLS APPLICATIONS

Skills Application 6-1: Satisfying Attributes of the Job

1. Working independently, rank the 12 items below in the order of their importance to you. Under column 1, place 1 next to the most important item, 2 next to the second most important, and so on through item 12.

2. Your instructor will establish teams of three to five students. The task for your team is to rank the items, according to the team's consensus, in order of importance. Do not vote or average the individual members' rankings; try to reach agreement on each item based on the concepts presented in this chapter, personal preferences, or the past experiences of group members. Enter the group's ranking in column 2.

3. When everyone is through, your instructor will aggregate the rankings of all groups. Enter the class's ranking in column 3.

4. Compare your individual rankings with those of the entire class. How do you explain the differences?

5. Why did perceptions differ among class members? What factors account for these differences?

What Do People Want from Their Jobs?	Self	Group	Class
Freedom to do my job	——	——	——
Supervisors and co-workers who care about me as a person	——	——	——
My ideas, suggestions, and opinions count	——	——	——
Opportunity to learn new skills	——	——	——
The resources to do the job right	——	——	——
A company that is family-friendly	——	——	——
Good wages	——	——	——
Opportunity to make work-related decisions	——	——	——
Job security	——	——	——
Appreciation for a job well done	——	——	——
Opportunity to use a variety of skills	——	——	——
Interesting and challenging work	——	——	——

Skills Application 6-2: Job Diagnostic Survey

Hackman and Oldham developed a self-report instrument for managers to use in diagnosing their work environment. The first step in calculating the "motivating potential score" (MPS) of your job is to complete the following questionnaire.

1. Use the scales below to indicate whether each statement is an accurate or inaccurate description of your present or most recent job. After completing the instrument, use the scoring key to compute a total score for each of the core job characteristics.

> 5 = Very descriptive   2 = Mostly nondescriptive
> 4 = Mostly descriptive   1 = Very nondescriptive
> 3 = Somewhat descriptive

_____ 1. I have almost complete responsibility for deciding how and when the work is to be done.

_____ 2. I have a chance to do a number of different tasks, using a wide variety of different skills and talents.

_____ 3. I do a complete task from start to finish. The results of my efforts are clearly visible and identifiable.

_____ 4. What I do affects the well-being of other people in very important ways.

_____ 5. My manager provides me with constant feedback about how I am doing.

_____ 6. The work itself provides me with information about how well I am doing.

_____ 7. I make insignificant contributions to the final product or service.

_____ 8. I get to use a number of complex skills on this job.

_____ 9. I have very little freedom in deciding how the work is to be done.

_____ 10. Just doing the work provides me with opportunities to figure out how well I am doing.

_____ 11. The job is quite simple and repetitive.

_____ 12. My supervisors or co-workers rarely give me feedback on how well I am doing the job.

_____ 13. What I do is of little consequence to anyone else.

_____ 14. My job involves doing a number of different tasks.

_____ 15. Supervisors let us know how well they think we are doing.

_____ 16. My job is arranged so that I do not have a chance to do an entire piece of work from beginning to end.

_____ 17. My job does not allow me an opportunity to use discretion or participate in decision making.

_____ 18. The demands of my job are highly routine and predictable.

_____ 19. My job provides few clues about whether I'm performing adequately.

_____ 20. My job is not very important to the company's survival.

_____ 21. My job gives me considerable freedom in doing the work.

_____ 22. My job provides me with the chance to finish completely any work I start.

_____ 23. Many people are affected by the job I do.

2. Scoring Key:

Skill variety (SV) (items 2, 8, 11*, 14, 18*) = _____ /5 = _____

Task identity (TI) (items 3, 7*, 16*, 22) = _____ /4 = _____

Task significance (TS) (items 4, 13*, 20*, 23) = _____ /4 = _____

Autonomy (AU) (items 1, 9*, 17*, 21) = _____ /4 = _____

Feedback (FB) (items 5, 6, 10, 12*, 15, 19*) = _____ /6 = _____

(Note: For each of the items with an asterisk, determine your score by taking 6 **minus** your score. For example, suppose you answered question #11 with a 5, indicating that this statement was "very descriptive" of your job. Your score on question #11 would then be 6 − 5 = 1. Use this formula for every question marked with an asterisk.)

Total the numbers for each characteristic and divide by the number of items to get an average score.

3. Now you are ready to calculate the MPS by using the following formula:

$$\text{Motivating Potential Score (MPS)} = \frac{(SV + TI + TS) \times AU \times FB}{3}$$

MPS scores range from 1 to 125.

4. You can compare your job characteristics with those of a fellow classmate or with norms that your instructor has. Is the MPS of your job high, average, or low?

5. What could be done to increase the motivating potential of your job?

Source: J. Richard Hackman and Greg R. Oldham, *Work Redesign* (adapted from pp. 80, 81, 90, and 303–306), ©1980 by Addison-Wesley Publishing Company, Inc. Reprinted by permission of Addison-Wesley Longman, Inc.

Skills Application 6-3: How Powerful is Money as a Motivator?

1. Imagine that you received a job offer today. The job will pay $150,000 per year and offers full benefits. You will work eight hours per day (9 A.M. to 5 P.M.) and your job duties will consist of absolutely nothing. Your job will be to come into work every day and sit at your desk. You will not have a telephone, computer, pen, or any reading material. You will be required to sit at the desk and do absolutely nothing. Discuss your reaction to this job offer. Would you accept the job? If so, how long do you anticipate you would remain in this job? Discuss your answers with other students. What can you conclude about the role of money as a motivator?

2. Go to a popular Internet search engine and type in "is money a motivator?" You will be provided with an extensive list of articles and opinions about the role of monetary rewards in motivating employees (see, for example, www.clemmer.net/excerpts/weak_leaders.shtml). Based on the results of your research, discuss the role money has in motivating employees. To what extent can problems with employee motivation be solved by offering more money?

3. You overheard a student say "I just don't buy this participative management idea. The majority of the people I've ever worked with just show up for a paycheque. If they were asked to contribute ideas and make more decisions, they'd just say that managers are the ones who are being paid to think. You'd never be able to get them to do more of anything unless you were willing to pay for it—and even then they'd do just enough to get by." How do you respond to this person's statement? Is there a way to "win over" workers who hold these attitudes about their work and to get them to want to excel in their jobs?

SKILLS DEVELOPMENT

Skills Development Module 6-1: Motivation

This video segment introduces Ken Foley, a production development supervisor with Carson Products, a manufacturing firm.

Questions for Discussion: The Ineffective Version

1. It is obvious that the road to employee motivation was not entirely clear to Ken Foley as he dealt with Jennifer Swanson, Alice Temprance, and J. C. Marko. List specific illustrations to support this observation.
2. Define motivation and explain why supervisor Foley should understand it.
3. Discuss what Foley can do to build trust between the employees and himself.
4. What can Foley do to effectively motivate his employees to work extra hours and finish up the project?

Questions for Discussion: The More Effective Version

1. Discuss how Foley motivated his employees to continuously improve.
2. Given the information in the video, would you say Foley focused on Herzberg's motivation factors or hygiene factors? Explain.
3. Discuss how Foley could broaden the scope and importance of each job.
4. What could Foley have done to be even more effective?

CASES

CASE 6-1

The Angry Outburst

Karen Flynn is the customer service supervisor of Canadian Online Auctions. The business was started four years ago and provides a way for Canadians to buy and sell a wide variety of merchandise using the Internet. Business has grown rapidly as people are becoming more comfortable entering into financial transactions online. Canadian Online Auctions provides a forum where sellers and buyers can "meet" electronically to negotiate the sale of goods. The customer service department is responsible for answering customer inquiries (both over the telephone and via email), as well as maintaining an up-to-date rating scale of all people who use the service. This rating is based on the person's track record with the company, and takes into account the person's payment record (when buying) and promptness of shipping goods (when selling).

Karen Flynn supervises three full-time workers and two contract staff. The full-time people have been with the company virtually since it began, while the contract staff were hired during the last year to help the department keep up with a rapidly escalating workload. The department is busy, and Flynn has had many "pep talks" with her staff to encourage them to "go the extra mile" to ensure that all customer inquiries and complaints are dealt with promptly.

Despite rapid business growth in the past year, upper management has insisted that no full-time staff will be hired until further notice is given. Management insists that this policy is necessary in order to maintain the company's flexibility should the level of business activity drop off unexpectedly. Any vacant positions must be filled with contract workers who are hired for a duration of six months. These employees earn, on average, only 75 percent of their full-time counterparts and receive no benefits. While there has been no guarantee of long-term employment, all contract workers have had their contracts renewed at least once and no one who has wanted to continue working with the company has been denied a contract extension.

Karen Flynn has always considered herself to be an approachable manager who encourages an open and participative work environment. She prefers to let her employees take much of the responsibility for their work and encourages a "team" approach. Staff are encouraged to share work and "pitch in" as needed to keep up with the hectic pace. The team appears to work well together, and all members of the department go out at least once a week after work to have dinner and socialize.

Today Karen Flynn witnessed a disturbing scene between two of her employees. Sheryl Vandekas, one of the full-time staff, approached Jenna Hughes, a contract worker, with a question about a customer file. Hughes pulled the relevant file from a stack on her desk and tossed it angrily at Vandekas and yelled, "I'm sick and tired of doing your work for you. Why don't you start pulling your own weight? You're the one getting paid the big bucks around here. I've been working just as hard as the rest of you and I'm still not even sure I'll have a job when my contract is finished. Why should I bother helping you?" With that, Hughes stormed out of the office saying that she was taking an early break. Everyone in the department stopped their work and watched as Hughes ran from the office.

Flynn knew that the contract workers have been surprised by the company's hiring freeze, but she had no idea that the ill-feeling had spread to such a degree in her department. Both of her contract workers had their contracts renewed recently, and Flynn had heard no direct complaints from them. She is dismayed by the incident she just witnessed and wonders what, if anything, she should do.

Questions for Discussion

1. Discuss the pros and cons of having Flynn step in at this point versus letting the two co-workers sort this situation out by themselves.
2. Many businesses hire temporary or contract workers to handle excess workload. Some contract workers choose to remain in a contract capacity because they like the flexibility and the variety of work settings that contract work provides. Other people accept contract jobs in the hope that, when a full-time position becomes available, they will be considered for the position.

    a. Using the Internet, type "motivating contract employees" into a popular search engine. Find at least three specific strategies that a supervisor can use to minimize the negative feelings that contract workers may experience while waiting for a full-time opportunity to arise.
    b. Based on your research and the information contained in this chapter, would equalizing the pay between the contract group and the full-time workers eliminate the potential ill-feelings among the contract workers? Explain.
3. What should Flynn do now? Develop an immediate and a longer-term action-plan to address the situation Flynn has just witnessed.

CASE 6-2

What Is Motivating Them?

Shirley Rice is the supervisor of the Packing Department of the Amcee Novelty Company. She supervises 15 employees, predominantly young workers in their twenties, whose job is to wrap finished products in tissue paper, put them into cardboard boxes, and then glue labels to the outside of the boxes. She is known as an experienced and firm supervisor. After observing and timing the operations frequently, she arrived at what she considered to be a fair standard of how many items each employee could box during an eight-hour day. However, this standard was seldom reached. In order to improve the situation, after additional studies she installed a different layout, rearranged the work benches, simplified the procedures, and did all she could to raise the output of the department. But output remained considerably below her expected standard.

As a last resort, Rice decided to try an idea that had greatly impressed her. During the last two months, once a week, the company had made it possible for all supervisors to attend a series of lectures given at a local college. These lectures covered the basics of good supervisory management. During the last lecture, the professor had discussed the advantages of group decision making and group discussion, including the advantages of decisions reached by those who will be concerned with the outcome. The professor stated that, in such cases, the employees usually will do their utmost to carry their decisions through to a successful conclusion. He compared them with decisions handed down unilaterally by supervisors, which employees often only grudgingly comply with.

Rice decided to apply this method and called a meeting of the workers in the department. She told them that a new standard of output had to be set. Instead of establishing the new production standard by herself, however, she wanted them to decide as a group what it should be. Of course, she hoped—but she did not say this—that they would arrive at a higher standard than the level at which they had been operating.

Several days later, much to Rice's amazement, the group arrived at a standard that was significantly lower than the level they had recently been achieving. The group claimed that even with the new work arrangements, the current standard was too high. Rice realized that she now had a more serious problem than before.

Questions for Discussion

1. Analyze Rice's style throughout this case in terms of McGregor's Theory X–Theory Y.
2. Could Rice have avoided the outcome of the group's decision by another approach? Explain.
3. Why did the group set a lower rather than a higher production standard?
4. Why does Rice now have a more difficult problem of getting group acceptance than she did before?
5. What should Rice do? What alternatives are open to her?

Chapter 7: Supervisory Leadership and the Management of Change

After studying this chapter you will be able to

1 Discuss the leadership component of supervision.

2 Identify and describe some of the elements of contemporary leadership thought.

3 Discuss the delegation process and define its three major components.

4 Discuss why some supervisors do not delegate, and describe the benefits of delegation.

5 Compare the autocratic (authoritarian) approach to supervision with the participative approach.

6 Suggest approaches for introducing change to employees and for proposing change to higher-level managers.

You are Lee McKenna, supervisor of the receiving and shipping department of a manufacturing plant of Tideway Corporation, a producer of paper products. You have supervised this department for two years after having worked as an employee in the department for about eight years. Fourteen employees report to you; all are members of the plant's labour union.

When you began your career as supervisor, you modelled your style after many of the managers you had worked for in the past. You had always worked for supervisors who would best be described as "autocratic"—they were "my way or the highway" type managers. You adopted this style when you became a supervisor because you believed it was the only way to show your employees that you were in control. You worried about being taken advantage of by your employees, especially since many of them had been your coworkers before you were promoted to supervisor. As supervisor, you perceived your job was to tell your employees what to do, how to do it, and to keep close control over the department so that the work would get done the way you wanted it.

Six months ago, you struck up a friendship with Maurice Leblanc, a new supervisor in the maintenance department of Tidewater Corporation. Leblanc was hired from outside the company, and quickly developed a reputation as an excellent supervisor. People in Leblanc's department have been very vocal about how much they enjoy working for him. In your two years as supervisor, you have never heard this said about you. You and Leblanc talk a lot about your jobs, and you have learned that he has a very different leadership style than you do. His employees make a lot of decisions about how the department is run. Leblanc's role seems to be more of a coach than a "boss," and you became curious about how he could maintain control over his workers with such a "laid-back" approach.

In an effort to learn more about supervision, you were able to attend a one-week supervisory management seminar delivered by a local consulting firm. You learned about theories and models of supervisory leadership, especially those urging a participative approach. You were taught techniques for giving directives to employees that were less authoritative than those you used previously. Participative styles were emphasized as being far more effective than just giving out orders.

It has been four weeks since you attended the seminar, and you have tried to implement what you learned. On a number of occasions you have asked employees—both individually and in groups—for their suggestions and opinions concerning what should be done. You have avoided giving direct orders and have tried to suggest to employees what needed to be done rather than spelling out your own objectives in detail. However, despite your best efforts, nothing seems to have changed. Work performance has not improved, and the employees seem to be going through the motions of their jobs just as before. The department shop steward even told you this morning that she did not think you understood how employees felt and that you had forgotten how it was to be a worker.

You wonder whether there is something wrong with your new approach. Is it just a waste of time? Is Leblanc able to use this style just because he is more of a natural leader than you are? Do your employees resent the fact that you were promoted to a supervisory position? You wonder whether you should just forget about the participative approach to management that you learned and go back to being a firm and authoritative supervisor. What should you do?

You make the call!

1   LEADERSHIP: THE CORE OF SUPERVISORY MANAGEMENT

Discuss the leadership
component of
supervision.

In this chapter's "You Make the Call" section, Lee McKenna is learning that becoming a supervisor does not automatically make a person a leader. Just because a supervisor occupies a position of responsibility and authority does not necessarily mean that he or she is a leader whom subordinates are willing to follow. In this chapter, we will explore the notion of leadership and examine ways that supervisors can begin to develop this very important set of skills.[1] We will discuss the process of delegation, as well as the introduction of change—two important aspects of leadership that an effective supervisor must consider.

The Test of Supervisory Leadership

Leadership
The ability to guide and influence the opinions, attitudes, and behaviour of others.

Leadership is the ability to guide and influence the opinions, attitudes, and behaviour of others. This means that anyone who can direct or influence others can function as a leader, no matter what position that person holds.

In the workplace, leaders can emerge from any level in the organizational hierarchy. Informal leaders—those who hold no official position of authority—can have a powerful impact on the people who choose to follow. From a supervisory perspective, informal leaders in the workgroup can have a very significant influence—either positive or negative—on the performance of the department. For example, employee resistance to changes in work arrangements, work rules, or procedures is quite common. Such resistance is usually the result of some informal leadership in the work group. On the other hand, if informal leaders in the work group are supportive of a supervisor's efforts, other employees will tend to follow suit and the supervisor's job can be made much easier.

Leadership is a process rather than just a positional relationship. Leadership includes not only what the supervisor does, but also what the followers think and do. The real test of supervisory leadership is how subordinates follow. Leadership resides in a supervisor's ability to obtain the work group's willingness to follow—a willingness based on commonly shared goals and mutual effort to achieve them. Leadership is associated with issuing instructions, assignments, and directives, but it also includes building an effective workforce by encouraging employees to work willingly and enthusiastically toward the accomplishment of organizational objectives.

Leadership Can Be Developed

When people are described by others as being "born leaders," the suggestion is that leadership is something a person either has or doesn't have. But does a person need to have certain natural qualities to be an effective leader? Research supports the notion that the ability to lead is something that can be learned. Successful supervisors tend to be well rounded in their interests and aptitudes, they are good communicators, they are mentally and emotionally mature, and they have strong inner drives. Most important, they tend to rely more on their supervisory skills than on their technical skills. These are essentially learned characteristics, not innate qualities.

Learning to be a leader is, however, an active process. One cannot just sit back and be taught how to be a leader. Author Peter Senge writes that "leadership has to do with how people are. You don't teach people a different way of being, you create conditions so they can discover where their natural leadership comes from."[2]

Supervisory leadership is something people can develop when they want to be leaders and not just people in charge of groups. As noted in the Appendix to Chapter 1, students can take advantage of volunteer opportunities, or participate in co-op or internship programs offered through their placement office. Look for volunteer projects that will help you to develop your managerial and human relations skills. Any activity that allows you to work with others toward the accomplishment of a goal is an opportunity to develop leadership skills. Involvement in campus clubs, community organizations, or industry associations can provide valuable experience. Seize every opportunity.

| **2** | **CONTEMPORARY THOUGHTS ON LEADERSHIP** |

Identify and describe some of the elements of contemporary leadership thought.

There is no shortage of books, articles, and seminars devoted to the topic of leadership. Many people are, apparently, looking for "words of wisdom" that will help them become more effective leaders (see Figure 7-1 as well as the accompanying Contemporary Issue box on page 203). One of the most noted writers on leadership, Warren Bennis, reported from his extensive research four things people want from their leaders:

1. **Direction:** People want leaders to have a purpose. The leader has a clear idea of what is to be done. Leaders love what they do. Followers want passion and conviction from a strong point of view.
2. **Trust:** The ability to trust a leader is essential. Integrity, maturity, and candour are required elements of building a relationship of mutual trust.
3. **Hope:** Leaders believe in what they are doing, and they kindle the fire of optimism in followers.
4. **Results:** Leaders accomplish difficult tasks. Success breeds success.[3]

We often hear employees say about management, "We don't trust them." The words "us versus them" are common in the workplace. But trust is the foundation of effective supervisory relations. Employees must absolutely believe that a supervisor will fulfill his or her commitments and always act with integrity. Similarly, the supervisor must be able to trust employees to work toward mutually agreed upon goals. Without trust, far too much time and effort is spent second-guessing people's motives and checking up on whether they've done what they agreed to do. Stephen R. Covey, author of *Principle-Centered Leadership*, notes that

Trust bonds management to labour, employees to each other, customers to supplier, and strengthens all other stakeholder relationships. With low trust, developing performance is exhausting. With high trust, it is exhilarating. The principle of alignment means working together in harmony, going in the same direction, supporting each other. [4]

Noted leadership researchers James Kouzes and Barry Posner contend that "leadership is an observable, learnable set of practices. Given the opportunity for feedback and practice, those with desire and persistence to lead can substantially improve their abilities to do so."[5] After examining the experiences of managers

FIGURE 7-1 The Banff Centre's top picks for reading about leadership.

The Banff Centre in Banff, Alberta, is a well-known Canadian learning centre dedicated to the arts and leadership development. The Banff Centre publishes *Leadership Compass Magazine* (available online at www.banffcentre.ca/departments/leadership/leadership_compass/). In addition to articles about leadership, each edition of the magazine provides a feature entitled "The *Leadership Compass* Top 5 Book Picks," which recommends and reviews current leadership titles. Below is a sample of some of the most recent "picks" that would be valuable reading for anyone who wants to expand his or her thinking in the area of leadership.

- *The Leadership Mystique—A User's Manual for the Human Enterprise* by Manfred Kets de Vries.
- *The Leader's Handbook: Making Things Happen, Getting Things Done* by Peter Scholtes.
- *Why Don't You Want What I Want? How to Win Support for Your Ideas Without Hard Sell, Manipulation, or Power Plays* by Rick Maurer.
- *The Five Dysfunctions of a Team: A Leadership Fable* by Patrick M. Lencioni.
- *The Encyclopedia of Leadership* by Murray Hiebert and Bruce Klatt.
- *Leadership Is an Art* by Max DePree.

This list is, of course, just a sampling of the hundreds of new books about leadership that are written every year. New supervisors should read widely in an effort to learn about many people's thoughts on leadership. Through this wide exposure, a supervisor can hone his or her own approach and clarify what style of leadership provides the best overall, individual "fit."

who were leading others to outstanding accomplishments, Kouzes and Posner identified practices and specific behaviours that can be learned and used by managers at all levels. These include

- Challenging the process (searching for opportunities, experimenting, and taking risks).
- Inspiring a shared vision (envisioning the future, enlisting the support of others).
- Enabling others to act (fostering collaboration, strengthening others).
- Modelling the way (setting an example, planning small wins).
- Encouraging the heart (recognizing contributions, celebrating accomplishments).[6]

Leadership Style Depends on Many Factors

While there is general agreement among researchers and theorists that leading is not the same as managing, there is still considerable debate regarding what the leader does and how the leader does it. A detailed discussion of various theories is beyond the scope of this text, but an overview can be found on our website at www.supervision2e.nelson.com. In spite of the variety of contemporary opinions about leadership, most supervisors and managers recognize that no single lead-

CONTEMPORARY ISSUE
Servant-Leadership

First put forward by Robert Greenleaf in 1970, the concept of servant-leadership is a model that is gaining increasing interest in the business community, as managers at all levels strive to understand the true meaning of leadership.

Simply put, the idea of servant-leadership is based on the notion that a true leader is a selfless servant whose passion is ensuring that other people's highest priority needs are being served. Rather than owning a position of leadership and being driven to lead by ego and ambition, servant-leaders are called to lead because they naturally want to be helpful. "They aren't possessive about their position. They view it as an act of stewardship rather than ownership."[1] A servant-leader's primary measure of success is "do those served grow as persons; do they, while being served, become healthier, wiser, freer, more autonomous, more likely themselves to become servants?"[2]

Servant-leadership is built on the belief that human beings are supremely valuable. While there's likely not a manager alive who would dare disagree with that statement, the servant-leader believes that people have an authentic value before they come to work, and therefore must be treated accordingly when they get there. "The work exists for the person as much as the person exists for the work ...The business exists as much to provide meaningful work to the person as it exists to provide a product or service to the customer."[3] The organization's people, then, are not merely a "valuable resource" that must be appreciated and recognized. The organization exists *so that* its people can have meaningful work.

Becoming a servant-leader is not about small changes in how one treats employees. Proponents of servant-leadership believe that "leadership starts on the inside with a servant heart, then moves outward to serve others. Real change in behaviour eventually requires a transformation of the heart. It is about character change, about being a good and caring person."[4]

The notion of a servant-leader is certainly different from the traditional take-charge, "I'll lead, you follow," results-oriented model of leadership. It is based on a more humble, thoughtful approach characterized by skilled listening, and a quest for understanding those people who are being served. Servant-leaders seek self-awareness and an "inner serenity" so that they can act according to their values. They persuade rather than direct. They are tirelessly committed to the growth of each and every person in the organization.[5]

People spend a great deal of their time and energy in their work life, and servant-leaders strive to ensure that the organization is a place where people can find meaning. Larry C. Spears, chief executive officer of The Greenleaf Center for Servant-Leadership (www.greenleaf.org) writes that "the servant-leader senses that much has been lost in recent human history as a result of the shift from local communities to large institutions as the primary shaper of human lives. This awareness causes the servant-leader to seek to identify some means for building community among those who work within a given institution."[6] The workplace has to be more than just a source of a paycheque, and even more than a "fun place to work." It must somehow feed the deeper craving that people have to make a difference in the world.

While servant-leadership may appear to be a tall order for the supervisor, Greenleaf and others believe that servant-leaders can be found at all organizational levels. Servant-leaders can emerge whenever a person consistently values service to others over self-interest. People can learn to be servant-leaders and can develop these characteristics and skills. "Recognize, however, the transition to servant-leadership is a gradual paradigm shift requiring life-long learning."[7]

Sources: (1) Ken Blanchard, "Leadership by the Book," *Executive Excellence* (March 2000), p. 4; (2) Robert Greenleaf from "Servant-leadership" at www.greenleaf.org/leadership/servant-leadership/What-is-Servant-Leadership.html (retrieved November 5, 2003); (3) Don Page, "Finding Meaning through Servant Leadership in the Workplace," as viewed at www.meaning.ca/pdf/2000proceedings/don_page.pdf (retrieved November 5, 2003); (4) Blanchard, p. 4; (5) and (6) Larry C. Spears, "On Character and Servant-Leadership: Ten Characteristics of Effective, Caring Leaders" at http://greenleaf.org/leadership/read-about-it/articles/On-Character-and-Servant-Leadership (retrieved November 5, 2003); (7) Max E. Douglas, "Servant-Leadership: An Emerging Supervisory Model," *Supervision* (February 2003), p. 6. See also Walter Kiechel III and M. Rosenthal, "The Leader as Servant," *Fortune* (May 5, 1992) p. 121.

ership style is effective in all situations. There is no simple set of do's and don'ts a supervisor can implement to achieve high motivation and excellent perform-ance. No one formula will apply in all situations and with all people.

Contingency-style leadership proponents suggest that the most effective lead-ership style depends on a multitude of factors, including the supervisor, the organization, the type of work, the employees involved, their ability and willing-ness to accomplish a task, the amount of time available to complete a task, and the situation and its urgency. In general, we conclude that effective leaders must be able to establish standards, develop a climate in which people become self-motivated, and adapt to constant change. The effective leader provides direction, instruction, guidance, support and encouragement, feedback and positive recog-nition, and enthusiastic help when necessary.

Contingency-style leadership
Approach to leadership based on the belief that no single leadership style is best; the appropriate style depends on a multitude of factors.

3   THE PROCESS OF DELEGATION

Discuss the delegation process and define its three major components.

One of the hallmarks of effective leadership is delegation. Successful leaders bring out the best in their people by carefully deciding what to delegate and to whom, and by delegating in a way that encourages success. Just as authority is a major component of management, the delegation of authority is essential to the creation and operation of an organization. In the broadest sense, **delegation** gives employees a greater voice in how the job is to be done; the employee is empow-ered to make decisions.[7]

Delegation
The process of entrusting duties and related authority to subordinates.

Unfortunately, some managers view delegation as a means of lightening their workloads. They assign unpleasant tasks to employees and subsequently find that the employees are not motivated to complete those tasks. The manager must look at delegation as a tool to develop employees' skills and abilities rather than as a way to offload unpleasant tasks.

A manager receives authority from a higher-level manager through delega-tion, but this does not mean the higher-level manager surrenders all accounta-bility. **Accountability** is the obligation one has to one's boss, as well as the expectation that employees will accept credit or blame for the results achieved in performing assigned tasks. When supervisors delegate, they are still ultimately accountable for the successful completion of the work.

Accountability
The obligation one has to one's boss. Also, the expectation that employees will accept credit or blame for the results achieved in performing assigned tasks.

Delegation is a supervisor's strategy for accomplishing objectives. It consists of the following three components, all of which must be present:

1. Assigning duties to immediate subordinates.
2. Granting authority to make commitments, use resources, and take all actions necessary to perform duties.
3. Creating an obligation (responsibility) on the part of each employee to per-form duties satisfactorily.

Unless all three components are present, the delegation process is incomplete. They are inseparably related; a change in one requires change in the other two.

Assigning Duties

Each employee must be assigned a specific job or task to perform. Job descrip-tions may provide a general framework through which the supervisor can examine duties in the department to see which tasks to assign to each employee. Routine duties can usually be assigned to almost any employee, but there are

A good leader uses delegation to develop employees' skills and abilities.

Getty Images/Photodisc Collection

other functions the supervisor can assign only to employees who are qualified to perform them. In other cases, the thoughtful assignment of challenging duties can result in self-development opportunities for some employees. There are also some functions a supervisor cannot delegate—those the supervisor must do. The assignment of job duties to employees is of great significance, and much of the supervisor's success depends on it.

Granting Authority

The granting of authority means that the supervisor confers upon employees the right and power to act, to use certain resources, and to make decisions within prescribed limits. Of course, the supervisor must determine the scope of authority that is to be delegated. How much authority can be delegated depends, in part, on the amount of authority the supervisor possesses. The degree of authority is also related to the employees and the jobs to be done. For example, if a sales clerk is responsible for processing items returned to the store, that clerk must have the authority to give the customer's money back with the understanding (limit) that the clerk should alert the supervisor if the returned item was used or damaged in some way. In every instance, enough authority must be granted to the employee to enable the employee to perform assigned tasks adequately and successfully. There is no need for the amount of authority to be larger than the tasks, but authority must be sufficient to meet the employee's obligations.

Throughout the process of delegation, employees must be reassured that their orders and authority come from their immediate supervisor. A supervisor must be specific in telling employees what authority they have and what they can or cannot do. It is uncomfortable for employees to have to guess how far their authority extends. For example, an employee may be expected to order certain materials as a regular part of the job. This employee must know the limits within which materials can be ordered, perhaps in terms of time and costs, and when permission from the supervisor is needed before ordering additional materials. If the supervisor does not state this clearly, the employee probably will be forced to test the limits and to learn by trial and error. If it becomes necessary to change an employee's job assignment, the degree of authority should be checked to ensure that the authority that is delegated is still appropriate. If it is less (or more) than needed, it should be adjusted.

Creating Responsibility

The third component of the process of delegation is creating obligation on the part of the employee to perform assigned duties satisfactorily. Acceptance of this obligation creates responsibility; without responsibility, delegation is incomplete.

Responsibility
The obligation to perform certain tasks and duties as assigned by the supervisor.

The terms *responsibility* and *authority* are closely related. Simply stated, **responsibility** is the obligation of a subordinate to perform duties as required by the supervisor. By accepting a job or accepting an obligation to perform assigned duties, the employee implies the acceptance of responsibility. Responsibility implies that the employee agrees to perform duties in return for rewards, such as paycheques. The most important facet of the definition is that responsibility is something a subordinate must recognize and accept if delegation is to succeed.

Supervisory Accountability Cannot Be Delegated

Although a supervisor must delegate authority to employees to accomplish specific jobs, the supervisor's own accountability cannot be delegated. Assigning duties to employees does not relieve the supervisor of the responsibility for those duties. Therefore, when delegating assignments to employees, the supervisor remains accountable for the actions of the employees carrying out those assignments. For example, when a high-level manager asks a supervisor to explain a mistake that was made in the department, the supervisor cannot plead that the responsibility was delegated to employees in the group. The supervisor remains accountable and must answer for the actions of his or her work group.

Being held accountable for the actions of others may worry some supervisors, but responsibility for the work of employees goes with the supervisory position. Even when the supervisor follows all of the right steps, there will be cases when employees will not always use the best judgment or perform in a superior fashion. If employees fail to carry out their assigned tasks, they are accountable to the supervisor, who must then redirect the employees as appropriate. When appraising a supervisor's performance, higher-level managers usually consider how much care the supervisor has taken in selecting, training, and supervising employees, and controlling their activities.

| **4** | **DELEGATION BY THE SUPERVISOR** |

Discuss why some supervisors do not delegate, and describe the benefits of delegation.

Good leaders are committed to developing the talents and skills of their employees. Effective supervisors understand that, through delegation, they are providing their employees with meaningful opportunities to learn and grow. However, many employees complain that their supervisors make all decisions and scrutinize their work because they do not trust the employees to carry out assignments. These complaints usually describe supervisors who are unable or unwilling to delegate, except minimally.

Reasons for Lack of Supervisory Delegation

A supervisor may be reluctant to delegate for several reasons. While some of these reasons can, at times, be valid, a good supervisor can almost always overcome these obstacles.

Shortage of Qualified Employees

Some supervisors cite a lack of qualified employees as an excuse for not delegating authority. Usually, many such supervisors believe that their employees cannot handle authority or are unwilling to accept it. If these supervisors refuse to delegate, employees will have little opportunity to obtain the experience they need to improve their judgment and to handle broader assignments. Supervisors must always remember that, unless they begin somewhere, they will probably always have too few employees who can and will accept more authority with commensurate responsibility. Supervisors in this situation must start by carefully selecting tasks that hold an appropriate degree of challenge for their employees and making themselves available for ample support and encouragement. By building on previous successes and gradually increasing the complexity of the tasks being delegated, the supervisor will eventually build a more effective work group with a broader range of skills and abilities.

Fear of Making Mistakes

Some supervisors think it best to make most decisions themselves because, in the final analysis, they retain overall responsibility. Out of fear of mistakes, such supervisors are unwilling to delegate, and, as a result, continue to overburden themselves. These supervisors quickly become "bogged down" by the sheer volume of work. By making decisions themselves, these supervisors are trying to save the time and money associated with the mistakes that they fear their employees might make. What they often don't see, however, is that the costs associated with delays and missed opportunities can quickly exceed the costs of any errors their subordinates might make. Also, by refusing to delegate, these supervisors are denying themselves and the organization the specialized expertise that employees can bring to the decision.

The "I'd-Rather-Do-It-Myself" Mentality

Supervisors sometimes complain that, if they want something done right, they have to do it themselves. They believe it is easier to do the job than to correct an employee's mistakes, or they may simply prefer to correct an employee's mistakes rather than taking the time to clearly explain what should have been done. Such supervisors may even believe that they can do the job better than any of the employees. While this may be true, these attitudes interfere with a supervisor's prime responsibility, which is to supervise others to get the job done.

The old stereotype of a good supervisor was that of one who pitched in and worked alongside employees, setting an example by personal effort. Even today, this type of supervision often occurs when a supervisor has been promoted through the ranks and the supervisory position is a reward for hard work and technical competence. By being placed in a supervisory position without managerial training, this type of supervisor is faced with many new challenges. These supervisors may retreat to their "comfort zone" and begin working alongside employees because this role is familiar and secure to them. Occasionally, the supervisor should pitch in, for example, when the job is particularly difficult or when an emergency arises. Aside from emergencies and unusual situations, however, the supervisor should be supervising and the employees should be doing their assigned tasks. Normally, it is the supervisor's job to get things done, not to do them.

A good supervisor occasionally shows employees how a job can be done more efficiently, promptly, courteously, and so forth. However, even if the supervisor's abilities to do the work exceed the employee's, it is almost never a good idea for the supervisor to do the work on a regular basis. By allowing the employee to do the job, the supervisor's time is reserved for supervisory responsibilities—for innovative thinking, planning, and more delegating. The effective supervisor strives to ensure that each employee, with each additional job, becomes more competent. Over time, the employee's performance on the job should be as good as or better than that of the supervisor.

Other Factors

Ineffective supervisors are afraid to let go. They may fear that if they share their knowledge with employees and allow them to participate in decision making, the employees will become so proficient at making good decisions that the supervisor will be unnecessary. Some organizations overcome this obstacle by making it clear to supervisors that they will not be promoted up the management ranks unless someone has been prepared to take the supervisor's place. This direct incentive ensures that the supervisor develops employees' skills by effective delegation.

Not everyone wants to take the responsibility for decisions. The supervisor must identify those employees who need the opportunity to grow and who want to be empowered. Employees may be reluctant to accept delegation because of their insecurity or fear of failure, or they may think the supervisor will be unavailable for guidance. Some employees are reluctant to accept delegation due to past managerial incompetence. Too often, employees have had boring, mundane, and unpleasant tasks given them from above. To overcome these obstacles, supervisors must ensure that they delegate meaningful tasks and that they are available to support and encourage employees along the way.

It is difficult for supervisors to create an environment of employee involvement and freedom to make decisions when their own managers do not allow them the same. An environment for delegation and empowerment must be part of the organization's culture. Upper-level managers must advocate delegation at all levels.

Benefits of Delegation

Effective delegation holds a number of benefits for the supervisor and the employees. First, the supervisor who delegates appropriately will have more time to plan, strategize, and lead—all of which are "higher level" activities that have a significant impact on the success of the department. Supervisors often complain that they are so busy with day-to-day operations of the department that they don't have time for longer-range thinking. By delegating any and all activities that can be done by other people, the supervisor is freed up for these other critical functions.

When a supervisor delegates appropriately, employees are given the opportunity to learn additional skills by taking on meaningful and challenging tasks, thereby improving their judgment and decision-making abilities. Employees are expected to make more decisions independently. This does not mean the supervisor is not available for advice. It means the supervisor encourages the employees to make many of their own decisions and to develop self-confidence in doing so. Effective delegation should cause employees to perform an increasing number of jobs and to recommend solutions that contribute to good performance.

Employees who are given the opportunity to perform a variety of meaningful tasks tend to be more motivated and more committed to better job performance. This may take time, and the degree of delegation may vary with each employee and with each department. However, in most situations, a supervisor's goal should be to delegate more authority to employees.

It must be reiterated that there are some supervisory areas that cannot be delegated. For example, it remains the supervisor's responsibility to formulate certain policies and objectives, to give general directions for the work unit, to appraise employee performance, to take disciplinary action, and to promote employees. Aside from these types of supervisory management responsibilities, the employees should be doing most of the departmental work.

5

Compare the autocratic (authoritarian) approach to supervision with the participative approach.

APPROACHES TO SUPERVISORY LEADERSHIP

Most employees accept work as a normal part of life. In their jobs, they seek satisfaction that wages alone cannot provide (see the Contemporary Issue box on page 203). Most employees probably would prefer to be their own bosses or at least have a degree of freedom to make decisions that pertain to their work. The question arises as to whether this is possible if an individual works for someone else. Can a degree of freedom be granted to employees if those employees are to contribute to organizational objectives? This is where the delegation of authority can help. The desire for freedom and being one's own boss can be enhanced by delegation, which, in the daily routine, essentially means giving directions in general terms. It means that the supervisor, instead of watching every detail of the employees' activities, is primarily interested in the results employees achieve and is willing to give them considerable latitude in deciding how to achieve those results.

Classifying Supervisory Leadership Styles

Organizational behaviour and management literature are replete with research studies and models that have sought to establish which leadership styles are most consistently associated with superior levels of performance.[8] The magnitude of these studies are beyond the scope of this text, and their findings and concepts are neither consistent nor conclusive.

Rather than debate the differences and nuances of various leadership theories, we believe they can all be classified into two styles or approaches. These styles range from essentially autocratic, or authoritarian supervisory styles (based on Theory X assumptions), to variations of general supervisory styles (based on Theory Y assumptions). These two styles can be presented as the extremes of a continuum (see Figure 7-2). However, in practice, a supervisor usually blends these approaches based on a number of considerations, including the supervisor's skill and experience, the employee or employees who are involved, the situation, and other factors. No one style of supervision has ever been shown to be correct in all situations. Consequently, supervisors must be sensitive to the needs and realities of each situation and to change their styles as necessary to accomplish objectives.

In Chapter 6, we discussed Theory X and Theory Y, as well as participative management. We expand these concepts in this chapter to relate them to a supervisor's day-to-day approaches to leading employees. While we focus primarily on supervisory leadership, recognize that a supervisory approach is not the only influence on employees' behaviour. Employees bring a host of innate factors and outside influences into the workplace that can significantly affect their behaviour and performance.

Autocratic (Authoritarian) Supervision

Autocratic (authoritarian) supervision
The supervisory style that relies on formal authority, threats, pressure, and close control.

Many supervisors still believe that emphasizing formal authority, or **autocratic (authoritarian) supervision,** is the best way to obtain results. A supervisor of this type often uses pressure to get people to work and may even threaten disciplinary action, including discharge, if employees do not perform as ordered.[9] Employees sometimes call these managers "taskmasters." Autocratic supervision means close control of employees in which supervisors issue directives with detailed instructions and allow employees little room for initiative. Autocratic supervisors

FIGURE 7-2
Leadership style continuum.

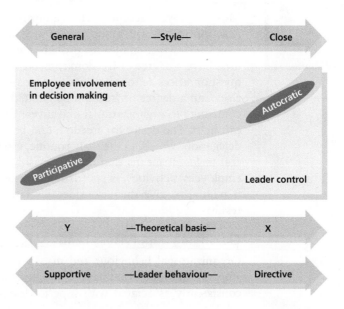

delegate very limited authority (or none at all). They believe they know how to do the job better than their employees and that employees are not paid to think but to follow directions. Autocratic supervisors further believe that, because they have been put in charge, they should do most of the planning and decision making. Because such supervisors are quite explicit in telling employees exactly how and in what sequence things are to be done, they follow through with close supervision and are focused on the tasks to be done.

Autocratic supervision is sometimes associated with what has been called the bureaucratic style of supervision. This style emphasizes an organizational structure and climate that require strict compliance with managers' policies, rules, and directives throughout the firm. Because bureaucratic managers believe that their primary role is to carry out and enforce policies and directives, they usually adopt an authoritarian approach. Their favourite sayings are "It's policy," "Those are the rules," and "Shape up or ship out!"

Autocratic supervisors do not necessarily distrust their employees, but they firmly believe that, without detailed instructions, employees could not do their jobs. Some autocratic supervisors operate from the premise that most employees do not want to do their jobs; therefore, close supervision and threats of job or income loss are required to get employees to work (Theory X). These supervisors think that, if they are not on the scene watching their employees closely, the employees will stop working or proceed at a leisurely pace.

When Autocratic Supervision Is Appropriate

Under certain circumstances and with some employees, autocratic supervision is both logical and appropriate. In times of crisis or when the risks associated with mistakes are very high, it may be essential for a supervisor to "take control" and give very explicit orders in an autocratic way. For example, most passengers and flight attendants would prefer that the pilot use an autocratic style when faced with an emergency during flight. The same is true in any organization when a situation requires immediate attention. It may also be true that there are a very limited number of employees who simply do not want to think for themselves and prefer to receive orders. Many leadership theorists claim, however, that virtually every human being seeks meaning from work and, given the opportunity, prefers to have some input into decisions.

Probably the major advantages of autocratic supervision are that it is quick and fairly easy to apply and that it usually gets rapid results in the short run. It may be appropriate when employees are new and inexperienced, especially if the supervisor is under major time pressures and cannot afford to have employees take time to figure out on their own how to get the work done.

Effects of Autocratic Supervision

For the most part, the autocratic method of supervision is not conducive to developing employee talents. It tends to frustrate employees who have ambition and potential. In an autocratic environment, such employees may lose interest and initiative and stop thinking for themselves because there is little need for independent thought. Those who believe in the sheer weight of authority and the "be strong" form of supervision tend to discount the fact that workers may react in ways that were not intended by the supervisor. Employees who strongly resent autocratic supervision may become frustrated rather than find satisfaction in their daily work. Such frustration can lead to arguments and other forms of discontent. In some cases, employees may become hostile toward an autocratic supervisor and resist the supervisor's directives. The resistance may not even be apparent to the supervisor when it takes the form of slow work, mistakes, absenteeism, and poor work quality. If the supervisor makes a mistake, these employees may secretly rejoice.

Participative Management and General Supervision

Because of the potential negative consequences associated with autocratic and close supervision, most supervisors prefer not to use it or to apply it sparingly. Is one leadership style better than another? Many research studies have suggested that effective supervisors tailor their leadership styles to situations and to the abilities and motivation of subordinates.

General supervision

The style of supervision in which the supervisor sets goals and limits but allows employees to decide how to achieve goals.

Effective supervisors who want to guide employees to higher levels of performance recognize that they cannot rely solely on managerial authority. **General supervision** means that the supervisor sets goals, discusses those goals with employees, and fixes the limits within which the work must be done. Within this framework, employees have considerable freedom to decide how to achieve their objectives. General supervision is based upon the belief that employees want to do a good job and will find greater satisfaction in making decisions themselves. The supervisor communicates the desired results, standards, and limits within which the employees can work, then delegates accordingly. General supervision is particularly applicable to routine tasks and daily assignments. By allowing employees to make decisions about how the work gets done, even the most routine jobs can become more meaningful and rewarding to the people who do them.

General supervision is closely linked to participative management. As discussed in Chapter 6, participative management means that the supervisor discusses with employees the feasibility, workability, extent, and content of a problem before making a decision and issuing a directive. Participative management involves gathering and placing significant emphasis upon employee input before making a decision that will affect those employees. General supervision and participative management are both grounded in Theory Y assumptions.

General supervision is not the same as what has been called free-rein (*laissez-faire*) supervision. Free-rein supervisors delegate virtually all authority and decision making to subordinates, perhaps even to the extent that such supervisors do not become involved in workplace decisions unless asked. For example, employees would be given freedom to do whatever they decided was necessary to accomplish their tasks without violating laws or company policies. The perceptive reader should ask, "If the supervisor essentially abdicates, why is the supervisor needed?" Free-rein leadership is typically not a viable approach given the true nature of most organizations.

Stretch targets

Targeted job objectives that present a challenge but are achievable.

For general supervision to work, employees should be trained and know the routine of their jobs and which results are expected, but the supervisor should avoid giving detailed instructions that specify precisely how results are to be achieved. Further, general supervision also means that the supervisor, or the supervisor and employees together, should set realistic standards or performance targets. These standards should be high enough to represent a challenge but not so high that they cannot be achieved. Such targets are sometimes referred to as **stretch targets**. Employees know that their efforts are being measured against these standards. If they cannot reach the targets, they are expected to inform the supervisor so that the standards can be discussed again and perhaps modified.

Regardless of one's preferred leadership style, the supervisor must ensure that the assigned work gets done efficiently and effectively. Many people wrongly assume that leaders who follow participative and general supervisory approaches never tell their subordinates what to do. While it is true that these supervisors prefer to involve employees in the decision-making process, there are times when even the most Theory Y supervisor will need to provide direction. Whether assigning tasks to subordinates or helping subordinates decide on how to do a task, the supervisor must provide directives. A directive is the means by which a supervisor conveys to employees what, how, and why something is to be accomplished. The degree to which the supervisor uses directives will, in part, vary with the task to be performed; the skill level, experience, and willingness of the subordinate; and the urgency of the situation. Figure 7-3 summarizes six major characteristics of good supervisory directives, and our website (www.supervision2e.nelson.com) provides even more detailed information.

A participative style does not lessen a supervisor's authority; the right to decide remains with the supervisor and the employees' suggestions can be rejected. *Participation* means that a supervisor expresses personal opinions in a manner that indicates to employees that these opinions are subject to critique. It also means sharing ideas and information between supervisor and employees and thoroughly discussing alternative solutions to a problem, regardless of who originates the solutions. A high degree of mutual trust must be evident.

More important than approach is the supervisor's attitude. Some supervisors are inclined to use a "pseudoparticipative" approach simply to give employees the impression that they have been consulted. These supervisors ask for suggestions even though they already have decided on a course of action. They use this approach to manipulate employees to do what will be required, with or without employees' consultation. However, employees can sense superficiality and will usually perceive whether a supervisor is genuinely considering their ideas. When employees believe their participation is false, the results may be worse than if the supervisor had practised autocratic supervision.

FIGURE 7-3 Guidelines for issuing good directives.

Reasonable—The supervisor should not issue a directive if the employee receiving it does not have the ability or experience and willingness to comply.

Understandable—The supervisor should ensure that an employee understands a directive by speaking in words that are familiar to the employee and by using feedback to ensure the employee understands.

Specific—The supervisor should state clearly what is expected in terms of quantity and quality of work performance.

Time limited—The supervisor should specify a time limit within which the work should be completed.

Compatible with organizational objectives—Supervisory directives must comply with policies, regulations, and ethical standards of the organization.

Appropriate tone and wording—Supervisors should state the directive, preferably as a request, using a polite and considerate tone.

If participative management is to succeed, the supervisor and the employees must want it. When employees believe the supervisor knows best and that making decisions is none of their concern, an opportunity to participate is not likely to induce higher motivation and better morale. Employees should be consulted in those areas in which they can express valid opinions and in which they can draw on their knowledge. The problems should be consistent with employees' experiences and abilities. Asking for participation in areas that are far outside employees' scope of competence may make employees feel inadequate and frustrated.

Advantages of Participative Management and General Supervision

Participative management and general supervision offer numerous advantages to both the supervisor and the employees (see Figure 7-4). Perhaps the greatest advantage is that a supervisor's directive can be transformed into a solution that employees have discovered or at least into a decision in which they have participated. This normally leads employees to cooperate with more enthusiasm in carrying out a directive, and their morale is apt to be higher when their ideas are valued. Active participation provides an opportunity to make worthwhile contributions. Still another advantage is that participative management and general supervision permit closer communication between employees and the supervisor so that they learn to trust and respect one another. For the most part, the workplace can become more enjoyable with less tension and conflict.

Participative Management and General Supervision as a Way of Life

When practised simultaneously, participative management and general supervision are a way of life that must be followed over time. A supervisor cannot expect sudden results by introducing these types of supervision into an environment in

FIGURE 7-4   The advantages of participative management and general supervision.

FOR SUPERVISORS
- Frees the supervisor from many details, which allows time to plan, organize, and control.
- Gives the supervisor more time to assume additional responsibility.
- Instills confidence that employees will carry out the work and develop suitable approaches to making decisions on the job when the supervisor is away from the department.
- The decisions made by employees may be better than the ones made by the supervisor, because the employees are closest to the details.

FOR EMPLOYEES
- Have a chance to develop their talents and abilities by making on-the-job decisions.
- May make mistakes, but are encouraged to learn from those mistakes and the mistakes of others.
- Are motivated to take pride in their decisions.
- May feel that they have a better chance to advance to higher positions.

which employees have been accustomed to authoritarian, close supervision. It may take considerable time and patience before positive results are evident.

The successful implementation of participative management and general supervision requires a continuous effort on a supervisor's part to develop employees beyond their present skills. Employees learn more when they can work out solutions for themselves. They learn best from their own successes and failures.

The participative supervisor spends considerable time encouraging employees to solve their own problems and to participate in and make decisions. As employees become more competent and self-confident, there is less need for the supervisor to instruct and watch them. A valid way to gauge the effectiveness of a supervisor is to study how employees in the department function when the supervisor is away from the job. This is the essence of employee empowerment.

While supervisors may use participative management and general supervision whenever possible, from time to time they will have to demonstrate some authority with those employees who require close supervision. Participative and general supervisors must be as performance conscious as any other type of supervisor. However, the style they use differentiates them from their more authoritarian counterparts.

6	**INTRODUCING CHANGE**

Suggest approaches for introducing change to employees and for proposing change to higher-level managers.

Change is expected as part of everyday life, and the survival and growth of most enterprises depend on change and innovation. Many books and articles have been written concerning the imperatives for change faced by most organizations. Indeed, it is recognized that the survival of a firm may depend on the abilities of its managers to make fundamental changes in virtually all aspects of operations while facing the risks of an uncertain future. The impact of change has become so commonplace that security and stability often are referred to as being concepts and practices related to the past.[10]

Making Change Means Supervisory Involvement

Our focus in the remaining part of this chapter is not to discuss comprehensive strategies for total organizational change.[11] Rather, it is to discuss the introduction and management of change from the supervisory perspective, which is another challenging aspect of a supervisor's leading function of management. As with so many other areas of concern, the introduction of change—such as a new work method, a new product, a new schedule, or a new human resources policy—usually requires implementation at the departmental level. In the final analysis, whether a change has been initiated by higher management or by the supervisor personally, it is the supervisor who has the major role in bringing about the change. The success or failure of any change is usually related to a supervisor's ability to anticipate and address the causes of resistance to change that are often present.

Reasons for Resistance to Change

Some supervisors are inclined to discount the existence and magnitude of human resistance to change. What may seem like a trifling change to the supervisor may bring strong reaction from the employees. Supervisors should remember that employees seldom resist change just to be stubborn. They resist because they believe a change threatens their positions socially, psychologically, or economically. Therefore, the supervisor should be familiar with the ways in which resistance to change can be minimized and handled successfully.

Most people pride themselves on being up to date. As consumers, they expect and welcome changes in material things such as new automobiles, convenience items, electronic appliances, or computers. But as employees, they may resist changes on the job or changes in personal relationships even though such changes are vital for the operation of the organization. If an organization is to survive, it must be able to react to prevailing conditions by implementing necessary adjustments.

Change disturbs the environment in which people exist. Prior to a change, employees become accustomed to a work environment in which patterns of relationships and behaviour have reached a degree of stability. When a change takes place, new ideas and new methods may be perceived as a threat to the security of the work group. Many employees fear change because they cannot predict what the change will mean in terms of their own positions, activities, or abilities. It makes no difference whether the change actually has a negative result. What matters is that the employees believe that the change will cause negative consequences.

For example, the introduction of new equipment is usually accompanied by employee fears of loss of jobs or skills. Even if the supervisor and higher-level managers announce that no employees will be laid off, rumours may circulate that layoffs will occur or existing jobs will be downgraded. Employee fears may still be present months after the change has been in place.

Changes affect individuals in different ways. A change that causes great disturbance to one person may create only a small problem for another. A supervisor must learn to recognize how changes affect different employees and observe how individuals develop patterns of behaviour that serve as barriers to accepting change.

Reducing Resistance to Change

Probably the most important factor in gaining employee acceptance of new ideas and methods is the personal relationship that exists between the supervisor who is introducing the change and the employees who are affected by it. If a relationship of confidence and trust exists, the employees are more likely to accept the change with minimal resistance.[12]

Provide Adequate Information

In the final analysis, it is not the change itself that usually leads to resistance. Rather, it is the manner in which the supervisor introduces the change. Thus, resistance to change that comes from fear of the unknown can be minimized by supplying all the information that the employees consciously and subconsciously need to know to minimize their fears.

Whenever possible, a supervisor should explain what will happen and why, and how the employees and the department will be affected by a change. If applicable, the supervisor should emphasize how the change will leave employees no worse off or may even improve their present situation. This information should be communicated to all employees who are directly or indirectly involved, either individually or collectively, and as early as appropriate. Only then can employees assess what a change will mean in terms of their activities.

Employee involvement is the key to overcoming resistance to change.

Corel Corporation

Employees who are well acquainted with the underlying factors that surround departmental operations usually understand the necessity for change. They probably will ask questions about a change but they then can adjust to it and go on. When employees have been informed of the reasons for a change, what to expect, and how their jobs will be affected, they usually make reasonable adaptations. Instead of insecurity, they experience feelings of relative confidence and willing compliance.

However, if the change definitely will involve closing certain operations and the loss of jobs, the impact of the change should be explained openly and frankly. It is especially important to discuss which employees are likely to be affected and how the job cuts will be made. If higher-level managers have decided not to identify which individuals will be terminated until it actually happens, the supervisor should explain this as a reality and not try to hide behind vague promises or raise unrealistic expectations.

Encourage Participation in Decision Making

Another technique for reducing resistance to change is to permit the employees affected by the change to share in making decisions about it. If several employees are involved in a change, group decision making is an effective way to reduce their fears and objections. When employees have an opportunity to work through new ideas and methods from the beginning, usually they will consider the change as something of their own making and give their support. The group may even apply pressure on those who have reservations about going along with the change, and it is likely that each member of the group will carry out the change once there is agreement on how to proceed.

Group decision making is especially effective when the supervisor is indifferent about the details as long as the change is implemented. In these cases, the supervisor must set the limits within which the group can operate and then turn the rest of the process over to the employees. For example, a supervisor may not care how a new departmental work schedule is divided among the group as long as the work is accomplished within a prescribed time, with a given number of employees, and without overtime.

Proposing Change to Higher-Level Managers

In many organizations, higher-level managers complain that supervisors are too content with the status quo and are unwilling to suggest new and innovative ways of improving departmental performance. Supervisors, on the other hand, complain that higher-level managers are not receptive to ideas that they have suggested for their departments. There is probably some truth to both allegations.

If supervisors wish to propose changes, it is important that they understand how to present ideas not only to their employees but also to higher-level managers. "Selling" an idea to a manager involves the art of persuasion, much as a good salesperson uses persuasion in selling a product or service to a customer.

Obtain Needed Information

A supervisor who has a good idea or who wishes to suggest a change should first ask, "What aspects of the idea or change will be of most interest to the boss?" Higher-level managers usually are interested if a change might improve production, increase profits, improve morale, or reduce overhead and other costs. It is important to do considerable homework to see whether a proposed change is feasible and adaptable to the departmental operation. By carefully thinking through the idea and getting as much information as possible, the supervisor will be in a better position to discuss the strong and weak points of the proposal. In addition, the supervisor should find out whether any other departments or organizations have used the proposed idea—either successfully or unsuccessfully. Doing this will impress the manager that the supervisor has invested time and effort in researching the idea in other work environments.

Consult with Other Supervisors

To get an idea or proposal beyond the discussion stage, the supervisor should consult with other supervisors and personnel who might be affected and get their reactions to the proposed change. Consultation gives them a chance to think the idea through, offer suggestions and criticisms, and work out some of the problems. Otherwise some supervisors may resist or resent the change if they feel they have been ignored.

If possible, it is helpful to get the tentative commitment of other supervisors. It is not always necessary to obtain their total approval, but higher-level managers will be more inclined to consider an idea if it has been discussed at least in preliminary form with knowledgeable people in the organization.

Formal Written Proposal

At times, a supervisor may be asked by a manager to put a proposed idea in writing, so that copies may be forwarded to higher-level managers, other supervisors, or other personnel. This requires effort. The supervisor may have to engage in considerable study outside normal working hours to obtain all the information needed. Relevant information on costs, prices, productivity data, and the like should be included in the proposal even if some data are only educated guesses. Highly uncertain estimates should be labelled as tentative, and exaggerated claims and opinions should be avoided. Risks, as well as potential advantages, should be acknowledged in the formal proposal.

Formal Presentation

If a supervisor is asked to make a formal presentation of the proposal to a committee or at a meeting, ample planning and preparation are required. The presentation should be made thoroughly and in an unhurried fashion, allowing sufficient time for questions and discussion.

A supervisor who has carefully thought through an idea should not be afraid to express it in a firm and convincing manner. The supervisor should be enthusiastic in explaining the idea, but at the same time be patient and empathetic with those who may not agree with it. A helpful technique in a formal presentation is to utilize some type of chart, diagram, or visual aid to dramatize it.

Acceptance or Rejection of Change by Higher-Level Managers

A supervisor who is able to persuade higher-level managers and other supervisors to accept a proposed change will feel inner satisfaction. Of course, any good idea requires careful implementation, follow-up, and refinement. Rarely does a change follow the exact blueprint suggested. Following up and working out the problems with others are important aspects of making a change effective.

Despite a supervisor's best efforts, the idea may be rejected, altered greatly, or shelved. This can be frustrating, particularly to a supervisor who has worked diligently to develop an idea that he or she believes would lead to positive results. The important thing here is to avoid becoming discouraged and developing a negative outlook. There may be valid reasons the idea was rejected, or the timing may not have been right. A supervisor should resolve to try again, perhaps to further refine and polish the idea for resubmission at a future date.

A supervisor who has developed an idea for change, even if it has not been accepted, usually will find that such efforts were appreciated by higher-level managers. Moreover, the experience of having worked through a proposal for change will make the supervisor a more valuable member of the organizational team, and there will be many other opportunities to work for the introduction of change.

SUMMARY

Supervisors spend the majority of their time leading. Supervisory leadership primarily resides in the ability of the supervisor to influence the opinions, attitudes, and performance of employees to accomplish organizational goals. The test of supervisory leadership is whether employees follow willingly. Supervisory leadership skills can be developed through practice, reading, and consulting with experienced leaders.

Several different thoughts on leadership have been identified and discussed in this chapter. Warren Bennis categorized four things people want from their leaders: (1) direction, (2) trust, (3) hope, and (4) results. Stephen Covey believes that the principle of alignment is essential for developing trust. James Kouzes and Barry Posner believe that successful leaders exhibit a series of five practices: (1) challenging the process, (2) inspiring a shared vision, (3) enabling others to act, (4) modelling the way, and (5) encouraging the heart. The chapter's Contemporary Issue box provides thoughts about "servant-leadership." The common threads are creating a corporate vision, communicating honestly with employees, holding employees accountable, and engendering mutual trust and respect. In addition, managers must develop a culture in which subordinates buy into the organization's purpose and values. Although no one supervisory leadership style is universally acceptable, the need to establish standards and develop a climate in which people are self-motivated and adapt to constant change are key traits of effective leaders.

The process of delegation is made up of three components: (1) assigning a job or duties, (2) granting authority, and (3) creating responsibility. For delegation to succeed, supervisors must give employees enough authority and responsibility to carry out their assigned duties. All three components are interdependent in that a change in one requires a corresponding change in the other two.

The supervisor must be specific in telling employees what authority they have and what they can and cannot do. The supervisor delegates authority to employees to accomplish specific jobs, but the supervisor's own accountability cannot be delegated.

 Included among the many reasons supervisors are reluctant to delegate are shortage of qualified employees, fear of making mistakes, the "I'd-rather-do-it-myself" mentality, fear of not being needed, reluctant employees, and lack of managerial support for decisions.

Effective supervisors see the benefits of delegation. Employees become more involved and gain knowledge and confidence in their skills. The supervisor benefits from greater flexibility, better decisions, higher employee morale, and better job performance.

 Participative management and general supervision promote delegation because they provide employees with considerable involvement in making decisions and doing their jobs to meet departmental objectives. These techniques offer many advantages to supervisors as well as employees. The supervisor saves time in the long term. By giving employees practice in making decisions and using their own judgment, the supervisor encourages employees to become more competent and more promotable.

Some supervisors believe that autocratic supervision is more likely than participative management or general supervision to get results from employees. While there are occasions when supervisors have to rely on their managerial authority, these should, for the most part, be the exceptions rather than the rule.

 To successfully cope with employees' normal resistance to change, supervisors must understand why resistance surfaces and what can be done to help employees adjust and accept necessary changes. A supervisor should also learn the principles of "selling" change to higher-level managers. This typically involves persuading the immediate superiors, higher-level managers, and other supervisors that the acceptance of a proposal will benefit them and the total organization.

QUESTIONS FOR DISCUSSION

1. Explain the concepts of responsibility, authority, and accountability and explain how they are closely related.
2. Identify the three steps of delegating successfully.
3. Explain why some supervisors are reluctant to delegate. Which, if any, are valid reasons why a supervisor should not delegate?
4. When the supervisor delegates effectively, what benefits can accrue to both the supervisor and the departmental employees?
5. Distinguish between autocratic (authoritarian) supervision on the one hand and participative management and general supervision on the other. What theoretical differences are implied in each of these approaches?
6. Is autocratic supervision always negative in its consequences? Why or why not?

7. Why are employee attitudes and expectations important if participative management is to be successful?
8. How does general supervision differ from "no supervision" (i.e., free-rein or *laissez-faire* style)?
9. Discuss the statement, "When practised simultaneously, participative management and general supervision are a way of life that must be followed over a period of time."
10. What are some of the advantages to supervisors and employees when participative management and general supervision are practised?
11. Discuss supervisory strategies for the effective introduction of change to employees.
12. Discuss the principles of proposing change to higher-level managers.

SKILLS APPLICATIONS

Skills Application 7-1: The Empire Club of Canada—Where Leaders Speak

Established in 1903, The Empire Club of Canada describes itself as "one of Canada's oldest and largest speakers' forums with a membership comprising some of Canada's most influential leaders from the professions, business, labour, education, and government." Over its history it has been addressed by more than 2,500 prominent Canadian and international leaders—men and women who have distinguished themselves in many fields of endeavour. Every Thursday from September to June, 200 to 1,000 Empire Club members and guests gather in Toronto to hear a prominent speaker. The text of these speeches, dating back to 1903, are available on the club's website, and provide an interesting historical record of important ideas that were being discussed by leaders at various times in Canada's history.

1. On 3 October 1991, Anita Roddick, president and founder of Body Shops International, addressed The Empire Club and talked about her views on business and leadership. Access the text of Roddick's speech at www.empireclub.org. Click the link to "The Speeches," type in "Roddick" as the speaker's name, and then click the link to the "full text" of the speech. Based on this speech, how would you classify Roddick's management style? What specific clues lead you to this conclusion?
2. On 15 April 1999, Marguerite Hale, Chair of Morrison Lamothe Inc., spoke to The Empire Club. Morrison Lamothe Inc. is Canada's largest manufacturer of frozen prepared foods and an award-winning supplier of "President's Choice" line of prepared foods. In 1998, Marguerite Hale was named "Canadian Woman Entrepreneur of the Year" in honour of her lifetime business achievement. Access the text of Hale's speech using the procedure described above and, using the concepts discussed in this chapter, comment on her leadership style.

Skills Application 7-2: Supervisory Styles

After reading each of the following scenarios, identify the type of supervisory style (i.e., autocratic supervision or participative management and general supervision) that you feel would be preferable, and why. Assume that for each scenario, only 10 individuals report directly to you at any one time.

Scenario 1: You are a supervisor in charge of work crews who lay track for a railroad line. Their basic duties are to lay railroad ties and secure the track to the ties.

Scenario 2: You are a supervisor in charge of a cancer research project in a pharmaceutical firm. The duties of your personnel vary greatly due to the experimental nature of the project. You supervise chemists, biologists, and technicians.

Scenario 3: You supervise a word-processing centre that provides numerous clerical and other services for a company of 300 employees. The work flow is extremely erratic. Some days there is little work, while on others there is an overload.

SKILLS DEVELOPMENT

Skills Development Module 7-1: Delegation

This video segment introduces Tony Roberts, the newly appointed supervisor in the accounting department at Lexicon Dynamics.

Questions for Discussion: The Ineffective Version

1. Discuss how Tony Roberts did not delegate and how it affected his department.
2. What should Roberts do to be more effective as department supervisor?
3. Explain why good communication skills are important for effective leadership.
4. In your opinion, how has the upper-level management at Lexicon Dynamics failed Roberts?

Questions for Discussion: The More Effective Version

1. Is Tony Roberts an effective supervisor? Why or why not?
2. How could Roberts do a better job of leading his subordinates?
3. Which of the leadership concepts in this chapter should Roberts know more about? Why?
4. Would you like to work for a supervisor like Roberts? Why or why not?

CASES

CASE 7-1

The Supervisor Who "Pitched In"

Anita Mathews has worked in the billing department of Concord Cable TV for 10 years. Two years ago she was promoted to supervisor of a data-processing section that sends cable television bills to customers. In a recent merger, Concord Cable acquired a smaller cable television operator in a neighbouring region. The billing department of the other company was eliminated, and Mathews's department was expected to handle all billing responsibilities without additional personnel. After integrating the different systems, the department still had an unusually large amount of work. To get the work done, Mathews decided to help. She now spends between two and four hours a day operating one of the statement collating machines to help get the statements out.

On a number of occasions Mathews has asked employees, individually and collectively, for their suggestions and opinions concerning what should be done. She has avoided giving direct orders and has tried to suggest to employees what needs to be done rather than spelling out the directions in detail. A number of years ago, her mentor suggested that her supervisory style should be one that "provides objectives and guidance rather than providing directions." Generally, the work performance of Mathews's four employees is good, and there is excellent camaraderie among the group members. However, this morning, one of the employees, Nancy Chan, complained about the workload and questioned whether any relief was on the way. Mathews understands how Chan feels but knows that the chances are slim that she will be authorized to post or recruit for additional help.

Mathews has neglected none of her supervisory duties, but while she is operating the machine, she is doing nothing else. This morning as she was operating one of the machines, she thought to herself, "I'm just swamped. This is our busiest time of the year. We're always behind and I don't know how much longer they can take the pressure." The continual battle of juggling family and work responsibilities has taken its toll on Mathews. She knows she is overloaded, and she is spending more time at work than ever before.

Art Roberts, Mathews's supervisor, has just returned from a long out-of-town trip. He does not yet know of her decision to help employees by running one of the machines. Mathews had planned to discuss this with him two days from now, which was the soonest she could schedule a meeting with him. However, Roberts came looking for her only a few hours after he was back in the office because he wanted to discuss some problems. As a result, he found Mathews operating a machine and not in her office. He became annoyed and called Mathews into his office. He proceeded to lecture Mathews, stating that it was a supervisor's job to get things done through and with people, and that did not mean she should be doing the work of the employees when the department is shorthanded. He accused her of neglecting her supervisory duties, and said that if she couldn't be a real leader he would find someone else who could do the job.

Mathews listened patiently to Roberts's statements and pondered her response.

Questions for Discussion

1. Evaluate Mathews' decision to assist her employees with their work. Should she have been operating the statement collating machines at all?
2. What options were available to Mathews when it first became apparent that her department was overloaded?
3. What should Mathews do now? What are her options if management refuses to hire additional staff?

CASE 7-2

Resistance to a Total Quality Management Plan

Merrill Dawe, plant manager of a major food processing plant, had attended a meeting of an industry association in which he had been impressed by several presentations on total quality management (TQM) and labour-management participation teams. Dawe was convinced that such approaches would be very appropriate in his plant, since he felt they could help improve the employee relations climate and perhaps assist in improving productivity and reducing quality problems. Dawe decided to call a number of his supervisors, along with the local union president and several of the plant's union shop stewards, to his office to discuss his plans to implement TQM. At the meeting in his office, Dawe outlined what he proposed to do. He said that he planned to have TQM meetings on a periodic basis, probably once a month, in which various departmental employee groups and committees, along with their supervisors, would discuss production problems, quality problems, and any other problems that needed attention. Dawe emphasized that employees would be paid for the time they spent in these meetings and that any ideas and suggestions would be given consideration and attention by supervisors and higher-level managers.

After listening patiently to Dawe's presentation, Jerry Bruno, the plant's local union president, responded as follows: "Mr. Dawe, our national and local union have heard about TQM and efforts of this nature. In general, we're skeptical about being part of them. We've heard that many companies simply use these as a way of trying to bypass the union contract and the grievance procedure. We feel that this can be just another tactic to lull employees into thinking that management is concerned about them. Frankly, I'd bet that TQM meetings will be little more than a place where the workers will say what's on their minds, and then company management will continue to ignore their concerns. Unless I'm convinced—and my fellow union representatives are convinced—that any such program in this plant will not be used to ignore the union and our labour agreement, we will not cooperate with you in this effort."

Dawe pondered how he should respond to Bruno's comments and whether he should seriously attempt to implement a TQM program.

Questions for Discussion

1. Evaluate how Dawe presented his ideas for a TQM program in the company plant. How might he have approached this in a way that would have gained greater support from the employees and the union? Discuss.
2. Evaluate the response of Bruno, the local union president. Can his objections be overcome in a short period of time?
3. At the end of the case, what should Dawe do? On the assumption that he decides to continue with the implementation of a TQM program, outline a series of steps or recommendations that would be helpful in overcoming union and worker opposition and making the program a worthwhile investment of time and management attention.

Chapter 8: Communication—The Vital Link in Supervisory Management

After studying this chapter you will be able to

1 Define communication and discuss its implications for effective supervisory management.

2 Discuss the major channels of communication available to the supervisor.

3 Explain the benefits of the various methods of communication.

4 Identify and discuss barriers to effective communication.

5 Describe ways to overcome communication barriers.

You are Paul Vaught, supervisor of the engineering group at Barry Automotive's Oshawa plant. While segments of the automotive industry have been in a slump, the Oshawa plant has been a beehive of optimism. New business and increased orders from existing customers have kept your group busy. Besides your company's day-to-day engineering work, your group is responsible for developing new products, improving existing products, and continuously improving production processes. Though your group is small—only five people—it has been very productive and contributed a great deal since its inception. Unfortunately, it is very underresourced.

As a quick but temporary fix, management consented to allow you to add one full-time engineering co-op student to your group. Vikram Kamil was selected from a group of very talented candidates. He was in the top percentile of his class in one of the top-ranked mechanical engineering programs in the country. During Kamil's first two months, everyone was impressed with his performance and his abundant energy.

After Kamil spent two months being mentored and shadowing key personnel, you decided to give Kamil his first real engineering challenge. Linda Burns, the lead operator on Line 14, had decided to run some trial (prototype) products on her line. Burns had been with the company for over 20 years and was one of the best operators on the production floor. She had been having production problems since the introduction of the prototype products on her line. In the past, Burns had asked for help resolving these production problems but, because of priorities elsewhere, you had been unable to assign anyone to investigate the problem. You introduced Kamil to Burns and the others on Line 14 and advised Kamil to coordinate with the production scheduler and Burns to manage time to run the prototypes.

For the past week, however, every time Kamil wanted to run a prototype, Burns refused to cooperate, saying she was more concerned about her regular production runs. On Wednesday, Kamil mentioned to you he was having problems, but you had been busy with a potential new customer visit and other priority issues. On Friday, you decided to meet with Jim Abrams, Burns's immediate supervisor, and Burns to discuss the prototype runs. Kamil was unable to attend the meeting because he was back at university attending a required co-op meeting.

According to Abrams and Burns, Kamil failed to communicate with Burns properly. As the conversation continued, you detected that part of the problem might stem from Burns's bias toward Kamil. Burns made it clear that she did not appreciate having to "babysit some know-it-all student." It became clear to you that a common ground had not been established between the two.

As you left work for what should have been a relaxing weekend, you begin to reflect on what you could have done differently, and, more important, what you could do now to get Burns and Kamil on the same page.

You make the call!

1

Define communication and discuss its implications for effective supervisory management.

NEED FOR EFFECTIVE COMMUNICATION

Communication

The process of transmitting information and understanding.

Communication is the process of transmitting information and understanding from one person to another. Effective communication means that there is a successful transfer of information, meaning, and understanding from a sender to a receiver. In other words, communication is the process of imparting ideas and making oneself understood by others. While it is not necessary to have agreement, there must be a mutual understanding for the exchange of ideas to be successful.

Most supervisory activities involve interaction with others, and each interaction requires skillful handling of the information process. The ability to communicate effectively is a key to supervisory success. Communication is the process that links all managerial functions. In managing their departments, supervisors must explain the arrangement of work. They must instruct employees, describe what is expected of them, and counsel them. Supervisors must also report to their managers, both orally and in writing, and discuss plans with other supervisors. All of these activities require communication.

Studies have indicated that supervisors generally spend between 70 and 90 percent of their time sending and receiving information. With the advent of electronic forms of communication and other convenient means of information flow, it seems that communication problems should be diminishing. Yet, supervisors still see communication difficulties as their most persistent challenge. A study called "Messaging Practices in the Knowledge Economy" was conducted in Canada, Germany, the United Kingdom, and the United States. The study revealed that an average office worker in Canada sends and receives 169 messages a day. These communications (via e-mail, voice mail, telephone calls, and paper-based memos, letters, etc.) create a significant workload, with 28 percent of the Canadian workers surveyed reporting that they "feel overwhelmed by the volume of messages exchanged daily."[1] The communication volume also creates constant interruptions. Of the survey respondents, "51 per cent experience six or more interruptions per hour, and 30 per cent are 'distracted' or 'very distracted' by the interruptions."[2] This escalation of communication, especially via e-mail, also raises important questions about privacy and ownership (see Contemporary Issue box). It appears that, while we are sending and receiving more messages than ever before, we may actually be communicating less effectively.

CONTEMPORARY ISSUE
Whose E-mail Is It Anyway? Check Your Corporate Policy

Internet and e-mail use in Canadian businesses continues to escalate. According to a 2000 Statistics Canada study, 63 percent of businesses use the Internet and 60 percent use e-mail.[1] For many employees, Internet and e-mail access is an essential part of their day-to-day life on the job.

But where there is e-mail and Internet use, there is potential for abuse, and Canadian organizations are waking up to the fact that what their employees do at their computers could place the organization at risk. "For example, employers are being held liable in courts for their employees' illegal use of office computers, such as transmitting child pornography."[2] Other employers have suffered embarrass-

(continued)

ment when e-mail messages intended for internal "eyes" only have somehow gone public. Even Bill Gates had his own e-mail used against him in Microsoft's highly publicized anti-trust hearings. Illegal activity aside, Canadian organizations are, at the very least, susceptible to tremendous productivity losses when employees use the Internet and e-mail for personal use on company time.

For some companies, electronic "surveillance" has become the answer to the risks associated with inappropriate employee use of the Internet and e-mail. Despite the illusion of privacy afforded by individual log-in passwords, the employer can electronically monitor which websites employees are visiting and "tap into" employee e-mail accounts—and do it legally. To date, Canadian case law upholds the notion that "e-mail sent and received on corporate equipment on employer-paid time belongs to the employer. Although of an intangible nature, email is employer property in the same way as personal effects at home belong to their owner."[3] While some people view e-mail to be very similar to using the telephone, the law does not agree. Under the Criminal Code of Canada, the interception of private telephone calls is an indictable offence. An employer may monitor employee telephone calls, but must first make it explicitly clear "so that the employees do not expect these calls to be private. As of yet, however, the Criminal Code provisions only apply to oral communications"[4] and not to electronic messages.

Many employees would be shocked to learn how much access their employer has to their "electronic life" on the job. A deleted e-mail can live on long after most people think it's gone. "There are several e-mail forensic experts who specialize in restoring deleted electronic messages and documents from magnetic tapes that have been overwritten several times."[5] These retrieved e-mail messages can (and have) been used as evidence in legal proceedings to support termination decisions and in other legal matters. A good rule of thumb, it appears, is that "if you know that you wouldn't want a particular e-mail message coming back to haunt you, then you probably shouldn't use e-mail to communicate the idea—pick up the phone."[6]

If an employer decides that monitoring e-mail and Internet use is needed to protect the organization's business interests, it is important that this monitoring is widely publicized to employees in the form of a corporate policy. While the law upholds the fact that electronic communication belongs to the employer, the employer should "address the potential impact that monitoring will have on the morale and dignity of its employees and how this will affect productivity and employee loyalty."[7] If there is a strong business case for this monitoring, then the surveillance should be limited to what is reasonably required to achieve the company's objective. A clearly worded and widely circulated computer use policy must be drafted. Employees should sign a copy of the policy to acknowledge that they understand that they are to expect decreased privacy in the workplace. In addition to guidelines about acceptable use of Internet and e-mail communications, the policy should also address the issue of e-mail retention—what messages should be retained by employees and for how long? This is particularly important if the company is subject to legal proceedings or, as in the case of government, is subject to requests for information under access-to-information legislation.

Should any personal use of Internet and e-mail be permitted at the workplace? Employers seem to acknowledge that some degree of personal electronic communication is to be expected on the job, "viewing it as an inevitable trade-off for the long hours their employees put in."[8] After all, an employee who has to work late might gain considerable peace of mind if he or she can send off a quick e-mail to a child—and take considerably less time doing it than if he or she called home. But there have to be guidelines. For example, there have been cases in which employees have been found to be using company time and computers to help run their own sideline businesses. Employees need to know what is and is not acceptable in terms of use of the company's electronic communication channels. The corporate policy must clearly address whether personal use of organizational computer resources are permitted and to what degree. A corporate policy is a must!

Sources: (1) Statistics Canada www.statcan.ca/english/research/56F0004MIE/56F0004MIE2001005.pdf (retrieved November 19, 2003); (2) "Privacy of E-Mail and Internet Use in the Workplace," *Labour Notes* (October 18, 1999); (3) Peter Bowal, "Stealing Time: It's in the Electronic Mail!" *Law Now* (October/November 1999), pp. 33–36; (4) "Privacy of E-Mail ..."; (5) Alex Du, "E-mail opens organizations to legal liabilities," *Computing Canada* (October 8, 1999), p. 13, 15; (6) Ibid; (7) "Privacy of E-Mail ..."; (8) Katie Hafner, "Your only e-mail's at work. Then you lose your job." *National Post* (June 27, 2003) p. PM 10F. See also Jim Carroll, "What Evil Lurks in E-Mail?" *CA Magazine* (July/July 2003) p. 16 and Reid Kanaley, "Resisting computer surveillance: Employees assume they have a right to privacy at work. Well that's not the case, as many firms monitor e-mail and Net use," *Financial Post/National Post* (September 10, 1999) p. C14.

Effective Communication Requires a Two-Way Exchange

Earlier in the chapter we defined communication as a process of transmitting information and understanding from one person to another. The significant point is that communication always involves at least two people, a sender and a receiver. For example, a supervisor who is alone in a room and verbally states a set of instructions does not communicate because there are no receivers present. While the lack of communication is obvious in this case, it may not be so obvious to a supervisor who sends an e-mail. Once the e-mail has been sent, the supervisor may believe that communication has taken place. However, this supervisor has not really communicated until and unless the e-mail has been received and read, and information and understanding have been transferred successfully to the recipient.

It cannot be emphasized too strongly that effective communication includes both sending and receiving information. A listener may hear a speaker because the listener has ears, but the listener may not understand what the speaker means. Understanding is a personal matter between people. If the idea received has the same meaning as the one intended, then we can say that effective communication has taken place. But if the idea received by a listener or reader is not the one intended, then effective communication has not been accomplished. The sender has merely transmitted spoken or written words. This does not mean that the sender and receiver must agree on a particular message or issue; it is possible to communicate and yet not agree.

Effective Communication Means Better Supervision

Some supervisors are more effective communicators than others. Usually these supervisors recognize that communication is vital, and they give it their major attention. Unfortunately, many supervisors simply assume that they know how to communicate, and they do not work at developing their communication skills.[3] Yet a supervisor's effectiveness will depend greatly on the ability to transfer information and ideas to employees. The employees must understand the supervisor's instructions to achieve their objectives. Similarly, the supervisor must know how to receive information and understand the messages sent by employees, other supervisors, and higher-level managers. Fortunately, the skills of effective communication can be developed. By using the techniques and suggestions in this chapter, you can become a more effective communicator and, ultimately, a more effective supervisor.

2	CHANNELS OF THE COMMUNICATION NETWORK

Discuss the major channels of communication available to the supervisor.

In every organization the communication network has two primary and equally important channels: (1) the formal, or official, channels of communication and (2) the informal channels, usually called the *grapevine*. Both channels carry messages from one person or group to another. In organizations, communication travels downward, upward, and horizontally through the formal and informal channels.

Formal Channels

Formal communication channels are established primarily by the organizational structure. The vertical formal channels can be visualized by following the lines of authority from the top-level executive down through the organization to supervisors and front-line employees.

Downward Communication

The concept of a downward formal channel of communication suggests that someone at the top issues instructions or disseminates information that managers at the next level in the hierarchy pass on to their subordinates, and so on down the line. The downward direction is the channel most frequently used by higher-level managers for communication. Downward communication helps to tie different levels together and is important for coordination. It is used by managers to start action by subordinates and to communicate instructions, objectives, policies, procedures, and other information to them. Generally, downward communication is mostly of an informative and directive nature and requires action on the part of subordinates. Downward communication from a supervisor involves giving instructions, explaining information and procedures, training employees, and engaging in other types of activities designed to guide employees in performing their work.

Upward Communication

Upward is an equally important direction of communication in the official or formal network. Supervisors who have managerial authority accept an obligation to keep their superiors informed and to contribute their own ideas to management.

No one knows the problems and possible solutions to those problems better than the employees who are doing the work.

Corel Corporation

Similarly, employees should feel free to convey their ideas to their supervisors and to report on activities related to their work. Managers and supervisors should encourage a free flow of upward communication.

Upward communication usually is of an informing and reporting nature, including questions, suggestions, and complaints. This is a vital means by which managers can obtain valuable insights from employees about problems and opportunities facing a unit. For example, by directing information upward through the formal channel, employees may report production results and also present ideas for increasing production in the future.

Supervisors should encourage upward communication among employees and give ample attention to the information transmitted. Supervisors must show that they want employee suggestions as well as the facts and then must evaluate and respond to them promptly. No one really knows the problems—and possible solutions—better than the employees doing the work.[4] To tap into this important source of information, supervisors must convey a genuine desire to obtain and use the ideas suggested by employees. The key word is *probe:* ask questions such as "How can we improve?" "What can we do better?" "What if …?" "What will make it work?" Effective supervisors will develop good rapport with their employees and other stakeholder groups—really listen to their ideas and suggestions—and act upon their suggestions. A supervisor who develops effective information-getting skills will win the respect and admiration of colleagues and employees.

Most supervisors will agree that it is often easier for them to converse with subordinates than to speak with their own manager. This is particularly true if they have ever had to tell their manager that they did not meet a schedule or that they made a mistake. Nevertheless, it is a supervisory duty to advise the manager whenever there are significant developments and to do this as soon as possible, either before or after such events occur. It is quite embarrassing to a manager to learn important news elsewhere. The manager can interpret this to mean that either the supervisor is not on top of his or her responsibilities or, even worse, that the supervisor is deliberately hiding important information.

Higher-level managers need to have complete information because they retain overall responsibility for organizational performance. Of course, this does not mean that supervisors need to pass upward every bit of trivial information. Rather, it means that supervisors should mentally place themselves in their managers' position and consider what information their managers need to perform their own jobs properly.

A supervisor's upward communication should be sent on time and in a form that will enable the manager to take necessary action. The supervisor should assemble and check the facts before passing them on. This may be quite difficult at times. A natural inclination is to "soften" the information a bit so that things will not look quite as bad in the manager's eyes as they actually are. However, when difficulties arise, it is best to tell the manager what is really going on even if this means admitting mistakes. Higher-level managers depend on the supervisor for reliable upward communication, just as the supervisor depends on his or her employees for the upward flow of information.

Horizontal Communication

There is a third direction of formal communication that is essential for the efficient functioning of an organization. This is lateral, or horizontal, communication, which is concerned mainly with communication between departments or people at the same levels but in charge of different functions. A free flow of horizontal communication is needed to coordinate functions among various departments.

Horizontal communication typically involves discussions and meetings to accomplish tasks that cross departmental lines. For example, a production manager may have to contact managers of the marketing and shipping departments to ascertain progress on a delivery schedule for a product. Or someone from the human resources department may have a meeting with a number of supervisors to discuss how a new medical leave policy is to be implemented at the departmental level. Still another example is the cashier who pages the stock clerk to inquire when a particular item will be available. Without effective horizontal communication, any organization would find it virtually impossible to coordinate specialized departmental efforts toward common goals.

Informal Channels—The Grapevine

Informal communication channels, referred to in Chapter 4 as the grapevine, are a normal outgrowth of informal and casual groupings of people on the job, of their social interactions, and of their understandable desire to communicate with one another. Every organization has its grapevine. This is a perfectly natural activity since it fulfills the employees' desires to know the latest information and to socialize with other people. The grapevine offers members of an organization an outlet for their imaginations and an opportunity to express their apprehensions in the form of rumours.

Understanding the Grapevine

The grapevine can offer considerable insight into what employees think and feel. An alert supervisor acknowledges the grapevine's presence and tries to take advantage of it whenever possible. The grapevine often carries factual information, but sometimes it carries half-truths, rumours, private interpretations, suspicions, and other bits of distorted or inaccurate information. Research indicates that many employees have more faith and confidence in the grapevine than in what their supervisors tell them.[5] In part, this reflects a natural human tendency to trust one's peers to a greater degree than people in authority, such as supervisors or upper-level managers.

The grapevine has no definite patterns or stable membership. Its workings cannot be predicted since the path followed yesterday is not necessarily the same as today or tomorrow. The vast majority of employees hear information through the grapevine but some do not pass it along. Any person within an organization may become active in the grapevine on occasion, although some individuals tend to be more active than others. They feel that their prestige is enhanced by providing the latest news, and they do not hesitate to spread and embellish upon the news. The rumours they pass on serve, in part, as a release for their emotions, providing an opportunity to remain anonymous and say what they please without the danger of being held accountable.

The grapevine sometimes helps clarify and supplement formal communications, and it often spreads information that could not be disseminated as well or as rapidly through official channels.

The Supervisor and the Grapevine

The supervisor should accept the fact that it is impossible to eliminate the grapevine. It is unrealistic to expect that all rumours can be stamped out, and the grapevine is certain to flourish in every organization. To cope with it, supervisors should tune in on the grapevine and learn what it is saying. They should determine who its leaders are and who is likely to spread information.

Many rumours begin in the wishful-thinking stage of employee anticipation. If employees want something badly enough, they may start passing the word along to one other. For instance, if production workers want a raise, they may start the rumour that management will offer an across-the-board raise. Nobody knows for certain where or how it started, but the story spreads rapidly because everyone wants to believe it. Of course, morale will suffer when hopes are built up in anticipation of something that does not happen. If such a story is spreading and the supervisor realizes it will lead to disappointment, the supervisor ought to move quickly to refute the story by presenting the facts. The best cure for rumours is to expose the true facts to all employees and to give a straight answer to all questions whenever possible.

Other frequent causes of rumours are uncertainty and fear. If business is slack and management is forced to lay off some employees, stories multiply quickly. During periods of insecurity and anxiety, the grapevine becomes more active than at other times. The rumours are often far worse than what actually will happen. If the supervisor does not disclose the actual facts to the employees, they will make up their own "facts," which may be worse than reality. Even if the news is bad, the supervisor must communicate openly and honestly (see Figure 8-1). Much of the fear caused by uncertainty can be eliminated or reduced if the truth of what will happen is disclosed. Continuing rumours and uncertainty may be more demoralizing than even the most disappointing facts presented openly.

Especially during periods of economic uncertainty, the grapevine carries bits of distorted information that flow quickly through the organization.

Ivy Images

FIGURE 8-1   Tips for communicating bad news.

- Communicate bad news as soon as possible to reduce the likelihood that rumours will develop and that employees will hear the news through the grapevine.
- Ensure that people inside the organization are informed about major developments before the news is communicated to outsiders.
- Whenever possible, speak to everyone who is affected by the news at the same time, rather than individually. It is best that everyone hears the news directly and simultaneously so that there is no distortion of the message.
- Decide in advance what you want to communicate.
- Be direct and honest. Do not attempt to "sugarcoat" the message or to "dole out" only certain pieces of information at a time. It is best that bad news be communicated in its entirety, clearly and openly.
- For significant bad news announcements that affect an entire organization, a senior-level manager should be responsible for communicating to all staff. This ensures that a consistent message is sent out to all stakeholders.
- Think carefully about what channel of communication to use. Face-to-face meetings are usually preferred, but written or electronic messages should be considered for follow-up.
- Communicate often. After the initial announcement, plan for follow-up communication to ensure that employees are kept up to date.

Rumours also arise out of dislike, anger, or distrust. Rumours spread through the grapevine can be about such topics as the company, working conditions, or events in the private or work life of its members. Rumours, like idle gossip or storytelling, are used to break the everyday boredom of organizational life or, in some extreme cases, used to personally harm someone. Occasionally, there is an employee who grows to hate the company, the supervisor, or a fellow worker. Out of malice and ill will, that employee may fabricate a sensational story and spread it through the grapevine. Rumours start small but are quickly spread by a few others who rush to fan the flames. Even if the rumour is ultimately proven to be false, the target of the rumour may suffer from a loss of credibility or respect.

The best supervisory strategy for dispelling rumours is to state the facts openly and honestly. If the supervisor does not have all the necessary information available, he or she should frankly admit this and then try to find out what the situation actually is and report it to the employees. One of the best ways to stop a rumour is to expose its untruthfulness. The supervisor should bear in mind that the receptiveness of a group of employees to rumours is inversely related to the quality of the supervisor's communications and leadership. If employees believe that their supervisor is concerned about them and will make every effort to keep them informed, they will tend to disregard rumours and look to the supervisor for proper answers to their questions.

As stated earlier, there is no way to eliminate the grapevine, even with the best efforts made through all formal channels of communication. The supervisor, therefore, should listen to the grapevine and develop skills in dealing with it. For example, an alert supervisor might know that certain events will cause undue anxiety. In this case, the supervisor should explain immediately why such events will take place. When emergencies occur, changes are introduced, or policies are modified, the supervisor should explain why and answer all employee questions as openly as possible. Otherwise, employees will make up their own explanations, which often will be incorrect.

There are situations, however, when the supervisor does not have the facts. Here the supervisor should seek out the appropriate higher-level manager to explain what is bothering the employees and to ask for specific instructions as to what information may be given, how much may be told, and when. Also, when something happens that might cause rumours, it may be helpful for supervisors to meet with their most influential employees to give them the real story directly. Then the employees can spread the facts before anyone else can spread the rumours.[6]

| **3** | **METHODS OF COMMUNICATION** |

Explain the benefits of
the various methods of
communication.

The preceding section described the various communication flows or channels of communication. The effective supervisor must be concerned with not only the content of communication directed at others but also the context of communication. The following sections explore various methods for delivering a message.

Behaviour Is Communication

Body language
All observable actions of either the
sender or the receiver.

Supervisors should realize that their behaviour as managers on the job is an important form of communication to their subordinates. **Body language** is the observable actions of either the sender or the receiver. The supervisor's body language communicates something to employees whether it is intended to do so or not. Gestures, a handshake, a shrug of the shoulder, a smile, even silence—all of these have meaning and may be interpreted differently by different people. For example, a supervisor's warm smile and posture slightly bent toward employees can send out positive signals to the employees. Conversely, a frown on a supervisor's face may send a much stronger message than the supervisor intends or is aware of.

A word of caution: body language does not have universal meaning, as illustrated in Figure 8-2. The message sent by different expressions or postures varies from situation to situation and particularly from culture to culture. Touching, as illustrated by the traditional "pat on the back," may be perceived differently by different people.[7] A supervisor must be sensitive to the fact that physical contact and other gestures might easily be misinterpreted.

A supervisor's inaction can send a very strong message to employees. For example, suppose a supervisor failed to have a piece of equipment repaired despite numerous employee requests. To the employees, who feared a shutdown, this lack of action on the part of the supervisor would communicate a message that the supervisor had no intention of sending.

Oral and Written Communication

Spoken and written words are the most widely used forms of communication in any organization. They also constitute a challenge to every supervisor who wishes to communicate effectively. Words can be tricky. Instructions that mean

FIGURE 8-2   Olympic Games staff working with international visitors were trained in what to say and how to gesture. This illustration shows several examples.

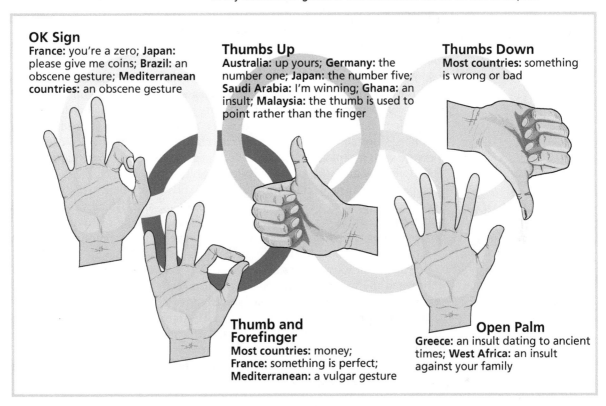

OK Sign
France: you're a zero; **Japan:** please give me coins; **Brazil:** an obscene gesture; **Mediterranean countries:** an obscene gesture

Thumbs Up
Australia: up yours; **Germany:** the number one; **Japan:** the number five; **Saudi Arabia:** I'm winning; **Ghana:** an insult; **Malaysia:** the thumb is used to point rather than the finger

Thumbs Down
Most countries: something is wrong or bad

Thumb and Forefinger
Most countries: money; **France:** something is perfect; **Mediterranean:** a vulgar gesture

Open Palm
Greece: an insult dating to ancient times; **West Africa:** an insult against your family

Source: Atlanta Committee for the Olympic Games as presented by Sam Ward, "The Olympic Don'ts of Gestures," *USA Today* (March 14, 1996), p. 7C.

one thing to one employee may have a different meaning to someone else. There is a story about a collection agency supervisor who told a new employee, "Get tough with Mr. Storm. His account is two months overdue." Upon checking an hour later, the supervisor found that the new employee had started foreclosure proceedings against Mr. Storm. Obviously, instructions such as "get tough" can be interpreted in several different ways!

Since words are the essence of oral and written communication, supervisors should constantly try to improve their skills in speaking, listening, writing, and reading. Although most messages are delivered orally, a well-balanced communication system uses both written and oral media. Supervisors do not have as many occasions to use the written medium since a high proportion of supervisory communication involves the spoken word.

Oral communication is generally superior to written communication because it facilitates better understanding and takes less time. This is true both with telephone and face-to-face communication. Face-to-face discussion between a supervisor and employees is the principal method of two-way communication. Employees like to see and hear the supervisor in person, and no written communication can be as effective as an interpersonal discussion. In a face-to-face discussion, both employees and supervisors can draw meaning from body language as well as from the oral message. Another reason for the greater effectiveness of oral communication is that most people can express themselves more easily and completely by voice than by a letter or memo.

Probably the greatest single advantage of oral communication is that it can provide an immediate opportunity for determining whether or not effective communication has been accomplished between the sender and receiver. Although the response may be only an expression on the receiver's face, the sender can judge how the receiver is reacting to what is being said. Oral communication enables the sender to determine immediately what the receiver hears and does not hear. Oral communication enables the receiver to ask questions immediately if the meaning is not clear, and the sender can clarify. The human voice can impart a message with meaning and nuances that pages of written words cannot convey. Body language and tone of voice help convey the message.

The principal problem with oral communication is that usually there is no permanent record of it, and, over time, speakers' and listeners' memories will blur the meaning of what was conveyed. This is why many supervisors follow up certain meetings and discussions with some type of memorandum or document to have a written basis for recalling what was discussed.

A supervisor must always remember that effective communication takes place only when the meaning received by the listener is the same as that which the sender intended. Supervisors who are effective communicators know how to speak clearly and be aware of the listener. They are sensitive to the many barriers to effective communication that can distort communication lines. They know how to overcome these barriers. Such supervisors recognize that a speaker and a listener are unique individuals and that many factors can interfere with messages that pass between them.

A Picture Is Worth a Thousand Words

The power of visual media in conveying meaning to people should never be underestimated. Pictures, charts, graphs, and symbols can be effective visual aids, and the supervisor should employ them where appropriate. They are particularly effective if used in connection with well-chosen words to complete a message. Businesses make extensive use of visual aids such as blueprints, charts, drafts, models, and posters to communicate information. Movies, videos, and comic strips demonstrate the power of visual media in communicating.

4   BARRIERS TO EFFECTIVE COMMUNICATION

Identify and discuss barriers to effective communication.

Noise
Obstacles that distort messages between people.

Human differences and organizational conditions can create obstacles that distort messages between people. These obstacles can be referred to as **noise**. Misunderstandings and conflicts can develop when communication breaks down. These breakdowns not only are costly in terms of money but also create dilemmas that hurt teamwork and morale. Many supervisory human relations problems are traceable to faulty communication. The way a supervisor communicates with subordinates constitutes the essence of their relationships.

Language and Vocabulary Differences

People vary greatly in their ability to convey meaning that others understand. For example, words in themselves can be confusing. People at different levels or in different departments sometimes seem to speak in different "languages" even though they are actually speaking English.[8] For example, an accounting department supervisor may use specialized words that may be meaningless when conversing with the plant manager. Similarly, if the plant manager uses highly technical engineering terms when conversing with the accounting supervisor, the latter will probably be confused. This is the communication problem known as **jargon,** or the use of words that are peculiar to a person's particular background or specialty.

Jargon
Words that are peculiar to an occupation or a specialty.

Another communication problem lies in the multiple meanings of words, known as **semantics.** Words can mean different things to different people, particularly in the English language, which is one of the most difficult in the world. The way some words are used in sentences can cause people to interpret messages in a manner other than the way that was intended. *Roget's Thesaurus,* a dictionary of synonyms, identifies the numerous meanings that commonly used words can have. For example, the word *smart* can be used in several ways. We speak of a "smart" person in the sense that the person is intelligent; a "smart aleck" is someone who is difficult to get along with; a person who dresses "smartly" is someone who dresses fashionably; and a "smarting" pain means a stinging or sharp pain. Many other words can also be used in many different ways. Where a word can have multiple meanings, the meaning intended must be clarified since listeners tend to interpret words based on their own perceptions, past experiences, and cultural backgrounds.

Semantics
The multiple meanings of words.

There are instances in which a frustrating conversation between a supervisor and employee ends with, "We are not talking the same language," even though both have been conversing in English. To avoid such breakdowns, supervisors should use words to which the employees are accustomed and that they can understand. The question is not whether the employee ought to understand the words; it is whether the employee does understand. Therefore, supervisors should strive to use plain, direct words in brief, uncomplicated statements. If necessary, they should restate messages in several ways to clarify the meaning or context that was intended.

Inappropriate Use of the Internet

In many businesses, Internet access gives employees the information that they need to do their jobs. But in some firms, Internet use can become time consuming and, if left unchecked, can ultimately impede productivity. The potential for unproductive and even illegal use of the Internet is a concern for many businesses, and some companies have gone to the extreme of restricting or forbidding employee Internet use altogether.[9]

Clearly, employees must be able to gather information. The key is that the information must be pertinent and useful to the employees' jobs. The supervisor should begin by asking "What information do my employees need to do their jobs?" The answer should be the foundation for policies and procedures governing information gathering. Employees must know what is expected, and what is and is not allowed with respect to electronic communication.

Status and Position

Status
Attitudes toward a person based on the position he or she occupies.

The organization's structure, with its several levels in the managerial hierarchy, creates a number of status levels among members of the organization. **Status** refers to the attitudes that are held toward a position and its occupant by the members of the organization. There is a recognized status difference between an executive level and a supervisory level, and between supervisors and employees. Differences in status and position become apparent as one level tries to communicate with another. For example, a supervisor who tries to convey enthusiasm to an employee about higher production and profits for the company may find that the employee is indifferent to these company goals. The employee may be primarily concerned with achieving higher personal wages and security. Thus, the supervisor and the employee may represent different points of view merely by virtue of their positions in the company. The differences in position may present an obstacle to understanding each other.

When employees listen to a message from the supervisor, several other factors affect the effectiveness of the communication. Employees evaluate the supervisor's words in light of their own backgrounds and experiences. They also take into account the supervisor's personality and position. It is difficult for employees to separate a message from the feelings that they have about the supervisor who sends the message. Therefore, the employees may infer nonexistent motives in the message. For example, union members may be inclined to interpret a management statement in very uncomplimentary terms if they are convinced that management is trying to weaken the union.

Obstacles due to status and position also can distort the upward flow of communication when subordinates are anxious to impress management. Employees may screen information passed up the line; they may tell the supervisor only what they think the latter likes to hear and omit or soften the unpleasant details. This problem is known as **filtering.** By the same token, supervisors are also anxious to make a favourable impression when talking to managers in higher positions. They may fail to pass on important information to their managers because they believe that the information would reflect unfavourably on their own supervisory abilities.

Filtering
The process of omitting or softening unpleasant details.

Resistance to Change or New Ideas

Many people prefer things as they are, and they do not welcome changes in their working situation. If a message is intended to convey a change or new idea to employees—something that will upset their work assignments, positions, or part of their daily routine—the natural inclination is for some employees to resist the message. It is normal for people to prefer that their environment not change. Consequently, a message that will change this equilibrium may be greeted with suspicion. The employees may screen out and reject new ideas if they conflict with a currently comfortable situation.

In the same fashion, most listeners are likely to receive only that portion of a message that confirms their present beliefs and will tend to ignore a message that conflicts with those beliefs. Sometimes beliefs are so entrenched that the listeners do not hear anything at all. The barriers can be so strong that the message will be immediately rejected as false, or the meaning will be twisted so that the message fits the listeners' own perceptions.

Receivers usually hear what they wish to hear. If they are insecure or fearful in their positions, this barrier becomes even more difficult to overcome. Supervisors often are confronted with situations in which their employees do not fully listen to what is being said. Employees become so preoccupied with their own thoughts that they give attention only to those ideas they want to hear and select only those parts of the total message that they can accept. Bits of information that they do not like or that are irreconcilable to their biases are brushed aside, not heard at all, or easily explained away. Supervisors must be aware of these possibilities, particularly when a message intends to convey some change that may interfere with the normal routine or customary work environment.

Perceptual Barriers

A message is often misunderstood because we all see the world differently. Thus, perception is one of the major barriers to effective communication. Barriers can arise from deep-rooted personal feelings, prejudices, and cultural or ethnic differences.

Stereotyping
The perception that all people in a certain group share common attitudes, values, and beliefs.

The perception that all people in a certain group share common attitudes, values, and beliefs is called **stereotyping.** Stereotyping influences how people respond to others. It becomes a barrier to effective communication when people are categorized into certain groups because of their sex, age, or race instead of being treated as unique individuals. For example, suppose that older employees consistently received poorer performance ratings from their supervisors despite doing a better job than their younger counterparts. Bias had led to ineffective communication between the older employees and their supervisors and this bias resulted in the supervisors' inability to accurately judge the workers' true contribution. Managers need to be aware of stereotyping because it can adversely affect communication.

Insensitive Words and Poor Timing

Sometimes, one person uses so-called "killer phrases" in a conversation. Comments such as "That's the stupidest idea I've ever heard!" "You do understand, don't you?" or "Do you really know what you're talking about?" can shut down communication. Often, the result is that the receiver of the "killer phrase" becomes silent and indifferent to the sender. Sometimes the receiver takes offence and directs anger back to the sender. Insensitive, offensive language or impetuous responses can cause difficulty in understanding. It is not difficult to think of many workplace illustrations of these occurrences. Often, the conflict that results impedes the accomplishment of organizational goals.

Another barrier to effective communication is the timing factor. Employees come to the workplace with extra "baggage"—that is, they sometimes carry to work events that have happened off the job. From personal experience, you can understand why it is hard to pay attention to someone else when you are anticipating an upcoming test. You pretend to listen politely but you probably are not listening carefully. Under these circumstances your attentiveness and responsiveness to information will not be as the other party expected.

Since barriers to effective communication are numerous and diverse, supervisors should not assume that the messages they send will be received as they were intended. In fact, supervisors should assume that most of the messages they send are likely to be distorted. If supervisors operate from this premise, they will be more likely to do everything within their power to overcome these barriers and improve the chances for mutual understanding.

5   OVERCOMING BARRIERS TO EFFECTIVE COMMUNICATION

Describe ways to overcome communication barriers.

Most techniques for overcoming communication barriers are relatively easy and straightforward. Supervisors will recognize them as techniques that they use sometimes but not as frequently as they should. Most are just common sense, but may not be commonly used. Supervisors are, as studies have shown over the years, very busy people whose work is often interrupted, and they rely on oral communication most of the time. As a result, supervisors must take a proactive approach to ensure that communication is effective.

Preparation and Planning

A first major step toward becoming a better communicator is to avoid speaking or writing until the message to be communicated has been thought through to the point that it is clear in the sender's mind. Only if supervisors can express their ideas in an organized fashion can they hope for others to understand. Therefore, before communicating, supervisors should know what they want and should plan the sequence of steps necessary to attain their objectives (see Figure 8-3). Rare is the activity that requires an instantaneous response.

FIGURE 8-3
Steps to achieving communication objectives.

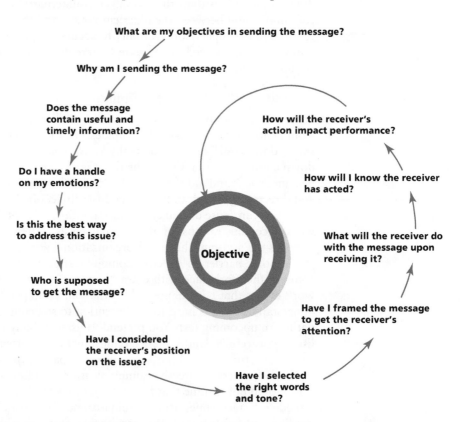

Sources: From ideas in Curtis Sittenfeld, "How to WOW an Audience—Every Time," *Fast Company* (September 1999), p. 84; Carol Leonetti Dannhauser, "Shut Up and Listen," *Working Women* (May 1999), p. 41; Sean Morrison, "Keep It Simple," *Training* (January 1999), p. 152; Douglas Stone, Bruce Patten, and Sheila Heen, *Difficult Conversations: How to Discuss What Matters Most* (New York: Viking, 1999); Paul A. Argenti, "Should Business Schools Teach Aristotle?" *Strategy & Business* (Third Quarter, 1998), pp. 4–6; and A. Blanton Godfrey, "Quality Management: Getting the Word Out," *Quality Digest* (June 1996), p. 7.

For example, if supervisors want to develop a job assignment, they should first analyze the job thoroughly so they are able to describe it properly. If supervisors want to explain the solution to a problem, they should study the problem until it is so clear in their minds that they will have little difficulty explaining the solution. When researching an issue, supervisors should determine in advance what information they need so that they can ask intelligent, pertinent, and precise questions. If a communication is to involve a disciplinary action, supervisors should have sufficiently investigated the case and compiled all relevant information before issuing a penalty. In other words, communication should not begin until supervisors know what they ought to say in relation to what they want to achieve.

Using Feedback

Feedback
The receiver's verbal or nonverbal response to a message.

Among the methods available to improve communication, **feedback** is by far the most important. In communication, feedback is the receiver's verbal or nonverbal response to a message. Feedback can be used to determine whether or not the receiver understood the message and to get the receiver's reaction to it. The sender can initiate feedback by using questions, discussion, signals, or clues. Merely asking the receiver, "Do you understand?" and receiving a "yes" as an answer may not be enough feedback. More information than this is usually required to ensure that a message was actually received as it was intended.

A simple way to encourage feedback is to observe the receiver and to judge that person's responses. Nonverbal clues such as an expression of bewilderment or understanding, a raised eyebrow, a frown, or the direction or movement of eyes can be very revealing. Of course, this kind of feedback is possible only in face-to-face communication, which is one of the major advantages of this form of communication.

Perhaps the best feedback technique is for the sender to ask the receiver to restate or "play back" the information just received. This is much more satisfactory than merely asking whether the instructions are clear. If the receiver can paraphrase the content of the message, then the sender will know what the receiver has heard and understood. At that time, the receiver may ask additional questions and request comments, which the sender can provide immediately.

Feedback is also important when a supervisor is on the receiving end of a message from an employee or a higher-level manager. To clear up possible misunderstandings, a supervisor can say, "Just to make sure I understand what you want, let me repeat in my own words that message you gave me." An employee or a manager will appreciate this initiative to improve the accuracy of communication. A similar technique to paraphrasing is reflective feedback. This is used when the supervisor reflects the feelings or emotions expressed by the sender. For example, the supervisor might say, "You feel _____ because _____." Reflective feedback emphasizes the supervisor's empathy for the speaker's feelings, and allows the sender to clarify or correct any misinterpretations.

Feedback can also be helpful when written communication is involved. Before sending a written message, the supervisor can have someone else—perhaps a colleague—read the message for comprehension. Most writing can be improved. It may be necessary to develop several drafts of a written message and have various people provide feedback as to which draft is the most clearly stated and most likely to be accurately interpreted by the intended audience.

Similarly, after sending a memo, fax, letter, or e-mail message, it often is desirable to discuss the written correspondence over the telephone or face to face to ensure that the receiver understands it. When a supervisor receives a written message from someone else and there is any doubt about its meaning, the supervisor should contact the sender to discuss and clarify the message.

Direct and Clear Language

Another sound approach to attaining effective communication is to use words that are understandable and as clear as possible. Supervisors should avoid long, technical, and complicated words. They should use language that the receivers will be able to understand without difficulty. Jargon or "shop talk" should be used only if the receiver is comfortable with it. The old "KISS" approach is usually a good motto to remember: KISS stands for "keep it short and simple."

A Calm Atmosphere

Tension and anxiety were mentioned previously as being serious barriers to effective communication. If a supervisor tries to communicate with an employee who is visibly upset, chances for mutual understanding are minimal. It is much better to communicate when both parties are calm and not burdened by unusual tension or stress. One of the best ways for a supervisor to ensure the proper atmosphere for communicating or discussing a problem with an employee is to set an appointed time for a meeting in a quiet room. This usually enables both parties to prepare to discuss the problem in a calm and unhurried fashion. Similarly, if supervisors want to discuss something with their managers, they should arrange for an appointment at a time and place that is conducive to having an uninterrupted discussion.

Taking Time to Listen

Another approach to overcoming barriers to communication is for both the sender and the receiver to take more time to listen, that is, to give the other person full opportunity to express what is on his or her mind. The supervisor who actively listens to what the employee is saying will learn more about the employee's values and attitudes toward the working environment. The supervisor should provide feedback by restating the employee's message from time to time and asking, "Is this what you mean?" A supervisor should always patiently listen to what the employee has to say. Intensive listening helps to reduce misunderstandings and, by listening, the supervisor will be better able to respond in ways that are appropriate to the concerns of the employee.

One of the worst things supervisors can do is to sit with faked attention while their minds are elsewhere. The supervisor can avoid this situation by politely stating, "Right now is not a convenient time for us to have this discussion. It needs my full attention, and if we can reschedule this meeting for 10:00 A.M., you will have my undivided attention." Attentiveness to the speaker will go a long way toward building a climate of trust. Figure 8-4 contains some practical do's and don'ts for effective listening.

Listening is a very important part of the supervisor's job, whether in one-on-one conversations or in meetings. The ability to listen is critical to success as a supervisor. Therefore, supervisors should work to develop their listening skills every chance they get.

FIGURE 8-4   The do's and don'ts of effective listening.

DO'S FOR LISTENING
- Do adopt the attitude that you will always have something to learn.
- Do take time to listen, give the speaker your full attention, and hear the speaker out.
- Do withhold judgment until the speaker is finished. Strive to locate the main ideas of the message.
- Do try to determine the word meanings within the context of the speaker's background. Listen for what is being implied as well as what is being said.
- Do establish eye contact with the speaker. Read body language. Smile, nod, and give an encouraging sign when the speaker hesitates.
- Do ask questions at appropriate times to be sure that you understand the speaker's message.
- Do restate the speaker's idea at appropriate moments to make sure that you understand correctly.

DON'TS OF LISTENING
- Don't listen with only half an ear by "tuning out" the speaker and pretending that you are listening.
- Don't unnecessarily interrupt the speaker or finish the speaker's statement because of impatience or wanting to respond immediately.
- Don't fidget or doodle while listening. Don't let other distractions bother you and the speaker.
- Don't confuse facts with opinions.
- Don't show disapproval or insensitivity to the speaker's feelings.
- Don't respond until the speaker has said what he or she wants to say.
- Don't become defensive.

Repetition of Messages

It is often helpful to repeat a message several times, preferably using different words or different methods. For instance, a new medical insurance claim process might be mentioned in a staff meeting, discussed in an article in the company newsletter, posted on the bulletin board, and maintained in a policy file available for employee use. The degree of repetition required will depend largely on the content of the message and the experience and background of the employees or other people involved in the communication. However, the message should not be repeated so much that it gets ignored because it sounds too familiar or boring. In case of doubt, some repetition probably is safer than none.

Reinforcing Words with Action

To succeed as communicators, supervisors need to complement their words with appropriate and consistent actions. Supervisors communicate a great deal through their actions; actions really do speak louder than words. Therefore, one of the best ways to give meaning to messages is to act accordingly. If verbal announcements are backed up by action, the supervisor's credibility will be enhanced. However, if the supervisor says one thing but does another, sooner or later the employees will be influenced primarily by what the supervisor does.

WHAT CALL DID YOU MAKE?

Communication is a two-way street. It is easy to tell another person what to do, but it takes real skill to listen to what that person is really saying. Skillful communication depends not only on what you say, but on how you say it and when you say it. It is easy for supervisors to become engrossed in the pressures of their work and to fail to listen effectively.

The "You Make the Call" scenario exemplifies the problems that occur when people take communication for granted. In short, the parties in this situation are communicating poorly. You, as Paul Vaught, probably believe you have communicated clear goals and expectations. Perhaps Vikram Kamil and Linda Burns heard what you said but did not understand the full meaning of your message. What feedback techniques did you use to ensure that your message was understood? In all likelihood, you believe you fulfilled your communication responsibility when you introduced Kamil to Burns and advised Kamil to coordinate the prototype runs. In reality, there is a perceptual problem between what you think you said and what the parties heard.

Clearly, it was "what was not being said" that was critical. Burns repeatedly called production problems to your attention. You either failed to understand their importance or determined they were not of the highest priority. By not immediately developing a plan of action to help Burns, you sent a message. By not acting on her call for help, you lost her respect and admiration. Remember that communication occurs between people. People have feelings and, no doubt, Burns's feelings were hurt. The unspoken message was that her problems with the prototype production run were unimportant. This set the stage for future problems. When you introduced Kamil to Burns, you anticipated that she would willingly cooperate with him to finish the assigned tasks. The notion of reciprocity was violated. You did not realize that your failure to respond to her earlier concerns would cause her to fail to respond to your request.

No evidence indicates that, after you introduced Kamil and Burns, you were available to help them.

Regardless of how busy you are, you must still help staff who are at the front lines. On the front line, you could have asked the right questions and encouraged feedback.

Most of the barriers to communication identified in this chapter contributed to the breakdown in communication in this scenario and prevented understanding. Kamil, a newcomer to the company, had been assigned the responsibility of working with Burns, a seasoned veteran. Burns's apparent unwillingness to cooperate fully might be explained by her perceptions of the situation. Burns may have lacked confidence and trust in Kamil. Burns might be intimidated by Kamil's educational background, or may perceive his presence as just another "burden" being added to her workday. In a sense, everyone in this dilemma shares responsibility for the problem.

As Vaught, you must assess, recognize, and accept the situation. You must also learn from this experience and develop a work culture in which all employees can speak their minds and you can count on everyone to be open and honest.

In this scenario, most principles of effective communication were violated. You did not appear to take enough time to give—or get—information. Kamil expressed his concerns to you, and you failed to respond in a timely manner. You met with Burns and her supervisor without speaking with Kamil. You must develop a strategy for gathering additional information from Kamil, and carry that strategy out.

Your ability to ask probing (information-getting) questions, regardless of their unpleasantness, will make you more effective as a supervisor. What else should you do? You should have another round of discussions with Kamil and Burns. You need to know all the facts behind this lack of cooperation. You must also apologize to Burns for failing to heed her earlier concerns about production.

Finally, you must assume responsibility for improving your communication skills. Nothing is gained by finger-pointing. The fault lies with you. To become a more effective supervisor, you should use this as a learning experience—a springboard for continuously improving your communication skills.

SUMMARY

1 Effective communication means that a successful transfer of information and understanding takes place between a sender and a receiver. The ability to communicate effectively is one of the most important qualities leading to supervisory success.

Communication is a two-way process. Communication is successful only if the receiver understands the message. The receiver need not agree with the message, just understand it as the sender intended.

2 Formal channels of communication operate downward, upward, and horizontally. These communication channels primarily serve to link people and departments in order to accomplish organizational objectives. Supervisors communicate downward to their employees, and employees communicate upward to supervisors. Equally important is the supervisor's duty to communicate upward to management and horizontally with supervisors in other departments. In addition to formal channels, every company has an informal channel, called the *grapevine*. The grapevine can carry rumours as well as facts. Supervisors should stay in touch with what is being transmitted on the grapevine and counteract rumours with facts where necessary.

3 Methods of communication range from oral, written, and visual to the unspoken body language. Spoken and written words are the most important means of communication. However, body language—a person's actions, gestures, posture, and so forth—also communicates, often in more powerful ways than words themselves. Oral communication is generally superior to other modes of communication because it enables face-to-face interaction. Feedback is instantaneous. Written words and visuals are sometimes preferred because of their permanency. Visual aids, such as pictures, charts, and videos, can be powerful tools in conveying meaning.

Human differences and organizational conditions can create obstacles, called *noise,* which distort messages between people. The use of jargon that the receiver does not understand can impede communication. Also, words have different meanings, so the sender must ensure that the receiver understood the intended meaning.

People who have different status or position levels within an organization bring different points of view to an interaction, which can distort meaning. People may "filter out" unpleasant information in communications with their managers. Also, people's natural resistance to change can cause them to avoid "hearing" messages that upset the status quo or conflict with their own beliefs.

4 Individuals perceive the world from the context of their own backgrounds and prejudices. Perceptual barriers between sender and receiver, such as biases and stereotyping, can impede communication, as can conversation-killing phrases and poor timing.

5 To overcome communication barriers, supervisors should adequately prepare what they wish to communicate. During face-to-face communication, the receiver's verbal and nonverbal responses, called *feedback,* can help the supervisor determine whether or not the receiver understood the message. Asking the receiver to restate the message is one feedback technique that helps verify understanding. For written communication, the supervisor can obtain feedback by asking a colleague to comment on the message before it is sent and by discussing it with receivers after it is sent to check understanding.

Using clear, direct language that the receiver can understand will facilitate communication. Also, both parties should agree on a time to talk when both parties will not be overly stressed and will have time to really listen to each other. Repeating the message in various words and formats can improve understanding, if not done to excess. Also, to be effective, words must be reinforced by consistent actions.

QUESTIONS FOR DISCUSSION

1. What is meant by effective communication? Why is mutual understanding at the heart of any definition of effective communication?
2. Discuss the techniques by which a supervisor can cope with the grapevine effectively.
3. How should a supervisor respond to a false rumour that is spreading through the organization?
4. Identify the strengths and weaknesses of oral versus written communication. Under what circumstances would a supervisor choose to communicate orally as opposed to in writing?
5. What specific challenges does a supervisor face as a result of the proliferation of electronic communication?
6. Identify the specific techniques a supervisor can use to overcome barriers to effective communication.
7. Explain how "reflective feedback" can improve communication between a supervisor and an employee.
8. What common mistakes do you make when listening to someone else? What specific steps do you need to take to improve your listening skills?

SKILLS APPLICATIONS

Skills Application 8-1: Is E-Mail Appropriate for Communicating Bad News?

It is a widespread belief that face-to-face communication is most appropriate for communicating bad news in an organizational setting. There has been some research, however, that suggests that using e-mail to communicate bad news messages might offer some advantages in some situations.

1. Using the Internet, research the potential benefits of e-mail for communicating bad news. Visit www.informs.org/Press/BadNews.html or find an alternate site of your own choosing. Based on your research, what are the potential benefits of using e-mail when communicating bad news?
2. Research the opposing side of this issue. Visit www.atkinson.yorku.ca/~hrresall/dbn.PDF (or a site of your own choosing) and list the potential disadvantages of using e-mail to communicate bad-news messages.
3. If you were the recipient of bad news at work, through which communication channel would you prefer to learn of that news? Why?
4. Discuss your results with a group of your fellow students. Under what circumstances do most people feel it is appropriate/inappropriate to communicate bad news via e-mail?

Skills Application 8-2: Unpleasant Situations

1. Read the following situations:
   a. An employee is performing a task improperly and you show him how you want it done. The employee says, "I was doing this before you were born and I don't need your advice."
   b. An employee has suddenly developed a tardiness problem. When you confront her, she says, "My husband is an alcoholic; I am worried about him. I have to get the kids breakfast and send them off to school before I can get here."
2. Decide on an appropriate response for each situation.
3. Pair up with a classmate. Decide which of you will play the supervisor and which will be the employee. (We suggest alternating roles for the situation so that both of you get an opportunity to play the supervisory role.) Pick up the action from where the situation leaves off.
4. Evaluate the interaction. As the supervisor, are you pleased with your follow-up to the situation? What did you do well? What could you have done more effectively?

Skills Application 8-3: Corporate E-mail and Internet Policies

This chapter's Contemporary Issue box (pages 228–29) focused on the need for clearly defined corporate e-mail and Internet use policies.

1. Using an Internet search engine, find at least two examples of corporate policies governing Internet and e-mail use. Some examples can be found at www.hrvs-rhsbc.ca/hr_practices/pg003b13_e.cfm, or find other examples of your own choosing.
2. Summarize the similiarities and differences between the policies that you reviewed.
3. What are the primary benefits associated with having clear policies about Internet and e-mail use in the workplace?

SKILLS DEVELOPMENT

Skills Development Module 8-1: Communication

This video segment features Ken Foley, production development supervisor at Carson Products. J. C. Marko, a systems designer, has encountered problems and needs Ken's help.

Questions for Discussion: The Ineffective Version

1. Discuss how Ken did not use effective communication skills to efficiently run his department.
2. What barriers hindered communication?
3. What specifically should Ken do to overcome the communication barriers?
4. Review Figure 8-4. What aspects of the Do's and Don'ts of Good Listening did Ken violate?

Questions for Discussion: The More Effective Version

1. Discuss how Ken used good communication skills to effectively run his department and solve problems.
2. Referring to Figure 8-4, identify the aspects of good listening that Ken exhibited.
3. What else could Ken Foley have done to be more effective?
4. How does this version reinforce the notion that good communication skills and good supervisory skills go hand in hand?

CASES

Don Hassad, supervisor of customer service at Software-n-More, was articulate and possessed a dry sense of humour. He could be counted on for occasional practical jokes, and he was not discriminating in his selection of targets.

Software-n-More was a major computer software, supplies, and services firm. The company had recently experienced some tough financial times. As a result, there had been layoffs of employees, several supervisors, and one middle-level manager. This restructuring had resulted in a consolidation of positions. The surviving supervisors were assigned additional employees and duties. Virtually everyone felt stressed from seeing colleagues depart and having more to do in the same amount of time.

Hassad decided that he would write a humorous news item to try to boost morale. He wrote an e-mail called "The Chopping Block" and circulated the message to all the employees in his department. A few excerpts follow:

Question: Rich, what is your reaction to the loss of your beloved supervisor, Karen Kates?

Response: Ding Dong, the Witch is Gone!!

Question: Sandra, how do you like taking on the responsibilities of the parts department while continuing to supervise the testing lab?

Response: My boss, Dave Kohenski, gave me a half-hour pep talk, and I was up to speed and on top of things at the end of the morning.

Question: Employees, how do you feel about our fearless leader's new motto, "Do More with Less!"?

Response: We feel that our president, Bob Swan, can teach us the true meaning of this motto, since he has lived it since birth.

By the end of the day, the e-mail had been circulated around the company. Someone had even forwarded it to upper-level managers. It was the talk of the company, and everyone was laughing—that is, everyone but the company president, Bob Swan.

Swan contacted Jean Mane, director of human resources, and asked her to arrange a meeting with Hassad and his boss, Bernie Collins. Swan told Mane that he was deeply concerned over the offensive remarks in the e-mail. He stressed that this type of humour was not acceptable. If carried to extremes, it could result in lawsuits by individuals who felt they were being ridiculed or defamed.

Later that day Hassad was summoned to Mane's office. Collins already was present when Hassad arrived. Mane said, "Don, your behaviour was unprofessional and inappropriate." Hassad replied, "It was just a joke. Company management needs to lighten up. Everyone is so uptight here. If we can't laugh at ourselves, then I think we've got a real problem." Mane replied, "Don, this is serious. You didn't exercise good supervisory judgment. Other supervisors and employees have been fired for less than this."

Collins told Mane that if Hassad was disciplined, it would alienate all of the other supervisors. He felt that the humour was "a bit sarcastic, but everyone is saying the same things in private."

When the meeting ended, Mane pondered what her recommendation to Swan should be.

Questions for Discussion

1. Was Hassad's e-mail just a bit of humour to improve morale, or was it a serious breach of a supervisor's responsibilities? Discuss.
2. Evaluate the general positions as stated by each individual in this case. Which of these do you find the most and which the least credible?
3. If you were Mane, what would you recommend, and why?

CASE 8-2

Abusive Rumours

John Jacobs was sales supervisor for the electronics department of Appliances Galore, a chain of large superstores specializing in appliance sales to both retail and commercial customers. The company had a reputation for extensive involvement in community activities. In fact, the company provided financial and other incentives to employees who volunteered their time in not-for-profit and other service activities.

Andy George, manager of marketing operations, just confided in Jacobs that he had heard "through the grapevine" that Steve Shepard's wife and two children showed up last night at the local women and children's shelter. George also indicated that Shepard's wife was reported to have been badly bruised and that this was not the first time she and her children had sought refuge.

Shepard was one of Jacobs's outstanding salespersons. Last year Shepard won the company's award for the most sales. George suggested to Jacobs that he should investigate the matter and make a recommendation about what the company should do.

Questions for Discussion

1. How should Jacobs respond to this report from the grapevine? What should he say right now to George?
2. If this report is true and Shepard's job performance was not affected by his personal life, should the company become involved in any way? Discuss.
3. What would you recommend that Jacobs do? Consider alternatives.

Chapter 9: Performance Appraisal and Managing the Outcomes of Performance Appraisal

After studying this chapter you will be able to

1 Define performance appraisal and clarify the supervisor's role in the process.

2 Explain how often performance feedback should be provided.

3 Discuss the advantages of a formal performance appraisal system.

4 Explain the concepts and techniques in using a written employee appraisal form.

5 Discuss the process of conducting an effective appraisal meeting.

6 Discuss coaching as a follow-up to performance appraisal.

7 Identify the benefits of a promotion-from-within policy.

8 Discuss the supervisor's role in employee compensation and outline the goals of an effective compensation program.

You are Franca Zulfi. You work as the advertising supervisor in the marketing department of a major retail department store chain. You have 14 direct reports. You know that the next few hours could be contentious. Sitting at your desk, you consider how to prepare for a performance appraisal session with Art Williams, one of your copywriting editors.

Several days ago, you completed a performance appraisal form for Williams. You were concerned about what you should say to Williams regarding his performance. You expected that there would be problems, because you had rated Williams as "average" on most of the categories on the appraisal form. Only on "attendance" and "relationships with other employees" had you rated Williams as "above average."

You believe that Williams has not performed at anything other than a general or an average level in most of his work responsibilities. In reviewing last year's appraisal form, you recognized that this was the same level at which you had appraised Williams at that time. During your interview with Williams last year, Williams had disagreed strongly with your evaluation; he thought he should have been rated "above average" or "excellent" in most categories. At that time, you had tried to explain to Williams why you had rated him as "average" in most categories and that you felt these were proper ratings. He had responded that your evaluation was unfair and discriminatory. You denied these accusations and let the evaluation form stand as you had completed it. Williams had refused to sign the form, because he was quite upset about it.

Now that another year has gone by, you recognize that you really had not given Williams any specific guidance as to how to improve his job performance. You also recognize that you had a limited number of conversations with Williams during the past year, most of which were about certain job situations and did not relate specifically to his performance. You recognize that, despite business pressures and the responsibilities of supervising a large group of employees, you should have kept better records and developed some specific examples to discuss with Williams.

Now you wonder what will happen this time and what you should say to Williams. You remain convinced that Williams is, at best, an average employee who has not improved over the past year. As you ponder what to say, Williams enters your office.

You make the call!

1 EMPLOYEE PERFORMANCE APPRAISAL

Define performance appraisal and clarify the supervisor's role in the process.

Performance appraisal
A systematic assessment of how well employees are performing their jobs, and the communication of that assessment to them.

From the time employees begin their employment with a firm, the supervisor is responsible for evaluating their job performance. **Performance appraisal** is a systematic assessment of how well employees are performing their jobs and the communication of that assessment to them. As discussed in earlier chapters, supervisors establish performance standards or targets that subordinates are expected to achieve. Performance appraisal includes comparing the employee's performance with the standards. Effective supervisors provide their subordinates with day-to-day feedback on performance. Regular feedback on performance is essential to improve employee performance and to provide recognition that will motivate employees to sustain good performance.

Most organizations also require supervisors to evaluate their employees' performance formally. These evaluations become part of an employee's permanent record and play an important role in management's decisions involving promoting, transferring, retaining, and compensating employees.

Supervisors should approach the appraisal process from the perspective that it is an extension of the planning, organizing, and leading functions. When employees understand what is expected of them and the criteria upon which they will be evaluated, and if they believe the process is fairly administered, performance appraisal serves as a powerful motivational tool. While performance appraisals are most frequently used in determining compensation, it is equally important that supervisors also use information from performance appraisals to provide feedback to employees so that they know where they stand and what they can do to improve performance and develop to their full potential.

Another reason that supervisors need to keep accurate records of employee performance is to document fulfillment of various employment regulations. The importance of documentation of personnel decisions cannot be overemphasized. It is becoming increasingly important for organizations to maintain accurate records to protect themselves against possible charges of discrimination in connection with promotion, compensation, and termination.

Although appraisal of employee performance is a daily, ongoing aspect of the supervisor's job, the focus of this chapter is on the formal system of performance appraisal. The purpose of the formal system is to evaluate, document, and communicate in understandable and objective terms the job achievements and the results of employee effort compared with job expectations. This is done by taking into consideration factors such as the job description, performance standards, specific objectives, and critical incidents for the evaluation period. The evaluation is based on direct observation of the employee's work over a period of time.[1]

The Supervisor's Responsibility for Performance Appraisal

A performance appraisal should be done by an employee's immediate supervisor, who is usually in the best position to observe and judge how well the employee has performed on the job. Effective supervisors should provide daily feedback on performance. Unfortunately, some supervisors fail to recognize performance problems or feel uncomfortable talking to employees about performance expectations. We contend that most employees want to know how well they have performed relative to the organization's expectations or performance standards. In order to provide this feedback, the supervisor should recognize and comment on a particular aspect of performance when that aspect occurs. The supervisor should gather information from direct observation of the employee's work or from other sources—customers, peers, attendance records, production data, sales data, and the like.

There are some situations in which a "consensus" or "pooled" type of appraisal may be done by a group of supervisors. An example of this would be if an employee works for several supervisors because of rotating shift schedules or because the organization has a matrix structure.

Some organizations have implemented work-team concepts that expand the supervisor's span of control, and some have become leaner and eliminated middle-level management positions. It may be impractical for a supervisor to track the performance of 20, 30, or even 50 workers and evaluate their performance objectively. In order to ensure that the performance appraisal is an accurate reflection of the employee's all-around performance, some organizations have expanded the formal appraisal system to include feedback from sources other than just the supervisor.

Peer Evaluations

Peer evaluation

The evaluation of an employee's performance by other employees of relatively equal rank.

A **peer evaluation** is the evaluation of an employee's performance by other employees of relatively equal rank. Peers usually have a closer working relationship with each other and are more knowledgeable about an individual's contribution to the team effort than the supervisor. However, safeguards must be built in to ensure that peers are basing their evaluations on performance factors and not on bias, prejudice, or personality conflicts. Having an individual's performance evaluated anonymously by a team of peers is one way to encourage candid evaluation. To protect appraisees from prejudice or vendettas, the organization should establish an appeals mechanism to allow review of ratings by upper-level managers.

Generally, employees work cooperatively to achieve common goals. Consider the situation in which members of work teams evaluate other team members' performance. On the one hand, since a peer-rating system uses a number of independent judgments, peer evaluations have the potential to be more reliable than supervisory evaluations. But on the other hand, if employees criticize their teammates via the performance appraisal system, their appraisals could have undesirable consequences for the cooperative culture and defeat the purposes of teamwork. Imagine what could happen to morale and esprit among team members when one worker gets a low evaluation from an unknown co-worker and wonders who was responsible. To safeguard the peer-rating process, supervisors can incorporate the input from all peers into a single composite evaluation. Thus, ratings that may be high because of friendship or low due to bias will cancel each other out. Safeguards to ensure confidentiality and minimize the possibility of bias are critical to the effective use of peer evaluations.[2]

360-degree evaluation

Performance appraisal based on data collected from all around the employee—from customers, vendors, supervisors, peers, subordinates, and so on.

Increasing numbers of organizations are using some form of 360-degree evaluation. A **360-degree evaluation** is based on evaluative feedback regarding the employee's performance collected from all around the employee—from customers, vendors, supervisors, peers, subordinates, and others. These 360-degree evaluations provide employees with feedback on their ability, skills, knowledge, and job-related effectiveness from sources who see different aspects of their work.[3] This approach provides employees with a complete picture from various perspectives of what they do well and where they need to improve. A form of 360-degree evaluation can also involve having subordinates appraise their own supervisor (see Contemporary Issue box on the next page).

Self-Evaluations

Many effective supervisors find it appropriate to supplement their own judgments with self-rating from the subordinate. About a week prior to the scheduled performance review, the employee is given a blank evaluation form to be used as a self-evaluation. Surprisingly, research has revealed that employees usually rate their own work less favourably than do their supervisors.[4] The supervisor compares the two evaluations to make sure to discuss all important performance specifics in the appraisal meeting. If the supervisor has provided ongoing feedback to the employee, the employee's self-ratings should be relatively close to the supervisor's ratings. Widely divergent ratings could mean that the supervisor is not giving enough feedback throughout the year for the employee to have a clear picture of how well he or she is doing. Ideally, in a system of participatory management, the formal appraisal should hold no surprises for the employee.

An employee's immediate supervisor is in the best position to observe and judge how well the employee has performed on the job.

John Henley/CORBIS

CONTEMPORARY ISSUE
Upward Appraisals—Where Employees Appraise the Supervisor

There is a great deal of debate about whether performance appraisals really result in better performance. Some people argue that "apart from those few employees who receive the highest possible ratings, performance review interviews, as a rule, are seriously deflating to the employee's sense of worth."[1] Other people argue that, while performance appraisals can be problematic if not done well, it is important to provide employees with formal feedback about their performance. One consultant writes that the "performance appraisal process is the only holistic assessment of corporate, departmental and individual, developmental progress and needs."[2]

A supervisor who worries that employees are fearful of appraisals should consider whether "upward appraisals" might improve the overall acceptance of the process. Upward appraisals allow employees to appraise their supervisors and to be on the "giving" rather than the "receiving" end of the rating. In addition to giving the supervisor valuable feedback about his or her own performance, upward appraisals can affect how employees feel about their own performance appraisals. Employees who have participated in the appraisal process by rating their supervisor gain valuable insight into the process. They see firsthand how difficult it can be to rate another person. Having been involved in creating a performance appraisal, they may be more open-minded when it comes time to participate in their own.

Upward appraisals are based on the assumption that, in many cases, the people who are in the best position to appraise the supervisor are the employees who work for him or her. Studies have shown that supervisors themselves agree that their own employees are "better evaluators of their leadership and information dissemination skills than they were themselves."[3] However, employees should be asked to rate only aspects of their own supervisor's performance that they are actually in a position to accurately assess. For example, while employees would certainly be able to evaluate the effectiveness of the supervisor's downward communication, they may not be well placed to comment on the supervisor's interactions with other supervisors or upper management. The employees' rating of the supervisor should, then, be only one aspect of the supervisor's own overall performance appraisal.

(continued)

While most supervisors welcome their employees' feedback, there have been concerns expressed about whether employees can be relied upon to provide accurate, unbiased ratings. For example, there may be a concern that subordinates will not be honest in their ratings for fear of repercussions from the supervisor, or that employees will give inflated ratings in the hopes that the manager will "go easy" on them when it comes time for their own performance appraisal.[4] Research indicates, however, that "these concerns are totally unfounded, in fact subordinate appraisals have been found to be widely accepted and more accurate than supervisory appraisals."[5]

Organizations should follow some simple guidelines when implementing an upward appraisal process. First, employees should be trained how to rate accurately. Lorne Sulsky, a professor at the University of Calgary's Faculty of Management notes that people conducting reviews should be trained to evaluate from the same frame of reference. "You think of figure skating at the Olympics and all these judges are giving different scores. It could be motivated by political factors, or it could be they all see the performance differently, so that five out of five doesn't mean the same thing to each judge. With proper training, if they see the same performance they're all going to say 4.8."[6] It should not be assumed that employees (or anyone for that matter) will instinctively know how to create an accurate rating. They need to be trained.

Upward appraisal should not be limited to the front line. In order to increase the likelihood that supervisors will "buy into" the process, upward appraisals should take place at every level of the organization. All managers, from top executives to front-line supervisors, should be appraised by the people who report to them. If upward appraisal takes place at all levels, the process becomes part of the organizational culture and less of a "checking up on" process.

Finally, it is worth considering simplifying the upward appraisal process. Rather than having subordinates complete a traditional appraisal form, it can be very useful to simply have them state whether, on specific measures, they want the supervisor to "do more of this," "do less of this," or "continue as now."[7] For example, subordinates can be given a list of supervisory behaviours such as "leads by example," "shows concern for employees' feelings," "provides specific instructions," and so on. By simply indicating whether they want to see more, less, or about the same degree of this behaviour, employees can send some very powerful feedback to the supervisor. The supervisor can use this information to actually change his or her behaviour in very specific ways to better suit the needs of the employees.

By implementing an upward appraisal system, the organization stands to benefit in a number of ways. Employees may be more receptive to their own performance being appraised, the supervisor will gain valuable feedback, and an organizational climate of open communication may be fostered. While performance appraisals continue to spark debate, upward appraisals may help to eliminate some of the "fear and loathing" that most people associate with the process.

Sources: (1) Tom Davis and Michael J. Landa, "A Contrary Look at Employee Performance Appraisal," *Canadian Manager* (Fall 1999) p. 18–19. (2) www.performanceappraisal.co.uk/pa_article2.htm (retrieved on November 19, 2003); (3) H. J. Bernardin and R. W. Beatty, "Can Subordinate Appraisals Enhance Managerial Productivity?" at www.sigmahr.com/sigmaradius/sigmaradius-article.htm (retrieved on November 21, 2003); (4) & (5) www.sigmahr.com/sigmaradius/sigmaradius-article.htm (retrieved on November 21, 2003); (6) Lorne Sulsky as quoted by Laura Ramsay, "Time to examine the exam: Mostly everyone dreads a performance appraisal, and for good reasons," *Financial Post/National Post* (October 18, 1999), p. C15. (7) Dr. Ron Forbes, "Upward Feedback: A New Power for the Learning Organisation," *HR Monthly* (November, 1996), p. 6–8.

Regardless of the approach used, the ultimate responsibility for completing the appraisal and conducting the appraisal meeting lies with the immediate supervisor. If peer evaluations are used, the supervisor must still reconcile the appraisals and communicate the information to the employee. The formal appraisal meeting usually takes place at a set time each year and should summarize what the supervisor has discussed with the employee throughout the year.

<table>
<tr><td>**2**</td><td></td></tr>
</table>

| **2** | **TIMING PERFORMANCE APPRAISALS** |

Explain how often performance feedback should be provided.

Upper-level management decides who should appraise and how often formal appraisals should be done. Most organizations require supervisors to conduct formal appraisals of all employees at least once a year. Traditionally, this has been considered long enough to develop a reasonably accurate record of the employee's performance and short enough to provide current, useful information. However, if an employee has just been hired or if the employee has been transferred to a new and perhaps more responsible position, it is advisable to conduct an appraisal within the first three to six months.

In the case of an employee who is new to the organization, the supervisor may have to do an appraisal at the end of the employee's probationary period. This appraisal usually determines whether or not the employee will be retained as a permanent employee. The performance evaluation of the probationary employee is critical. Employees are usually on their best behaviour during the probationary period, and if their performance is less than acceptable, the organization should not make a long-term commitment to them. Consider the following example. A supervisor tolerated a probationary employee whose attendance record was not acceptable. Extensive efforts to develop better attendance habits failed. Even so, the supervisor felt that if the employee was terminated, upper management might use the opportunity to cut costs by eliminating the position altogether. The supervisor's theory of "half an employee is better than none" cost the company dearly in the long run. The employee never became a satisfactory performer, and eventually had to be terminated after the company had invested significantly in training.

After the probationary period, the timing of appraisals varies. In some organizations, appraisals are done on the anniversary of the date the employee started; in others, appraisals are done once or twice a year on fixed dates. Any time an employee exhibits a performance problem during the evaluation period, the supervisor should schedule an immediate meeting with the employee. This meeting should be followed by another formal evaluation within 30 days to review the employee's progress. If the performance deficiency is severe, the supervisor should conduct regular appraisals to completely document the performance deficiency and the supervisor's efforts to help the employee.

As stated before, performance evaluation should be a normal part of the day-to-day relationship between a supervisor and employees. If an employee is given ongoing feedback, then the annual appraisal should contain no surprises. The supervisor who frequently communicates with employees concerning how they are doing will find that the annual appraisal is primarily a matter of reviewing much of what has been discussed during the year. Regular feedback can reduce the natural apprehension surrounding performance appraisals by removing the uncertainty.

Ongoing feedback throughout the year, both positive and negative, rewards good performance and guides improvement. Over time, ongoing feedback, as well as formal appraisals, can become an important influence on employee motivation and morale. Appraisals reaffirm the supervisor's genuine interest in employees' growth and development. Most employees would rather be told how they are doing—even if it involves some criticism—than receive no feedback from their supervisor.

3	## ADVANTAGES OF A FORMAL APPRAISAL SYSTEM
Discuss the advantages of a formal performance appraisal system.	

A formal appraisal system provides a framework to help the supervisor evaluate performance systematically. It forces the supervisor to scrutinize the work of employees from the standpoint of how well they are meeting previously established standards and to identify areas that need improvement.

Most large firms use some type of formal appraisal system. Management scholar Douglas McGregor identified three reasons for using performance appraisal systems:

1. Performance appraisals provide systematic judgments to support salary increases, promotions, transfers, layoffs, demotions, and terminations.
2. Performance appraisals are a means of telling subordinates how they are doing and of suggesting needed changes in behaviour, attitudes, skills, or job knowledge. Performance appraisals let subordinates know where they stand with the supervisors.
3. Performance appraisals are used as a basis for coaching and counselling of employees by supervisors.[5]

Organizations that view their employees as a long-term asset worthy of development adopt the philosophy that all employees can improve their current level of performance.

Employees have the right to know how well they are doing and what they can do to improve. Most employees want to know what their supervisors think of their work. This desire can arise for different reasons. For example, some employees realize that they are doing a relatively poor job, but they hope that the supervisor is not too critical and they are anxious to be assured of this. Other employees feel that they are doing an outstanding job and want to make certain that the supervisor recognizes and appreciates their contribution.

Formal appraisals usually become part of an employee's permanent employment record. These appraisals serve as documents that are likely to be reviewed and even relied on in future decisions concerning promotion, compensation, training, disciplinary action, and even termination. Performance appraisals can generate answers to questions such as the following:

- Who should be promoted to department supervisor when the incumbent retires?
- Who should get merit raises this year?
- What should be the raise differential among employees?
- Who, if anyone, needs training?
- What training do they need?
- An employee is continuing to fall short of expectations. Does the employee need additional coaching, or is it serious enough for disciplinary action?
- An employee is appealing his termination. Does the company have adequate documentation?

A formal appraisal system serves another important purpose. An employee's poor performance and failure to improve may be due, in part, to the supervisor's inadequate supervision. Thus, a formal appraisal system also provides clues to the supervisor's own performance and may suggest where the supervisor needs to improve.

Even when designed and implemented with the best intentions, performance appraisal systems are often a source of anxiety for employee and supervisor alike. Formal performance appraisal systems can be misused as disciplinary devices rather than being used as constructive feedback aimed at rewarding good performance and helping employees improve. Employees need to be reassured that the primary aim of the appraisal system is to reward good performance and, when needed, to help employees identify strategies for improvement. Remember that actions speak louder than words. Employees will trust the performance appraisal process only if they see that it is consistently being used constructively rather than strictly as a tool for justifying future disciplinary action.

4	**THE PERFORMANCE APPRAISAL PROCESS**

Explain the concepts and techniques in using a written employee appraisal form.

Typically, a formal employee performance appraisal by a supervisor involves (a) completing a written appraisal form and (b) conducting an appraisal interview.

Completing a Written Appraisal Form

To facilitate the appraisal process and make it more uniform, most organizations use performance appraisal forms. There are numerous types of forms for employee evaluation. These rating forms are usually prepared by the human resources department with input from employees and supervisors. Once the forms are in place, the human resources department usually trains supervisors and employees in their proper use. Supervisors are often responsible for informing new employees about the performance appraisal process as part of their orientation.

Factors in Measuring Performance

Most appraisal forms include factors that serve as criteria for measuring job performance, skills, knowledge, and abilities. The following are some of the factors that are most frequently included on employee appraisal rating forms:

- Job knowledge.
- Quantity of work.
- Quality of work.
- Timeliness of output.
- Effectiveness of resource use.
- Ability to learn.
- Dependability (absenteeism, tardiness, work done on time).
- Amount of supervision required (initiative).
- Quality of suggestions and ideas generated.
- Cooperation (effectiveness in dealing with others).
- Safety.
- Customer service orientation.
- Aptitude.
- Judgment.
- Adaptability.
- Appearance.
- Ability to work with others.

Regardless of the factors used, the appraisal form must be relevant to the employee's actual job. Factors that enable the supervisor to make performance evaluations rather than personality judgments should be used whenever possible. For each of these factors, the supervisor may be provided with a "check the box" choice or a place to fill in the achievement of the employee. Some appraisal forms offer a series of descriptive sentences, phrases, or adjectives to assist the supervisor in understanding how to judge the rating factors. Generally, the "check the box" forms are somewhat easier and less time consuming for supervisors to complete. Ideally, the supervisor should also write a narrative to justify the evaluation. There should be no shortcuts to performance appraisal. Supervisors should give it as much time as it needs.

Figure 9-1 is an example of a typical appraisal form that requires the supervisor to check the appropriate box for each rating factor. The supervisor identifies the outstanding aspects of the employee's work as well as specific performance characteristics that need improvement, and suggests several things that might be done to improve performance. The form provides space for additional comments about the various aspects of an employee's performance. Examples of other appraisal forms can be found on our website at www .supervision2e.nelson.com.

Many organizations continue to search for the "one best form" that will vastly improve their performance appraisal process. However, an effective performance appraisal system is not based on a form. It requires the supervisor to be conscious of employee performance on an ongoing basis and to regularly reflect upon what each employee is doing well and what areas need to be improved. We recommend that the supervisor start with a blank sheet of paper and record vital information that needs to be conveyed during the appraisal process (see Figure 9-2 on page 264). Once the supervisor has clarified his or her thoughts, the formal appraisal form can be completed.

If the system calls for employee self-appraisal, the employee's form is usually identical to the regular appraisal form except that it is labelled as a self-appraisal. Self-appraisals give employees an opportunity to think about their own specific achievements and to prepare for the appraisal meeting.

Performance Appraisal Software

There are numerous software packages designed to facilitate the completion of performance appraisal forms. Existing evaluation forms can be imported into the software, or an entirely new appraisal form can be developed. The software can weight each job performance factor according to its importance to the employee's job. Then, to determine whether the employee has met, exceeded, or failed to meet the performance standard, the supervisor can rate a series of statements and an overall "score" will be tabulated. According to freelance technology writer George Hulme, "The leading programs guide users through the process of performance appraisal, provide on-screen tutorials that answer frequently asked questions, and steer managers clear of potential legal problems."[6] Various programs will scan the supervisor's appraisal to locate sensitive words and suggest alternatives, and assist with the production of the appraisal form.

The use of specialized software does not reduce the supervisor's responsibility for the appraisal process. Even if such software is being used, the supervisor must still make a concerted effort to regularly observe and record employee performance (both positive and negative) as incidents occur throughout the appraisal

FIGURE 9-1

A "check-the-box" type of performance appraisal form.

Sanders Supermarkets

Employee Appraisal Form

Employee's Name: _____

Occupation: _____

The following general definitions apply to each factor rated below.

Satisfactory:	The employee's performance with respect to a factor meets the full job requirements as the job is defined at the time of rating. A satisfactory rating means good performance. THIS IS THE BASIC STANDARD FOR RATING ANY FACTOR BELOW.
Fair: The employee's performance with respect to a factor is below the requirements for the job and must improve to be satisfactory.	**Very Good:** The employee's performance with respect to a factor is beyond the requirements for satisfactory performance for the job.
Unsatisfactory: The employee's performance with respect to a factor is deficient enough to justify release from present job unless improvement is made.	**Exceptional:** The employee's performance with respect to a factor is extraordinary, approaching the best possible for the job.

Rate on Factors Below	Unsatisfactory	Fair	Satisfactory	Very Good	Exceptional
	☐	☐	☐	☐	☐
Personal Efficiency: Speed and effectiveness in performing duties assigned.	Efficiency too poor to remain in job without improvement.	Efficiency below job requirements in some respects.	Personal efficiency fully satisfies job requirements.	Superior efficiency.	Extraordinary degree of personal efficiency.
Job Knowledge: Extent of job information and understanding possessed by employee.	Knowledge inadequate to remain in job without improvement.	Lacks some required knowledge.	Knowledge fully satisfies job requirements.	Very well informed on all phases of work.	Extraordinary. Beyond scope that present job can fully utilize.
Judgment: Extent to which decisions and actions are based on sound reasoning and weighing of outcome.	Judgment too poor to remain in job without improvement.	Decisions not entirely adequate to meet demands of job.	Makes good decisions in various situations arising in job.	Superior in determining correct decisions and actions.	Extraordinary. Beyond that which present job can fully utilize.
Initiative: Extent to which employee is a "self-starter" in attaining objectives of job.	Lacks sufficient initiative to remain in job without improvement.	Lacks initiative in some respects.	Exercises full amount of initiative required by the job.	Exercises initiative beyond job requirements.	Extraordinary. Beyond that which present job can fully utilize.
Job Attitude: Amount of interest and enthusiasm shown in work.	Attitude too poor to remain in job without improvement.	Attitude needs improvement to be satisfactory.	Favourable attitude.	High degree of enthusiasm and interest.	Extraordinary degree of enthusiasm and interest.
Dependability: Extent to which employee can be counted on to carry out instructions, be on the job, and fulfill responsibilities.	Too unreliable to remain in job without improvement.	Dependability not fully satisfactory.	Fully satisfies dependability demands of job.	Superior to normal job demands.	Extraordinary dependability in all respects.
Overall Evaluation of Employee Performance:	Performance inadequate to remain in present job.	Does not fully meet requirements of the job.	Good performance. Fully competent.	Superior. Beyond satisfactory fulfillment of job requirements.	Extraordinary. Performance approaching the best possible for the job.

(OVER)

period. Simply having a software package available at performance appraisal time will not be a significant benefit if the supervisor has neglected to keep accurate records. Software can facilitate the clerical aspects of the performance

FIGURE 9-1
(continued)

Use This Item Only If the Employee Is Still in the Learning Stage on the Job

Evaluation of Trainee Performance:	Unsatisfactory	Fair	Satisfactory	Very Good	Exceptional
Considering the length of time on the job, how do you evaluate the employee's performance so far?	Progress too slow to retain job.	Progressing but not as rapidly as required.	Making good progress.	Progressing very rapidly.	Doing exceptionally well. Outstanding rate of development.
	☐	☐	☐	☐	☐

1. Outstanding abilities and accomplishments.	2. Weaknesses.
	Recommendations for Improvement:
3. General remarks concerning employee's performance.	
4. Specific suggestions for further development.	
Rated by: Date	Reviewed by: Date

TO RATER: Initial and date this space when you have discussed this rating with the employee.

_____
SUPERVISOR

*Signature of Employee _____

*This signature merely verifies that this evaluation has been discussed with the employee, and it does not express approval or disapproval of the above.

appraisal process, but it is not a substitute for the supervisor's ongoing efforts to provide employees with regular feedback throughout the year.

FIGURE 9-2
Begin with a blank sheet
of paper and answer these
questions.

Problems with Appraisal Forms

Despite the uncomplicated design of most performance appraisal forms (either paper based or computerized), supervisors encounter a number of problems when filling them out. For one thing, not all raters agree on the meaning of such terms as "exceptional," "very good," "satisfactory," "fair," and "unsatisfactory." While descriptive phrases or sentences added to each of these adjectives are helpful in choosing the level that best describes the employee, the choice of an appraisal term or level depends mostly on the rater's perceptions. This may be an inaccurate measure of actual performance.

The performance appraisal process will suffer when supervisors do not make accurate ratings of employee performance. For example, one supervisor may be more severe than another in the appraisal of employees. When one supervisor gives lower ratings than other supervisors for the same performance, employees will perceive that they have been judged unfairly and morale will be affected. Some supervisors feel that, since no one is perfect, no one should ever receive an "above average" evaluation. Other supervisors believe that if employees are rated too highly, they will receive promotions and be lost to the department. A supervisor who is concerned about "losing people" may rate employee performance lower than it actually was. In the long run, these supervisors will lose the employees' trust and respect and/or lose them to other firms entirely.

On the other hand, some supervisors tend to be overly generous or lenient in their ratings.[7] The **leniency error** occurs when supervisors give employees higher ratings than they deserve. Some supervisors give high ratings because they believe that poor evaluations may reflect negatively on their own performance, suggesting that they have not been able to elicit good performance from the employees. Other supervisors do not give low ratings because they are afraid that they will antagonize the employees and thus make them less cooperative. Some

Leniency error
Supervisors giving employees higher ratings than they deserve.

supervisors are so eager to be liked by their employees that they give out only high ratings, even when such ratings are undeserved.

Supervisors also should be aware of the problem of the halo effect or horns effect (described in Chapter 5) which causes a rating on one factor to result in similar ratings on other factors. One way to avoid the halo or horns effect is for the supervisor to rate all employees on only one factor at a time and then go on to the next factor for all employees, and so on. This suggestion works only if the supervisor is rating several employees at the same time. If that is not the case, then the supervisor should pause and ask, "How does this employee compare on this factor with other employees?" The supervisor must rate each employee in relation either to a standard or to another employee on each factor.

The supervisor should ask what conditions exist when the job is done well. These conditions are **performance standards.** They should be described in terms of "how much," "how well," "when," and "in what manner." Effectiveness and efficiency measures are part of these standards. The positive and negative effects of performance should also be considered. Consider, for example, the most prolific salesperson in a store. His product knowledge and selling ability are second to none and he received a very positive performance appraisal. However, he always expects the cashiers to set other orders aside and ring up his sales first. The cashiers are frustrated, and the other salespeople are not as able to give good service. In addition, he always has the stockroom personnel running errands for him. The salesperson receives accolades on selling, but every one of his sales is a rush project, and other people are expected to juggle their schedules to accommodate him. While the salesperson is proficient in his own job performance, in the process of getting his job done he creates negative impacts elsewhere in the organization. The supervisor needs to broaden the performance standards to include more than product knowledge and selling.

Performance standards
The job-related requirements by which an employee's performance is evaluated.

Appraisal Should Be Job Based

Every appraisal should be made within the context of each employee's particular job, and every rating should be based on the total performance of the employee. It would be unfair to appraise an employee on the basis of a single assignment that had been done recently, done particularly well or done very poorly. Random impressions should not influence a supervisor's judgment. The appraisal should be based on an employee's total record for the appraisal period. All relevant factors need to be considered. Moreover, the supervisor must continuously strive to exclude personal biases for or against individuals, which can be a serious pitfall in appraisal.

Although results of performance appraisal are by no means perfect, they can be quite objective and serve as a positive force in influencing an employee's future performance.

5	**THE APPRAISAL MEETING**

Discuss the process of conducting an effective appraisal meeting.

The second major part of the appraisal process is the evaluation or appraisal meeting. After the supervisor has completed the rating form, he or she arranges a time to meet with the employee to review the ratings. Since this meeting is the most vital part of the appraisal process, the supervisor should develop a general plan for carrying out the appraisal discussion. If handled poorly, this meeting can lead to considerable resentment and misunderstanding. The conflict that develops may not be reparable.

The Right Purpose

The primary purpose of the appraisal meeting is to let the employee know how he or she is doing. The supervisor formally praises the employee for his or her past and current good performance. This recognition increases the likelihood that the employee's good behaviours will be maintained. The appraisal meeting is also used by the supervisor to help the employee develop good future performance. The supervisor can explain the opportunities for growth that exist within the organization and encourage the employee to develop the required skills. Finally, the supervisor should use the appraisal meeting to explain past behaviours that need correcting and the need for future improvement. Even when improvement is needed, the supervisor should take the positive approach that he or she believes in the employee's ability to improve and will do everything possible to help.

The Right Time and Place

Appraisal meetings should be held shortly after the performance rating form has been completed, preferably in a private setting. It is a good idea for the supervisor to complete the rating form several days in advance and then review it a day or two before the meeting to analyze it objectively and to ensure that it accurately reflects the employee's performance. Privacy and confidentiality should be assured since this discussion could include criticism, personal feelings, and expressions of opinion.

The supervisor should make the appointment with the employee several days in advance. This enables the employee to be prepared for the appraisal meeting and to consider in advance what he or she would like to discuss.

Conducting the Appraisal Meeting

Although appraisal meetings tend to be directive, in many situations an appraisal meeting can take on characteristics of a nondirective interview since the employee may bring up issues that the supervisor did not expect or was unaware of. It is

At an appraisal meeting, the supervisor emphasizes an employee's strengths to help that employee develop good future performance.

Corel Corporation

easy for most supervisors to communicate positive aspects of job performance, but it is difficult to communicate major criticisms without generating resentment and defensiveness. There is a limit to how much criticism an individual can absorb in one session. If there is a lot of criticism to impart, dividing the appraisal meeting into several sessions may ease the stress.

The manner in which the supervisor conducts the meeting influences how the employee reacts. After a brief, informal opening, the supervisor should state that the purpose of the meeting is to assess the employee's performance in objective terms. During this warm-up period, the supervisor should state that the purpose of the performance appraisal is to congratulate the employee on his or her achievements and, if necessary, to help the employee improve performance. The supervisor should review the employee's achievements during the review period, compliment the employee on those accomplishments, identify the employee's strengths, and then proceed to the areas that need improvement. A secret of success is to get the employee to agree on the strengths that he or she brings to the workplace because it is easy to build on strengths.

Unfortunately, not every employee performs at the expected level. Limiting criticism to just a few major points, rather than dumping a "laundry list" of minor transgressions on the employee, draws attention to the major areas that need improvement without overwhelming him or her. The supervisor must get the employee to agree on the areas that need correction or improvement. If there is agreement, then the supervisor and employee can use a problem-solving approach to jointly determine ways that the employee can improve performance.

If the employee absolutely refuses to acknowledge the need for improvement, the supervisor should review the specific examples of deficient performance that occurred during the review period. By highlighting actual examples of the employee's past performance, the supervisor can emphasize the fact that the review process is not based on opinions, personality, or other factors not related to actual job performance.

When dealing with an employee who is performing at substandard levels, the supervisor must clearly communicate to the employee that the deficiencies are serious and that substantial improvement must be made. The supervisor should mix in some positive observations so that the employee knows that he or she is doing some things right. The supervisor should work with the employee to create an action plan for improvement with clear expectations and progress checkpoints along the way. It is important that the employee leave the meeting feeling capable of meeting the expectations.

Performance appraisals have been increasingly scrutinized by the legal system in recent years. It is essential that organizations ensure that their performance appraisal systems are legally defensible. Employees often disagree with negative aspects of the performance appraisal because the ratings can affect their pay or opportunities for advancement later on. The supervisor must be certain that each employee fully understands the standards of performance that serve as the basis for appraisal. Also, the appraisal must accurately represent the employee's performance and be free of bias. The employee must know that the review is fair, is based on job performance factors, and is supported by proper documentation.

Most mature employees are able to handle deserved, fair criticism. By the same token, those who merit praise want to hear it. Figure 9-3 offers suggestions for relieving the uncertainty of the performance appraisal process.

FIGURE 9-3   Comprehensive performance appraisal checklist.

❏ Supervisors are trained in the performance appraisal system:

   ❏ The forms.   ❏ Rating scales and dimensions.
   ❏ Use of job standards.   ❏ Linkages with personnel
   ❏ Timing of appraisal.   decisions.
   ❏ Monitoring employee progress.   ❏ Objective performance
   ❏ Contracting for performance   assessment.
       improvement.   ❏ Documentation.
   ❏ Using developmental methods   ❏ Interviewing techniques.
       and action plans.   ❏ Rewarding performance.
   ❏ Providing feedback.

❏ Both the supervisor and the employee understand the purpose of the appraisal process.

❏ The supervisor clarifies employee expectations through a job description that lists duties and responsibilities.

❏ An updated job description serves as the foundation for the appraisal.

❏ The supervisor makes the employee aware of performance standards and specific areas of accountability.

❏ The supervisor provides ongoing feedback on performance (e.g., "There is no substitute for daily feedback on performance").

❏ Supervisor gives at least one official performance appraisal per year—within the first 30 workdays for new employees or transfers and as required for "problem" employees.

❏ As soon as a performance problem is observed, the supervisor works with the employee to try to determine the cause of the problem and identify the corrective action required.

❏ The supervisor keeps a regular record of all unusual behaviour—a critical incident file.

❏ The supervisor schedules the appraisal meeting several days in advance.

❏ The supervisor puts the employee at ease at the beginning of the appraisal meeting.

❏ The supervisor allows the employee to engage in self-evaluation. (The supervisor may ask the employee to complete a self-rating form.)

❏ The supervisor reviews the written appraisal with the employee, stating both standards and/or objectives met and not met.

❏ The supervisor criticizes performance, not the person (tells the employee specifically what he or she did wrong).

❏ The supervisor objectively emphasizes work behaviours rather than personal traits (the *O* of OUCH).

❏ The supervisor provides positive as well as negative feedback.

❏ The supervisor uses specific examples to illustrate the employee's accomplishments. (The employee knows that the supervisor is using factual information that is well documented.)

FIGURE 9-3 *(continued)*

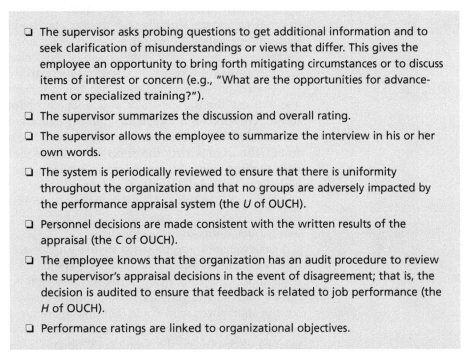

- ❏ The supervisor asks probing questions to get additional information and to seek clarification of misunderstandings or views that differ. This gives the employee an opportunity to bring forth mitigating circumstances or to discuss items of interest or concern (e.g., "What are the opportunities for advancement or specialized training?").
- ❏ The supervisor summarizes the discussion and overall rating.
- ❏ The supervisor allows the employee to summarize the interview in his or her own words.
- ❏ The system is periodically reviewed to ensure that there is uniformity throughout the organization and that no groups are adversely impacted by the performance appraisal system (the *U* of OUCH).
- ❏ Personnel decisions are made consistent with the written results of the appraisal (the *C* of OUCH).
- ❏ The employee knows that the organization has an audit procedure to review the supervisor's appraisal decisions in the event of disagreement; that is, the decision is audited to ensure that feedback is related to job performance (the *H* of OUCH).
- ❏ Performance ratings are linked to organizational objectives.

Critical incident method
Supervisors record specific examples of outstanding and below-average performance on the part of each employee.

During the appraisal meeting, the supervisor should emphasize that everybody in the same job in the same department is evaluated using the same standards and that no one is singled out for special scrutiny. The supervisor must be prepared to support or document ratings by citing specific illustrations and actual instances of good or poor performance. In particular, the supervisor should indicate how the employee performed or behaved in certain situations that were especially crucial or significant to the performance of the department. This is sometimes referred to as the **critical incident method.** To use this method, the supervisor must keep a file during the appraisal period of written notes describing situations when employees performed in an outstanding fashion and, conversely, when their work was clearly unsatisfactory. An example of a positive critical incident would be the following. "Shortly before closing on October 22, an employee realized that a customer had received an item of lesser value than she had paid for. The employee called the customer to verify that a mistake had been made, apologized for the error, and offered to either credit the customer's account or come to her residence to make the proper exchange. Identification and correction of the problem enabled the store to maintain customer confidence and to develop a system to prevent recurrence." When the critical incident method is used, employees know that the supervisor has a factual record upon which to assess performance.

If the supervisor has chosen to use the employee self-rating approach mentioned earlier, the discussion primarily centres on the differences between the employee's self-ratings and the appraisal of the supervisor. This may involve considerable back-and-forth discussion, especially if there are major differences of opinion regarding various parts of the appraisal form. Typically, however, this is not a major difficulty unless the employee has an exaggerated notion of his or her ability or feels that the supervisor's ratings were unjustified. The current spate of downsizing and the shrinking job market may lead to greater disagreement over performance appraisal than in previous years since there are now more people competing for fewer jobs. Conflict will be particularly likely if the employee perceives that the supervisor's appraisal may jeopardize his or her job.

As part of the appraisal meeting, the supervisor must include a discussion about plans for improvement and possible opportunities for the employee's future. The supervisor should mention any educational or training plans that may be available. The goal of every employer should be to have a better-skilled workforce. This means that the supervisor should be familiar with advancement opportunities open to employees, requirements of future jobs, and each employee's personal ambitions and qualifications. In discussing the future, the supervisor should be careful not to make any promises for training or promotion that are not certain to materialize in the foreseeable future. Making false promises is a quick way to lose credibility.

The evaluation meeting also should provide the employee with an opportunity to ask questions, and the supervisor should answer them as fully as possible. If the supervisor is uncertain about the answer, it is better to say, "I don't know, but I'll find out and get back to you with an answer tomorrow." Employees lose trust in supervisors who evade the subject, are not truthful, and do not respond with answers in a timely fashion. In the final analysis, the value of an evaluation meeting depends on the employee's ability to recognize the need for self-improvement and the supervisor's ability to stimulate in the employee a desire to improve. It takes sensitivity and skill for a supervisor to accomplish this, and it is frequently necessary for the supervisor to adapt what is said to each employee's reactions as they surface during the meeting.

Difficult Responses During the Appraisal Meeting

Many supervisors try to avoid conducting appraisal meetings. They believe they need only fill out the form. With the increased demands placed on supervisors to do more with less, to increase productivity, and to find ways to continuously improve quality, many supervisors fail to find adequate time to evaluate the performance of their employees properly. As one manager recently stated, "We don't have time to evaluate around here. As you can see, we're up to our necks in things to do." However, supervisors *must* evaluate their employees' performance.

People react to performance appraisals in different ways. Figure 9-4 lists some of the responses that have been encountered by supervisors conducting performance meetings. Previous discussions regarding communication and interviewing should be reviewed for ideas on how to cope with such behaviours. Difficult responses can cause headaches for a supervisor, but they should not cause the supervisor to ignore or short-circuit the appraisal process.

Closing the Appraisal Meeting

When closing the appraisal meeting, the supervisor should be certain that the employee has a clear understanding of his or her performance rating. Where applicable, the supervisor and employee should agree on some mutual goals in areas in which the employee needs improvement. The supervisor should set a date with the employee—typically in a few weeks—to discuss progress toward

FIGURE 9-4   Difficult responses the supervisor may encounter during the appraisal meeting.

- "You hired me. Therefore, how can I be so bad?"
- "You're just out to get me!"
- "You don't like my lifestyle. This has nothing to do with my on-the-job performance."
- "This evaluation is not fair!"
- "I didn't know that was important. You never told me that."
- "Look, my job depends on getting good-quality material from others. I can't turn out quality work because I have to constantly inspect their work first."
- "You never say anything nice to me. You just make me feel so bad."
- The employee fails to comprehend what you've said.
- The employee refuses to talk, sits silently, or fails to respond to your open-ended questions.
- The employee rambles.
- The employee explodes and vents deep-seated hostilities toward you, his or her spouse, a parent, a coworker, and so on.
- The employee accuses you of gender, racial, religious, age, or other bias.

meeting the new goals. This reinforces the supervisor's stated intent to help the employee improve and gives the supervisor an opportunity to praise the employee for progress made.

Many organizations request that employees sign their performance appraisal form after the meeting. If a signature is requested as proof that the supervisor actually held the appraisal meeting, the supervisor should so inform the employee. The supervisor should ensure the employee understands that signing the form does not necessarily indicate agreement with the ratings on the form. Otherwise, the employee may be reluctant to sign the form, especially if he or she disagrees with some of the contents of the appraisal. Some appraisal forms have a line above or below the employee's signature stating that the signature confirms only that the appraisal meeting has taken place and that the employee does not necessarily agree or disagree with any statements made during the appraisal.

Some organizations require the supervisor to discuss employee appraisals with a manager or the human resources department before the appraisal documents are placed in the individual's permanent employment record. A supervisor may be challenged to justify certain ratings—if, for example, he or she has given very high or very low evaluations to the majority of departmental employees. For the most part, if the supervisor has appraised employees carefully and conscientiously, such challenges will be infrequent.

The employer should have an audit process to review supervisors' appraisal decisions. The purposes of this audit are to ensure that evaluations are done fairly and to provide employees with a means of resolving conflicts arising from the appraisal process. If the supervisor bases the appraisal on actual behaviour and approaches the appraisal with sensitivity, serious conflicts should be relatively rare.

6	**MANAGING PERFORMANCE APPRAISAL RESULTS: COACHING EMPLOYEES**

Discuss coaching as a follow-up to perform-ance appraisal.

Coaching
The frequent activity of the supervisor to provide employees with information, instruction, and suggestions relating to their job assignments and performance.

Effective supervisors use periodic performance evaluations as a way to develop their employees' competence. **Coaching** occurs when the supervisor provides employees with information, instructions, and suggestions relating to their job assignments and performance. The supervisor must be a coach, a cheerleader, and a facilitator to guide an employee's behaviours toward the desired results.[8] In this role the supervisor must reinforce the employee's positive behaviours and correct the negative behaviours in a positive way.

The supervisor's follow-up role in performance appraisal varies with the assessment. As a rule, supervisors use a coaching approach to help superior employees prepare for greater responsibility as well as to improve the perform-ance of all employees. In both cases, the purpose of coaching is to help the employee become more productive by developing an action plan. Even though a plan may be jointly determined with the employee, the supervisor is ultimately responsible for finalizing the plan and the necessary instructions for carrying it out. The questions presented in Figure 9-5 may serve as guidelines for the super-visor's coaching effort.

Effective supervisors recognize that ongoing employee skill development is critical to the organization's success. Instruction, practice, and feedback are essential elements of development. Imagine playing golf without first receiving instruction and having a chance to practise newly learned techniques. Most golfers seek instruction because they want to improve their game. Athletes such as Tiger Woods, who in 1996 made a swift transition from amateur golf to the professional circuit, are gifted with fundamental ability, yet they continually seek advice from their coaches.

In business, as in sports, employees benefit from coaching. The coach observes the employee's current performance and communicates what went well and what specifically needs to be improved. The plan for improvement usually includes defining the expected level of performance, recommending specific steps for improvement, and observing performance. After developing the plan, the coach instructs the employee, allows the employee time to practise the skills, and then observes the employee's performance, providing feedback about the effectiveness of the performance and offering further instruction and encouragement, if needed.

Generally, the employees who benefit most from coaching are the average performers, not the superstars. Average employees need to develop their skills and learn the fundamentals. The coach must provide constructive feedback on an ongoing basis. Remember, improvement does not occur instantly. The supervisor should be patient with the employee in the skill development process and allow for different learning styles and speeds.

Employee performance usually improves when specific improvement goals are established during the performance appraisal. It is important that the super-visor realize that he or she is responsible for improving the performance of a defi-cient employee. The supervisor must remember that an employee cannot improve performance unless he or she knows exactly what is expected. The supervisor should maintain close contact with the employee and provide instruction when needed. Supervisors also provide suggestions for improvement and serve as men-tors. Performance improvements should be supported by positive feedback and reinforcement.

FIGURE 9-5
Questions to determine coaching strategies.

The effective supervisor uses these questions to help the employee improve performance.

1. Have you identified specific areas of performance that need improvement?

2. Is it worth your time and effort to help the employee improve?

3. Does the employee understand that his or her performance needs improvement?

4. Does the employee know what is expected (standards of performance)?

5. Are there barriers beyond the employee's control that influence current performance?

6. Does the employee know how to do the job?

7. Could the employee do the job if his or her life depended on it? (If not, training is necessary.)

8. What happens when the employee does the job well?

9. What do you do when performance is deficient?

10. Have you considered alternative courses of action?

11. Have you and the employee mutually agreed on a course of action (e.g., set specific objectives and a timetable, developed improvement plans, identified training program, etc.)?

12. Have you provided information, instruction, and suggestions?

13. Does the employee fully understand the consequences if unacceptable performance continues?

14. What follow-up measures will you use and how will you measure improvements?

15. How will you reward and reinforce improvement?

16. What will you do if performance does not improve?

In rare circumstances when the action plan does not result in improved performance and unsatisfactory performance continues, termination may be necessary. Replacement of an employee is a very expensive proposition. Good coaching can avoid termination in many cases. The role of the supervisor in the positive discipline of less proficient employees is discussed in Chapter 10.

7   MANAGING PERFORMANCE APPRAISAL RESULTS: PROMOTING EMPLOYEES

Identify the benefits of a promotion-from-within policy.

Given the proper encouragement, many employees strive to improve their performance and eventually be promoted. A promotion usually means advancement to a job with more responsibility, more privileges, higher status, greater potential, and higher pay.

Although the majority of employees want to improve or advance, this is not true of everyone. Some employees have no desire to advance any further. They may feel that an increase in responsibility would demand too much of their time and energy—which they prefer to devote to other interests—or they may be content with the security of their present positions. But employees who do not want to improve or advance tend to be in the minority. Most employees want promotions. For them, starting at the bottom and rising in status and income over time is part of a normal career path.

Promoting from Within

Most organizations have policies for promoting employees. The policy of promotion from within is widely practised, and it is important to both an organization and its employees. For the organization, it means a steady source of trained personnel for higher positions; for employees, it is a major incentive to perform better. If employees have worked for an organization for a long time, more is usually known about them than even the best selection processes and interviews could reveal about outside applicants for the same job. Supervisors should know their own people well, but they do not know individuals hired from the outside until those individuals have worked for them a while.

Occasionally a supervisor might want to bypass an employee for promotion because the productivity of the department would suffer until a replacement is found and trained. This kind of thinking is short sighted. In the long run, it is better for the organization to have the best people in positions where they can make the greatest contribution to the organization's success.

Similarly, there would be little reason for employees to improve themselves if they believed that the better and higher-paying jobs were reserved for outsiders. Employees tend to be more satisfied when they know that stronger efforts on their part may lead to more interesting and challenging work, higher pay and status, and better working conditions. Most employees are better motivated if they see a link between excellent performance and promotion.

When considering promotion for an employee, the supervisor should recognize that what management considers a promotion may not always be perceived as such by the employee. For example, an engineer may believe that a promotion to managerial work is a hardship, not an advancement. The engineer may feel that managerial activities are less interesting or more difficult than technical duties and may be concerned about losing or diluting professional engineering skills. Such an attitude is understandable, and the supervisor should try to suggest promotional opportunities that do not require unacceptable compromises.

The supervisor should be sensitive to employees who appear to be satisfied in their present positions. They may prefer to stay with their fellow employees and retain familiar and comfortable responsibilities. These employees should not be pressured by the supervisor to accept higher-level positions. However, if the supervisor believes that such an employee has excellent qualifications for promotion, the supervisor should offer encouragement and support.

Modifying a Promotion-from-within Policy

Generally, it is preferable to apply a promotion-from-within policy whenever possible. However, situations will arise in which strict adherence to this policy would not be sensible and might even be harmful to an organization. If there are no qualified internal candidates for a position, then someone from the outside has to be recruited. For example, if an experienced computer programmer is needed and no existing employee has programming expertise, the departmental supervisor will have to hire from outside the organization.

At times, bringing a new employee into a department may be desirable since this person brings different ideas and fresh perspectives to the job. Another reason for recruiting employees from the outside is that an organization may not be in a position to train its own employees in the necessary skills. A particular position may require long, specialized, or expensive training, and the organization may be unable either to offer or to afford such training. In these situations, an absolute promotion-from-within policy must be modified. This is why most written policy statements concerning promotion from within include a qualifying clause such as "whenever possible" or "whenever feasible."

Criteria for Promotion from Within

Typically, more employees are interested in being promoted than there are openings available. Since promotions should serve as an incentive for employees to perform better, some supervisors believe that employees who have the best records of production, quality, and cooperation are the ones who should be promoted. In some situations, however, it is difficult to measure such aspects of employee performance accurately or objectively, even when there has been a conscientious effort by supervisors in the form of performance appraisals.

Seniority

Seniority

An employee's length of service within a department or organization.

One easily measured and objective criterion that has been applied extensively in an effort to reduce favouritism and discrimination is seniority. **Seniority** is an employee's length of service within the department or organization. Labour unions have emphasized seniority as a major promotion criterion, and its use is also widespread among organizations that are not unionized and for jobs that are not covered by union agreements. Many supervisors are comfortable with the concept of seniority as a basis for promotion. Some supervisors feel that an employee's loyalty, as expressed by length of service, deserves to be rewarded. Basing promotion on seniority also assumes that an employee's abilities tend to increase with service. Although this assumption is not always accurate, it is likely that with continued service an employee's skills and knowledge do improve. If promotion is to be based largely on seniority, then the initial selection procedure for new employees must be particularly careful, and each new employee should receive considerable training in various positions.

Probably the most serious drawback to using seniority as the major criterion for promotion is that it discourages employees who have less seniority. Less senior employees may believe that they cannot advance until they, too, have accumulated years of service on the job. Consequently, they may lose enthusiasm and perform at only an average level since they feel that no matter what they do, they will not be promoted for a long time. They may use this organization as a training ground and then move to another for a more senior job. Another serious drawback is that the best performer is not always the most senior. If seniority is the only criterion, then there is no incentive to perform well. Employees can be promoted for simply "sticking around."

Merit and Ability

Although labour unions have stressed the seniority criterion in promotion, seniority alone does not guarantee that an individual either deserves promotion or is capable of advancing to a higher-level job. In fact, some employees with high seniority may lack the necessary skill or educational levels needed for advancement. Consequently, most unions understand that length of service cannot be the only criterion for promotion. They agree that promotion should be based on seniority combined with merit and ability, and this type of provision is included in many union contracts.

Merit usually refers to the quality of an employee's job performance. **Ability** means an employee's capability or potential to perform, or to be trained to perform, a higher-level job. Supervisors often are in the best position to determine the degree to which merit and ability are necessary to compensate for less seniority. However, seniority is frequently the decisive criterion when merit and ability are relatively equal among several candidates seeking a promotion.

Merit
The quality of an employee's job performance.

Ability
An employee's potential to perform assigned tasks.

Balancing the Criteria

Good supervisory practice attempts to attain a workable balance between the concepts of merit and ability on the one hand, and seniority on the other. When selecting from among the most qualified candidates available, the supervisor may make the decision primarily on the basis of seniority. Or, the supervisor may decide that, to be promoted, the employee who is most capable but who has less seniority will have to be far better than those with more seniority. Otherwise, the supervisor will promote the qualified employee with the greatest seniority, at least on a trial basis.

Because promotion decisions can have great significance, the preferred solution would be to apply all criteria equally. However, promotion decisions often involve "grey" areas or subjective considerations that can lead rejected employees to be dissatisfied and file grievances. Realistically, unless there are unusual circumstances involved, it is unlikely that a supervisor will choose to promote an employee over other eligible candidates solely on the basis of merit and ability without giving some thought to seniority.

8	MANAGING PERFORMANCE APPRAISAL RESULTS: COMPENSATING EMPLOYEES

Discuss the supervisor's role in employee compensation and outline the goals of an effective compensation program.

Although it is not always recognized as such, a supervisor's staffing function includes helping to determine the relative worth of a job. Typically, wage rates and salary schedules are formulated by higher-level management, the human resources department, union contract, or government legislation or regulation. In this respect, the supervisor's authority is limited. Nevertheless, within such limitations, the supervisor is responsible for determining appropriate compensation for departmental employees.

The question of how much to pay employees has posed a problem for many organizations. It is possible, however, to establish a compensation program that is objective, fair, and relatively easy to administer. The objectives of a compensation program should be to

- Eliminate pay inequities to minimize dissatisfaction and complaints among employees.
- Establish and/or maintain sufficiently attractive pay rates so that qualified employees are attracted to and retained by the company.
- Conduct periodic employee merit ratings to provide the basis for comparative performance rewards.
- Control labour costs with respect to gains in productivity.
- Reward employees for outstanding performance or the acquisition of additional skills or knowledge.

Every supervisor has some responsibility for establishing compensation standards that will attract and retain competent employees. Too often, wage rate schedules simply follow historical patterns, or they are formulated haphazardly. At the departmental level, wage rate inequities often develop over time due to changes in jobs, changes in personnel, and supervisors who use varying standards for administering compensation. Supervisors should immediately address any wage inequities or concerns, and strive for a wage system that is consistent and fair.

The Supervisor's Role in Compensation Decisions

Although an equitable compensation structure should be of great concern to everyone in management, it is an area in which supervisors typically have little direct authority. However, supervisors should make an effort to make higher-level managers aware of serious compensation inequities at the departmental level. This can often be done when supervisors make their recommendations for wage and salary adjustments for individual employees.

Unfortunately, supervisors often recommend automatic wage increases rather than seriously considering whether each employee deserves such a raise. Here is where employee performance evaluation becomes crucial. If an employee's work has been satisfactory, then the employee deserves the normal increase. But if the employee has performed at an unsatisfactory level, the supervisor should suspend the recommendation for an increase and discuss this decision with the employee. The supervisor might outline specific targets for job improvement that the employee must meet before the supervisor will recommend a wage increase at a future date. If an employee has performed at an outstanding level, the supervisor should not hesitate to recommend a generous, above-average wage increase if this can be done within the current wage structure. Such a tangible reward will encourage the outstanding employee to continue striving for excellence.

Employee Incentives

Many organizations attempt to directly link an employee's pay to his or her performance. Performance-based or incentive compensation systems are designed to motivate employees to perform at a higher level.[9] In this section we present an overview of incentive systems.

Piecework

Piecework

Piecework
System in which the employee earns a certain amount of pay for each piece produced.

In a straight **piecework** system the employee earns a certain amount of pay for each piece produced. Difficulties arise when jobs are interdependent and the employee must rely on others in order to complete his or her assigned task.

Pay for Performance

Pay for performance is compensation given strictly on the basis of achieving employee or corporate performance goals. Among these approaches are special cash awards, bonuses for meeting performance targets, team (departmental) incentive bonuses, profit sharing, and gain sharing for meeting production or cost-saving goals. **Gain-sharing plans** are group incentive plans. Group or team plans are usually used when either the contribution of an individual employee is not easily measurable or when performance depends on team cooperation. Employees share the monetary benefits (gains) of improved productivity, cost reductions, or improvements in quality or customer service. Most plans use an easy-to-understand formula to calculate productivity gains and the resulting bonus.

Skill-Based Pay

A **skill-based pay** or knowledge-based pay system rewards employees for acquiring additional skills or knowledge within the same job category. Employees are rotated through a variety of tasks associated with the job until they learn them all. The rewards are based on acquisition of and proficiency in new skills, regardless of the employee's length of service.[10] Employees are rewarded in accordance with the number of skills they have mastered. Skill-based pay has become popular as a way to reward employees when promotional opportunities are scarce.

Skill-based pay is most successful in organizations in which a participatory management philosophy prevails. The supervisor is usually the key to the success of a skill-based pay plan. Other attributes of a skill-based pay system are

1. The need for deep commitment to training to achieve success.
2. The necessary use of job rotation.
3. The fact that the choice of plan is tied to business needs.
4. The support of supervisors.
5. The fact that it is not for every company.[11]

For a skill-based pay plan to succeed, the company must require and directly benefit from the skills it pays for. A closed-end questionnaire is used by employees to identify the activities, skills, knowledge, and abilities required by their jobs. All jobs are assigned a pay grade based on the value of their required activities, skills, and knowledge.[12] All employees then know what they must be able to do in order to be eligible for a promotion or a lateral transfer.

Suggestion Plans

In earlier chapters, we discussed the fact that employees may be motivated by the sense of achievement that comes from seeing their ideas implemented. Suggestion plans are one way to solicit employee ideas; typically employees are paid based on the value of their suggestions. Suggestion systems, however, may fail if they are evaluated on the basis of the savings alone.[13] For example, an employee might suggest a way that the company could become more environmentally responsible. This suggestion may not result in any direct cost savings to the company, but would have many indirect benefits in terms of corporate image and goodwill.

Employee Benefits

In addition to monetary compensation, most organizations provide supplementary benefits for employees, such as vacations with pay, holidays, retirement plans, insurance and health programs, tuition-aid programs, employee assistance programs (EAPs), and numerous other services. Supervisors have little involvement in establishing benefits, but they are obligated to see that departmental employees understand how their benefits operate and that each employee receives his or her fair share.

When employees have questions about benefits, supervisors should consult with the human resources staff or higher-level managers. For example, a supervisor often has to make decisions involving employee benefits, such as scheduling departmental vacations and work shifts during the holidays. In these circumstances, the supervisor must be sure that what is done at the departmental level is consistent with the organization's overall policies, as well as with federal and provincial laws, and union contract provisions.

Compensation Concerns

It is common for employees to compare their own compensation with that of others. This becomes a serious motivational problem for the supervisor when the organization has wages or benefits that are lower than those for similar jobs at other firms in the community.

Two-tier wage systems and the use of contract employees are additional challenges for the supervisor in trying to maintain a perception of fairness. A two-tier wage system means that new employees are paid less than present employees performing the same or similar jobs. Unfortunately, lower-paid employees can have feelings of inequity when working under these systems.

Regardless of the compensation system used, employees must perceive that the program is fair. Supervisors should make every effort to stay informed about their organization's compensation system and should consult the human resources or benefits office when questions arise. Supervisors should permit and even encourage employees to visit the human resources department—or the appropriate manager—for advice and assistance concerning benefits. This is particularly desirable when individual employees have personal problems or questions about sensitive areas such as medical and other health benefits or retirement and insurance programs.

WHAT CALL DID YOU MAKE?

As Franca Zulfi, advertising supervisor in the marketing department for a major retail department chain, informal appraisals of employees such as Art Williams should have been an accepted part of your normal supervisory routine. Effective supervisors provide their employees with frequent feedback on performance. Unfortunately, you have violated almost every rule of performance appraisal discussed in this chapter. Your communication with Williams during the year has been minimal, and you have treated performance appraisal as a task to be completed only once a year as opposed to an ongoing responsibility.

You must recognize that the success of a performance management system depends, in part, on how well you communicate expectations, provide daily feedback on performance, and train and develop your employees to their full potential. A performance appraisal system will help you make better decisions in the areas of compensation, training, promotion, retention, and termination. While having performance appraisal discussions with people such as Williams can be uncomfortable, avoiding the issue and avoiding your responsibilities for performance management in your department will only make matters worse.

You have neglected your supervisory responsibilities this year. Your responsibility is to assess, inform, guide, and develop your employees. Last year, you assessed Williams's performance and communicated that assessment to him, but when there was a substantive difference of opinion, you abandoned those efforts. Williams left the appraisal meeting without signing the form, and you did not identify future performance goals. You did not follow up with Williams, and you have taken no action to help guide his performance this year.

For his part, Williams has done nothing this year to address the performance issue. Williams failed to take the initiative to communicate openly with you. He disagreed with your evaluation of his performance and he, too, has avoided the issue. He should have asked you to identify performance improvement goals and asked for specific suggestions on ways to improve.

Moving forward, you must now address what you should do as Williams enters your office. You

should courteously welcome him in, ask him to sit down, review with him the purposes of the company's formal appraisal process, and give him a blank copy of the evaluation form. Ask him to take the form away and complete it so that you and he will have a basis for starting a discussion about his contribution to the department. Ask him to set up a meeting with you when his self-assessment is complete. This will enable you to get some things in order. Of course, you could always improvise the appraisal meeting, but employees want to work for supervisors they can respect and trust. During the past year, you left Williams alone to do the work that must be done. If you improvise in the appraisal meeting, the doors of communication may become permanently closed between you and Williams.

Clearly, you should learn from this experience. When conducting a formal appraisal meeting, be sure to focus on job performance standards and specific objectives that have been communicated to the employee. Avoid the various rating errors mentioned in this chapter. Focus on the job Williams is doing, then pause. Williams could be a better employee than you believe. If so, he should have an opportunity to point out specific areas where he believes he performed in a superior manner. Get input from coworkers, colleagues, customers, and others who have had an opportunity to observe Williams's performance over the past year. You may be correct in your assessment, but without documentation, your case lacks credibility. Finally, put yourself in Williams's position and try to anticipate his questions and concerns.

When you meet with Williams again, start by reviewing his self-assessment. Discuss areas of performance where you agree that he deserves an "above average" rating. This will build some common ground. Then, address the most important areas where you feel Williams's performance has not deserved an "above average" rating. Be specific, and use examples from his work to reinforce your point. The toughest part of the appraisal meeting will be if Williams accuses you of being unfair. Because you anticipated this accusation, however, you will have checked all the records and have specific dates and instances in which William's performance was, indeed, average.

You should review with Williams the meaning of an "average" rating. He may see this as a criticism of

(continued)

his work when, in fact, it usually means that the employee is "meeting expectations." Provide specific examples of what "above average" performance would actually look like in Williams's job. Be sure that he understands exactly what it would take to achieve an "above average" rating in the specific areas that he is most concerned with. Perhaps Williams has never had a clear understanding of the performance standards in his job. He may legitimately have felt that he was going "above and beyond the call of duty" when, in fact, he was just meeting the normal expectations.

Ensure that you have a follow-up plan. After the appraisal meeting, it is essential that you make a point of regularly checking in with Williams. Be sure that he knows that you are available to help him and give him positive feedback when you see his performance beginning to improve. Schedule a follow-up meeting and ensure that you have documented specific examples of his recent work to discuss with him.

In the future, you must give your employees regular feedback on performance so there will be no surprises during appraisal meetings. Positive feedback on performance is an effective tool for developing employees. Make the performance appraisal of all your employees a high priority. This means carefully monitoring your employees, having periodic meetings and discussions with them to discuss performance and progress, establishing goals for performance, and providing feedback when employees perform exceptionally well or do not meet standards. A written record of performance indicators is highly recommended.

SUMMARY

A formal performance appraisal system is the process of periodically rating an employee's performance against standards and communicating this feedback to the employee. Supervisors are responsible for appraising employee performance both on an informal, day-to-day basis and formally at predetermined intervals. To ensure that appraisals are based on facts rather than opinions, supervisors need to keep accurate records of employee performance.

To ensure that employees feel that the appraisal process is fair, each evaluator must understand what is necessary for successful job performance. Peer evaluations and 360-degree performance evaluations are ways to provide performance feedback from perspectives other than just the supervisor's, and they can contribute to a more complete performance picture. Including self-rating in the process can facilitate open discussion of an employee's own perceptions of his or her strengths and weaknesses.

Most organizations require formal performance appraisals at least once each year. In addition to formal appraisals, supervisors should provide their employees with frequent feedback on performance throughout the year. Because the decision to retain or not retain a new employee is critical, performance assessment of probationary employees should be done at the end of the probationary period. For every employee, the supervisor should provide immediate feedback anytime there is a performance problem. Ongoing feedback, both positive and negative, should be a regular part of the supervisor's routine. If the employee is given ongoing feedback, then the annual appraisal should contain no surprises. It should be a review of what the supervisor and employee have discussed during the year.

If properly done, formal performance appraisals benefit both the organization and the employee. Organizations use performance appraisals as a basis for making important decisions concerning promotions, raises, and terminations. Performance appraisals reward employees' good performance and inform them about how they can become more productive.

3 The major advantage of a formal system is that it provides a framework to help the supervisor systematically evaluate performance and communicate to the employees how they are doing. Formal appraisals can be an incentive to employees. They get positive feedback about their performance, and they know that the formal system provides documentation of their performance.

Much of the criticism of performance appraisals dwells on the fact that they often focus only on past accomplishments or deficiencies. Supervisors can overcome this criticism by emphasizing the developmental aspects of performance appraisal. Ensure that employees see the performance appraisal process as a way of developing plans and goals for the future.

4 Appraisal forms may vary in format and approach, but they should all allow supervisors to identify the outstanding aspects of the employee's work, specify performance areas that need improvement, and suggest ways to improve performance.

Supervisors should be consistent in applying the terms used to describe an employee's performance. Not all supervisors judge employees' performance accurately, and sometimes a supervisor can damage an employee's morale by giving lower ratings than the employee deserves. Additional perceptual errors include the leniency error, the halo and horns effects, and other personal biases.

When completing the appraisal form, the supervisor should focus on the employee's accomplishments. The results should be described in terms of "how much," "how well," and "in what manner." Whatever the choice of appraisal form, it is important that every appraisal be made within the context of the employee's particular job and be based on the employee's total performance.

5 Although the appraisal meeting may be a trying situation, the entire employee performance appraisal system is of no use if this aspect is ignored or is carried out improperly. The supervisor should begin by stating that the overall purpose of the appraisal meeting is to let the employee know how he or she is doing. The supervisor should recognize and praise good performance, emphasize strengths that the employee can build upon, and identify areas of performance that need improvement.

The meeting should be conducted shortly after the form is completed, and in private. How the supervisor conducts the meeting depends to a large extent on the employee's performance. Supervisors should address those areas that most need correction or improvement. An employee performing at a substandard level must clearly understand that the deficiencies are serious and that substantial improvement is needed. An employee is more likely to agree with the appraisal when he or she understands the standards of performance and recognizes that the appraisal is free of bias.

The supervisor should emphasize that all employees in the same job are evaluated using the same standards and process. Supervisors may use a critical incident method for documenting employee performance that is very good or unsatisfactory. Employees should be given an opportunity to ask questions, and the supervisor should answer them honestly. The supervisor should anticipate questions, potential areas of disagreement, and difficult responses that may arise during the appraisal meeting.

The employee should clearly understand his or her evaluation. New objectives should be set and areas for improvement identified. Generally, the employee is asked to sign the appraisal form to prove that the meeting took place. Organizations should have an audit process to resolve conflicts arising from the appraisal.

6 All supervisors should fulfill the role of coach in the conduct of their daily activities. During the performance appraisal process, supervisors provide employees with information, instruction, and suggestions relating to their job assignments and performance.

Supervisors can use a coaching approach to prepare superior employees for greater responsibility as well as to improve the performance of all employees. Ongoing employee skill development is essential. Based on the performance appraisal, the coach develops a plan for improvement and sets specific improvement goals with the employee's input. The employee receives instruction and is given an opportunity to practise. The coach provides feedback and encouragement.

7 Most employees want to improve and advance in the organization. Promotion from within is a widely practised personnel policy that is beneficial to the organization and to the morale of employees. Supervisors know their employees' strengths and abilities; they do not know as much about individuals hired from the outside. If employees know that they have a good chance of advancement, they will have an incentive to improve their job performance. In short, promotion from within rewards employees for their good performance and serves notice to other employees that good performance can lead to advancement.

Strict adherence to a promotion-from-within policy would not be sensible. If internal employees have not received the necessary training, an external candidate may be preferred. Sometimes, an outsider may be needed to inject new and different ideas. However, organizations should promote from within whenever possible.

Since promotions should serve as an incentive for employees to perform better, it is generally believed that employees who have the best performance records should be promoted. Nevertheless, seniority still serves as a basis for many promotions. Seniority is easily understood and withstands charges of favouritism and discrimination. However, a promotional system based solely on seniority removes the incentive for junior employees who want to advance. Although it is difficult to specify exactly what should be the basis for employee promotion, there should be appropriate consideration of ability and merit on the one hand, and length of service on the other.

8 The supervisor's staffing function includes ensuring that employees of his or her department are properly compensated. Many compensation considerations are not within the direct domain of a supervisor.

Tangible monetary rewards serve, in part, to reward employees who perform at an outstanding level. However, supervisors must become aware of other compensation arrangements that may better meet their employees' needs. Pay for performance, skill-based pay, suggestion systems, and other benefit plans should be considered.

Since supervisory responsibility and authority are limited in these areas, supervisors should work closely with the human resources staff to maintain equitable compensation offerings and to ensure that departmental employees are informed and fairly treated in regard to benefits and any bonus plans that may be available.

QUESTIONS FOR DISCUSSION

1. What are the purposes of a formal performance appraisal system?
2. Discuss why many employees are uncomfortable with formal performance appraisals. What can the supervisor do to eliminate much of the discomfort that employees experience around the issue of appraisals?
3. What are the benefits of using peer ratings, 360-degree evaluations, and an employee self-rating approach?
4. Outline what a supervisor should do before, during, and after the appraisal meeting to ensure that the performance appraisal process improves rather than hinders the employee's motivation to perform.
5. Discuss and evaluate the issues related to promotion based on seniority on the one hand, and merit and ability on the other. Are there clear guidelines that a supervisor can use to ensure a workable balance between these criteria?

SKILLS APPLICATIONS

Skills Application 9-1: Controversy Surrounding Performance Appraisals

There is significant disagreement in the business and educational communities about whether formal performance appraisals, even when done well, ever have a positive impact on the organization. Some people argue that no matter how well planned or conducted, the formal performance appraisal process will always leave employees feeling demoralized. Other people feel that the formal appraisal system can be an effective means of improving overall performance in the organization and motivating employees toward higher achievement.

1. Using an Internet search engine, type in "abolishing performance appraisals" or "scrapping performance appraisals" to find opinions that support the discontinuation of formal performance appraisals. Also try www.businessknowhow.com/manage/abolish/feedback.htm, www.hrmsllc.com/news/00art2.htm and http://home.att.net/~nickols/scrap_it.htm for articles that put forward this opinion.
2. Using an Internet search engine, find articles that support the continuation of the formal appraisal process. One example can be found at www.workforce.com/section/01/feature/23/48/77/.
3. Identify the strongest arguments on each side of this issue.
4. Based on your research, which opinion do you support? Why?

Skills Application 9-2: Role-Play Exercise

1. Form into groups of three, with one person acting as the employee, a second as the supervisor, and the third as observer. The supervisor will evaluate the employee using the information contained in one of the situations listed below. The supervisor role will require you to use your imagination in providing feedback. It is suggested that you review the "Check-the-Box" Appraisal Form in Figure 9-1.

   The observer will observe the interview relationship using the Observer Recording Form (provided by your instructor) At the end of each interview, the observer will provide feedback on the effectiveness/ineffectiveness of the interview.

2. Rotate roles. Continue the exercise by switching roles until all participants have played each of the roles.

Situation A: "Nowhere to Go." Allison Adams is an above-average performer with high potential for advancement. She was promoted three years ago to her current position as produce department manager for Sanders Supermarkets. She has worked for Sanders for the past seven years. She won a supervisory management contest sponsored by the local college last summer. Her strengths lie in personal efficiency, job knowledge, and dependability. On occasion, she is "too customer service oriented"; for example, she makes substitutions of more expensive produce for a lower price. You approach the interview knowing the following circumstances:
a. There are roadblocks ahead for the employee such that her opportunity for advancement is limited for the foreseeable future.
b. There are several opportunities for advancement in the organization, but they require relocation or rotating shift work (both undesirable alternatives from the employee's perspective).

Situation B: "The Expert." Ahmed Shamara had been a regional supervisor for Sanders Supermarkets. When the organization consolidated operations, Shamara was demoted and transferred to an assistant's position at the Pridemore location. Shamara has been with Sanders for over 30 years and is much older than his supervisor. He shows up for work early and stays late, and his knowledge of the supermarket industry is second to none. However, he is unwilling to share it with anyone. He is very angry about the demotion. In general, he is very difficult to work with. He is belligerent toward younger employees, resents your authority, and insists on doing things "Ahmed's way." You have constantly counselled Shamara on his inappropriate behaviours, and he reminds you that he started at Sanders "before you were born." Some employees try to avoid him. Several have threatened to quit unless he changes his ways. As well, Shamara has made some serious errors in scheduling of deliveries. You approach the interview knowing the following circumstances:
a. Shamara's performance is unsatisfactory on most factors.
b. You question whether he should be retained as an employee. Your perspective is clouded because you know that your immediate supervisor trained under Shamara and has said on several occasions that Shamara taught him everything he knows. Your supervisor feels that if Shamara hadn't helped him back then, he wouldn't have such a great job today.

Situation C: "Miss Cue." Mary Cue has an entry-level data-processing position at Sanders Supermarkets. She has been on the job for six months and is generally performing at "less than a satisfactory level." She has an attendance problem. She usually misses work once every two weeks—either on a Monday or Friday. On five occasions, something happened that required her to leave work early to check on her elderly parents. She has a tendency to rush work, thus causing errors in payment and shipments. She often can be found in other parts of the building chatting with other employees. She is a great storyteller. You sent her to a Windows XP class but she has trouble progressing beyond the basics. Her attention span is limited, and she does not readily grasp new concepts. You approach the interview knowing the following circumstances:
a. Mary is a single parent.
b. Mary believes that she is underpaid for the work she is expected to do.

Source: The format for this role-play exercise was adapted from Don Harvey and Robert Bruce Bowin, *Human Resource Management: An Experiential Approach* (Upper Saddle River, NJ: Prentice Hall, 1996), p. 151. The situations were developed by Professors Leonard and Hilgert for use in this edition. The Observer Rating Form in the *Instructor's Manual* may be reproduced for use with Skills Application 9-2 only.

Skills Application 9-3: What Is the Right Way to Pay Employees?

1. Using the Internet, find information about incentive compensation programs. (At the time of publication, www.workopolis.com/servlet/Content/fasttrack/20031029/RWAGES29?section=HR was a link to one article. Typing "incentive pay plans" into a popular search engine will provide other sources.)
2. Based on your research, how common are incentive pay plans in Canada? What types of incentives are most commonly used?
3. Would an incentive pay system be appropriate for college or university employees? Why or why not?
4. With a group of your classmates, discuss the following:
   a. If an incentive program would be appropriate for college or university employees, should there be more than one plan, each tailored to different job classifications?
   b. What should be the basis of incentive payments?
   c. What kinds of incentives should be included?
5. Why is it important for employees to be compensated on some basis other than seniority?
6. Compare your responses with those of other groups. What common views do you have? What are areas of difference? Discuss the basis for your differences.

SKILLS DEVELOPMENT

Skill Development Module 9-1: Coaching and Performance Appraisal

This video segment features Ken Foley, a production development specialist with Carson Products, as he tries to handle a situation with Jennifer Swanson, a systems designer, who comes to him for advice and guidance.

Questions for Discussion: The Ineffective Version

1. Discuss Foley's coaching pitfalls.
2. In some organizations employees rate their supervisors. If you were Swanson, how would you rate Foley as a supervisor? Why?
3. How do you think Swanson will continue to perform on the job—more effectively or less? Why?
4. If you were Foley, what would you do to be more effective in helping Swanson with her concerns?

Questions for Discussion: The More Effective Version

1. Discuss Foley's appraisal and coaching technique.
2. How would you rate Foley's performance as a supervisor? Illustrate with specific examples to support your rating.
3. If you were Foley, what would you do to be even more effective in helping Swanson with her concerns?
4. Why should Foley strive to provide his employees with daily feedback on performance?

CASES

CASE 9-1

I Hate Performance Appraisals

Patrick James was distribution centre supervisor for Barry Automotive's Oshawa plant. When the 12-year veteran was promoted to supervisor six years ago, there was no resentment on the part of the employees, because he was generally well liked and viewed as deserving the supervisory position. James had practised open and honest communication with his employees and developed a climate of mutual trust and respect. The employees would "go to the wall" to get their jobs done effectively and efficiently. However, there was little possibility for James to advance beyond his present position. A lateral move within the company might be possible, but a promotion would require moving to the U.S. facility, and James did not want to uproot his family.

Several years ago, a formal appraisal system was instituted at Barry Automotive. It consisted primarily of having each supervisor complete a rating scale evaluation form with space for comments, then discuss the appraisal with each employee. In three weeks, James would have to conduct appraisals with all his employees in order to meet the deadline set by the head office. He looked forward to doing the appraisals, with one exception: Brigitta Swensen.

The 33-year-old Swensen was promoted to assistant supervisor about two years ago. She was regarded as an effective supervisor. She was knowledgeable about the technical aspects of the job and had shared her expertise with all employees. She emphasized that the success of Barry Automotive depended on how quickly an employee could learn new processes and apply them to better serving customers. A perfectionist, Swensen demanded no less from other employees. A few employees considered her to be pushy and strong willed.

Swensen was to receive her diploma in Business Administration at the end of this term, and James knew that she expected to advance in the organization to a position with additional responsibility.

Generally, Swensen's employees got their work done in an exceptional manner, but every once in a while, she overstepped her bounds. She required strict adherence to company rules, at all times and in all circumstances. She was particularly upset when employees told jokes that she considered to be "off colour." Twice in the past two months, Swensen had called James in to reprimand employees for this behaviour. James knew that Swensen had expected him to do more to eliminate the jokes.

Barry Automotive's sales and profits had been declining over the last 15 months. People in other industries in the area had been laid off, and the unemployment level in the region was at a five-year high. James had four unfilled positions in the plant because upper management would not allow him to hire replacements for people who had retired. The consolidation of duties forced managers and supervisors to find creative solutions to problems and to do more with fewer resources.

James knew that Swensen's performance was very good and that she very much wanted to become a full-fledged supervisor. There was little likelihood that such a position would become available any time soon at the Oshawa plant. James was not looking forward to the performance appraisal.

Questions for Discussion

1. According to some experts, employee appraisals are detested by both management and employees. Outline a process that might help James feel more comfortable in conducting the performance appraisal of Swensen.
2. Having direct reports, peers, and customers provide assessments of a manager's performance has gained in popularity. If James decides to solicit the input of others (a 360-degree evaluation), how should he go about doing it?
3. How should James conduct Swensen's performance appraisal?
4. What should James do to help Swensen meet her career goals?

CASE 9-2

The Psychological Assessment

Nelson Financial Group has 41 insurance and mortgage loan offices located throughout Canada. Colette Dupuis worked as application processing clerk at the home office for three years prior to being promoted to group leader. Group leaders at Nelson Group were working members of the team who had responsibility for assigning work and training new employees. In a recent conversation with her supervisor, John Townsend, Dupuis expressed an interest in being considered for a supervisory position in the future.

Nelson Group used the services of a psychological testing firm to profile each supervisory and managerial candidate. Townsend sent Dupuis to the human resources department to make arrangements to have her profiled. About a week later, Dupuis spent a day at the office of Psychological Diagnostics, a local consulting firm. She was given a battery of assessment tests and was interviewed by two of this firm's psychologists. Two weeks later, the following report was sent to Shelley Schwarz, human resources manager for Nelson Group.

Summary Assessment Profile for Colette Dupuis

She has average problem-solving and reasoning ability. Although learning ability is average, repetition may still be an effective training method, particularly if the work is complicated and technical. Management can assign Ms Dupuis to special projects that will help her improve her problem-solving and reasoning ability. Any effort she makes to increase reading speed or enhance her memory skills should be encouraged.

Ms Dupuis has had very little exposure to business terminology. Her observational skills are weak. She also may have a short attention span. Her language skills are below average, but she is bilingual. When working under pressure, she feels much more comfortable relying on her French vocabulary. She has obtained a great deal of computer literacy. She appears to be consistent and honest, and flexible enough to handle emergencies. She is a fair and reliable individual who could easily win the trust of her co-workers.

Ms Dupuis is a reserved person who does not feel comfortable around people she does not know. At first, others may find her distant and detached. As they become better acquainted, they will see that she is a good listener who has difficulty expressing herself around strangers.

Ms Dupuis is very competitive and is prepared to meet or beat any challenge. She has an intense desire to excel and takes pride in her accomplishments. She is efficient and works hard to achieve her goals. However, she is not a team player and is often reluctant to contribute to a group project. She wants her work to stand on its own merits. Relationships with co-workers may suffer because of her strong desire to win. Ms Dupuis does not handle criticism or rejection well. She often becomes discouraged for short periods of time. Ms Dupuis becomes remotivated when the "right" rewards are offered. She will take risks if the potential for personal gain and recognition are evident.

Townsend and Schwarz reviewed Dupuis's performance appraisal results and the psychological assessment profile. Schwarz commented to Townsend that, "with proper coaching," Colette Dupuis could be prepared for a group leader or supervisory position.

Questions for Discussion

1. What should Townsend do to assist Dupuis if she pursues a supervisory position?
2. Describe how Townsend should develop Dupuis's potential.
3. Using the factors in determining training needs and the questions that supervisors should ask in formulating an employee development program, outline a development program for Dupuis.

Chapter 10: Positive Discipline

After studying this chapter you will be able to

1 Discuss the basis and importance of positive discipline in an organization.

2 Identify disciplinary situations that violate standards of conduct, and discuss the need to confront those situations appropriately.

3 Discuss the disciplinary process and approaches that ensure disciplinary action for just cause.

4 Define and discuss the application of progressive discipline.

5 Explain the "hot-stove rule" for disciplinary actions.

6 Discuss the need to document disciplinary actions and to provide the right of appeal.

7 Explain the discipline-without-punishment approach as an alternative to progressive discipline.

You are Linda Capelli, a departmental supervisor for a major aerospace firm. You currently manage a group of six accountants and financial analysts, and a clerk who is responsible for maintaining all contract records for one of the company's aircraft programs. All of the accountants and financial analysts have bachelors' degrees and most are currently pursuing or have completed requirements for a master's degree. Over the past year, two of your employees left the company. Because the company was facing difficult times, these individuals were not replaced. Consequently, the remaining members of the department had to keep up with heavy workloads. Considerable overtime and Saturday work were necessary. About a month ago, higher-level management agreed to move an available person from another division to your department. This employee, Scott Morino, had worked for the company for five years since graduating with an accounting degree. During this time he also completed his master's degree through night courses at the local university. He came to the department with excellent credentials, and he had a high recommendation from his previous supervisor in corporate accounting.

Thursday at 5:30 P.M. Devica Florence, one of your financial analysts, came into your office and said,

"Well I don't really know where to start, Linda, so I guess I'll just jump right in. Quite a few of us in the department are upset with Scott. I don't know if you're aware of the situation or not, but the bottom line is he just doesn't do anything. He's great at reading *The Financial Post* and making weekend and evening plans. But when the rest of us are hustling to get the job done, it's a bit frustrating to watch him relaxing at his desk. He even went so far as to give out his office telephone number when he listed his car for sale. Then, because he was on the phone all the time, most calls went to our department clerk, John. John was really angry, and I don't blame him. He has enough to do just supporting the rest of us. I know Scott's still pretty new in our department but the job here is not that different from the work he did in corporate accounting. Given how shorthanded we are, department morale is certainly going to drop further if he continues this way. One last thing. He's called in sick three days this month. None of us believes that he was sick since all of his absences were on Friday or Monday."

After Devica leaves, you wonder how to handle the situation. You have never experienced a problem quite like this in three years of supervising this department.

You make the call!

---

1 | THE BASIS AND IMPORTANCE OF POSITIVE DISCIPLINE

Discuss the basis and importance of positive discipline in an organization.

Discipline
State of orderliness; the degree to which employees act according to expected standards of behaviour.

Positive discipline
Condition that exists when employees generally follow the rules and meet the standards of the organization.

The term *discipline* is used in several different ways. Many supervisors associate it with the use of authority, force, or punishment. In this text, however, we prefer to consider **discipline** as a condition of orderliness, that is, the degree to which members of an organization act properly and observe the expected standards of behaviour. **Positive discipline** exists when employees generally follow the rules and meet the standards of the organization. Discipline is negative (or bad) when they follow the rules reluctantly or when they actually disobey regulations and violate the prescribed standards of acceptable behaviour.

Discipline is not identical to morale. Morale is a state of mind, whereas discipline is primarily a state of affairs. However, there is some relationship between morale and discipline. Normally there are fewer disciplinary problems when morale is high; conversely, low morale is usually accompanied by more disciplinary problems. Yet a high degree of positive discipline could be present in spite of low morale; this could result from insecurity, fear, or sheer force. However, it is unlikely that a high degree of positive employee discipline will be maintained indefinitely unless there is an acceptable level of employee morale.

Positive self-discipline
Employees regulating their own behaviour out of self-interest and their normal desire to meet reasonable standards.

The best type of discipline is **positive self-discipline** in which employees essentially regulate themselves out of their own self-interest. This is based on the normal human tendency to do what needs to be done, to do one's share, and to follow reasonable standards of acceptable behaviour. Even before they start to work, most people accept the idea that following instructions and fair rules of conduct are normal responsibilities in any job.

Positive self-discipline relies on the premise that most employees want to do the right thing and can be counted on to exercise self-control. They believe in performing their work properly; coming to work on time; following the supervisor's instructions; and refraining from fighting, using drugs, drinking alcohol, or stealing. They know that it is natural to subordinate some of their own personal interests to the needs of the organization. As long as company rules are communicated and are perceived as reasonable, most employees usually will observe the rules.

Unfortunately, there are always some employees who, for one reason or another, fail to observe established rules and standards even after having been informed of them. For example, employee theft from employers is an escalating problem. The Retail Council of Canada estimates that retail losses due to employee theft in Canada amounted to over $3 million per day or an astounding $1.2 billion annually. These losses were attributed to dishonest employee activities such as fraudulent use of customer credit cards, unauthorized price reductions at point of sale, and theft of cash. In 2003, losses in the retail sector due to employee theft were estimated to be even higher than external theft by non-employees.[1] These alarming numbers do not even include the effect of employee theft in the non-retail sector of the economy. When added to other forms of employee dishonesty—including habitual misuse or "stealing" of company time by unwarranted absenteeism, tardiness, doing personal business, and socializing on company time—the cost of employee theft to businesses in Canada has been estimated to be in the multiple billions of dollars each year!

Positive Employee Discipline Requires Supervisory Example

Despite such unfortunate statistics, supervisors should maintain a balanced perspective that employees at the departmental level are, for the most part, honest and reliable. Employees will take most of their cues for self-discipline from their supervisors and managers. Ideally, positive self-discipline should exist throughout the entire management team, beginning at the top and extending through all supervisors. Supervisors should not expect their employees to practise positive self-discipline if they themselves do not set a good example. As we have stated several times previously, a supervisor's actions and behaviour are easy targets for the employees to either emulate or reject. Further, if the supervisor is able to encourage the vast majority of the employees in the department to show a strong sense of self-discipline, usually these employees will exert group pressure on the dissenters. For example, if a no-smoking rule is posted for a building, usually someone in the work group will enforce this rule by reminding smokers to leave the premises before lighting a cigarette. Thus, the need for corrective action by the supervisor is reduced when most employees practise positive self-discipline.

Oren Harari, a professor and management consultant, has commented that good employee discipline mostly depends on the supervisor's daily behaviour, decisions being aligned in the same positive direction, and on consistency of supervisory actions. He states: "Discipline is the daily grind that makes things happen and lets people know that you're worthy of your word. In short, it's about honour and integrity."[2]

| 2 | **IDENTIFYING AND CONFRONTING DISCIPLINARY SITUATIONS** |

Identify disciplinary situations that violate standards of conduct, and discuss the need to confront those situations appropriately.

Because individuals do not always agree on what should be acceptable standards of conduct, top-level managers must define the standards for supervisors and employees. In many companies, standards are defined in statements of ethical codes and rules of conduct.

Ethical Codes and Policies

In Chapter 3 we presented a series of "ethical tests" to be applied in decision making, and we mentioned that many organizations have developed statements of ethical standards or ethical codes.[3] Such codes usually outline in broad, philosophical terms the norms and ideals that are supposed to guide everyone within the organization. Figure 10-1 is an example of a code of ethics. The nine principles within this code are expanded upon in a policy manual that provides guidance for employees concerning the meaning of the principles and how to comply with them.

Because ethical standards and ethical behaviour are often subject to varying interpretations, some firms have found it desirable to develop their ethical codes and policies with substantial participative input from teams of employees and supervisors.[4] Further, some major firms have established so-called "hot lines" or ethics reporting systems by which employees are encouraged to report questionable situations or individuals whom they believe are acting unethically, improperly, or illegally. These firms may have a corporate ombudsman who investigates the allegations and takes appropriate actions when justified. The person who reported the alleged wrongdoing, usually referred to as a *whistle blower,* should

FIGURE 10-1   Corporate code of ethics.

CODE OF ETHICS

Integrity and ethics exist in the individual or they do not exist at all. They must be upheld by individuals or they are not upheld at all. In order for integrity and ethics to be characteristics of the corporation, we must strive to be

- Honest and trustworthy in all our relationships.
- Reliable in carrying out assignments and responsibilities.
- Truthful and accurate in what we say and write.
- Cooperative and constructive in all work undertaken.
- Fair and considerate in our treatment of fellow employees, customers, and all other people.
- Law abiding in all our activities.
- Committed to accomplishing all tasks in a superior way.
- Economical in utilizing company resources.
- Dedicated in service to our company and to improvement of the quality of life in the world in which we live.

be afforded anonymity. There is supposed to be no retaliation, regardless of whether or not the report is supportable by facts and evidence.[5] In this regard, it is generally recognized that a hot line or ethics reporting system requires top-level management's commitment to make the system credible, that is, both to deal firmly with wrongdoing when it is reported and, further, not to retaliate against a messenger who delivers an unwelcome message.[6] Of course, if someone has made an unfounded or false report with malice, this may require a disciplinary response by management.

Some firms also have developed statements and policies for dealing with "conflicts of interest"; these may be part of, or in addition to, their ethical codes. Conflict-of-interest statements usually define situations and employee behaviours that would be inconsistent with an individual's primary obligations to his or her employer. Figure 10-2 is an excerpt from a major firm's statement on conflicts of interest. In the final analysis, a firm's commitment to high standards of ethical behaviour must go far beyond just codes and policy statements. An ethical commitment requires everyone in the organization, especially those in management and supervision, to show daily, by word and action, that behaving ethically at work is not optional.

Rules of Conduct

Not every organization has a published code of ethics or conflict-of-interest statement. However, virtually every large firm, and probably the majority of other firms and organizations, have some formal statement or list of rules of behaviour to which employees are expected to conform.

In Chapter 2, we discussed the need for policies, procedures, methods, and rules as standing plans that cover many aspects of ongoing operations. These are

FIGURE 10-2   Excerpt from a conflict-of-interest policy statement.

CONFLICTS OF INTEREST
- Employees have the duty and the obligation to act—at all times—in the best lawful and ethical interests of the company.
- Employees are specifically prohibited from using their positions with the company for personal gain, favour, or advantage. For example, this specifically prohibits any unauthorized or personal use of the official stationery, news release masthead, logo, or any other forms, labels, envelopes, etc., bearing the name or logo of the company.
- Employees are expected to avoid relationships that might interfere with the proper and efficient discharge of their duties, or that might be inconsistent with their obligations of loyalty to the company. For example, if an employee, close relative, or any other person with whom the employee has a close personal relationship has a financial interest in an organization that does business or competes with the company, a conflict of interest may exist. Also, there may be a conflict if an employee, close relative, or any other person with whom the employee has a close personal relationship engages in certain transactions with; renders services to; or accepts payments, loans, or gifts from customers, vendors, contractors, or competitors of the company.

particularly vital in informing employees of the standards of behaviour that are expected and those that are unacceptable.

Most organizations provide employees with a written list of rules or code of conduct. These are sometimes included in an employee handbook; otherwise, they are provided as a separate booklet or as a memorandum posted in each department. The supervisor must ensure that employees read and understand the general and departmental rules, which may include safety and technical regulations, depending on the activity of a department.

Written rules and regulations provide a common basis and standards that should assist the supervisor in encouraging employee self-discipline. Some organizations spell out very detailed lists of rules and infractions, and they may include examples of the likely penalties for violations. Other organizations—probably the majority—prefer to list their major rules and regulations without tying down the consequences for violations of various rules. An example of such a list is shown in Figure 10-3. Regardless of what type of list is used, the supervisor is the person most responsible for the consistent application and enforcement of both company and departmental rules. In fact, the degree to which employees follow the rules in a positive, self-disciplined way is usually more attributable to the supervisor's role and example than to any other factor.

FIGURE 10-3 Partial list of company rules and regulations.

COMPANY RULES AND REGULATIONS

The efficient operation of our plants and the general welfare of our employees require the establishment of certain uniform standards of behaviour. Accordingly, the following offences are considered to be violations of these standards, and employees who refuse to accept this guidance will subject themselves to appropriate disciplinary action:

- Habitual tardiness and absenteeism.
- Theft or attempted theft of company or other employee's property.
- Fighting or attempting bodily injury upon another employee.
- Horseplay, malicious mischief, or any other conduct affecting the rights of other employees.
- Intoxication, drinking on the job, or being in a condition that makes it impossible to perform work in a satisfactory manner.
- Refusal or failure to perform assigned work, or refusal or failure to comply with supervisory instructions.
- Inattention to duties; carelessness in performance of duties; loafing on the job, sleeping, or reading newspapers during working hours.
- Violation of published safety or health rules.
- Possessing, consuming, selling, or being under the influence of illegal drugs on the premises.
- Unauthorized possession of weapons, firearms, or explosives on the premises.
- Requests for sexual favours, sexual advances, and physical conduct of a sexual nature toward another employee on the premises.

Rules of conduct and policy statements in employee handbooks and manuals often are subject to review and change because of legal problems and interpretations. Although review and revision of employee handbooks and manuals are usually the responsibility of human resources staff, supervisors, too, should be very familiar with the content of employee handbooks. Supervisors should not hesitate to offer suggestions for revisions when changes appear to be justified or needed.

Confronting Disciplinary Situations

Despite a supervisor's best efforts to prevent infractions, it is almost inevitable that he or she will, at times, be confronted with situations requiring some type of disciplinary action. Among the most common situations requiring supervisory disciplinary actions are

- Infractions of rules regarding time schedules, rest periods, procedures, safety, and so forth.
- Excessive absenteeism or tardiness.
- Defective or inadequate work performance.
- Poor attitudes that influence the work of others or damage the firm's public image.

At times, a supervisor might experience open insubordination, such as an employee's refusal to carry out a legitimate work assignment. A supervisor may even be confronted with disciplinary problems that stem from employee behaviour off the job. For example, an employee may have a drinking problem or may be taking illegal drugs. Whenever an employee's off-the-job conduct has an impact on his or her job performance, the supervisor must be prepared to respond to the problem in an appropriate fashion.

Every supervisor will confront situations that require some type of disciplinary action.

Ryan McVay/Photodisc Red/Getty Images

Situations that call for disciplinary action are not pleasant, but the supervisor must have the courage to deal with them. Ignoring the situation is rarely the right strategy. If the supervisor does not take responsible action when required, some borderline employees might be encouraged to try similar violations.

A supervisor should not be afraid to draw on some of the authority inherent in the supervisory position, even though he or she might prefer to overlook the matter or "pass the buck" to higher-level managers or the human resources department. A supervisor who expects the human resources department to take over all departmental disciplinary problems is shirking responsibility and undermining his or her own position of authority.

Normally, a good supervisor will not have to take disciplinary action frequently. But whenever it becomes necessary, the supervisor should be ready to take the proper action no matter how unpleasant the task may be.

3	THE DISCIPLINARY PROCESS AND JUST CAUSE

Discuss the disciplinary process and approaches that ensure disciplinary action for just cause.

Supervisors must initiate any disciplinary action with sensitivity and sound judgment. The purpose of a disciplinary action should not be to punish or seek revenge but to improve the employees' future behaviour. In other words, the primary purpose of a disciplinary action is to prevent similar infractions in the future.

In this chapter we do not consider directly those situations in which union contractual obligations may restrict the supervisor's authority in taking disciplinary action. Special considerations involving labour unions will be discussed in Chapter 12. Nevertheless, the ideas discussed here are generally applicable in most unionized as well as nonunionized organizations.

Disciplinary Action Should Have Just Cause

Just cause
Standard for disciplinary action requiring tests of fairness and elements of normal due process, such as proper notification, investigation, sufficient evidence, and a penalty commensurate with the nature of the infraction.

Most employers accept the general premise that disciplinary action taken against an employee should be based on "just cause." **Just cause** (or "proper cause") means that the disciplinary action meets certain tests of fairness and elements of normal due process, such as proper notification, investigation, sufficient evidence, and a penalty commensurate with the nature of the infraction. Figure 10-4 lists seven questions that arbitrators or arbitration boards apply in union/management disciplinary-type grievance matters. A "no" answer to one or more of these questions in a particular case means that the just-cause standard was not fully met, and the arbitrator or arbitration board might then set aside or modify management's disciplinary action.

The overwhelming preponderance of labour union contracts specify a just-cause or proper-cause standard for discipline and discharge. Similarly, many cases decided by government agencies and by the courts have required employers to prove that disciplinary actions taken against employees were not discriminatory but were for just cause (see Contemporary Issue box on pages 298–99).

The guidelines presented in this chapter are consistent with the principles and requirements necessary to justify any disciplinary or discharge action. The supervisor who follows these guidelines in a conscientious way normally should be able to meet a just-cause standard in either a unionized or a nonunionized environment.

FIGURE 10-4   Seven tests for just cause.

1. Did the company give the employee forewarning or foreknowledge of the possible or probable disciplinary consequences of the employee's conduct?
2. Was the company's rule or managerial order reasonably related to (a) the orderly, efficient, and safe operation of the company's business and (b) the performance that the company might properly expect of the employee?
3. Did the company, before administering discipline to an employee, make an effort to discover whether the employee did in fact violate or disobey a rule or an order of management?
4. Was the company's investigation conducted fairly and objectively?
5. Did the investigation reveal that there was substantial evidence or proof that the employee was guilty as charged?
6. Has the company applied its rules, orders, and penalties even-handedly and without discrimination to all employees?
7. Was the degree of discipline administered by the company in a particular case reasonably related to (a) the seriousness of the employee's proven offence and (b) the record of the employee's service with the company?

Source: These seven tests for just cause were originally suggested by arbitrator Carroll R. Daugherty. They are included in many texts and arbitral citations. See Raymond L. Hilgert and Sterling H. Schoen, *Cases in Collective Bargaining and Industrial Relations,* 10th ed. (Boston: Irwin/McGraw-Hill, 2002), pp. 198–99.

CONTEMPORARY ISSUE
Wrongful Dismissal—A Sampling of Canadian Decisions

The popular wisdom in today's workplace is that it is "virtually impossible" to fire anyone. Many people believe that, even if an employee is extremely incompetent, it is difficult for an employer to win when a discharged employee sues the employer for wrongful dismissal.

Wrongful dismissal cases in Canada provide an interesting insight into the way the courts and adjudicators view the employee/employer relationship and the requirements that must be met in order for a dismissal to be upheld. Nonunionized employees who do not have access to a formal grievance procedure can appeal to the courts when they feel that they have been wrongfully terminated. In unionized environments, employees must follow the established grievance procedures outlined in the collective agreement. The final decision about a dismissal case in a unionized environment is usually heard by an outside adjudicator whose decision is considered to be final and binding. The courts and adjudicators draw on a long history of past decisions when

weighing the merits of a particular case. They will hear the facts and make a decision about whether the dismissal was warranted or, alternately, whether the employee should be reinstated or paid damages.

Labour lawyers and human resource professionals keep a close watch on the new cases that the courts and arbitrators are deciding. Summaries of current cases and the decisions that have been made provide valuable insights into the current "thinking" of the adjudicators and the courts and the expectations that must be met in order for a dismissal to be upheld. Below are summaries of some recent Canadian decisions that dealt with wrongful dismissal cases.

Female Firefighter Reinstated[1]

Tawney Meiorin, a female firefighter, was dismissed from her job when she could not pass minimum physical fitness standards established by the British

(continued)

Columbia government. Meiorin had, in the past, satisfactorily performed her job as a forest firefighter. Her case was heard by the Supreme Court of Canada, which ruled that the fitness standards imposed by the government were not proven to be necessary for either men or women to perform the work of a forest firefighter safely and efficiently. The court ruled that standards imposed by an employer must be rationally connected to the performance of the job, and that the employer must prove that it is impossible to accommodate individual employees who cannot meet that standard without imposing undue hardship on the employer. In Meiorin's case, the court decided that the fitness standards imposed were not rationally connected to the performance of the job. The court reinstated Meiorin to her former position and ordered compensation for lost wages and benefits.

Innocent Absenteeism[2]

A 40-year-old worker with 15 years of seniority was dismissed due to a long history of "innocent" absences from work. The worker had no disciplinary record, but had suffered from a string of accidents and illnesses that had resulted in short- and long-term absences from work over a 9½-year period. The employer accepted these absences as legitimate, and genuinely related to accidents or illnesses. The employee was considered "intelligent, conscientious, and a hard worker," and it was noted that he lived with a terminally ill sister.

Records indicated that the employer had repeatedly counselled the employee about his attendance, and had repeatedly offered him assistance through the company's health centre and its employee assistance program. The employee promised to improve his attendance to equal or better than the plant average. This did not happen. The employee was given a final warning, followed by a six-month period in order to improve his attendance. Following the six-month review, he was dismissed.

The arbitrator decided that the employer did have the right to dismiss this employee. The arbitrator ruled that the employer had the right to expect regular attendance and cannot be faulted for terminating the employee after having tried for so long in so many different ways to accommodate his

personal needs. The arbitrator said that because there was no evidence to suggest that the employee would be capable of regular future attendance, the employer was justified in dismissing him even though the past absences were for legitimate reasons. The arbitrator ruled that it would be up to the employee to prove that the past circumstances that had prevented his regular attendance were no longer present. The employee could not prove that there was a foreseeable likelihood of change in his future attendance, and his termination was upheld.

High Workload and Poor Supervision[3]

An Ottawa-area social worker with two years of experience was terminated after several incidents of misconduct, including falsifying expense claims and pocketing money that had been given to her by a child who was making a restitution payment. In addition to these thefts, The Children's Aid Society of Ottawa-Carleton also claimed that the employee's work performance was poor and that documentation on a number of files was incomplete or inaccurate.

The arbitrator in this case concluded that the employee had shown poor judgment and carelessness, and had lied to cover up how far behind she was in her work. Although she deserved to be disciplined for misconduct, dismissal was excessive, and no discipline was warranted for the job performance issues.

In making the ruling, the arbitrator emphasized that the social worker's misconduct was "closely related to the emotional state she was in as a result of her workload and lack of support." She was carrying a workload that would have been heavy even for an experienced social worker. The arbitrator stated that "there is an expectation that Social Workers, particularly inexperienced ones, will receive close supervision … It is easy, it seems to me, for inexperienced employees to become snowed under by their weighty responsibilities … These employees need to be carefully monitored and they need support…. The employer must bear some responsibility for allowing this situation to have developed."

The arbitrator ruled that the social worker should be reinstated but, because she had lied to cover up her poor job performance, no award was made for lost wages or benefits.

Sources: (1) www.opseu.org/legal/legalupdate8.htm (retrieved November 28, 2003); (2) www.opseu.org/legal/legalupdate4.htm (retrieved November 28, 2003); (3) www.opseu.org/legal/legalupdate36.htm (retrieved November 28, 2003). See also www.duhaime.org/Employment/ca-wd.htm.

Precautionary Questions and Measures

As a first consideration in any disciplinary situation, a supervisor should guard against undue haste or taking unwarranted action based on emotional response. There are a number of precautionary questions and measures that a supervisor should follow before deciding on any disciplinary action in response to an alleged employee offence.

Investigate the Situation

Before doing anything, the supervisor should investigate what happened and why. The questions in Figure 10-5, while not comprehensive, might be used as a checklist as the supervisor considers what should be done.

For certain gross violations, such as stealing, illegal substance use, and violence, an organization may call in law enforcement authorities to conduct an investigation and to take appropriate action. There even may be situations where it is decided that investigation of possible wrongdoing requires some form of personnel surveillance. An outside private investigator may be hired to conduct electronic surveillance or perhaps become part of the workplace as an undercover "employee." The supervisor may or may not be informed that such surveillance is taking place.[7]

When an employee is injured on the job, many firms require the employee to take a drug and alcohol screening test. The Ontario Human Rights Commission has ruled that "following accidents or reports of dangerous behaviour ... an employer will have a legitimate interest in assessing whether the employee in question had consumed substances ... which may have contributed to the incident."[8] Such tests usually are given by a qualified person in the firm's first-aid room or by someone at a health clinic where the employee is treated. Safeguards concerning employee privacy and test-result validation usually are followed, although the results may be utilized as part of management's investigation and decision-making process.

FIGURE 10-5   Checklist of questions to ask during a disciplinary investigation.

1. Are all or most of the facts available, and are they reported accurately? That is, can the alleged offence be proven by direct or circumstantial evidence, or is the allegation based merely on suspicion?
2. How serious is the offence (minor, major, or intolerable)? Were others involved in or affected by the offence? Were company funds or equipment involved?
3. Did the employee know the rule or standard? Does the employee have a reasonable excuse and are there any extenuating circumstances?
4. What is the employee's past disciplinary record, length of service, and performance level? Does the offence indicate carelessness, absentmindedness, loss of temper, and so forth? How does this employee react to criticism?
5. Should the employee receive the same treatment others have had for the same offence? If not, is it possible to establish a basis for differentiating the present alleged offence from past offences of a similar nature?
6. Is all the necessary documentation available in case the matter leads to outside review?

Investigatory Interviews

As part of the supervisor's investigation of an alleged infraction, it may be necessary to question the employee involved as well as other employees who may have relevant information. In general, such interviews should be conducted in private and on an individual basis—perhaps with a guarantee of confidentiality. This is usually less threatening to an employee who otherwise may be reluctant to tell what he or she knows. Conducting individual interviews helps to prevent having what employees say unduly influenced by another's versions and interpretations.

If a union employee is to be interviewed concerning a disciplinary matter, the employee may request that a union representative or co-worker be present during the interview. Normally the supervisor should grant such a request.

In conducting an investigatory interview, most of the principles of interviewing discussed in Chapter 5 are applicable. The supervisor should ask both directive and nondirective questions that are designed to elicit specific answers concerning what happened and why. Above all, the supervisor should avoid making any final judgments until all the interviews have been held and other relevant information has been assembled.

Maintaining Self-Control

Regardless of the severity of an employee violation, a supervisor must not lose self-control. This does not mean that a supervisor should face a disciplinary situation half-heartedly or indifferently. But if a supervisor feels in danger of losing control of temper or emotions, the supervisor should delay the investigatory interviews and not take any action until he or she calms down. A supervisor's loss of self-control or display of anger could compromise fair and objective judgment.

Generally, a supervisor should never lay a hand on an employee in any way. Except for emergencies, when an employee has been injured or becomes ill, or when employees who are fighting need to be separated, any physical gesture could easily be misunderstood. A supervisor who engages in physical violence, except in self-defence, normally will be subjected to disciplinary action by higher-level management.

Privacy in Disciplining

When a supervisor finally decides on a course of disciplinary action, she or he should communicate the decision to the offending employee in private. A public reprimand not only humiliates the employee in the eyes of co-workers but also can lead to loss of morale in the department or even a grievance. If, in the opinion of the other employees, a public disciplinary action is too severe for the violation, the disciplined employee might emerge as a martyr in the view of every employee in the department.

Many union contracts require that employees who are to be disciplined for an infraction have the right to have a union representative present. If this is the case, it is desirable to have more than one management person present—for example, the supervisor, the supervisor's manager, and perhaps the human resources director. Thus, both management and the union have witnesses to the disciplinary action, even when it takes place in a private area.

Only under extreme circumstances should disciplinary action be taken in public. For example, a supervisor's authority may be challenged directly and openly by an employee who repeatedly refuses to carry out a reasonable work request. Or an employee may be drunk or fighting on the job. In these cases, it is necessary for the supervisor to reach a disciplinary decision quickly—for example, by sending the offending employee home on suspension pending further investigation. The supervisor may even have to do this in the view of other employees in order to maintain their respect and to regain control of the situation.

Disciplinary Time Element

When a supervisor decides to impose a disciplinary action, the question arises as to how long the violation should be held against an employee. Generally, it is desirable to disregard minor or intermediate offences after a year or so has elapsed since they were committed. Thus, an employee with a poor record of defective work might be given a "clean bill of health" by subsequently compiling a good record for six months or one year. Some companies have adopted "point systems" to cover certain infractions—especially absenteeism and tardiness. Employees can have points removed from their records if they have perfect or acceptable attendance during later periods.

There are situations when the time element is of no importance. For example, if an employee is caught brandishing a knife in a heated argument at work, the supervisor need not worry about any time element or previous offences. This act is serious enough to warrant immediate discharge.

4   PRACTISING PROGRESSIVE DISCIPLINE

Define and discuss the application of progressive discipline.

Progressive discipline
System of disciplinary action that increases the severity of the penalty with each offence.

Unless a serious wrong, such as stealing, physical violence, or gross insubordination, has been committed, the offending employee rarely is discharged for a first offence. Although the type of disciplinary action appropriate to a situation will vary, many organizations practise a system of **progressive discipline,** which provides for an increase in the severity of the penalty with each offence. The following stages comprise a system of progressive disciplinary action: informal talk, oral warning (or verbal counselling), written warning, disciplinary layoff (suspension), transfer or demotion, and discharge. Figure 10-6 illustrates a progressive discipline policy.

Early Stages in Progressive Discipline

Many disciplinary situations can be handled solely or primarily by the supervisor without escalating into a difficult confrontation. In the early stages of progressive discipline, the supervisor communicates with the employee concerning the problem and how to correct it.

Informal Talk

If the offence is relatively minor and if the employee has had no previous disciplinary record, a friendly and informal talk will clear up the problem in many cases. During this talk, the supervisor should try to determine the underlying reasons for the employee's unacceptable conduct. At the same time, the supervisor should reaffirm the employee's sense of responsibility and acknowledge his or her previous good behaviour.

FIGURE 10-6   A hospital's progressive disciplinary policy.

CORRECTIVE ACTION POLICY

Corrective action shall progress from verbal counselling to written reprimand, suspension, and termination. All corrective actions shall make reference to the policy or procedure that has been violated, the adverse consequence resulting from the violation, the type of behaviour expected in the future, and the corrective action that will be taken if further violations occur. A copy of the completed corrective action form shall be given to the employee. Following are guidelines for the corrective action procedure:

- **Verbal counselling:** Verbal counselling shall be given for all minor violations of hospital rules and policies. More than two verbal counsellings in the past 12-month period regarding violations of any rules or policies warrants a written reprimand.
- **Written reprimand:** Written reprimands shall be given for repeated minor infractions or for first-time occurrences of more serious offences. Written reprimands shall be documented on the "Notice of Corrective Action" form, which is signed by the department head or supervisor and the employee.
- **Suspension:** An employee shall be suspended without pay for one to four scheduled working days for a critical or major offence or for repeated minor or serious offences.
- **Termination**: An employee may be terminated for repeated violations of hospital rules and regulations or for first-time offences of a critical nature.

Oral Warning

If a friendly talk does not take care of the situation, the next step is to give the employee an oral warning (sometimes known as *verbal counselling*). Here the supervisor emphasizes the undesirability of the employee's repeated violation in a straightforward manner. Although the supervisor should stress the preventive purpose of discipline, he or she should also emphasize that, unless the employee improves, more serious disciplinary action will be taken. In some organizations, a record of this oral warning is made in the employee's file. Alternately, the supervisor may simply write a brief note in a supervisory log book to document the fact that an oral warning was given on a particular date. This can be important evidence if the same employee commits another infraction in the future.

If oral warnings are carried out skillfully, many employees will respond and improve at this stage. The oral warning should leave the employee with the feeling that there must be improvement in the future, but that the supervisor believes the employee can improve and stands ready to help the employee do so.

Written Warning

A written warning contains a statement of the violation and the potential consequences of future violations. It is a formal document that becomes a permanent part of the employee's record. The supervisor should review with the employee the nature of this written warning and again stress the necessity for improvement.

The employee should be placed on clear notice that future infractions or unacceptable conduct will lead to more serious discipline, such as suspension or discharge.

Written warnings are particularly necessary in unionized organizations because they can serve as evidence in grievance procedures. The employee usually receives a duplicate copy of the written warning, and another copy is sent to the human resources department. Figure 10-7 is an example of a written warning used by a supermarket chain. This form provides space for the supervisor to note if the employee refuses to sign it.

Even at this stage in the disciplinary process, the supervisor should continue to express a belief in the employee's ability to improve and the supervisor's willingness to help in whatever way possible. The primary goal of disciplinary action up until discharge should be to assist the person to improve and to become a valuable employee.

FIGURE 10-7
Example of a written warning used by a supermarket chain.

EMPLOYEE CORRECTIVE ACTION NOTICE

Employee's name_____ Date of notice_____

Store address_____ Store #_____ Dept._____ Job Classification_____

This notice is a: First warning   Second warning   Third warning   Final warning
                          ☐   ☐   ☐   ☐

Reason for corrective action: (Check below)

☐ Lack of cooperation   ☐ Cash register discrepancy   ☐ Insubordination

☐ Quality/quantity of work   ☐ Dress code   ☐ Time-card violation

☐ Tardiness/absenteeism   ☐ Disregard for safety   ☐ Other cause(s) (Explain)

Explanation must accompany reason checked above:

_____

_____

_____

I HEREBY SIGNIFY THAT I HAVE RECEIVED A FULL EXPLANATION OF MY FAILURE TO PERFORM AS EXPECTED. THE COMPANY AND I UNDERSTAND THAT FURTHER FAILURE ON MY PART WILL BE DUE CAUSE FOR DISCIPLINARY ACTION UP TO, AND INCLUDING, DISCHARGE.

_____   _____   _____   _____
Employee's signature   Date   Supervisor's signature   Date

                                            _____   _____
                                            Store manager's signature   Date

REFUSAL OF EMPLOYEE TO SIGN THIS NOTICE SHOULD BE SO NOTED HEREON.

Note: Prepare original and four copies. Send original and one copy to the human resources director. Send one copy to the store manager and one copy to the employee. Retain one copy.

Advanced Stages in Progressive Discipline

Unfortunately, not every employee will respond to the counselling and warnings of the supervisor to improve job behaviour. In progressive discipline, more serious disciplinary actions may be administered for repeated violations, with discharge being the final step.

Disciplinary Layoff (Suspension)

If an employee has committed offences repeatedly and previous warnings were of no avail, a disciplinary layoff would probably constitute the next disciplinary step. Disciplinary layoffs involve a loss of pay and usually extend from one day to several days or weeks. Because a disciplinary layoff involves a loss of pay, some organizations limit a supervisor's authority at this stage. Some supervisors can only initiate or recommend a disciplinary layoff, which then must be approved by higher-level managers after consultation with the human resources department.

Employees who do not respond to oral or written warnings usually find a disciplinary layoff to be a rude awakening. The layoff may restore in them the need to comply with the organization's rules and regulations. However, managers in some organizations seldom apply layoffs as a disciplinary measure. They believe that laying off a trained employee will hurt their own production, especially in times of labour shortages. Further, they reason that the laid-off employee may return in an even more unpleasant frame of mind. Despite this possible reaction, disciplinary layoffs can be an effective disciplinary measure in some situations.

Transfer

Transferring an employee to a job in another department typically involves no loss of pay or skill. This disciplinary action is usually taken when an offending employee seems to be experiencing difficulty in working for a particular supervisor, in working at a current job, or in associating with certain other employees. The transfer may bring about a marked improvement if the employee adjusts to the new department and the new supervisor in a positive fashion. If a transfer is made simply to give the employee a last chance to retain a job in the company, the employee should be told that he or she must improve in the new job or else be subject to discharge. Of course, the supervisor who accepts the transferred employee should be informed about the circumstances surrounding the transfer. This will help the supervisor in assisting the transferred employee to make a successful transition.

Demotion

Another disciplinary measure, the value of which is open to serious question, is demotion to a lower-paying job. This course of action is likely to bring about dissatisfaction and discouragement since losing pay and status over an extended period of time is a form of constant punishment. The dissatisfaction of the demoted employee can also spread to other employees. Therefore, most organizations avoid demotion (or downgrading) as a disciplinary action.

Demotion should be used only in unusual situations in which a disciplinary layoff or a discharge is not a better alternative. For example, a long-service employee may not be maintaining the standards of work performance required in a certain job. In order to retain seniority and other accrued benefits, this employee may accept a demotion as an alternative to discharge.

Discharge (Termination)

The most drastic form of disciplinary action is discharge (or termination). The discharged employee loses all seniority standing and may have difficulty obtaining employment elsewhere. Discharge should be reserved only for the most serious offences and as a last resort.

A discharge involves loss and waste. It means having to train a new employee and disrupting the makeup of the work group, which may affect the morale of other employees. In unionized companies, discharging an employee may result in prolonged grievance and arbitration proceedings. Management knows that labour arbitrators or arbitration boards are unwilling to sustain discharge except for severe offences or for a series of violations that cumulatively justify the discharge. Therefore, because of the serious implications and consequences of discharge, some organizations have taken the right to discharge away from supervisors and have reserved it for higher-level managers. Other organizations require that any discharge recommended by a supervisor be reviewed and approved by higher-level managers or the human resources department, often with the advice of legal counsel.

Because of legal and other such concerns, the final termination interview with the discharged employee may be conducted by a human resources staff person. However, if the supervisor conducts the termination interview, he or she should be careful to focus on the reasons for the termination and be responsive to the questions of the person being terminated. The supervisor should not lose emotional control or engage in a heated debate about the fairness of the termination decision. Hopefully, the supervisor will be able to close the termination interview by suggesting avenues or options that the individual should consider for possible future employment elsewhere.[9]

It should be noted by supervisors that after terminating an employee not covered by a collective agreement, the employer may be accused of wrongful dismissal. In general, the basis for these cases is that the supervisor was arbitrary or unfair in discharging the employee. The courts have made it clear that employees have certain rights in pursuing their jobs and are entitled to a fair hearing before management, including the right to progressive discipline.

5

Explain the "hot-stove rule" for disciplinary actions.

APPLYING THE HOT-STOVE RULE

Taking disciplinary action may place the supervisor in a strained, difficult position. Disciplinary action tends to generate employee resentment, and it is not a pleasant experience. To assist the supervisor in applying the necessary disciplinary measure so that it will be least resented and most likely to withstand challenges from various sources, some authorities have advocated the use of the **hot-stove rule**. This rule compares touching a hot stove with administering disciplinary measures. Both contain four elements: advance warning, immediacy, consistency, and impersonality.

Everyone knows what will happen if he or she touches a red-hot stove *(advance warning)*. Someone who touches a hot stove gets burned right away, with no questions of cause and effect *(immediacy)*. Every time a person touches

Hot-stove rule

Guideline for applying discipline analogous to touching a hot stove: advance warning and consequences that are immediate, consistent, and applied with impersonality.

a hot stove, that person gets burned *(consistency)*. Whoever touches a hot stove is burned because of the act of touching the stove, regardless of who the person is *(impersonality)*. These four elements of the hot-stove rule can be applied by the supervisor when maintaining employee discipline.

Advance Warning

For employees to accept disciplinary action as fair, it is essential that they know in advance what is expected of them and what the rules and regulations are. Employees must be informed clearly that certain acts will lead to disciplinary action. Many organizations use orientation sessions, employee handbooks, and bulletin board announcements to inform employees about the rules and how they are to be enforced. In addition, supervisors are responsible for clarifying any questions that arise concerning rules and their enforcement.

Some firms print their rules in an employee handbook, which every new employee receives. As part of orientation, the supervisor should explain to each new employee the departmental rules and the rules that are part of the employee handbook. Some organizations require employees to sign a document stating that they have read and understood the rules and regulations.

Unfortunately, in some organizations there are rules on the books that have not been enforced. For example, there may be a rule prohibiting smoking in a certain area that the supervisor has not previously enforced. Of course, it would be improper for the supervisor to suddenly decide that it is time to enforce this rule strictly, and try to make an example by taking disciplinary action against an employee found smoking in this area.

However, the fact that a certain rule has not been enforced in the past does not mean that it can never be enforced. To enforce such a rule, the supervisor must inform and warn the employees that the rule will be strictly enforced from this point on. It is not enough just to post a notice on the bulletin board since not everyone looks at this board every day. The supervisor must issue a clear, written notice and supplement it with oral communication.

Immediacy

After noticing an offence, the supervisor should take disciplinary action as promptly as possible. At the same time, the supervisor should avoid undue haste, which might lead to unwarranted reactions. The sooner the discipline is imposed, the more closely it will be seen to be connected with the offence.

There will be instances when it appears that an employee is guilty of a violation, but the supervisor needs time to consider what degree of penalty should be imposed. For example, incidents such as fighting, intoxication, or insubordination often require an immediate response from the supervisor. In these cases the supervisor may place the employee on temporary suspension, which means being suspended pending a final decision. The temporarily suspended employee is advised that he or she will be informed about the ultimate disciplinary decision as soon as possible or at a specific date.

Temporary suspension in itself is not a punishment. It protects both management and the employee. It provides the supervisor with time to make an investigation and an opportunity to cool off. If the ensuing investigation indicates that no disciplinary action is warranted, then the employee is recalled and does not suffer any loss of pay. If a disciplinary layoff eventually is applied, then the time during which the employee was temporarily suspended will constitute part of the disciplinary layoff. The advantage of temporary suspension is that the supervisor can act promptly. However, it should not be used indiscriminately.

Consistency

Appropriate disciplinary action should be taken each time an infraction occurs. The supervisor who feels inclined to be lenient every now and then is, in reality, not doing the employees a favour. Inconsistency in imposing discipline will lead to employee anxiety and create doubts as to what employees can and cannot do. This type of situation can be compared to the relations between a motorist and a traffic police officer in an area where the speed limit is enforced only occasionally. Whenever the motorist exceeds the speed limit, the motorist experiences anxiety because he or she knows that the police officer can enforce the law at any time. Most motorists would agree that it is easier to drive in a location where the police force is consistent in enforcing or not enforcing speed limits. Employees, too, find it easier to work in an environment in which the supervisor is consistent in applying disciplinary action.

However, being consistent in applying disciplinary action does not necessarily mean treating everyone in exactly the same manner. Special considerations surrounding an offence may need to be considered, such as the circumstances, the employee's productivity, job attitudes, length of service, etc. The extent to which a supervisor can be consistent and yet consider the individual's situation can be illustrated with the following example. Assume that three employees become involved in some kind of horseplay. Employee A just started work a few days ago, Employee B has been warned once before about this, and Employee C has been involved in numerous cases of horseplay. In taking disciplinary action, the supervisor could decide to have a friendly, informal talk with Employee A, give a written warning to Employee B, and impose a two-day disciplinary layoff on Employee C. Thus, each case is considered on its own merits, with the employees being judged according to their work history. Of course, if two of these employees had the same number of previous warnings, their penalties should be identical.

Imposing discipline consistently is one way a supervisor demonstrates a sense of fair play. Yet, this may be easier said than done. There are times when the department is particularly rushed and the supervisor may be inclined to conveniently overlook infractions. Perhaps the supervisor does not wish to upset the workforce or does not wish to lose the output of a valuable employee at a critical time. This type of consideration is paramount, especially when it is difficult to obtain employees with the skill that the offending employee possesses. Most employees will see an exception as fair if they know why the exception was made and if they consider it justified. However, the employees must feel that any other employee in exactly the same situation would receive similar treatment.

Impersonality

All employees who commit the same or a similar offence should be penalized. Penalties should be connected with the offensive act, not with the person or personality of the employee involved. It should not make any difference whether the employee is male or female, young or old, or a member of any other group. The same standards of disciplinary expectations and actions should be applied uniformly.

When a supervisor is imposing discipline, impersonality can help reduce the amount of resentment that is likely to be felt by an employee. At the same time, supervisors should understand that employee reactions to discipline will vary, just as individuals who get burned by touching a hot stove will react differently. For example, one person may shout, another may cry, another may reflexively inhale, or another may push away from the point of stimulus of pain with the opposite hand. Regardless of the individual, there will always be a reaction to being burned.

The optimal reaction to discipline would be the acceptance of responsibility for the wrongdoing and a change in behaviour by the employee to the desired standards, with no severe side effects such as loss of morale, disruption of other employees, or a negative portrayal of the company to customers or external business associates. Making a disciplinary action impersonal may reduce the level of resentment felt by the employee, but it is difficult to predict each employee's specific reaction. Personality, acceptance of authority, the job situation, and circumstances of the offence will all factor into an employee's reactions. A supervisor may have to deal with an employee's reactions if these are of a detrimental nature. However, assuming that the employee's reactions are not severe, the supervisor should treat the employee the same as before the infraction and disciplinary action, without being apologetic about what had to be done.

6   DOCUMENTATION AND THE RIGHT TO APPEAL

Discuss the need to document disciplinary actions and to provide the right of appeal.

Documentation
Keeping records of memoranda, documents, and meetings that are relevant to a disciplinary action.

Right to appeal
Procedures by which an employee may request high-level management to review a supervisor's disciplinary action.

Whenever a disciplinary action is taken, the supervisor must keep records of the offence committed and the decision made, including the reasoning involved in the decision. This is called **documentation,** and it may include keeping files of memoranda, documents, minutes of meetings, and the like that were part of handling the case. Documentation is necessary because the supervisor may be asked at some future time to justify the action taken, and the burden of proof is usually on the supervisor. It is imprudent for the supervisor to depend on memory alone. This is particularly true in unionized firms where grievance-arbitration procedures often result in a challenge to disciplinary actions imposed on employees.

The **right to appeal** means that it should be possible for an employee to request a review of a supervisor's disciplinary action from higher-level management. If the employee belongs to a labour union, this right is part of a grievance procedure. In most firms, the appeal is first directed to the supervisor's boss, thereby following the chain of command. Many large firms have provided for a hierarchy of several levels of management through which an appeal may be taken. The human resources department may become directly involved in an appeal procedure. Grievance procedures in unionized organizations are discussed in Chapter 12.

The right of appeal must be recognized as a real privilege and not merely a formality. Some supervisors tell their employees that they can appeal to higher-level management but that it will be held against them if they do so. This attitude is indicative of a supervisor's own insecurity. Supervisors should not be afraid to encourage their employees to appeal to higher-level management if the employees feel that they have been treated unfairly. Nor should supervisors feel that an appeal threatens or weakens their position as departmental managers. For the most part, a supervisor's manager will be inclined to support the supervisor's

When a supervisor is imposing discipline, impersonality can help reduce the resentment the employee feels.

Getty Images/Photodisc Collection

original action. If supervisors do not foster an open appeal procedure, employees may enlist aid from outside, such as a union would provide. Management's failure to provide a realistic appeal procedure is one of the reasons some employees have resorted to unionization.

In the course of an appeal, the disciplinary penalty imposed or recommended by a supervisor may be reduced or reversed by the higher-level manager. The supervisor's decision might be reversed because the supervisor has been inconsistent in imposing disciplinary action or has not considered all the necessary facts. Under these circumstances, the supervisor may become discouraged and feel that the manager has not backed him or her up. Although this situation is unfortunate, it is better for the supervisor to be disheartened than for an employee to be penalized unjustly. Situations such as these can be avoided if supervisors adhere closely to the principles and steps discussed in this chapter before taking disciplinary action.

7   DISCIPLINE WITHOUT PUNISHMENT

Explain the discipline-without-punishment approach as an alternative to progressive discipline.

Discipline without punishment

Disciplinary approach that uses coaching and counselling as preliminary steps and a paid decision-making leave for employees to decide whether to improve and stay, or quit.

In recent years, a growing number of companies have adopted disciplinary procedures usually called **discipline without punishment.** The major thrust of this approach is to avoid confrontation by stressing extensive coaching, counselling, and problem solving. A significant (and controversial) feature is the so-called paid "decision-making leave" in which an employee is sent home for a day or more with pay to decide whether or not he or she is willing to make a commitment to meet the expected standards of performance previously not met. If the employee makes a commitment to improve but fails to do so, the employee is then terminated.

In general, this approach replaces warnings and suspensions with coaching sessions and reminders by supervisors of the expected standards. The decision-making leave with pay is posed as a decision to be made by the employee, namely, to improve and stay, or quit.

Organizations that have implemented this approach successfully have reported various benefits, particularly in the area of reduced complaints and grievances and improved employee morale. It is questionable whether discipline-without-punishment programs will be adopted extensively since it is not clear that these programs are all that different in concept and outcome from progressive disciplinary action as discussed in this chapter. What is clear is that a discipline-without-punishment approach requires commitment from all management levels—especially from supervisors—if it is to be carried out successfully.[10]

WHAT CALL DID YOU MAKE?

As Linda Capelli, you recognize that following the principles discussed in this chapter is sometimes easier said than done. The situation in your department first requires investigation before you take action. You should make an extra effort to observe Scott Morino to see if you can verify any of Devica Florence's allegations. At the same time, you probably should talk with your own manager or the director of human resources for their suggestions on how to proceed. Then you should talk with several other employees in your department to get their versions of Morino's behaviour to see how they compare with Florence's report.

If other employees' perceptions mirror Florence's, you should meet with Morino to inform him of the allegations and hear his side of the story, even if his explanation is primarily self-serving. If, after this discussion, you believe that there is a major disciplinary problem, you should review the relevant rules of the department with Morino so that he is clear about your expectations concerning rules, attendance, and work performance. You need to remind him of the importance of good work habits, including a specific admonition that most personal business should not be performed during work hours. Urge him to establish better relationships with his co-workers, and point out that if he does not, his contributions to the department will be minimal. Try to get him to agree to some specific target objectives for various components of his job that you then can evaluate directly. Tell Morino that he should consider this discussion as a verbal or informal warning and that you will be monitoring his performance closely in the weeks to follow.

Tell Morino that you hope his performance will improve considerably and that his relationships with his co-workers will foster teamwork. At the same time, ensure he understands that if similar complaints continue and his performance is not satisfactory, you will have to consider future disciplinary action. If he asks what such disciplinary action might be, do not be specific but be sure that he understands that it will be more than a verbal warning and that it even could, ultimately, result in his termination.

Finally, after your interview with Morino, write a memorandum that summarizes the interview. This memorandum should be kept confidential and in a safe place. It could be valuable as documentation if future disciplinary action becomes necessary.

SUMMARY

Employee discipline can be thought of as the degree to which employees act according to expected standards of behaviour. It is likely that if employee morale is high, discipline will be positive and there will be less need for the supervisor to take disciplinary action. Supervisors should recognize that most employees want to do the right thing. Positive self-discipline means that employees essentially regulate their own behaviour out of self-interest and their normal desire to meet reasonable standards. Supervisors should set a positive example for their employees to emulate.

Many employers have codes of ethics that describe, in broad terms, the ideals and ethical requirements of the enterprise. Ethical codes and conflict-of-interest policies usually include procedures for reporting possible violations.

2 Most organizations have written rules and regulations with definitions of infractions and possible penalties for infractions. Rules of conduct typically address areas of attendance, work scheduling, job performance, safety, improper behaviour, and other matters. When infractions do occur, supervisors must take appropriate disciplinary action. If ignored, the problems will not go away.

3 When infractions occur, the supervisor should take disciplinary action with the objective of improving employees' future behaviour. Before disciplining, the supervisor first needs to investigate the situation thoroughly. Disciplinary actions should be for just cause. Emotional and physical responses should be avoided. The supervisor should determine whether there is sufficient evidence to conclude that the employee knew about the rule or standard and in fact violated it. The supervisor should consider the severity of the violation, the employee's past service record, and other relevant factors. If a disciplinary action is necessary, it normally should be discussed in private.

4 A number of progressively severe disciplinary actions, ranging from an informal talk to a warning, a suspension, and discharge, are open to a supervisor as alternative choices, depending on the circumstances and the nature of the infraction. The supervisor's purpose in taking disciplinary action should be to improve the employee's behaviour and to maintain proper discipline within the entire department.

5 Taking disciplinary action can be an unpleasant experience for both the employee and the supervisor. To reduce the distasteful aspects, disciplinary action should fulfill the requirements of the hot-stove rule. These are advance warning, immediacy, consistency, and impersonality.

6 Documentation of a disciplinary action is important in order to substantiate the reasons for the action taken by a supervisor. This is especially important if there is appeal of the disciplinary decision to higher-level management through a grievance or complaint procedure. In the interest of fairness, an appeal procedure provides the employee with a review process by which the supervisor's disciplinary decision may be upheld, modified, or set aside.

7 The discipline-without-punishment approach utilizes extensive coaching and counselling as preliminary steps. If there is no improvement, a paid decision-making leave may be given to the employee to decide whether he or she will make a commitment to improvement or be terminated.

QUESTIONS FOR DISCUSSION

1. Define the concept of employee discipline as a part of the working environment in a firm. In this context, differentiate between positive discipline and negative discipline.
2. Discuss the relationship between discipline and morale.
3. What are the differences among a code of ethics, a conflict-of-interest policy, and written rules and regulations? What are their purposes?
4. What is meant by just cause?
5. What should be the purpose of any disciplinary action?
6. Why is demotion considered to be the least desirable form of disciplinary action?
7. Under what circumstances might a transfer be an appropriate disciplinary strategy?
8. Define and evaluate each of the following elements of the hot-stove rule:
   a. Advance warning.
   b. Immediacy.
   c. Consistency.
   d. Impersonality.
9. Why should a supervisor document any disciplinary action that is taken?
10. What is meant by the right to appeal? How can this right be implemented in a nonunion organization? Discuss.
11. Is a discipline-without-punishment approach significantly different from regular progressive discipline? Discuss.

SKILLS APPLICATIONS

Skills Application 10-1: Employee Dress and Appearance Standards

One of the difficult current areas of discipline involves employee dress and appearance. In Canada, this issue became front-page news when Baltej Singh Dhillon challenged the dress code of the Royal Canadian Mounted Police and ultimately won the right to wear a turban instead of the traditional Stetson hat. Dress codes are especially important when employees deal directly with the public, such as in banks, retail stores, and restaurants. There also is concern about individual rights because of racial/gender/ethnic and other differences that often cause problems or potential issues of favouritism or discrimination.

1. Using the Internet, research the rights an employer has to establish a dress code. For example, can an employer demand that an employee not show tattoos or body piercings while on the job? Can an employer demand that an employee not wear extreme hair styles or colours? (For example, visit www.albertahumanrights.ab.ca/publications/Videos/Understand_Gender/Appendix_3.asp and read Case #7, "The Case of Samantha." Also visit www.workrights.ca and visit the FAQ link for information about dress codes.)
2. What alternatives are open to an employer if an employee consistently violates a company dress code?
3. What alternatives are open to an employee who does not wish to comply with a corporate dress code? Is your answer influenced by the underlying reason behind the employee's concerns? Explain.

Skills Application 10-2: Rules of Conduct

Reproduced on page 314 is a list of rules of conduct of the Acme Company as it appears in the company's employee handbook. The firm is not unionized. Review these rules and then answer the questions that follow.

RULES OF CONDUCT

Rules and guidelines have been established for the mutual benefit of Acme Co. and all employees. We ask your cooperation in following these rules. Our purpose is not to prohibit your rights but to help you be as productive and effective as possible. The following list summarizes rule and policy violations subject to disciplinary action:

First Offence—Suspension or Immediate Discharge

1. Absence from work two consecutive days without authorization.
2. Intoxication and/or use of drugs.
3. Theft or unauthorized possession of Acme property.
4. Careless, negligent, or improper use of Acme property.
5. Falsifying employment application.
6. Refusal to work.
7. Abusive or threatening language to staff, supervisors, employees, or customers.
8. Fighting.
9. Falsifying work records or time cards.
10. Punching another employee's time card.
11. Releasing confidential information without proper authority.

First Offence—Verbal and/or Written Warning

1. Insubordination.
2. Unauthorized absence.
3. Excessive absenteeism.
4. Repeated tardiness.
5. Failure to report to work.
6. Failure to maintain satisfactory relationships with other employees.
7. Smoking in unauthorized areas.
8. Failure to punch the time clock.
9. Sleeping on the job.
10. Inefficiency, incompetency.
11. Disregard of personal appearance, dress.
12. Leaving assigned place of work without supervisory permission.

Second and/or Third Offence—Suspension or Immediate Discharge

Any of the above rule violations listed under "First Offence—Verbal and/or Written Warning" that occur a second or third time may result in a disciplinary suspension or immediate discharge.

The above rules of conduct are meant only to serve as a guide. Variations in disciplinary actions taken may depend on the severity and intent of the offence and other circumstances.

1. How does the list of violations illustrate a progressive discipline system?
2. Do you agree that the list of violations leading to possible immediate discharge after the first offence is appropriate? Why or why not? If not, which items should be dropped, or what should be added?
3. Should the disciplinary action for second and/or third offences be more specifically detailed? Why or why not?
4. If you were to rewrite or edit this list of rules, what would you propose?

Skills Application 10-3: Drug & Alcohol Testing

W W W

Testing for drug and alcohol use is a sensitive area of the law in Canada. Some employers feel that testing for drug and alcohol use is important to ensure a safe workplace, especially when employees are in safety-sensitive jobs. Other people question whether an employer has the right to control or monitor what an employee does off the job.

Visit the website of the human rights commission for your province or territory and find information about policies for drug and alcohol testing in the workplace. Also, use a popular search engine to find information about actual cases that the courts or arbitrators have ruled on in this area (an example can be found at www.emond-harnden.com/entrop.html.)

1. Is it legal for an employer to use drug and alcohol testing as a screening tool when hiring new employees?
2. Is it legal for an employer to use random drug and alcohol testing for existing employees? Explain.
3. If an employee arrived on the job and was suspected of being under the influence of drugs or alcohol, could that employee be dismissed? Explain.

CASES

CASE 10-1

Under the Influence?

Carl Kloski had been employed as a labourer for eight years in the warehouse division of a wholesale appliance distributor. His record over the years indicated the following disciplinary actions:

1. Three written reprimands for unexcused absences.
2. One one-day suspension for reporting to work under the influence of alcohol.
3. One five-day suspension for reporting to work under the influence of alcohol.
4. One one-day suspension for failure to report to work.

On a Friday morning, Kloski reported to work at about 7:30 A.M. Sometime prior to the beginning of the shift, Kloski's lead person, George Keong, noticed that Kloski appeared to be under the influence of alcohol, since he was talking loudly and walking about in a confused manner. Keong reported this to his boss, warehouse supervisor Steven Bell. Bell sent Keong and the rest of the crew out to perform their normal duties, but he ordered Kloski to stay behind to do clean-up work in the employee lunch room. About an hour or so later, Bell noticed that Kloski had done very little clean-up work. Bell approached Kloski and asked him why he had not followed his instructions. Kloski objected to this questioning, and he continued in a loud manner that the supervisor was always "picking on him" and "being discriminatory."

In response to these accusations, Bell took Kloski into his office to review his file for past performance appraisals and disciplinary actions. A lengthy discussion followed in which Kloski continued talking in a loud and angry manner. Both Bell and the office clerk, Marilyn O'Toole, believed that they could smell alcohol on Kloski's breath.

Finally, Bell said, "Carl, I think you're under the influence of alcohol again, and with your past record, I ought to terminate you immediately!"

Kloski exploded, "What do you mean 'under the influence'? You assigned me to work over an hour ago, and you've got no proof whatsoever. You're just mad because I don't jump when you say, 'Jump!'"

Bell pondered his next response.

Questions for Discussion

1. What should Keong or Bell have done when they first believed that Kloski might have been under the influence of alcohol? Discuss alternatives.
2. Evaluate Bell's decision to assign Kloski to clean up the employee lunchroom.
3. Discuss Kloski's comment that the company had no proof whatsoever that he was under the influence of alcohol.
4. What should Bell do? Consider alternatives.

CASE 10-2

On Parole

Bascomb Manufacturing Company had a major plant that manufactured parts for the automotive industry. Local No. 428 of the United Production and Maintenance Workers represented several hundred employees in manufacturing areas of the plant.

Kyle Craver, the grievant in this case, had been employed by the company for 22 years prior to his discharge. During that time, Craver had compiled a satisfactory work record; he had not received any major disciplinary warning or penalty during his employment.

Eight weeks ago, Craver had been apprehended and charged by police with the "delivery of a controlled substance." In a plea bargain arrangement made with the court, Craver was placed on a special "probation/parole work release program." Through his union, Craver requested that he be returned to his job as a production line inspector while he served his three-month probation/parole work release program. The company's human resources director, Marjorie Florman, after consulting with higher management, refused to permit Craver to work under such an arrangement. The union filed a grievance complaining that the company was treating Craver unfairly since the company had previously allowed another employee to work on the job under a work release program following a drunk-driving conviction.

After examining the situation further, the company discharged Craver, stating that it had "just cause." The union then amended its grievance to include a protest against the company's "unjust discharge." After proceeding through the several steps of the grievance procedure, the company and the union agreed to submit the case to an arbitrator for a decision.

The following were the provisions of the parties' labour/management agreement relevant to the positions of the parties.

Article XIV—Management

Section 1. The Union recognizes the management of the plant and the direction of the working forces are exclusively the prerogatives of the Company. These prerogatives include but are not limited to:

The right to suspend or discharge for just cause; subject, however, to review thereof as provided in the grievance procedure contained herein.

Section 2. The Company agrees that in the exercise of management prerogatives, there shall be no violations of the terms of this Agreement.

Article XIX—Safety and Health

Section 7. Alcohol and Drug Abuse. Without detracting from the existing rights and obligations of the parties recognized in the other provisions of this

Agreement, the Company and the Union agree to cooperate at the plant level in encouraging employees afflicted with alcohol and/or drug dependency to undergo a coordinated program directed to the objective of their rehabilitation.

Position of the Company

In the arbitration hearing, the company primarily contended that there was ample just cause to discharge Craver. The company claimed that the plant operated within a larger community in which the company had a moral obligation to take actions that showed that the distribution or use of illegal drugs by employees would not be tolerated. The company claimed that there were many employees and generations of families and relatives of employees who objected to any form of drug use.

If the company retained Craver after his conviction for distributing drugs, this would be detrimental to the company's reputation and adversely affect employee morale and the company's business. The company said it would have a problem of credibility if customers learned of the company's willingness to continue employment of someone who had been convicted of off-duty drug dealing.

In summary, the company claimed that Craver was guilty of a major felony. To continue his employment would cast a serious shadow on the company's reputation, employee morale, and the company's ability to deal with customers and the community at large. The company urged that the union grievance should be denied.

Position of the Union

The union claimed that the company did not meet a proper burden of proof to support the claim that just cause existed for discharging Craver. The union claimed that there was no validity to the company's allegation that Craver's reinstatement would cause morale problems in the workplace. The fact that the union and union employees were supporting Craver's grievance showed that most employees felt that Craver should be returned to the job, especially in view of his long years of good service with the company. The union further claimed that Craver had not violated any known work rule, policy, or provision of the collective bargaining agreement. He did make a mistake, for which he paid an appropriate penalty. The union felt that there was no basis on which to terminate Craver since his discharge involved something that happened off the job. The union also claimed that the company was inconsistent in having allowed another employee to work during a work release program while on probation and not giving the same consideration to Craver. The union urged that the arbitrator should reinstate Craver and award him all lost pay, seniority, and benefits.

Questions for Discussion

1. Evaluate the contentions of the company in support of the position that the discharge of Craver was justified. Which do you find the most compelling and which do you find the least compelling?
2. Evaluate the contentions of the union in support of the position that Craver should be reinstated. Which of these do you find the most compelling and which do you find the least compelling?
3. If you were the arbitrator in this case, how would you decide? Explain the basis for your decision.
4. What are some of the broader implications of a case of this nature?

Chapter 11: Building Effective Work Teams and Maintaining Morale

After studying this chapter you will be able to

1 Explain why work groups form and function.

2 Classify work groups and their relevance for supervisors.

3 State some important research findings about work groups.

4 Discuss the importance of employee morale and its relationship to teamwork and productivity.

5 Understand the factors that influence employee morale and the supervisor's role in dealing with both external and internal factors.

6 Discuss techniques to assess employee morale, including observation and employee attitude surveys.

7 Understand why counselling is an important part of the supervisor's job.

8 Identify programs that organizations use to assist employees with personal and work-related problems, including workplace violence.

You are Charlie Graham, director of operations for Belmont Manufacturing. The company's 250 nonunionized employees manufacture plastic interior parts for the auto industry.

When you joined Belmont, employee turnover was over 75 percent. Belmont was scraping the "bottom of the barrel" when hiring employees. Some employees could barely read or write and had difficulty following basic instructions. The productivity problems alienated customers. Belmont was scrapping more product than it was shipping. That was when you and Elaine Knight, the new director of marketing, attended a total quality management (TQM) seminar.

When you returned from the seminar, you and Knight began calling customers and vendors; visiting manufacturing plants known for their total quality commitment; and analyzing production processes, methods, and costs. Working with Horst Watters, the newly hired personnel manager, you and Knight conducted an in-depth analysis of employee morale, followed by an identification of the costs, savings, and potential benefits of improving morale.

The three of you and seven other employees formed the Belmont Excellence Team. The team's mission was to make Belmont a better place to work. After several starts and stops, and a few glitches, the team came up with several ideas.

"The real key," you recall, "was learning how to listen carefully to our people." Those people told you what they needed to be satisfied at work and in life. Additional data from the attitude surveys, exit interviews, and customer service indexes played a role in your restructuring. Watters served as the conduit for all employee concerns. The Belmont Excellence Team instituted a basic literacy program for employees and eliminated two management layers: (1) plant superintendent and (2) foreperson. Removing those layers showed that you and the rest of the team were serious about the future—front-line workers would be empowered.

"When I came in here, corporate management had directed us to bring about improvement or they would close the plant," you reflect. "I knew from experience that there is no instant quality improvement program that will produce miraculous results overnight. Elaine, Horst, and I had a commitment from top management that they would give us 30 months to show progress before the plant would be shut down. The three of us agreed to follow Covey's 'Law of the Farm' model—we must plow and plant in the spring and tend the crops during the summer so we can harvest in the fall."

"We instituted job skills and process training," Knight continues. "After the classroom training, all employees attended an employee 'day camp' where they swung on ropes, climbed trees, and helped colleagues through a challenge course. It is common in a high output, just-in-time production plant for workers not to communicate with others outside their work areas. The team training really helped to bring people from different departments together. As a result, new teams were formed to deal with specific projects—work processes, scrap, defects, productivity, and the like."

All the team's plans resulted in a scrap rate less than the industry average; in the most recent quarter, customer complaints plummeted to just 4 from 350 the year before your arrival; individual productivity jumped more than 50 percent; and overtime in the past quarter dropped to less than 8 hours.

You recount, "People really want to come here and work now. We now have a reputation as a good place to work. Cross-functional team members act like Belmont is their personal company. We've built a continuous improvement process into our culture. Increased employee wages and benefits have more than been covered by the savings generated through employee suggestions."

As director of operations, you know that more changes will be needed. Where do you go from here? How can you help sustain the momentum you have helped build over the past four years?

You make the call!

1	**UNDERSTANDING WORK GROUPS AND THEIR IMPORTANCE**

Explain why work groups form and function.

In Chapter 4 we presented an overview of the *informal organization* with particular reference to the supervisor's relationship with informal work groups and their leaders. We mentioned that informal work groups can exert a positive or negative influence on employee motivation and performance. Throughout this book we have emphasized that a supervisor's decisions must be concerned not only with employees as individuals, but also with how they relate to groups both within and outside the supervisor's own department.

Clues to an individual's motivations and behaviour are often found in the context of the person's associates, colleagues, and peers. On the job, an employee's attitudes and morale can be shaped to a large degree by co-workers, at times even more so than by the supervisor or other factors in the work environment. Therefore, a supervisor should be aware of work groups and how they function. Moreover, a supervisor needs to develop a keen understanding of how morale influences employee performance and what can be done to maintain a high level of morale at the departmental level.

Why Work Groups Form and Function

There are many reasons work groups form and function in work settings.[1] Among the most commonly identified reasons are the following:

- **Companionship and identification:** The work group provides a peer relationship and a sense of belonging, which help satisfy the individual employee's social needs.
- **Behaviour guidelines:** People tend to look to others, especially their peers, for guides to acceptable behaviour in the workplace.
- **Problem solving:** The work group may be instrumental in providing a viable means by which an individual employee may solve a personal problem.
- **Protection:** The old adage of "strength in numbers" is not lost on employees, who often look to the group for protection from outside pressures, such as those placed by supervisors and higher-level managers.

Much behavioural research has focused on factors that make work groups tightly knit, cohesive, and effective. Work groups usually are most cohesive when

- The group members perceive themselves to have a higher status as compared with other employees, as, for example, in matters of job classification or pay.
- The group is generally small in size.
- The group shares similar personal characteristics, such as age, sex, ethnic background, off-the-job interests, and the like.
- The group is located relatively distant from other employees, such as geographically dispersed work groups or groups located away from the home office.
- The group has been formed due to outside pressures or for self-protection, such as a layoff or disciplinary action taken by management.
- Group members can communicate with one another relatively easily.
- The group has been successful in some previous group effort, which encourages the members to seek new group objectives.

Of course, a supervisor will never be completely aware of the kinds of forces that are most prevalent in the group dynamics of the department. However, sensitivity to the considerations just described can help the supervisor deal with work groups more effectively.

2 | CLASSIFICATIONS OF WORK GROUPS

Classify work groups and their relevance for supervisors.

Four major types of employee work groups can be identified in most organizations.[2] Groups can be classified as command groups, task groups, friendship groups, and special-interest groups. Since there is some overlap in these classifications, a supervisor should recognize that individual employees may be members of several such groups simultaneously.

Command Group

Command group
Grouping of employees according to authority relationships on the formal organization chart.

The **command group** is a grouping of employees according to the authority relationships shown on the formal organizational chart. Members of this group work together daily to accomplish regularly assigned work. For example, at the departmental level a command group consists of the supervisor and the employees who report to this supervisor. Throughout the organization there will be interrelated departments or divisions of command groups that reflect the formal authority structure.

Task Group or Cross-Functional Team

Task group or cross-functional team
Grouping of employees who come together to accomplish a particular task.

Consisting of employees from different departments, a **task group** or **cross-functional team** comes together to accomplish a particular task. For example, for a telephone to operate in a customer's home, the telephone company's employees and supervisors from a number of departments—such as customer service, construction, plant installation, central office equipment, accounting, and test centre—may come into contact with one another to accomplish the job. Another example would be a hospital, where numerous interdepartmental task relationships and communications take place among hospital personnel from departments such as admitting, nursing, laboratory, dietary, pharmacy, physical therapy, and medical records in order to care for a patient. Simply put, the purpose of task groups or cross-functional teams is to bring groups of people together so they can apply their combined talents to solve problems or better serve customers.

Friendship Group

Friendship group
Informal grouping of employees based on similar personalities and social interests.

The **friendship group** is an informal group of people who have similar personalities and social interests. Many friendship groups are related primarily by common factors such as age, sex, ethnic background, and outside interests. Of course, the presence of command and task groups may be instrumental in bringing clusters of friendship groups together.

Special-Interest Group

Special-interest group
Grouping of employees that exists to accomplish something in a group that individuals do not choose to pursue individually.

The **special-interest group** exists to accomplish in a group something that individuals feel incapable of or unwilling to pursue individually. Such a group can be either temporary or permanent. A temporary special-interest group might be a committee of employees who wish to protest an action taken by a supervisor or management, to promote a charitable undertaking, or to organize an employee event. A labour union is an example of a more permanent special-interest group since it is legally and formally organized. A labour union brings together employees from different departments and divisions to unite them in striving for economic gains and other objectives.

As stated earlier, an employee may be a member of a number of groups in the workplace, and the supervisor who understands the nature of these different groups is more likely to be in a position to influence them. Some research studies have suggested that a supervisor has a better chance to influence an individual employee's behaviour as a member of a work group than to deal with that employee individually (that is, without having the work group's influence in mind). Some concepts in this regard will be presented later in this chapter.

3 | RESEARCH INSIGHTS FOR MANAGING WORK GROUPS

State some important research findings about work groups.

Numerous behavioural studies have been made of work groups and how they function. From these, a number of approaches for managing work groups effectively have been suggested. While these approaches are not certain to produce desired results, they are consistent with behavioural research findings concerning work group dynamics and group behaviour.

Insights from the Hawthorne Studies

The work-group studies that probably have had the most lasting influence were conducted in the late 1920s and early 1930s at the Western Electric Company's Hawthorne plant near Chicago, Illinois.[3] Known as the **Hawthorne Studies,** they remain even today a comprehensive and definitive source on the subject of work group dynamics as related to employee attitudes and productivity.

Hawthorne Studies
Comprehensive research studies that focused on work-group dynamics as related to employee attitudes and productivity.

A brief synopsis of two of the major experiments at the Hawthorne plant is given here. These are the relay assembly room experiment and the bank wiring observation room experiment.

Relay Assembly Room Experiment

In the relay assembly room experiment, a group of six female employees assembled electrical relay equipment. They were closely observed in a special room while being subjected to various working conditions. For about two years, researchers experimented with a number of scheduling arrangements, such as changes in rest and lunch periods, in workday arrangements, and in the work week. Regardless of whether the changes instituted were favourable or unfavourable to the group, the outcome was that the employees' performance generally improved. By the end of this experiment, overall productivity had risen by about 30 percent over the pre-experiment level.

The researchers found that the primary reasons for the marked improvement in work performance were the attitudes and morale that had developed the employees into a solid, cohesive group. The employees became involved in the changes that were implemented, and the women felt that they were part of a team. The employees said that they felt that their supervision was much more informal and relaxed than they had experienced previously. Equally important was the fact that the employees considered the experiment to be an important part of a major project in the company. Since their work took on new importance, they developed their own norms for doing their jobs better. The research results clearly showed that a work group can be a positive influence on job performance if the group believes that it is part of a team and that what they are doing is important.

Bank Wiring Observation Room Experiment

A second group research experiment at the Hawthorne plant occurred a little later and lasted for almost a year. It involved 14 male employees whose work was to attach and solder banks of wires to telephone equipment. These employees and an observer were placed in a special room. The purpose of this experiment was to determine the impact of a series of wage incentive plans on employee productivity. The results of this experiment, however, revealed that a work group can have a negative influence on job performance. It turned out that the bank wiring observation room employees, as a group, developed an entirely different approach to their jobs than did the women in the relay assembly room experiment. The men decided to restrict output and keep it at a constant standard (or norm), which they referred to as the "bogey." It was learned from observation and interviews with the men in this group that there was strong pressure on the group members not to do anything more than the standard agreed upon by them. In effect, their approach was to maintain production at a level considered sufficient to keep the company satisfied, but not nearly as much as the employees could do. In fact, the employees believed that if they increased production significantly, it would not mean higher wages but would instead lead to a management "speed-up" without additional compensation, and some employees might be laid off.

In many organizations, supervisors complain that their employees would perform at higher levels if it were not for work groups that place considerable pressure on individual employees not to do too much. The ongoing challenge to today's supervisor is to encourage positive attitudes among work groups to perform at superior levels, such as that exhibited many years ago by the relay assembly room group at the Hawthorne plant.

Additional Insights from Team Research

In a number of chapters we have mentioned various organized participative management programs. These have been called by many names—most prominently quality circles, employee involvement, and total quality management (TQM). Many firms have developed their own versions, but these programs all have certain characteristics in common. For the most part, they try to build effective work teams that will foster continual improvement of work processes, project tasks, and service to customers. Because of the power of teams to positively or negatively affect work performance, many researchers and writers have studied how organizations can harness the power of the team toward organizational goals.

The Wisdom of Teams

One of the most comprehensive surveys of what makes teams effective was conducted by Jon Katzenbach and Douglas Smith, two management consultants who interviewed hundreds of team members in dozens of organizations that had used teams to address various problems. Katzenbach and Smith identified principles that are most closely associated with effective work teams, including

- Team members must be committed to the group and to the performance of the group.
- Teams function better when they are small, usually 10 members or fewer.
- Teams should be composed of individuals who have skills that are complementary and sufficient to deal with the problem.
- Teams should be committed to objectives that are specific and realistic.[4]

Much can also be learned from the case studies reported in Steven Jones's and Michael Beyerlein's *Developing High Performance Work Teams*. One such study, which describes Eastman Chemical Company's decision to move to a team management approach at its Kingsport, Tennessee, facility, delivered the following findings:

- Because supervisors must take on more responsibility and receive less recognition, they may feel threatened by transitions to teams. Therefore, supervisors must be coached, supported, and encouraged in their new roles.
- Team members must be held accountable for their actions to increase feelings of personal responsibility for the team's success.
- New team leadership roles for supervisors include coaching and facilitating.
- Communication becomes more important. Team leaders must be process oriented and have meetings to clarify team roles.[5]

Collaborative Workplace

Teamwork
People working cooperatively to solve problems and achieve goals important to the group.

None of the great sports teams or business organizations of the past could have succeeded without **teamwork**—people working cooperatively to solve problems and achieve goals important to the group. A **collaborative workplace** means that, throughout the organization, there is shared authority for decision making between employees and management. Teamwork processes are utilized to promote trust and integrity and to build consensus and shared ownership in striving to achieve common objectives. Collaboration is based on a work ethic that recognizes that people want and need to be valued for their contributions, and that improvements and changes are best achieved by those who are responsible for implementing them and committed to making them work.[6]

Collaborative workplace
Work environment characterized by joint decision making, shared accountability and authority, and high trust levels between employees and managers.

Figure 11-1 is a statement excerpted from a major company's training manual in regard to its total quality management (TQM) program. This policy statement demonstrates the firm's commitment to a collaborative workplace and to developing teams throughout the organization that will make major contributions toward improvement in various areas. Like many other firms, this company has organized teams from all parts of its organization consisting of employees, supervisors, professionals, and others. These teams grapple with and find solutions to problems that cross departmental lines.

Teams That Work

Another series of studies, conducted among work teams in a large financial services company, reached the conclusion that teams were most effective (1) when the focus was on managing the team as a group and having the team itself manage its individual members and (2) when the work teams were designed to be effective in terms of both improving productivity and improving satisfaction of the team members. These studies emphasized that the success of teams was largely attributable to the careful design and focus of the teams at the outset of their functioning.[7] Figure 11-2 summarizes the characteristics of effective work teams.

FIGURE 11-1   Excerpts from a policy statement concerning a firm's total quality management program.

ELEMENTS OF A TOTAL QUALITY MANAGEMENT SYSTEM

People—Teams and Partnerships

People are obviously the primary drivers in reaching customer satisfaction. People develop the systems and the processes and in turn use them to perform their jobs.

How can we best work together? In complex operations like ours, we need to bring groups of people together so that they can apply their combined talents to develop and improve processes. As more and more companies are learning, we need to work in teams. Teams enable the company to bring every ounce of intelligence and motivation and experience to bear on a process or problem or opportunity.

Every employee is empowered. This is one of the key elements of our TQM system. All employees have both the responsibility and the authority for performing their work, for the quality of their work, and for improving the way their work is done. They have the responsibility and authority to improve processes, procedures, and systems that will improve the way their work is done.

Probably no element of our TQM system is more misunderstood than empowerment. It doesn't mean that employees can act totally independently of their supervisors; employees are empowered within defined boundaries. It doesn't mean that supervisors have no control over their areas of responsibility. Supervisors must still know what's going on and must set directions for the department; and among other duties, they must give people regular and constructive feedback.

Management, employees, union members, suppliers, customers—all are important constituencies for our company, and one of our goals is to build teams among them in order to achieve our goal of total customer satisfaction.

A partnership or team in which all members accept responsibility for their work, a team that gets the kind of support and coaching it needs to accomplish its tasks, is a team that produces impressive results.

Not all participative management programs have been successful. In fact, a considerable number of firms have abandoned these programs for a variety of reasons. Perhaps the primary reason organized participative management programs fail is because management is looking for a "quick fix." Stated another way, a program such as TQM will work only to the degree that top-level management gives its full support, effort, and resources over a period of time to make the program a major part of ongoing organizational life.[8]

Self-Directed (Self-Managed) Work Teams: The "Ultimate" in Teamwork?

There is a growing phenomenon of self-directed (or self-managed) work teams, also known as autonomous work teams. In some respects, these could be considered the "ultimate" in efforts to maintain a collaborative workplace by having

FIGURE 11-2   Characteristics of effective work teams.

16 KEYS TO EFFECTIVE WORK TEAMS

- Group members agree on team goals and objectives and commit to those goals.
- All members participate actively in team meetings and discussions.
- All team members follow team rules, guidelines, and procedures.
- All members are valued and treated with respect and dignity.
- Team members share vital information and ensure that everyone is informed on a need-to-know basis.
- Members express their ideas without fear of retribution—team members also feel free to disagree—and the group grows with differences of opinion.
- The team uses a systematic problem-solving approach, but members are encouraged to think "outside the box" (i.e., alternative ways of thinking are encouraged).
- All members are included in solving problems, developing alternatives, and institutionalizing decisions.
- Decisions are made by consensus (i.e., all team members support decisions, even though they may not totally agree with those decisions; therefore, every team member feels ownership for the team's decisions and responsibility for the team's success).
- The team is cohesive—openness, trust, support, and encouragement are always present.
- Conflict is viewed as healthy—conflict is brought out into the open and addressed in a timely manner.
- Group members give each other honest feedback on performance; constructive feedback is used to improve performance.
- Team training and peer helping are essential elements of the team process. Peers help team members who may need individualized attention.
- The team continually evaluates its performance and uses that information as the basis for improvement.
- Pride in team accomplishments motivates team members.
- Members enjoy their team affiliation.

employees made largely responsible for managing themselves and their work. Much has been written about self-directed work teams, and organizations have taken a number of approaches. In general, these types of teams set their own targets or goals after consultation with higher management, and the team more or less determines how work is to be accomplished in order to achieve these objectives. In their most advanced form, teams may be given wide latitude to carry out responsibilities that formerly belonged to supervisors and/or human resource department staff. These responsibilities include such areas as selecting and dismissing team members and leaders, assigning tasks within the group, training team members, appraising team members, allocating pay adjustments, disciplinary actions, and work scheduling.[9] There have been few comprehensive studies concerning the effectiveness of self-managed work teams, but preliminary evidence—much of which is anecdotal—suggests that they can be very effective in improving efficiency, morale, and customer service.[10]

Members of a cohesive work group enjoy their group affiliation.

Tom & Dee Ann McCarthy/CORBIS

Virtual team
Geographically separated people who are working on a common project and are linked by communication technologies.

The accompanying Contemporary Issue box describes another variant of work teams that presents unique challenges at every stage of development and performance. In a **virtual team**, members share a purpose but are dispersed geographically. With these teams, the managers' challenge is to build commitment, cooperation, and collaboration through effective communication.

4 UNDERSTANDING AND MAINTAINING EMPLOYEE MORALE

Discuss the importance of employee morale and its relationship to teamwork and productivity.

Morale
A composite of feelings and attitudes that individuals and groups have toward their work, environment, supervisors, top-level management, and organization.

Most definitions of *morale* recognize that it is essentially a state of mind. For example, the *Nelson Canadian Dictionary* defines the word *morale* as "the state of the spirits of a person or group as exhibited by confidence, cheerfulness, discipline, and willingness to perform assigned tasks." For our purposes we will consider **morale** as consisting of the attitudes and feelings of individuals and groups toward their work, environment, supervisors, top-level management, and organization. Morale is not a single feeling but a composite of feelings and attitudes. It affects employee performance and willingness to work, which in turn affect individual and organizational objectives. When employee morale is high, employees usually do what the organization wants them to do; when it is low, the opposite tends to occur.

Numerous articles have suggested that today's employees are unhappier with many aspects of their jobs than were employees of earlier decades. Much of this lowered morale is attributed to a belief that many employers do not trust and are not loyal to their employees; as a result, employees do not trust and are not loyal to their employers. It long has been recognized and documented that the reasons employees either stay with or leave an employer are frequently attributable to factors other than pay.[11]

CONTEMPORARY ISSUE
Managing Virtual Teams: How Different Is It?

As many companies have expanded their operations domestically and internationally, they have found that virtual teams can help them focus on meeting customer requirements. A virtual team is one that has members who rarely, if ever, meet face to face, even though they work on a project or in an area of operations with a common goal.

Virtual teams function primarily through technological tools that enable them to communicate. Most prominent are e-mails, video conferences, teleconferences, and video phone calls. Virtual teams require their members to receive specialized training in technology use, and they necessitate careful planning and organization to establish regular times for group interaction as well as other communication needs. One advantage of virtual teams is that members can communicate quickly when needed to bring team members up to date on events and to keep each other informed.

The requirements of virtual team managers and supervisors are slightly different than those for conventional teams. Virtual teams are geographically dispersed, which typically means that managers and supervisors have less direct control over team members. Nevertheless, the need for supervisory feedback and evaluation is paramount. One recommended approach is that team members be brought together initially or at some point to help them become better acquainted and to strengthen their relationships. The challenge for a manager or supervisor of a virtual team is to hold team members together and keep them motivated even though they are separated physically and are often very different. The focus must be on overall results rather than on the specific activities of team members. Managers of virtual teams have tried various techniques to help team members stay focused on their projects and to strengthen their functioning and team spirit. Among these are giving the project team a name or logo, rotating the hosting of conference calls, sharing information about personal events (e.g., birthdays and weddings), and recognizing accomplishments.

In essence, managing virtual teams, while it has some unique challenges and problems, differs only slightly from managing teams that are close geographically. Both types of teams require supervisors and managers who are adept at applying their managerial skills with effective human relations approaches that serve the individual and group needs of team members.

Managers of virtual teams must help team members communicate with one another in the absence of nonverbal cues and body language. Karim Ladak is an associate director with Proctor & Gamble in Toronto. He leads a virtual team of 50 people located in Toronto, Cincinnati, Brussels, Manila, Warsaw, Singapore, San Jose, and Geneva. Ladak stresses the need for careful communication among the members of a virtual team. "On a call, I use subtle listening. I listen for a quiver or a pause. And even then I know that I can very quickly miss something." Ladak also points out the particular challenges faced by global virtual teams. "You have to value diversity. You can't jump the first time someone says something different. Some cultures are slower to respond or more passive than others. Even between Canada and the U.S. there are cultural nuances."

Sources: Excerpted and adapted from Carla Joinson, "Managing Virtual Teams," *HRMagazine* (June 2002), pp. 69–73 and Sharda Prashad, "Building trust tricky for 'virtual' teams," *Toronto Star* (October 23, 2003), p. K06.

There should be little doubt that employee morale is an important supervisory consideration. Some supervisors simply believe that morale is something that employees either have or do not have. Actually, morale is always present in some form, and it can be positive (high), negative (low), or varied. High morale, of course, is desirable. Employees with high morale find satisfaction in their positions, have confidence in their abilities, and usually work with enthusiasm and to the full extent of their abilities. High morale cannot be ordered, but it can be fostered by conditions in the workplace that are favourable to its development. High morale is not the cause of good human relations; it is the result of good human relations. High morale is the result of positive motivation, respect for people, effective supervisory leadership, good communication, participation, counselling, and desirable human relations practices. The state of employee morale reflects, to a large degree, how effectively a supervisor is performing his or her managerial responsibilities.

Morale Should Be Everyone's Concern

Every manager, from the chief executive down to the supervisor, should be concerned with the morale of the workforce. It should be a priority to develop and maintain employee morale at the highest level possible.

Because of widespread concern about deteriorating employee morale and alienation of many workers toward their employers, many firms have embarked on various programs and efforts that collectively have been called **workplace spirituality.** These organizational efforts are designed to make the work environment more meaningful and creative by recognizing and tapping into people's deeply held values and spiritual beliefs. Some believe that spirituality can improve employees' personal lives and mental outlook and that this might translate to a better work environment.[12]

Our concern in this chapter is not to analyze these and other organization-wide efforts aimed at improving morale. Rather, we primarily will discuss the role played by the first-line supervisor, who, probably more than anyone else, influences the level of morale in day-to-day contacts with employees.

Bringing morale to a high level and maintaining it there is a continuous process; it cannot be achieved simply through short-run devices such as pep talks or contests. High morale is slow to develop and difficult to maintain. The level of morale can vary considerably from day to day. Morale is contagious in both directions because both favourable and unfavourable attitudes spread rapidly among employees. Unfortunately, it seems to be human nature that employees quickly forget the good and long remember the bad when it comes to factors influencing their morale.

The supervisor is not alone in desiring high morale. Employees are just as much concerned with morale since it is paramount to their work satisfaction. High morale helps to make the employee's day at work a pleasure and not a misery. High morale also is important to an organization's customers. They usually can sense whether employees are serving them with enthusiasm or just going through the motions.

Morale, Teamwork, and Productivity Relationships

Teamwork is often associated with morale, but the two terms do not mean the same thing. Morale refers to the attitudes and feelings of employees, whereas teamwork primarily relates to the degree of cooperation among people in solving problems and accomplishing objectives. Good morale is helpful in achieving teamwork, but teamwork can be high even when morale is low. Such a situation might exist in times when jobs are scarce and employees tolerate bad conditions and poor supervision for fear of losing their jobs. On the other hand, teamwork may be absent when morale is high. For example, employees working on a piecework basis or salespeople being paid on a straight commission basis typically are rewarded for individual efforts rather than for group performance.

Workplace spirituality
Organizational efforts to make the work environment more meaningful and creative by relating work to employees' personal values and spiritual beliefs.

Many supervisors believe that high morale usually is accompanied by high productivity. Much research has been done to study this assumption. Although there are some contradictions in research results, there is substantial evidence to suggest that in the long run, high-producing employees do tend to have high morale. That is to say, well-motivated, self-disciplined groups of employees tend to do a more satisfactory job than those from whom the supervisor tries to force such performance. Furthermore, when supervisors are considerate of their employees and try to foster positive attitudes among them, there tends to be greater mutual trust, lower absenteeism and turnover, and fewer grievances.[13] Regardless of its other effects, there is little question that a high level of morale tends to make work more pleasant, particularly for the supervisor!

<table>
<tr><td>5</td><td></td></tr>
</table>

| 5 | **FACTORS INFLUENCING MORALE** |

Understand the factors that influence employee morale and the supervisor's role in dealing with both external and internal factors.

Virtually anything can influence the morale of employees either positively or negatively. Some of these influences are within the control of the supervisor; others are not. These factors generally can be classified as two broad types: external and internal.

External and Internal Factors Influencing Morale

Influences outside the organization are generally beyond the supervisor's control. Nevertheless, they may significantly affect the morale of employees at work. Examples of external factors are family relationships, care of children or elderly parents, financial difficulties, problems with friends, a car breakdown, sickness or death in the family, outside pressures, and the like. What happens at home can change an employee's feelings very quickly. An argument before leaving for work may set an emotional tone for the rest of the day. Even headlines in the morning newspaper may be depressing or uplifting.

Conditions within the company can also influence morale. Examples of internal factors are compensation, job security, the nature of work, relations with co-workers, working conditions, recognition, and so on. These factors are partially or fully within the supervisor's control. For example, when compensation is adequate, other factors may assume a more significant role. But even when wages are good, morale can sink quickly if working conditions are neglected. The critical factor here is whether or not the supervisor attempts to improve working conditions. Employees often will perform very well under undesirable conditions and still maintain high morale if they believe that their supervisor is seriously trying to improve work conditions.

All aspects of good supervision affect employee morale in relation to conditions on the job. However, perhaps the most significant day-to-day influence on employee morale is the supervisor's general attitude and behaviour in departmental relationships. If a supervisor's behaviour indicates suspicion about the employees' motives and actions, low morale will likely result. If the supervisor acts worried or depressed, employees tend to follow suit. If the supervisor loses his or her temper, some employees may also lose theirs. Conversely, if the supervisor shows confidence in the employees' work and commends them for good performance, this reinforces their positive outlook.

This does not mean that a supervisor should overlook difficulties that are present from time to time. Rather, it means that if something goes wrong, the supervisor should act as a leader who has the situation in hand. For example, supervisors often will be called upon to mediate conflict among their employees. The supervisor should demonstrate the attitude that the employees will be relied on to correct the situation and to do what is necessary to prevent occurrence of a similar situation.

Supervisors should not relax their efforts to build and maintain high employee morale. However, they should not become discouraged if morale drops from time to time because many factors beyond their control can cause this. Supervisors can be reasonably satisfied if employee morale is high most of the time.

Workplace Incivility

Rude behaviour is on the rise both in the workplace and in society at large. The findings of two recent studies indicate that workplace incivility can have a negative impact on worker morale. Specifically, these studies have found that

- Incivility has worsened in the past 10 years.
- Rude people are three times more likely to be in higher positions than their targets.
- Men are seven times more likely to be rude or insensitive to the feelings of their subordinates than to the feelings of their superiors.
- Twelve percent of people who experience rude behaviour quit their jobs to avoid the perpetrators.
- Twenty-two percent of respondents deliberately decreased their work efforts as a result of rudeness.[14]

Supervisors should be aware of the longer-term impact of workplace incivility on team morale. In the workplace, the clear expectation should be that everyone will be treated with civility and respect.

The Downside of Downsizing on Morale

According to a 1996 survey of about 1,000 corporations employing more than 25,000 workers, a decade of downsizing left a "legacy of fear" among workers. Some 46 percent of the employees surveyed indicated that they worried about being laid off, and 53 percent expressed concerns about the future of their firms. Both of these percentages were significantly higher than those from just four years previously. Further, only 40 percent of the surveyed workers indicated that they felt their companies valued long-term employees.[15]

It is apparent that employee morale in many organizations can suffer from what has been termed *survivors' syndrome*. Most companies do not seem to be prepared to deal with widespread employee fears and insecurities. However, some firms have developed training programs and have provided counselling services in order to plan and implement job reductions and to assist remaining employees to cope with the aftereffects. Among the recommended strategies are (1) early, clear, and ample communication with specific details concerning which jobs have been eliminated and, more importantly, why; and (2) working with remaining employees to develop new short-term objectives that will enable them to focus on activities and targets over which they have a semblance of control.[16] Here, too, first-line supervisors have a crucial role in influencing the direction of employee morale.

| 6 | ASSESSING EMPLOYEE MORALE |

Discuss techniques to
assess employee morale,
including observation
and employee attitude
surveys.

Although most firms believe that employee morale is important in the long run if the organization is to be successful, good measurements of employee morale are somewhat elusive. Some firms rely on statistical comparisons to assess the state of morale in their company. They look at data that compare their employees with industry standards for employee attendance, turnover, use of sick leave, and other broad indicators.[17]

These comparisons are useful, but for supervisors they may or may not be relevant to the departmental situation. Some supervisors pride themselves on their ability to size up morale intuitively. However, most supervisors would be better advised to approach the measurement of morale in a more systematic fashion. Although it may not be possible to measure morale precisely, there are techniques for assessing prevailing levels and trends. The two most frequently used techniques are (1) observation and study and (2) attitude surveys.

Observing and Studying Indicators of Morale

By observing, monitoring, and studying patterns of employee behaviour, a supervisor can often discover clues to employee morale. The supervisor should closely monitor such key indicators as job performance levels, tardiness and absenteeism, the amount of waste or scrap, employee complaints, and accident and safety records. Any significant changes in the levels of these indicators should be analyzed since they often are interrelated. For example, excessive tardiness and absenteeism seriously interfere with job performance. The supervisor should determine why employees are often tardy or absent. If reasons are related to morale, are the causes within the supervisor's control, or should the employee be referred somewhere for counselling or assistance?

It is relatively easy to observe the extremes of high and low morale. However, it is quite difficult to differentiate among intermediate degrees of morale—or to assess when morale is changing. For example, an employee's facial expression or shrug of the shoulder may or may not reflect that person's level of morale. Only an alert supervisor can judge whether this employee is becoming depressed or frustrated. Supervisors must sharpen their powers of observation and be careful not to brush aside indicators of change.

The closeness of daily working relationships offers numerous opportunities for a supervisor to observe and analyze changes in employee morale. However, many supervisors do not take time to observe, and others do not analyze what they observe. It is only when an extreme, obvious drop in the level of morale has taken place that some supervisors recall the first indications of change. By then, the problems that led to this lowered state of morale probably will have magnified to the point where major corrective actions will be necessary. As so often is the case in supervision, addressing issues proactively can prevent small problems from escalating.

Exit interview
Interview with individuals who leave a firm to assess morale and reasons for employee turnover.

Many companies conduct **exit interviews** with individuals leaving their employment. Exit interviews are usually conducted by a human resources staff person, although sometimes, especially in a small firm, the supervisor may fill this role. The interviewer asks questions about why the person is leaving and about conditions within the firm as that person sees them. Results of exit interviews are used to assess the morale in the firm or in certain departments of the firm, as well as to identify reasons for employee turnover. Because they are conducted when a person is leaving the organization, exit interviews can reveal insights into employee morale that current employees may be unwilling to express.

Employee Attitude Surveys

Attitude survey
Survey of employee opinions about major aspects of organizational life used to assess morale.

Another technique used to assess employee morale is an **attitude survey,** also called an *opinion* or *morale* survey. All employees—or a sample of the employees—are asked to express their opinions about major aspects of organizational life, usually in the form of answers to questions on a survey form. The survey questionnaire elicits employee opinions about such factors as management and supervision, job conditions, job satisfaction, co-workers, pay and benefits, job security, advancement opportunities, and so on.

Employee attitude surveys are rarely initiated by a supervisor. Usually they are undertaken by top-level management and are prepared with the help of the human resources department or an outside consulting firm.[18] The survey questionnaire should be written in language that is appropriate for most employees.

Attitude surveys, or questionnaires, may be completed on the job or in the privacy of the employee's home. Some organizations prefer to have employees answer these questionnaires on the job because a high percentage of questionnaires that are mailed out are never returned. On the other hand, a possible advantage of filling out the questionnaire at home is that employees may give more thoughtful and truthful answers. Regardless of where they are completed, questionnaires should not be signed so that they remain anonymous, although some surveys may request employees to indicate their departments.

Many attitude survey forms offer employees the choice of answering questions from a given list of answers. Other forms are not so specific and provide employees the opportunity to answer as freely as they wish. Since some employees may find it too time consuming or cumbersome to write down their opinions in sentences, better results usually are obtained with a survey form on which the employees simply check the printed responses that correspond to their answers.

Follow-up of Survey Results

Responsibility for tabulating and analyzing questionnaires is usually given to the human resources department or to an outside consulting firm. Survey results are first presented to top-level and middle-level managers and eventually to departmental supervisors. In some organizations, survey results are used as discussion materials during supervisory training, especially when they provide clues about ways to improve employee morale.

Attitude surveys may reveal deficiencies that the supervisor can eliminate. For example, a complaint about a lack of soap in the washroom can be resolved easily. But frequently the responses are difficult to evaluate, as, for example, a complaint that communication channels are not open to employees. Such complaints raise more questions than answers and may necessitate a careful study of existing policies and procedures to see whether corrective actions are warranted.

If the attitude survey reveals a correctable problem at the departmental level—perhaps with an individual supervisor—the solution should be developed and implemented by the supervisor involved. On the other hand, a broader problem that requires the attention of higher-level managers should be reported to the appropriate manager for action. If supervisors and higher-level managers do not make needed changes as a result of a survey, the survey was a waste of time and money. In fact, if no changes materialize, or if changes are not communicated to the employees, a decline in morale may occur after the survey. Employees may feel that their problems and suggestions have been ignored. Thus, whenever possible, dissatisfactions expressed in an attitude survey should be addressed promptly by managers and supervisors, or at least employees should be informed that management is aware of the dissatisfactions and is investigating ways to resolve them by some future date.

Organizational Development

Many companies follow up their attitude surveys with feedback meetings and conference sessions with groups of employees and supervisors. Typically these meetings are conducted by an outside consultant, or by a staff person from the human resources or some other department. In these meetings, results of attitude surveys are discussed and debated openly. The groups are expected to develop recommendations for improvement, which are forwarded anonymously to higher-level management for consideration and possible implementation.

Organizational development (OD)

Meetings with groups under the guidance of a neutral conference leader to solve problems that are hindering organizational effectiveness.

This approach is often part of a broader concept that also has become widespread in many large enterprises. Known as **organizational development (OD)**, *team building,* or *process consultation,* it usually involves having scheduled group meetings under the guidance of a neutral conference leader. The groups may consist of just employees, employees and supervisors, just supervisors, just higher-level managers, or whatever composition is appropriate. For the most part, the meetings focus on solving problems that may be hindering effective work performance or causing disruption, poor coordination, fouled-up communications, and strained personal relations. When there is frank discussion in a relatively open and informal atmosphere, individuals tend to open up about what really is on their minds and what might be done to resolve problems and reduce conflict. Organizational development can take numerous patterns that are beyond the scope of this text.[19] Suffice it to say, however, that many supervisors will be involved in organizational development efforts since these programs can contribute to the improvement of morale and organizational effectiveness.

| 7 | **THE SUPERVISOR'S COUNSELLING ROLE** |

Understand why counselling is an important part of the supervisor's job.

Counselling is not the same as coaching. In counselling, the supervisor tries to address on-the-job performance problems that result from an employee's personal problems.[20] As mentioned in Chapter 9, an employee's performance problems may stem from a job-related personal problem, such as the failure to get a promotion, or from an off-the-job situation, such as a financial crisis due to divorce. When left unaddressed, these problems can impede morale and the quality of work. Therefore, the supervisor must help the employee return to productivity. The most effective way to get an employee back on track is to counsel—to ask, listen, reflect, and encourage. A counselling interview is essentially nondirective (as described in Chapter 5); the supervisor serves primarily as an empathetic listener, and the employee is encouraged to discuss the problem frankly and to develop solutions. Figure 11-3 illustrates the steps in the counselling process.

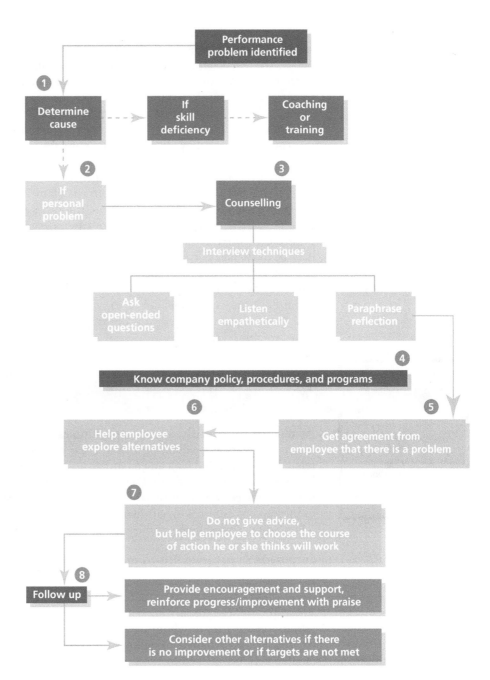

FIGURE 11-3
Steps in the counselling process.

By being a good listener, the supervisor can help the employee develop alternatives. For example, perhaps Laura, one of the employees at Belmont Manufacturing (from this chapter's You Make the Call), is upset because of a sudden financial crisis, and her work performance shows a marked decline. She spends more of her time thinking about how to solve her financial problems than she does thinking about her work. In short, a counselling interview might begin when the supervisor addresses a performance problem and expresses concern: "Laura, I'm concerned about your performance. You were late for work two days last week, and the Finegan report did not get done. Could you explain?" The supervisor should listen carefully and without interruption to understand Laura's perspective. In Chapter 8, we discussed the importance of paraphrasing and reflecting to improve understanding. Paraphrasing involves expressing, in different words, Laura's response (e.g., "Let me see if I understand what you're saying ..."). A follow-up question might be, "Why do you feel that way?" Through reflection, the supervisor can help Laura talk about her feelings.

The supervisor may discuss with Laura possible ways to obtain financial assistance. The supervisor should not offer specific advice, because it might bring unwanted repercussions. If Laura is dissatisfied with the results of following a supervisor's advice, for example, she might blame the supervisor, which would complicate an already difficult situation. If Laura's problem is beyond the supervisor's expertise, perhaps the supervisor can arrange for Laura to get help from a professional or refer her to the human resources department, where assistance may be available. For example, many employers provide assistance and referral services for employees with personal problems. Many large employers also have employee assistance programs (EAPs), which are discussed later in this chapter. Regardless, the supervisor's job is to help the employee explore alternatives and find the help that is needed in order to get the employee's performance back to an acceptable level.

8	**PROGRAMS FOR ASSISTING EMPLOYEES WITH PERSONAL AND WORK-RELATED PROBLEMS**
Identify programs that organizations use to assist employees with personal and work-related problems, including workplace violence.	

As discussed previously, supervisors at times hold counselling interviews with employees who are exhibiting low morale or experiencing personal or work-related problems. By being an empathetic and sincere listener, the supervisor may help such employees work out their own solutions or may suggest avenues of professional advice or assistance. Alternatively, the supervisor may refer an employee to the human resources department or some designated management person who will hold the counselling interview and suggest possibilities for help.

Employee Assistance Programs

Employee assistance program (EAP)

Company program to assist employees with certain personal or work-related problems that are interfering with job performance.

In recent years, many organizations—especially large corporations and major government agencies—have adopted **employee assistance programs (EAPs).** These programs typically involve a special department or outside resources retained by the firm to whom supervisors may refer employees with certain types of problems. Alternatively, employees may seek help on their own from the EAP, or they may be referred to the EAP by other sources such as their union. Most employee assistance programs provide help for alcoholism and substance abuse; marriage, child-care, and family problems; financial questions; and other personal, emotional, or psychological problems that may be interfering with job performance. Figure 11-4 is a policy statement included in the EAP booklet provided to employees of a major corporation. It illustrates the typical elements of this type of program.

The supervisor's role in an EAP is essential for its effectiveness. The supervisor needs to be alert to signs that an employee may be troubled, even though the supervisor has tried to respond to the employee's work performance using normal supervisory procedures. For example, a supervisor may be concerned

FIGURE 11-4 Policy statement for an employee assistance program (EAP).

EMPLOYEE ASSISTANCE PROGRAM

Introduction

The employee assistance program (EAP) was adopted to provide confidential, professional assistance to employees and their families. The program also provides managers and union representatives with a constructive way to help employees and to reduce the adverse economic impact on the company that occurs when personal problems interfere with job performance.

How the Program Works

There are essentially four ways that a person may enter the EAP:
1. Self-referral.
2. Management referral.
3. Union referral.
4. Medical referral.

Self-Referral

Any employee or family member may call the EAP office for information or to make an appointment to discuss a personal problem. The contact, as well as what is discussed, is handled in the strictest confidence.

Management Referral

Managers and supervisors may suggest to an employee that he or she seek help when there is a noticeable decline in the employee's work performance that is not correctable through usual supervisory procedures or where there are specific on-the-job incidents that indicate the presence of a personal problem.

Union Referral

Official union representatives are encouraged to ask their members to make use of the services provided by the EAP. Union officials may call the EAP office and speak with the counsellor or provide the employee or family member with the EAP office telephone number.

Medical Referral

Medical referrals to the EAP are based either upon the identification of a medical symptom or disorder that is normally associated with a personal problem or upon a request from the employee for advice or assistance regarding a personal problem.

about an employee's recent poor attendance and low production while at work. The supervisor suspects that something is amiss—perhaps an alcohol-related problem or substance abuse. When talking with the employee, the supervisor should focus primarily on the person's poor or deteriorating job performance and then suggest to the employee the EAP services that might be of some help. Figure 11-5 is a procedural statement excerpted from a supervisory policy manual within a major firm's EAP. The procedural guidelines for supervisors in this policy are representative of types of approaches that most major organizations have adopted in their EAP efforts.

FIGURE 11-5   A firm's procedural guidelines for EAP case handling by supervisors.

SUPERVISORY PROCEDURES FOR EAP CASE HANDLING

The employee assistance program is for all employees—management and occupational—who want help with their personal problems. The EAP is prepared to accept referrals from many sources, including supervisors and union representatives, who believe that personal problems are causing an employee's job performance to deteriorate. Experience has shown that many employees will seek assistance once they realize that help is readily available. But the decision to seek help must always be the employee's, and actual counselling should be left to professionals.

The following procedures generally apply when trying to help an employee improve job performance:

- Talk about job performance in an initial discussion with the employee. Only deteriorating job performance should be discussed. Opinions and judgments about possible personal problems should be avoided—leave that to the professional counsellor. Specific instances of deteriorating job performance, such as unsatisfactory attendance, quality of work, or productivity, will be the basis for the initial discussion.
- Employees who initiate discussion of personal problems with either supervisors or union representatives should be informed of the EAP and encouraged to participate on a voluntary basis.
- Describe the EAP after job performance has been discussed. Tell the employee about the service available through the EAP. Stress that EAP contacts are confidential; no information concerning the nature of the problem or the specific treatment will be revealed without the employee's consent. Usually, the employee will not be terminated for the unsatisfactory job performance until an opportunity to use the EAP has been offered.
- If the employee chooses to accept help, referral will be made directly to the EAP counsellor to determine the nature of the problem and develop a course of action.
- To help the EAP counsellor, any information pertaining to the employee's job performance or behaviour should be provided by the supervisor or union representative at the time of referral.
- The EAP counsellor may determine that outside resources are appropriate. If so, these referrals will be made as necessary.
- The employee will be allowed a reasonable period to improve job performance with the aid of counselling and supervisory support.
- If the employee rejects the offer of assistance and the job performance problems do not continue or recur, nothing further need be done.
- If the offer is rejected by the employee and job performance problems continue or recur, appropriate action may then be taken in accordance with existing company policy and the union agreement for handling problems of deteriorating job performance.

Most EAPs emphasize the confidential nature of the services. Supervisors should discuss this with employees and assure them that no stigma will be associated with their seeking EAP help. However, the supervisor should inform an employee who refuses EAP assistance and whose work performance continues to deteriorate that such a refusal might be a consideration in a termination decision.

Wellness Programs

Wellness program

Organized efforts by a firm to help employees to get and stay healthy in order to remain productive.

Another approach used by some firms, often where an EAP is in place, has been called a wellness program. A **wellness program** essentially is an organized effort by a firm designed to help employees stay healthy both physically and mentally and to reduce costs associated with absenteeism and stress. Programs are varied, but they often focus on areas of recovery and staying free of certain problems such as stress, substance abuse, injury, and the like. Wellness programs can include providing exercise facilities, counselling, and other resources either on company premises or elsewhere. In some firms, corporate wellness programs are viewed as a type of employee benefit, but for the most part they are directed efforts by the firm to improve employee health and safety, which in turn should have a positive impact on morale and work performance.[21]

Ombudsman

Ombudsman

Staff person who serves as a neutral mediator in resolving conflicts on the job.

Still another approach for assisting employees with special work-related problems is to use an **ombudsman** (or *corporate ombudsman*). Typically, the ombudsman is a staff person who serves as a neutral mediator in resolving conflicts on the job. Only large companies are likely to have an ombudsman. The person serving in the ombudsman role may or may not be human resources staff or part of an EAP program. In some firms the ombudsman is part of a separate department, which might be identified as the "personnel communications department" or the "liaison department." Employees who have work-related problems are encouraged to

Wellness programs provide exercise facilities, counselling, and other resources on company premises and elsewhere.

CORBIS

come to this department to be interviewed confidentially. Perhaps the employee has a conflict with his or her supervisor that the employee is afraid to discuss with the supervisor. Or perhaps the employee is dissatisfied about something that has happened—for example, being passed over for a promotion, being disciplined, being given unfair work assignments or schedules, and the like. The ombudsman listens to the employee's concerns and then may choose to follow a number of alternatives in an effort to resolve the problem. The ombudsman does not have any direct authority, but acts as a "third party" or "neutral service" when, for example, he or she meets with the employee's supervisor to discuss the matter and to see what—if anything—might be done. In this regard, the ombudsman is acting as a communications link, which often becomes the most important aspect of resolving or at least reducing the magnitude of a conflict.

Dealing with Workplace Violence

In recent years, violence has increased dramatically. Although experts agree that it is impossible to accurately predict violent behaviour, some studies have identified certain behavioural problems that may be precursors to violence on the job. Supervisors typically are in the best position to identify the warning signals, which include "paranoid" behaviour such as panicking easily or perceiving that the "whole world is against me"; reacting to or failing to take any criticism either from a supervisor or a colleague; and unexplained dramatic changes in an individual's productivity, attendance, or hygiene.[22] Studies of violent acts in the workplace have shown that these typically start as verbal disputes and involve persons who know each other. Disputes may be over trivial matters or minor disagreements with supervisors or fellow employees. The disagreement intensifies in spite of reasonable efforts to resolve the problem.[23]

Supervisors should be alert to these types of warning signals and report them to higher management, the human resources department, or the EAP staff if this type of service is available. Some firms have established oversight committees or programs—often in connection with security personnel—in order to have policies and procedures in place both to prevent and deal with individuals and work situations that have a potential for serious or violent consequences. Any situation that explodes into violence on the job can have a devastating impact on employee morale. Here, too, the sensitivity and actions of supervisors in coordinating efforts throughout the firm to prevent workplace violence are among the most important elements of a firm's response to this unfortunate problem.

WHAT CALL DID YOU MAKE?

As Charlie Graham, director of operations for Belmont Manufacturing, you realize that you have accomplished much during the past four years. Since coming to Belmont, you have been impressed with the many successes you have had. The major problems have been eliminated or reduced. On the surface, it appears that you have been able to get most employees on board with the work-team concept. Most of the concepts and principles discussed in this chapter were relevant to your success.

To ensure Belmont's teams are still on track, you, Elaine Knight, and Horst Watters, the management trio, must review the characteristics of effective teams. Employee morale should be continually monitored. Ask employees questions like the following:

- What can we do to enhance the success of your team? Your individual performance?
- What additional skills do you need or want?
- What can we do to help you be the very best employee?

It might be appropriate to implement a regular employee attitude and needs survey. Understanding employees' needs and their perceptions about the workplace is critical. By analyzing and acting on the information you receive, the management trio can ensure that success is sustained.

Perceptive students realize that even the best teams can get complacent. It is difficult to sustain high performance over long periods. Review the following chapters, which can serve as foundations for Belmont's continual search for improvement:

- Chapter 3 (problem solving).
- Chapter 6 (motivation).
- Chapter 7 (leadership).
- Chapter 8 (communication).

In short, you can help your team become more effective by ensuring that all employees know what is expected of them. The use of stretch targets is one approach. Hire employees who are or can be team players and have senior employees (high performers) help those employees acclimate. Ensure employees know they can ask for help, and recognize that all employees have off-the-job problems. If Belmont lacks an EAP (Employee Assistance Plan), it should study the feasibility of implementing one. Teams should seek input from customers and suppliers to help identify problems, develop more efficient processes and procedures, and address issues in a timely manner. Last, but not least, you must recognize and reward the efforts of your teams. Remember: there is no substitute for daily feedback on performance.

SUMMARY

Work groups typically are formed to provide companionship and identification, behaviour guidelines, problem-solving help, and protection. Various factors can contribute to the cohesiveness and functioning of the work group, such as the group's status, size, personal characteristics, location, and previous success. Work groups can exert significant influences upon employee attitudes and job performance, which supervisors must recognize and be prepared to deal with.

At any time, an employee may be a member of a command group, task group, friendship group, or special-interest group. Command and task groups are formed primarily based on job-related factors; friendship groups primarily reflect personal relationships and interests; special-interest groups focus on an activity that individuals feel incapable of or unwilling to pursue on their own. Supervisors should be sensitive to all of these clusters and how they affect employees.

3 The Hawthorne research studies demonstrated that work groups can have either a positive or a negative influence on employee performance. To influence work groups in a positive direction, supervisors should review the keys to effective team building. Teams should be relatively small, and members must have the necessary skills and be committed to specific and realistic objectives. Work teams are called self-directed, or self-managed, when they are given wide latitude and autonomy for making decisions concerning workplace operations. Organized participative management programs primarily involve building effective work teams to tackle tasks that will improve work performance and customer service. For such programs to be effective, top-level and other managers must give their full, ongoing support.

4 Employee morale is a composite of feelings and attitudes of individuals and groups toward their work environment, supervisor, and the organization as a whole. Morale can vary from very high to very low and can change considerably from day to day. Everyone in the organization should be concerned about morale. Morale and teamwork are not synonymous, but high morale usually contributes to high teamwork and productivity.

5 Morale can be influenced by factors from outside the organization as well as by on-the-job factors. There is relatively little a supervisor can do to change the existence of external factors. The supervisor can listen empathetically to the employee's concerns and perhaps refer the employee to a source of assistance. If an employee requests a leave of absence because of sickness or certain types of family considerations, the supervisor should refer this to higher-level management or the human resources department.

Many internal factors associated with the job can influence employee morale. Good supervisory management practices can do much to positively influence these factors. The supervisor's general attitude and behaviour in departmental relationships with employees will have the most influence on the day-to-day direction of employee morale. This also extends to helping employees cope with any insecurities and fears that are a result of the massive job displacements and downsizing of firms in recent years.

6 Astute supervisors can sense a change in the level of morale by observing employee behaviours and key indicators, such as absenteeism and performance trends. Another means of assessing levels of employee morale is to conduct an attitude survey. Supervisors and higher-level managers should—if possible—correct problems that have been brought to their attention through the survey. It is also desirable to discuss the results of an attitude survey in meetings with groups of employees and supervisors, and encourage them to recommend improvements.

7 Counselling is an effort by the supervisor to deal with on-the-job performance problems that are the result of the employee's personal problems. When left unattended, these problems may decrease morale and eventually erode quality and productivity. The counselling process includes identifying the performance problem, asking questions, listening empathetically to employee concerns, and perhaps referring the employee to a source of assistance. Sound interviewing and communication practices are the foundation of counselling.

To assist employees with personal and work-related problems that a supervisor would not be competent to handle, some organizations have employee assistance programs, wellness programs, or ombudsmen. EAP efforts typically assist employees to solve problems that detract from their job performance with the goal of restoring them to full capabilities to meet acceptable work standards. Wellness programs aim at promoting and maintaining proper physical conditioning and other personal/health habits that will tend to keep employees healthy and on the job. Because of increased concerns about workplace violence, some firms have established programs and procedures to assist supervisors in recognizing symptoms displayed by problem employees that could lead to violent behaviour, and to outline what supervisors should do in such circumstances.

QUESTIONS FOR DISCUSSION

1. What are some of the most common reasons for forming work groups? What are some factors that make a work group cohesive? Is cohesiveness of a work group always desirable? Discuss.
2. Define each of the following classifications of work groups:
   a. Command group.
   b. Task group.
   c. Friendship group.
   d. Special-interest group.
3. What were the principal aspects and results of the relay assembly room experiment and the bank wiring observation room experiment conducted as part of the Hawthorne Studies? Discuss the relevance of these findings to modern supervision.
4. Define employee morale. Differentiate between external and internal factors influencing employee morale. What should a supervisor do to minimize the influence of external factors on an employee's work?
5. Discuss the relationships between (a) morale and teamwork and (b) morale and productivity. Is it possible for employees to have low morale and still achieve a high level of work performance? Discuss.
6. Explain the use of employee attitude surveys in assessing employee morale. Why is follow-up of survey results vital if an attitude survey is to be beneficial? What types of follow-up can managers and supervisors utilize? Discuss.
7. Discuss the use of employee assistance programs and ombudsmen, especially in large enterprises.
8. Discuss what a supervisor should do if he or she is concerned that an employee is exhibiting behaviour patterns that have been associated with subsequent workplace violence.

SKILLS APPLICATIONS

Skills Application 11-1: Canadian Companies Promoting Work/Life Balance through Wellness Programs

Many Canadian companies are designing wellness programs and other initiatives to help their employees better manage the balance between work and outside commitments. Canadian workers are spending more time on the job and are struggling to find a balance in their lives. Using the Internet, find examples of Canadian companies that offer innovative wellness programs to help their employees achieve work/life balance (see, for example, organizational profiles on the Human Resources and Skills Development Canada website at http://labour.hrdc-drhc.gc.ca/worklife/experiencesll-en.cfm). Find at least two examples of Canadian companies using wellness programs, then answer the following questions:

1. Write a brief summary of the most innovative wellness initiatives you read about.
2. Most wellness initiatives are financed by the company itself. How do these corporations justify the expense associated with these programs?
3. Is it realistic to think that wellness programs such as the ones you found could be implemented in the majority of Canadian organizations? Why or why not?

Skills Application 11-2: An Employee Attitude Survey

Below are data from an attitude survey conducted with 150 employees in a small industrial plant. There were 15 first-line supervisors in the plant. The question posed to employees was "What attention or emphasis is given to the following by your supervisor?"

	Too Much Attention	About Right	Too Little Attention	Does Not Apply
The quality of your work	21%	65%	11%	3%
Costs involved in your work	45%	38%	12%	5%
Meeting schedules	36%	41%	15%	8%
Getting your reactions and suggestions	19%	26%	53%	2%
Giving you information	16%	69%	13%	1%
Making full use of your abilities	15%	31%	45%	8%
Safety and housekeeping	25%	60%	8%	7%
Development of employees	27%	38%	32%	3%
Innovations, new ideas	17%	35%	47%	1%
Effective teamwork among employees	21%	68%	8%	3%

After reviewing the data, answer the following questions:

1. What overall observations would you make about the style of supervision that generally is in place according to the survey data? Why?
2. What positive factors were revealed by the survey data?
3. What specific actions would you suggest to respond to potential problems revealed by the survey data?
4. What role could a supervisory training and development program play in responding to the survey data?

Skills Application 11-3: Preventing Violence in the Workplace

Unfortunately, violent acts in Canadian workplaces are not unheard of. In 1999, a disgruntled employee of the Ottawa transit system, OC Transpo, arrived at work and shot and killed four employees before turning the gun on himself. As described in this chapter, alert supervisors can often recognize signs that an employee is potentially dangerous. Using the Internet, conduct a search for additional resources about the prevention of workplace violence (for example, visit the Canadian Centre for Occupational Health and Safety at www.ccohs.ca/oshanswers/psychosocial/violence.html). Based on your research, answer the following questions:

1. What are the most common signs that an employee may be dangerous in the workplace?
2. Are certain occupational groups more at risk for workplace violence than others? Discuss.
3. What specific, practical steps can an employer take to minimize the risk of workplace violence?
4. What are the advantages of having a written policy concerning workplace violence?

CASES

<table>
<tr><td>

CASE 11-1

The Problem Employee

</td><td>

Phyllis Walker, human resources manager at Marsh Electric Company, looked through her in-basket for a memo Steve Graziani had mentioned briefly to her that morning. Graziani, the contracts manager, was a relatively new, inexperienced supervisor, who had been with the office for only seven months. Happy that Graziani had asked for guidance on how to handle what he had referred to as a touchy situation, Walker located the memo and read it immediately.

</td></tr>
</table>

TO: Phyllis Walker, HR Manager
FROM: Steve Graziani, Contracts Manager
SUBJECT: Stephanie Barkwell—Problem Employee

We've got a problem, Phyllis, and I need some advice on how to handle it. One of my department assistants, Stephanie Barkwell, is beginning to pose a problem. For the last couple of months she has been late to work almost a third of the time, and she regularly takes 45 minutes or more for lunch when the allotted time is only half an hour. Her frequent absences are disrupting office efficiency. Her 13-year-old boy is her usual excuse.

However, there are some recent unfavourable rumours that I've heard circulating through the department. I'm a bit uncomfortable mentioning them to you, although I have a gut feeling they might be true. The Monday before last, Stephanie called me at home around 9:30 at night, and she told me that she had some personal business to take care of and probably wouldn't be in the following day. She wasn't; nor did she show up at the office on Wednesday or Thursday. Friday she called and said she was too emotional to function at work, but she would be in on Monday.

On Monday she told me that her son was having trouble with the police. However, the rumour mill has it that Stephanie herself was arrested and held on drug charges. I've not discussed the issue with her; I would like your input first.

I'm a single parent too, so I know first-hand how difficult it can be to balance work and family. However, we have a job to do here at Marsh, and people depend on Stephanie for administrative support. When at work, Stephanie is very productive and pleasant to work with. Her prior work record apparently has been excellent. We're already shorthanded, and her recent absences and tardiness are now affecting the overall performance of my department. I've tried to be tolerant, but it is becoming a continuing problem. I've been getting complaints from her co-workers.

Let's sit down and talk about this soon, before I approach Stephanie. Please call me when you have had a chance to review her file, and we'll figure out the best way to handle this situation.

"Steve wasn't kidding," thought Walker as she completed her review of Stephanie's file. "It's a shame that this firm doesn't have an employee assistance program; in this case it might have been the answer."

Walker pondered the situation and wondered what the best course of action would be.

Questions for Discussion

1. If you were Walker, what advice would you offer Graziani about how to proceed?

2. If Graziani determined that Barkwell had a drug problem or some other type of serious personal problem, would the company be obligated to offer some form of personal assistance to her? Why or why not?

3. Once Graziani is fully aware of Barkwell's situation, how much information should he share with her co-workers?

4. Would you try to retain Barkwell as an employee? Would it make a difference if the police are indeed involved in this situation?

5. If you decided to keep Barkwell at this time, what steps would you take to ensure that her work performance improved?

| CASE 11-2 |
| Mary's Disability |

Mary Nadjiwon, about 30 years old, was first hired by Eldorado Insurance Company as an accounting assistant. The responsibilities of an accounting assistant were mainly administrative and clerical and involved processing various forms and returns. Nadjiwon performed very well in this position. She was dedicated, worked considerable overtime hours as needed, and was considered to be an accurate and thorough employee. At first, Nadjiwon got along well with the rest of the accounting department staff. She was a mother with two children, and she had enrolled on a part-time basis at a local college to continue her work toward a diploma.

The accounting department included three professionals who held the titles of either junior accountant or senior accountant. One junior accountant had just graduated with her bachelor's degree in accounting and had worked for the company two previous summers. Another junior accountant had graduated four years previously; he had two years of insurance experience before joining Eldorado. The third professional accountant recently had been promoted to senior accountant. She attended a local university on a part-time basis to pursue an MBA degree, and she was anxious to progress to a managerial position somewhere in the company.

The Promotion of Mary Nadjiwon

After Nadjiwon had been at her job for about two years, Tess Wilson, the accounting department supervisor, decided to promote Nadjiwon to a junior accountant position. Wilson felt that Nadjiwon had performed very well, and she was pleased with her work on corporate tax returns. Wilson believed that promoting Nadjiwon would be a less expensive option since Nadjiwon did not have a diploma at this time. Wilson also had been urged by the human resources department to expedite promotions for individuals who were members of minority groups. The human resources department was delighted to approve the promotion, since Nadjiwon's work was exemplary and she also was a First Nations woman. Wilson also felt that promoting Nadjiwon would keep her with the company since her skills could be in demand from other firms in the area. When Wilson told Nadjiwon about her promotion, Wilson also gave her the responsibility to find her replacement and to supervise the new accounting assistant.

The promotion of Nadjiwon was not met with favour by the professional accountants in the department. Nadjiwon had not yet completed her diploma, and previously all junior or senior accountants were required to be college graduates. The accountants talked with Wilson about this in a private meeting during which they asked Wilson why Nadjiwon had been promoted without having her accounting diploma. Wilson's response was that she needed someone to fill the position, that Nadjiwon had worked hard, and that she expected the rest of the accountants to cooperate with Nadjiwon and be supportive of her promotion.

Unfortunately, the professional accountants did not welcome Nadjiwon as a fully qualified professional. She was still about four courses away from completing her diploma, and she was making slow progress by taking only one or two courses each year. Nadjiwon did not improve her popularity with the other accountants when she hired George Keeshig, the son of a close friend, to fill the position of accounting assistant. Keeshig was enrolled on a part-time basis in a local community college, and he had taken only a few accounting courses. Nadjiwon justified her hiring of Keeshig by stating that he was a very quick learner who had considerable motivation to complete his diploma.

The Disability of Mary Nadjiwon

After Nadjiwon had been in the position of junior accountant for about six months, problems began to appear that suggested the promotion might have been a mistake. The accountants believed that Nadjiwon was not cooperating with other members of the department as needed. When work required overtime and teamwork was necessary to meet deadlines, she no longer was available. The problem was further complicated by the fact that Nadjiwon was absent from work excessively. She continually was calling in sick or reporting late to work although her excuses did not seem to be suggestive of anything severe in nature. To everyone's dismay, Nadjiwon announced one November afternoon that she had developed a rare illness that was causing loss of sight. One eye was close to being blind, and she was losing her peripheral vision. Because of this, she was now unable to drive in the dark. Nadjiwon lived about an hour away from work, and therefore she could not work overtime, especially during the winter months. These were the months when demands on the department were very high, and other accountants were expected to work 50, 60, or 70 hours per week.

Because of her eyesight problems, Nadjiwon's work no longer was as accurate or timely as it had been in the past. She had difficulties researching information on the computer screen, analyzing data, and reviewing the work of others, including that of Keeshig. Even though the other accountants felt sorry for Nadjiwon's condition, they now resented her and they were quite unhappy about her unwillingness and inability to perform the necessary work. They complained to Wilson about having to redo much of Nadjiwon's and Keeshig's work because of inaccuracies and improper information.

Morale Problems Require a Decision

It was late January, and the morale of the accountants in the department had deteriorated to a low level. Much of their dissatisfaction focused on Nadjiwon, who was viewed as an unqualified and unfriendly individual who was not contributing to the performance of the department. The accountants went to Wilson in another private meeting to speak their minds. In effect, they claimed that Nadjiwon was now a problem who—if she was to remain in the position of junior accountant—at least should be required to work the hours necessary to deserve the title. Regardless of her disability and the fact that she was a First Nations woman, she was not measuring up to the demands of the position. The accountants felt that it was not fair to the rest of them who had their diplomas and who had to work more than their share to compensate for Nadjiwon and her protégé, Keeshig.

Following the meeting with the accountants, Wilson realized that she had to make a decision. On the one hand, she could ignore the complaints and lowered morale of her professional accountants, some of whom might leave the company if the situation did not improve. On the other hand, Wilson was concerned that if she demoted Nadjiwon and/or perhaps terminated her, the company could be faced with discrimination charges and would be subject to negative publicity in the First Nations community in which the company operated. Wilson knew that something had to be done, and she decided that the time had come to discuss the matter with the director of human resources.

Questions for Discussion

1. Was the promotion of Nadjiwon to the position of junior accountant an advisable one? How could Wilson have made this promotion decision more acceptable to the other professional accountants in the department? Discuss.

2. Consider the discrimination prohibitions within the Human Rights legislation. Would it be advisable/possible to demote or terminate Nadjiwon for not being able to fulfill the responsibilities associated with her position? Discuss.

3. Assume that you are director of human resources. How would you advise Wilson, the accounting department supervisor who had promoted Nadjiwon, concerning the actions that should be taken in this situation? Speculate about why Wilson may have waited so long to address the problem.

Chapter 12: The Labour Union and the Supervisor

After studying this chapter you will be able to

1 Explain why and how labour unions continue to affect organizations and the supervisory position.

2 Identify aspects of good management that are likely to deter a union organizer's appeal.

3 Outline procedures for supervisors to follow if confronted with a union organizing effort.

4 Discuss the importance of good union–management relationships and the supervisor's key role in maintaining those relationships.

5 Discuss the limited but important role of the supervisor in negotiating the labour agreement.

6 Discuss the major role of the supervisor in the interpretation and application of the labour agreement at the departmental level.

7 Describe the nature and importance of a good relationship between a supervisor and the union shop steward.

You are Leslie Brown, supervisor of environmental services at the Northside General Hospital, a 300-bed facility located in the downtown core of the province's largest city. You are responsible for what was formerly known as housekeeping services. You have several assistants (working supervisors) who report to you. There are about 80 full- and part-time employees in your department.

In recent weeks, rumours have been circulating about a major organizing campaign being undertaken by the Service Workers Union. Union organizers have been reported at several of the other hospitals in the city, but you have not noticed any union organizers at your own hospital. This morning, however, Tom Mayes, one of your best employees, who has worked for you for seven years, came into your office. This is what he said:

"Leslie, I need your advice. Several of my co-workers have cornered me on three occasions, trying to get me to sign union authorization cards. They're trying to organize all of the housekeeping employees into a union bargaining unit. They are saying we're being treated unfairly, both in wages and benefits, and we need a union to get a fair shake. They really are putting the pressure on me and others to sign. They have even been going after me and others while we're trying to get our work done in the hospital. Perhaps we do need a union here, but at this point I really don't know whom to believe. What do you think? I know the names of most of the individuals who want the union here in the hospital. Perhaps you could talk to them to see if you can resolve some of their complaints. What should I do in the meantime?"

You know that you must respond to Tom. What should you say and do?

You make the call!

LABOUR UNIONS ARE STILL PART OF SUPERVISORY ORGANIZATIONAL CONCERNS

Explain why and how labour unions continue to affect organizations and the supervisory position.

Labour organizations are a significant consideration for supervisors in Canada. In 2003, there were over 4 million unionized workers in Canada, representing approximately 30.4 percent of the entire workforce.[1] The absolute number of unionized workers in Canada has been on a generally upward trend since the 1960s (see Figure 12-1). Unionization activity in Canada far exceeds that of the United States, where unions have lost significant ground in terms of absolute union membership and unionization rates.

Despite the increasing numbers of workers who belong to unions, however, **union density** or the rate of unionization in Canada has declined from a peak of 37 percent in the mid-1980s to the current rate of 30.5 percent. The reduction in union density is due to the fact that the size of the overall Canadian workforce increased proportionately more than the increase in the number of unionized workers. Unions must add between 150,000 and 200,000 new members a year in Canada in order to maintain the rate of overall union density—a goal that unions have been unsuccessful in achieving in recent years.[2]

There are some technical distinctions in their designations, but in this text we will use the terms **labour union** and **labour organization** interchangeably to describe any legally recognized organization that exists for the purpose of representing a group or "bargaining unit" of employees and that negotiates and administers a labour agreement with an employer. A **labour agreement,** also called a **union contract,** is the negotiated document between the union and the employer that covers terms and conditions of employment for the represented employees.

Union density
The percentage of the total labour force that is represented by a union.

Labour union (labour organization)
Legally recognized organization that represents employees and negotiates and administers a labour agreement with an employer.

Labour agreement (union contract)
Negotiated document between union and employer that covers terms and conditions of employment for the represented employees.

FIGURE 12-1   Historical Rates of Unionization in Canada vs. U.S.

YEAR	UNION MEMBERSHIP IN CANADA	UNION MEMBERSHIP IN U.S.	UNION DENSITY IN CANADA	UNION DENSITY IN U.S.
1960	1,459,000	15,516,000	32.3%	28.6%
1970	2,173,000	20,990,000	33.6%	29.6%
1980	3,397,000	20,968,000	35.7%	23.2%
1990	4,031,000	16,740,000	34.8%	15.2%
2000	4,058,000	16,257,000	31.9%	13.5%
2002	4,174,000	16,100,000	31.1%	13.2%

Sources: Jon Peirce, *Canadian Industrial Relations*, 2nd edition, (Toronto: Prentice Hall, 2003), p. 123–24; U.S. Bureau of Labour Statistics at www.bls.gov/news.release/union2.nro.htm (retrieved December 15, 2003); Human Resources Development Canada Workplace Information Directorate, *Union Membership in Canada—2002* at http://www.hrsdc.gc.ca/en/lp/wid/oa/26Union_Membership_in_Canada_2002.shtml (retrieved March 23, 2004).

Historically, labour unions most often were identified with so-called blue-collar employees. In recent years labour organizations have made gains in obtaining representational rights for white-collar employees such as office workers, salespeople, nurses, teachers, and engineers. With their membership base decreasing in the traditional manufacturing sectors, unions have been increasing their organizing efforts in sectors of the economy that have not traditionally been unionized (see the Contemporary Issue box on page 352).

Although many unions have lost members and the percentage of workers in labour organizations has declined over the past two decades, unions remain an important element of the workforce that supervisors should know about and be prepared to deal with appropriately. This is especially true where employees are represented by a labour union and supervisors must abide by the requirements of a union agreement.

The Labour Relations Framework

Most unionized employees are members of local unions that are affiliated with national and international labour organizations. In Canada, the Canadian Labour Congress (CLC) is the dominant federation of unions federally and provincially. The CLC is an "umbrella" organization to which the majority of unions in Canada belong. As the major federation of organized labour, the CLC continues to play a significant role in political, legislative, and other areas, even though many of its unions have undergone significant changes and mergers.

Historically, most labour unions adopted an adversarial posture toward employers in order to obtain economic and other gains through collective bargaining. In recent years, the adversarial approach has been tempered with more cooperative efforts. Nevertheless, unionized employees still have divided or dual loyalties concerning their unions and their employers, which a supervisor must understand and accept.

It is beyond the scope of this text to cover the history of labour relations or to discuss the federal and provincial labour laws that govern union–management relations. Suffice it to say that most employees in the private sector of the

CONTEMPORARY ISSUE
Wal-Mart Narrowly Escapes Union Drive

With over 200 stores and 57,000 workers in Canada,[1] Wal-Mart has become one of the nation's largest employers. The retail giant employs over 1.3 million people worldwide, and recently surpassed General Motors and Exxon as the world's largest company with sales of $244.5 billion for the year ended January 31, 2003.[2] With such staggering employment numbers, it is natural that Wal-Mart has attracted the attention of union organizers who would dearly love to add Wal-Mart workers to their membership base. To date, however, Wal-Mart has been successful in keeping the unions at bay. As of the end of 2003, no Wal-Mart store in North American was unionized.

That's not to say that there haven't been some close calls. In August 2003, workers at a Thompson, Manitoba, Wal-Mart rejected representation by the United Food and Commercial Workers (UFCW) union. The vote was close; the final tally was 54 votes in favour of the union versus 61 votes against. Michael Fraser, the National Director of the UFCW Canada says, "The vote was very close and shows we have a lot of support. We'll continue to campaign and monitor the situation in Thompson."[3] Under Manitoba labour laws, the UFCW must wait six months before applying again for a certification vote at the Thompson store.

In February 2000, meat cutters at a Jacksonville, Texas, Wal-Mart voted in favour of representation by the United Food and Commercial Workers. Just one month later, Wal-Mart announced that it had decided to replace freshly cut meat with case-ready meat—eliminating the need for meat cutters in every one of its stores.[4] This decision caused the meat cutting jobs to be eliminated, and the workers to be reassigned to the position of "sales associate." The union claimed the company's decision was strictly aimed at circumventing the union organizing campaign. "Changing the way all of its stores sell meat shows the extent to which Wal-Mart will go to keep the union out of its stores," says UFCW Executive Vice President Mike Leonard.[5] Three years later, in 2003, a National Labor Relations Board Administrative Law Judge ordered the company to recognize and bargain with Local 540 over the effects of the change to pre-packaged meat.[6]

One indication of the interest that the UFCW has in unionizing Wal-Mart workers is the use of a website targeted at current Wal-Mart workers. The UFCW maintains a site called "Wal-Mart Workers Canada" at www.walmartworkerscanada.ca. The site contains a direct link to a union organizer who will answer questions and assist workers who are interested in launching an organizing campaign. The site also provides links to information about pending litigation against Wal-Mart, as well as a planned "day of action" protesting the company's labour practices. Wages, working hours, job security, and benefits are key issues.

With union membership dwindling in the traditionally unionized sectors of the Canadian economy, it will be interesting to watch the progress of the UFCW and its efforts to unionize Wal-Mart workers. According to UFCW's National Director, Michael Fraser, "It's not a question of 'if' but 'when.'"[7]

Sources: (1) "Wal-Mart Canada Launches "Canadian Idol" Line of Apparel," August 14, 2003 at www.ctv.ca/generic/WebSpecials/Shows/CanadianIdol/Press/Release-Aug14-WalMart.html (retrieved December 19, 2003); (2) Andreas Knorr and Andreas Arndt, "Why Did Wal-Mart Fail in Germany?" Institute for World Economics and International Management (June 2003), at www.iwim.uni-bremen.de/publikationen/pdf/w024.pdf (retrieved December 19, 2003); (3) Michael Forman, "Wal-Mart Narrowly Escapes Union Drive," UFCW Canada Communications (August 20, 2003) at www.walmartworkerscanada.ca/news.php?articleID=00081 (retrieved December 19, 2003); (4), (5), & (6) "Wal-Mart Ordered to Recognize UFCW Local" at www.union-network.org/unisite/sectors/commerce/Multinationals/Wal-Mart_ordered_to_recognise_UFCW_Local.htm (retrieved December 19, 2003); (7) Op. cit., Forman.

Canadian workforce have the legal right to join or not to join labour unions under the various provisions of federal and provincial labour relations laws. Labour law is very complicated, and it addresses many areas of concern such as those employees who are and who are not covered, their protected rights, unfair labour practices, and a host of requirements concerning collective bargaining.

A supervisor must understand that unionized employees have divided or dual loyalties concerning their unions and their employers.

Chuck Stoody/CP

Because of the many legal and other ramifications, most firms find it desirable to have human resources staff specialists handle many or most of the labour relations matters, typically with the assistance and advice of legal counsel.

This chapter will discuss only some of the most important organizational considerations, obligations, and rights of supervisors who are confronted with (1) employee attempts to unionize and (2) union activities in a firm whose employees are already represented by a union. This chapter's discussion will represent a composite of considerations that generally are valid regardless of the nature of the work setting.

In the discussion to follow, it should be noted that under Canadian labour relations laws, those supervisors who are not part of management—such as working supervisors and lead persons—may join the same labour union as their fellow employees. But most supervisors who are part of management do not have the legal right to join and be represented by labour unions. As management's first-line representatives, supervisors play a major role in determining whether or not the employees will turn to a labour union in an effort to improve wages and other conditions of employment.

2	UNDERSTANDING EMPLOYEE EFFORTS TO UNIONIZE

Identify aspects of good management that are likely to deter a union organizer's appeal.

A major union official once made the following comment to one of the authors of this text: "Labour unions don't just happen; they're caused. And it's the management, not the unions, that causes them!" This labour official was quite candid about his opinion that labour unions were a direct response to failures of management to respond to employee needs. Further, he implied that the sentiments of workers are usually determined more by the conditions existing in their work situations than by a union organizer's campaign. Many studies of employee and labour relations have generally verified the opinion of this union official. These studies recognize that good management and supervision, particularly as exemplified by positive human relations approaches, are usually the most important determinants in preventing the unionization of a work group.

Numerous aspects of good management that contribute to "union avoidance" or a climate that deters unionizing efforts have been discussed previously throughout this text. The consistent use of good employee relations practices make it more difficult for a union organizer's appeal to succeed. These include the following:

- Wages and benefits that are fair and reasonable comparable to those offered by other companies.[3]
- Personal facilities for employees that are generally satisfactory or improving.
- A stable employment pattern (that is, no severe ups and downs in hiring and layoffs of large numbers of employees).
- Supervisors who communicate well with their employees and treat them with dignity and respect.
- Employees who have been well trained and see opportunities for advancement to higher-paying or upgraded positions. This is especially important for employees in low-level jobs who do not like to feel that they will be in "dead-end" positions forever.
- Supervisors who demonstrate a participative approach to management that encourages employees to share in making decisions about their jobs.[4]
- Employees who feel that they are treated fairly by being given an opportunity to resolve their complaints through a complaint procedure.

For the most part, the economic conditions surrounding wages, benefits, and employment patterns are not within a supervisor's direct control. However, the supervisor has a significant role in most of the other factors that may cause employees either to join or not to join a labour union.

It does happen that some employees turn to a labour union even though their employer has worked diligently to develop and implement policies and procedures consistent with those listed above. Employees may join a labour union primarily to achieve economic objectives such as higher wages and greater benefits. Or they may join to satisfy objectives of a psychological or sociological nature. For example, some employees feel that membership in a labour union provides them with greater security and better control over their jobs through a seniority system. Other employees feel that it is important for a union to be present in processing grievances and complaints in order to get a fairer settlement of their disputes. Still others find a greater sense of identity when they are part of a labour union.

Union Security Arrangements

Union security clause
The part of the collective agreement (contract) that describes whether employees must belong to the union in order to maintain their employment.

Union shop
A labour agreement provision in which employees are required to join the union as a condition of employment, usually after 30 days.

When a labour union gains representational rights, or if a union already is in place, employees may have to join it as a requirement under a union security provision of the labour agreement. A **union security clause** in the collective agreement outlines whether employees are required to be union members as a condition of employment. In a **union shop**, an employee is required to join the union after a certain period of time, usually 30 days. Even though such employees initially are required to join the union through the union shop provision, eventually most of them become loyal to the union because they believe that they can

Closed shop
A labour agreement provision that specifies that only people who are already union members will be eligible for employment.

achieve more collectively than they would individually. In a **closed shop,** only people who are already members of the union are eligible to be hired. In Canada, closed shops are typically associated with the construction and longshoring industries. Employers contact the union when they need to hire employees, and the union selects from its roster of eligible members.

It should also be noted that the Charter of Rights and Freedoms in the Constitution Act, 1982, regulates the relationship between employees and their union. Any action or activity by the union that contravenes or restricts an individual's freedom is prohibited. For example, some people's religious convictions may prevent them from joining a union or paying union dues. In such a case, the employee may be exempted from union membership, so long as the amount that he or she would have been paying in union dues is paid by the employee to a registered charity mutually agreed on by the employee and the union.[5]

3	UNION ORGANIZING EFFORTS AND THE SUPERVISOR

Outline procedures for supervisors to follow if confronted with a union organizing effort.

Union organizing efforts can take place both outside and within a firm. If a supervisor notices that union organizing activities are taking place among employees, the supervisor should report what he or she observes to higher-level managers or to the human resources department. This must be done so that the company's response to the union organizing efforts can be planned. In the meantime, the supervisor should be very careful not to violate—by either actions or statements—the labour laws governing union organizing activities. Since these labour laws are quite complicated, many companies hire a consultant or lawyer to advise higher-level managers and supervisory personnel about what they should and should not do or say under these circumstances. It is important that supervisors and upper management abide by the law, since any actions that are deemed to be unfair to the workers' rights can, in some provinces, result in automatic certification of the union in the workplace.

The following guidelines, although not comprehensive, are recommended for supervisors during a union organizing period:

1. Supervisors should not question employees either publicly or privately about union organizing activities in the department or elsewhere in the company. Doing this—even merely out of curiosity—can violate labour laws, which provide employees the right to choose a union to represent them without interference or discrimination by the employer.
2. Supervisors should not make any threats or promises related to the possibility of unionization. Any statement that can be construed as a threat (for example, loss of job or loss of privileges if the union succeeds) or a promise (for example, some favour or benefit to the employee if the union fails) is a violation of most labour laws.
3. Supervisors should respond in a neutral manner when employees ask for their opinions on the subject of unionization.
4. Supervisors have the right to prohibit union organizing activities in work areas if these take place during work hours and interfere with normal work operations. Supervisors may also prohibit outside union organizers from coming into the department to distribute union bulletins and information. However, employees who support the union have the right to distribute these

materials to other employees during lunch and break periods so long as this does not interfere with work operations. If in doubt about what can be done to control union organizing activities within the department, supervisors should first consult higher-level managers or the human resources department.

5. Supervisors should not look at union authorization cards that employees may have signed. This, too, may be considered illegal interference with the employees' rights to organize.

6. Supervisors should continue to do the best supervisory management job possible.

A union-organizing campaign often results in a representational election conducted by the provincial Labour Relations Board or some other government agency. If the majority of the employees vote for the union, the union becomes the exclusive bargaining representative for these employees. If the union loses the representational election, this means only that the employees will not have a union for the immediate future—perhaps for a minimum of one year. Many companies have found that, after rejecting a union in previous elections, employees may later vote it in. The transition from a nonunion to a unionized workplace can be a trying period of change for all concerned. If the organizing campaign is successful, most supervisors eventually accept the place and role of the union and learn to adjust their supervisory practices accordingly.

4	THE SUPERVISOR'S INVOLVEMENT IN UNION–MANAGEMENT RELATIONSHIPS

Discuss the importance of good union-management relationships and the supervisor's key role in maintaining those relationships.

Labour unions are a permanent part of our free-enterprise economy. A union, just like any other institution, has the potential for either advancing or interfering with the common efforts of an organization. Thus, it is in management's self-interest to develop a union–management climate that is conducive to constructive relationships. However, there is no simple formula for fostering such a climate. It takes patience, sensitivity, and hard work for all managers in an organization to show in their day-to-day relationships that the union is accepted as the official and responsible bargaining representative for the employees.

In any mutual efforts to maintain a constructive relationship between management and the union, the most important link is often the supervisor. It is the supervisor's daily relationships with employees and union representatives that make the labour agreement a living document for better or for worse. This is why it is essential that supervisors be well informed about the fundamentals of collective bargaining and be knowledgeable about the labour agreement. For the most part, the supervisor's involvement in union–management relations consists of two phases: (1) a limited role in negotiating the labour agreement and (2) a major role in applying the terms of the agreement on a day-to-day basis.

5

Discuss the limited but important role of the supervisor in negotiating the labour agreement.

Labour agreement negotiations (collective bargaining)
The process of discussion and compromise among representatives from labour and management leading to an agreement governing wages, hours, and working conditions for union employees.

THE SUPERVISOR'S LIMITED ROLE IN LABOUR AGREEMENT NEGOTIATIONS

Labour agreement negotiations, also called **collective bargaining**, are the discussions and compromises among representatives from labour and management leading to an agreement governing wages, hours, and working conditions for union employees. Negotiations often involve meetings between the parties extending over a period of many months. On occasion, a union may threaten or call a work stoppage in an attempt to pressure the employer to agree to certain proposals or make concessions. Because collective bargaining can be complicated, an employer may hire a lawyer or consultant to work with human resources department staff and management to develop and carry out its negotiating strategy.

Labour negotiations in a previously nonunionized company may be a stressful experience for employees, supervisors, and higher-level managers. Usually emotions run high, and the grapevine is active with rumours and speculation. Because of this climate, negotiations between management and union representatives are usually held away from the company premises, perhaps at a lawyer's office or a conference room in a hotel. If a committee of union employees is participating in the negotiations, a line of communication with the other employees will be established. Supervisors usually are excluded from this line of communication, although higher-level managers may keep them informed of important developments.

Most labour agreements cover a period of one, two, three, or more years. As time goes on and new agreements are negotiated, the supervisor's role becomes an increasingly important one. Most supervisors do not sit at the negotiating table, but it is desirable for higher-level managers to consult with them about

Employers usually hire a lawyer or consultant to help the human resources staff and management develop a plan for collective bargaining.

Rob Lewine/CORBIS

(1) how provisions of the existing agreement have worked in the past and (2) what changes they would like to see in the next agreement. This exchange of information between higher-level managers and supervisors is essential prior to negotiations, and at times it may be needed as negotiations proceed.

Supervisors should have some influence on negotiations because they bear a major responsibility for carrying out provisions of the agreement in the day-to-day operations of their departments. Many issues discussed during contract negotiations stem from relationships that the supervisors have experienced with their employees. For example, problems concerning work assignments between job classifications, work-shift schedules, seniority rights, working conditions, and transfer and promotion of employees can become important issues for negotiation. Therefore, it is to the supervisors' as well as the firm's advantage that provisions in the agreement be written in such a way that supervisors have as much flexibility as possible in running their departments.

To supply relevant information, supervisors should be keenly aware of what has been going on in their departments. Their views will be considered more credible if they have facts available to substantiate their observations. Records of prior grievances, productivity, and disciplinary problems are important, as these will highlight areas of the collective agreement that may need to be revised. Supervisors should discuss with higher-level managers and the human resources department problems that management should consider in developing an overall bargaining strategy. Thus, even though the primary responsibility for negotiating a labour agreement rests with higher-level managers, supervisors should be prepared to provide relevant input to the negotiations. Supervisors must be willing to express their opinions and substantiate them with documents and examples so that management's representatives can negotiate desirable changes in the agreement at the bargaining table.

6 | THE SUPERVISOR'S MAJOR ROLE IN APPLYING THE LABOUR AGREEMENT

Discuss the major role of the supervisor in the interpretation and application of the labour agreement at the departmental level.

The labour agreement or contract that has been agreed on by representatives of management and the union becomes the document under which both parties will operate during the life of the agreement. Although no two labour agreements are exactly alike, most agreements cover wages, benefits, working conditions, hours of work, overtime, holidays, vacations, leaves of absence, seniority, grievance procedures, and numerous other matters.

A labour agreement outlines union–management relationships. In essence, it is a policy manual that provides rules, procedures, and guidelines—as well as limitations—for both management and the union. To make it a positive instrument for fostering constructive relationships, the agreement must be applied with appropriate and intelligent supervisory decisions. The best-written labour agreement will be of little value if it is poorly applied by the supervisor.

Compliance with the Labour Agreement

Wherever it applies, supervisors are obliged to manage their departments within the framework of the labour agreement. This means that supervisors should know the provisions of the agreement and also how to interpret them. One way to accomplish this is for higher-level managers or the human resources department to hold meetings with supervisors to brief them on the contents of the agreement and to answer questions about any provisions that they do not understand. Copies of the contract and clarifications of various provisions should be furnished to the supervisors so that they know what they can and cannot do while managing their departments.

Supervisors should recognize that a labour agreement has been negotiated, agreed upon, and signed by both management and union representatives. Even if a provision in the agreement causes inconveniences, the supervisor should not try to circumvent the contract in the hope of doing the firm a favour. For example, assume that a provision specifies that work assignments must be made primarily on the basis of seniority. Although this provision may limit the supervisor in assigning the most qualified workers to certain jobs, the supervisor should comply with it or be prepared to face probable conflict with the union. If a labour agreement provision is clear and specific, the supervisor should not attempt to ignore what it requires. If supervisors do not understand certain provisions, they should ask someone in higher-level management or the human resources department to explain them before they attempt to apply the provisions that are in question.

Adjusting to Unionization

A labour agreement does not fundamentally change a supervisor's position as a manager. Supervisors still must accomplish their objectives by planning, organizing, staffing, leading, and controlling. Supervisors retain the right to require employees to comply with instructions and to get the jobs done in their departments. The major adjustment required when a union is present is that supervisors must perform their managerial duties within the framework of the labour agreement. For example, a labour agreement may spell out some limitations to the supervisor's authority, especially in areas of disciplinary action, job transfers, and assignments. Or the labour agreement may specify procedures concerning the seniority rights of employees with regard to shift assignments, holidays, and vacations. Supervisors may not like these provisions. However, they must manage within them and learn to minimize the effects of contractually imposed requirements or restrictions by making sound decisions and relying on their own managerial abilities. Figure 12-2 shows selected provisions from a labour agreement that cover various areas where seniority considerations must be followed.

As members of management, supervisors have the right and duty to make decisions. A labour agreement does not take away that right. However, it does give the union a right to challenge a supervisor's decision that the union believes to be in violation of the labour agreement. For example, virtually all labour agreements specify that management has the right to discipline and discharge for "just" (or "proper") cause. Thus, taking disciplinary action remains a managerial responsibility and right, but it must meet the just-cause standard. Since a challenge from the union may occur, the supervisor should have a sound case before taking disciplinary action. If a supervisor believes that disciplinary action is called for when an employee breaks a rule, the supervisor should examine thoroughly all aspects of the problem, take the required preliminary steps, and think through the appropriateness of any action. In other words, unless there is a contractual requirement to the contrary, the supervisor normally will carry out the disciplinary action independently of union involvement. However, some labour agreements require that a supervisor notify a union representative prior to imposing discipline or that a union representative be present when the disciplinary action is administered.

FIGURE 12-2   An example of labour agreement seniority provisions.

ARTICLE IV—SENIORITY

SECTION 1. The purpose of seniority is to provide a declared policy of right of preference in regard to layoff and recall and promotion and transfer. Length of service for seniority purposes shall be determined to start from the original hiring date at the Company plant, except as interrupted for reasons set forth in Section 5 of this Article.

SECTION 2. Seniority shall be plantwide with respect to the entire bargaining unit.

SECTION 3. In cases of layoff or recall, seniority shall govern, provided the employee is capable (with incidental training not to exceed 40 hours) of performing the job to which he or she may be transferred by reason of the layoff of an employee with less seniority.

The Company agrees that in the event that layoffs—other than disciplinary layoffs or temporary emergency shutdowns—are deemed necessary, the employees affected will be notified as far in advance as practicable, in no case less than (2) days.

SECTION 4. Transfers and promotions within the bargaining unit shall be made on the basis of seniority provided the employee is qualified and able to do the job. Requests for transfers will be honoured only after an employee has completed a probationary period. An employee shall be considered a probationary employee during his or her first three (3) months, and the Company shall have the right to discharge an employee in such status and no grievance shall arise therefrom.

In no case shall the Company be under obligation to promote, transfer, or assign work because of preferred seniority status to an employee who is not capable (with incidental training not to exceed 40 hours) of doing the job.

SECTION 5. An employee shall cease to have seniority and be on the seniority list if the employee:
   A. Quits
   B. Is discharged for just cause.
   C. Is absent three (3) days without notifying the Company, except if the employee furnishes an explanation in writing satisfactory to the Company.
   D. Fails to return to work within two (2) days upon completion of a vacation, leave of absence, or recall from layoff notice, except if the employee furnishes an explanation in writing satisfactory to the Company.

If an employee whose seniority has been broken by any of the causes mentioned above is again hired, he or she shall begin as a new employee for seniority purposes.

Supervisory Decision Making and the Labour Agreement

In practice, the supervisor may amplify provisions of the labour agreement by decisions that interpret and apply them to specific situations. In so doing, the supervisor might establish precedents that arbitrators consider when deciding grievances.

A **grievance** is a complaint that has been formally presented by the union to management and that alleges a violation of the labour agreement. Most labour agreements specify several steps as part of a grievance procedure before a griev-

Grievance
A formal complaint presented by the union to management that alleges a violation of the labour agreement.

Arbitrator

Person selected by the union and management to render a final and binding decision concerning a grievance.

Arbitration board

Three-person board with a company nominee, union nominee, and a mutually agreed-upon chairperson to render a final and binding decision concerning a grievance.

ance goes to arbitration (see Figure 12-3). An **arbitrator** is someone who is selected by the union and management to render a final and binding decision concerning a grievance when the union and management are unable to settle the grievance themselves. Arbitration may also be handled by an **arbitration board** made up of a company nominee, a union nominee, and an impartial chairperson chosen by the two nominees. Procedures for arbitrating grievances are included in virtually all labour agreements.

FIGURE 12-3 Grievance and arbitration procedure in a labour agreement for a retail store's unionized employees.

ARTICLE 4—GRIEVANCES AND ARBITRATION

4.1 Should any differences, disputes, or complaints arise over the interpretation or application of the contents of this agreement, there shall be an earnest effort made on the part of both parties to settle the same promptly through the following steps:

Step 1: By conference between the aggrieved employee, the union steward and/or business agent, or both, and the store manager or owner. Store management shall make its decision known within two (2) working days thereafter. If the matter is not resolved in Step 1, it shall be referred to Step 2 within two (2) working days.

Step 2: By conference between the business agent and the owner or a supervisor of the employer. The employer shall make its decision known within three (3) working days thereafter. If the matter is not resolved in Step 2, it shall be reduced to writing and referred within three (3) working days to Step 3.

Step 3: By conference between an official or officials of the union and a designated representative of the employer.

Step 4: In the event the last step fails to settle the complaint, it shall be referred within seven (7) working days to arbitration.

4.2 In any case in which an employee is aggrieved and the union promptly notifies the employee that it does not intend to request arbitration after the Step 3 meeting, the time for requesting arbitration shall be stayed pending the employee's exhaustion of internal union appeals to the union's executive board.

4.3 The employer and the union shall mutually agree to an impartial arbitrator to hear said arbitration case. Said arbitrator will be chosen within three (3) days. The expenses of the arbitrator shall be paid for jointly. Such arbitrator shall not be empowered to add to, detract from, or alter the terms of this agreement.

4.4 The employer may, at any time, discharge any worker for proper cause. The union or the employee may file a written complaint with the employer within seven (7) days after the date of discharge, asserting that the discharge was improper. Such complaint must be taken up promptly. If the employer and the union fail to agree within five (5) days, the matter shall be referred to arbitration. Should the arbitrator determine that it was an unfair discharge, the employer shall abide by the decision of the arbitrator.

(continued)

FIGURE 12-3 *(continued)*

4.5 Grievances must be taken up promptly. No grievance presented later than seven (7) days after such has happened will be considered, discussed, or be eligible for arbitration.

4.6 The employer shall have the right to call a conference with a union steward or officials of the union for the purpose of discussing a grievance, criticisms, or other problems.

4.7 Grievances will be discussed only through the outlined procedures; except that by mutual agreement between the union and the employer, the time limits may be waived.

4.8 There shall be no lockout or cessation of work pending the decision of the arbitrator.

It would be impossible for management and the union to negotiate an agreement that specified how to solve every possible situation that could occur in union–management relations. Therefore, the supervisor's judgment becomes paramount in applying the agreement to actual situations. Since the supervisor is part of management, an error in the supervisor's decisions becomes management's error. By interpretation and application, a supervisor's decisions may take on dimensions that go well beyond the department and may have a long-lasting impact. A decision may set a precedent that could become binding on both management and the union in the future. Supervisors should bear in mind that unions often base their claims on precedents, and arbitrators or arbitration boards often base their decisions on previous decisions made by both sides. If a supervisor is uncertain about how the contract should be interpreted in a particular situation, he or she should consult with higher-level management or the human resources department in order to avoid setting an unfavourable precedent.

A labour agreement usually contains provisions that specify how certain situations should be handled. Examples are provisions associated with work schedules, distribution of overtime, transfers, promotions or demotions, and other recurring matters. Usually the labour agreement identifies certain limits or procedures for handling these types of issues. For example, many agreements have provisions that require the supervisor to consider both seniority and ability in decisions that involve promotion, transfer, and layoff (see Figure 12-2). In these situations, the supervisor's personal appraisal of the abilities of the employees involved becomes vitally important. Often the opinion of the union will be at odds with the opinion of a supervisor concerning certain contractual meanings. A supervisor should not be afraid to risk the possibility that the union will file a grievance so long as the supervisor believes that he or she understands the provisions and is complying with them. If an employee files a grievance, the supervisor should not see this as a personal attack, but rather should work to resolve the issue quickly and fairly (see Figure 12-4).

Labour agreements also contain broadly stated clauses, such as those associated with the assignment of work between various job classifications, nondiscrimination, management rights, and disciplinary or discharge actions for just cause. In these areas, supervisors often encounter difficulty in applying a general

FIGURE 12-4 Guidelines for Resolving Grievances.

- Make time available.
- Listen patiently and with an open mind.
- Distinguish facts from opinions.
- Determine the real issue(s).
- Check and consult with others who might have additional information or advice.
- Avoid setting precedents.
- Exercise self-control.
- Minimize delays in reaching a decision.
- Explain decisions clearly and sensitively.
- Keep records and documents.
- Do not fear a challenge.

statement in the agreement when the situation requires a specific interpretation. If the supervisor has doubts about the meaning of a broadly stated provision, he or she should first consult higher-level managers or the human resources department. Even though the supervisor may be well versed in the content of the labour agreement, problems can develop that necessitate an interpretation beyond the supervisory level.

Maintaining Employees' Compliance with the Labour Agreement

It is also the supervisor's duty to take action whenever employees do not comply with provisions of the labour agreement. Employees may interpret lack of action to mean that the provisions are unimportant or not to be enforced. For example, if a contractual provision specifies that employees are entitled to a 15-minute rest period at designated times during a work shift, the supervisor should see to it that the employees take a 15-minute rest period—no more and no less—during the designated times. Supervisors should make certain that employees observe the provisions of the labour agreement just as supervisors themselves must operate within the agreement. Inaction on the supervisor's part could set a precedent or be interpreted to mean that the provision has been set aside.

| 7 | **THE SHOP STEWARD AND THE SUPERVISOR** |

Describe the nature and importance of a good relationship between a supervisor and the union shop steward.

Shop steward
Employee elected or appointed to represent employees at the departmental level, particularly in grievance processing.

Supervisors probably will have most of their union contacts with the union shop steward. A **shop steward,** also called a *shop committeeperson,* usually is a full-time employee who is elected or appointed to represent the employees at the departmental level, particularly in processing of their grievances. Supervisors may also have to discuss certain issues and grievances with a **union business representative** or business agent. This person is a paid, full-time official of the local or national union. Some shop stewards prefer to have the business agent present when discussing significant union-related problems with the supervisor.

For the most part, a shop steward is recognized by fellow employees to be their official spokesperson to management and for the union. This can be a difficult position since the shop steward must serve two masters. As an employee,

Union business representative
Paid official of the local or national union who may be involved in grievance processing.

the shop steward is expected to perform satisfactory work for the employer. As a union representative, the shop steward has responsibilities to other employees and to the union. The supervisor must understand this dual role of the shop steward because a good relationship with the shop steward can create an effective link between the supervisor and the employees.

The Shop Steward's Rights and Duties

Unless the labour agreement contains special provisions pertaining to the shop steward's position, the shop steward is subject to the same standards and regulations for work performance and conduct as every other employee of the department. The labour agreement may specify how much company time the shop steward can devote to union matters, such as meetings or discussions with members and grievance handling. The labour agreement may also grant the shop steward the right to take time off to attend union conventions and handle other union matters.

A major responsibility of the shop steward is to process complaints and grievances on behalf of employees. The shop steward will communicate these to the supervisor, who then must work with the shop steward to settle the complaints. Labour agreements usually outline procedures for handling complaints and grievances, and the shop steward and the supervisor are obligated to follow those prescribed steps.

Supervisory Relations with the Shop Steward

Some shop stewards are unassuming; others are overbearing. Some are helpful and courteous; others are aggressive and militant. Some take advantage of their position to do as little work as possible; others perform an excellent day's work in addition to their union duties. The day-to-day behaviour of the shop steward depends considerably on his or her individual personality and approach.

At times the supervisor may feel that the shop steward processes petty grievances in order to harass management. This may happen because the shop steward wants to assure workers that the union is working on their behalf. However, an experienced shop steward knows that normally there are enough valid grievances to be settled that it is not necessary to submit minor complaints that rightfully will be turned down by the supervisor.

Supervisors should bear in mind that the shop steward, as the official union representative, learns quickly what the employees are thinking and what is being communicated through the grapevine. Moreover, the national or local union will likely train the shop steward to be informed about the content of the labour agreement, management's prerogatives, and employee rights. The local union will expect the shop steward to submit grievances in such a way that they can be carried to a successful conclusion. Before submitting a grievance, the shop steward will ascertain which provisions of the labour agreement allegedly have been violated, whether the company acted unfairly, or whether the employee's health or safety was jeopardized. Once a grievance has been formally submitted, the shop steward will try to win it. In most grievance matters, the union is "on the offensive," and the supervisor must be prepared to respond. If the shop steward challenges a supervisor's decision or action, the supervisor must be ready to justify what he or she did or otherwise develop a remedy and resolve the grievance.

Since shop stewards are necessarily interested in satisfying the union members, their behaviour may at times antagonize supervisors. A supervisor may not care to discuss certain matters with the shop steward because, on a day-to-day basis, the shop steward is an employee in the department. But a shop steward is also the designated representative of union members and should be treated as an "equal" by a supervisor in matters pertaining to the union. If a sound relationship is developed, the shop steward will keep the supervisor alert and will literally force the supervisor to be a better manager![6]

WHAT CALL DID YOU MAKE?

As Leslie Brown, your best response at this point is to tell Tom Mayes that you really don't know how to advise him until after you have checked out his questions with the human resources director and your own manager. Under no circumstances should you ask Mayes or anyone else to provide you with the names of the employees who are involved in the union-organizing efforts or who favour the union. Doing this would be a violation of labour law and could result in a union becoming automatically certified in the workplace. After adjourning your meeting with Tom, you should immediately report your conversation to the human resources director and your manager and ask for guidance. They most likely will counsel you along the lines of the concepts and principles presented in this chapter. In particular, you should continue to treat all employees fairly, have them participate in some departmental decisions, and be willing to listen to and act on their legitimate complaints. You should not question, threaten, or interfere with your employees' efforts to organize. However, you should inform all of them that union organizing efforts must not take place in hospital working areas during regular work times. Hospital management may or may not decide to conduct a countercampaign; if management decides to do so, you will receive additional instructions about what you should and should not do and say.

SUMMARY

About one in three employees in Canada is represented by a labour union. Unions continue in their efforts to organize, especially among white-collar, public-sector, and service industry employees. Supervisors need to know how to respond to employee efforts to unionize and how to manage if departmental employees are represented by a union.

Good management practices can help deter a labour union from gaining representational rights. Employees may turn to a labour union for representation if they see the union as a vehicle for satisfying certain needs, including economic gains and fair treatment of their concerns. If management addresses employees' needs, then employees are less likely to feel the need for a union to promote their interests.

Confronted with a union organizing campaign, the supervisor should report the campaign to higher-level managers or the human resources department. The supervisor must not interfere with or threaten employees or promise any benefits in an effort to influence their choice of whether or not to join the union. The supervisor does have the right to prohibit union organizing activities that directly interfere with job performance during working hours and in work areas.

4 Labour unions are a part of our economic system, and they can either advance or interfere with the objectives of an organization. Thus, good union–management relations are essential to the success of a unionized firm. The supervisor is the key to good relations since he or she applies the labour agreement in day-to-day contact with employees.

5 Most supervisors do not participate directly in labour agreement negotiations. Yet many demands that a union presents during negotiations stem from issues that supervisors have encountered with the union and departmental employees during day-to-day operations of their department. Therefore, supervisors should make their opinions and suggestions known to higher-level managers so that management can attempt to negotiate needed changes to the labour agreement.

6 The supervisor's major role in union–management relations lies in the day-to-day interpretation and application of the labour agreement. Although a labour agreement does not in itself change a supervisor's job as a manager, it does give a union the right to challenge supervisory decisions. The supervisor still must carry out managerial duties within the terms of the labour agreement. It is to the supervisor's advantage to seek advice from higher-level managers or the human resources department in interpreting certain clauses of the agreement. The supervisor's actions can set precedents that bind management and the union in the future.

7 Supervisors have most of their union contacts with the union shop steward who represents employees at the departmental level. The shop steward is an employee as well as a union spokesperson for processing employee grievances. The shop steward should be treated as an equal by the supervisor in matters relating to the labour agreement. If a proper relationship is developed, a shop steward primarily will challenge only those actions of the supervisor that seem to be unfair or in violation of the agreement. In effect, this will force the supervisor to do a better job of managing the department.

QUESTIONS FOR DISCUSSION

1. Discuss the trends in union membership and union density in Canada as compared to the United States.
2. What are some of the principal reasons employees join labour unions?
3. What are some of the major factors that are typically crucial in preventing the formation of a labour union? Over which of these does a supervisor have the most direct control?
4. Discuss the proper role of the supervisor regarding union organizing activities. How should a supervisor respond to employees' questions about the union organizing effort?
5. What is the supervisor's role in labour agreement negotiations? What input should a supervisor have in the negotiating process?
6. Discuss why the supervisor should not attempt to ignore the labour agreement or circumvent it even if it seems like the smart thing to do.
7. Why should supervisors consult higher-level managers or the human resources department when they need interpretation of a clause in the labour agreement?
8. How does a labour agreement complicate a supervisor's job?
9. What should a supervisor do when employees do not comply with provisions of the labour agreement?

10. Discuss the role of the shop steward within a department. Why is this person in a key position of influence?

SKILLS APPLICATIONS

Skills Application 12-1: Attitudes About Labour Unions

Before compiling this survey, visit the website for the Canadian Automotive Workers at www.caw.ca or other unions to learn about the issues and concerns for labour unions in Canada.

1. The following are statements regarding labour unions. Respond to each statement, applying the following rating scale:

Strongly Agree	Agree	Undecided	Disagree	Strongly Disagree
1	2	3	4	5

Scoring

———— 1. Unions are necessary to protect employees from job favouritism and discrimination.

———— 2. Job seniority is the fairest way to reward employees for their services with a firm.

———— 3. Unions are needed to ensure that workers are paid good wages and receive adequate benefits.

———— 4. Without a labour union, employees have little chance to have their complaints handled fairly.

———— 5. Every employee who benefits from the union should be required to join and support the union (i.e., a union shop).

———— 6. Most employees join a labour union because they want to join and they agree with the union's objectives.

———— 7. The best form of employee job participation occurs when a union can negotiate a labour agreement with an employer to cover terms and conditions of employment.

———— 8. Stronger unions and wider representation of employees by unions are needed in order to counter corporate greed and management's indifference toward workers.

———— TOTAL

2. Add up your scores and compare your total with the following:

8–19　　You generally do not agree with or approve of labour unions.
20–27　　You have mixed attitudes about labour unions.
28–40　　You generally support unions and their objectives.

Do you agree with the results? Why or why not?
Optional: Compare your scores with those of another student (or students). Can you explain any differences in the respective perceptions?

Skills Application 12-2: Political Lobbying by Unions in Canada

In addition to representing the individual interests of their members, unions in Canada are actively involved in current political issues. Unions will often publicize an issue that is deemed to be important to their members, and will lobby for political change that they believe would be favourable to the union membership as a whole.

1. Visit the websites for some of the largest unions and federations in Canada. For example,
   a. Canadian Auto Workers at www.caw.ca

b. Canadian Union of Public Employees at www.cupe.ca

c. United Food and Commercial Workers Union at www.ufcw.ca

d. Canadian Labour Congress at www.clc-ctc.ca

2. Identify two political issues that are addressed on these websites. Briefly summarize the two issues you have selected and outline the position the union has taken on each issue.

3. Do you agree with the union positions on these issues? Why or why not?

Skills Application 12-3: Management and Union Views in a Unionized Work Location

1. Supervisors and managers often differ in their viewpoints concerning what a labour union does for its members. Visit a plant or office that is unionized. Interview a supervisor, manager, or director of human resources using the first set of questions. Then interview a shop steward or union member using the second set of questions.

   a. Management Questions
      (i) How would you describe overall relations between the union and the management in this company?
      (ii) In general, what things would you say the union members like most here? Least?
      (iii) In your opinion what most needs improvement in the union–management relationship?
      (iv) What would you do differently if the union did not exist?

   b. Union Questions
      (i) How would you describe overall relations between your union and the management in this company?
      (ii) In general, what things would you say your members like most here, and what things do they like least?
      (iii) In your opinion what most needs improvement in the union–management relationship?
      (iv) If the union did not exist, what do you think management would do differently?

2. a. What similarities and differences between the responses to each question were the most significant? Most surprising?

   b. Were any of your prior viewpoints about labour unions changed or influenced as a result of these interviews?

CASES

CASE 12-1

Showdown with the Shop Steward

Neko Ogaki supervised a group of 20 employees in the communication services division of a major university. All employees in this division were represented by a local chapter of the Public Employees Office and Professional Union.

One day Ogaki called Eleanor Kane into her office. Kane was a technical specialist who served as union shop steward. "Elly," said Ogaki, "it's time that we had a showdown about the amount of time you've been spending on union matters in this office. For the last two weeks you've averaged over two hours each day away from your job, allegedly to handle union grievances. This is entirely too much. I won't tolerate this anymore!"

"What do you mean, too much?" responded Kane. "The union contract says I'm allowed a reasonable time to handle union grievances, and it does not specify an upper time limit. I take only the time necessary to do my job as union steward. And lately there's been a flock of complaints and grievances that have come to my attention."

"I don't care about your union affairs," replied Ogaki. "You've got a job to do, and being away from your job this much of the time is unreasonable by any standard. From now on, if you're gone more than one hour each day on union matters, I'm going to dock your pay accordingly."

"Neko," snapped Kane, "If you do that, I'll file a grievance right away and will fight you all the way to arbitration if necessary. You haven't got a leg to stand on, and you know it. Go see Larry Niland, your director of human resources. He'll tell you the same thing. In the meantime, I'm going to report this harassment to our union business agent at the local union office!" With that, she left Ogaki's office.

Ogaki pondered what her next move, if any, should be. She also reviewed Article 3, Section 1, of the current labour agreement, which in part stated as follows:

A Union shop steward shall be permitted reasonable time to investigate, present, and process grievances on the Employer's property without loss of time or pay during regular working hours, provided that the steward obtains permission from his or her supervisor prior to such absence from assigned duties. Such time spent in handling grievances during the steward's regular working hours shall be considered working hours in computing daily or weekly overtime if within the regular schedule of the steward.

Questions for Discussion

1. Whose responsibility is it to determine what is meant by the word "reasonable" in Article 3, Section 1 of the labour agreement? Does this have to be negotiated with the union in more specific terms? Discuss.
2. Should Ogaki attempt to handle this problem on her own, or should she refer it to Niland, the director of human resources? Why?
3. Outline a series of recommendations for Ogaki and/or Niland in order to reach a satisfactory resolution of the problem.

CASE 12-2

Reported to Work in Error

Central Container Company manufactured various types of metal container products on a three-shift basis. One of the maintenance employees, Art Glenn, reported for work at 11:00 P.M. on a Friday night shift through an error on his part. He had not been scheduled to work and he had not been called in, although a small crew was scheduled to work this shift.

At about midnight, Glenn's regular supervisor, Gerry Fresno, entered the plant on a trouble call and questioned Glenn regarding his presence in the plant. After some discussion, both realized that Glenn had reported in error.

However, Fresno told Glenn that he could finish the shift. Glenn worked eight hours. This was Glenn's sixth consecutive day of work, and by union contract, Glenn was to be paid at a rate of time and one half for this shift.

The next day, however, another maintenance employee, Willie Flanders, filed a grievance because Glenn had worked on a sixth day, although Glenn was junior to Flanders in seniority. Flanders claimed equal pay for the time Glenn worked (eight hours at time and one half, i.e., 12 hours of pay). Flanders and his union steward claimed that in accordance with a well-established practice at the company, overtime had to be offered first to employees in accordance with their seniority and their ability to perform the work.

Several days later, at a grievance meeting held in Fresno's office, Jana De Waal, the union business representative, argued that if Fresno had sent Glenn home after he found him working, no grievance would have been filed. However, since the past practice had been and still was to let the most senior employees work overtime, the union position should be upheld in this case, and Flanders should be paid for all time at the appropriate rate that the junior employee (Glenn) was paid.

Fresno responded that the company should not be required to pay 12 hours of pay to another employee. Out of consideration for the employee who reported by mistake, Fresno had allowed Glenn to work the full shift instead of sending him home with only one hour's pay. The claim of the union was unjust and inequitable. No union employee, neither Flanders nor anyone else, suffered any loss of work or income because Fresno had acted in a considerate manner. If Glenn had not erroneously reported for work, no one would have worked in that job. Fresno claimed that his decision to allow Glenn to continue to work after he was discovered in the plant should be commended and not criticized.

De Waal ended the meeting with this comment, "If that's your decision, we'll have to pursue this case further, even to arbitration if necessary. You goofed on this one, and you ought to recognize it right now!"

After De Waal left his office, Fresno decided that he had better take up the grievance with his manager and the director of human resources.

Questions for Discussion

1. If Glenn had worked the entire Friday evening shift in error without having met his supervisor, would Glenn have been entitled to payment for the unscheduled work on his part? Why or why not?
2. Should Flanders be entitled to overtime pay under the practice of offering overtime to employees in accordance with their seniority and ability? Why or why not?
3. Evaluate Fresno's statement that the claim of the union was unjust and inequitable. Evaluate his contention that no union employee, including Flanders, had suffered any loss of work or income because he had acted in a considerate manner.
4. Should the company grant the union grievance and pay Flanders, or should the company deny the grievance and go to arbitration, if necessary?

Chapter 13: Fundamentals of Controlling

After studying this chapter you will be able to

1 Describe the nature and importance of the managerial controlling function.

2 Identify three types of control mechanisms based on time.

3 Explain the essential characteristics of effective controls.

4 Describe the essential steps in the control process.

5 Discuss the supervisor's role in controlling through budgets.

6 Discuss the supervisor's role in maintaining cost consciousness and in responding to higher-level managers' orders to reduce costs.

7 Identify additional control areas and explain how the controlling function is closely related to the other managerial functions.

YOU MAKE THE CALL

You are Gil Pietro, accounting department supervisor for a manufacturing plant that employs approximately 600 people. Reporting to you are two accountants and four data-entry clerks. They work in an office area that is separate from other departments. Your department is involved in virtually all aspects of internal and external accounting responsibilities, although some work has been outsourced to local consulting firms.

Several new software packages have been successfully implemented in your department. A new streamlined software system for processing accounts payable and receivable was a recent project given top priority. It was so important that you decided to develop and carry out the project yourself. Your boss, the controller, specified a deadline date for completion that was very tight. In developing the software package, you met with the data-processing manager, the controller, and outside consultants you hired to write the software package. Your staff, who will be the software's primary users, were told only recently

about the project, its implementation date, and scheduled training sessions.

This morning, a day after the second training session, several members of your staff walked into your office quite upset. They claimed that the project's proposed implementation date was "totally unrealistic" and could not be met due to "serious flaws" in the new software package. They asserted that the new package would create more work than the old system, would confuse some customers, and would require extra time that simply was not available with existing staff. Anika Hakomaki, a data-entry clerk in the group, summed up the group's feelings by stating, "All this could have been avoided if we had been part of the project planning from the start!"

The group has just left your office, and you are now rather distressed. The project's scheduled implementation date is two weeks away, only one training session remains, and it would be impossible to rewrite the package in time. As Pietro, how should you respond to your staff? What should you do to rectify the situation? How could this type of issue be avoided in the future?

You make the call!

---

1 | THE SUPERVISOR'S ROLE IN CONTROLLING

Describe the nature and importance of the managerial controlling function.

Although the word *control* often elicits negative reactions, control is a normal part of daily life. At home, at work, and in the community, everyone is affected by a variety of controls, such as alarm clocks, thermostats, fuel and electronic gauges, traffic lights, and police officers directing traffic. Controls also play an important role in all organizations. Controls assure that results match what was planned. Every manager—from the chief executive down to the supervisor—must develop and apply controls that regulate the organization's activities to achieve the desired results.

Controlling
The managerial function aimed at determining whether actual performance conforms to expected standards and taking corrective action when it does not conform.

The managerial function of **controlling** consists of checking to determine whether operations are adhering to established plans, evaluating whether proper progress is being made toward objectives, and taking appropriate actions where necessary to correct any deviations from established plans. In other words, the supervisor takes action to make things happen the way they were planned. Controlling is essential whenever a supervisor assigns duties to employees because the supervisor remains responsible for assigned work. If all plans set in motion proceeded according to plan without interference, there would be no need for the controlling function. As every supervisor knows, this is not the case in real life. Thus, it is part of the supervisor's job to keep activities in line and, where necessary, to get them back on track. This is done by controlling.[1]

Nature of the Controlling Function

Controlling is one of the five primary managerial functions. It is so closely related to the others that a line of demarcation between controlling and the other functions is not always clear. However, the controlling function is most closely related to the planning function. In planning, the supervisor sets objectives that become standards against which performance is appraised. If there are deviations between performance and standards, the supervisor must carry out the controlling function by taking corrective action, which may involve establishing new plans and different standards.

Since controlling is the last managerial function discussed in this book, it might be perceived as something that the supervisor performs after all other functions have been executed. This might imply that controlling is concerned only with events after they have happened. It is true that the need for controlling is evident after a mistake has been made. However, it is much better to view controlling as a function that goes on simultaneously with the other managerial functions. As we discuss later in this chapter, there are control mechanisms that are utilized before, during, and after an activity takes place.

Employee Responses to Controls

Employees often view controls negatively because the amount of control that exists within their department may determine how much freedom of action they have in performing their jobs. Yet most employees understand that a certain amount of control is essential to regulate performance. They know that without controls, confusion, inefficiency, and even chaos would result.

In a behavioural sense, controls and on-the-job freedom seem to conflict. However, when controls are well designed and properly implemented, they can be a positive influence on employee motivation and behaviour. The supervisor should try to design and apply control systems that employees will accept without resentment but that also will be effective in monitoring performance in the department.[2]

Controlling Should Be Forward-Looking

There is nothing a supervisor can do about the past. For example, if work assigned to an employee for the day has not been accomplished, controlling cannot correct the day's results. Yet some supervisors believe that the main purpose of controlling is to find out who is responsible for mistakes and to assign blame. This attitude is not sound since supervisors primarily should look forward rather than backward. Of course, supervisors must also study the past to learn what and why something happened and then take steps so that future activities will not lead to the same mistakes.

Since supervisors should be forward-looking while controlling, it is essential that they discover any deviations from established standards as quickly as possible. Setting up controls within a process or within an activity's established time frame—rather than at its end—will enable the supervisor to take prompt corrective action. For example, instead of waiting until the day is over, the supervisor could check at midday to see whether a job is progressing satisfactorily. Even though the morning is past and nothing can change what has already happened, there may be time to correct a problem before the damage becomes excessive.

Controlling and Closeness of Supervision

Supervisors need to know how closely to monitor employees' work. The closeness of supervisory follow-up is based on such factors as an employee's experience, initiative, dependability, and resourcefulness. Permitting an employee to work on an assignment without close supervision is both a challenge and a test of a supervisor's ability to delegate. This does not mean that the supervisor should leave the employee completely alone until it is time to inspect the final results. It does mean that the supervisor should avoid watching every detail of every employee's work. By becoming familiar with each employee's abilities, the supervisor can develop sensitivity as to how much leeway to give and how closely to follow up and control.

2	TIME-FACTOR CONTROL MECHANISMS

Identify three types of control mechanisms based on time.

Before we discuss the steps of the controlling process, it is important to distinguish among three types of control mechanisms. These are classified according to time as (a) feedforward (or preliminary, preventive, anticipatory) controls, (b) concurrent (or in-process) controls, and (c) feedback (or after-the-process) controls.

Feedforward (Preliminary, Preventive, Anticipatory) Controls

Feedforward control
Anticipatory action taken to ensure that problems do not occur.

Since controlling has forward-looking aspects, the purpose of a **feedforward control** is to anticipate and prevent potential sources of deviation from standards by considering in advance the possibility of any malfunction or undesirable outcomes. A preventive maintenance program, designed so that equipment will not break down at the height of production, is an example of a feedforward control. The produce clerk who checks samples of bananas to ensure their acceptability is another example. The clerk selects a sample from the crates before the crates are unloaded and the merchandise is placed on display. Requiring assemblers to evaluate the quality of components prior to installation and to signify that they have done so is becoming increasingly commonplace. Other examples of feedforward controls include devices such as safety posters; fire drills; disciplinary rules; checklists to follow before starting up certain equipment; and the policies, procedures, and methods drawn up by managers when planning operations. Everyone uses feedforward control at one time or another. For example, a person who checks tires, oil, and gas gauge before beginning a trip is using feedforward control.

Concurrent (In-Process) Controls

Concurrent control
Corrective action taken during the production or delivery process to ensure that standards are being met.

A control that is applied while operations are going on and that spots problems as they occur is called a **concurrent control**. The traveller who notices that the fuel warning light has just come on and pulls into the next gas station for a fill-up is using a concurrent control. Examples of concurrent control mechanisms are online computer systems, numerical counters, automatic switches, gauges, and warning signals. To illustrate, suppose a retail store optically scans customers' purchases. The customer gets a printout of what was purchased and the price paid (the sales receipt). At the same time, the store's count of the number of items in inventory is automatically decreased by the number just sold. The store's computer records the items sold and stores the information. The computer has been programmed either to alert the purchasing supervisor or to automatically place a purchase order when the store's inventory falls to a specified level. Thus, the stock is replenished as needed and the store does not risk running out. Where these types of aids are not in place, supervisors monitor activities by observation, often with the assistance of departmental employees.

Even though feedforward controls have been set up, concurrent controls are still necessary to catch problems that feedforward controls were not able to anticipate. Consider the situation of the traveller who filled the fuel tank prior to the trip and estimated, based on past experience, that she should be able to travel the 500 km to her destination without having to refuel. Unexpectedly, the weather turns unseasonably warm and the traveller experiences a lengthy delay due to a highway accident. The traveller allows the car to run with the air conditioner on while tied up in traffic. The expected six-hour trip takes longer due to the delay, and the unexpected need for the air conditioner increases fuel consumption. Unless the traveller periodically checks the fuel gauge or is alerted by the low-fuel warning light (concurrent controls), she will run out of fuel before she reaches her destination.

Feedback (After-the-Process) Controls

Feedback control
Action taken after the activity, product, or service has been completed to prevent future problems.

The purpose of a **feedback control** is to evaluate the results of a process or operation when it is finished to determine ways to prevent future deviations from standard. The traveller who calculates average kilometres per litre and uses that feedback when planning the budget for the next trip is using feedback control. Other examples of feedback controls include measurements of the quality and quantity of units produced, various kinds of statistical information, accounting reports, and visual inspections. Since these controls are applied after a task, process, service, or product is finished, they are the least desirable control mechanisms if damage or mistakes have occurred. If damage or mistakes took place, feedback controls are used as a basis for further improvement of the process or the finished product. Feedback controls are probably the most widely used category of controls at the supervisory level. Too often, however, they are used primarily to determine what went wrong and where to place blame rather than to prevent recurrence of the problem in the future.

3	**CHARACTERISTICS OF EFFECTIVE CONTROLS**
Explain the essential characteristics of effective controls.	

For control mechanisms to work effectively, they should be understandable, timely, suitable and economical, indicational, and flexible. These characteristics are required of the controls used in all supervisory jobs—in manufacturing, retailing, office work, health care, government service, banks, and other services. Supervisors have to tailor control mechanisms to the particular activities, circumstances, and needs of their departments.

Understandable

All control mechanisms—feedforward, concurrent, and feedback—must be understood by the managers, supervisors, and employees who are to use them. At higher management levels, control mechanisms may be rather sophisticated and based on management information systems, mathematical formulas, complex

A factory worker inspects computer components for any deviations from company standards.

Ed Kashi/CORBIS

charts and graphs, and detailed reports. At the top levels, such controls should be understandable to all of the managers who utilize them. However, controls should be much less complicated at the departmental level. For example, a supervisor might use a brief, one-page report as a control device. In a dry-cleaning store, this report might show the number of different garments cleaned and the number of employee hours worked on a given day. It is uncomplicated, straightforward, and understandable. If the control mechanisms in use are confusing or too sophisticated to be truly useful, the supervisor should devise new control systems that will meet departmental needs and be understandable to everyone who uses them.

Timely

Control mechanisms should indicate deviations from standard without delay, and such deviations should be reported to the supervisor promptly even if they are substantiated only by approximate figures, preliminary estimates, or partial information. It is better for the supervisor to know when things are about to go wrong than to learn that they already are out of control. The sooner a supervisor is aware of deviations, the more quickly the deviations can be corrected.

For example, assume that a project that requires the installation of equipment must be completed within a tight schedule. The supervisor should have reports on a daily or weekly basis showing where the project stands at that time and how this progress compares to the schedule. Potential roadblocks (e.g., missing parts or employee absences from work) that might delay the completion of the project should be included in these reports. The supervisor needs this type of information early in order to take corrective steps before the situation gets out of hand. This does not mean that the supervisor should jump to conclusions and resort to drastic action hastily. Generally, the supervisor's experience and familiarity with the job will be helpful in sensing when a job is not progressing the way it should.

Suitable and Economical

Controls must be suitable for the activity to be observed. A complex information system control approach that is necessary for a large corporation would not be applicable in a small department. The need for control exists in the small department, but the magnitude of the control system will be different. Whatever controls the supervisor applies, they must be suitable and economical for the job involved. There is no need to control a minor assignment as elaborately as a manager would control a major capital investment project.

For example, the head nurse in a hospital will usually control the supply of narcotics with greater care and frequency than the number of bandages on hand. Or, in a small company with three clerical employees, it would be inappropriate and uneconomical to have someone assigned full time to check their work for clerical mistakes. It is better to make each employee responsible for checking his or her own work or, possibly, to make employees responsible for checking each other's work. However, in a large department involving the work of several hundred employees who are mass producing a small-unit product, it makes considerable sense to employ full-time inspectors or quality control specialists to check the results. Typically, this is done on a sampling basis since it may not be feasible to check every item that goes through the production process.[3] There are many in-between situations in which supervisors must use good judgment as to the suitability of the controls utilized.

Controls also must be economical; that is, they must be worth their expense, even though it may be difficult to determine how much a control system costs and how much it is worth. In such a situation, it is advisable to consider the consequences that could result if controls were not in place. For example, think of the value of an elaborate, expensive control system in a company producing pharmaceuticals as compared to an enterprise manufacturing rubber bands. Defective rubber bands would be an inconvenience, but defective drugs could kill people! The risks for the pharmaceutical company make elaborate controls worth the expense.

Indicational

It is not enough for controls just to expose deviations as they occur. A control mechanism should also indicate who is responsible for the deviation and where the deviation occurred. If several subassemblies or successive operations are involved in a work process, it may be necessary for the supervisor to check performance after each step has been accomplished and before the work moves on to the next workstation. Otherwise, if end results are not up to standards, the supervisor may not know where to take corrective action.

Flexible

Since work operations occur in a dynamic setting, unforeseen circumstances can play havoc with even the best-laid plans and systems. Therefore, controls should be flexible enough to cope with unanticipated changes and problems. Control mechanisms must permit changes when such changes are required. For example, if an employee encounters significant changes in conditions early in a work assignment—such as an equipment failure or a shortage of materials—the supervisor must recognize this and adjust the plans and standards accordingly. If these difficulties are due to conditions beyond the employee's control, the supervisor also must adjust the criteria by which the employee's performance will be appraised.

4

STEPS IN THE CONTROL PROCESS

Describe the essential steps in the control process.

The control process involves three sequential steps. The first step (which usually is part of the planning function) begins with the setting of appropriate standards for what should be accomplished. Next, actual performance must be measured against these standards. If performance does not meet the standards, the third step is to take corrective action. These three steps must be followed in the sequence presented if controlling is to achieve the desired results (see Figure 13-1). Figure 13-2 provides selected tips for supervisors as they carry out control responsibilities with their employees.

Setting Standards

Standards
Units of measurement or specific criteria against which to evaluate results.

Standards may be defined as units of measurement or specific criteria against which to judge performance or results. **Standards** indicate the targets that should be achieved; they are criteria against which performance will be compared for exercising control. Standards must be set before any meaningful evaluations can be made about a person's work, a finished product, or a service. In Chapter 2 we described goals and the establishment of objectives as foundations of planning. Objectives give specific targets for employees to aim for. However, just having specific targets does not mean they will be attained. The effective supervisor needs to follow up to ensure that the actions that are supposed to be taken are, indeed, being taken and that the objectives are being achieved.

Tangible standards
Standards for performance results that are identifiable and measurable.

Intangible standards
Standards for performance results that are difficult to measure and often relate to human characteristics (e.g., attitude, morale, satisfaction).

Many types of standards can be established, depending on the areas of performance or results that need to be measured. **Tangible standards** are performance targets for results that are identifiable and measurable. For example, tangible standards can be set to measure such things as quantity of output, quality of output, labour costs, overhead expenses, time spent in producing a unit or providing the service, and the like. (Tangible standards included on employee appraisal rating forms were identified in Chapter 9.) **Intangible standards** are tar-

FIGURE 13-1
Steps in the control process.

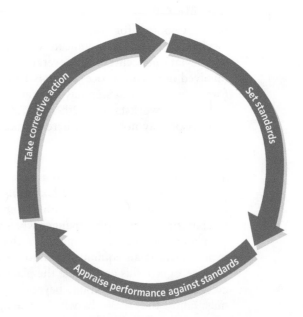

FIGURE 13-2   Supervisory tips for positively controlling employee performance.

- Be very clear when communicating the objectives and specifics of work assignments.
- Get agreement, if possible, on the standards and measures of performance assessment.
- Solicit employees' ideas for improvement; use their ideas whenever appropriate.
- Concentrate on those issues that most need attention.
- Take corrective action with improvement as the primary goal; do not just try to assign blame.
- Demonstrate consistently with all personnel that you consider budgets, standards, and controls to be necessary components of effective management and supervision.
- Convey, by words and actions, that in no area of your supervisory responsibilities will you compromise or accept any work performance that is unsatisfactory.

gets for results that have no physical form; they may cover such areas as an organization's reputation; employee morale; or the quality of humane, loving care of patients in a health care centre or nursing home. It is usually more difficult to establish intangible standards in numerical or precise terms.

The most frequent tangible standards that supervisors establish pertain to the operations of their departments. For example, in a production department, standards can be set for the number of units to be produced; the labour hours per unit; and the quality of the product in terms of durability, finish, and closeness of dimensions.[4] In a sales department, standards might be set for the number of customers contacted, the sales dollars realized, and the number and types of customer complaints.[5]

In setting standards, a supervisor can be guided by experience and knowledge of the jobs to be performed. Through experience and observation, most supervisors have a general idea of how much time it takes to perform certain jobs, the different resources required, and what constitutes good or poor quality. By study and analysis of previous budgets, past production, and other departmental records, supervisors should be able to develop workable standards of performance for most aspects of their departments' operations.

Motion and Time Studies

A more thorough and systematic way to establish standards for the amount of work employees should accomplish within a given period is to have industrial engineers perform motion and time studies.[6] A **motion study** is an analysis of how a job currently is performed with a view to improving, eliminating, changing, or combining steps to make the job easier and quicker to perform. After a thorough analysis of the work motions and layout, the industrial engineer will develop what he or she considers to be the best current method for doing this job.

Motion study
An analysis of work activities to determine how to make the job easier and quicker to do.

Time study
A technique for analyzing jobs to determine the standard time needed to complete them.

Once the best current method has been designed, a **time study** is performed to determine a time standard for the job. This is accomplished in a systematic and largely quantitative manner by selecting certain employees for observation; observing the times used to accomplish various parts of the job; applying correction factors; and making allowances for fatigue, personal needs, and unavoidable delays. When all these factors are combined properly, the result is a time standard for performing the job.

Although this approach attempts to be objective, considerable judgment and approximations are part of the established time standard. A time standard determined by motion and time study is neither wholly scientific nor beyond dispute, but it does provide a sound basis on which a supervisor can set realistic standards.[7] Standards developed by motion and time studies can help the supervisor distribute work more evenly and judge each employee's performance fairly. Such standards also assist the supervisor in predicting the number of employees required and the probable cost of a job to be done.

Most supervisors work in organizations without industrial engineers. When a new job is to be performed in the department, the supervisor can set tentative standards based on similar operations in this or other departments. When no comparison standard is readily available, the supervisor should identify the key tasks necessary to accomplish the job and then directly observe the employees or ask them to record the time required to complete the tasks. From these data a reasonable standard can be calculated.

To illustrate, suppose a shift supervisor in a fast-food restaurant needs to determine how long it takes employees to prepare a new menu item. The supervisor lists all the steps necessary to complete the job. Then the supervisor can perform the task under several different circumstances and record the required time. The supervisor can also select several employees to perform the task under a variety of conditions. From among the several observations, the supervisor can determine the average time required to complete the task. Not only will realistic standards be established, but also such an approach might uncover better ways of doing the job.

Employee Participation

Some employees resent standards, especially those arrived at through motion and time studies. This resentment is part of a longstanding fear that so-called "efficiency experts" and supervisors use motion and time studies primarily to speed up the workers' output. However, the main purpose for setting performance standards should be to create realistic targets—that is, objectives that can be achieved and that are considered fair by both the supervisor and the employees. Workers are more apt to accept standards as reasonable and fair if they have played an active role in the formulation of those standards.[8]

One technique for having employees participate in establishing standards is to form a committee of workers to assist the supervisor and/or industrial engineer in carrying out a work measurement program. The employees selected for this committee should be those who, in the supervisor's judgment, consistently do a fair day's work.

In addition, the supervisor and industrial engineer should explain to all employees what is involved in motion and time studies, including areas in which judgment is involved. Employees should be given opportunities to challenge any standard that they consider to be unfair, perhaps even to have a job restudied and retimed if necessary. Most workers will accept performance standards if they feel that the supervisor has tried to help them understand the basis for the standards and is willing to reconsider and adjust standards that appear to be unreasonable.

Strategic Control Points

The number of standards needed to determine the quantity and quality of performance may become larger as the department expands. As operations become more complex and as functions of a department increase, it becomes time consuming and impractical for the supervisor to constantly check against every conceivable standard. Therefore, the supervisor should concentrate on certain strategic control points against which overall performance can be monitored. **Strategic control points,** or strategic standards, consist of a limited number of key indicators that give the supervisor a good sampling of overall performance. There are no specific rules on how to select strategic control points. Because the nature of the department and the makeup of the supervisor and employees are different in each situation, only general guidelines can be suggested.

A major consideration in choosing one standard as being more strategic than another is its timeliness. Time is essential in control; therefore, the sooner a deviation can be discovered, the better it can be corrected. A supervisor needs to recognize at what critical step operations should be checked during a given process. For example, a strategic control point might be established when a subassembly operation is finished but before the product is put together with other parts and spray painted. A similar approach can be applied in the process of dry-cleaning a stained suit for a customer. A strategic control point is established shortly after the stain remover is applied. If the stain is still present, the dry-cleaner will avoid wasted time and effort by preventing the suit from progressing through the remaining processing steps until the stain is properly dealt with.

A supervisor should be careful that the selection of a strategic control point does not have a significant adverse effect on another important standard. For example, excessive control to increase the quantity of production might have an adverse effect on the quality of the product.[9] Likewise, if labour expenses are selected as a strategic control point, supervisors might try to hold down wage expenses by not hiring enough workers, causing both quality and quantity standards to deteriorate. To illustrate, a laundry department supervisor in a nursing home must not sacrifice high infection-control standards simply to achieve a goal of reducing the cost of laundering linen to a certain price per kilogram. Thus, decisions about strategic control points depend to some extent on the nature of the work performed. What serves well as a strategic control point in one department will not necessarily apply in another.

Another example of applying the concept of strategic control points is the supervisor who wishes to assess the quality of departmental employee relations. The supervisor might decide to use the following indicators as strategic control standards:

- Number of employees' voluntary resignations and requests for transfer.
- Levels of absenteeism and tardiness.
- Accident frequency and severity rates.
- Number and types of employee grievances and complaints.
- Number and types of customer complaints.
- Amount of scrap and rejects, and unexplained losses of materials and inventory.

Strategic control points
Performance criteria chosen for assessment because they are key indicators of overall performance.

By closely watching trends and changes in these indicators, the supervisor should be able to spot problems requiring corrective action. If the trend of most or all of these selected indicators is unfavourable, significant supervisory attention is needed.

Consider the example of a wire manufacturer that used simple statistics to track the productivity of machine operators. It was noted that during the preceding hour, scrap exceeded the acceptable standard by 10 percent. Using strategic control points in a timely fashion, the supervisor working with the operators and the maintenance department knew it was time to check the production process. A check of the diamond dies, pressure settings, and quality of the raw stock led to action so that scrap rates did not increase further and could be returned to their previous lower levels. Strategic control points should be established so that corrective action can be taken early in the production process.[10]

As mentioned previously, there are also areas of an intangible nature that should be monitored closely, even though it is difficult to set precise standards for them. For example, the state of employee morale is typically an important element of departmental operations that a supervisor may decide to monitor and assess as a strategic control standard. Techniques for measurement and evaluation of employee morale were discussed in Chapter 11.

Checking Performance against Standards

The second major step in the control process is to check actual performance against established standards. This is an ongoing activity for every supervisor. The primary ways for a supervisor to do this are by observing, studying oral and written reports, making spot checks, and using statistical sampling techniques.

Personal Observation

For monitoring employee performance, there is no substitute for direct observation and personal contact by a supervisor. The opportunity for inspection and close personal observation of employee performance is an advantage the supervisor has over top-level managers. This is because the farther removed a manager is from where the employees actually carry out the organization's work, the more the manager will have to depend on reports from others. The supervisor, however, has ample opportunity for direct observation.

When supervisors find deviations from expected standards, they should assume a questioning attitude but not necessarily a fault-finding one. It is possible that the problem is due to something outside the employees' control, such as a malfunctioning machine or faulty raw materials. Supervisors should raise questions about mistakes in a positive, helpful manner. For example, instead of just criticizing what happened, a supervisor first should ask what caused the problem and whether there is any way in which he or she can help the employees do their jobs more easily, safely, or efficiently. Supervisors also should elicit suggestions from employees concerning what should be done to correct existing problems. When standards are stated primarily in general terms, supervisors should look for specific unsatisfactory conditions, such as inadequate output, sloppy work, or unsafe practices. It is not enough just to tell an employee that his or her work is "unacceptable" or "not satisfactory." If the supervisor can point to specific instances or cite actual recent examples, the employee is more likely to acknowledge the deficiencies that must be corrected.[11]

Also, supervisors can use personal observation and questioning to turn up causes of poor performance that are not the employees' fault, such as inadequate training, problems with work-flow design, or an unusual increase in workload. For example, if a retail store supervisor discovers that customers are not being processed through the cashier quickly enough, the reason may be that an unusually large number of customers entered the store at one time. Instead of chastising employees, the proper corrective action may be to open up another checkout lane. Also, the supervisor may need to find a better way to predict customer traffic or hire a backup cashier. The supervisor may build alternative ways of doing the job into future plans. Employees may have valuable ideas about how to prevent the problem from recurring.

Checking employee performance through personal observation does have limitations. It is time consuming, and it may require the supervisor to spend hours away from his or her desk. Also, it may not be possible to observe some important activities at critical times. There always will be some employees who perform well while being observed but revert to poorer, less diligent habits when the supervisor is not around. Nevertheless, personal observation still is the most widely used and probably the best method of checking employee performance at the supervisory level.

Oral and Written Reports

If a department is large, operates in different locations, or works around the clock, oral and written reports are necessary. For example, if a department operates around the clock and its supervisor has the overall responsibility for more than one shift, the supervisor must depend on reports submitted by employees to appraise the performance of shifts that occur when the supervisor is not present. When a department operates multiple shifts and different supervisors are in charge on different shifts, each supervisor should arrive early to get a firsthand report from the supervisor who is completing the previous shift.

Whenever reports are required, the supervisor should insist that they be clear, complete but concise, and correct. If possible, written reports should be submitted along with an oral presentation. Reports are more effective when they are substantiated with statistical or comparative data.

Most employees submit reasonably accurate reports even when they contain unfavourable outcomes. Report accuracy depends a great deal on the supervisor's reaction to reports and his or her existing relations with employees. If the supervisor handles adverse reports in a constructive and helpful manner, appreciating honesty instead of just assigning blame, employees will be encouraged to submit accurate reports even if the reports show them in an unfavourable light.

Exception principle
Concept that supervisors should concentrate their investigations on activities that deviate substantially from the standard.

In checking reports, supervisors usually find that many activities have been performed according to standards and can be passed over quickly. As a result, many supervisors use the **exception principle** by concentrating on those areas in which performance is significantly above or below standard. Supervisors may even ask employees to forgo reporting on activities that have for the most part attained the established standards, and to report only on activities that are exceptionally below or above standard. If performance is significantly below standard, the supervisor will have to move to the third stage of the control process, taking corrective action. If performance is significantly above standard, the supervisor should praise the employees and study how such exceptional performance was achieved to determine whether what was done can be repeated in the future. The supervisor should also ensure that employees have not sacrificed product quality or customer service standards in their efforts to achieve exceptional results in other areas.

Spot Checks

If the employees' work routine does not lend itself to reports, the supervisor may have to rely on periodic spot checks. For example, a data systems supervisor who is responsible for a centralized computer department that works around the clock six days a week should occasionally come to work at varying times to see what goes on in the department during the different shifts. Supervisors who have little or no opportunity to perform spot checks usually have to depend on reports.

Sampling Techniques

Sampling techniques are really supplements to strategic control points and spot checks. In some firms, each part or product is inspected to determine whether it meets the prescribed standards. Inspecting every item is a time-consuming and costly process. It is becoming increasingly crucial for supervisors, particularly in production facilities, to acquaint themselves with statistical process control (SPC). SPC is a method to help supervisors determine not only which products, product components, or services to inspect, but also how many of each to inspect.[12] **Sampling** is the process of inspecting some predetermined number of products from a batch to determine whether the batch is acceptable or unacceptable.

Sampling
The technique of evaluating some number of items from a larger group to determine whether the group meets acceptable quality standards.

To illustrate, suppose that a store manager has been concerned with the quality of produce received from a distributor. The store manager and the produce manager use SPC to determine how many individual boxes of an incoming shipment should be inspected. Rather than inspecting the entire load of produce, they compare random samples against a predetermined acceptable quality standard. If a certain number of the samples do not meet the standard, then they reject the entire load. Note that if the distributor used this technique prior to shipping the produce, it would be feedback control. The same process used by the store manager would be feedforward control. While SPC saves time and money in inspection costs, the supervisor must ensure that the sample of units inspected is randomly selected and accurately represents the quality of all the units.

Taking Corrective Action

When no deviations from established standards occur, the process of control is fulfilled by the first two steps—setting standards and checking actual performance against the standards. But if discrepancies or deviations have been noted through personal observation, reports, or spot checks, then the supervisor must take the third step of taking corrective action to bring performance back into line.

Prior to taking specific corrective action, the supervisor should bear in mind that there are various reasons discrepancies or deviations from standards can occur in any job. Among these are the following:

- The standards could not be achieved because they were based on faulty forecasts or assumptions or because an unforeseen problem arose that distorted the anticipated results.
- Failure already occurred in some other job (or activity) that preceded the job in question.

- The employee who performed the job either was unqualified or was not given adequate directions or instructions.
- The employee who performed the job was negligent or did not follow required directions or procedures.

Therefore, before taking corrective action, the supervisor should analyze the facts of the situation to determine the specific causes for the deviation. Only after identifying the specific causes can the supervisor decide what remedial actions are necessary to obtain better results in the future. For example, if the reason for the deviation lies in the standards themselves, the supervisor must revise the standards accordingly. If the employee who performed the job was not qualified, additional training and closer supervision might be the answer. Or if the employee was not given the proper instructions, then the supervisor should accept the blame and improve his or her own techniques for giving directives. In the case of sheer negligence or insubordination on the part of the employee, corrective action may consist of a discussion with the employee or a verbal or written reprimand. At times, more serious forms of disciplinary action may have to be taken, including suspending or replacing the employee. Under such circumstances, the disciplinary procedures discussed in Chapter 10 should be followed.

| 5 | **BUDGETARY CONTROL** |

Discuss the supervisor's role in controlling through budgets.

Establishing a budget falls under the managerial function of planning, but carrying out the budget—or living within the budget—is part of the controlling function. Supervisors must manage their departments within budget limits and refer to their budgets to monitor their expenditures during the operating period. When a budget is approved by higher-level management, the supervisor is allocated specific amounts of money for each item in the budget. Expenditures in the supervisor's department must be charged against various budget accounts. At regular intervals (e.g., weekly), the supervisor must review the budgeted figures and compare them with the actual expenses incurred.

Incremental budgeting
A technique for projecting revenues and expenses based on history.

Zero-based budgeting
The process of assessing, on a benefit and cost basis, all activities to justify their existence.

Most annual budgets are projections for the following year based on the previous year's budget. This approach for making a budget is known as **incremental budgeting.** Another approach, which has gained some acceptance, is **zero-based budgeting,** in which all budgets must begin "from scratch," and each budget item must be individually justified and substantiated. In zero-based budgeting, the previous budget does not constitute a valid basis for a future budget. The advantage of zero-based budgeting is that all ongoing programs, activities, projects, and products are reassessed in terms of their benefits and costs to the organization. This avoids the tendency of automatically continuing expenditures from a previous budget without much review or consideration. The disadvantage of zero-based budgeting is that it is more time consuming than incremental budgeting.[13]

If the supervisor notes that actual expenditures for a specific item greatly exceed the budgeted amount, he or she must find out what happened. Investigation could reveal a logical explanation for the discrepancy. For example, if the amount spent on labour in a manufacturing department exceeded the budgeted amount, this could be due to an unanticipated demand for the firm's product that required working overtime. If the excessive deviation from the budgeted amount cannot be justified, the supervisor must take whatever actions are necessary to bring the out-of-control expenditures back to where they should be, at least from that point on. Excessive deviations usually have to be explained by the supervisor to higher-level managers or the accounting department. To avoid this unpleasant task, a supervisor is well advised to make regular comparisons of actual expenditures with budgeted amounts and to keep expenses close to the budget.

Supervisors need to understand accounting tools so that they can forecast objectives and assess results. Virtually everything the organization does will be reflected in monetary terms. While the accounting department may do a good job of preparing the income statement and balance sheet, the supervisor and employees need to fully appreciate what the information means and how it can be used to more effectively manage the business.

A supervisor's budget should not be so detailed and rigidly applied that it becomes a burden. The budget should allow the supervisor some freedom to accomplish departmental objectives. Flexibility does not mean, however, that the supervisor can change budget figures unilaterally. Rather, it means that the supervisor can retain some discretion in decision making. Budgets are guides for management decisions, not substitutes for good judgment.

To prevent budgets from becoming a burden, most organizations have supervisors and higher-level managers or the accounting department regularly review budgets. These reviews should take place every three months, when operating conditions change, or whenever there is a valid indication that the budget cannot be followed and a revision is in order. For example, unexpected price increases or major fluctuations in the general economic climate might be reasons to review and revise a budget.

| **6** | ## COST CONTROL AND THE SUPERVISOR |

Discuss the supervisor's role in maintaining cost consciousness and in responding to higher-level managers' orders to reduce costs.

Competition from domestic companies and those abroad, as well as the changing economic environment, requires most organizations to strive continuously to control costs. Sooner or later most supervisors become involved in some way with cost control because higher-level managers expect them to control costs at the department level to help meet organizational cost goals. Thus, cost consciousness should be an ongoing concern of supervisors. Economy drives, crash programs, and sporadic efforts to curtail costs seldom have lasting benefits. Although many large organizations employ consultants trained in work efficiency and cost control, in the final analysis it remains the supervisor's duty to look at cost consciousness as a permanent part of the managerial job.

Sharing Information and Responsibility with Employees

While there have been many lists of companies that practise management excellence, author Robert Levering, from his examination of a number of large firms, concludes that any manager can turn a bad workplace into a good one by granting employees more responsibility for their jobs. "Management's new approach involves establishing a partnership with employees rather than acting as adversaries."[14] In forging a partnership with its employees, a firm must be willing to share financial information with them. Information sharing is becoming common in small as well as large firms (see the Contemporary Issue box).

In one such company, employees are provided with weekly information on all aspects of the business, from revenue and purchasing costs to labour and management expenses. Every employee learns to understand the information and knows that part of his or her job is to move those numbers in the right direction. It seems to be a good way to involve employees in the organization.[15]

Traditionally, managers, particularly those in closely held or privately owned businesses, have been reluctant to share financial information. The following illustration cited by management consultant Ken Blanchard shows how a consultant overcame a restaurant chain president's reluctance to share important financial information with employees:

The consultant went to the firm's largest restaurant one night at closing time. After dividing the employees—cooks, dishwashers, waiters, buspeople, and hostess—into groups of five or six, he asked each group to come to an agreement about the answer to the question: "Of every dollar that comes into this restaurant, how many cents fall to the bottom line—money that can be returned to investors as profit or reinvested in the business?"

The lowest amount any group suggested was 40 cents. The reality in the restaurant business is that if you keep 5 cents on the dollar, you're excited. After sharing the actual figures, the consultant was impressed when a chef asked, "You mean if I burn a $6 steak, with a 5 percent profit, we have to sell 20 more steaks for essentially nothing to make up for my wastage?"[16]

However, it is not enough for a firm to simply share financial information with employees. Employees must have an understanding of what the financial data mean and a basis for comparing their firm's current financial information with that of previous years and competitors.

CONTEMPORARY ISSUE
Open-Book Management: Sharing the Controlling Function with Employees

Robert Frances, CEO of PEAK Investment Services Inc. of Montreal (www.peakgroup.com), is a strong proponent of open-book management, the regular sharing of key financial information with employees at all levels of the organization. Frances says, "If my employees right across the organization don't know where the revenues come from, what the numbers are, what the targets are, what the expenses are, where the money's going and how we're going to grow ... then they can't move fast enough to suit our needs."[1] By opening the books to employees, Frances encourages them to become actively involved in the control process. "If only top management, or even just certain top management, controls the process," says Frances, "you end up with a hierarchy of financial influence. That's not desirable in a fast-growing company where people need to be able to deal with change quickly."[2] Open-book management has had tangible rewards at PEAK, where employees can see clearly how their own efforts affect the company's overall performance. The company has ranked for six consecutive years in *Profit Magazine*'s prestigious list of fastest-growing Canadian companies (www.profitguide.com).

Open-book management appears to be a growing trend in Canadian companies. The idea is that by opening financial records to employees and getting them to think and act as business owners, higher profits, greater efficiency, better morale, and a more competitive workforce can result. Employees are encouraged to be involved in the process of setting targets and take an active role in the monitoring and control function. What used to be confidential financial information is opened up for all to see, and "employees are expected to return the favour by working with management to help the

(continued)

company meet its financial goals."[3] Open-book management is often accompanied by profit-sharing or bonus plans that reward employees when key targets are met. By giving them a financial stake in the process, employees are encouraged to participate in the achievement of the company's overall goals.

The term *open-book management* is usually credited to John Case, who wrote a book titled *The Open-Book Experience*. A leading proponent of open-book management is Jack Stack, chief executive of SRC Holdings Corporation in Springfield, Missouri, who used the approach to bring about major improvements and profits in his company. According to Stack, it requires education to teach employees about how to succeed in business. Opening the financial books to them is part of that educational process. Stack contends that when employees understand the business and are actively involved in setting goals and monitoring the results, they can all contribute to the company's success. He advocates that having employees act as owners is a way to get employees focused on building a company's value and competitive position.

The approach seems to work at Eagle's Flight Creative Training Excellence Inc. of Guelph, Ontario (www.eaglesflight.com). The company was founded in 1988 and provides experiential training programs for clients around the world. The company has practised open-book management since 1995. Co-founder Dave Loney says, "We have no secrets. People can ask any questions about what's going on in terms of profit or how the business is run."[4] A bulletin board prominently displays budgeted sales, expenses, and profit on a bar graph, and the information is updated weekly. Loney says the emphasis is on making the information accessible and enjoyable. "When it's coming in a way that shows it's fun," he says, "employees get excited about learning. They look forward to having a hand in the health of the business ... Being able to see that the company is healthy gives people the confidence to work for the team and stay with the team."[5]

But open-book management may not be for everyone. There must be a lot of trust between management and employees and a deeply ingrained belief that employees have something to offer. Additionally, some companies have found that employees are not receptive to full financial disclosure, and are unsettled by the day-to-day ups and downs of a company's financial performance. Robert Herjavec is an entrepreneur and founder of BRAK Systems Inc., a Mississauga-based computer security company that he recently sold to AT&T Canada. When he was CEO and president of BRAK, Herjavec found that open-book management was actually a destructive force. "We completely opened the books, every line item, and we went to great lengths to teach people what everything was. It didn't work for us."[6] When the company experienced one bad quarter, knowing the full details was too much information for some staff. "They didn't think we'd survive, and when people are worried it creates an overall mood of trepidation."[7] One key employee felt the risk was too great and left the organization, and new employees became harder to attract. In response to this experience, Herjavec adapted his approach and filtered the information that he provided to his staff. "[Staff] wanted to know that the company was moving ahead," says Herjavec, "but whether we had enough cash to pay our bills that month and how close we came to not being able to, they just didn't want to know that stuff."[8]

On balance, though, it appears that open-book management is a viable option to help some companies increase the commitment of staff and encourage their participation in the control function. Rather than having supervisors and upper management be seen as the holders of the chequebook, employees can become fully involved in the budgeting and control process. The numbers become their numbers, rather than directives from above. Employees can see the direct impact that their actions have on the company's bottom line, and are encouraged to perform in a way that will help the organization meet its goals. Employees will need training and guidance to learn how to interpret and use the information that is made available to them, but once this is done, open-book management may help turn employees into long-term business partners with a real stake in the organization's success.

Sources: (1) & (2) Richard Wright, "21 Ways to Build Great People—Profit 100 CEO's Reveal Their Best Tips for Finding and Keeping Top-Notch Talent," *Profit: The Magazine for Canadian Entrepreneurs* (June 2000), pp. 122–32; (3), (4), & (5) Michela Pasquali, "Opening the Books to Better Biz: Letting Everyone in on Your Financial Game Plan Can Increase Trust, Accountability and Perhaps Profits," *Profit: The Magazine for Canadian Entrepreneurs* (September 1997), p. 69; (6), (7), & (8) Op. cit., Wright. See also: Ron Hall, "Open Your Books for Profit," *Landscape Management* (January 2002), pp. 22–25 and Rich Maurer, "Open-Book Management," *Journal for Quality & Participation* (Spring 2001), p. 64.

Maintaining Cost Awareness

Because cost consciousness is of ongoing concern to the supervisor, plans should be made for achieving cost awareness throughout the department. Here is where planning and controlling again become closely interrelated. By setting objectives and defining specific results to be achieved within a certain time frame, cost priorities can be set.

In setting cost objectives, the supervisor should involve the employees who are in positions that will be most affected. Employees can often make valuable contributions. The supervisor should fully communicate cost-reducing objectives to employees and get as much input from them as possible. The more employees contribute to a cost-control program, the more committed they will be to meeting objectives. It may also be advisable to point out to employees that eventually everyone benefits from continuous cost awareness. Supervisors should help employees see cost containment as part of their jobs and as being in their own long-term interest. Firms that do not control costs cannot remain competitive, which could mean loss of jobs. Most employees will try to do the right thing and seek to reduce waste and costs if their supervisors approach them in a positive way.

Responding to a Cost-Cutting Order

Reducing costs is a natural concern of most organizations, and it is frequently brought on by competition. It is likely that within an enterprise, at one time or another, an order will come from top-level managers to cut all costs across the board by a certain percentage. At first glance, such a blanket order could be considered fair and just; however, this may not be so since it could affect some supervisors much more severely than others. Some supervisors are continuously aware of costs and operate their departments efficiently, while others are lax and perhaps even wasteful. How should a supervisor react to such a blanket order?

The more employees contribute to the development of a cost control program, the more committed they will be to meeting objectives.

Getty Images/Photodisc Collection

There are some supervisors who will read the order to mean that everything possible should be done immediately to bring about the desired percentage of cost reduction. They might hold "pep rallies" with employees or, at the other extreme, engage in harsh criticism of employees and others. Some supervisors might stop buying supplies, leading eventually to work delays. Others might eliminate preventive maintenance work even though this eventually could lead to equipment breakdowns and interruptions of the work flow. Although these actions might bring about some immediate cost reductions, they could be more expensive in the long run.

Other supervisors will merely follow the cost-cutting directive halfheartedly. They will make minimal efforts here and there to give the appearance that they are doing something about costs. Such efforts are not likely to impress the employees, who in turn will also make only a halfhearted effort. This type of supervisory response will not contribute adequately to a cost-control program.

An across-the-board cost-reduction order may present a hardship to the diligent, cost-conscious supervisor whose department is already working efficiently. Nevertheless, this supervisor should strive to take some action by looking again at areas where there is still room to reduce expenses. This supervisor should call for suggestions from employees because they are the ones who can bring about results. For example, there may be some paperwork that can be postponed indefinitely. Or there may be certain operations that are not absolutely necessary even if they are performed efficiently. The supervisor should point out to the employees which are the most expensive operations and let them know what these actually cost. An employee might suggest a less expensive way of doing a job; if so, the supervisor should welcome the suggestion. The supervisor should be committed to the cost-reduction campaign and should set a good personal example whenever possible. Although it may be difficult for such a supervisor to come up with large savings, at least he or she will have made a diligent effort to support the organization's cost-cutting drive. While supervisors play a key role in cost reduction, they cannot succeed without employee involvement and commitment.

Elimination of things that cost money is one way to save money. Effective supervisors are constantly on the lookout for ways to eliminate excess costs by questioning the necessity of everything that is done in their departments.

Even if an organization does not have a formal suggestion program, supervisors can establish a climate of mutual trust and respect that encourages suggestions from their employees. The supervisor can use formal and informal encouragement during departmental meetings to emphasize the value of making suggestions. Whether for changing policies or controlling costs, employee suggestions can be a valuable source of ideas. Employees like to see their ideas put into effect and are more committed to goals they helped to set.

7   OTHER CONTROLS

Identify additional control areas and explain how the controlling function is closely related to the other managerial functions.

In addition to accounting and budgetary controls, other areas of management control exist in many organizations. Typically, these control areas are supervised by specialized departments and are outside the realm of most supervisors' direct authority and responsibility. Nevertheless, supervisors should be aware of these control areas, and, if necessary, should familiarize themselves with the methods employed by the specialists who perform these control activities. Often such specialists are attached to the organization in staff positions.

Specialized Controls

Inventory control is concerned with keeping watch over raw materials, supplies, work in process, finished goods, and the like. Maintaining sufficient but not excessive inventory on hand, keeping status records of all inventory, ordering economic lot sizes, and many other problems connected with inventory policy are part of inventory control.[17]

Quality control consists of maintaining the quality standards set by a firm for its products or services. These must be continually tested to make certain that quality is maintained. Quality control of products is often accomplished by testing randomly selected samples to determine whether or not quality standards are being met.

Production control usually consists of a number of activities to maintain overall operations on schedule. It involves routing of operations, scheduling, and, if necessary, expediting of the work flow. Elaborate charts and network analyses may be utilized. For example, the production control department may start with a Gantt chart, which is a diagram or pictorial representation of the progress and status of various jobs in production. If practical, this can lead to a computerized network analysis. Two of the most widely used analyses are PERT (program evaluation review technique) and CPM (critical path method), which were discussed in Chapter 2.[18]

Controlling and the Other Managerial Functions

Throughout this book, we have discussed numerous aspects of effective managerial controls from different perspectives. At this point we will review several of them as they relate specifically to the controlling function.

In Chapter 2, we discussed the system of MBO (management by objectives) in connection with motivation and planning. The MBO process involves setting objectives and standards, evaluating results, following up, and revising previous objectives if necessary. Evaluation of results, follow-up, and establishment of new objectives are elements of control.

In Chapter 2, we also discussed standing (repeat-use) plans, such as policies, procedures, methods, and rules, primarily in regard to managerial planning. However, when standing plans are not working or are not followed, the supervisor must take the necessary corrective actions to bring the department's operations back in line. Thus, these types of standing plans may be seen as forward-looking control devices.

Performance appraisal, which we discussed in Chapter 9, also has a place as a control mechanism. During a performance appraisal meeting, the supervisor evaluates an employee's performance against predetermined objectives and standards. At the same time, the supervisor and the employee may agree on steps for corrective action, as well as on new objectives and standards. The element of supervisory control can be detected throughout a performance appraisal cycle.

In Chapter 10 we discussed the subject of employee discipline as part of the controlling function. If a supervisor takes disciplinary measures when established rules are not followed by employees, such measures serve as control techniques.

These managerial activities show how intrinsically related the controlling function is to all the other managerial functions. As stated previously, controlling typically is performed simultaneously with the other managerial functions. The better the supervisor plans, organizes, staffs, and leads, the better will be his or her ability to control the activities and employees in the department. Thus, controlling takes a forward-looking view, even though it has been discussed as the "final" managerial function in this book.

WHAT CALL DID YOU MAKE?

As Gil Pietro, you should not become angry or defensive when responding to your staff but thoughtfully weigh their comments. One option is to call a staff meeting to discuss the situation. To prepare for the meeting, you should investigate the allegations of program flaws and increased workload. The meeting should be a discussion in which you explain the reasoning behind the implementation decision. Give your staff ample opportunities to express and discuss their feelings about the new software. After this meeting, and perhaps after further discussing the issues, decisions will need to be made. If the flaws and increased workload due to the software seem real, you could try to persuade your boss and upper management to delay the project's implementation date until the software is ready. If, however, you decide to go forward with the implementation plan for the new software, such a decision should be reported to upper managers so

they know the implications and adjustments that may be required, such as overtime. If you believe your staff's allegations are unfounded and are based on their resistance to change, you must try to reduce this resistance. This means trying to persuade your staff that it is a sound decision, then involving those staff in decisions on how to proceed with the implementation. Without staff involvement and some support, the project may be doomed to failure or, at best, will be replete with problems and inefficiencies.

As for the future, learn from this experience and vow never to repeat these mistakes. Be sure to involve your staff in all the planning phases of any project that will have a major impact on the staff's work situations. Then, as discussed in this chapter, there will be far less chance that such projects will be out of control and will require major adjustments. The best control is usually a good plan in which all affected parties have participated and to which they are committed.

SUMMARY

Controlling is the managerial function that determines whether or not plans are being followed and performance conforms to standards. Every manager must develop and apply controls that regulate the organization's activities to achieve the desired results. The controlling function is most closely related to the planning function. Supervisors set objectives and, in turn, these objectives become standards against which performance is checked. Well-designed controls can be a positive influence on employee motivation. Control should be forward-looking since nothing can be done about the past. The closeness of supervisory control depends, in part, on the employees' experience, initiative, dependability, and resourcefulness.

Control mechanisms can be categorized as feedforward, concurrent, and feedback based on when they are implemented in the process. Feedforward, or preliminary, controls are used to anticipate and prevent undesirable outcomes. The person who checks the tires, oil, gas gauge, and the like before beginning a trip is using feedforward control. The traveller who notices that the fuel warning light has just come on and pulls into the next gas station for a fill-up is using concurrent control. Feedback controls are employed after the fact—they are used as a basis for further improvement. The traveller who calculates average kilometres per litre and uses that information when planning the budget for the next trip is using feedback control. Generally, effective supervisors rely on all three types of control mechanisms to improve the process or prevent recurrence of a problem in the future.

To be effective, controls must be understandable to everyone who uses them and must yield timely information so that problems can be corrected before the situation gets out of hand. Also, controls should be suitable and economical for the situation. The more serious the consequences of mistakes, the tighter the controls should be, despite the expense. Finally, controls should indicate where the trouble lies in the process and be flexible enough to adjust to changing conditions.

In performing the controlling function, a supervisor should follow three basic steps: setting standards, checking actual performance against standards, and taking corrective action if necessary. Standards may be set for both tangible and intangible areas. A supervisor's own experience and knowledge can serve to develop certain performance standards. More precise work standards can be accomplished through motion and time studies. Employee participation in setting standards is crucial to their acceptance. Many supervisors focus their control efforts on selected strategic control points (or strategic standards) that provide major indicators of performance.

The supervisor should check performance against the established standards. In some instances, the supervisor has to depend on reports, but in most cases personal observation and inspection are appropriate for checking employee performance. At times, the supervisor may apply the exception principle, which means concentrating on areas where performance is significantly below or above the expected standards. Sampling can be used to help the supervisor determine whether or not products meet prescribed standards. When unfavourable discrepancies from standards are revealed, the supervisor must take the necessary corrective actions to bring the performance back in line and to prevent future deviations.

The most widely used financial control device is the budget. The preparation of a budget is primarily a planning function. However, applying, monitoring, and living within the budget are part of the controlling function. When significant deviations from the budget occur, the supervisor must investigate and take whatever actions are appropriate to bring expenditures back in line.

Cost control and cost consciousness should be a continuing concern of all supervisors. When top-level managers issue cost-cutting orders, supervisors should avoid taking extreme measures that may in the long run be more costly than the immediate savings.

Involving employees in cost-reduction efforts is one way that the effective supervisor can create cost awareness. Suggestion programs can be used to solicit ideas for potential areas of cost reduction. The supervisor should constantly be on the lookout for ways to eliminate excess costs. Periodically, the supervisor should look at the department through the eyes of a stranger and question the necessity of everything that is done in the department.

7 Many organizations have specialists who concentrate on inventory control, quality control, and production control. These types of control systems usually are not under the direct authority of most departmental supervisors but are handled by staff specialists. Other managerial concepts, techniques, and approaches used by departmental supervisors contain aspects of the controlling function. Among these are MBO, use of standing plans, maintenance of discipline, and employee performance appraisal. Thus, controlling is intimately interrelated with all the other managerial functions.

QUESTIONS FOR DISCUSSION

1. Define the managerial function of controlling and discuss its relationship to the other managerial functions.
2. Why do many people view controls negatively? How can a supervisor minimize employees' resistance to controls?
3. Define and give examples of each of the following:
   a. Feedforward controls.
   b. Concurrent controls.
   c. Feedback controls.
4. Define and discuss each of the primary steps in the control process:
   a. Setting standards.
   b. Checking actual performance against standards.
   c. Taking corrective action.
5. Define and provide an example of a strategic control point.
6. Describe the differences between incremental and zero-based budgeting. What are the relative strengths and weaknesses of each approach?
7. Discuss the supervisor's duty to take appropriate action when accounting reports indicate that actual expenditures are significantly above or below budget allocations. How do effective supervisors reduce costs?

SKILLS APPLICATIONS

Skills Application 13-1: Analysis of Examination Results

Tests and exams are a control mechanism designed to assess whether learning has taken place to an identified standard. Think about your most recent test in the context of Figure 13-1. The test gave you a chance to appraise your performance.

1. What standards of performance did you set for yourself in the course?
2. Did the test results reflect your knowledge? Why or why not?
3. Look over the learning objectives (standards) listed in the text or presented by your professor. Did the test adequately cover the standards? Why or why not?
4. What corrective action might be indicated by the test results?

Skills Application 13-2: Zero-based Budgeting

In this chapter, we introduced the concept of zero-based budgeting. Using an Internet search engine, type in "benefits of zero-based budgets" to find sites that deal with this topic. After reviewing several sources of information (for example, www.accts.com/baseline.htm), answer the following questions:

1. Suppose you were creating your own personal budget for this year. Describe how your budgeting process would unfold if you were using zero-based budgeting as a model.

2. What are the primary advantages and disadvantages associated with zero-based budgeting?

3. From your research, what types of companies would most benefit from the use of zero-based budgeting? What organizational characteristics would make a company a good candidate for this approach?

Skills Application 13-3: Effective Controls and Cost-Cutting

During times of rapid change and increased competition, many Canadian companies have been faced with cost-cutting mandates. For example, in July 2003, pilots at Air Canada approved a new contract that would result in a 15 percent wage cut and a total savings of $250 million per year for the struggling airline (see www.cbc.ca/stories/2003/06/30/aircan_030630). Using an Internet search engine, perform a search using "cost cutting in Canadian companies" as your search term. Look for examples of Canadian companies that have undertaken significant cost-cutting exercises. Based on your research, answer the following questions:

1. What similarities in approach to cost cutting did you find among the examples you researched? What differences did you uncover in terms of how these companies went about cutting costs?

2. Cost-cutting measures usually have an impact on the employees in an organization, either through reduced job security, reduced hours, or pay cuts. How can an organization undertake cost-cutting measures and still retain the support of the employees who will be affected?

3. Write a short profile of one of the companies that you read about. Outline how the company went about cutting its costs. Compare your profile to that of another student. Which company appears to have undertaken this difficult exercise most successfully? Why?

CASES

CASE 13-1

Resistance to a Work-Sampling Program

Debbie Quarter, a new staff engineer for the C.W.S. Manufacturing Company, had been assigned the responsibility of administering the plant's work-sampling program. This was the first assignment of this nature in her career. Her only knowledge of the program until this time came in the form of comments from friends working as plant supervisors. She recalled that they referred to the work-sampling program as "bird-dogging." They seemed universally to regard the program as unfair, a waste of time, and a personal affront. Quarter sensed widespread resistance to the work sampling program at C.W.S. Even those people who supported the program referred to it as "a necessary evil."

Details of the Program

The work-sampling program, or ratio-delay as it was sometimes called, involved the statistical sampling of the activities of hourly production and maintenance department employees, which included approximately two-thirds of the plant's 2,000 employees. The sampling was conducted on a continuous basis by a full-time observer who walked through the plant via a series of randomly selected, predetermined routes. The observer's job was to record the activity of each worker as the worker was first observed. An activity could fall into one of seven categories, which in turn were subclasses of either "working," "travelling," or "nonworking." The data were compiled monthly, and results were charted for each group and sent to the various supervisors and superintendents.

The program had been in effect for about five years at the plant. At the time it was initiated, management stated the purpose of the program as threefold: (1) it was to be used as an indication of supervisory effectiveness; (2) it was to help identify problems interfering with work performance; and (3) it was to be a control measure of the effect of changes in work methods, equipment, facilities, or supervision.

Meetings on the Program

Realizing the widespread resistance to the program, Quarter began immediately to conduct informational meetings for all line supervisors. In these sessions she discussed the purpose of the program and the mechanics of conducting it. She also attempted to answer any questions raised. The supervisors were most vocal in expressing their negative opinions about the program, and after a few meetings she noted that certain comments were being repeated in some form by almost every group.

Most supervisory groups identified particular aspects of the sampling program that they thought biased its results against them. The most common complaint of this type was that the sampling was too often conducted during periods when work was normally lightest, that is, during coffee breaks and early or late in the day. Since the method of scheduling visits was quite complex, efforts to explain the concept of randomness and how fairness was ensured had never been accepted. Some basic statistical training had been attempted in the past but with little success—especially among the supervisors who had traditionally come up through the ranks and had little technical background.

Another frequently repeated complaint was that activities normally considered as "work" were not recorded as such. Examples of this were going for tools or carrying materials. The reason for this, as had been explained to the supervisors, was to allow identification of those factors not directly accomplishing work, since these were areas where improvements could be made.

Several maintenance supervisors complained that results were repeatedly used to encourage them to pressure their workers. When they would tighten down, they said, the workers would resist, and less was accomplished than before. One supervisor quoted his boss as saying, "These figures [work-sampling results] better be up next month, or I'm going to have three new supervisors in here!" It was general knowledge that the superintendents placed quite a bit of emphasis on these results when appraising the supervisors.

Virtually no one at any level of supervision had a good understanding of how results could be affected by sample size. Small groups with few samples said they had experienced wide fluctuations in results that "just couldn't happen." This, of course, reinforced their distrust of sampling methods.

There had been few, if any, changes initiated by first-line supervisors as a result of work sampling results. Several staff projects had been generated—some of which were quite popular with the workers (for example, motorized personnel carriers)—but these were not generally associated with work-sampling results.

After the first few sessions, Quarter wondered whether her meetings with the supervisors were perhaps doing more harm than good. The meetings seemed to get everyone upset, and anything that was learned was probably lost in the emotional discussion. She pondered what she should do next.

Questions for Discussion

1. Evaluate the work-sampling program in view of the principles of a sound control system as outlined in this chapter.
2. Outline a course of action for Quarter.

CASE 13-2

Frederick, Where Art Thou?

It was early morning on March 18 and the line was ready to run at Great Lakes Coating. Frederick Hall, however, was a "no-show." As the minutes ticked by and he waited for Hall to show, Emilio Kerba, Hall's supervisor, fumed. Per their agreement, Hall had taken the previous 10 days off from work. He was scheduled to return today but had not called. No one had heard from him. Kerba wanted to fire Hall immediately, but he knew he should do nothing rash. Had Hall had an accident? Was he sick? Why couldn't he get to a phone and call in? Kerba sighed, doubting anything drastic had happened, but he was unsure what the appropriate steps were in this sort of situation.

Hall had been a difficult employee. He had worked on the line at Great Lakes Coating for over six years and was, at best, a marginal employee. When Hall put some effort into his work, he was above average, but he had been known to be insubordinate and to ignore written instructions, and he was not particularly liked by his coworkers. He had been tardy a few times, and Kerba had recently given him a written warning.

Great Lakes Coating was a small manufacturing firm employing only 10 people. The firm used Lang Temp Services to provide seasonal and replacement personnel as needed. Andy Simmons, Great Lakes' owner, also served as director of sales. Karin Mitchell served as receptionist, bookkeeper, and office manager. Like many small firms, Great Lakes Coating had few policies governing employee behaviour.

In his third year with the firm, supervisor Kerba had responsibility for all production, maintenance, receiving, and shipping functions. Simmons had given Kerba the authority to hire and direct the production force as necessary. Kerba was particularly good at diagnosing and solving production problems. He was well liked and respected by all—except Hall—for his expertise. As Kerba pondered the situation with Hall, he thought of how the adage, "Twenty percent of your employees will cause you 80 percent of your problems" applied to him.

A few weeks before this incident, Hall had been stopped on a traffic violation. He was detained temporarily when a police check uncovered that he had two outstanding arrest warrants in another province. Kerba had arranged for Hall to take time off work to attend the court sessions for these legal problems. In return, Hall had agreed to work extra hours to make up for this time off, and he did.

During his court appearances, however, Hall was given a jail sentence. He had a choice: two months of weekend jail time with work release during the weekdays or 10 consecutive days of jail time. As Hall put it, he "liked his weekends off to party and relax," so he chose the 10 consecutive days of jail time.

Kerba agreed to give Hall time off with the condition that, when Hall returned to work, he would be on probation. Hall agreed to these terms. He was to serve his time from March 8 through March 17. During Hall's incarceration, Kerba contracted with Lang Temp Services to provide a temporary employee. When March 18 came and Hall did not show, Kerba called Hall's home phone but got no response. The day ended and Kerba had still not heard from Hall. March 19 arrived, but Hall did not. Kerba had to decide how to respond to Hall's apparent job abandonment.

Source: Case adapted with permission for use in this edition. "Frederick, Where Art Thou?" was prepared by Professor Claire McCarty Killian of the University of Wisconsin–River Falls. See the *Society for Case Research 2002 Proceedings* (www.sfcr.org), pp. 18–21.

Questions for Discussion

1. What are the pros and cons of Great Lakes Coating's lack of formal policies for employee behaviour?
2. What are the main issues Kerba must address?
3. What do you think Kerba should do about this matter?
4. What is your contingency plan in case your recommendation fails?

Chapter 14: Supervising a Diverse Workforce

After studying this chapter you will be able to

1 Recognize how effective diversity management can lead to better business results.

2 Identify demographic changes that are making the Canadian workforce more diverse.

3 Explain the issues involved in the supervision of a diverse workforce.

4 Discuss factors that are particularly important when supervising female employees.

5 Discuss considerations involved when supervising workers with disabilities, older workers, and employees with religious beliefs.

6 Explain the issue of reverse discrimination.

7 Discuss the overriding concern in supervision of all employees in a diverse workforce.

You are Charlie Willow, supervisor in a small printing plant. You have just had two interviews that left you confused. This morning one of your fairly new printing press assistants, Zenaida Nurdin, came into your office and accused her lead person, George Cholakis, of sexual and other forms of harassment. She claimed that Cholakis resented her as a woman on his otherwise male work crew, and that he continually criticized her for being unable to do her work in the way that he wanted it done. She claimed that Cholakis had told her that she was "too small and weak" to handle the job; further, Cholakis had used a number of obscene words when "yelling" at her to get the job done. Nurdin stated that either it had to stop or she would file harassment and discrimination charges against the company.

About an hour later, however, you interviewed Cholakis. His version was quite different. He denied ever having used any obscene words toward Nurdin. He acknowledged that he had not been satisfied with her work since she came to work at the firm several months ago. However, he said he had gone to great lengths to help her whenever he could. Cholakis did not think that Nurdin was able to handle the demands of the job, and he said that she had "a poor attitude." He denied ever having made any reference to her as being physically unable to do her work. Cholakis claimed that Nurdin was simply out to get him in order to save her own job.

You frankly don't know whom to believe. You believe that there may be some merit in the statements of both employees, but you don't know how to determine the truth. You know that your company has a strong policy prohibiting harassment, similar to the policy statement shown in Figure 14-2 in this chapter. You don't know how to apply the policy in this situation. What should you do?

You make the call!

| 1 | **BENEFITS OF EFFECTIVE DIVERSITY MANAGEMENT** |

Recognize how effective diversity management can lead to better business results.

In Chapter 1 we presented an overview of some of the principal demographic and societal trends that have an impact on organizations in general and on supervision in particular. As the Canadian population grows more diverse, so does the workforce. The most notable factors in the workforce are changes in the employment of women, older people, ethnic minorities, people with disabilities, and employees who are openly gay or lesbian.

The effective management of a diverse workforce can provide an organization with significant benefits. By embracing diversity, an organization is assured of maximizing the pool of talented workers from which it can draw. For example, a business that makes a proactive decision to ensure that all its facilities are wheelchair accessible not only becomes more attractive to a wider customer base, but also will benefit from attracting talented employees who may not otherwise have had the opportunity to work there.

Diversity management encompasses many considerations, including legal, demographic, economic, and political factors. The dimensions of diversity management touch virtually all aspects of a firm's operations, especially the supervisory level. Initiatives and efforts to better manage a diverse workforce are growing significantly, not just because of legal requirements or social considerations, but because there is a recognition that this has become an area of vital importance to a firm's long-term success and bottom-line results.[1]

2	**DEMOGRAPHIC CHANGE IN THE CANADIAN WORKFORCE**

Identify demographic changes that are making the Canadian workforce more diverse.

As discussed in Chapter 1, the Canadian workforce is changing. As the workforce becomes more diverse, supervisors will need to be particularly skilled in leading a heterogeneous group of people toward the achievement of organizational goals. While good supervisory practices are universal regardless of the makeup of the workforce, increased workforce diversity can sometimes make the supervisor's job more complex. In this section, we review some of the major demographic changes that are contributing to the increased diversity of the Canadian workforce.

Women

In 2001, women represented 47 percent of the total workforce, up dramatically from just 22 percent of the workforce in the early 1950s.[2] There are now over 7.4 million women in the workforce in Canada, in virtually all industries and occupations. Women are also widely represented at the managerial level of Canadian business. In 2001, Statistics Canada reported that women made up 35 percent of managers in Canadian organizations, up from only 17 percent in 1972.[3]

Belinda Stronach, CEO and president of Magna International, is one of Canada's powerful female executives.

CP Picture Archive

Some of the most influential Canadian executives are women, including Belinda Stronach, CEO and president of Magna International; Louise Wending, senior vice president and general manager of Costco Wholesale Canada; and Heather Reisman, CEO and chair of Indigo Books and Music.

Older Employees

The median age of the workforce continues to grow. In the 1980s, the median was approximately 31 years of age, while in 2001 the average age of the Canadian workforce was 39 years of age. As the baby boom generation continues to age, it is projected that the average age of the Canadian workforce will reach 41 by the year 2008.[4] The growth in the number of people in the mature age category will provide an ample supply of experienced individuals who are promotable to supervisory and other management positions and who may wish to remain in those positions beyond retirement age. It is also of note that workers, for various reasons, are now spending more years in the workforce.

Traditional retirement is not appealing to many of today's older workers. Effective January 1, 2005, Ontario employers will no longer be permitted to enforce mandatory retirement at age 65. According to Ontario's former Citizenship Minister, Carl DeFaria, mandatory retirement deprives the workforce of valuable employees. "It robs our economy of skilled workers. It denies seniors the opportunity of contributing to our economy."[5]

Ethnic Minorities

Until 1967, the vast majority of immigrants to Canada came from Europe or Great Britain. These immigrants had received a special status in comparison with applicants from the rest of the world. In 1967, Canada changed its immigration policy to one that awards points based on education, skills, ability to speak one of the official languages, and economic criteria. Now most immigrants arrive from developing countries. These new immigrants are dramatically changing the country's racial and cultural mix, especially in Canada's large urban centres where most immigrants choose to settle. It is estimated that, by 2005, Vancouver and Toronto will have a visible minority population in excess of 40 percent of their total population. For more details see Figures 1-5 and 1-6 in Chapter 1.

People with Disabilities

Changes in both technology and attitude have allowed more people with disabilities to fully participate in the workforce. Miniaturization, computer chips, voice recognition software, and rapidly decreasing costs for this type of equipment have all contributed to providing people with disabilities the means to communicate and work effectively in virtually all sectors of the Canadian economy.

Gay and Lesbian Workers

Historically, it has been difficult to estimate the number of gay or lesbian workers as many were not prepared to identify themselves due to the possibility of discrimination or harassment. Slowly, more gays and lesbians are choosing to be open about their sexual orientation, both in their personal and work lives. Human rights legislation and other practices are being challenged to include these groups, especially in the extension of benefits to same-sex couples.

Legislation on Diverse Workforces

Considering the previously noted factors, it is in the self-interest of any organization to embark on a proactive diverse staffing program. When staffing, supervisors must keep in mind some of the major federal and provincial laws that affect employment of all people in Canada.

Figure 14-1 presents highlights of Canadian legislation that influences various aspects of staffing with a diverse workforce, especially prohibited discriminatory practices. Since the requirements of employment discrimination laws can be quite complicated, supervisors normally should refer questions that are of a legal or compliance nature to the appropriate human resources staff person.

The OUCH Test in Supervision of All Employees

The OUCH test is a guideline for selecting employees (discussed in Chapter 5), but it also applies to day-to-day supervision. This test should remind supervisors to make their actions

O—*O*bjective.
U—*U*niform in application.
C—*C*onsistent in application.
H—*H*ave job relatedness.

For example, assume that an organization's policy specifies a disciplinary warning for being late three times in one month. The supervisor should give the same warning to *every* employee who is late the third time in one month, regardless of his or her sex, race, religion, etc. This supervisory approach would meet the OUCH test because tardiness is an observable behaviour that is objectively measured for all employees. The penalty is the same for all employees, is consistent, and is clearly job related.

A myth occasionally voiced by some people is that certain categories of employees cannot be disciplined or discharged because of their status. That view is false. Laws and regulations do not prevent a supervisor from taking disciplinary action against any employee. However, they do require that all employees be treated equally whenever disciplinary action is taken. Therefore, it is extremely important that supervisors be careful in meeting the OUCH test and in justifying their actions through adequate documentation. Good supervisory practices in this regard are universally applicable, regardless of the composition of the workforce.

| 3 | **SUPERVISING A DIVERSE WORKFORCE** |

Explain the issues involved in the supervision of a diverse workforce.

Canada has a long tradition of multiculturalism and upholding and celebrating the characteristics that make various groups unique. This fundamental value in Canadian society has, in general, resulted in relatively harmonious relationships as people from different backgrounds come together to participate in all aspects of daily life.

Canadian organizations have benefited from the wide range of expertise, education, and life experience that people from all walks of life bring to the workplace. For the most part, Canadian organizations reflect the diversity of the communities in which they do business. Leaders of progressive organizations

FIGURE 14-1 Major federal employment legislation.

The Canadian Charter of Rights and Freedoms: The Charter was passed as part of the Constitution Act, 1982. It applies to individuals dealing with the federal government, provincial governments, and agencies under their jurisdictions. The Charter provides the following fundamental rights to every Canadian: freedom of conscience and religion; freedom of thought, belief, opinion, and expression, including freedom of the press and other media of communication; freedom of peaceful assembly; and freedom of association. See http://laws.justice.gc.ca/en/charter for more information.

Canadian Human Rights Act: This legislation became effective in 1978. Intended to give individuals equal opportunities, the act prohibits discrimination on the grounds of race, national or ethnic origin, colour, religion, age, sex, marital status, conviction for an offence for which a pardon has been granted, or physical handicap. The act applies to all federal departments, agencies, Crown corporations, banks, railways, airlines, and businesses that operate in federal jurisdictions, such as insurance and communications companies. A guide to the Canadian Human Rights Act can be found under the "Publications" tab on the Canadian Human Rights Commission's website at www.chrc-ccdp.ca.

Canadian Federal Equal Pay for Equal Work Legislation: In 1951, the International Labour Organization (ILO) passed the Equal Remuneration Convention, 1951, which called for governments to ensure "the application to all workers of the principle of equal remuneration for men and women workers for work of equal value."[1] In practice, the application of equal pay for equal work began in Canada in the 1950s, but the Canadian government did not ratify the ILO convention until 1972.[2] Equal pay for equal work legislation prohibits paying different wages to men and women who perform the same or substantially similar work. The Canadian Human Rights Commission maintains links to various sites about pay equity legislation in Canada. Visit www.chrc-ccdp.ca/pe-ps for more information.

Employment Equity Act, 1986: This act was intended to remove discriminatory barriers to employment for four designated groups: women, visible minorities, people with disabilities, and Aboriginal peoples. Every employer with 100 or more employees, working under federal jurisdiction, must submit an annual report showing the statistics for each of the four designated groups. Federal contractors who bid on contracts worth more than $200,000 also have to pledge to carry out an employment equity program. For more information about employment equity legislation in Canada, visit Human Resources and Skills Development Canada's website at http://info.load-otea.hrdc-drhc.gc.ca/workplace_equity/home.shtml.

(**Note:** All the provinces and territories have their own human rights legislation. Some also have employment equity and pay equity legislation.)

Sources: (1) and (2) Government of Canada Pay Equity website at www.payequityreview.gc.ca/1100-e.html (retrieved March 24, 2004).

recognize that to exclude any individual or group on the basis of non-job-related factors is not only illegal, but also a bad business decision that can seriously hinder the organization's ability to attract and retain the best employees.

As the organization's first tier of management, supervisors are in the best position to ensure that all employees are treated fairly and with respect, regardless of their race, ethnic background, sex, age, sexual orientation, or other factors. The purpose of the following sections is to highlight some of the specific ways that supervisors can foster an environment in which all employees feel valued and respected.

Appreciating Cultural Differences

Rather than allowing cultural differences among employees to be a barrier, supervisors should find ways to ensure that the rich traditions and distinctive values of various ethnic groups are appreciated and respected in the organization. This is often achieved when the supervisor shows a genuine interest in learning about the cultural heritage of the people who work in the department. For example, a supervisor who takes the time to learn and use a few words in an employee's native language is showing respect for that person's cultural background. Similarly, a supervisor who finds a workable solution to accommodate an employee's request for a day off to observe a cultural celebration is demonstrating that the organization values the diversity of its workforce.

A supervisor should also be sensitive to the fact that some employees may require specific coaching or guidance in order to become familiar with organizational norms and expectations. For example, if an employee comes from a culture in which punctuality is not considered a necessity in the workplace, the supervisor should ensure that expectations about hours of work are made clear so that the employee is given the opportunity to meet those expectations. Regardless of any cultural differences that exist in the workforce, it is the supervisor's job to ensure that all employees fully understand the requirements of the work environment. A good supervisor will communicate clearly with all employees to ensure that everyone in the department has been given the opportunity to contribute fully to organizational goals.

Understanding Discrimination's Effects

Minority employees who have experienced prejudicial treatment may resent supervisors of different racial/ethnic backgrounds. Supervisors must be sensitive to the feelings of employees who may have experienced discriminatory treatment in the past or who believe that they are currently experiencing discrimination. Supervisors should not enter into debates with employees who display lingering resentment and suspicion. Rather, supervisors should always strive to be fair and considerate when making decisions that affect these employees. By demonstrating that all employees will be supervised fairly and with respect, a supervisor can reduce the negative effects of past discrimination. In the event that an employee's feelings of resentment interfere with job performance or department relations, the supervisor should refer the employee to the human resources department or to an EAP counsellor, when available.

Overcoming Language Difficulties

Another consideration in supervising minority employees relates to different languages that may be spoken in a work environment.

According to Statistics Canada, over 90 percent of the visible minority population reported that they could carry on a conversation in either French or English.[6] Nevertheless, a small number of employees may come to the workplace with limited fluency in Canada's official languages.

Some employers hold training programs to encourage supervisors and managers to better understand minority language patterns. For example, one large firm held a series of one-day training sessions for supervisors, managers, and professional staff to make them more knowledgeable about the cultural and language backgrounds of certain employees. The training program focused on language expressions and speech habits with which people from other backgrounds are generally unfamiliar.

Some employers sponsor courses in English improvement and business English for employees. These programs focus on the development of writing and speaking skills needed for job improvement and advancement.

At one time, some employers attempted to prevent employees from using their native languages at work. However, such restrictions today are viewed with skepticism unless interpersonal communication is a critical part of the job. For example, a manufacturing company's refusal to hire a worker who speaks no English on an assembly line might be ruled as prejudicial since, on this job, communication skills may be much less important than manual dexterity skills. However, for a nurse working in an emergency room, fluency in the language spoken by the majority of patients and other staff would be considered essential.

Fairness in All Supervisory Actions and Decisions

Supervisors should always endeavour to be scrupulously fair. In work assignments, training opportunities, performance appraisals, disciplinary actions—in virtually all supervisory actions and decisions—supervisors must make every effort to make decisions on objective and job-related grounds. If an employee complains of harassment or discriminatory treatment by the supervisor, a fellow employee, or some other person, the supervisor must treat that complaint as a priority concern. In most cases, the supervisor should listen carefully to the nature of the complaint and report it to a higher-level manager or the human resources department for further consideration and direction concerning what to do. In no way should a supervisor retaliate against the complainant, even if the supervisor believes that the discrimination or harassment allegation is without merit. The supervisor is responsible for ensuring that the human rights of all employees are genuinely protected. In summary, supervising any group of employees requires understanding, sensitivity, and scrupulous fairness.

| 4 | **SUPERVISING WOMEN** |

Discuss factors that are particularly important when supervising female employees.

Throughout the last several decades, both the number and the percentage of women in the labour force have increased dramatically. Among the reasons cited most often are changed values regarding personal fulfillment through work, wider career opportunities, higher educational levels, growth in single-parent and single-adult households, and economic pressures.

Both male and female supervisors should be aware of a number of important concerns that affect the supervision of women. While not all-inclusive, the areas to be discussed here represent a range of issues that supervisors should recognize and deal with appropriately.

Entry of Women into Many Career Fields

The increasing number of women in the workforce has led to the movement of women into many jobs that were traditionally dominated by men. Women are working in virtually all occupational sectors and emerging to lead some of the country's top business, educational, and community organizations.

While women may have faced historical barriers in some occupations, those challenges are virtually a thing of the past. At a 2004 conference for female managers and MBA students, "some of Canada's most successful businesswomen were direct, confident and refreshingly optimistic about the future prospects for women in management."[7] Ethel Taylor is group vice president of full-line stores at Sears Canada Inc., and was the first-ever female manager of a department store in Canada. Speaking at the 2004 conference, Taylor says that "corporate culture is 'changing by exposure' as more women and people from diverse cultural backgrounds move up the ranks and prove their mettle."[8] Mary Aitken, CEO and co-founder of Toronto-based Renaissance Securities Inc., asserts that "For the younger generations entering the work force, gender is almost a non-issue. [Younger workers are] very collegial. They look at each other and say 'let's get this job done'... I think we're looking at a really exciting landscape."[9]

Ensuring employment and advancement opportunities for all qualified workers, it appears, makes good business sense. A recent study of *Fortune* 500 companies in the United States revealed that "the group of companies with the highest representation of women in their senior management teams has a 35 per cent higher return on equity and a 34 per cent higher total return to shareholders than companies with the lowest women's representation.[10]

While historical barriers to employment and advancement have all but disappeared for women, this chapter's "You Make the Call" section illustrates that a supervisor may occasionally encounter an individual employee who may not welcome women into traditionally male-dominated fields. The supervisor plays a pivotal role in ensuring that all employees understand that everyone in the workplace must be treated equally and with respect. For example, if a woman is hired to work in a previously male-dominated environment, the supervisor must make it clear that no form of unfair treatment or harassment of any employee will be tolerated.

Female supervisors may occasionally encounter some resistance to their own leadership and may find lingering barriers to advancement based solely on their gender. Most successful female leaders advise women to seek out organizations with people and corporate cultures that will value their contribution. Beth Wilson, a chartered accountant and audit partner with KPMG, says that women need to move on if they find their route to advancement blocked. "If it's not working, move somewhere it will work."[11]

Issues of Sexual Harassment and Sexual Stereotyping

Sexual harassment
Unwelcome sexual advances, requests, or conduct when submission to such conduct is tied to the individual's continuing employment or advancement, unreasonably interferes with job performance, or creates a hostile work environment.

A growing number of human rights cases in Canada have dealt with problems of sexual harassment. We generally define **sexual harassment** as sexual advances, requests for sexual favours, and other verbal or physical conduct of a sexual nature when

- Submission to such conduct is made either explicitly or implicitly a condition of an individual's employment.
- Submission to or rejection of such conduct by an individual is used as the basis for employment decisions affecting that person.
- Such conduct has the purpose or effect of unreasonably interfering with an individual's work performance or creating an intimidating, hostile, or offensive working environment.

Harassment may also include verbal abuse or threats, unwelcome remarks or jokes, displaying pornographic or other offensive pictures, practical jokes that cause awkwardness or embarrassment, and leering or other gestures.

While the majority of cases dealing with sexual harassment in the courts have been brought forward by women who were subjected to inappropriate behaviours or comments in the workplace, it is important to note that the law protects both men and women. There have been cases in which women have been charged with sexual harassment of men, as well as cases in which both parties are of the same sex. The law protects all employees from inappropriate behaviour or comments.

Many firms have developed sexual harassment policy statements. Figure 14-2 is an example of such a statement by a printing company that defines the term *harassment* even beyond gender terms. The statement informs employees what to do if they encounter what they consider to be harassment.

Court decisions have generally held that an employer is liable if sexual harassment of employees is condoned, overlooked, or does not lead to corrective actions by management. Reprimand and discipline of offending employees and supervisors are recommended courses of action.[12] Supervisors should avoid and strongly discourage sexual language, innuendoes, and behaviour that is inappropriate in the work environment. Supervisors who use their positions improperly in this regard are engaging in conduct that is unacceptable and that could lead to their own dismissal.

Many firms have required their managers, supervisors, and employees to attend training programs or seminars designed to prevent and deal with sexual harassment. These programs typically are developed and presented by the human resources staff and/or by outside training consultants. Information and discussion focus on prohibited types of conduct, how employees can deal with offensive comments and behaviour, and remedies that are available.[13] Such programs also may cover certain aspects of sexual stereotyping that can be problematic.

Sexual stereotyping
Use of language or judgments that demean someone, usually by men toward women.

Sexual stereotyping means the use of language or judgments to demean someone, usually by men toward women. For example, a department store supervisor may find that women sales associates strongly resent being referred to as "the girls." Or a supervisor may imply that women are more emotional, less rational, or less reliable than men.

Many traditionally held assertions comparing female employees with male employees are inaccurate. Thus, the supervisor should not make supervisory decisions based on sexual stereotypes.

FIGURE 14-2   No-harassment policy statement of a printing company.

NO-HARASSMENT POLICY

This company does not and will not tolerate harassment of our employees. The term "harassment" includes, but is not limited to, slurs; jokes; and other verbal, graphic, or physical conduct relating to an individual's race, colour, sex, religion, national origin, citizenship, age, or disability. "Harassment" also includes sexual advances; requests for sexual favours; unwelcome or offensive touching; and other verbal, graphic, or physical conduct of a sexual nature.

VIOLATION OF THIS POLICY WILL SUBJECT AN EMPLOYEE TO DISCIPLINARY ACTION, UP TO AND INCLUDING IMMEDIATE DISCHARGE.

If you feel that you are being harassed in any way by another employee or by a customer or vendor, you should make your feelings known to your supervisor immediately. The matter will be thoroughly investigated and, where appropriate, disciplinary action will be taken. If you do not feel that you can discuss the matter with your supervisor or if you are not satisfied with the way your complaint has been handled, please contact either the human resources director or the company president. Your complaint will be kept as confidential as possible, and you will not be penalized in any way for reporting such conduct. Please do not assume that the company is aware of your problem. It is your responsibility to bring your complaints and concerns to our attention so that we can help resolve them.

Training and Development Opportunities

Female employees should be offered equal access to available training and development opportunities. This is especially important with regard to promoting women to supervisory and other managerial positions. A number of research studies have found that women often benefit from special training and development activities that focus on enhancing their self-esteem, communication skills, and career development. For women who already are managers and supervisors, many firms provide programs that include such topics as personal awareness, assertiveness training, managerial barriers to success, time management, delegation, and specific problems encountered by women in managerial positions.

Despite the entry of women into supervisory and lower-level management positions, upward mobility for women in organizations is still quite slow. In 2003, women held only 14 percent of corporate officer positions in Canada. While this is up from 12 percent in 1999, the movement toward parity in Canada's executive ranks is a slow process.[14] As mentioned in Chapter 1, the barrier to upward progression of women and minorities has been called the *glass ceiling*. Firms that make serious efforts to shatter the glass ceiling and bring more women and minorities into higher levels of management usually do so because their top management has a strong commitment to make this happen. Promotion of women and minorities is part of these firms' diversity management initiatives within their strategic business plans and a wise business choice to ensure that they are getting the best employees from the widest possible range.[15]

Many firms find that a well-conceived and implemented mentoring program is essential. Mentoring efforts usually involve having senior-level managers—both male and female—serve as mentors or advisors for employees who have been identified as having potential for higher management positions. Mentors provide assistance in various ways including feedback on job performance, career counselling, and networking with other mentors, advisees, and others to make them better known to people who can be influential in promotion and career decisions.[16]

Equity in Compensation

Statistically, the pay received by women employees in Canada generally has been below that of men. In 1996, women's compensation was 64.8 percent of that for men while in 2002, female employees earned 82 cents for every dollar earned by men. While some progress is being made, women are continuing to struggle for fair pay for the work they do in Canadian organizations.

Equal pay for equal work has been part of the Canada Labour Code since 1971, as well as part of many of the provinces' Employment Standards acts. It requires the employer to pay men and women the same wage or salary when they do the same work. Thus, male and female electricians in the same company must be paid the same rate if they are performing the same work. Exceptions are allowed when a valid seniority or merit pay system exists. Merit systems provide for higher rates when the worker performs better than others. Other exceptions include commission pay systems, commonly used for salespeople.

In 1978 the Canadian Human Rights Act made it illegal to discriminate on the basis of similar job content or similar value. This results in a different approach to equal pay for equal work. A job is generally measured by the skills, effort, responsibility, and working conditions. In effect, jobs with the same "job value" are to be paid the same rate or salary. This is frequently referred to as **pay equity.** Thus, if a groundskeeper and a call-centre employee have the same job value, they are to be paid the same rate or salary. Some differences are allowed, considering factors such as seniority, performance ratings, rehabilitation assignments, training positions, or phase-in wage increases or reductions. These factors justify differences, but it is implied that the job evaluation is still carried out in an equitable fashion.

Pay equity
Concept that jobs should be paid at the same level if they require similar skills, effort, responsibility, and working conditions.

---

5 | SUPERVISING WORKERS WITH DISABILITIES

Discuss considerations involved when supervising workers with disabilities, older workers, and employees with religious beliefs.

When hiring, organizations should focus on finding the very best candidate for the job. In order to do this, it is important that all potential candidates, including those with various disabilities, are considered and given fair opportunities. In 2001, Statistics Canada reported the number of working-age Canadians with disabilities at more than 1.9 million or 9.9 percent of Canada's population. However, only a small fraction of that total is actually employed in the workforce.[17] Many organizations are recognizing that people with disabilities represent a valuable pool of qualified candidates, and are taking steps to ensure that workers with disabilities are given fair access to employment opportunities (see the accompanying Contemporary Issue box on page 414). In addition, various levels of government have established agencies and online resources to ensure that workers with disabilities can obtain information and support when entering the job market. (For example, see the Canadian Council on Rehabilitation and Work website at www.ccrw.org.)

The Canadian Human Rights Act stipulates that employers have a duty to accommodate workers with disabilities. The act states that employers must take appropriate steps to eliminate discrimination resulting from a rule, practice, or barrier that has an adverse impact on individuals with disabilities. The law requires that employers must make **reasonable accommodation** and take whatever steps are required to accommodate employees, potential employees, or clients, short of undue hardship.[18]

The term *undue hardship* is purposely vague, in recognition of the fact that smaller organizations with fewer resources should not be held to the same requirements as large organizations with vast financial resources. For example, it may not be financially viable for a small company to install an expensive lift or elevator to accommodate a candidate with a mobility issue. A large corporation, however, would very likely be required to make this accommodation, since the expense would not place undue hardship on the organization. While some accommodation requirements can be expensive, studies indicate that the vast majority of workers can be accommodated with expenditures of $500 or less.[19]

Good supervisory practices are universal, and apply to workers with or without disabilities. In some instances, however, a supervisor may need to be flexible and creative in order to ensure that workers with disabilities are given fair opportunities in the workplace. For example, some workers might benefit from flexible work arrangements that allow some home-based work. Similarly, small technological adaptations might vastly improve a worker's comfort and productivity on the job. Once reasonable accommodations have been made, however, the supervisor should apply the same supervisory practices that are used with other workers. Figure 14-3 provides some answers to common questions about the hiring and supervision of workers with disabilities. Figure 14-4 (page 413) provides some basic points of etiquette that can help ensure that all people with disabilities are treated with respect.

Reasonable accommodation
Altering the usual ways of doing things so that a qualified person with a disability can perform the essential job duties, but without creating an undue hardship for the employer.

FIGURE 14-3   Frequently asked questions about employing workers with disabilities.

The Canadian Human Rights Commission has compiled answers to frequently asked questions that employers may have about employing workers with disabilities.

Q: Isn't there a high cost to integrating people with disabilities into my office?

A: No. The cost of accommodation is reasonably modest. Employers can accommodate most adaptation needs for $500 or less. These costs are even more reasonable when you consider them amortized over the entire duration of the employee's stay in your organization. The cost of adapting a workstation to the needs of a person with a disability can sometimes be high, but not prohibitively high—accommodation is just one part of the continuum of meeting the needs of your employees.

Q: My existing staff are already extremely busy; do I have sufficient resources to train people with disabilities?

A: Some flexibility and creativity is required in integrating people with disabilities into the workplace; however, it's a misconception that extra job-related training is

(continued)

FIGURE 14-3 *(continued)*

always required for people with disabilities. Introducing a new and qualified colleague to a busy staff will be helpful and a morale-booster.

Q: I'm not opposed to the idea of hiring people with disabilities, but what kind of work can they do and not do?

A: Like other employees, people with disabilities bring education, expertise, and experiences to your workplace; providing an accommodation ensures that you and your organization benefit from that experience and expertise. Advertise your job openings in the disability community—you may be surprised how many qualified people you'll find.

Q: What are the potential consequences if I fail to accommodate people with disabilities in my workplace?

A: Employees or potential employees who feel that an employer has not met the duty to accommodate may make a claim to the applicable provincial or federal human rights tribunal or commission. The case will be heard and if it is found that the employer has discriminated against the employee and not met the duty to accommodate, awards of compensation for lost wages and emotional hardship may be made.

Q: What if I have provided accommodation for an employee, and the situation is still not working out?

A: Employment accommodation is not always a one-time provision; individuals' needs can change over the course of their employment, as can the job itself. If an employee approaches you to tell you that he or she cannot perform well enough without further accommodation, this may be entirely legitimate. However, if an employee arrives continually late for work, this is a management issue, and not an accommodation requirement of flexible work hours. It is important to ensure that all employees understand what performance level is expected of them, and what workplace ethics are a part of your corporate culture. Accommodation is a means of enhancing an individual's abilities, and of ensuring that workplace performance standards are met, not compromised.

Q: How do I introduce a new employee with a disability, and how do I prepare my staff for his or her arrival?

A: When someone with a disability joins your staff, you introduce him or her exactly the same way you would introduce anyone else. An individual's disability should not define him or her any more than sex, race, or any other personal characteristic. Drawing attention to a new employee's disability should be avoided, since it focuses on an aspect of that employee that—if properly accommodated—is irrelevant to his or her function in the workplace.

Source: Adapted from *Barrier-Free Employers—Practical Guide for Employment Accommodation for People with Disabilities,* Canadian Human Rights Commission at www.chrc-ccdp.ca/ee/bfe-eso.asp?l=e#faq (retrieved January 3, 2004).

FIGURE 14-4   Points of Etiquette to Ensure That People with Disabilities Are Treated with Respect.

BASIC POINTS OF ETIQUETTE

1. Avoid asking personal questions about someone's disability. If you must ask, be sensitive and show respect. Do not probe if the person declines to discuss it.
2. Be considerate of the extra time it might take for a person with a disability to do or say something.
3. Be polite and patient when offering assistance, and wait until your offer is accepted. Listen or ask for specific instructions.
4. When planning a meeting or other event, try to anticipate specific accommodations a person with a disability might need. If a barrier cannot be avoided, let the person know ahead of time

WHEN SPEAKING OR WRITING ABOUT A DISABILITY

1. Refer to a person's disability only when necessary and appropriate.
2. Refer to the individual first, then to his or her disability. (It is better to say "the person with a disability" rather than "the disabled person."
3. Avoid terms that may disempower people or have negative meanings (e.g., "invalid," "able-bodied," "wheelchair-bound," "victim," "handicap")
4. Avoid terms that imply that people with disabilities are overly courageous, brave, or special.

WHEN MEETING AND TALKING WITH A PERSON WHO HAS A DISABILITY

1. A handshake is not a standard greeting for everyone. When in doubt, ask the person whether he or she would like to shake hands with you. A smile along with a spoken greeting is always appropriate.
2. Speak directly to the person with a disability, not just to the person accompanying him or her.
3. Don't mention the person's disability, unless he or she talks about it or it is relevant to the conversation.
4. Treat adults as adults. Don't patronize or talk down to people with disabilities.
5. Be patient and give your undivided attention, especially when someone speaks slowly or with great effort.
6. Never pretend to understand what a person is saying. Ask the person to repeat or rephrase, or offer him or her a pen and paper.
7. Relax. Anyone can make mistakes. Offer an apology if you forget some courtesy. Keep a sense of humour and a willingness to communicate.

Source: From disABLEDperson Inc. at www.disabledperson.com/articles/etiquette.asp (retrieved March 24, 2004).

CONTEMPORARY ISSUE
A Successful Hiring Program Provides Food for Thought

The right partnership can benefit everyone involved. And for Loblaws Supermarkets Limited, that fact has been proven over and over again in the past 10 years.

During that time, Loblaws stores in Ontario have worked with local Community Living Associations to successfully train and hire more than 100 people with intellectual disabilities. The Work Experience Program is based on the belief that, under the right circumstances, all people are capable of some form of meaningful work. This has been a "win-win" recruitment partnership program, with Loblaws, its employees, and the community all benefiting. Al Barnett, senior manager of Industrial Relations for Loblaws, says, "There is a mistaken belief that people with disabilities who are not in the labour force are either unable or unwilling to work. People with disabilities face a number of barriers that make it difficult for them to participate in the labour force … Many of these barriers, while challenging, are not insurmountable."

The Process

Community Living Employment Services staff begin the process by assessing potential candidates to determine their fit. Any candidate with appropriate skills completes an eight-week training program paid for by Community Living. During that time, the trainee is placed in a Loblaws store to receive instruction by staff on such skills as grocery bagging, price checks, and housekeeping. If the training period is successful, the trainee becomes a unionized, part-time employee. The union supported the creation of this special job classification, and a special clause was written into the collective agreement to support the Work Experience Program. The employee is initially supported by a Community Living job coach who gradually decreases his or her involvement until the employee no longer needs the support. "We work with business owners and employees to make sure that the employment opportunity is a success. We don't set people up for failure; employers expect the same from our clients as any other employee," says

Dave Jenkins, employment consultant and vocational counsellor with Toronto's Association for Community Living.

Employer and Employee Benefits

The Work Experience Program offers Loblaws, its employees, and its customers many benefits:

- The Work Experience employees fill a newly created "Front-End Clerk" position, which allows Loblaws to provide customers with extra services at the front end of the store.
- Loblaws is provided with prescreened applicants and on-the-job training of employees at no cost.
- Customers see Loblaws as a company willing to give people job opportunities, not only behind the scenes but also dealing with customers on a one-to-one basis.
- The program provides a great opportunity for Loblaws stores to become involved with their local communities.
- Loblaws has benefited from enhanced staff morale and the hiring of dedicated, long-term employees.
- Employees with intellectual disabilities have the opportunity to demonstrate their skills and abilities, build their self-esteem, become more independent, and therefore improve their quality of life.

An Award-Winning Employer

Loblaws has been awarded the Canadian Association for Community Living Employment Award, in recognition of its contribution to the employment of Canadians with intellectual difficulties. Yvonne Rensen of the Community Living Association in London, Ontario, says that "Loblaws is an exemplary employer. It recognized the barriers that separate companies and disability organizations from each other. The Work Experience Program has resulted in a direct link between local Loblaws stores, local service providers, and people with intellectual disabilities."

Source: Ontario Ministry of Citizenship at www.equalopportunity.on.ca/eng_g/subject/index.asp?action=search-7&file_id=5351 (retrieved May 13, 2004).

Loblaws Supermarkets Limited has been recognized for its contribution to the employment of Canadians with intellectual disabilities.

Ryan Remiorz/CP

SUPERVISING OLDER WORKERS

The Canadian Human Rights Act and corresponding provincial acts state that every person has a right to freedom from discrimination on the grounds of age. In the area of employment, "age" has historically meant from 18 to 65 years, thereby allowing employers to enforce mandatory retirement at age 65. In the last few years, however, most of the provinces have introduced legislation that will end the ability of employers to implement and rely on mandatory retirement policies. In general, the legislation redefines the term "age" in the employment context to mean 18 years of age and over, with no upper limit.

A supervisor's decisions in the areas of hiring, promotion, and discharge must be made on the basis of job-related factors. A person's age is almost never considered a job-related factor and should therefore not enter into decisions the supervisor makes. For example, a supervisor who must choose between a 35-year-old job candidate and a 55-year-old candidate must evaluate the skills and abilities of each person objectively and hire the best person for the job, regardless of his or her age. If any part of the hiring decision is based upon age, the supervisor may be not only overlooking a potentially valuable candidate, but also placing the organization at risk for an age-discrimination lawsuit.

While studies indicate that older workers exhibit lower turnover, more dedication to the workplace, and have more positive work values than younger workers, there will certainly be times when a supervisor must discipline or even discharge an older worker.[20] However, the decision to discipline or terminate any worker must be firmly based upon job performance factors and must be documented with objective performance appraisals. All employees, regardless of their age, must know the standards that are expected of them, and must receive regular feedback about their performance. A person's age must not enter into the evaluation process or any decisions with respect to discipline or termination.

In some cases, the performance of a worker may change as he or she ages. Some studies note that older workers may work more slowly and may not make quick decisions as easily as their younger counterparts.[21] However, this change is balanced by the fact that older workers tend to be more accurate in their work and make more correct decisions than faster, younger co-workers. The supervisor must be careful to look at all aspects of an employee's performance, not just speed of work or other isolated factors.

In terms of health and safety on the job, studies point to some differences among older and younger workers. Older workers tend to have fewer accidents than younger employees, but when older workers do get injured, their injuries are often more severe and require longer recovery times. Younger workers tend to get more eye or hand injuries, while older workers who have been working for many years report more back injuries and repetitive-strain problems.[22]

Adaptations to working conditions for different workers may be needed to meet the needs of any employee, not just one who is older. The supervisor should ensure that workstations and job tasks are matched to the needs of the individual worker as much as possible. For example, a modification to a piece of equipment that allows an older employee to work more efficiently and safely would probably be a modification that all people who do the job would benefit from, regardless of their age.

Older employees who are contemplating retirement present another issue that requires sensitivity on the part of supervisors. Some employees who have worked for 30 years or more look forward to retirement as a time to enjoy a greater variety of leisure activities. However, others may view retirement with anxiety, even when they are voluntarily choosing to retire. They may worry about the prospect of losing an established daily routine and valued social relationships that they have developed in the workplace.

Supervisors should be supportive and understanding as older employees near retirement. These employees should be encouraged to take advantage of preretirement planning activities that may be available in the company or through outside agencies. Some companies allow employees contemplating retirement to attend retirement-related workshops during working hours without loss of pay. Members of the human resources department or a benefits specialist may spend considerable time with each employee nearing retirement to discuss pensions, insurance, and other financial matters. Supervisors should also encourage recent retirees to attend company social functions and to maintain contact with their former supervisors and co-workers wherever possible. Such contacts are valuable aids in making the transition to retirement more comfortable.

ACCOMMODATION FOR RELIGIOUS VIEWS

Under the Human Rights acts, most employers are required to afford nondiscriminatory treatment to employees who hold religious views. Although court decisions have not always clearly defined religious discrimination, the principle has evolved that employers must make reasonable accommodation for employees who have religious beliefs. Employers generally may not discriminate in employment practices because of an individual's religious beliefs, and they are obligated to prevent practices or actions that might constitute a "hostile environment" for someone because of his or her religion.[23]

Relatively speaking, charges of religious discrimination in Canada have been limited. Reasonable accommodation in holiday and other work scheduling has been the most recurring area where employers have had some problems of compliance. For example, Orthodox Jews hold religious observance on Saturday. Requiring such employees to work on Saturday would be the same as requiring employees who are members of some Christian sects to work on Sundays. A supervisor might be able to accommodate the religious views of such employees by scheduling their workweeks to take into account their religious beliefs. Allowing Jewish employees to take holidays on Rosh Hashana and Yom Kippur instead of Christmas and Easter is another example of accommodation, as is recognition of Ramadan for Muslims.

Supervisors may be confronted with situations in which it is difficult to accommodate all employees' religious preferences and still schedule the work. If this happens, a supervisor would be well advised to discuss the problem with his or her manager and with the human resources staff to determine whether scheduling alternatives are available that might accommodate the employees and yet not be too costly or disruptive for the organization as a whole.

6	UNDERSTANDING REVERSE DISCRIMINATION

Explain the issue of reverse discrimination.

Reverse discrimination
Preference given to minority group members in hiring or promotion over other more qualified or more experienced workers.

The use of employment equity plans by organizations may sometimes lead to charges of **reverse discrimination**. Normally, these charges arise when an employer hires or promotes a member of a minority group over an individual who is better qualified but not a member of a minority group. While the courts have ruled that employment equity programs that attempt to correct past discrimination may be allowed even if they result in reverse discrimination, these programs often raise questions of fairness.

Employment equity programs most often negatively affect white male employees. Some white males feel that they do not have an equal or fair opportunity to compete for promotions or higher-paying jobs. They consider and interpret the existence of numerical goals in these programs as "quotas" that have to be met by hiring and promoting unqualified or less qualified minorities.

Supervisors of integrated racial groups and male and female employees may be apprehensive about their situations. For example, supervisors may become reluctant to discipline anyone so as to avoid charges of favouritism or discrimination. Another difficulty is that conflicts and distrust among these various groups may arise that place stress on interpersonal relationships and may affect the performance of the department. Such problems are not easily overcome. However, communication between the supervisor and all groups of employees is absolutely essential, and the supervisor should try to correct misperceptions about any employee's abilities and qualifications as they occur. Most important is the supervisor's response to the feelings of all groups and individuals in an understanding, fair, and objective manner.

7   GOOD SUPERVISION: THE OVERRIDING CONSIDERATION

Discuss the overriding concern in supervision of all employees in a diverse workforce.

The purpose of this chapter was to familiarize practising and potential supervisors with some of the particular issues associated with the management of a diverse workforce. However, supervisors should always recognize that the best way to manage *all* employees in their departments is to consistently apply the principles of good supervision as presented throughout this book. Regardless of gender, ethnic background, disability, age, or any other personal characteristic, every employee should be treated equally, fairly, and with respect by everyone in the organization. Figure 14-5 provides some additional suggestions for the positive and professional handling of diversity issues.

We stated at the outset of this chapter that management of a diverse workforce is a reality that affects most aspects of organizational operations and has an impact on a firm's bottom line.[24] Because of its importance, specialized training programs in diversity management are expanding.[25] But, in our view, supervision of diversity should not be viewed as something extra or separate. Supervision of diversity is and will continue to be an integral and significant component of good supervision generally, which effective supervisors recognize as part of their ongoing responsibilities.

FIGURE 14-5   Suggestions for managing diversity.

- Ensure that the organization's policy statement on discrimination and harassment is posted in a prominent, visible place in the department or elsewhere.
- Periodically review this policy statement with employees, including procedures to be followed if an employee wishes to report a perceived violation or to lodge a complaint. Assure employees that any such complaint will initially be handled confidentially.
- Discuss diversity issues at department meetings with employees. Provide examples of behaviours that are unacceptable and that will not be tolerated, as well as the consequences of violations.
- Whenever an employee alleges discrimination or harassment, investigate the matter thoroughly and identify the appropriate course of action.
- If a matter cannot be resolved at the supervisory level, expeditiously report the case to the director of human resources or other such person who is designated to handle discrimination complaints at the company or corporate level.
- Do not in any way react negatively or adversely to an employee who has filed a discrimination or harassment charge.
- Always supervise on a scrupulously fair and objective basis and with equitable performance standards. Try to find ways by which all employees have the same or comparable opportunities at work assignments and training and development programs.

WHAT CALL DID YOU MAKE?

As supervisor Charlie Willow, you have just experienced a classic "she said, he said" situation where truth is difficult to ascertain. First, interview other employees in the department to see whether or not any of them will back up either Zenaida Nurdin's allegations or George Cholakis's denials. In these types of cases, often no one else in the department will have seen or heard anything or other employees do not want to get involved, so they refuse to say anything. If you are unable to get any further information that would support either version, you should immediately report the case to the human resources department or the manager who is responsible for handling issues of sexual harassment or discrimination. Since this situation may have serious legal implications, further handling of the case probably should be left to those individuals.

However, as supervisor, you should again talk to Cholakis and warn him to be very careful in what he says and does in relation to Nurdin. Tell him that you will be watching very closely to ensure that Nurdin is being treated fairly, and that no type of harassment of her will be tolerated. You also should talk to Nurdin to tell her what you have done, and to reinforce the fact that her performance is being appraised based on her ability to meet the requirements of the job. Ensure that she understands the performance standards of her job and that she receives regular performance appraisals just like every other employee. Assure her that if she needs any help, she should not hesitate to discuss her situation with you. Finally, you should be sure that your future actions are consistent and fair toward all employees.

SUMMARY

1 The diverse nature of the Canadian workforce requires that supervisors be prepared to manage many different people in the workforce to the firm's overall advantage and bottom-line results. Diversity management can impact on virtually all aspects of a firm's operations and should be viewed by supervisors as both a challenge and an opportunity.

2 Statistics reveal that the Canadian workforce is changing. More women, older workers, ethnic minorities, people with disabilities, and openly gay or lesbian workers are now part of the workforce than ever before.

3 When supervising minority employees, supervisors should be aware of cultural factors and recognize language differences. Both are important aspects of a supervisor's sensitivities toward minority employees. Being scrupulously fair in all aspects of supervision and striving to prevent any type of discriminatory treatment toward minorities are essential.

4 Supervisors must ensure that women are provided fair opportunities as they move into a greater variety of career fields and positions. Avoidance of sexual harassment and stereotyping is mandatory. Human resources policies should stress training and development opportunities for women, nondiscriminatory treatment, and equity in compensation.

5 The Canadian Human Rights Act and the corresponding provincial acts require that employers make accommodations for people with disabilities. Employees, prospective employees, and customers should not be adversely affected by rules, procedures, or barriers. Employers have a responsibility to accommodate workers with disabilities to the point of undue hardship—a standard that will vary depending upon the resources of the individual employer.

When making decisions concerning older employees, supervisors should appraise older workers' qualifications and performance objectively. Supervisors should try to adjust to any reduced abilities of older workers if possible and find ways to tap into the older worker's vast experience. Also, supervisors should assist employees who are nearing retirement to prepare for it.

The principle of reasonable accommodation also should be followed when supervising employees of different religious beliefs. Reasonable adjustments in work scheduling should be afforded individuals who have specific religious requirements.

6 Supervisors should be sensitive to the feelings of some employees—most often white males—about the issue of reverse discrimination. Employees may accuse the company of reverse discrimination if a person from a designated or minority group is hired or promoted over a more experienced or more qualified employee.

7 The best way to manage will always be to apply the principles of good supervision to *all* employees.

QUESTIONS FOR DISCUSSION

1. Why has management of a diverse workforce become both a reality and business necessity for many firms? Some people view diversity management primarily as being "politically correct." Do you agree or disagree with this type of assessment?
2. What are some of the major considerations that supervisors of minority employees should keep in mind?
3. What is meant by sexual harassment and sexual stereotyping? Give an example of sexual harassment and describe what a supervisor should do to deal with it.
4. Assume that a supervisor has a 60-year-old administrative assistant whose performance has slipped recently. What considerations should affect the supervisor's actions toward this employee?
5. How does the concept of reasonable accommodation apply to employees with religious beliefs? Are there limits to reasonable accommodation? Discuss.
6. Suppose an employer advertises a job opening for a purchasing clerk. The most qualified applicant is in a wheelchair, but the purchasing department is in an area of the building that is not wheelchair accessible. Would the employer be required to hire this candidate? Explain.

SKILLS APPLICATIONS

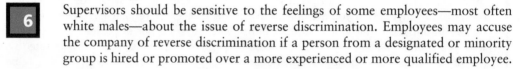

Skills Application 14-1: A Review of Decisions by Provincial Human Rights Commissions
Go to the University of Ottawa's Virtual Human Rights Research Library at www .uottawa.ca/hrrec/links/sitescan_e.html. Under the title "Human Rights Jurisprudence" on the site's main page, click the link to recent decisions that have been made by human rights tribunals in the province of your choice.

1. Click the link to the most recent year's case summaries. Scan the recent decisions that have been made by the human rights commission in the province you selected.
2. Select one recent case that interests you and write a brief summary of the issue and the decision that was made. Be sure to carefully summarize the reasoning behind the decision.

3. Team up with three other students who have chosen other cases and share your summaries. Compare the issues and decisions that were made. What are the points of similarity and difference among the cases?
4. What benefit would a supervisor realize by regularly reviewing the decisions being made by the human rights commission in his or her province?

Skills Application 14-2: Sexual Harassment Policies

Sexual harassment can take many forms. While some types of sexual harassment are quite obvious, others are more subtle and not as obviously identified. As a supervisor, it is important that you become familiar with the wide range of behaviours that can be considered sexual harassment so that you can take appropriate action if these behaviours occur in the workplace.

1. Using a popular Internet search engine (www.google.ca for example), perform a search for "sexual harassment policy." Use the "Canadian search" option in order to return examples of sexual harassment policies from a wide variety of Canadian organizations.
2. Review the sexual harassment policies from three Canadian organizations, preferably from different sectors of the economy.
3. Create a list of behaviours that are defined as being examples of sexual harassment.
4. Other than the policy itself, what other measures have these Canadian organizations instituted to deal with sexual harassment in the workplace?

Skills Application 14-3: Guide to Workplace Accommodation

The Government of Canada maintains a website called the "Workplace Accommodation Toolkit" that summarizes the various products available to accommodate workers with disabilities.

1. Go to www.apt.gc.ca. Select the icon labelled "Products for people with disabilities" and view the product categories that are available to assist workers with disabilities.
2. From the list, identify and describe five products that you were previously unaware of that can be used to accommodate various categories of disability.
3. Would every employer be required to purchase the products that you have identified if they could assist a particular employee? Explain.

CASES

CASE 14-1

Unwanted Attention from the Supervisor

Beth Conners was a recent electrical engineering graduate of a major university. She went to work for the Wilcox Engineering Company, and was assigned to work on projects designing electrical systems for automated and computerized equipment. Conners enjoyed her work and developed a rapport with other engineers in the firm.

The department supervisor was Terry Wells. Wells had been with the firm for six years, and he had been a supervisor for two years. He was 30 years old; like Beth, he was single.

Conners had been with the firm about four months when Wells called her into his office to review her progress. He told her that she was doing a great job, and that he was very pleased with her work performance. He discussed a few suggestions that he felt would further her development technically. When he was finished, he looked at his watch and said, "Wow, it's already lunchtime. Would you like to join me?" Hesitating at first, Conners agreed to have lunch with him at a local restaurant. Wells paid the bill for both of them.

Early the next morning, Conners was working on a computer-aided drawing system, when Wells came into her office to chat. He made a lot of small talk, and then he asked her whether she again would accompany him for lunch. A little uncomfortable, Conners again agreed. She thought that this second luncheon offer was unusual, but she passed it off, thinking that maybe she was being overly sensitive.

However, Conners grew very concerned during the next several weeks when the invitations for lunch continued. Furthermore, on several occasions Wells asked her out on dates for which she made up excuses to decline. Conners felt that she couldn't refuse the luncheon invitations since Wells was her supervisor. But she didn't want to have any kind of off-the-job relationship with her supervisor, even though she did enjoy working in his department.

The situation became very stressful when several of her colleagues told her at a coffee break that some members of the department felt she was getting special treatment from their supervisor. One engineer even asked, "Are you and Terry seeing each other?"

Conners became even more distressed when one day Wells came into her office and made the following remark: "Beth, I don't know why you won't let me take you out some evening. I know we hit it off well at lunch, and I know we both are attracted to each other." Conners told Wells that she would think it over and let him know later.

She realized that the situation was getting out of hand, and that she had to do something. She knew the company had a policy on sexual harassment, but she didn't know whether this situation applied. She was concerned that if she reported this matter in confidence to the human resources director or to someone in higher-level management, it might jeopardize her position in the company. She pondered what she should do.

Questions for Discussion

1. Is this a situation of sexual harassment? Why or why not?
2. Should Conners refuse any further luncheon invitations from her supervisor? Discuss.
3. What options are open to Conners? What would you recommend that she do?

CASE 14-2

Overtime Denied to the Older Painter

Local No. 134 of the Maintenance Workers' Union represented carpenters, painters, mechanics, and other workers employed by the Board of Education of the Rolling Hills District School Board. The school board operated 20 school facilities located in the suburbs of a large city.

A meeting was held at a school district office to hear a grievance filed by the union on behalf of Bernie Custolo, a painter. Present at the hearing besides Custolo were the union shop steward, Arnie Meredith; Terry Wu, supervisor of the maintenance department; and Sergiy Berecz, director of human resources for the district. Custolo's written grievance alleged a violation of two provisions of the collective bargaining agreement between the union and the Board of Education. These provisions were as follows:

ARTICLE II—DISCRIMINATION

Section 2.1 There shall be no discrimination, coercion, or intimidation of any kind against any employee of the board for any reason whatsoever, including marital status, sex, race, religious belief, age, disability, sexual orientation, or union activity, by the board or by the union.

ARTICLE V—HOURS OF WORK

Section 5.8 All overtime shall be distributed equally in so far as this is possible on an annual basis among eligible employees in the school district.

Six months ago, Bernie Custolo had celebrated his 65th birthday. He considered retiring at that time, but decided to avail himself of the new legislation in his province that eliminated mandatory retirement. While he was happy to still be working, Custolo claimed that he had been denied overtime for the last six months since turning 65. Other painters had been assigned overtime work as needed, but Custolo was told by his supervisor that he would not be assigned any overtime in the future. Custolo's specific grievance related to a Saturday work situation when two younger painters were assigned to work an entire day on an overtime basis. This was despite the fact that Custolo had worked far less overtime hours prior to this situation than had the two younger painters, both of whom had fewer years of service with the school board than Custolo. Custolo claimed that this was discrimination based solely on his age, and it was a violation of the parties' bargaining agreement that required overtime to be divided equally among employees.

However, Terry Wu, Custolo's supervisor, said that Bernie Custolo simply was not able to work as efficiently as his coworkers. Wu claimed that Custolo was slower and made more mistakes than any other painter in his crew, and this problem had become more serious during the last several years. Wu said that allowing Custolo to work overtime would be a burden to the school board since it was under great pressure to hold costs down. Taxpayers should not be required to pay time-and-a-half premium pay to workers who were not efficient. Wu said that Custolo no longer had the energy to work an eight-hour work shift as he frequently became fatigued during the day. During the previous several years, Custolo usually refused overtime that had been offered to him, claiming that he was "burnt out." Wu stated that it was unfair to other workers to be expected to "carry" Custolo even though Custolo had more seniority. Wu further claimed that Custolo often had talked about retirement when he turned 65, but apparently Custolo had changed his mind and now wanted to continue to work indefinitely. As to the specific Saturday in question, Wu stated that the two painters he assigned were the best and most efficient he had for the project. The project could not have been completed on Saturday if Custolo had been permitted to work overtime on that day.

After about a half hour of discussion, Sergiy Berecz, director of human resources, stated: "Let's adjourn the meeting. I need to discuss the case with the Director of Education. We will have a reply to the grievance tomorrow by 10 A.M." Arnie Meredith, the union shop steward, responded: "Okay, Sergiy. We feel that your answer should go our way, or we are likely to take this case all the way to arbitration. I might add that Bernie also is thinking about filing age discrimination charges with the Human Rights Commission, so you better keep that in mind when you make your decision."

Questions for Discussion

1. Was the school board obligated to assign Bernie Custolo to overtime work on an equal basis with other employees if Custolo in fact was much slower and made more mistakes in his work performance? Why or why not?
2. Could Bernie Custolo file an age discrimination complaint to the Human Rights Commission in his province in addition to filing a union grievance? Why or why not?
3. What should be the school board's response to the union grievance?
4. Discuss what the school board should do in order to prevent future complaints of age discrimination.

PARTIAL LISTING OF FEDERAL EMPLOYMENT LEGISLATION THAT AFFECTS SUPERVISORS

Canadian Charter of Rights and Freedoms

It provides essential rights and protection to every Canadian in the following areas:

1. Fundamental freedoms such as opinion, belief, religion, expression, association, etc.
2. Democratic, legal, and equality rights for all individuals.
3. The right to live and seek employment anywhere in Canada and adhere to recognized languages of Canada.
4. Canada's multicultural heritage.
5. Minority language and education rights along with Aboriginal peoples' rights.

For more information about the Charter, visit http://laws.justice.gc.ca/en/charter/.

Public Service Employment Act

Under this act, candidates from the public service employment competition can request an investigation if they believe their qualifications were not properly reviewed during the application process. For more information, visit http://laws.justice.gc.ca/en/P-33/.

Canadian Human Rights Act

It is an equal employment law that applies to government departments and agencies, Crown corporations, and businesses and industries under federal jurisdiction such as banks, airlines, and railway companies. The act prohibits discrimination on the grounds of race, national or ethnic origin, colour, religion, age, sex, marital status, mental or physical handicap, conviction of an offence for which pardon has been granted, and harassment. For more information about the act, visit http://laws.justice.gc.ca/en/H-6/.

Canada Labour Code

The code identifies the rights of employees under federal jurisdiction to organize trade unions and bargain collectively with employers. It also includes health and safety issues in the workplace, as well as minimum wage stipulations for organizations under federal jurisdiction (provinces have their own minimum wage acts). For more information, visit http://laws.justice.gc.ca/en/L-2/.

Employment Equity Act

The Employment Equity Act requires employers under federal jurisdiction with 100 employees or more to establish plans for the employment of designated groups, those being women, Aboriginal people, people with disabilities, and visible minorities. For more information, visit http://laws.justice.gc.ca/en/E-5.401/.

The Parliamentary Employment and Staff Relations Act

The act provides assistance in collective bargaining between the federal government as the employer and various unions representing federal workers. For more information, visit http://laws.justice.gc.ca/en/P-1.3/.

Canadian Centre for Occupational Health and Safety Act

This act established a public corporation by the Parliament of Canada to administer such tasks as promoting health and safety in Canadian workplaces, establishing and maintaining high standards of occupational health and safety, and harmonizing federal, provincial, and territorial jurisdictions. For more information, visit http://laws.justice.gc.ca/en/C-13/.

Fair Wages and Hours of Labour Act

This act applies to all contracts made with the government of Canada. It requires that all contractors pay reasonable wages and set forth eight-hour workdays. For more information, visit http://laws.justice.gc.ca/en/L-4/56393.html.

Canada Pension Plan and Quebec Pension Plan (CPP and QPP)

It relates to all self-employed persons and employees in Canada. In both plans, both employer and employee contribute. The plans' rights do not vary with cost-of-living changes. Each plan pays retirement, disability, and pension for surviving spouses.

Employment Insurance Act

Employment insurance is a program designed to monetarily assist individuals changing from one job to another. Most salaried and hourly workers (excluding self-employed) employed for at least 15 hours a week are covered by employment insurance. For more information, see http://laws.justice.gc.ca/en/E-5.6/.

Workers Compensation Acts

The federal government and all of the provinces and territories have an act or regulations that entitle workers to compensation for workplace injuries.

Old Age Security (OAS) and Guaranteed Income Supplement (GIS)

These are supplementary pension payments available from the federal government. Unlike CPP, both pensions are given under restricted circumstances, one case being where an individual's income was too low to receive CPP or QPP.

Pay Equity Acts

All employees with the same job content will be eligible for the same pay rate or range with some limited exceptions such as seniority. A number of provinces and the federal government have pay equity acts.

Hazardous Products Act

The major objective of this act is protection for all consumers by regulating the sale of hazardous goods. For more information, see http://laws.justice.gc.ca/en/H-3/.

Workplace Hazardous Material Information System (WHMIS)

WHMIS requires suppliers to label all dangerous material and provide a Material Safety Data Sheet (MSDS) on all of these products. For more information, visit www.hc-sc.gc.ca/hecs-sesc/whmis/.

Transportation of Dangerous Goods Act

The act allows Transport Canada (a federal government agency) to regulate the hazardous material of federally controlled shipping companies. It requires that all carriers be informed of such material and that they be coded according to a standardized system. For more information, visit http://laws.justice.gc.ca/en/T-19.01/.

Personal Information Protection and Electronic Documents Act

This act sets out ground rules for how private sector organizations may collect, use, or disclose personal information in the course of commercial activities. The law gives individuals the right to see and ask for corrections to information an organization may have collected about them. The act applies to personal information about customers or employees that is collected, used, or disclosed by organizations subject to the act. For more information, visit www.privcom.gc.ca/legislation/02_06_01_e.asp.

G Glossary

A

Ability An employee's potential to perform assigned tasks.

Accountability The obligation one has to one's boss. Also, the expectation that employees will accept credit or blame for the results achieved in performing assigned tasks.

Arbitration board Three-person board with a company nominee, union nominee, and a mutually agreed-upon chairperson to render a final and binding decision concerning a grievance.

Arbitrator Person selected by the union and management to render a final and binding decision concerning a grievance.

Attitude survey Survey of employee opinions about major aspects of organizational life used to assess morale.

Authority The legitimate right to direct and lead others.

Autocratic (authoritarian) supervision The supervisory style that relies on formal authority, threats, pressure, and close control.

B

Baby-boomers A large wave of the population born between 1946 and 1963.

Behaviourally based interview questions Questions that ask a job applicant to describe his or her performance in a past situation.

Benchmarking The process of identifying and improving on the practices of the leaders.

Biological needs The basic physical needs, such as food, rest, shelter, and recreation.

Body language All observable actions of either the sender or the receiver.

Brainstorming A free flow of ideas within a group, while suspending judgment, aimed at developing many alternative solutions to a problem.

Budget A plan that expresses anticipated results in numerical—usually financial—terms for a stated period of time.

C

Closed shop A labour agreement provision that specifies that only people who are already union members will be eligible for employment.

Coaching The frequent activity of the supervisor to provide employees with information, instruction, and suggestions relating to their job assignments and performance.

Collaborative workplace Work environment characterized by joint decision making, shared accountability and authority, and high trust levels between employees and managers.

Command group Grouping of employees according to authority relationships on the formal organization chart.

Communication The process of transmitting information and understanding.

Competitive advantage The ability to outperform competitors by increasing efficiency, quality, creativity, and responsiveness to customers and effectively utilizing employee talents.

Concurrent control Corrective action taken during the production or delivery process to ensure that standards are being met.

Contingency-style leadership Approach to leadership based on the belief that no single leadership style is best; the appropriate style depends on a multitude of factors.

Contingent worker A part-time, temporary, or contract employee supplied on an "as needed" basis by an external agency for a specified period of time and for a fee.

Controlling Ensuring that actual performance is in line with intended performance and taking corrective action if necessary.

Corporate culture Set of shared purposes, values, and beliefs that employees hold about their organization.

Critical incident method Supervisors record specific examples of outstanding and below-average performance on the part of each employee.

Critical path The chain of activities in the PERT network that will take the longest time to complete.

D

Decision criteria Standards or measures to use in evaluating alternatives.

Decision making Defining problems and choosing a course of action from among alternatives.

Decision-making process A systematic, step-by-step process to aid in choosing the "best" alternative.

Delegation The process of entrusting duties and related authority to subordinates.

Department An organizational unit for which a supervisor has responsibility and authority.

Departmentation The process of grouping activities and people into distinct organizational units.

Directive interview Interview approach in which the interviewer guides the discussion along a predetermined course.

Discipline State of orderliness; the degree to which employees act according to expected standards of behaviour.

Discipline without punishment Disciplinary approach that uses coaching and counselling as preliminary steps and a paid decision-making leave for employees to decide whether to improve and stay, or quit.

Diversity Differences in culture, ethnic background, gender, age, educational level, race, and life-style characteristics among employees.

Division of work (specialization) Dividing work into smaller components and specialized tasks to improve efficiency and output.

Documentation Keeping records of memoranda, documents, and meetings that are relevant to a disciplinary action.

Downsizing (restructuring, right-sizing) Large-scale reduction and elimination of jobs in a company that usually results in reduction of middle-level managers, removal of organizational levels, and a widened span of management for remaining supervisors.

E

Employee assistance program (EAP) Company program to assist employees with certain personal or work-related problems that are interfering with job performance.

Empowerment Giving employees the authority and responsibility to accomplish organizational objectives.

Enabler The person who does the things necessary to enable employees to get the job done.

Ethical "tests" Considerations or guidelines to be addressed in developing and evaluating ethical aspects of decision alternatives.

Exception principle Concept that supervisors should concentrate their investigations on activities that deviate substantially from the standard.

Exit interview Interview with individuals who leave a firm to assess morale and reasons for employee turnover.

Expectancy theory Theory of motivation that holds that employees perform better if they believe such efforts will lead to desired rewards.

External stressors Causes of stress that arise from outside the individual, such as job pressures, responsibilities, and work itself.

Extinction Good behaviour occurs less frequently or disappears because it is not recognized.

F

Feedback The receiver's verbal or nonverbal response to a message.

Feedback control Action taken after the activity, product, or service has been completed to prevent future problems.

Feedforward control Anticipatory action taken to ensure that problems do not occur.

Filtering The process of omitting or softening unpleasant details.

Flextime Policy that allows employees to choose their work hours within stated limits.

Friendship group Informal grouping of employees based on similar personalities and social interests.

Functional authority The right granted to specialized staff people to give directives concerning matters within their expertise.

G

Gain-sharing plans Group incentive plans that have employees share in the benefits from improved performance.

Gantt chart A graphic scheduling technique that shows the activity to be scheduled on the vertical axis and necessary completion dates on the horizontal axis.

General supervision The style of supervision in which the supervisor sets goals and limits but allows employees to decide how to achieve goals.

Glass ceiling Invisible barrier that limits advancement of women and minorities.

Glass walls Invisible barriers that compartmentalize or segregate women and minorities into certain occupational classes.

Grapevine The informal, unofficial communication channel.

Grievance A formal complaint presented by the union to management that alleges a violation of the labour agreement.

H

Halo effect The tendency to allow one favourable aspect of a person's behaviour to positively influence judgment on all other aspects.

Hawthorne Studies Comprehensive research studies that focused on work-group dynamics as related to employee attitudes and productivity.

Hierarchy of needs Maslow's theory of motivation, which suggests that individuals' needs are arranged in priority order such that lower-order needs must be satisfied before higher-order needs become motivating.

Horizontal corporation A very flat firm resulting from restructuring by customer process.

Horns effect The tendency to allow one negative aspect of a person's behaviour to negatively influence judgment on all other aspects.

Hot-stove rule Guideline for applying discipline analogous to touching a hot stove: advance warning and consequences that are immediate, consistent and applied with impersonality.

Human resources (HR) department Department that provides advice and service to other departments on human resource matters.

Human resources management (HRM) Organizational philosophies, policies, and practices that strive for the effective use of employees.

Hygiene factors Elements in the work environment that, if positive, reduce dissatisfaction but do not tend to motivate.

I

Incremental budgeting A technique for projecting revenues and expenses based on history.

Informal organization Informal gatherings of people, apart from the formal organizational structure, that satisfy members' social and other needs.

Innovative duties Creative activities aimed at finding a better way to do something.

Intangible standards Standards for performance results that are difficult to measure and often relate to human characteristics (e.g., attitude, morale, satisfaction).

Internal stressors Pressures that people put on themselves, such as feeling a need to be outstanding in everything.

ISO 9000 A rigorous series of manufacturing quality standards created by the International Organization for Standardization.

J

Jargon Words that are peculiar to an occupation or a specialty.

Job description Written description of the principal duties and responsibilities of a job.

Job enlargement Increasing the number of tasks an individual performs.

Job enrichment Job design strategy that helps fulfill employees' higher-level needs by giving them more challenging tasks and more decision-making responsibility for their jobs.

Job redesign The process of changing the structure of a job in order to improve employee motivation.

Job rotation The process of switching job tasks among employees in the work group.

Job sharing Policy that allows two or more employees to perform a job normally done by one full-time employee.

Job specification Written description of the personal qualifications needed to perform a job adequately.

Just cause Standard for disciplinary action requiring tests of fairness and elements of normal due process, such as proper notification, investigation, sufficient evidence, and a penalty commensurate with the nature of the infraction.

L

Labour agreement (union contract) Negotiated document between union and employer that covers terms and conditions of employment for the represented employees.

Labour agreement negotiations (collective bargaining) The process of discussion and compromise among representatives from labour and management leading to an agreement governing wages, hours, and working conditions for union employees.

Labour union (labour organization) Legally recognized organization that represents employees and negotiates and administers a labour agreement with an employer.

Law of effect Theory that behaviour with favourable consequences is repeated; behaviour with unfavourable consequences tends to disappear.

Lead person Employee placed in charge of other employees who performs limited managerial functions but is not considered to be part of management.

Leadership The ability to guide and influence the opinions, attitudes, and behaviour of others.

Leading The managerial function of guiding employees toward accomplishing organizational objectives.

Leniency error Supervisors giving employees higher ratings than they deserve.

Line and staff organizational structure Structure that combines line and staff departments.

Line authority (scalar authority) The right to direct others and to require them to conform to decisions, policies, rules, and objectives.

Line department Department whose responsibilities are directly related to making, selling, or distributing the company's product or service.

Line organizational structure A structure that consists entirely of line authority arrangements with a direct chain of authority relationships.

M

Management Getting objectives accomplished with and through people.

Management by objectives (MBO) A process by which the supervisor and employee jointly set the employee's objectives and the employee receives rewards upon achieving those objectives.

Matrix (project management) organizational structure A hybrid structure in which regular functional departments co-exist with project teams comprising people from different departments.

Mentoring The guiding of a newer employee by an experienced employee in areas concerning job and career.

Merit The quality of an employee's job performance.

Mission statement A statement of the organization's basic philosophy, purpose, and reason for being.

Morale A composite of feelings and attitudes that individuals and groups have toward their work, environment, supervisors, top-level management, and organization.

Motion study An analysis of work activities to determine how to make the job easier and quicker to do.

Motivation A willingness to exert effort toward achieving a goal, stimulated by the effort's ability to fulfill an individual need.

Motivation factors Elements intrinsic in the job that promote job performance.

Motivation-hygiene theory Herzberg's theory that factors in the work environment influence only the degree of job dissatisfaction, while intrinsic job-content factors influence the amount of job satisfaction.

N

Negative reinforcement Making behaviour occur more frequently by removing an undesirable consequence.

Noise Obstacles that distort messages between people.

Nominal group technique (NGT) A group brainstorming and decision-making process by which individual members first identify alternative solutions privately and then share, evaluate, and decide on them as a group.

Nondirective interview Interview approach in which the interviewer asks open-ended questions that allow the applicant greater latitude in responding.

Nonprogrammed decisions Solutions to unique problems that require judgment, intuition, and creativity.

O

Ombudsman Staff person who serves as a neutral mediator in resolving conflicts on the job.

Operational plans Short-range plans developed by supervisors to cover specific activities and areas of accountability.

Optimizing Selecting the "best" alternative.

Organization Group structured by management to carry out designated functions and accomplish certain objectives.

Organization chart Graphic portrayal of a company's authority and responsibility relationships.

Organization manual Written description of the authority and responsibilities of managerial and supervisory positions, as well as formal channels, major objectives, and policies and procedures.

Organizational development (OD) Meetings with groups under the guidance of a neutral conference leader to solve problems that are hindering organizational effectiveness.

Organizing Arranging and distributing work among members of the work group to accomplish the organization's goals.

Orientation The process of smoothing the transition of new employees into the organization.

P

Participative management Supervisory approach that gives employees an active role in making decisions about their jobs.

Pay equity Concept that jobs should be paid at the same level if they require similar skills, effort, responsibility, and working conditions.

Pay for performance Compensation, other than base wages, that is given for achieving employee or corporate goals.

Peer evaluation The evaluation of an employee's performance by other employees of relatively equal rank.

Performance appraisal A systematic assessment of how well employees are performing their jobs, and the communication of that assessment to them.

Performance standards The job-related requirements by which an employee's performance is evaluated.

Personality The knowledge, attitudes, and attributes that combine to make up the unique human being.

PERT A flowchart for managing large programs and projects showing the necessary activities with estimates of the time needed to complete each activity and the sequential relationship among them.

PERT activity A specific task to be accomplished.

PERT event The beginning and/or ending of an activity.

Piecework System in which the employee earns a certain amount of pay for each piece produced.

Planning Determining what should be done.

Policy A standing plan that serves as a guide to making decisions.

Positive discipline Condition that exists when employees generally follow the rules and meet the standards of the organization.

Positive reinforcement Making a behaviour occur more often because it is linked to a positive consequence.

Positive self-discipline Employees regulating their own behaviour out of self-interest and their normal desire to meet reasonable standards.

Principle of compulsory staff advice (service) Situation in which supervisors are required by policy to consult with specialized staff before making certain types of decisions.

Principle of organizational stability Principle that holds that no organization should become overly dependent upon one or several "indispensable" individuals.

Procedure A standing plan that defines the sequence of activities to be performed to achieve objectives.

Program A major single-use plan for a large undertaking related to accomplishing the organization's goals and objectives.

Programmed decisions Solutions to repetitive and routine problems provided by existing policies, procedures, rules, and so on.

Progressive discipline System of disciplinary action that increases the severity of the penalty with each offence.

Project A single-use plan for accomplishing a specific nonrecurring activity.

Punishment Making behaviour occur less frequently because it is linked to an undesirable consequence.

R

Realistic job preview (RJP) Information given by an interviewer to a job applicant that provides an honest view of both the positive and the negative aspects of the job.

Realistic organizational preview (ROP) Sharing of information by an interviewer with a job applicant concerning the mission, values, and future direction of the organization.

Reasonable accommodation Altering the usual ways of doing things so that a qualified person with a disability can perform the essential job duties, but without creating an undue hardship for the employer.

Re-engineering Concept of restructuring a firm on the basis of processes and customer needs and services, rather than by departments and functions.

Regular duties The essential components of a supervisor's job, such as giving directives and checking performance.

Responsibility The obligation to perform certain tasks and duties as assigned by the supervisor.

Reverse discrimination Preference given to minority group members in hiring or promotion over other more qualified or more experienced workers.

Right to appeal Procedures by which an employee may request high-level management to review a supervisor's disciplinary action.

Routine duties Minor tasks, done daily, that make a minor contribution to achievement of objectives.

Rule A directive that must be applied and enforced wherever applicable.

S

Sampling The technique of evaluating some number of items from a larger group to determine whether the group meets acceptable quality standards.

Satisficing Selecting the alternative that minimally meets the decision criteria.

Scheduling The process of developing a detailed list of activities, their sequence, and the required resources.

Security needs Desire for protection against danger and life's uncertainties.

Selection The process of choosing the best applicants to fill open positions.

Selection criteria Factors used to choose among applicants who apply for a job.

Self-directed (self-managed) work teams (SDWTs) Employee groups who are given wide latitude and considerable authority to make many of their own job-related decisions.

Self-fulfillment needs Desire to use one's abilities to the fullest extent.

Self-respect needs Desire for recognition, achievement, status, and a sense of accomplishment.

Semantics The multiple meanings of words.

Seniority An employee's length of service within a department or organization.

Sexual harassment Unwelcome sexual advances, requests, or conduct when submission to such conduct is tied to the individual's continuing employment or advancement, unreasonably interferes with job performance, or creates a hostile work environment.

Sexual stereotyping Use of language or judgments that demean someone, usually by men toward women.

Shop steward Employee elected or appointed to represent employees at the departmental level, particularly in grievance processing.

Single-use plans Plans developed to accomplish a specific objective or to cover only a designated time period.

Situational interview questions Questions that ask a job applicant to describe what the applicant thinks he or she might do in a given hypothetical situation.

SKAs Skills, knowledge, and abilities that a person has.

Skill-based pay System that rewards employees for acquiring new skills or knowledge.

Social needs Desire for love, affection, and affiliation with something worthwhile.

Span of management principle Principle that there is an upper limit to the number of subordinates a supervisor can manage effectively.

Special duties Tasks not directly related to the core tasks of the department, such as meetings and committee work.

Special-interest group Grouping of employees that exists to accomplish something in a group that individuals do not choose to pursue individually.

Staff authority The right to provide counsel, advice, support, and service in a person's areas of expertise.

Staff department Specialized department responsible for supporting line departments and providing specialized advice and services.

Staffing The tasks of recruiting, selecting, orienting, training, appraising, promoting, and compensating employees.

Standards Units of measurement or specific criteria against which to evaluate results.

Standing plans Policies, procedures, and rules that can be applied to recurring situations.

Status Attitudes toward a person based on the position he or she occupies.

Stereotyping The perception that all people in a certain group share common attitudes, values, and beliefs.

Strategic control points Performance criteria chosen for assessment because they are key indicators of overall performance.

Strategic planning The process of establishing goals and making decisions that will enable an organization to achieve its long- and short-term objectives.

Strategic plans Long-term plans developed by top management.

Stress A person's nonspecific bodily reactions to demands and conditions that he or she encounters.

Stretch targets Targeted job objectives that present a challenge but are achievable.

Supervisor First-level manager in charge of entry-level and other departmental employees.

T

Tactical plans Annual or intermediate-range plans developed by middle managers and staff specialists.

Tangible standards Standards for performance results that are identifiable and measurable.

Task group or cross-functional team Grouping of employees who come together to accomplish a particular task.

Teamwork People working cooperatively to solve problems and achieve goals important to the group.

Telecommuting Working at home with links to the office via computer and modem.

Theory X Assumption that employees dislike work, avoid responsibility, and must be coerced to do the job.

Theory Y Assumption that employees enjoy work, seek responsibility, and are capable of self-direction.

360-degree evaluation Performance appraisal based on data collected from all around the employee, from customers, vendors, supervisors, peers, subordinates, and so on.

Time study A technique for analyzing jobs to determine the standard time needed to complete them.

Total quality management (TQM) An organizational approach involving all employees in the effort to satisfy customers by continual improvement of goods and services.

Two-tier wage system Paying new employees at a lower rate than more senior employees.

U

Underemployment Situation in which people are in jobs that do not utilize their skills, knowledge, and abilities (SKAs).

Union business representative Paid official of the local or national union who may be involved in grievance processing.

Union density The percentage of the total labour force that is represented by a union.

Union security clause The part of the collective agreement (contract) that describes whether employees must belong to the union in order to maintain their employment.

Union shop A labour agreement provision in which employees are required to join the union as a condition of employment, usually after 30 days.

Unity of command principle Principle that each employee should report to only one immediate supervisor.

V

Virtual corporation Companies linked temporarily to take advantage of marketplace opportunities.

Virtual team Geographically separated people who are working on a common project and are linked by communication technologies.

W

Wellness program Organized efforts by a firm to help employees to get and stay healthy in order to remain productive.

Workplace spirituality Organizational efforts to make the work environment more meaningful and creative by relating work to employees' personal values and spiritual beliefs.

Z

Zero-based budgeting The process of assessing, on a benefit and cost basis, all activities to justify their existence.

E Endnotes

Chapter 1

1. "You Win Some ... You Lose Some," *Canadian Business* (July 7, 2003), p. 42; "Can Buffeted Air Canada Rebound as a National Carrier?" *Maclean's* (April 14, 2003), p. 13; Laura King, "Air Canada to Cut More Jobs," *The Daily Deal* (April 23, 2003); Dave Knibb, "Air Canada Takes Action to Counter Business Slump," *Airline Business* (September 1, 2001), p. 20; Luke McCann, "Silicon Valley North chills," *Toronto Star* (September 16, 2003), p. C4.

2. Timothy D. Schellhardt, "Off the Ladder: Want to Be a Manager? Many People Say No, Calling Job Miserable," *The Wall Street Journal* (April 4, 1997), p. A1.

3. The statistics and projections included in this and other sections are drawn from various Canadian Government Publications: Statistics Canada, *Labour Force, Employed and Unemployed, Numbers and Rates by Sex, Canada and the Provinces, Annual Averages, 2001*, website: www.statcan.ca/english/pgdb/people/labour/labour07a.htm (retrieval date n.a.); Statistics Canada, *Perspectives*; various daily releases of Statistics Canada on the following website: www.statcan.ca/daily/english/960416/d960416.htm#art/ (retrieval date n.a.); *News and World Report*, p. 6 and p. 17.

4. Morley Gunderson, "Are You for or against Mandatory Retirement?" *HR Professional* (August/September 2003), p. 38.

5. Ann Ironside in an interview with Gillian Shaw, "Young people must change expectations of work, expert says," *The Vancouver Sun* (September 12, 1995), p. B4.

6. Neil Howe and William Strauss, *Millennials Rising: The Next Generation* (New York: Vintage Books, 2000), p. 45.

7. From the Families and Work Institute as reported by Alison Ashton, "When It's Work vs. Family, Work Usually Wins," *Working Mother* (December 2001/January 2002), p. 10.

8. Vanessa Lu, "Skilled newcomers get work," *Toronto Star* (September 10, 2003), p. B1.

9. Ibid., p. B1.

10. Dana Flavelle, "Glass ceiling more visible in U.S.," *Toronto Star* (January 31, 2002), p. C1.

11. Ibid., p. C11.

12. "Women at Work: Executive Summary—A Special Report on the Status and Satisfaction of Working Women and Initiatives for Their Advancement," conducted by Fortune Marketing Research for Deloitte & Touche LLP (1995). A complete copy of the report is available by contacting Deloitte & Touche LLP.

13. Don Clark, "Managing the Mountain: For Many People, Information Is Proving to Be More of a Burden than a Resource," *The Wall Street Journal* (June 21, 1999), p. R4.

14. Rebecca Blumenstein and Gabriella Stern, "Man of Many Parts: How a Tough Boss Managed to Salvage a Messy Unit at GM," *The Wall Street Journal* (June 3, 1996), pp. A1 and A8.

15. See Merrill Goozner, "Longtime Temporary Employees Are Rebelling," reprint of article in *St. Louis Post-Dispatch* that originally was published in the *Chicago Tribune* (July 1, 1999), p. C7. Also see Aaron Bernstein, "A Leg up for the Lowly Temp," *Business Week*, (June 21, 1999), pp. 102–3.

16. Adapted from *Hewlett-Packard Statement of Corporate Objectives and Annual Reports*. Also see "Hewlett-Packard: Where Slower Growth Is Smarter Management," *Business Week* (July 9, 1975), pp. 50–58. The statement was first put in writing in 1957, has been modified occasionally since then, and has been a significant part of the "HP Way."

17. Ibid.

18. See Christine M. Pearson, Lynn M. Andersson, and Christine L. Porath, "Assessing and Attacking Workplace Incivility," *Organizational Dynamics*, 29, 2 (2000), pp. 123–37; Jenny McCune, "Civility Counts," *Management Review* (March 2000), pp. 6–8; and Michael A. Verespej, "A Call for Civility," *Industry Week* (February 12, 2001), p. 17.

19. Robert M. Bramson, *Coping with Difficult People* (New York: Dell Publishing Company, 1989).

20. A 1994 survey indicated that 75 percent of employers had incorporated some means of employee involvement to empower employees. For another twist on the employee involvement issue, see Mary E. Pivec and Howard Z. Robbins, "Employee Involvement Remains Controversial," *HR Magazine* (November 1996), pp. 145–50.

21. Following on the works of others, Hendrie Weisinger identified four building blocks that help one to develop skills and abilities. They are to (1) accurately perceive, appraise, and express emotion; (2) access the ability or generate feelings on demand when they can facilitate understanding of yourself or another person; (3) understand emotions and the knowledge that derives from them; (4) regulate emotions to promote emotional and intellectual growth. See Weisinger, *Emotional Intelligence at Work* (San Francisco: Jossey-Bass, 1998). Also see John D. Mayer and Peter Salovey, "Emotional Intelligence and the Construction of Regulation and Feelings," *Applied and Preventive Psychology* (4, 1995), pp. 197–208; Mayer, Salovey and Caruso, *Emotional IQ Test: CD-ROM Version* (Needham: MA: Virtual Entertainment, 1997); and Steve Bates, "Your Emotional Skills Can Make or Break You," *Nation's Business* (April 1999), p. 17.

22. For additional information on Pandolfini's principles for making the right decision under pressure, see "All the Right Moves," *Fast Company* (May 1999), p. 34.

23. The Hagberg Consulting Group survey results as reported in Albert R. Karr, "Work Week: A Special New Report About Life on the Job—and Trends Taking Shape There," *The Wall Street Journal* (November 26, 1996), p. A1.

24. Eldrick (Tiger) Woods became the first person to hold all four major golf championships at the same time. For information on his career and his tips for improvement, see www.tigerwoods.com.

25. As reported in Ann Harrington, "Make That Switch," *Fortune* (February 4, 2002), p. 162.

Chapter 2

1. See Peter F. Drucker, *Management: Tasks, Responsibilities, and Practices* (New York: Harper & Row, 1974), p. 611. Also see Drucker, *The Practice of Management* (New York: Harper Brothers, 1954), pp. 62–65, 126–29; Drucker, "Plan Now for the Future," *Modern Office Technology* (March 1993), pp. 8–9, and Peter F. Drucker as quoted in the article by Mike Johnson, "Drucker Speaks His Mind," *Management Review* (October 1995), pp. 11–14.

2. Numerous books and articles discuss strategic management. For example, see Jeffrey S. Harrison and Caron St. John, *Foundations in Strategic Management*, 2nd ed. (Cincinnati: South-Western/Thomson Learning, 2002); Lester A. Digman, *Strategic Management: Concepts, Processes, Decisions*, 5th ed. (Houston: Dame Publications, Inc. 1999); Terrence Fernsler, "Strategic Planning in 150 Pages or Less," *Nonprofit World* (November/December 1998), p. 51; Timothy C. Hoerr, "Strategic Planning: The Seven Foundations of High-Performing Organizations," *Agency Sales Magazine* (January 1999),

pp. 27–28; and Bill Merrick, "How to Avoid These Seven Strategic Planning Pitfalls," *Credit Union Magazine* (February 1999), p. 45.

3. See Richard W. Oliver, *Seven Imperatives for Winning in the New World of Business* (New York: McGraw-Hill, 1999), or Ian Mitroff, *Smart Thinking for Crazy Times: The Art of Solving the Right Problems* (San Francisco: Berrett-Koehler Publishers, 1998).

4. For expanded discussions on planning time horizons, see John R. Schermerhorn, Jr., *Management,* 6th ed. (New York: John Wiley & Sons, 1999), pp. 140–42; or Stephen P. Robbins, *Managing Today!* (Upper Saddle River, New Jersey: Prentice-Hall, 1997), pp. 130–32.

5. For additional information on MBO, see George S. Odiorne, "MBO Means Having a Goal and Plan—Not Just a Goal," *Manage* (September 1992), pp. 8–11, and David Halpern and Stephen Osofsky, "A Dissenting View of MBO," *Public Personnel Management* (Fall 1990), pp. 59–62.

6. We have found that most small firms lack personnel policies, a finding confirmed in a 2002 study by SHRM and CareerJournal.com. See Betty Sosnin, "Packaging Your Policies," *HR Magazine* (July 2001), pp. 66–72.

7. Due to its proactive, consumer-oriented response to the Tylenol scare, Johnson & Johnson became one of the world's most respected companies. See Robert F. Hartley, *Management Mistakes and Successes,* 7th ed. (London: Wiley, 2002), Chapter 8; Ian I. Mitroff and Gus Anagnos, *Managing Crises Before They Happen* (New York: AMACOM, 2001); and Matthew Boyle, "The Shiniest Reputations in Tarnished Times," *Fortune* (March 4, 2002), pp. 70–82.

8. For additional information on TQM and continuous improvement, see George Eckes, "Making Six-Sigma Last (and Work), *Ivey Business Journal* (January/February 2002), pp. 77–81; Donald S. Miller, "Q-u-a-l-i-t-y: Realities for Supervisors," *Supervision* (May 2000), pp. 3–5; A. Blanton Godfrey, "Is Quality Dead?" *Quality Digest* (December 2000), p. 14; W. J. Duncan and J. G. Van Matre, "The Gospel According to Deming: Is It Really New?" *Business Horizons* (July–August 1990), pp. 3–9; and Richard M. Hodgetts, *Implementing TQM in Small and Medium-Sized Organizations: A Step-by-Step Guide* (New York: AMACOM Division of American Management Association, 1996).

9. Stratford Sherman, "Are You as Good as the Best in the World?" *Fortune* (December 13, 1993), p. 95.

10. *ISO 9000: Handbook of Quality Standards and Compliance* (Waterford, Conn.: Bureau of Business Practice, 1992). Also see Frank Voehl, Peter Jackson, and David Ashton, *ISO 9000: An Implementation Guide for Small to Mid-Sized Businesses* (Delray Beach, Fla.: St. Lucie Press, 1994). Also see C. W. Russo, "10 Rules for Successful ISO Registration," *Quality Digest* (May 1996), pp. 28–31; and Scott M. Paton, Alen Karolyi, and Dirk Dusharme, "ISO 9000 Registrar Directory and Consultants Buyers Guide," *Quality Digest* (May 1996), pp. 33–44.

11. For additional information concerning Gantt charts, see Andrew J. DuBrin and R. Duane Ireland, *Management and Organization,* 2nd ed. (Cincinnati: South-Western Publishing Co., 1993), p. 34; or James A. F. Stoner and R. Edward Freeman, *Management,* 5th ed. (Englewood Cliffs, NJ: Prentice-Hall, 1992), pp. 288–89.

12. For additional information on PERT networks, see Li-Chih Wang and Wilbert E. Wilhelm, "A PERT-Based Paradigm for Modeling Assembly Operations," *IIE Transactions* (March 1993), pp. 88–103; DuBrin and Ireland, *Management and Organization,* pp. 415–18; and Stoner and Freeman, *Management,* pp. 289–91.

13. For expanded discussions on time management, particularly for supervisors, see R. Alex Mackenzie, *The Time Trap: The New Version of the 20 Year Classic on Time Management* (New York: AMACOM division of American Management Association, 1990); "Developing a Time Budget: How to Live with Tight Deadlines," *Supervisory Management* (November 1995), pp. 34–36; William Keenan, Jr., "Time Management Made Simple," *Sales and Marketing Management* (September 1995), pp. 34–36; Christina Maccherone, "The Secrets of

Managing Yourself," *Office Systems* (January 1998), p. 16; Steve Kaye and Irene Kim, "Time Management," *Chemical Engineering* (February 1998), pp. 129–37; Linda R. Dominguez, "Putting an End to Putting It Off," *HR Magazine* (February 1999), pp. 124–29.

14. See R. Wayne Mondy and Robert M. Noe, *Human Resource Management,* 6th ed. (Englewood Cliffs, NJ: Prentice-Hall, 1996), p. 444.

15. From Randall S. Schuler, "Managing Stress Means Managing Time," *Personnel Journal* (December 1979), pp. 22–25. For expanded discussions concerning stress and coping with stress, the following are recommended: John Marks, "Time Out," *U.S. News & World Report* (December 1995), pp. 85–96; Susie Carlton, "Getaways from Stress," *Working Woman* (January 1996), pp. 70–74; Catherine Green, "Dealing with the Stress of Change," *People Management* (November 30, 1995), p. 40; and Suzanne M. Crampton, John W. Hodge, and Jitendra M. Mishra, "Stress and Stress Management," *SAM Advanced Management Journal* (Summer 1995), pp. 10–18.

Chapter 3

1. In addition to the sources listed in the "Contemporary Issue" box, see Jane E. Henry, "Lessons from Team Leaders," *Quality Progress* (March 1998), pp. 57–59; Ben Nagler, "Recasting Employees into Teams," *Workforce* (January 1998), pp. 101–6; Cynthia Stohl and George Cheney, "Participatory Processes/Paradoxical Practices," *Management Communication Quarterly* (February 2001), pp. 349–407; Rick Delbridge and Keith Whitfield, "Employee Perceptions of Job Influence and Organizational Participation," *Industrial Relations* (July 2001), pp. 472–89.

2. See Harold Koontz and Heinz Weirich, *Management,* 9th ed. (New York: McGraw-Hill, 1988), p. 143, or James A. F. Stoner and R. Edward Freeman, *Management,* 5th ed. (Upper Saddle River, NJ: Prentice-Hall, 1992), pp. 251–52.

3. See Andrew J. DuBrin and R. Duane Ireland, *Management and Organization,* 2nd ed. (Cincinnati: South-Western Publishing Co., 1993), pp. 90–100, or John R. Schermerhorn, Jr., *Management,* 6th ed. (New York: John Wiley & Sons, 1999), pp. 59–64.
For a detailed study on effectiveness of decision making, see James W. Dean, Jr., and Mark P. Sharfman, "Does Decision Process Matter? A Study of Strategic Decision-Making Effectiveness," *Academy of Management Journal* (April 1996), pp. 368–96.

4. "Harnessing Employee Creativity," *The Worklife Report* (2001), p. 14.

5. For more information on brainstorming and creative problem solving, see Alex F. Osborn (with Alex Faickney), *Applied Imagination,* 3rd rev. ed. (Buffalo: Creative Education Foundation, 1993). Also see Alan G. Robinson and Sam Stern, *Corporate Creativity: How Innovation and Improvement Actually Happen* (San Francisco: Berrett-Koehler Publishers, 1997). For a list of ways to disrupt a brainstorming session, see Tom Kelley, "Six Ways to Kill a Brainstormer," *Across-the-Board* (March/April 2002), p. 12.

6. For an expanded discussion on NGT, see David H. Holt, *Management: Principles and Practices*, 3rd ed. (Upper Saddle River, NJ: Prentice-Hall, 1993), pp. 139–41. Still another group-type of brainstorming approach that has gained some acceptance in recent years is called storyboarding. Originally attributed to Walt Disney and his organization in developing animated cartoons, storyboarding can be especially helpful in generating alternatives and choosing among them. Depending on the nature of the problem, it may be appropriate to use a neutral party to manage the team process when alternatives, ideas, and other information are listed on index cards and arranged on "storyboards." For more information on storyboarding, see James M. Higgins, "Story Board Your Way to Success," *Training and Development* (June 1995), pp. 13–17, or "Putting the Bang Back in Your TQM Program," *Journal for Quality and Participation* (October/November 1995), pp. 40–45.

7. See Charles W. Prather and Lisa K. Gundry, *Blueprints for Innovation: How Creative Processes Can Make You and Your Company More Competitive* (New York: American Management Association, 1995); Oren Harari, "Turn Your Organization into a Hotbed of Ideas," *Management Review* (December 1995), pp. 37–39; Ralph D. Stacey, *Complexity and Creativity in Organizations* (San Francisco: Berrett-Koehler Publishers, 1996).

8. In the wake of numerous business scandals, many job seekers and recent hires are now more concerned about whether their employers have high ethical standards and practices. See Kris Maher, "Wanted: Ethical Employer," *The Wall Street Journal* (July 9, 2002), pp. B1, B8. For a study of various sociodemographic, personal, and other factors influencing ethical decision making, see Irene Roozen, Patrick DePelsmacker, and Frank Bostyn, "The Ethical Dimensions of Decision Processes of Employees," *Journal of Business Ethics* (September 2001), pp. 87–99.

9. For excellent discussions on both the theory and practice of sound business ethics, see O. C. Farrell and Hohn Fraedrich, *Business Ethics: Ethical Decision Making and Cases*, 3rd ed. (Boston: Houghton-Mifflin Company, 1997); Laura Pincus Hartman, *Perspectives in Business Ethics* (Chicago: Irwin/McGraw-Hill, 1997); Marianne M. Jennings, *Business Ethics: Case Studies and Selected Readings*, 3rd ed. (Cincinnati: West Educational Publishing Company, 1999).

For more general discussions on ethics and morality, see William H. Capitan, *The Ethical Navigator* (Blue Ridge Summit, PA: University Press of America, 2002), and E. Hammond Oglesby, *Ethical Issues That Matter* (Blue Ridge Summit, PA: University Press of America, 2001).

10. Some management theorists distinguish between the terms *risk* and *uncertainty* in decision making. According to Stephen Robbins, *risk* involves conditions in which the decision maker can estimate the likelihood of certain alternatives occurring, usually based on historical data or other information that enables the decision maker to assign probabilities to each proposed alternative. *Uncertainty* involves a condition in which the decision maker has no reasonable probability estimates available and can only "guesstimate" the likelihood of various alternatives or outcomes. See Stephen P. Robbins, *Managing Today* (Upper Saddle River, NJ: Prentice-Hall, 1997), pp. 64–65.

11. See J. G. March and H. A. Simon, *Organizations* (New York: John Wiley & Sons, 1958), pp. 10–12.

12. See Russ Holloman, "The Light and Dark Sides of Decision Making," *Supervisory Management* (December 1989), pp. 33–34.

13. See Jim Perrone, "Moving from Telling to Empowering," *Healthcare Executive* (September/October 2001), pp. 60–61.

14. The guidelines were adapted from Robert Kreitner and Angelo Kinicki, *Organizational Behavior*, 3rd ed. (Homewood, IL: Richard D. Irwin, 1995), pp. 312–13.

15. For a general overview of several quantitative approaches to decision making, see Andrew J. DuBrin and R. Duane Ireland, *Management and Organization*, 2nd ed. (Cincinnati: South-Western Publishing Co., 1993), pp. 436–42, and Ricky W. Griffin, *Management*, 5th ed. (Boston: Houghton-Mifflin, 1996), pp. 702–21. For a comprehensive discussion of problem solving and decision making that includes a number of applied quantitative models and examples, see William J. Altier, *The Thinking Manager's Toolbox: Effective Processes for Problem Solving and Decision Making* (New York: Oxford University Press, 1999).

Chapter 4

1. See Jeffrey Pfeffer and John F. Veiga, "Putting People First for Organizational Success," *Academy of Management Executive* (May 1999), pp. 37–48. This article was adapted from the book by Jeffrey Pfeffer, *The Human Equation: Building Profits by Putting People First* (Boston: Harvard Business School Press, 1998).

2. See Michael R. Carrell, Daniel F. Jennings, and Christina Heavrin, *Fundamentals of Organizational Behavior* (Upper Saddle River, NJ: Prentice-Hall, 1997), pp. 342–45, or David A. DeCenzo, *Human Relations* (Upper Saddle River, NJ: Prentice-Hall, 1997), pp. 201–7.

3. In Chapter 12 we discuss supervisory relationships with the departmental union shop steward where a labour union represents employees in a firm. Some of the same types of supervisory considerations should apply to a union shop steward as to an informal work group leader.

4. More employees are working from their homes, automobiles, hotel rooms, and the like. Offices are becoming more open, with fewer walls and more temporary partitions. These arrangements usually save firms money, but many problems can also be associated with them. See Barbara Ettorre, "When the Walls Come Tumbling Down," *Management Review* (November 1995), pp. 33–37; Sandra E. O'Connell, "The Virtual Workplace Moves at Warp Speed," *HR Magazine* (March 1996), pp. 50–57; and Joan Hamilton, with Stephen Baker and Bill Vlasic, "The New Workplace," *Business Week* (April 29, 1996), pp. 107–17.

5. The outsourcing of human resources management functions has created a growth industry of *professional employer organizations (PEOs)*. PEOs are subcontractors who assume numerous human resources management responsibilities, primarily for firms of from 10 to 500 employees. Depending on the nature of the contractual agreement, the PEO typically will handle payroll, taxes, benefits, insurance, and regulatory compliance. Some PEOs also provide recruitment, selection, and job-training services. Fee charges are negotiable; 3 to 4 percent of a client's payroll costs is a typical fee arrangement. See William Flannery, "PEOs change the face of human resources," *St. Louis Post-Dispatch* (August 24, 1999), p. C6.

6. See J. E. Osborne, "Job Descriptions Do More Than Describe Duties," *Supervisory Management* (February 1992), p. 8, or Danny G. Langdon and Kathleen S. Whiteside, "Redefining Jobs and Work in Organizations," *HR Magazine* (May 1996), pp. 97–101. For more information about developing a job description, see Ethan A. Winning, "Building the Job Description," retrieved February 24, 2004, from www.ewin.com/articles/jdq.htm.

7. See Wayne F. Cascio, "Downsizing: What Do We Know? What Have We Learned?" *Academy of Management Executive* (February 1993), pp. 95–104, or Alex Markels and Matt Murray, "Call It Dumbsizing: Why Some Companies Regret Cost-Cutting," *The Wall Street Journal* (May 14, 1996), pp. A1, A6.

8. See K. S. Cameron, S. J. Freemand, and A. K. Mishra, "Best Practices in White Collar Downsizing: Managing Contradictions," *Academy of Management Executive* (August 1991), pp. 57–73, and Susan Sonnesyn Brooks, "Managing a Horizontal Revolution," *HR Magazine* (June 1995), pp. 52–58.

9. See Sandra O'Neal, "Reengineering and Compensation: An Interview with Michael Hammer," *ACA Journal* (Spring 1996), pp. 6–11.

10. See "Management's New Gurus," *Business Week* (August 31, 1992), pp. 44–47, 50–52, and Robert B. Blaha, "Forget Functions, Manage Processes," *HR Magazine* (June 1995), pp. 52–58.

11. See John A. Byrne, "The Horizontal Corporation," *Business Week* (December 20, 1993), pp. 76–81, and Frank Ostroff, *The Horizontal Corporation: What the Organization of the Future Actually Looks Like and How It Delivers Value to Customers* (New York: Oxford University Press, 1999).

12. See "The Virtual Corporation," *Business Week* (February 8, 1993), pp. 98–99, 100–3, and Roger Nagel, as quoted in *Challenges* (published by the Council on Competitiveness, June 1993), p. 4.

13. For a comprehensive view of trends that will likely impact organizational structures and practices, see Maureen Minehan, "SHRM—Futurist Task Force," *HR Magazine* (1998 50th Anniversary Issue), pp. 77–84.

Chapter 5

1. For an excellent overview of the history and future of human resources management, see Michael Losey, "HR Comes of Age," *HR Magazine* (50th anniversary publication, 1998), pp. 40–53. For an extended discussion of human resource management in today's dynamic, changing environment, see David A. Decenzo and Stephen P. Robbins, *Human Resources Management* (New York: John Wiley & Sons, 2002), pp. 2–32.

2. See Figure 4-7 on pp. 119–21 for an example of a combined job description and job specification. For an extended discussion on job analysis, including job descriptions and job specifications, see Michael Harris, *Human Resources Management: A Practical Approach* (Orlando, FL: Dryden Press, 2000), pp. 133–40.

3. The following are recommended for discussions of sources for job candidates, both internal and external to a firm. John Byrne, "The Search for the Young and Gifted: Why Talent Counts," *BusinessWeek* (October 4, 1999), pp. 108–10; Robert D. Mulberger, "How to Find, Attract, Hire and Keep the Winners," *AFP Exchange* (May/June 2001), pp. 18–20; Sarah Fister, "Online Recruiting: Good, Fast, and Cheap," *Training* (May 1999), p. 26; Shannon Peters Talbott, "How to Recruit Online," *Personnel Journal* (March 1999), pp. 14–17; Elma Harris, "Hire Power," *Sales and Marketing Management* (October 2000), pp. 88–98; Bridget McCrea, "When Good Employees Retire," *Industrial Distribution* (March 2001), pp. 63–64; and Phillip M. Perry, "Hiring the I've Never Held a Job Before Worker," *Rural Telecommunications* (January/February 2001), pp. 64–67. For a discussion of employee turnover costs associated in large part with recruitment and selection deficiencies, see William G. Bliss, "Cost of Employee Turnover Can Be Staggering," *Fairfield County Business Journal* (May 7, 2001), pp. 20–21.

4. For an extensive discussion of selection test validity, see N. Schmidt and F. J. Landry, "The Concept of Validity," in Neal Schmidt and Walter Borman (eds.), *Personnel Selection in Organizations* (San Francisco: Jossey-Bass, 1993), pp. 275–309. For interesting approaches to selection testing, see Alessandra Bianchi, "The Character-Revealing Handwriting Analysis," *Inc.* (February 1996), pp. 77–79, and William Poundstone, "Beware the Interview Inquisition," *Harvard Business Review* (May 2003), p. 18.

5. This concept was part of a training program developed by Jagerson Associates, Inc. for the Life Office Management Association.

6. For an overview of selection testing concepts and various types of employment tests being used, see Gary Dressler, *Human Resources Management* (Upper Saddle River, NJ: Prentice-Hall, 2000), pp. 174–86.

7. Bradford Smart as interviewed by Geoffrey Colvin, "How GE Topgrades: Looking to Hire the Very Best? Ask the Right Questions. Lots of Them," *Fortune* (June 21, 1999), p. 194. Also see Smart, *Topgrading: How Leading Companies Win by Hiring, Coaching, and Keeping the Best People* (Englewood Cliffs, NJ: Prentice-Hall, 1999), and Michael Barrier, "References: A Two-Way Street," *Nation's Business* (May 1999), p. 19.

8. From "Beware of Resumania," *Personnel Journal* (April 1996), p. 28. See also Kenneth Bredemeier, "Credit Checks Are Fair Game for Employers," *Fort Wayne Journal-Gazette* (August 19, 2001), p. 1D, and Max Messmer, "A Closer Look at Résumés," *Strategic Finance* (September 2001), pp. 8–10.

9. For lists of questions that might be asked during the employment interview, see Michael Barrier, "Hire Without Fear," *Nation's Business* (May 1999), pp. 15+; Christopher Caggiano, "HR Red Herrings: Interview Questions," *Inc.* (August 1999), pp. 107–8; Caggiano, "What Were You in For? And Other Great Job-Interview Questions of Our Time," *Inc.* (October 1998), p. 177. In addition, visit www.collegegrad.com/jobsearch/16-15.shtml (retrieved October 22, 2003) for a list of 50 common interview questions.

10. John P. Wanous, "Installing a Realistic Job Preview: Ten Tough Choices," *Personal Psychology* (Spring 1989), pp. 177–33. Also see Carol Hymowitz, "How to Avoid Hiring the Prima Donnas Who Hate Teamwork," *The Wall Street Journal* (February 15, 2000), p. B1.

11. For a general discussion on making the hiring decision, see Max Messmer, "Finalizing the Hiring Decision," *Strategic Finance* (November 2001), pp. 8–10.

12. Aaron Bernstein, "Making Teamwork Work—And Appeasing Uncle Sam," *BusinessWeek* (January 25, 1993), p. 101.

13. For an expanded discussion of employee orientation, see Don Anderson, "Orienting the New Employee," *Agency Sales* (August 2001), pp. 63–65.

14. Franklin J. Lunding, "Everyone Who Makes It Has a Mentor," *Harvard Business Review* (July–August 1978), pp. 91–100.

15. For a general overview of the mentoring process, see George Bohlander, Scott Snell, and Arthur Sherman, *Managing Human Resources* (Cincinnati: Southwestern College Publishing, 2001), pp. 288–90. See also Pam Slater, "Careers Can Be Made or Derailed Over Choice or Absence of a Mentor," *Knight-Ridder Tribune Business News: The Sacramento Bee* (August 9, 1999), and Mary Curtuis, "Careers/Playing Politics: New Alliances Finding the Right Mentors—Inside and Outside Your Workplace—Can Be a Key to Success," *Los Angeles Times* (August 10, 1998), pp. 2–8D.

16. For discussions on training and approaches to training, see "Training Employees as Partners," *HR Magazine* (February 1999), pp. 64–70; Candice G. Harp, Sandra C. Taylor, and John W. Satzinger, "Computer Training and Individual Differences: What Really Matters?" *Human Resources Development Quarterly* (Fall 1998), pp. 271–83; Judith N. Mottl, "Online Training Gets Good Grades," *Internet Week* (October 5, 1998), p. 35; and Suzanne Kapner, "Virtual Training Takes Foodservice into the Future," *Nation's Restaurant News* (April 15, 1996), p. 7. For information on the depth and breadth of training, see Donald V. McCain, "Aligning Training with Business Objectives," *HR Focus* (February 1999), pp. 51–53, and Mark McMaster, "Is Your Training a Waste of Money?" *Sales & Marketing Management* (January 2001), pp. 40–48.

17. For a general discussion on career development, see Cassandra Hayes, "Choosing the Right Path," *Black Enterprise Magazine* (April 2001), pp. 108–10.

18. See George Kimmerling, "How Is Training Regarded and Practiced in Top-Ranked U.S. Companies?" *Training & Development* (September 1993), pp. 29–36. For a detailed discussion of training program evaluation, see Donald L. Kirkpatrick, *Evaluating Training Programs* (Washington, D.C.: American Society for Training and Development, 1975), and "Four Steps to Measuring Training Effectiveness," *Personnel Administrator* (November 1983), pp. 57–62. Also see Dean R. Spitzer, "Embracing Evaluation," *Training* (June 1999), pp. 42–47, and Kathryn Tyler, "Evaluating Evaluations," *HR Magazine* (June 2002), pp. 85–93.

19. Daniel H. Pink, "Richard Bolles: What Happened to Your Parachute?" *Fast* (September 1999), p. 241. See Bolles's latest annual edition of "What Color Is Your Parachute?" (Berkeley, CA: Ten Speed Press, 2003) or visit his website at www.jobhuntersbible.com.

Chapter 6

1. From www.jobquality.ca/indicator_e/dem.stm retrieved on October 29, 2003.

2. Many companies rely in part on personality assessment programs to evaluate employees. One of the more widely recognized approaches to the identification of individual differences is the Myers-Briggs Type Indicators. If your college or university has the Myers-Briggs test, use it to identify your basic personality type. You can also use it to identify personality types that do not complement yours. You can take an online test based on Myers-Brigg personality types at www.humanmetrics.com/cgi-win/JTypes1.htm. For additional information on personality development, see J. M. George, "The Role of Personality in Organizational Life: Issues and Evidence," *Journal of

Management (Volume 18, 1992), pp. 185–213; R. D. Arvey, T. J. Bouchard, N. L. Segal, and L. M. Abraham, "Job Satisfaction: Environmental and Genetic Components," *Journal of Applied Psychology* (Volume 74, 1989), pp. 187–92; and R. C. Carson, "Personality," *Annual Review of Psychology* (Volume 40, 1989), pp. 227–48.

3. As quoted in Rebecca Meany, "What a Pain?" *Successful Meetings* (February 2001), p. 72. See Sandra A. Crowe, *Since Strangling Isn't An Option … Dealing with Difficult People: Common Problems and Uncommon Solutions* (New York: Perigee, 1999). Also see the classic by Margaret Henning and Anne Jardim, *The Managerial Woman* (New York: Anchor Press/Doubleday, 1977), p. 82. The social grouping of children at an early age can have lifelong psychological consequences. See Hara Estroff Marano, "The Friendliness Factor," *Working Mother* (November 1998), pp. 42ff. Additional research supports the contention that early influence is important in leadership development. See Sandra J. Hartman and Jeff O. Harris, "The Role of Parental Influence in Leadership," *Journal of Social Psychology* (April 1992), pp. 153–67.

4. See Abraham H. Maslow, *Motivation and Personality,* 2nd ed. (New York: Harper & Row, 1970), Chapter 4. Also see Ron Zemke, "Maslow for a New Millennium," *Training* (December 1998), pp. 54–58.

5. The complete dual-factor theory is well explained in Frederick Herzberg, Bernard Mausner, and Barbara Bloch Snyderman, *The Motivation to Work,* 2nd ed. (New York: John Wiley & Sons, 1967), and in Herzberg's classic article, "One More Time: How Do You Motivate Your Employees?" *Harvard Business Review* (Volume 46, January–February 1968), pp. 53–62.

6. For a discussion of expectancy theory, see Victor H. Vroom, *Work and Motivation* (New York: John Wiley & Sons, 1964), and Terrence R. Mitchell, "Expectancy Models of Job Satisfaction, Occupational Preference, and Effort: A Theoretical, Methodological, and Empirical Appraisal," *Psychological Bulletin* (Volume 81, 1974), pp. 1053–77.

7. The thoughts and ideas for the section on the ABCs were adapted from Aubrey C. Daniels, Ph.D., *Performance Management: Improving Quality and Productivity through Positive Reinforcement,* 3rd ed. (Atlanta: Performance Management Publications, Inc., 1989).

8. Ibid., pp. 14, 75+.

9. E. L. Thorndike, *Educational Psychology: The Psychology of Learning, Vol. II* (New York: Teachers College Columbia University, 1913). B. F. Skinner built on the works of Thorndike and identified S-R and R-S behaviours. The latter is known as operant conditioning and infers that individuals behave, in large part, to receive desired consequences. See Skinner, *The Behavior of Organisms* (New York: Appleton-Century Crofts, 1938).

10. Daniels, *Performance Management,* p. 45.

11. Douglas McGregor, *The Human Side of Enterprise* (New York: McGraw-Hill, 1960), pp. 45–57.

12. J. Richard Hackman, Greg R. Oldham, Robert Janson, and Kenneth Purdy, "A New Strategy for Job Enrichment," *California Management Review* (Summer 1975), pp. 51–71; J. R. Hackman and G. R. Oldham, *Work Redesign* (Reading, MA: Addison-Wesley, 1980); and Carol T. Kulik, Greg R. Oldham, and Paul H. Langner, "Measurement of Job Characteristics: Comparison of the Original and the Revised Job Diagnostic Survey," *Journal of Applied Psychology* (August 1988), pp. 462–66.

13. Hackman, Oldham, Jenson, and Purdy, p. 58.

14. Ibid.

15. Robert Levering, *A Great Place to Work* (New York; Random House, 1988).

16. Ken Blanchard, "Empowerment Is the Key," *Quality Digest* (April 1996), p. 23. Also see Ken Blanchard, Alan Randolph, and John Carlos, *Empowerment Takes More Than a Minute* (San Francisco: Berrett-Koehler, 1996); and Ken Blanchard, John P. Carlos, and Alan Randolph, *The Three Keys to Empowerment: Release the Power Within People for Astonishing Results and Make Success Measurable! A Mindbook-Workbook for Setting Goals and Taking Action* (San Francisco: Berrett-Koehler, 1999).

17. The oldest documented system of formal employee involvement is Eastman Kodak's employee suggestion program, established in 1898. The Employee Involvement Association (EIA) annually reports suggestion system information. Contact EIA, Fairfax, VA 22030 (703) 303-1010, or visit their website, www.eianet.org. Numerous suggestions for getting employees involved in improvement activities can be found in Norman Bodek and Bunji Tozawa, *The Idea Generator: Quick and Easy Kaizen*, (Vancouver, WA: PCS Press, 2001).

Chapter 7

1. For general discussions on leadership, the following are recommended: James M. Kouzes and Barry Z. Posner, "Exemplary Leaders," *Executive Excellence* (June 2001), pp. 5–7; Ronald A. Heifetz and Donald L. Laurie, "The Work of Leadership," *Harvard Business Review* (December 2001), pp. 131–41; Kennard T. Wing, "Become a Better Leader," *Strategic Finance* (February 2001), pp. 65–68; and Sherwood Ross, "The best leaders learn to tune in to employees and resonate ideas," *St. Louis Post-Dispatch* (March 25, 2002), p. BP2.

2. Stratford Sherman, "How the Best Leaders Are Learning Their Stuff," *Fortune* (November 27, 1995), pp. 90–102. Also see Peter Senge, *The Fifth Discipline: The Art and Practice of the Learning Organization* (New York: Doubleday, 1990) and Senge et al., *The Fifth Discipline Handbook: Strategies and Tools for Building a Learning Organization* (Doubleday, 1994).

3. As reported in Gerald Graham, "Results among four traits workers want in their leadership," *The Fort Wayne, IN News Sentinel* (July 8, 1996), p. 11B. The literature is replete with the need for developing trust. We concur that mutual trust and respect are the foundation of effective supervision. Also see Warren Bennis, "Learning to Lead," *Executive Excellence* (January 1996), p. 7, and Sherman E. Afholderbach, "Supervisory Techniques: A Supervisor's Perspective," *Supervision* (June 1998), pp. 11–13. Ram Charan and Geoffrey Colving, "Why CEOs Fail," *Fortune* (June 21, 1999), pp. 69–78, identified eight qualities that characterize successful CEOs. Not surprisingly, integrity was at the top of their list. Kevin Cashman, author of *Leadership from the Inside Out* (Executive Excellence, 1998), argues that there are three core qualities to leadership: (1) authenticity, (2) self-expression, and (3) value creation.

4. Stephen R. Covey, "Principle-Centered Leadership," *Quality Digest* (March 1996), p. 21. Authors Richard L. Daft and Robert H. Lengel, *Fusion Leadership* (San Francisco: Berrett-Koehler, 1998), describe a method for bringing people together to accomplish mutual goals based on shared vision and values. The principles of fusion (joining together) rather than fission (splitting apart) support individual employee growth and ingenuity.

5. A more complete discussion can be found in James M. Kouzes and Barry Z. Posner, *The Leadership Challenge: How to Get Extraordinary Things Done in Organizations* (Jossey-Bass, 1987) and *Leadership Practices Inventory (LPI): A Self-Assessment and Analysis* (available from Pfeiffer & Company, San Diego).

6. James M. Kouzes and Barry Z. Posner, *Credibility: How Leaders Gain and Lose It, Why People Demand It* (San Francisco: Jossey-Bass, 1993).

7. For general discussions on delegation and the benefits of effective delegation, the following are recommended: W. H. Weiss, "The Art and Skill of Delegating," *Supervision* (September 2000), pp. 3–5; Ted Pollock, "Secrets of Successful Delegation," *Automotive Design & Production* (September 2001), pp. 10–12; Sheila Murray Bethel, "Productive Delegating," *Executive Excellence* (January 2000), p. 16,

and Joyce M. Rosenberg, "Delegating is difficult, but necessary for growth," *St. Louis Post-Dispatch* (July 2, 2001), p. BP10.

8. Ronald E. Merrill and Henry D. Sedgwick, in their article "To Thine Own Self Be True," *Inc.* (August 1994), pp. 50–56, identified six styles of entrepreneurial management" (1) the Classic, (2) the Coordinator, (3) the Craftsman, (4) the Team Manager, (5) the Entrepreneur plus Employee Team, and (6) the Small Partnership. Like us, they contend that any one of them can be effective. For a discussion on seven essential leadership skills, see Kennard T. Wing, "Become a Better Leader," *Strategic Finance* (February 2001), pp. 65–68.

9. Much of this is based on our personal observations and inferences drawn from articles like that by Sue Shellenbarger, "The Care and Feeding (and the Avoiding) of Horrible Bosses," *The Wall Street Journal* (October 20, 1999), p. B1; Stanley Bing, "Hail and Farewell, Chainsaw Al! Don't Let the Door Hit You on the Way Out, Y'Hear," *Fortune* (July 20, 1998), pp. 43–44; and Brian Dumaine, "America's Toughest Bosses," *Fortune* (October 18, 1993), pp. 38–50. For a research study concerning employee creativity as it relates to managerial styles of leading, see Maria M. Clapham, "Employee Creativity: The Role of Leadership," *Academy of Management Executive* (August 2000), pp. 138–39.

10. For general discussions on change and overcoming resistance to change, the following are recommended: Peter de Jager, "Resistance to Change: A New View of an Old Problem," *Futurist* (May/June, 2001), pp. 24–28; David Foote, "The Futility of Resistance to Change," *Computerworld* (January 15, 2001), p. 36; and Devid Geisler, "Bottom-Feeders: People Who Reject Change," *Executive Excellence* (December 2001), pp. 19–20.

11. For overviews of strategic organizational change approaches, see Peter L. Brill and Richard Worth, *The Four Levels of Corporate Change* (AMACOM, 1997); Rick Maurer, *Beyond the Wall: Unconventional Strategies That Build Support for Change* (Bard Press, 1996); and T. L. Stanley, "Change: A Common Sense Approach," *Supervision* (January 2002), pp. 7–9. For information on bringing about quality improvement initiatives, see Don Harrison, "Accelerating Change," *Quality Digest* (December 1999), p. 33.

12. For discussions on building trust between supervisors and employees when changes are being made, see Parry Pascarella, "Fifteen Ways to Work for You," *HR Magazine* (April 1996), pp. 75–81; Max Messmer, "Leading Your Team through Change," *Strategic Finance* (October 2001), pp. 8–10; and Copley News Service, "Older Workers Embracing Change," *Northeast Indiana Careers* (July 11, 2001), p. 1.

Chapter 8

1. "Get the message? As the number of Internet access options grows, pace of work expectations increase dramatically," *Computer Dealer News* (October 22, 1999), p. 22.

2. Ibid.

3. There has been discussion regarding the inability of school systems to adequately prepare students for the business world. See Paul A. Argenti, "Should Business Schools Teach Aristotle?" *Strategy & Business* (Third Quarter, 1998), p. 4, and Anne Fisher, "Readers Speak Out on Illiterate MBAs," *Fortune* (March 1, 1999), p. 242. Research by Business Intelligence reported that the three most important competencies for managers and directors responsible for internal communication are strategic thinking, internal communication practice, and change management. Unfortunately, the study found that less than half the people occupying these positions have relevant professional qualifications. See "Communications Is Critical to Business Success," *Management Services* (October 2001), p. 3.

4. Tom Peters has strongly advised managers to become highly visible and to do better jobs of listening to subordinates. We agree. For additional information on "management by wandering around (MBWA)," see Tom Peters, *Thriving on Chaos* (New York: Alfred A. Knopf,

1988), pp. 423–40. For an example of MBWA in practice, see Polly LaBarre, "The Agenda—Grassroots Leadership," *Fast Company* (April 1999), pp. 114+.

5. The grapevine cuts across the formal channels of communications. See Stanley J. Modic, "Grapevine Rated Most Believable," *Industry Week* (May 15, 1989), pp. 11 and 14, and Walter Kiechel III, "In Praise of Office Gossip," *Fortune* (August 19, 1985), pp. 253, 254, and 256. The classic article on this subject is Keith Davis's "Management Communication and the Grapevine," *Harvard Business Review* (September–October 1953), pp. 43–49.

6. For further discussion of informal channels of communication and the grapevine, see Rudolph F. Verderber and Kathleen S. Verderber, *Inter-Act: Using Interpersonal Communication Skills* (Belmont, CA: Wadsworth Publishing Company, 1995); William W. Hull, "Beating the Grapevine to the Punch," *Supervision* (August 1994), pp. 17–19; "Stopping Those Nasty Rumors," *HR Focus* (November 1990), p. 22; J. Mishra, "Managing the Grapevine," *Public Personnel Management* (Summer 1990), pp. 213+; Keith Davis and Curtis Sittenfield, "Good Ways to Deliver Bad News," *Fast Company* (April 1999), pp. 58+.

7. Brenda Major, "Gender Patterns in Touching Behavior," in Nancy M. Henley, ed., *Gender and Non-Verbal Behavior* (New York: Springer-Verlag, 1981). See Rich McGuigan, "Communication: Your Most Valuable Tool," *Supervision* (November 2001), pp. 3–5, for tips on how managers can interpret body language.

8. Quality guru Joseph Juran used the simple explanation that managers needed to be bilingual—that is, they had to speak the language of both upper management and of the workforce. See A. Blanton Godfrey, "Speak the Right Language," *Quality Digest* (July 1998), p. 18. The English language is estimated to contain some 750,000 words, but the vocabulary of the average person is only 20,000 to 40,000 words. While English is generally recognized as the world's primary business language, not all employees will understand the common tongue. In one section of their book, Rodin and Hartman observe that IT staff use technical terms because at most companies "they're herded into one, isolated department." The authors argue that "the best IT professionals live with the business units." Rob Rodin and Curtis Hartman, *Free, Perfect, and Now: Connecting to the Three Insatiable Customer Demands* (New York: Simon & Schuster, 1999), pp. 49, 56.

9. Respondents to the March 1997 "Where I Stand" poll in *Nation's Business*. Also see Tim McCollum, "Preventing a Productivity Drain," *Nation's Business* (March 1998), p. 56.

Chapter 9

1. Many employees dislike performance reviews. See "Gentler Reviews & Other Responses to Forced Rankings," *Ioma's Pay for Performance Report* (June 2002), pp. 7+; Max Messmer, "Performance Reviews," *Strategic Finance* (December 2000), pp. 10–12; Tom Coens and Mary Jenkins, *Abolishing Performance Appraisals: Why They Backfire and What to Do Instead* (Berrett-Koehler, San Francisco: 2000); Michael Barrier, "Reviewing the Annual Review," *Nation's Business* (September 1998), pp. 32–34; Timothy D. Schellhardt, "Annual Agony: It's Time to Evaluate Your Work, and All Involved Are Groaning," *The Wall Street Journal* (November 19, 1996), pp. A1, A5. For an expanded discussion of performance monitoring, see Gordon M. Amsler, Henry M. Findley, and Earl Ingram, "Performance Monitoring: Guidance for the Modern Workplace," *Supervision* (October 2001), p. 3+.

2. For a discussion of peer appraisals, see "Multi-Rater Feedback and Performance Evaluation Programs Do Not Mix," *Supervision* (March 1998), p. 25; Daniel Kanouse, "Why Multi-Rater Feedback Systems Fail," *HRFocus* (January 1998), p. 3; David A. Waldman, "Predictors of Employee Preferences for Multirater and Group-Based Performance Appraisal," *Group & Organizational Management* (June 1997), pp. 264–87; Carol W. Timmreck and David W. Bracken, "MultiSource Feedback: A Study of Its Use in Decision Making,"

Employment Relations Today (Spring 1997), pp. 21–27; and Martin L. Ramsey and Howard Lehto, "The Power of Peer Review," *Training & Development* (July 1994), pp. 38–41. Also see Irene Buhalo, "You Sign My Report Card—I'll Sign Yours," *Personnel* (May 1991), p. 23, and G. M. McEvoy, P. F. Buller, and S. R. Roghaar, "A Jury of One's Peers," *Personnel Administrator* (May 1988), pp. 94–98.

3. The 360-degree appraisals are controversial. Dennis Coates says, "You can use 360-degree feedback for performance management, but not for performance appraisal. Why not? Because it undermines trust." See Coates, "Don't Tie 360 Feedback to Pay," *Training* (September 1998), pp. 58–78. For an extended discussion of the pros and cons of 360-degree appraisals, see Tammy Galvin, "Technology Meets 360-Degree Evaluations," *Training* (February 2001), p. 24; Susan J. Wells, "A New Road: Traveling beyond 360-Degree Evaluation," *HRMagazine* (September 1999), pp. 82–91; and David A. Waldman and David E. Bowen, "The Acceptability of 360-Degree Appraisals: A Customer-Supplier Relationship Perspective," *Human Resource Management* (Summer 1998), pp. 117–29; Scott Wimer and Kenneth M. Nowack, "13 Common Mistakes Using 360-Degree Feedback," *Training & Development Journal* (May 1998), pp. 69+.

4. Patricia J. Hewitt, "The Rating Game," *Incentive* (August 1993), pp. 39–41. Also see Michael Rigg, "Reasons for Removing Employee Evaluations from Management Control," *Industrial Engineering* (August 1992), p. 17.

5. Douglas McGregor, "An Uneasy Look at Performance Appraisal," *Harvard Business Review* (September–October 1972), pp. 133–34. For an expanded discussion on how supervisors can make more effective use of performance appraisals, see Charles N. Painter, "Ten Steps for Improved Appraisals," *Supervision* (June 1999), pp. 11–13.

6. Excerpted and adapted from George V. Hulme, "Using Software for Worker Reviews," *Nation's Business* (September 1998), pp. 35–36. At the time of publication, PerformanceNow! can be obtained from KnowledgePoint in Petaluma, CA (1-800-727-1133) and Employee Appraiser 3.0 from Austin-Hayne Corp. (1-800-809-9920). Current issues of personnel and human resources management journals will periodically carry advertisements for other computerized software products. Check the following websites for information on other products: www.businessdecisions.com or www.sap.com/solutions/hr.

7. Barbara Holmes, "The Lenient Evaluator's Hurting Your Organization," *HRMagazine* (June 1993), pp. 75–77.

8. One of the supervisor's important roles is to coach, that is, to help employees learn how to become better employees. For an enlightening discussion on the supervisor's role as a coach, see Dianne Molvig, "Yearning for Learning," *HRMagazine* (March 2002), pp. 67+; Lynda C. McDermott, "Developing the New Young Managers," *Training & Development* (October 2001), pp. 42+; Diane Franklin, "Coaching for Success," *Credit Union Management* (December 2000), pp. 50–53; Clinton O. Longenecker and Gary Pinkel, "Coaching to Win at Work," *Manage* (February 1997), pp. 19–21; Jeremy Lebediker, "The Supervisor's Role as Coach: 4 Essential Models for Setting Performance Expectations," *Supervision* (December 1995), pp. 14–16; and Bill Halson, "Teaching Supervisors to Coach," *Personnel Management* (March 1990), pp. 36–53. Also see Marianne Minor, *Coaching for Development* (Menlo Park, CA: Crisp Publications, Inc., 1995). This book is self-instructional and forces the reader to get involved through a variety of exercises and problems. For a discussion of new training methods, see Sue Shellenberger, "New Training Methods Allow Jobs to Intrude Further into Off Hours," *The Wall Street Journal* (July 11, 2002), p. B1.

9. The Compensation Planning 2002 study found that 77.2 percent of companies reported having short-term incentive plans, and half had equity compensation programs. See "Seven Out of Ten Companies Now Use Variable Compensation," *Ioma's Pay for Performance* (July 2002), pp. 7+. Their findings were consistent with those reported by World at Work 2001–2002 Total Salary Increase Budget Survey,

which found seven out of ten companies were using alternative pay strategies. These alternative compensation plans include skill- and competency-based pay, group and team pay incentives, gain sharing, lump-sum merit increases, and broad-banding.

Also see Joanne Summer, "The Incentive Comp Quandary," *Business Finance* (December 1998), pp. 83–86. Also see Jeffrey Pfeffer, "Six Dangerous Myths About Pay," *Harvard Business Review* (May/June 1998), pp. 108–19, and Don Barksdale, "Leading Employees through the Variable Pay Jungle," *HRMagazine* (July 1998), pp. 110–18.

For additional information on compensation concerns, see Michael G. Stevens, "Serve up Cafeteria Plans," *The Practical Accountant* (May 2002), pp. 46–48; Charlotte Garvey, "Steer Teams with the Right Pay," *HRMagazine* (May 2002), pp. 70–78; Marc Knez and Duncan Simester, "Making Across-the-Board Incentives Work," *Harvard Business Review* (February 2002), pp. 16–17; Edward P. Lazear, "Performance Pay and Productivity," *The American Economic Review* (December 2000), pp. 1346–61; Harry J. Paarsch and Bruce Shearer, "Piece Rates, Fixed Wages, and Incentive Effects: Statistical Evidence from Payroll Records," *International Economic Review* (February 2000), pp. 59–92; Patricia K. Zingheim, *Pay People Right* (San Francisco: Jossey-Bass, 2000); Edward E. Lawler III, *Rewarding Excellence* (San Francisco: Jossey-Bass, 2000); Glenn Parker, Jerry McAdams, and David Zielinski, *Rewarding Teams: Lessons from the Trenches* (San Francisco: Jossey-Bass, 2000).

10. For an expanded discussion of skill-based pay, see George E. Ledford, Jr., "Three Case Studies on Skill-Based Pay: An Overview," *Compensation Review* (March/April 1991), pp. 11–23; Richard L. Bunning, "Models for Skill-Based Plans," *HRMagazine* (February 1991), pp. 62–64; and Earl Ingram II, "Compensation: The Advantage of Knowledge-Based Pay," *Personnel Journal* (April 1990), p. 138.

11. Nina Gupta, Timothy P. Schweizer, and Douglas Jenkins, Jr., "Pay-for-Knowledge Compensation Plans: Hypotheses and Survey Results," *Monthly Labor Review* (October 1987), pp. 40–43.

12. R. Bradley Hill, "How to Design a Pay-for-Skills-Used Program," *Journal of Compensation and Benefits* (September/October 1993), pp. 32–38.

13. Pamela Bloch-Flynn and Kenneth Vlach, "Employee Awareness Paves the Way for Quality," *HRMagazine* (July 1994), p. 78, and John Allen, "Suggestion Systems and Problem-Solving: One and the Same," *Quality Circles Journal* (March 1987), pp. 2–5.

Chapter 10

1. From Retail Council of Canada, 2003 Canadian Security Report Executive Summary, at www.retailcouncil.org/rpn/asr/2003_Security_Report_ExecSum.pdf (retrieved November 27, 2003).

2. From Oren Harari, "U2D2: The Rx for Leadership Blues," *Management Review* (August 1995), pp. 34–36.

3. In a survey of large employers in the United States, 60 percent of those surveyed indicated that they had codes of ethics in place and a third provided training on ethical business conduct. See "Boost in Ethical Awareness," *HRMagazine* (February 1995), p. 19.

4. See Mary G. Rendini, "Team Effort at Maguire Group Leads to Ethics Policy," *HRMagazine* (April 1995), pp. 63–66.

5. See Kate Walter, "Ethics Hot Lines Tap into More Than Wrongdoing," *HRMagazine* (November 1995), pp. 79–85.

6. For example, see Debra R. Meyer, "More on Whistleblowing," *Management Accounting* (June 1993), p. 26; and Marcy Mason, "The Curse of Whistleblowing," *The Wall Street Journal* (March 14, 1994), p. A14.

7. See James G. Vigneau, "To Catch a Thief ... and Other Workplace Investigations," *HRMagazine* (January 1995), pp. 90–95.

8. From the Ontario Human Rights Commission "Policy on Drug and Alcohol Testing" at www.ohrc.on.ca/english/publications/drug-alcohol-policy.pdf (retrieved on December 3, 2003).

9. See Dennis L. Johnson, Christie A. King, and John G. Kurutz, "A Safe Termination Model for Supervisors," *HRMagazine* (May 1996), pp. 73–78; and Gary Bielous, "How to Fire," *Supervision* (November 1996), pp. 8–10.

10. For a thorough discussion of the pros and cons and applications of discipline-without-punishment approaches, see Dick Grote, *Discipline without Punishment* (New York: American Management Association, 1995). See also Dick Grote, "Discipline without Punishment," *Across-the-Board* (September/October 2001) pp. 52–57.

Chapter 11

1. For an expanded discussion of group processes in organizations, see Jennifer M. George and Gareth R. Jones, *Understanding and Managing Organizational Behavior* (Reading, MA: Addison-Wesley, 1999), pp. 330–400.

2. See David H. Holt, *Management: Principles and Practices* (Englewood Cliffs, NJ: Prentice-Hall, 1993), pp. 351–52. Also see Natasha Calder and P. C. Douglas, "Empowered Employee Teams: The New Key to Improving Corporate Success," *Quality Digest* (March 1999), pp. 26–30, for a discussion of empowered teams.

3. For a discussion of the Hawthorne Studies and their impact, see Andrew J. Dubrin and R. Duane Ireland, *Management and Organization* (Cincinnati: South-Western Publishing, Co., 1993), pp. 39–40.

4. Jon R. Katzenbach and Douglas K. Smith, *The Wisdom of Teams: Creating the High-Performance Organization* (Boston: Harvard Business School Press, 1993).

5. "From Supervisor to Team Manager," by Allen Ferguson, Amy Hicks, and Steven D. Jones, is one of the case studies in *Developing High-Performance Work Teams*, edited by Jones and Michael M. Beyerlein, (Washington, D.C. ASTD, Part 1, 1998, and Part 2, 1999). Also visit the Center for Collaborative Organizations' website at www.work-teams.unt.edu (retrieved March 24, 2004) for additional information.

6. See Edward M. Marshall, "The Collaborative Workplace," *Management Review* (June 1995), pp. 13–17.

7. From Michael A. Campion and A. Catherine Higgs, "Design Work Teams to Increase Productivity and Satisfaction," *HRMagazine* (October 1995), pp. 101–7.

8. See Priscilla M. Elsass, "When Teammates Raise a White Flag," *Academy of Management Executive* (February 1996), pp. 40–49.

9. For a comprehensive review of what self-directed work teams do, see "1995 Industry Report," *Training* (October 1995), p. 72.

10. See Stephanie Overman, "Teams Score on the Bottom Line," *HRMagazine* (May 1994), pp. 82–84.

11. See "Why I Do This Job," reporting survey data developed by William M. Mercer, Inc.–Yankelovich Partners, Inc., in *BusinessWeek* (September 11, 1995), p. 8.

12. See George Gallup, Jr., and Tim Jones, *The Next American Spirituality* (Gallup Organization: National Opinion Research Center, 2000); Michelle Conlin, "Religion in the Workplace: The Growing Presence of Spirituality in Corporate America," *BusinessWeek* (November 1, 1999), pp. 153+; and Nancy K. Austin, "Does Spirituality at Work Work?" *Working Women* (March 1995), pp. 26–28.

13. For a comprehensive source on how to develop and maintain a positive work environment, see Jim Harris, *Getting Employees to Fall in Love with Your Company* (New York: AMACOM, 1996).

14. In Kate N. Grossman, "Boys Behaving Badly: Men Mostly at Fault for Rising Incivility at Work," *Associated Press* (August 11, 1999). This news release summarized the work of University of North Carolina professor Christine M. Patterson et al., *"Workplace Incivility: The Target's Eye View,"* presented at the Academy of Management's Annual Meeting (Tuesday, August 10, 1999). Alice Ann Love, "Survey Finds Workplace Angst: Colleagues, Communications Equipment Sources of Anger," *Associated Press* (September 6, 1999), reports on the Gallup Organization's telephone survey of workers for Marlin to assess the extent of workplace anger and stress. Also see Noa Davenport, Ruth Distler Schwartz, and Gail Pursell Elliott, *Mobbing: Emotional Abuse in the American Workplace* (Ames, IA: Civil Society Publishing, 1999).

15. "Decade of Downsizing Has Left Its Mark," Associated Press story concerning a survey conducted by the International Survey Research Corporation, as reported in the *St. Louis Post Dispatch* (December 26, 1996), p. 13D.

16. Robert J. Grossman, "Damaged, Downsized Souls: How to Revitalize the Workplace," *HRMagazine* (May 1996), pp. 54–61.

17. From "Checking Your Firm's Morale," *Communication Briefings* (April 1993), p. 3.

18. See Elaine McShulkis, "Employee Survey Sins," *HRMagazine* (May 1996), pp. 12–13.

19. For a detailed explanation of OD, see Warren G. Bennis's classic, *Organizational Development: Its Nature, Origins, and Perspectives* (Reading, MA: Addison-Wesley, 1969).

20. See Marianne Minor, *Coaching and Counseling: A Practice Guide for Managers* (Crisp Publications, Inc., 1989), and Arthur Sherman, George Bohlander, and Scott Snell, *Managing Human Resources* (Cincinnati: South-Western College Publishing, 1998), pp. 550–53.

21. One study found that 85 percent of surveyed companies offered wellness programs. See "Here's to Your Health," *HRFocus* (January 1996), p. 18, and Paul L. Cerrato, "Employee Health: Not Just a Fringe Benefit," *Business and Health* (November 1995), pp. 21–26.

22. See Sandra J. Kelley, "Making Sense of Violence in the Workplace," *Risk Management* (October 1995), pp. 50–57.

23. See Christine McGovern, "Take Action, Heed Warnings to End Workplace Violence," *Occupational Hazards* (March 1999), pp. 61–63, and John W. Kennish, "Violence in the Workplace," *Professional Safety* (November 1995), pp. 34–36.

Chapter 12

1. Statistics regarding unionization rates in Canada were obtained from Workplace Information Directorate, Labour Program, Human Resources Development Canada, "Union Membership in Canada—2003," *Workplace Gazette* (Vol. 6, No. 3) at www.110hrdc-drhc.gc.ca/millieudetravail_workplace/gazette/pdf/en/Union%20Membership%20in%20Canada%972003%2D12.pdf (retrieved March 24, 2004).

2. Virginia Galt, "Unions Covering Fewer of Canada's Workers," at http://record.workopolis.com/servlet/Content/fasttrack/20031013/RLABO13?section=Trades (retrieved December 15, 2003).

3. According to Statistics Canada (http://erl.bibliocentre.ca:2066/content/english/articles/daily/020926i.shtml (retrieved March 24, 2004) in 1999 average hourly earnings of unionized workers were higher than those of nonunionized workers. The average hourly rate for full-time unionized workers in Canada in 1999 was $20.36 compared to $17.82 for nonunionized workers.

4. In a major 1995 study of 2,400 workers, approximately 63 percent said they would like to have more influence in workplace decisions involving such areas as production, training, equipment, and working conditions. By about a 2-to-1 majority, the workers indicated a preference for "nonunion participation" or "nonunion representation." At the same time, however, most surveyed workers indicated that they wanted workplace organizations that were "employee selected" and that had some real "power" in being able to influence managerial decisions that affected workers. See "Workers Want Nonunion Participation," *Issues in HR* (January/February 1995), pp. 1–2.

5. See Canadian Legal Information Institute at www.canlii.org/ca/sta/l-2/sec70.html (retrieved December 15, 2003).

6. Some authorities believe that the time has arrived for union–management relationships to become far more cooperative than adversarial. A comprehensive book that advocates such an approach, including the important roles played by supervisors, is Warner P. Woodworth and Christopher B. Meek, *Creating Labor–Management Partnerships* (Reading, MA: Addison-Wesley, 1994).

Chapter 13

1. For expanded discussions on the controlling function, see John R. Schermerhorn, Jr., *Management*, 6th ed. (New York: John Wiley & Sons, Inc., 1999), pp. 180–99, and Ricky W. Griffin, *Management*, 5th ed. (Boston: Houghton Mifflin Company, 1996), pp. 600–31. See also Jim Dismukes, "Quality Control: A Job for All Seasons," *Real Estate Investor* (June 2002), p. 116.

2. See W. H. Weiss, "Organizing for Quality, Productivity, and Job Satisfaction," *Supervision* (February 2002), pp. 13–15.

3. Often this is accomplished through some form of statistical quality control (SQC) or statistical process control (SPC), which is discussed later in this chapter. See Lloyd S. Nelson, "Test on Quality Control Statistics and Concepts," *Journal of Quality Technology* (January 2001), pp. 115–17.

4. A major survey of over 700 manufacturing firms revealed that, among the identified "leading" firms, the following areas of performance measurement were used by over 90 percent of firms: manufactured/delivered costs per unit, inventory levels, worker productivity, manufacturing cycle time, and cost efficiencies in operations. See "Survey in Manufacturing," *Management Review* (September 1999), pp. 18–19.

5. See Dara Mirsky, "Good, Bad, and Close Customer Service as 2001 Ends," *Customer Interaction Solutions* (February 2002), pp. 44–45.

6. For expanded descriptions of job design and work-measurement techniques, see Richard B. Chase and Nicholas J. Aquilano, *Production and Operations Management: Manufacturing and Services*, 7th ed. (Chicago: Irwin/McGraw-Hill, 1995), pp. 432–79, or Benjamin W. Niebel, *Motion and Time Studies*, 9th ed. (Homewood, IL: Richard D. Irwin, 1993).

7. See Rick Rutter, "Work Sampling: As a Win/Win Management Tool," *Industrial Engineering* (February 1994), pp. 30–31.

8. See Alberto Bayo-Moriones and Javier Marino-Diaz de Cerio, "Quality Management and High Performance Work Practices: Do They Coexist?" *International Journal of Production Economics* (October 13, 2001), p. 251.

9. For additional information on productivity measurement, see Robert O. Brinkerhoff and Dennis E. Dressler, *Productivity Measurement: A Guide for Managers and Evaluators* (Newbury Park, CA: Sage Publications, Applied Social Research Methods Series, Volume 19, 1990). Also see Otis Port, "How to Tally Productivity on the Shop Floor," *BusinessWeek* (November 23, 1998), p. 137, and Kostas N. Dervitsiotis, "Looking at the Whole Picture in Performance Improvement Programmers," *Total Quality Management* (September 2001), pp. 687–700.

10. In the major manufacturing survey mentioned in Endnote 4, manufacturers were asked to identify the "critical practices" they used to compare their operations with those of competitors. The five most often cited were (1) cost efficiencies in operations, (2) speed of time-to-market, (3) research and development, (4) rapid supply from suppliers, and (5) delivery logistics. See *Management Review*, (Sept. 1999), op. cit., p. 18. For interesting discussions of matching production levels to the rapidly changing automotive industry, see Katherine Hobson, "The Good, the Fad, and the Ugly," *U.S. News & World Report* (April 1, 2002), p. 31; Thomas K. Grose, "License to Thrill," *U.S. News & World Report* (April 1, 2002), p. 30; and Darren Fonda, "Going Topless," *Time* (April 1, 2002), pp. 50–52.

11. See Susan Oakland and John S. Oakland, "Current People Management Activities in World-Class Organizations," *Total Quality Management* (September 2001), pp. 773–88.

12. For expanded discussions on statistical quality control, see Roberta S. Russell and Bernard W. Taylor III, *Operations Management*, 3rd ed. (Upper Saddle River, NJ: Prentice-Hall, Inc., 2000), pp. 131–81, or James R. Chapman and Jacek Koronacki, *Statistical Process Control for Quality Improvement* (New York: Chapman & Hall, 1993).

13. For a discussion comparing incremental versus zero-based budgets and several other budgeting approaches, see Stephen P. Robbins, *Managing Today* (Upper Saddle River, NJ; Prentice-Hall, 1997), pp. 178–80.

14. From Beth Brophy, "Nice Guys (and Workshops) Finish First," *U.S. News & World Report* (August 22, 1988), p. 44. Also see Robert Levering and Milton Moskowitz, "The 100 Best Companies to Work For," *Fortune* (February 4, 2002), pp. 72–80; or visit their website at www.fortune.com/fortune/bestcompanies/0,15126,,00.html (retrieved March 24, 2004); and "Special Report: The Best (& Worst) Managers of the Year," *BusinessWeek* (January 13, 2003), pp. 58–92.

15. See John Case, "The Open-Book Revolution," *Inc.* (June 1995), pp. 26–43; David Whitford, "Before and After," *Inc.* (June 1995), pp. 44–50; John Case, *The Coming Business Revolution* (New York: HarperBusiness, 1995); Willard I. Zangwill, "Focusing All Eyes on the Bottom Line," *The Wall Street Journal* (March 21, 1994), p. A12; and Timothy L. O'Brien, "Company Wins Workers' Loyalty by Opening Its Books," *The Wall Street Journal* (December 20, 1993), pp. B1, B2.

16. Ken Blanchard, "Sharing Information Is Key," *Quality Digest* (July 1996), p. 17.

17. For expanded information on inventory control, see Richard J. Tersine, *Principles of Inventory and Materials Management*, 4th ed. (New York: North-Holland, 1994), or Jan B. Young, *Modern Inventory Operations: Methods for Accuracy and Productivity* (New York: Van Nostrand Reinhold, 1991).

18. For expanded information on production control, see Fred Aslup and Ricky M. Watson, *Practical Statistical Process Control: A Tool for Quality Manufacturing* (New York: Van Nostrand Reinhold, 1993); T. E. Vollmann, W. L. Berry, and D. C. Whybark, *Manufacturing and Control Systems*, 3rd ed. (Homewood, IL: Richard D. Irwin, 1992); or E. M. Goldratt and J. Cox, *The Goal: A Process of Ongoing Improvement* (Great Barrington, MA: North River Press, 1992). For information on total performance and measurement model systems, see Jiju Antony, Graeme Knowles, and Tolga Taner, "10 Steps to Optimal Production," *Quality* (September 2001), pp. 45–49, and Gopal K. Kanji and Patricia Moura e Sa, "Kanji's Business Scorecard," *Total Quality Management* (December 2001), pp. 898–905.

Chapter 14

1. Don McNerny, "The Bottom-Line Value of Diversity," *HRFocus* (May 1994), pp. 22–23. See also Kathleen Melymuka, "Diversity Pays Off," *Computerworld* (January 18, 2001), pp. 32–43.

2. Status of Women Canada website at www.swc-cfc.gc.ca/dates/whm/2000/whm2000_e.html (retrieved December 30, 2003).

3. Virginia Galt, " 'Go for it,' female executives told," *The Globe and Mail* (March 15, 2004), p. B1.

4. Canadian Centre for Occupational Health & Safety at www.ccohs.ca/oshanswers/psychosocial/aging_workers.html (retrieved March 24, 2004).

5. "Ont. Retirement Law to Take Effect in 2005," *Workplace Diversity Update* (July 2003), p. 8 at www.diversityupdate.com/WDUJul03E.pdf (retrieved March 24, 2004).

6. "Visible Minorities in Canada," Statistics Canada, Catalogue no. 85F0033MIE at www.statcan.ca/english/freepub/85F0033MIE/85F0033MIE01009.pdf (retrieved March 25, 2004).

7. Virginia Galt, "'Go for it,' female executives told," *The Globe and Mail* (March 15, 2004), p. B1.

8. Ibid.

9. Ibid.

10. Ibid.

11. Ibid.

12. See "Tips for Policies on Personal Relationships in the Workplace," *Public Management* (May 2000), pp. 38–43; Tim Barnett, Amy McMillan, and Winston McVea, Jr., "Employer Liability for Harassment by Supervisors," *Journal of Employment Discrimination Law* (Fall 2000), pp. 311–16; Laura Lawson and Karen Caldwell, *HRMagazine* (October 2000), pp. 217–18; and Steven C. Millwee, "I Just Want It to Stop," *Security Management* (March 2001), pp. 101–7.

13. See Anne Fisher, "Did the Bill-and-Monica Debacle Teach Us Nothing?" *Fortune* (December 30, 2002), p. 206; David Rubenstein, "Harassment Prevention Is Now a Must for U.S. Companies," *Corporate Legal Times* (August 1999), pp. 31–32; Patricia M. Buhler, "The Manager's Role in Preventing Sexual Harassment," *Supervision* (April 1999), pp. 16–18; Rebecca Ganzel, "What Sexual Harassment Training Really Prevents," *Training* (October 1998), pp. 86–94; and George F. Simons, "Using Drama for Intercultural and Diversity Training," *Managing Diversity* (June 1998), pp. 1, 3.

14. Janet McFarland, "Women still find slow rise to power positions," *The Globe and Mail* (March 13, 2003) p. B1.

15. See "Glass Ceiling Report Is No Surprise to SHRM," *Mosaics* (April 1995), p. 4. See also William B. Irvine, "Beyond Sexual Harassment," *Journal of Business Ethics* (December 2000), pp. 353–60, and John A. Pearce, II, and Samuel A. DiLullo, "A Business Policy Statement Model for Eliminating Sexual Harassment and Related Employer Liability," *S.A.M. Advanced Management Journal* (Spring 2001), pp.12–21.

16. See Anne Fisher, "Ask Annie: Readers Weigh in on Finding Mentors," *Fortune* (July 5, 1999), p. 192, and Marilyn J. Haring, "Mentoring to Support Gender Equity," *Purdue Alumnus* (October 1999), p. 48. For a broad overview of women's issues in the workplace, including mentoring programs, see "Making Equal Pay a Reality in Your Workplace," *Facts on Working Women,* published by the U.S. Department of Labor Women's Bureau (March 27, 2002).

17. "Workopolis Partners with The Canadian Council on Rehabilitation and Work (CCRW) to Assist Canadians with Disabilities to Find Work" at www.workink.com/workink/national/articles.asp?subsection=986 (retrieved January 3, 2004).

18. From the Canadian Human Rights Act, at www.chrc-ccdp.ca/ee/bfe-eso.asp?l=e#duty (retrieved January 3, 2004).

19. Paths to Equal Opportunity, Government of Ontario, Ministry of Citizenship and Immigration at www.equalopportunity.on.ca/eng_t/subject/index.asp?action=search_7&file_id=25210 (retrieved March 24, 2004).

20. Canadian Centre for Occupational Health & Safety at www.ccohs.ca/oshanswers/psychosocial/aging_workers.html (retrieved March 24, 2004).

21. Ibid.

22. Ibid.

23. Michelle Conlin, "Religion in the Workplace," *BusinessWeek* (November 1, 1999), p. 158. See also Georgette F. Bennett, "Religious Diversity in the Workplace," *Diversity Factor* (Winter 2001) pp. 15–20.

24. Some research studies have statistically linked effective diversity management efforts by certain firms to positive economic results. For example, see Peter Wright, Stephen Ferris, Janine Hiller, and Mark Kroll, "Competitiveness through Management of Diversity: Effects on Stock Price Valuations," *Academy of Management Journal* (January/February 1995), pp. 272–87.

25. See Iris Taylor, "Winning at Diversity," *Working Women* (March 1999), p. 36, for a discussion of what several organizations have done to create informal diversity plans. Also see "Diversity Training on the Rise," *Human Resources Forum* (December 1995), p. 3, or Alice Starke, "Diversity Training Program to Develop In-House Trainers," *HRNews* (March 1996), pp. 21+.

Index

P · Photo Credits for Chapter Openers